The Cytotoxics Handbook

Fourth Edition

Edited by

Michael Allwood BPharm, PhD, FRPharmS
Director, Pharmacy Academic Practice Unit,
School of Health and Community Studies,
University of Derby, Derby

Andrew Stanley BSc, MSc, MRPharmS
Director of Oncology and Palliative Care Pharmacy and
Honorary Senior Lecturer in Medical Oncology,
City Hospital, Birmingham

and

Patricia Wright BPharm, MPhil, MRPharmS
Chief Operating Officer
West Middlesex University Hospital,
Isleworth, Middlesex

Radcliffe Medical Press

Radcliffe Medical Press Ltd
18 Marcham Road
Abingdon
Oxon OX14 1AA
United Kingdom

www.radcliffe-oxford.com
The Radcliffe Medical Press electronic catalogue and online ordering facility.
Direct sales to anywhere in the world.

First edition 1990
Second edition 1993
Third edition 1997

Every effort has been made to ensure the accuracy of this text, and that the best information available
has been used. This does not diminish the requirement to exercise clinical judgement, and neither the
publishers nor the authors can accept any responsibility for its use in practice.

British Library Cataloguing in Publication Data

A catalogue record for this book is available from the British Library.

ISBN 1 85775 504 9

Typeset by Advance Typesetting Ltd, Oxon
Printed and bound by Biddles Ltd, Guildford and King's Lynn

Contents

Chemotherapeutic agents

Biologicals

Adjuvant therapies

Introduction

The development of drug treatment of cancer continues to dominate research and understanding in oncology practice. Important breakthroughs in our understanding of the nature of neoplastic disease are now contributing to the development of new and better targeted cancer chemotherapeutic drugs, which are able to kill or impair susceptible tumour cells by blocking a drug-sensitive biochemical or metabolic pathway. Furthermore, we are poised at the point of massive breakthroughs in the biological and genetic treatment of cancer. These therapies and their new and respective challenges will, we are sure, dominate the fifth edition. However, our increasing understanding of these drugs has also resulted in the increasingly effective employment of agents in combination, improving clinical outcomes in a variety of conditions.

However, cytotoxic therapy inevitably has its limitations, and little progress has been made in overcoming drug toxicity, which commonly imposes severe limitations on tolerable dosing. Enhancing selectivity between neoplastic and normal cells, especially in the bone marrow and reproductive organs, remains an important challenge. Many of the agents are inevitably carcinogens and mutagens, and have been implicated in causing secondary neoplasms in patients who are being treated for cancer, and most agents cause local damage to skin and mucous membranes due to their irritant, vesicant or allergenic action.

The obvious toxicity of these drugs continues to concern staff at all levels of involvement, because of the possible hazard to healthcare workers who prepare and administer the drugs and care for patients during treatment. Guidelines for the safe handling of antineoplastic drugs continue to be strengthened as our understanding of the risks and mechanisms of exposure is further enhanced by the emergence of new evidence. There now exists worldwide a consensus view that all handling of cytotoxic drugs must be restricted to controlled environments specifically designed to minimise the risk of any form of contact, and that handling requires expertise and skills which can only be attained by adequate training. Pharmacy-operated and controlled reconstitution and preparation services in dedicated facilities – be they centralised or satellite based – should be regarded as the optimum approach to ensure staff safety and product quality at the point of administration.

Much time has been spent on researching the literature for information on drug stability, designing documentation, establishing training programmes and ensuring that facilities comply with health and safety requirements. *The Cytotoxics Handbook*, first published in 1990, was and continues to be prepared by a number of experts in the UK and elsewhere with the aim of providing a complete source of information and guidance on the provision of cytotoxic services and drug administration in oncology. In this fourth edition we have retained the core structure and content, but again the material has been extensively updated.

The compendium of monographs on injectable cytotoxic drugs has, as in previous editions, been prepared for specific use by those pharmacists and experienced pharmacy technicians who are responsible for the provision of reconstituted and ready-to-administer cytotoxic drugs. Information on stability refers to preparation in controlled environments, where the sterility of the final product can be assured. The object of each monograph is to provide the basic information relevant to the preparation, stability during storage in the primary container, stability in secondary packaging systems, administration and disposal of each drug. Use of the monographs should obviate the need for extensive literature searching and interpretation of data. The author of each monograph is named and can be consulted on specific queries. The section of monographs on Biologicals used in cancer treatment and related clinical management, such as interferon, interleukins and granulocyte-stimulating factors, has been enhanced. Finally, we have retained and updated the section on specific adjuvant therapies.

The section on investigational agents has been removed, but key drugs currently in clinical trials but unlicensed (in the UK) are now incorporated in the main list. Readers are referred to the National Cancer Institute book, *Investigational Drugs* (available from The Pharmaceutical Resources Branch, National Cancer Institute, Executive Plaza North, Suite 18, Bethesda, Maryland 20892, USA), and to specialist oncology centres for further information.

Michael Allwood
Andrew Stanley
Patricia Wright
September 2001

ACKNOWLEDGEMENT

This fourth edition is sadly to be Trish's last one as she has moved on to greater and more exciting things in the broader world of hospital management. It is true to say that we would not have reached this point without her encouragement, expertise and attention to detail. She has by her own admission moved away from the cytotoxics and cancer treatment fields. We wish her well and every success in her career, and trust she will continue to be a keen supporter of oncology pharmacy practice.

Good luck and thank you.

Michael Allwood
Andrew Stanley
September 2001

Michael Allwood
Director
Pharmacy Academic Practice Unit
University of Derby
Kingsway House
Derby DE22 3HL
e-mail: m.c.allwood@derby.ac.uk

Yaacov Cass
Regional Pharmaceutical Officer
Ministry of Health
PO Box 12052
Jerusalem
Israel 91120
e-mail: ildyaakov@mail.cc.health.gov.il

Lynnette Ferguson
Director, Centre for Mutagen Testing
Cancer Research Laboratory
Faculty of Medicine and Health Sciences
University of Auckland
Private Bag 92019
Auckland
New Zealand
e-mail: l.ferguson@auckland.ac.nz

Gerard Lee
Group Manager, Laboratories and Licensing
Medicines Control Agency
Market Towers
1 Nine Elms Lane
London SW8 5NQ
e-mail: ged.lee@mca.gov.uk

Tony Moore
Principal Pharmacist
Pharmacy Department
Royal Hallamshire Hospital
Glossop Road
Sheffield S10 2JF
e-mail: tony.moore@csuh-tr.trent.nhs.uk

Paula Myers
Drug Information Pharmacist
Pharmacy Department
The Royal Marsden Hospital
Fulham Road
London SW3 6JJ
e-mail: paula.myers@rmh-nthames.nhs.uk

Richard Needle
Chief Pharmacist
Colchester General Hospital
Turner Road
Colchester CO4 5JL
e-mail: richardneedle@essexrivers.nhs.uk

Graham Sewell
Professor of Pharmacy Practice
School of Pharmacy and Pharmacology
University of Bath
Claverton Down
Bath BA2 7AU
e-mail: prsgjs@bath.ac.uk

Robert Shaw
Director
Academic Pharmacy Practice Research Centre
The Queen's Building
University of East Anglia
Norwich NR4 7TJ
e-mail: ea.appu@uea.ac.uk

Andrew Stanley
Director of Oncology and Palliative Care Pharmacy
City Hospital
Dudley Road
Birmingham B18 7Q
e-mail: 5lewis@tinyworld.co.uk

Max Summerhayes
Principal Oncology Pharmacist
Pharmacy Department
Guy's Hospital
St Thomas Street
London SE1 9RT
e-mail: maxwell.summerhayes@gstt.sthames.nhs.uk

Alexander Tabachnik
Clinical Oncology Pharmacist
Pharmacy Division
Hadassah University Hospital
Ein Heren
Jerusalem
Israel
e-mail: tabac@hadassah.org.il

Jayne Wood
Chief Pharmacist
North Manchester General Hospital
Delauney's Road
Crumpsall
Manchester M8 5RB
e-mail: jayne.wood@mail.nmanhc-tr.nwest.nhs.uk

Patricia Wright
Chief Operating Officer
West Middlesex University Hospital
Twickenham Road
Isleworth
Middlesex TW7 6AF
e-mail: patricia.wright@wmuh-tr.nthames.nhs.uk

PART ONE: Cytotoxic services

Introduction to cytotoxic services

INTRODUCTION

When *The Cytotoxics Handbook* was first conceived over 10 years ago, there was huge variation in the way in which cytotoxics were prescribed, reconstituted and administered in the UK and worldwide.

One of the main aims of the book was to provide pharmacists with the information and tools to enable them to convince doctors, nurses, managers and pharmacy colleagues that cytotoxics should be prepared in a controlled environment, ideally under the direct control of a pharmacist.

Within the UK, the publication of the Calman–Hine Report on cancer services[1] and the recently published NHS Cancer Plan and the standards for cancer services[2] supported by Control of Substances Hazardous to Health (COSHH) regulations[3] and the development of clinical practice guidelines for the administration of cytotoxic chemotherapy,[4] have essentially established the place of cytotoxic reconstitution services. Similar developments have occurred in a number of developed countries.[5-8]

However, it is recognised that pharmacists and clinicians in other countries may still be struggling to convince hospital administrators of the importance of a cytotoxic reconstitution service. The bulk of this and the associated chapters is aimed at them. Pharmacists running established services may wish to refer to some of the sections when reviewing the scope of their service, particularly if this may involve significant capital/revenue costs, as part of large-scale development or reconfiguration.

The following sections outline a proposed, stepwise process for establishing a cytotoxic reconstitution service.

IS THERE A NEED FOR A CYTOTOXIC RECONSTITUTION SERVICE?

There are a number of areas that need to be studied in order to justify to doctors, nurses, managers and pharmacy staff the introduction of such a service. Before proceeding, the following issues should be addressed in order to establish need.

1 Range of current service and workload

▼ What is the workload?
It will be necessary to establish:
the type of preparations used
the number of individual doses administered annually

the stability of the preparations administered
the identity of the prescriber
who prepares the reconstitution and who administers the drug (is it the same person?)
how long it takes to reconstitute the preparation
if there is adequate time allowed for documentation
the preferred method of administration.
▼ Competence issues.
Are doctors and nurses adequately trained to prepare cytotoxic drugs?
▼ Health and safety.
Are existing arrangements satisfactory and appropriate for patient safety and operator protection?
▼ Risk/medicine management.
Is there a risk management approach to drug ordering, preparation and delivery?
▼ Cost.
What is the current expenditure in terms of drugs, equipment, facilities and staff?
Are there sufficient amounts of nursing and medical time which could be better utilised by providing direct patient care?
Can the value of some of the time saved be attached to the pharmacy budget?
Is drug wastage a significant financial issue (e.g. paediatrics)?
Will the provision of a pharmacy-led service reduce or increase expenditure?
▼ Quality issues.
Are preparation areas suitable?
Are there checks for drug compatibility?
What is the administration time vs. the prescribed time?
Are there interruptions in preparation or administration?
Are medication errors documented?
Are vial/ampoule contents stored and reused?
Are administration methods appropriate?
Is the duration of the injection appropriate?

2 Problems with the current service

▼ Identify existing problems and their importance.

3 Potential benefits of a reconstitution service

▼ Standardisation of drug concentration and administration route and method.
▼ Consequent reduction in errors of administration.
▼ Drug administration at the correct time and rate.
▼ Improved monitoring and control of health and safety issues.
▼ Comprehensive documentation.
▼ Increased confidence in drug stability and sterility.

4 Potential disadvantages of a reconstitution service

▼ Capital expenditure.
▼ Communication of requirements to colleagues.
▼ Distribution and storage of drugs.
▼ Increase in staff.
▼ Out-of-hours service.
▼ Increase in expenditure if commercial services are employed.

SETTING UP A WORKING PARTY

A multidisciplinary working party should be appointed. Clear objectives should be set, which are then backed up by information gathered locally to help to evaluate whether the introduction of a reconstitution service is appropriate.

1 Membership

Membership of the working party should include the following.

▼ *Clinicians*:
    medical oncologists
    clinical oncologists
    haematologists.
▼ *Nurses*:
    specialists
    nurse managers
    tutors
    community/homecare.
▼ *Pharmacy staff*:
    pharmacists (including a quality-control pharmacist)
    technicians.
▼ *Management*:
    general manager or representative
    risk manager, or member of risk management team.
▼ *Occupational health*:
    senior representative.

2 Objectives

▼ To establish and co-ordinate a pilot study in accordance with previously agreed aims and objectives.
▼ To assess the capital and revenue implications of a service and allocate resources as appropriate.
▼ To decide what type and level of service is required.
▼ To monitor the performance of the service.
▼ To formulate policy and provide advice on relevant issues.

DETERMINING WHAT TYPE OF SERVICE IS REQUIRED

When deciding on the type of service to be provided, certain areas need to be considered.

1 Workload

The volume of work, measured as individual patient doses per annum, and annual expenditure on cytotoxic chemotherapy are key considerations.

2 Range and presentation of doses

The range and pattern of cytotoxic prescribing need to be determined. The key areas to consider include the following:

▼ range of cytotoxics used
▼ stability in solution of the drugs used
▼ methods of administration (e.g. bolus injections, infusions and continuous infusions)
▼ whether treatment regimens are established
▼ whether there is any standardisation of doses.

3 Level of service

▼ Determine the level of service that pharmacy can provide.
▼ Can a total service be provided during normal working hours, or does a 24-hour service need to be established?
▼ Will 'on-call' arrangements be required?

The skill level on wards will need to be addressed as there may be a loss of skills due to the reduction or disappearance of medical or nursing preparation.

4 Quality assurance and sterility assurance

Quality assurance procedures should be agreed, documented and adhered to. In order to achieve high levels of sterility assurance, procedures should include rigorous standards for equipment maintenance, operator training and environmental monitoring.

5 Facilities

Utilise existing facilities if these are available. If they are not, convert the current facilities and purchase appropriate equipment.

6 Health and safety needs

Local and national guidelines must be adhered to (*see* Chapter 3 on health and safety).

7 Risk management

Modern risk management methods which are complementary to and compatible with the institution's clinical governance policy should be employed.

8 Funding

Resources should be identified.

▼ Can potential savings on medical and nursing time or savings on drug expenditure be utilised?
▼ Is the hospital prepared to pay for increased safety, quality and proactive risk management?

9 Personnel

Are there staff available? What is their level of expertise? Are funds available for recruitment and training?

10 Logistics

Points for consideration include the following:

▼ the physical geography of the site
▼ the number of sites that are being serviced
▼ communication and transport systems
▼ consultants' prescribing habits
▼ recovery and reuse
▼ distribution
▼ weekends
▼ costing arrangements
▼ location of inpatients and outpatients in relation to pharmacy.

11 Clinical commitment

The level of clinical involvement by pharmacy can be enhanced by providing a service. However, the level of involvement with patient care should not detract from the efficiency of the service, and will depend on the attitudes of local personnel and their managers.

RUNNING A PILOT SCHEME

A pilot scheme can provide the opportunity to test proposed procedures, gain valuable feedback from staff and collect 'local' data.

A reconstitution service is a major development, and thorough planning and research should be completed before such a service is introduced. Additional resources may well be required, or existing resources may need to be redeployed. An awareness of strategic plans is vital to ensure that an appropriate balance of commitments to resources is achieved.

SERVICE OPTIONS

A list of the possible service options (with the advantages and disadvantages of each) follows.

1 Pharmacy-controlled centralised unit

Advantages	*Disadvantages*
Existing facilities	Potential large capital cost
High sterility/stability assurance	Extended lines of communication between pharmacy/nurse/doctor
Cost/efficiency savings on a high workload	Problems of distribution to clinical areas and off-site locations
Planned workload	Slower reaction/lead times
Suitably trained/skilled staff	Out-of-hours service may not be provided
High level of operator/product protection	Potential long-term pharmacy staff exposure
Easier supervision	High level of long-term pharmacy commitment
Standardisation of presentation of doses	Loss of expertise at ward level
Comprehensive documentation	

2 Pharmacy-controlled satellite unit

Advantages	*Disadvantages*
Workload centralised in designated hospital areas	Deployment of staff away from pharmacy, with potential for increased staff requirements and labour costs
Short lines of communication	Increased stock holdings
Reduced distribution problems	Potential for greater wastage
Increased interprofessional contact	Fragmentation of pharmacy service
Ability to respond more quickly to requests	Negotiating space within another department
Cost/efficiency savings on high workload	May also be required to supply oral medication and adjuvant therapy
High sterility/stability assurance	Potential long-term pharmacy staff exposure
Easier to provide an extended-hours service	
Potential for access by non-pharmacy staff out of hours (working to strict pharmacy procedures)	
High level of operator/product protection	

3 Ward/clinic-based in an uncontrolled environment (nurse/doctor operated)

Advantages	*Disadvantages*
Status quo	Health and safety aspects/operator protection
	No product protection
	High level of wastage
	High stock holdings
	Limited pharmacy control
	No record of preparation process, and therefore no recall traceability
	Possibility of untrained staff preparing doses

4 Ward/clinic-based in a controlled environment (nurse/doctor operated)

Advantages	*Disadvantages*
Reduced pharmacy labour costs	High nursing and medical staff turnover, leading to increased training requirements
Rapid response, 24-hour service	Less time for direct patient care
Short lines of communication	Decreased assurance of sterility/stability
No distribution or delivery problems	Higher level of wastage
	Limited pharmacy control
	No record of preparation process; therefore no recall traceability
	Increased stock holdings
	Difficult to maintain high standard of quality assurance
	Pharmacy activity undertaken by non-pharmacy staff
	Management responsibilities and level of control poorly defined
	Formal accreditation/validation system would be required, which would lead to increased quality assurance costs

5 Commercial service

Advantages	Disadvantages
No additional capital or staff costs (full off-site service)	Potential for increased revenue expenditure
Provision of a full range of drugs in a ready-to-use form	
Health and safety aspects of a local reconstitution eliminated	Communication and supply logistics (if service is off site)
Standardisation of presentation of doses	Further distribution of drugs from a central delivery point to the ward/clinic
Planned workload	
Comprehensive documentation	
Minimal stock holdings	
Reduced wastage	
High sterility/stability assurance	
Existing staff can be deployed elsewhere	

SERVICE OPERATION

The following operational areas need to be considered in the cytotoxic reconstitution service. For further information, see the chapters listed in parentheses.

▼ Facilities and equipment (*see* Chapter 2).
▼ Health and safety issues (*see* Chapter 3).
▼ Documentation and training (*see* Chapter 4).

REFERENCES

1 Department of Health (1995) *A Policy Framework for Commissioning Cancer Services: a Report by the Expert Advisory Group to the Chief Medical Officers of England and Wales.* Department of Health, London.
2 Department of Health (2000) *Improving the Quality of Cancer Services.* HSC 2000/021. Department of Health, London.
3 Anon. (1999) *The Control of Substances Hazardous to Health Regulations.* HMSO, London.
4 Royal College of Nursing (RCN) (1998) *Clinical Practice Guidelines: the administration of cytotoxic chemotherapy (recommendations and technical report).* Nursing Standard Publications, Harrow.
5 Anon. (1990) AHSP technical assistance bulletin on handling cytotoxic and hazardous drugs. *Am J Hosp Pharm.* **47**: 1033–49.
6 Joint Commission on Accreditation of Healthcare Organisations (JCAHO) (1994) *Accreditation Manual for Hospitals.* JCAHO, Oakbrook Terrace, IL.
7 Daly L (1998) Safe handling of cytotoxic drugs. *Austr Nurs J.* **5**: 21–4.
8 Canadian Society of Hospital Pharmacists (1993) *CSHP Guidelines for the Safe Handling and Disposal of Hazardous Pharmaceuticals.* Canadian Society of Hospital Pharmacists, Ottawa, Canada.

2

Facilities

INTRODUCTION

The risks associated with handling and administering cytotoxic drugs have resulted in the widespread use of safety cabinets for the preparation and dispensing of these products. Such cabinets must achieve a balance between operator and product protection in order to provide adequate levels of safety for both the patient and the staff preparing and administering the drug. There are two broad options for facilities and equipment that can be used for the preparation of sterile cytotoxic doses. These are as follows:

▼ conventional cleanroom with a vertical laminar flow cabinet (VLFC)
▼ isolators in a suitable environment.

Vertical laminar flow cabinets with similar operating characteristics to Class II microbiological safety cabinets have limitations which have led to an increased use of isolators. Isolators have an advantage over cleanrooms in that they only need to be located in an EC GMP Grade D environment, and they do not need costly and time-consuming gowning procedures.

The selection of equipment and the working environment is dependent on a number of factors, including the following:

▼ expected workload
▼ existing facilities and commitments
▼ resources available (capital/revenue, personnel, etc.).

Health and safety considerations have, up until now, required cytotoxic and carcinogenic substances to be handled in negative-pressure environments, since this provides the optimum balance between operator and product protection. However, there are facilities which have used positive-pressure isolators for preparing cytotoxic injections.

There are currently ongoing discussions between the Medicines Control Agency, NHS and Health and Safety Executive on the relative merits and safety of positive- and negative-pressure isolators for this purpose. At the time of publication no definitive advice is forthcoming. Therefore this chapter is written from the standpoint of current practice, which is to use negative-pressure cabinets.

1 Vertical laminar flow cabinets

1.1 Standards

There are no nationally agreed standards in the UK for vertical laminar flow drug safety cabinets. The British Standard for Microbiological Safety Cabinets, BS 5726,

1992,[1] which is being updated and partially superceded by EN 12469, makes reference to vertical laminar flow protection cabinets, but this standard is not readily applicable to hazardous drugs for the following reasons.

▼ Bacteria have a defined mass or bulk and are of known particle size, whereas cytotoxic contaminants are of variable size and may be in a solid, liquid or gaseous state.
▼ For the materials handled in microbiological safety cabinets, operator protection is more critical than product protection.

The Australian Standard, AS 2567, 1982[2] has been written to apply only to cytotoxic cabinets. Some of the features of this standard are as follows:

▼ all potentially contaminated zones are under negative pressure
▼ all filter seals which may come into contact with potentially hazardous material are under negative pressure with respect to the uncontaminated zones
▼ stainless steel construction
▼ incorporation of carbon exhaust filter.

In Germany, a 'cytostatic workstation' is defined in a document describing principles of operation and test procedures, GS-GES-04, published by the Professional Association of Health Service and Welfare Care[3] (GS DIN 12590). Filters are tested to DIN standard 24184 and are of 99.99% efficiency. These work stations are essentially compact laminar downflow cabinets with a front visor that has two apertures for the worker to access the work zone. Although manufacturers vary the machine dimensions and number of filters used, the principles and tests in GS-GES-04 are common to all. In the USA, the American Society of Hospital Pharmacists has produced guidelines on cytotoxic drug handling.[4] Laminar downflow safety cabinets that comply with US National Sanitation Foundation Standards[5] are described.

1.2 Operating principles

A vertical downflow of laminar-flow air, filtered through a High Efficiency Particle Entrapment (HEPA) filter (efficiency 99.997% in UK and 99.990% in Germany), passes over the work surface. The air then passes through vents at the front and back of the cabinet and is recirculated. Depending on the manufacturer, there may be one or more filters in the recirculation and exhaust air flows. Approximately 30% of the recirculated air is exhausted from the cabinet and, to compensate for this, air is drawn in through the front opening. This creates a negative pressure within the cabinet. The balance between the cabinet downflow and the air drawn in at the front of the cabinet produces an air curtain, which is the basis of the operator and product protection properties of the cabinet. The air exhausted from the cabinet may be recirculated into the room or ducted to the outside, subject to local health and safety guidance.

A carbon exhaust filter is not a true filter, but rather a gas adsorption cell that can be subject to channelling. It can release carbon particles into the room, and it is not possible to test the adsorption capacity non-destructively. There seems to be little need for a carbon exhaust filter, particularly if the air exhaust is ducted to the outside.

1.3 General comments on VLFCs

Where cabinets are sited in aseptic suites, product protection is simplified because the cabinet itself is in an EC GMP Grade B environment.[6] If it is situated in a dispensary or on a ward, local air turbulence will be a more critical factor in determining operator and product protection than the cabinet's design. Since isolators are now commonly available, it is recommended that they should be the cabinets of choice in such areas. UK, US, Australian and German cabinets are not strictly comparable, and it is necessary to ensure that equipment complies with regulatory requirements in the country of use.

Recent reports on exposure to cytotoxic drugs have questioned the effectiveness of using HEPA filters alone for exhaust filtration from cytotoxic cabinets. This may be of particular concern where recycling of air into the room is involved.[7] As no conclusions have yet been drawn from the studies, it is premature to give definitive advice. It is therefore advisable to refer to the most recent literature available at the time of reading.

2 Isolators

2.1 Standards

Within the UK there is now a guidance document on isolators for pharmaceutical applications.[8] This refers to design principles and operational characteristics for negative-pressure (type 2) isolators that can be used for handling cytotoxic drugs. BS 5726[1] includes a reference to Class III containment microbiological safety cabinets. The International Standards Organisation Committee ISO TC 209 is currently reviewing the standard for cleanrooms and clean air equipment to include isolators within a section on enhanced separation devices.

2.2 Operating principles

Isolators are enclosed workstations supplied with filtered air which should meet EC GMP Class A[6] in the controlled workspace. Operators use either glove ports or a half-suit arrangement to access the working area, and materials are introduced through a transfer device. Isolators can be of a rigid or flexible structure, and their design can have a considerable impact on their potential use, as well as on operating, monitoring and disinfection procedures.

Transfer devices include rigid boxes (filtered or unfiltered air supply), rapid-transfer docking ports or another isolator which can be connected to the main working enclosure. Many different designs exist and are acceptable. The choice of device will depend on the design of the isolator, the application for which it is to be used, and the external environment of the isolator. Appendix 1 provides information on UK isolator manufacturers.

2.3 Flexible film isolators

The dimensions and configurations of flexible isolators are variable, as there are a large number of working, bank, transfer and sterilisation chambers marketed. Companies will meet the design needs of the customer.

Design characteristics: Flexible film isolators have an enclosure made entirely of flexible PVC film supported on a chrome or stainless-steel framework. Sizes can vary, and two-, three- or four-glove-port models, and half-suit or double-half-suit designs are available. Inlet and outlet air is HEPA filtered (99.997% efficiency in UK models), and the air supply can be designed so that the working environment is under positive or negative pressure. The air supply is not necessarily laminar flow, and it normally provides the controlled workspace with no fewer than 20 air changes per hour. By their very nature, flexible isolators are more easily damaged and therefore require care during use.

The half-suit system offers greater flexibility and all-round movement, but appears at first to be claustrophobic. The suits are double-layered and are fed with an air supply that both inflates and lifts the suit so that it does not press against the operator, while providing a flow of air across the face and body.

When operating under negative pressure, flexible film isolators may require extra support frames, and the relative pressures may cause ingress of contaminated air if the PVC canopy is damaged. Monitoring procedures must therefore be capable of detecting pin-hole leaks.

Flexible film isolators are available from a large number of cleanroom equipment manufacturers, to a wide range of specifications.

2.4 Rigid isolators

The walls of the cabinet are rigid with an enclosed workspace. The inlet air and outlet air supplies are HEPA filtered (99.997% efficiency in UK models), and the air can be turbulent or laminar flow. The front panel is typically constructed of clear plastic and may be fitted with up to four glove ports. Standard models available from UK manufacturers are listed below.

Amercare Ltd:

A range of standard and bespoke negative- and positive-pressure units is available, including the following.

Compact range (CIN): a two-module isolator consisting of a transfer chamber and a process isolator, which is fitted with two, three or four glove ports, and is available in both exhaust and recirculating models.

Code	Width (mm)	Depth (mm)	Height (mm)	Work surface area w × d (mm)
CIN22P	1220	600	2000	800 × 600
CIN23P	1620	600	2000	1200 × 600
CIN24P	2020	600	2000	1600 × 600

Compact throughflow range (CTN): a three-module isolator consisting of two transfer chambers and a process isolator, which is fitted with two, three or four glove ports, and is available in both exhaust and recirculating models.

Code	Width (mm)	Depth (mm)	Height (mm)	Work surface area w × d (mm)
CTN22P	1640	600	2000	800 × 600
CTN23P	2040	600	2000	1200 × 600
CTN24P	2420	600	2000	1600 × 600

Full compact range (FCN): a three-module isolator consisting of two-glove-port manipulating transfer chamber and a process isolator, which is fitted with two, three or four glove ports and is available in both exhaust and recirculating models.

Code	Width (mm)	Depth (mm)	Height (mm)	Work surface area w × d (mm)
FCN24P	2020	600	2000	800 × 600
FCN25P	2420	600	2000	1200 × 600
FCN26P	2820	600	2000	1600 × 600

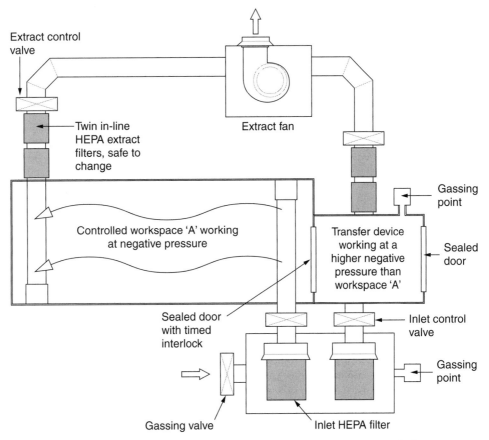

Figure 2.1: *Schematic diagram of airflow within an Amercare negative pressure isolator*

Filters: Filters are cylindrical cartridge filters, 145 mm in diameter and 160 mm in length (two in line, sealed top and bottom, safe change).

Design characteristics: These isolators are rigid 4-mm-thick stainless steel constructions. The inlet air supply is HEPA filtered (99.997% efficient). All enclosures are under negative pressure, air being drawn through the system into the controlled workspace through small-bore distribution tubes, creating rapid turbulent flow. Air is either ducted to outside, or units can be designed to recirculate air. Inner and outer door sets are fitted with timed interlocks and are pneumatically sealed.

The air change rate in the work zone of each of the cabinets is 100 m³/hour and in the transfer chamber is 70 m³/hour.

Figure 2.1 shows the airflow pattern of a compact isolator with Class D transfer device.

Amercare isolators are suitable for gaseous sterilisation with formaldehyde, Citanox® and vapourised hydrogen peroxide. They are also compatible with 70% aqueous industrial methylated spirit, 70% aqueous isopropyl alcohol and peracetic acid.

Envair UK Limited:

CDC 'C'

Cabinet dimensions:

	Width (mm)	Depth (mm)	Height (mm)
Two-glove recirculating	2432	695	2430
Two-glove ducted	2432	695	2280
Four-glove recirculating	3030	695	2430
Four-glove ducted	3030	695	2280

Work surface area:

	Width (mm)	Depth (mm)
Two glove	1097	480
Four glove	1700	480

Filters:

	Width (mm)	Depth (mm)	Height (mm)
Downflow HEPA (minipleat):			
Two glove	1220	508	66
Four glove	1828	508	150
Main (primary exhaust) HEPA (minipleat)			
Two glove	1130	456	66
Four glove	860	456	124 (×2)
Secondary exhaust HEPA (minipleat)	590	420	66
Hatch HEPAs	460	320	66
Pre-filters	600	180	25

The filters are sealed on the upstream and downstream faces

Design characteristics: The CDC 'C' is a rigid, polyester-coated mild steel carcase with an electropolished 316 stainless-steel work surface. Two or four glove ports are fitted into the front viewing panel, which is pneumatically assisted and may be lifted to allow the installation of large pieces of equipment. The cabinet is supplied with vertical laminar flow HEPA-filtered air (99.997% efficient), and is fitted with dual-exhaust HEPA filters. The air supply provides approximately 1800 air changes per hour in the two- and four-glove unit.

Transfer devices constructed of polyester-coated stainless steel are fitted on the side panels of the cabinet and are independently flushed with HEPA-filtered air, providing 3400 changes per hour.

Airflow patterns for controlled work zone and the transfer hatch of the Containair cabinet with a C2-type[7] transfer hatch are shown in Figure 2.2.

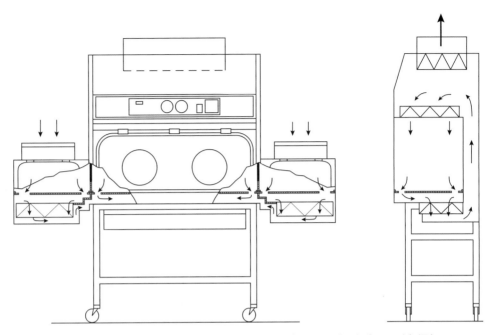

Figure 2.2: *Airflow diagrams for Envair CDC 'C' two-glove negative isolator with 'D'-type transfer chambers*

Medical Air Technology Limited (MAT)

Isomat 2

Cabinet dimensions:

	Width (mm)	Depth (mm)	Height (mm)
Two glove	2400	630	2040
Four glove	3200	630	2040

Work surface area:

	Width (mm)	Depth (mm)
Two glove approximately	1200	600
Four glove approximately	2000	600

Filters:

	Width (mm)	Depth (mm)	Height (mm)
Downflow HEPA (minipleat)	1090	500	66
Exhaust HEPA (minipleat)	900	305	88

The filters are sealed (gel-seal) on the upstream and downstream faces

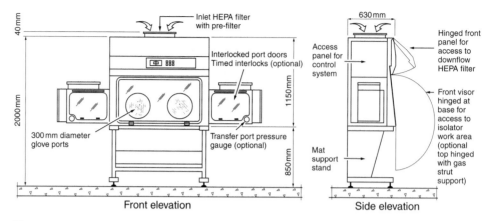

Figure 2.3: *MAT type 1 pharmaceutical isolator*

Design characteristics: The Isomat is a rigid, powder-coated mild steel carcase with a stainless-steel work chamber and work surface. The front viewing panel is hinged, and may be opened to allow the installation of large pieces of equipment. The cabinet is available in recirculating or total exhaust versions, the recirculating version having a second exhaust HEPA filter in-line. The air supply to the controlled workspace provides 1800 air changes per hour, and 400 changes per hour to the transfer device.

The airflow to the controlled work zone and the transfer device is shown diagrammatically in Figure 2.3.

TPC Microflow

Cytoflow isolators

The standard range of isolators that is available includes a two-glove model with either one or two transfer chambers, and a four-glove model with two transfer chambers.

Cabinet dimensions:

	Width (mm)	Depth (mm)	Height (mm)
Two glove	1700	550	2100
Four glove	2700	550	2100

Work surface area:

	Width (mm)	Depth (mm)
Two glove	900	550
Four glove	1900	550

Filters: Inlet HEPA filters (99.995% efficient) are sealed downstream. There are dual-exhaust HEPA filters (99.995% efficiency). The first of these filters is downstream sealed and the second is upstream sealed. All filters are safe change. Air change rates to the transfer devices are 200/hour.[1]

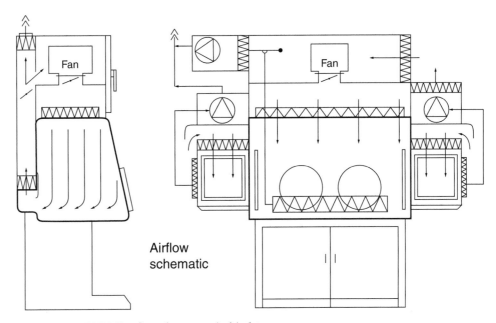

Airflow
schematic

Figure 2.4: *TPC Microflow pharmaceutical isolator*

Design characteristics: The cytoflow isolator work zone operates at low positive pressure (20 Pa) with unidirectional airflow. The two transfer chambers run at low negative pressure. An emergency button will switch the isolator to negative pressure and sound an audible alarm.

The work chamber is manufactured from polished stainless steel, and the front visor is 10-mm toughened glass.

Filters are changed from within the isolator using a safe-change bagging technique. Power supplies can be fitted to the chamber. Sterilisation and disinfection can be achieved with formaldehyde, Citanox®, or by alcoholic surface treatment. *See* Figure 2.4.

Bassaire Containments Ltd

Bassaire high-integrity isolator

Cabinet dimensions:

	Width (mm)	Depth (mm)	Height (mm)
Two glove	1600	775	2000
Three glove	2000	775	2000
Four glove	2500	775	2000

Work surface area:

	Width (mm)	Depth (mm)
Two glove	800	650
Three glove	1200	650
Four glove	1700	650

Filters: Downflow HEPA

	Width *(mm)*	Depth *(mm)*	Height *(mm)*
Two glove	525	457	66
Three glove	915	457	66
Four glove	1425	457	66

Design characteristics: The Bassaire isolator is a rigid cabinet constructed of 316 stainless steel and fitted with Class D hatches.[8] The front visor is bolted on and the hatches are fitted with vertical sliding doors. The cabinet is available in a recirculating or total exhaust version. The air supply to the controlled workspace provides 1800–2000 air changes/hour.

A schematic diagram of the airflow to the controlled workspace and the transfer device of the total exhaust version is shown in Figure 2.5.

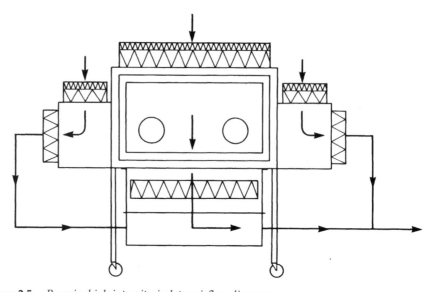

Figure 2.5: *Bassaire high integrity isolator airflow diagram*

2.5 *General comments on isolators*

Rigid isolators are relatively easy to clean and disinfect using hard-surface disinfectants. As they may be used in an unclassified environment and will operate under negative pressure, high-efficiency seals in all cabinets are essential.

In addition, units with non-unidirectional airflow may have dead spots within the EC GMP Grade A area.[6] Purging of contaminants from the cabinets is largely dependent on air turbulence created within the cabinet.

3 Sterilisation and sanitisation of internal surfaces

Gaseous sterilisation is a practical method of sterilising isolators, some of which are designed with this purpose in mind. The filtered output air is ducted to the outside above the roof of the building, or the exhaust air is passed through a suitable chemi-sorbant filter pack, which adds considerably to the cost.

It is possible to link two or more flexible isolators via the transfer ports. Components, containers and equipment can be surface-sterilised by gaseous sterilisation in one isolator overnight, and then transferred the following day to the adjoining isolator prior to use.

Formaldehyde, peracetic acid and hydrogen peroxide vapour are the usual sterilants. Peracetic acid is the most effective and easy to use, but is also the most toxic sterilant. Formaldehyde is absorbed by PVC, and therefore time must be allowed for the gas to desorb from the canopy.

It is possible to validate sterilisation cycles that use gaseous sterilants, but many problems are associated with this process, and there is still little information about it in the published literature.

Gaseous sterilisation cannot be recommended for the surface sterilisation of articles within isolators unless the user can fully validate the system with regard to gas desorption from packaging, closures, syringes, etc. There is also a risk of gas entry into drug or diluent containers if stress cracks are present, or if the closure of individual containers is not guaranteed to be impervious to gas ingress.

Any sterilisation process will be ineffective unless adequate cleaning has preceded it. Any spillages of nutrient solutions will provide ideal growth media for bacteria, and will also protect bacteria from the effects of sterilants.

In the UK, COSHH regulations[9] require that a safe and effective means of gas desorption, removal and disposal must be included in any protocol for use of sterilisation equipment.

Sanitisation of small flexible film isolators by hard-surface disinfectants is not precluded, but the effect of the alcoholic sprays on PVC film needs to be evaluated. Chlorhexidine-based alcoholic sprays should be used with caution, or not at all, as a film of chlorhexidine residue builds up on surfaces, which can potentially cause contamination of solutions.

For rigid isolators, surface sanitisation with an alcoholic solution is the simplest and quickest option, but some manufacturers do not advocate the practice. However, direct questioning has revealed that the reservations which have been expressed relate to long-term soaking in alcoholic solutions leading to crazing of some types of clear plastic. The routine use of alcohol solutions by swab or spray applications with subsequent rapid evaporation is not regarded as problematic.

Sanitisation is not a validated sterilisation process, and is not guaranteed to leave surfaces free from viable micro-organisms. Although alcohols are very effective against vegetative organisms, they have no sporicidal activity.

4 Gauntlets and glove ports (*see also* Chapter 3)

All isolators, whether they be rigid, flexible film or half-suit isolators, are accessed via a glove port. These are glove/sleeve arrangements designed to maintain the aseptic environment within the isolator. Several types of gauntlets and glove/sleeve systems, made from various materials, are available, and careful selection will be necessary.

Gloves and gauntlets used with isolators should at the very minimum comply with the limits for perforations specified in BS 4005: 1984, the British Standard for sterile latex gloves[10] or its equivalent international standard. Because pin-holes are unavoidable, the integrity of the gloves and gauntlets should be tested frequently. Most manufacturers of isolators have a simple, relatively inexpensive device available for this purpose.

4.1 Gauntlets

These are one-piece, full-arm-length gloves. They are available in a range of materials. Pin-holes do occur, as manufacturers are not always aware of the need for stringent testing for perforations during manufacturing.

Gauntlets are usually changed on a weekly (or less frequent) basis due to the high cost, resulting in a potential risk of drug penetration and poor general hygiene, as a number of operators will use the same gloves. For these reasons, double-gloving is generally used. However, as gauntlets do not fit well, particularly under conditions of negative pressure, operator sensitivity will be reduced. They are normally thicker than surgeons' latex gloves, which may offset the risk of drug penetration to some extent. They are not normally available pre-sterilised.

4.2 Glove/sleeve systems

These are multi-component systems that generally consist of a replaceable sleeve piece, a connecting cuff piece and the glove. The sleeve should be mechanically strong enough to remain in position without deterioration for a number of weeks. It should not be too rigid to allow comfortable working, and it should be resistant to chemical attack. The cuff piece should allow an easy, safe, aseptic glove change-over.

A glove/sleeve system allows gloves of an appropriate specification, particularly with regard to perforations and pin-holes, to be used. It will, if correctly designed, allow the individual operator to fit and change gloves of correct size as frequently as necessary and enable the glove material to be altered without jeopardising the isolator environment. The risk of drug penetration can be minimised in this way, and general hygiene is improved, as each operator can fit a fresh sterile pair of gloves each time the equipment is used.

5 Monitoring

Aseptic preparation facilities in hospitals enable the preparation of injections in controlled environments with greater assurance of sterility. The *British Pharmacopoeia* currently recommends that unpreserved injections, prepared aseptically from sterile ingredients, should have a 24-hour shelf-life. Furthermore, the product licences of lyophilised injections often restrict their shelf-lives to 24 hours after reconstitution. The overriding reason for the 24-hour shelf-life is the risk of microbial contamination of the product during preparation or reconstitution. However, in centralised cytotoxic dispensing facilities, where a licensed sterile product is used for the preparation of sterile medication and is prepared under conditions of good manufacturing/dispensing practice in suitably monitored and audited premises, the shelf-life may be extended beyond 24 hours, provided that the microbiological integrity of the process has been validated and the physicochemical stability of the product justifies it.

It is therefore essential that a monitoring programme is implemented to:

▼ confirm that aseptic dispensing facilities continuously meet performance requirements
▼ indicate and identify system breakdown before product sterility is affected.

Such a programme will include physical tests of the cabinets and isolators and the surrounding environment, in addition to active and passive microbial sampling of the controlled environment.

Units should determine their optimum programme for monitoring of facilities. The frequency of testing will be a function of the design of the facility, and will be dependent on the workload and frequency of service use. Data obtained during commissioning studies will help to decide the frequency of monitoring. Each unit should agree a programme of daily, weekly, monthly, quarterly and annual testing, which should be implemented and all of the results documented. Each of these programmes should be a combination of the following tests.

5.1 Physical tests

These should include the following:

▼ pressure differentials
▼ alarm checks
▼ integrity tests
▼ airflow
▼ particle counts
▼ leak tests
▼ operator protection test (KI Discus test).

5.2 Microbiological tests

These should include the following:

▼ settle plates
▼ surface swabs
▼ airborne viable counts
▼ finger dab plates.

For some tests (e.g. pressure differentials), daily data will be expected. Tests such as the installation leak tests need only be undertaken annually. However, other tests should be carried out at more frequent intervals.

Testing of VLFCs is similar to that for horizontal LFCs, but in addition to particle counts and filter challenge tests, operator protection factors should be measured regularly. Particle counts and filter challenge tests are equally applicable to isolators. Furthermore, there is a need to monitor for pin-holes and defects in gloves, and in the canopies of flexible isolators, so regular leak tests are also required. Suggested limits for the monitoring results are given in Table 2.1. These limits are based on those in the EC GMP guide,[6] in BS 5295,[11] and on those in the Parenteral Society's technical monograph on environmental microbiological contamination in controlled environments.[12] Because of the imprecision of the methods, expected low

Table 2.1: *Environmental monitoring: centralised cytotoxic dispensing services – limits for physical testing and target microbiological levels*

	Controlled areas		Laminar flow	Isolators	
	Filling room	Change area		Controlled workspace	Transfer device
Pressure differentials[11]	>10 Pa between classified area and adjacent area of lower classification >15 Pa between classified and unclassified area				
Airborne particle counts[6,11] (particles/m³)					
> 0.5 μ	3500	350 000	3500	3500	350 000
> 5 μ	0	2000	0	0	2000
> 10 μ	0	450	0	0	450
Airflow velocity/ exchange rate[1,7,11]	>20 air changes/ hour				
Installation leak test[11]			Vertical 0.30 ± 0.05 m/s Maximum concentration 0.001%	Maximum concentration 0.001%	
Settle plates[12] (90 mm: 4-hour exposure)	5	20	1 per 2 plates	1 per 2 plates	5
Surface swabs[12] (55-mm plate)	5		2	2	
Airborne viable[6,12] counts (cfu/m³)	10	100	<1	<1	10

Notes:

1 Where a number of classified areas are connected in cascade, the differential over-pressure need not exceed 30 Pa so long as an over-pressure can be demonstrated between each classified area.[11]
2 Airborne particle counts will only be possible in transfer devices that allow access by monitoring equipment.
3 If settle plates are exposed for less than 4 hours, target levels should be adjusted accordingly.
4 The source documents for each of the limits are referenced. Where no reference is indicated, the limit is suggested best practice.

levels of contamination and the natural variability of the levels, the microbiological data require extremely careful analysis. It is recommended that the levels shown in Table 2.1 are regarded as target levels. Exceeding target levels on isolated occasions may not require more action than examination of control systems. However, the frequency with which the limit is exceeded should be examined, and should be low. If the frequency is high or shows an upward trend, then action should be taken.

6 Summary

Isolators offer significant advantages over cleanrooms for small-scale, aseptic operations. They can be housed in an EC GMP Grade D cleanroom, and a minimum of gowning is required. Revenue and maintenance costs are substantially lower than for conventional cleanrooms. Rigid isolators are generally fairly compact and not designed for industrial-scale use. However, these cabinets are very suitable for small-scale operations, and particularly for one-off aseptic dispensing operations, since sanitisation is quick and easy and materials can be introduced very simply.

Flexible isolators address the problem of space but create other problems, such as the detection of pin-holes (particularly when under negative pressure), sanitisation, and loading ready for use. Ideally they need to be loaded for a complete session of work, and rapid, aseptic transfer of items that have been omitted is not easy.

The problems of turbulence due to the immediate environment or to the operator limit the effectiveness of VLFCs as cytotoxic dispensing cabinets. Isolators offer an enclosed work area. Aseptic transfer into and out of isolators is more complicated than for VLFCs, as there is no simple front aperture. In this respect the transfer hatches of the rigid isolators have an advantage over docking ports.

Isolators should be sited within a designated room which provides an appropriate external environment to the isolator.[8] When installing VLFCs and isolators with external ducting, there may be problems with regard to filtration of the air supply to the cabinet and balancing of air pressures within the room in which the cabinet is sited. Adequate consideration should also be given to the discharge of the exhaust duct.

Gaseous sterilisation should only be used on those cabinets that are fitted with external ducting or other appropriate means of removal of the toxic sterilant gas. Isolators that lend themselves to sanitisation with hard-surface disinfectants and do not require fumigation with formaldehyde or peracetic acid are generally preferred by users and allow more flexibility.

For very large-scale operations and for batch manufacturing, a traditional cleanroom may be preferable because of the flexibility it allows, but the costs of operation will be higher and the increased risk potential should be recognised.

The choice of gloves and glove changing procedures is an important practical consideration, and should be thoroughly investigated before purchasing decisions are made.

It should be possible to change gloves without loss of EC GMP Grade A[6] conditions within the isolator.

FACILITIES FOR NON-STERILE CYTOTOXIC DRUG MANIPULATION

Cytotoxic chemotherapy regimens often include oral cytotoxic preparations, and healthcare personnel should be aware of the potential hazards when handling them. Care in the supply and administration of solid dosage forms is essential to ensure that staff and (when appropriate) patients and their carers are given suitable advice on the safe handling of cytotoxic drugs.

Developments in paediatric oncology have resulted in more babies and young children receiving cytotoxic chemotherapy. The treatment regimens for these patients can result in doses being prescribed that cannot be administered in commercially available solid oral dosage forms. In addition, liquid oral preparations are often required for babies and children, and also for adult patients who are unable to swallow solid dosage forms.

The extemporaneous preparation of medicines containing cytotoxic drugs must be avoided whenever possible. In addition, any manipulation of dosage forms on wards which may cause release of a drug into the atmosphere should be discouraged.

Any dosage manipulation or extemporaneous preparation must be restricted to the pharmacy department.

The extemporaneous preparation of any liquid oral or other non-parenteral cytotoxic drug should be performed in such a way that the operator is protected from dust from capsules, tablets and powders, and from aerosols of liquids.

Facilities for non-sterile manipulation of cytotoxic preparations need to provide satisfactory levels of operator protection, but product protection is less critical as product sterility is no longer necessary.

The use of appropriate personal protective clothing is essential, and the preparation should be performed in fume cupboards or containment enclosures.

1 Fume cupboards

Fume cupboards and exhaust hoods with a negative air inflow and a filtered or ducted exhaust airflow will provide suitable working environments. In the UK, fume cupboards should comply with the British Standard for fume cupboards BS 7258, 1990.[13] This standard, in its various parts, covers safety and performance, design and installation and use and maintenance of laboratory fume cupboards. An ancillary document, BS DD191,[14] describes methods for testing such equipment. However, such installations are not always appropriate to hospital pharmacy departments, since they are bulky, of fixed construction, and require ducted exhaust airflow. Some smaller benchtop designs are now available that have a filtered air outlet, but their size and bulk can still be a problem.

2 Enclosed workstations

Another option is the use of glove-box containment cabinets. These are simplified, smaller designs of isolators with sealed glove ports. Inlet and outlet air supplies are HEPA filtered, and they also have activated carbon exhaust filters. Such cabinets are available from Amercare Ltd, Envair and Miller-Howe. They can be freestanding or benchtop units. However, they are bulky (typically (w × d × h) 600 × 600 × 800 mm), expensive and not easily moved, and their class F[11] environment is an unnecessary luxury for handling non-sterile cytotoxic manipulations.

The Envair Micro Iso workstation can be fitted with a type D transfer chamber, and in this format may be suitable for small-scale aseptic manipulations.

3 Portable containment or extraction systems

Benchtop, negative-pressure extraction systems which are portable or movable and allow flexibility are preferred. They should have a filtered exhaust air supply, and the velocity of the inlet airflow should give satisfactory operator protection. Systems are available that provide a localised contained workstation or localised extraction at low cost.

It should be recognised that these systems are not designed to the same specification as clean air devices, and they may not provide total containment of any dust generated. The system should be evaluated and its suitability for its intended task confirmed.

Gelman Sciences

Safetech fume bubble FX1 (see Figure 2.6)

Dimensions: (w × d × h) 500 × 600 × 580 mm.

Weight: 15 kg.

Volume: 0.053 m³.

Work surface area: 1500 cm².

Filters: Exhaust filter cartridges are available as either HEPA, activated carbon, or a combination. Filter cartridges have a 5-μ pre-filter. The HEPA filter is 99.997% efficient.

Design characteristics: This safety cabinet is a spherical, clear, acrylic construction with two hand ports. Air is drawn through the hand ports and is exhausted via the filter. The minimum negative air velocity at the hand ports is 0.7 m/s.

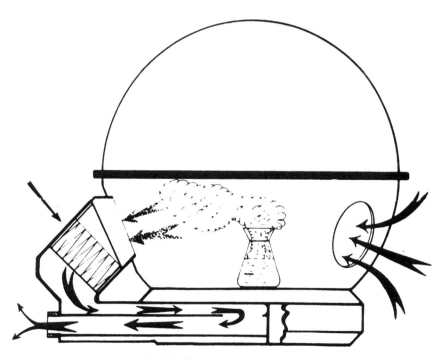

Figure 2.6: *Safetech fume bubble FX1 (Gelman Sciences)*

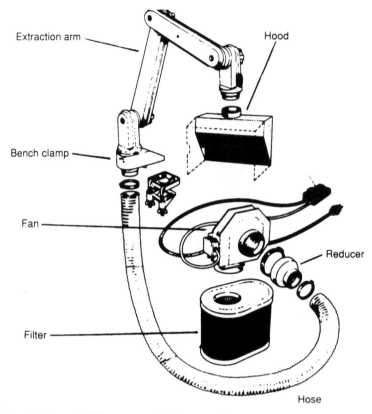

Figure 2.7: *Nederman 2000 extractor (Nederman Ltd)*

Nederman Ltd

Nederman 2000 extractor (see Figure 2.7)

Dimensions: (w × d × h) 385 × 175 × 272 mm.

Weight: 10 kg.

Filters: The filter consists of a particle filter and an activated carbon filter, of dimensions (w × d × h) 288 × 388 × 285 mm. The particle filtration is 99.97% efficient.

Design characteristics: The extractor is a multicomponent system. An aluminium rectangular hood which covers the work area clips onto a polypropylene extraction arm, which in turn is clamped to the working surface and can be pivoted about its foot for manoeuvrability. It is connected via a 2.5 m PVC flexible hose to the fan which is attached to the exhaust filter. The fan fits directly onto the filter element, and the total depth of the fan and filter is 555 mm.

Industri Filter UK

Alsident system

Work surface area: dome 350 mm in diameter; canopy 150 × 200 mm.

Filters: Available both as a two-stage filter (which consists of a pre-filter and a HEPA filter) and a three-stage filter (which has a carbon filter as well as a pre-filter and HEPA filter).

Design characteristics: A filter unit is connected by flexible tubing to an extraction tube. This consists of short lengths of 50-mm-diameter rigid aluminium or polypropylene tubes connected together with polypropylene swivel joints. The extraction tube is clamped onto the work surface and terminates in a circular extraction dome or a rectangular extraction canopy.

DISPOSABLES

1 Introduction

Despite the range of items available for drug reconstitution, transport and disposal, the overriding aim when selecting disposables for use with cytotoxic drugs should be suitability, safety and simplicity. The devices listed in this chapter meet all three criteria, although the choice of particular items will depend on the level of service provided. The cost of many of the devices may seem prohibitive, but their use can be justified for health and safety reasons. No one particular manufacturer is recommended – the choice is left to each individual. Most hospital supplies departments stock a wide range of disposables.

2 Syringes and administration systems

It is recommended that syringes used for cytotoxic drugs be luer-lock and made of polypropylene, as the material is chemically inert.[15,16] Styrene syringes are specifically not recommended for cytotoxic drugs. Standards for syringes are given in BSEN ISO 7886.[17]

Syringes are usually made in three parts, namely the barrel and piston of plastic materials and the plunger of rubber. Certain grades of rubber have been found to release water-soluble materials on prolonged contact with drug solutions.[18,19] Therefore, chemical interactions between rubber extractives and the drugs may occur. If it is intended to store drugs in a particular brand of syringe for prolonged periods, it is advisable to check that there are no such interactions. Two-piece polypropylene luer-lock syringes are available, which overcome the possibility of an interaction between plunger and drug. In addition to ensuring that a drug is stable on storage, it is necessary to check that there is not an unacceptable degree of water loss from the syringe.[20]

Syringes must be fitted with blind-hub closures, not needles, when prepared in the pharmacy. The blind hubs should be luer-lock and a good fit, and must not permit leakage. They should be of a suitable size for medical and nursing staff to be able to remove them safely.

Instillations of cytotoxic drugs are better presented in syringes or containers with catheter tips. Some bladder syringes have luer-lock connections in addition to the usual catheter tip. However, the addition of a luer-lock fitting to a bladder irrigation container may be potentially hazardous, as it could facilitate intravenous administration of the bladder irrigation solution. Catheter-tip adaptors with luer-lock connections which can be used with syringes, and fittings to convert a mini-bag into a bladder instillation device are available in some countries. Several closed-system devices which allow the reconstitution and direct administration of the drug are also available.

Information on disposables used in ambulatory pumps can be found in Chapter 5.

3 Needles and filtration systems

3.1 Needles and quills

When removing solutions from vials or ampoules, it is essential to use a needle with as wide a bore as possible in order to prevent undue pressure building up in the system. This is particularly important with viscous solutions such as etoposide. Specifications for needles are included in BSEN ISO 7864.[21] The length of the needle used will depend on the nature of the procedure being performed.

Butterfly needles, which consist of a winged needle attached to a length of tubing with a luer-lock connector at the end, can be useful for multiple additions or withdrawals from infusion bags or vials. They are available in standard needle sizes. However, devices with one-way valves and luer-lock connections are easier and safer to use than systems such as butterfly needles for multiple additions and withdrawals.

Quills are useful for drawing up solutions from ampoules, the rate of flow being greater than with a needle.

3.2 Filtration systems

Sterilising filters are not recommended for use with solutions of cytotoxic drugs because of the risk of pressurising the system (*see* section below on reconstitution devices and air vents). If a solution requires clarification, a filter with a pore size of not less than 5 µm can be used, but with great caution. Filter straws are quills with a 5- or 10-µm filter attached. Filters are not recommended for use with etoposide as there is a potential chemical interaction with the material of which most filters are made.[22]

4 Reconstitution devices and air vents

The hazard of aerosol production during the preparation of cytotoxic drugs is well recognised. To prevent the risk of exposure to individuals performing cytotoxic drug reconstitution, substantial positive or negative deviations from atmospheric pressure within drug vials and syringes should be avoided.[15,16,23] The practice of using needles to 'vent' cytotoxic drug vials is not recommended because the risk of exposure is high. 'Venting' of cytotoxic drug vials can be performed in any of the following ways.

▼ *Using a negative-pressure procedure:* The negative-pressure procedure described by Wilson and Solimando[24] requires consistent and impeccable technique. Some operatives find it difficult to maintain, and it may not always be possible with partially pressurised vials.
▼ *Using a non-filtered air vent:* Even though these equilibrate the pressure within the system, they are not recommended because of the risk of escape of cytotoxic drug.

▼ *Using a reconstitution device:* A number of reconstitution devices are available, but not all of them are suitable for use with cytotoxic drugs. The devices usually have a short, fine plastic spike attached to a filter. Spikes can make large holes in rubber bungs, with the possibility of leakage of the solution from around the spike. In addition, there is a risk of producing a 'core' of rubber. Where devices with spikes are used for cytotoxic drug reconstitution, they should be single-use only and the spike should not constitute more than 50% of the surface area of the rubber bung of the vial. Reconstitution devices are useful for the repeated aspiration of measured volumes of diluent by syringe.

▼ *Using a hydrophobic filter-needle unit:* Several types are available that incorporate a 0.2-μ hydrophobic filter supplied as a reconstitution device or a unit which can be used separately. The latter type can be difficult to use with smaller vials, as both the filter unit and the needle of the reconstituting syringe need to be accommodated in the rubber bung of the vial. Hydrophobic filter-needle units are relatively expensive, but it is prudent to balance cost against increased safety to the individual.

5 Incidental items

5.1 Cleaning equipment

All cleaning equipment should only be used in the designated cytotoxic reconstitution area. Any cloths, sponges or mop-heads can be used provided that they are low-lint. Cleaning equipment should be disposable. If there are several areas to be cleaned, the use of colour coding may be applicable.

5.2 Trays

These can be used for many purposes, including collection of waste inside an isolator or VLFC, as a confined environment for cytotoxic drug reconstitution and for setting up each preparation prior to reconstitution. Trays are available in a variety of materials and sizes, and it is important that they can be easily cleaned or sterilised, depending on their use.

5.3 Absorbent mats

These are used for lining work surfaces. Their use in VLFCs is not ideal, because recirculation of air is hampered, but they may have a use in isolators. Their ease of disposal once contaminated is an advantage. Any absorbent material of suitable size can be used so long as it can be sterilised for use within an aseptic area.

5.4 Tamper-evident seals

The injection ports of infusion bags and the tops of infusion bottles should ideally be sealed after addition of a drug or reconstitution. This prevents the further addition of drugs, and indicates any loss of integrity during storage and transport. A variety of caps and seals are commercially available.

5.5 Packaging

All cytotoxic preparations should be packed in leak-proof containers after preparation. Polythene tubing, which can be heat sealed to give an air/water-tight seal and which can be cut to enclose any size or shape of container, is recommended.

Grip-top bags should be avoided, as the seal is easily broken. Opaque polythene can be used for drugs that require light protection. Polythene of gauge 200–250 g is suitable for most purposes. However, 500 g polythene may be required for outer packaging of items that are being transported to off-site centres.

Heat sealers are available from a number of sources. The sealer selected must create an adequate seal and be durable enough to withstand repeated use. Domestic heat sealers are not suitable for the grades of plastic recommended.

REFERENCES

1 Anon. (1992) *Microbiological Safety Cabinets, BS 5726*. British Standards Institute, London.
2 Anon. (1982) *Cytotoxic Drug Safety Cabinets, AS 2567*. Standards Association of Australia, Sydney.
3 Professional Association of Health Service and Welfare Care (1988) *Deutsche Industrie Norm Standard 24184*. GS-GES-04. Professional Association of Health Service and Welfare Care, Bonn.
4 Anon. (1990) ASHP technical assistance bulletin on handling cytotoxic and hazardous drugs. *Am J Hosp Pharm.* **47**: 1033–49.
5 Anon. (1987) *National Sanitation Foundation Standard: class II (laminar flow) biohazard cabinetry. Standard 49*. National Sanitation Foundation, Ann Arbor, MI.
6 European Commission (1992) *Good Manufacturing Practice for Medicinal Products. Vol. IV*. European Commission, Brussels.
7 Anon. (1999) Occupational exposure to cytotoxic drugs. *Pharm J.* **263**: 65–7.
8 Lee MG and Midcalf B (1994) *Isolators for Pharmaceutical Applications*. HMSO, London.
9 Anon. (1999) *The Control of Substances Hazardous to Health Regulations*. HMSO, London.
10 Anon. (1984) *Sterile Latex Surgeons' Gloves, BS 4005*. British Standards Institute, London.
11 Anon. (1989) *Environmental Cleanliness in Enclosed Spaces. Parts 1, 2 and 3, BS 5295*. British Standards Institute, London.
12 Anon. (1989) *Environmental Contamination Control Practice. Technical Monograph No. 2*. The Parenteral Society, Swindon.
13 Anon. (1990) *Laboratory Fume Cupboards. Parts 1, 2 and 3, BS 7258*. British Standards Institute, London.
14 Anon. (1990) *Method for Delimitation of the Containment Value of Laboratory Fume Cupboards, BS DD191*. British Standards Institute, London.
15 Anon. (1983) Guidelines for the handling of cytotoxic drugs – working party report. *Pharm J.* **230**: 230–1.
16 Anon. (1983) *The Safe Handling of Cytotoxic Drugs*. Association of Technical, Scientific and Managerial Staff, Health and Safety Office, Special Report.
17 Anon. (1997) *Sterile Hypodermic Syringes for Single Use, BSEN ISO 7886 (Parts I and II)*. (Available through the Standards Institute of the relevant country).
18 Petersen MC *et al.* (1981) Leaching of 2-(2-hydroxyethylmercapto)benzothiazole into contents of disposable syringes. *J Pharm Sci.* **70**: 1139–43.
19 Reepmeyer JC and Juhl YH (1983) Contamination of injectable solutions with 2-mercaptobenzothiazole leached from rubber closures. *J Pharm Sci.* **72**: 1302–5.

20 Parkinson R *et al.* (1989) Stability of low-dose heparin in pre-filled syringes. *Br J Pharm Pract.* **11**: 34–6.
21 Anon. (1996) *Sterile Hypodermic Needles for Single Use, BSEN ISO 7864.* (Available through the Standards Institute of the relevant country.)
22 Forrest SC (1984) Vepesid injection. *Pharm J.* **232**: 88.
23 Anon. (1996) Controlling occupational exposure to hazardous drugs. *Am J Health Syst Pharm.* **52**: 1669–85.
24 Wilson JP and Solimando DA (1981) Aseptic technique as a safety precaution in the preparation of antineoplastic agents. *Hosp Pharm.* **16**: 575–81.

APPENDIX 1

Manufacturers of isolators

Isolators in flexible film and rigid formats are available from a number of manufacturers, including the following:

La Calhene (GB) Ltd, 2 Stephenson Road, St Ives, Cambridgeshire PE17 4WJ.
Bassaire Ltd, Duncan Road, Swanwick, Southampton SO3 7ZS.
Envair Ltd, York Avenue, Haslingdon, Rossendale, Lancashire BB4 4HX.
Amercare, Thame Park Road, Thame, Oxfordshire OX9 3UH.
MAT, Canto House, Wilton Street, Denton, Manchester M34 3LZ.
TPC Microflow, 11 Minster Park, Cottam, Preston PR4 0BY.
Atlas Clean Air Ltd, 176 Lomeshaye Business Village, Nelson, Lancashire BB9 7DR.

3

Health and safety aspects of cytotoxic services

INTRODUCTION

It is now well recognised that most anticancer drugs are potentially hazardous substances, since they are mutagenic, teratogenic and/or carcinogenic.[1,2] There is also substantial evidence to show that patients may develop reproductive defects and secondary neoplasms as a result of treatment with cancer chemotherapeutic agents,[3–12] indicating the potential threat to the health of any individuals who are exposed to this class of drugs. Such risks may be acceptable for patients with life-threatening diseases. However, they are clearly unacceptable to hospital personnel who are exposed to such chemicals in the workplace. There is now a large body of evidence to show that healthcare personnel who are involved in the preparation and manipulation of anticancer drugs can, if not adequately protected, absorb potentially harmful quantities of such compounds. Much of the evidence comes from epidemiological studies on such diverse groups as nurses, pharmacists and pharmacy technicians, and it has been extensively reviewed.[13–18] There is also evidence that not only workers who are involved directly with the cytotoxic drugs but also those in adjacent areas may absorb potentially hazardous amounts of these drugs.[19,20] The potential dangers are, therefore, well established. For example, studies have shown an association between infertility, spontaneous abortions and malformations in the offspring of nurses who are subject to occupational exposure to cytotoxic agents.[11,21–25] Nurses who handle these drugs have often shown increased mutagenic activity in their urine compared with unexposed personnel.[26–29] Similar patterns have also been reported in the serum of oncology nurses.[30–32] Pharmacists and technicians who regularly handle cytotoxic drugs have also shown some evidence of an excess of acute adverse effects, including chronic throat irritation and diarrhoea[33] and menstrual dysfunctions.[34] Physicians who regularly handle antineoplastic drugs appear to be at increased risk of leukaemia and lymphoma,[35] while it was suggested that antineoplastic drugs were causal in the development of bladder cancer in a pharmacist.[15] Sessink and Bos[18] have calculated that staff who handle cytotoxic drugs have a significantly increased risk of cancer. These and other studies indicate the potential high level of risk to staff working with anticancer drugs. A number of relevant safety measures have been introduced – many of them as a result of regulatory requirements – to protect healthcare personnel who prepare or administer cytotoxic drugs. A number of studies have now been reported that highlight the fact that such improvements can substantially reduce staff exposure levels. For example, improved care in handling has been shown to reduce mutagenic activity detected in nurses' urine.[14,29,36] Pharmacy staff who prepared cytotoxic agents in a vertical laminar flow cabinet (biological safety cabinet Type 2b) with 30% recirculation, while wearing gloves and arm protection, did not show any evidence of increased urine mutagenic activity compared with non-exposed controls.[37]

However, the development of more sensitive techniques for detecting traces of cytotoxic drugs in air and surface samples in a range of preparation and treatment areas has raised new concerns about the safety of personnel handling these agents. Of particular concern is the detection of significant quantities of cytotoxic drugs in air and surface samples in hospital pharmacy preparation and clinical areas, even when protective measures were taken and safety guidelines were followed.[38-42] The contamination appears to arise from three main sources, namely surface contamination of drug vials when they arrive from the manufacturer,[43] leakage of cytotoxics during preparation and administration leading to transfer to gloves and surfaces, and vaporisation of cytotoxic drugs, which allows them to pass through HEPA filters, leading to contamination of working areas supplied with recycled air.[43] The use of closed transfer systems (*see* Chapter 2) has been shown to reduce environmental contamination dramatically,[43,44] and studies are in progress to develop polymer filters which will prevent the egress of vaporised drugs.[45]

In conclusion, there is sufficient evidence to indicate that any staff who are involved in the handling of cytotoxic drugs (e.g. pharmacists, nurses, doctors, stores staff, porters and laundry staff) are potentially at risk from occupational exposure. It is not possible to establish maximum safe exposure levels, and all necessary measures should be adopted to prevent, or at least reduce to a minimum, exposure to these hazardous substances. As all of the available approaches are, by the very nature of the problem, of an indirect form, many different aspects of service operation must be included to ensure adequate, state-of-the-art staff protection.

These should include the following.

▼ Staff education and training:
  – how cytotoxic drugs are used
  – hazards of cytotoxic drugs
  – preventing exposure
  – controlling exposure.
▼ Provision of adequate protective environments:
  – suitable safety cabinets, isolators or hoods
  – suitable protective equipment.
▼ National/local risk management guidelines:
  – effective written procedures for all stages in the process of delivering chemotherapy
  – ongoing staff training and reassessment of competence
  – environmental monitoring
  – regular audit of activities.
▼ Health surveillance:
  – regular monitoring by occupational health staff
  – maintenance of exposure records
  – responding to acute contamination episodes.

This chapter reviews a number of the areas of health and safety listed above. Information on approaches to education and training and service operation for pharmacy staff is outlined in Chapter 4. Specific information on facilities can be found in Chapter 2.

STAFF MONITORING

It is essential to maintain a system of health surveillance for staff who are directly involved in handling cytotoxic agents on a routine basis. This may consist of regular general health screening together with the use of specific biochemical, mutagenic and/or cytogenetic tests to determine whether an individual has been exposed to harmful levels of mutagenic substances.

1 Health surveillance

Four data-gathering elements have been identified as contributing to a medical surveillance programme for staff working with cytotoxic drugs.[46]

1.1 Medical history

The employee's medical and occupational history is rightly the prerogative of the occupational health department. Their staff have a key role to play in record-keeping and counselling. The concept of an individual exposure record has been postulated as an attempt to quantify the drug 'burden' to which the individual has been exposed. A record of length of time for which hazardous materials have been handled is logistically simpler to produce and arguably more valid than a cumulative record of doses prepared. The scientific case for such records remains unproven, and the problems of data interpretation are vast. Individual agents vary in their acute toxicity, particularly with regard to irritant effects, but differentiating between exposure to different drugs on a chronic basis is unlikely to be possible.

1.2 Physical examinations

These should be routine pre-employment practice. For staff involved in cytotoxic drug handling, they should be repeated at regular intervals in order to identify symptoms which could be associated with acute exposure (e.g. irritation of mucous membranes, dizziness, light-headedness).[33,46] Documentation of untoward events such as spills and accidents, together with estimations of potential exposure 'doses', will form part of the individual health surveillance record. One aim should be to determine whether abnormal findings or test results are associated with longer handling times.

1.3 Laboratory tests

Full blood and differential white-cell counts are performed routinely in many centres. Such data provide little information except in the case of high levels of exposure, and must be interpreted with care. Tests for changes in liver and renal function have also been advocated[46] in the light of the toxicity profiles of many cytotoxic drugs. There is also some evidence to link any such changes with adverse effects reported in healthcare workers who have been handling cytotoxic drugs without adequate protection.[33,47]

1.4 Biological monitoring

The measurement of concentrations of specific cytotoxic agents in body fluids (e.g. in blood and urine) has been reported for certain drugs or their known metabolites.[19,20,41,48–50] However, the value of monitoring such levels is limited, due to the increasing range of potential agents, and the likelihood that the extremely low concentrations of drug anticipated in an occupational exposure setting will be below the limits of sensitivity of many assay procedures. Nevertheless, the measurement of individual drugs, such as cyclophosphamide, using highly sensitive gas chromatography methods has proved informative in recent studies.[18,41] Measures of mutagenicity or of the thioether content of urine provide an indirect measure of a general property of many anticancer drugs.[16,18,26,51] An alternative approach is to estimate accumulative effects at either the DNA or chromosomal level on body tissues such as buccal cells, sperm or blood.[52,53]

1.5 Health surveillance in practice

In practice, the cornerstone of an occupational health-monitoring process is to give all new staff working with cytotoxic drugs a confidential interview (which is designed to review their medical history) and a physical examination. Simple laboratory tests, such as blood counts and differential white-cell counts, together with urine and liver function tests, may also be performed in order to confirm their current state of good health. This interview should also be used as an opportunity for the staff member to discuss any fears they may have concerning work with such agents. In this way, all new staff can be educated about the risks involved. This should reinforce the information that is imparted during the training programme. This interview should be repeated at suitable intervals when the employee's exposure record can also be updated. Such interviews are usually recommended on an annual basis. The exposure record is an essential part of staff surveillance programmes. It should include a record of all time spent by each staff member working with cytotoxic agents, together with a specific record of involvement with accidental spillages or other events which could increase that person's exposure. In addition, all incidents involving accidental exposure, such as gross spillages or needlestick incidents, must be reported to the occupational health department. Following such incidents, blood testing and a physical examination should be undertaken to identify signs of acute toxicity to skin, mucous membranes, eyes, etc. Records should be maintained centrally, ideally by occupational health or personnel departments. Computerisation of these records allows for rapid data entry and recall, especially if linked to the pharmacy system used in the operation of the service. Exposure and incident records should be retained with the employee's personal record. A copy should be made available on request to any employee who leaves the service or transfers to another hospital. If a local occupational health policy exists, this should be made available to general practitioners whose patients include such staff, for reference.

Many authorities now recommend that staff who are pregnant or contemplating pregnancy, or who are breastfeeding, should be excluded from duties that involve the preparation or administration of cytotoxic drugs.

2 Biological monitoring of staff

The need to monitor staff for specific biological evidence of enhanced exposure to cytotoxic drugs is controversial.[16–18,54] Baker and Connor[16] argued that none of the currently available biological or analytical methods is sufficiently reliable or repro-ducible for routine monitoring of exposure in the workplace, and therefore recom-mended that their use should be discontinued. They suggested that efforts should instead focus on improving the implementation of better practices for handling cytotoxic drugs. However, Sessink *et al.*[41] showed that even with an intensified hygienic regimen, absorption of cyclophosphamide by occupational staff was still occurring. These observations would appear to justify consideration of an ongoing or periodic monitoring programme.

There is some question as to whether the monitoring methods that are currently available can offer adequate assurance of their ability to identify the real risk.[5,6,14,16,18,46] These methods may be either insufficiently sensitive or poorly validated. The following tests are available and, in theory at least, offer a monitoring test for staff. These methods have been assessed by various authors in the context of hospital staff exposure to cytotoxic drugs.[14,16–18,41,54] Several of these methods have been more generally reviewed with regard to environmental exposure to mutagens and carcinogens.[13,53,55–63] More recently, the significance of chromosomal aberrations in circulating lymphocytes as predictors of cancer incidence has been confirmed in prospective studies within Europe.[64,65]

2.1 Tests for urine mutagenicity

The *Salmonella/mammalian* microsome mutagenicity test (Ames' test) can be used as a routine method to measure mutagenic activity in the urine of pharmacy staff.[26,29] The test relies on the measurement of mutations in bacterial cells caused by carcinogenic agents. This test, although relatively simple and cheap to perform, lacks both sensitivity and specificity as a means of measuring staff exposure to cytotoxic agents in normal practice.[14,16,18] It is now considered to be unsuitable for staff monitoring.

2.2 ^{32}P-postlabelling and other assays to detect altered DNA bases

The alkylating anticancer drugs act through the formation of DNA adducts, which can be detected by a range of physicochemical or immunochemical techniques.[57,61] Chemical-specific techniques (e.g. using antibodies)[55] rely on knowledge of the structure and properties of the particular DNA adducts, whereas non-specific techniques such as ^{32}P-postlabelling are much more generally applicable.[66] There is epidemiological evidence that DNA adducts can be predictive of cancer risk.[56] These methods are highly sensitive, and it has been suggested that they are applicable to biomonitoring of oncology personnel, although they have not been reported in this context to date. However, they have the following disadvantages.

▼ They are specific to alkylating agents.
▼ They vary in quantitation between different laboratories.
▼ Their use for monitoring occupational exposure to cytotoxic drugs has not been validated to date.

2.3 HPRT assay for gene mutation

The *hprt* gene controls the enzyme hypoxanthine-guanine phosphoribosyltransferase (HPRT), which is involved in purine salvage. In addition to its normal substrates, HPRT catalyses the conversion of purine analogues such as 6-thioguanine into a toxic form. Thus, resistance to the toxicity of 6-thioguanine provides a selective assay that can be used to measure mutation to HPRT deficiency in T-lymphocytes from blood cultures. Studies of *in-vivo* T-cell HPRT mutations have found associations with cancer and induction of mutants by known carcinogens in animals, and have shown potential in epidemiology.[60] This assay has been successfully applied to the biomonitoring of nurses and pharmacists.[67]

2.4 Assays for DNA breakage

Many if not most of the anticancer drugs in common use are effective DNA-breaking agents. Highly sensitive assays which can measure DNA breaks include alkaline elution[68] and the comet assay.[59,69] Both of these assays have been applied to various studies with anticancer drugs, and the alkaline elution assay has been used to demonstrate the effectiveness of protective clothing and procedures in reducing anticancer drug absorption by oncology nurses.[68] Collins et al.[59] reviewed specifically the application of the comet assay to human biomonitoring. Using this technique, virtually any accessible cell population, including blood leucocytes, granulocytes or lymphocytes, and buccal, bladder, gastric or nasal epithelial cells, can be evaluated for DNA damage. The comet assay in particular is becoming one of the sensitive methods of choice in biomonitoring studies, and would be highly applicable to monitoring for cytotoxic exposure.

2.5 Assay for chromosomal aberrations

This method provides the most direct estimate of heritable changes, but is relatively insensitive and laborious to perform. Its main importance lies in the fact that it measures long-lasting lesions, and therefore provides an index of cumulative damage. It is also the only one of these assays that has been validated as a long-term predictor of cancer incidence.[64,65] In fact, if the test indicates that a particular individual does show an increase in chromosomal aberrations with time, this probably suggests that hazardous substances are being absorbed and urgent preventive measures are required.

In addition to classical cytogenetic methods for scoring chromosomal aberrations in metaphase cells, structural and numerical damage may be detected in either metaphase- or interphase-stage lymphocytes and a range of other cell types[53] using fluorescence in situ hybridisation (FISH).[70] This technique may considerably improve biomonitoring sensitivity.

2.6 Micronucleus assay

This is a more indirect method of detecting exposure to cytotoxic substances. It is less time-consuming to perform than chromosomal aberration tests, and it does not require the same high level of technical skill. However, it is too variable to identify real differences in individuals,[71] although it may be useful when applied to sufficiently large groups of workers to identify differences between populations or between working conditions. It may be improved by the use of the cytochalasin block method.[72]

2.7 Sister chromatid exchange (SCE)

This method detects reciprocal exchanges between chromatids. It is a sensitive method and detects changes that could be caused by very low levels of mutagenic compounds. However, it must be realised that SCE lesions are short-lived and decline substantially within a few days. The test must be performed immediately after the sample has been collected. It will clearly have relevance to the testing of personnel who are working with cytotoxic drugs, and it has been successfully applied in several such studies.[30,31] It has also been related to cancer incidence,[58] but has no retrospective value.

3 Should blood/urine tests be used to monitor staff?

Whether or not routine testing of staff for evidence of exposure to mutagenic substances should be undertaken remains controversial.[16,17,54] It has been claimed that these tests are not sensitive enough and as yet not sufficiently well validated to provide meaningful information about the levels of risk to which staff have been exposed.[14,46] Although recent validation studies have confirmed the value of estimating chromosomal aberrations as a predictor of human cancer,[65] these tests need to be applied with care.[73] In particular, the study design requires detailed consideration.[74] Ferguson[54] argues that a monitoring programme would provide a means of assessing whether a relationship might exist between consistent detection of abnormalities and occupational exposure to cytotoxic agents. Such testing may also provide a warning of equipment failure, poor technique practised by an individual, or inadequacies in protective clothing.[54] The knowledge base relating to oncology staff testing remains insufficient to allow firm guidance to be offered on the value of or necessity for such testing. McDairmid[46] warns that, since it is not yet possible to interpret accurately the results of these various tests or to link any single 'positive' result to occupational exposure, such a 'positive' result may provoke unjustifiable anxiety in individuals for whom its importance cannot be adequately explained. Ferguson *et al.*[72] suggest that the cytokinesis-blocked micronucleus test is most readily applied to the testing of personnel who are actively working in cytotoxic services. However, if tests are performed routinely on all staff, irrespective of their current duties, the chromosomal aberrations test may be the most appropriate method. For new monitoring services, the use of the comet assay should be seriously considered. It has been suggested that the analysis of blood or urine for the presence of specific cytotoxic drugs or metabolites could represent an alternative or additional valuable tool for monitoring staff exposure.[17,18] Both chromatographic and spectrophotometric methods have been investigated. These analytical methods have shown minor amounts of cyclophosphamide in the urine of pharmacy nurses and technicians, even where they were handling drugs while observing special safety precautions. Sorsa *et al.*[75] calculated an increased cancer risk of 1×10^{-5} in these circumstances. Sessink and Bos[18] also calculated that, even with substantially improved drug-handling conditions, the possibility of drug absorption and cancer risk still remains.

CONTROL OF EXPOSURE

1 Regulations controlling exposure of staff to hazardous substances

Many countries now have statutory controls concerning the protection of staff who work with potentially hazardous substances. Specific examples include the following:

▼ UK – Control of Substances Hazardous to Health Regulations (COSHH) (1999)[76]
▼ UK – Personal Protective Equipment at Work Regulations (1992)[77]
▼ USA – Federal Occupational Health and Safety Administration (OHSA)[5]
▼ USA – National Institute for Occupational Safety and Health (NIOSH).

Such regulations require employers to prevent or control exposure of their employees (or visitors to their premises) to any substance that is potentially or actually hazardous to health.

All employers should undertake a risk assessment of the potential hazards associated with each step of the handling of cytotoxic drugs, and should ensure (within the current state of knowledge) that hazards to staff are reduced to the lowest possible level.

One way of approaching this is to establish national or local guidance/guidelines on the safe handling of cytotoxics. By their very nature, these can only provide recommendations on good practice. Adaption to a local setting may be required in order to gain ownership. However, safe practice ultimately depends on the organisation's commitment to minimising risk in the workplace, individual practitioners' understanding of the hazards, the quality of initial and ongoing training and the provision of protective equipment. Examples of guidelines on handling cytotoxic drugs include the following:

▼ USA – American Society of Hospital Pharmacists (ASHP) technical assistance bulletin on handling cytotoxic and hazardous drugs (1990)[6]
▼ USA – Joint Commission on Accreditation of Healthcare Organisations (JCAHO) accreditation manual for hospitals (1994)[78]
▼ Australia – New South Wales College of Nursing and WorkCover Authority of NSW guidelines on safe handling of cytotoxic drugs (1997)[79]
▼ UK – Royal College of Nursing, Clinical Practice Guidelines: the administration of cytotoxic chemotherapy (recommendations and technical report) (1998).[80]

Guidelines should be evidence based and represent the most up-to-date information at that time. Regular review is essential.

Safety information may also be sought from other national regulatory bodies, including (in the UK) the Health and Safety Executive and the Medical Devices Agency.

2 The working environment

There is sufficient evidence in the literature of the dangers to staff of handling cytotoxic drugs for it to be recommended that they are handled in a controlled manner at all stages of the process of delivery to a patient.[43]

2.1 Storage areas

Stores staff, porters and ward staff must be aware of the hazards of handling cytotoxic drugs, even in their original containers. They should be provided with education and training to a level that is appropriate to their responsibilities.

Cytotoxic drugs should be segregated from other medicines, and storage areas should be clearly labelled with appropriate hazard warnings.

Storage areas should be equipped with hand-washing facilities, eye irrigation solutions and a spill kit. Details of the protective clothing required are provided later.

2.2 Controlled environments in pharmacy or clinical areas

All aseptic preparative work involving the handling of cytotoxic drugs must be performed within a suitable safety cabinet or isolator. A review of the equipment options is given in Chapter 2. Cabinets, including isolators, should ideally be situated within a dedicated area, with access restricted to authorised personnel, in order to prevent the possible spread of contamination to other working areas. Standard operating procedures, such as those listed within the section on audit (see later) need to be in place. Strict adherence to these procedures ensures maximum operator protection.

2.3 Uncontrolled environments in wards and clinics

It is recommended that cytotoxic drugs should not be prepared or administered in an uncontrolled environment. However, it is accepted that in some circumstances (which should be rare) drugs may have to be prepared in less than ideal conditions. In these situations, every effort should be made to segregate the activity from normal ward/clinic activities. The preparation and administration process should only be undertaken by suitably qualified and competent staff, and all staff should wear appropriate protective equipment (see later). Ready-prepared cytotoxics should be used wherever possible, or reconstitution equipment should aim to minimise the risk of aerosols or spills, and preparation and reconstitution equipment should be disposed of in a safe manner. Appropriate spill kits and safety equipment must be available at all times.[80]

3 Monitoring of the working environment

There is increasing evidence that, despite the use of rigorous validation procedures and preparation of cytotoxic drugs in contained environments, significant levels of cytotoxic drug have been detected in the air and on surfaces in cytotoxic preparation areas.[38-43] Accidental cytotoxic spillage can also occur during preparation or administration, with resultant contamination of the working environment. In addition, there may be a need to confirm the absence of contamination on equipment prior to disposal.

A number of techniques have been developed for identifying spilt material and validating cleaning and inactivation procedures. These include direct fluorescence measurement,[81,82] bioluminescent estimation of residual mutagenic activity,[83] high-performance liquid chromatography (HPLC)/tandem mass spectrometry,[40] gas chromatography (GC)/tandem mass spectrometry,[38,42] HPLC[38,39,42,84,85] and adsorptive voltammetry.[86]

In the UK, two relatively simple methods for monitoring the working environment have been developed and validated in a number of laboratories.[87] In looking for a monitoring method, certain important criteria were identified. The methods needed to:

▼ detect cytotoxic agents prepared routinely or regularly. Such products could be used as markers to, at the very minimum, give a yes/no indication of whether residues have been deposited
▼ detect products at normal handling concentrations
▼ use simple and reproducible laboratory methods.

The two methods are described below. Both methods are sufficiently simple that any quality assurance laboratory with basic equipment and experienced staff should be able to carry them out.

The environmental sampling and extraction stages are common to both methods.

3.1 Environmental sampling

1 Decide on the area of the working environment to be sampled and divide it into 10-cm squares.
2 Swab each square with a separate Steret IPA swab. Place each swab in a test-tube.
3 Include an unused Steret as a control.

3.2 Extraction

1 Add 0.5 mL of methanol to each test-tube.
2 To extract, agitate with a clean glass rod for 30 seconds.

3.3 Thin-layer chromatography (TLC) method

1 Set up a TLC tank using a freshly prepared mobile phase of chloroform: methanol: glacial acetic acid 75: 20: 5.
2 Prepare fresh standard solutions as follows: vincristine 1 mg/10 mL; cyclophosphamide 500 mg/25 mL and methotrexate 5 mg/2 mL.
3 Use silica-gel plates. Condition by heating at 110°C for 1 hour. Cool.
4 Apply 10-µL spots for each sample, each standard and the control. Allow to dry.
5 Run the chromatogram for 10 cm, dry and spray with potassium iodobismuthate solution BP.

3.4 Spot method

1 Prepare fresh standard solutions as follows: vincristine 1 mg/10 mL; cyclophosphamide 500 mg/25 mL and methotrexate 5 mg/2 mL.
2 Use either a silica-gel TLC plate or a fine filter paper.
3 Apply 10-µL spots for each sample, each standard and the control. Allow to dry.
4 Spray with potassium iodobismuthate solution BP.

3.5 Interpretation of results

1 For either method, note the colour and intensity of any spots. For the TLC method also record the position of each spot, and calculate the R_f value.
2 Compare any spots from samples with those of the standard solutions.
3 Refer to the sampling plan, and for each square record whether or not contamination is detected.
4 If spots are detected, appropriate action should be agreed. This should include identification of the substance detected, examination and revalidation of the premises and equipment and examination of the operating procedures.
5 Results and actions should be documented in detail and a full report kept on file.

Experience from using the methods: Spot colours are yellow-brown, with methotrexate giving the most intense colour. Vincristine is not detected on filter paper, but should be detected on silica-gel plates. No spot colour is found with the control. Use of the TLC method enables spot colours and R_f values to be used in identification. R_f 100 values are as follows:

▼ vincristine – approximately 70–75 (approximately 90 with benzyl alcohol)
▼ cyclophosphamide – approximately 85–95
▼ methotrexate – approximately 10–20.

The method can also be used for fluorouracil. Yellow-brown spot colours are obtained and the R_f 100 value is approximately 60–70.

The detection limit of the methods is approximately a 10-µL spot of each of the standard solutions. The sensitivity can be increased by using repeat spot applications.

HANDLING CYTOTOXIC DRUGS

Exposure to cytotoxic materials may arise as a result of ingestion, inhalation,[38-40,88,89] absorption through the skin[38-40,48,49,90] or direct splashing (e.g. into the eye).[91]

The safe handling of cytotoxic materials is dependent on attention to a number of factors that were described earlier. A breakdown in any of these areas will compromise safe working practice.[39,40,42] It should be emphasised that failure of a member of the team to perform in a safe and competent manner will create a potential risk, not only for that person, but also for the other staff working in the area.

1 Preparation

1.1 Parenteral cytotoxic drugs

Practical experience in basic aseptic technique is essential before staff are involved in cytotoxic manipulation. All staff who reconstitute cytotoxic drugs should understand the theory behind their use in the treatment of cancer, and the risks associated with drug handling. Handling techniques should be taught and assessed using non-hazardous materials until the operator's technique has been validated. Harrison *et al.*[92] demonstrated that simulation testing significantly improved competence in the preparation of cytotoxic agents. The following standard tests exist for such validation.

▼ A 1% quinine hydrochloride or 0.5 mg/mL fluorescein sodium solution[92] can be used in aseptic transfers. These fluoresce under UV light, indicating spilt material and poor cleaning technique.
▼ The transfer of dye solutions such as amaranth or methylene blue between pressurised vials is a useful method of demonstrating aerosol formation.

Another key question to be discussed by clinical managers is whether or not to rotate staff through the service and other duties. A number of factors need to be considered when making such a judgement. The advantages of employing staff specifically to work in the cytotoxic service include assurance that a high level of expertise is established, that speed and efficiency of operations are optimised and that such personnel can also fulfil training roles. The disadvantages are that the same staff are exposed to the hazards associated with cytotoxic handling over longer periods, and it is more difficult to cover for staff absences. Finally, boredom due to carrying out the same activities over long periods can lead to lowering of performance. If a rotational scheme is operated, this ensures that the maximum number of staff are trained and that the levels of exposure to potentially harmful substances are reduced. However, overall competence may be lower, and a higher level of supervision and monitoring may be deemed necessary.

1.2 Non-parenteral cytotoxic drugs

Extemporaneous preparation

Requests for extemporaneous preparation of oral or topical medicines may arise whenever a dose regimen falls outside commercially available dose forms. This is particularly true of paediatric doses. There may also be demands for liquid formulations if patients have difficulty in swallowing tablets or capsules.

The extemporaneous preparation of medicines containing cytotoxic drugs should be avoided wherever possible. If unavoidable, any manipulation of dosage forms, such as attempting to divide tablets, must be restricted to a controlled environment, ideally within a pharmacy department. Such activities should be discouraged at ward/clinic level. Recommendations for the preparation and dispensing of non-injectable cytotoxic drugs have been promulgated by the American Society of Hospital Pharmacists (ASHP).[6]

Preparation should be in accordance with strict operating procedures and should ideally be undertaken in specialised containment cabinets (*see* Chapter 2). Isolators or cabinets used for aseptic preparation should not be employed for non-sterile work.

Dispensing

Healthcare staff are often unaware that oral and topical cytotoxic drugs pose a potential health hazard if handled carelessly.

The following precautions should be observed in all healthcare settings and the patient's home.

▼ Staff/carers should wear appropriate gloves (see later) when handling products containing cytotoxic drugs or equipment used to manipulate them.
▼ The 'no-touch' principle should apply. Whenever possible, tablets should be used in preference to solutions, and tablets/capsules should be foil or blister packed.
▼ All counting of tablets/capsules must be undertaken using designated equipment. Automated tablet-counting machines must not be used for cytotoxic drugs.
▼ Labels should warn all users of the hazards of touching tablets or liquids directly.
▼ Advice on dealing with skin contact or inhalation should be provided with the patient information sheet.
▼ Nursing/medical staff and carers should be explicitly advised not to crush tablets.

2 Administration

Administration of cytotoxics in wards/clinics and in the patient's home should be in accordance with national/local evidence-based guidelines.[6,78–80] The points listed below highlight some of the key issues in these guidelines, and readers are referred to their national/local policies for more detailed information.

▼ Systems for (re)validating staff competence described in the section on parenteral cytotoxic drugs above apply equally to nursing/medical staff or carers administering cytotoxic drugs to patients.
▼ Strict aseptic technique is as essential when administering parenteral drugs as during preparation, and should help to minimise the risk of spills, aerosol formation or needlestick injuries.

▼ Wherever possible, drugs should be prepared in a pharmacy or by a commercial manufacturer and presented in a form that is ready to administer.
▼ Administration should be carried out in quiet, designated areas away from thoroughfares, waiting or eating areas.
▼ Facilities should include easy access to expert help and all of the equipment necessary for the management of emergencies, including anaphylaxis, extravasation, acute medical emergencies and accidental spillage, and for the disposal of waste.

3 Managing accidental spillage and contamination

All personnel involved in the handling of cytotoxic drugs, or who are in an area where these drugs are handled, should be aware of the policies and protocols required for handling spillage of such drugs or contamination of individuals or surfaces with cytotoxic preparations.

Separate procedures are required for the following:

▼ spillage within the cytotoxic reconstitution area
▼ spillage within the wider environs of the pharmacy department
▼ spillage within the ward/clinic areas of the hospital or in the patient's home.

Procedures and protocols should be developed by a multidisciplinary team and should be in line with appropriate risk management guidance.

General procedures for dealing with spillages are covered in the ASHP technical assistance bulletin (1990)[6] and the Royal College of Nursing Clinical Practice Guidelines (1998).[80] In summary, the key elements are as follows:

▼ adequate protective clothing for all individuals involved in the cleaning operation
▼ containment of spillage as far as possible
▼ prompt action to remove the hazard
▼ adequate, clearly labelled containers for the disposal of waste associated with the clean-up operation
▼ the provision of emergency spill kits at appropriate locations
▼ documentation of all spillages
▼ reports of spillages which have resulted in skin contact, inhalation or ingestion to be forwarded to the occupational health department and the health and safety officer.

More specific monitoring of the contaminated and surrounding areas may be required if there has been a significant spill or there is a suspicion of continual low-level contamination. The monitoring systems described earlier in the chapter may provide a quantitative approach to estimating the exposure risk from spillage incidents.

4 Disposal of waste and cytotoxic contaminated materials and equipment

4.1 Patient waste

There is evidence to suggest that handling excreta (urine, faeces, sweat, saliva and vomit), or laundry which may be contaminated with excreta, puts handlers at risk of exposure to cytotoxic drugs. Potentially hazardous amounts of cytotoxic drugs or their active metabolites have been identified in excreta.[93–96]

The period over which staff who are handling patient waste are potentially at risk depends on the following:

▼ the particular drug involved
▼ pharmacodynamic factors (dose, route of administration, duration of therapy, renal and/or hepatic function)
▼ concomitant drug therapy which may influence elimination rates.

Guidance on the potential hazard from patient excreta has been collated in Table 3.1, which summarises the time over which additional protective measures are required for specific drugs.

Table 3.1: *Details of drugs that require extended precautionary periods for handling excreta after chemotherapy*[94,95]

Drug	Route	Duration (days) after completion of therapy for which precautions are necessary when handling	
		Urine	Faeces
Bleomycin	Injection	3	?
Cisplatin	IV	7 (7/7)	?
Cyclophosphamide	Any	3 (7/14)	5
Dactinomycin	IV	5	7
Daunorubicin	IV	2	7
Doxorubicin	IV	6 (7/14)	7
Epirubicin	IV	7	5
Etoposide	Any	4	7
Melphalan	Oral	2	7
Mercaptopurine	Oral	3	?
Methotrexate	Any	3	7
Mitomycin C	Injection	? (7/14)	?
Mitoxantrone	IV	6	7
Thiotepa	Injection	3	?
Vinca alkaloids	IV	4	7

? = no information available. Numbers in parentheses refer to data in reference 94, which investigated the drug stability and mutagenicity in urine for up to 14 days. The first figure in parentheses relates to stability and the second refers to mutagenicity.

As a general rule, the excreta from patients who are receiving cytotoxic drugs should be assumed to be hazardous *for a minimum of 48 hours* after the completion of treatment, in the absence of any more specific information.[81] Such patients should be clearly identified to ward staff, and chemical inactivation (*see* Table 3.2) should be considered if the patient has received high doses of chemotherapy and nursing staff are handling large quantities of patient excreta.

Strict procedures for handling patient waste in clinical areas and in the home should be applied, and staff/carers should be provided with suitable education on the hazards.

Apart from the standard precautions relating to prevention and control of exposure, the following additional precautions apply.[5,93,95]

▼ Patients and staff should use different toilet facilities.
▼ Double sluicing of bedpans, vomit bowls and other items that are heavily contaminated with waste materials should be carried out. Disposable items are preferable, and should be treated as hazardous clinical waste and disposed of accordingly.
▼ Contaminated linen and uniforms may pose a threat to laundry staff. Lightly contaminated linen may be treated as 'infected waste' and dealt with by the normal laundry process. Heavily contaminated items may need to be quarantined to allow the drugs to degrade, or may need to be incinerated. Soaking of linen in sodium hypochlorite solution has been recommended for drugs such as doxorubicin.[93,94]

Each institution should have a policy on the safe handling and disposal of cytotoxic drugs and materials contaminated with the latter. Clear and concise procedures for the collection, segregation and disposal of waste should be established, and all staff involved, including non-pharmacy staff, should be trained in their use. Procedures should be updated at regular intervals and there should be a system of audit to ensure compliance with the procedures at all times.

Suitable containers, clearly labelled and reserved solely for cytotoxic waste, should be available in all areas where the drugs are handled. They should be brightly coloured, with space to indicate the nature of the contents both during use and while awaiting disposal. 'Sharps' containers should be robust enough to contain any sharps and leaked solution. They should be constructed of plastic (not lined cardboard), with tightly fitting lids which can be sealed when the container is full. Absorbent material (paper or absorbent granules) should be placed in the bottom of the container to mop up any leaked solution. It is essential to carry out quality assurance on all disposal containers in order to check that they are suitable for use and can be disposed of safely and in the appropriate manner.

Facilities for the storage of the cytotoxic waste awaiting destruction must safeguard the integrity of the packaging and not expose personnel to any risk. Waste should not be allowed to accumulate in either clinical or storage areas.

In the UK, prescription-only medicines are listed in Schedule 1 of the Control of Pollution (Special Waste) Regulations (1980)[97] as substances which are to be regarded as special waste. There is no specific reference to cytotoxic drugs in these regulations, but their disposal will be subject to the general controls set out therein.

The risks associated with pharmaceutical wastes which might enter the water cycle have been discussed in detail in a review by Richardson and Bowron.[98] They calculated that the major source of pharmaceutical chemicals as contaminants in potable water would be from domestic sources, including homes and hospitals, with only a marginal contribution to the load from industry. The authors concluded, from analytical and biodegradation data, that few drugs were likely to survive treatment in sewage works, river retention, reservoir retention and waterworks. Those drugs that did survive would be unlikely to pose a health risk at the concentrations likely to be found in water supplies. It can therefore be concluded that disposal to sewer may be used for small quantities of pharmaceuticals.

Disposal via the domestic sewerage system should not be used for large quantities of pharmaceutical waste. The Royal Pharmaceutical Society of Great Britain, in their guidelines, recommend pharmacists to use their professional judgement when deciding on the disposal of substances which may be particularly toxic, insidious or persistent.[99]

The relationship between hazard and the quantities of any particular cytotoxic substance requiring disposal is not generally addressed. However, in the USA this issue is covered by regulations from the Environmental Protection Agency. These have been summarised by Gallelli.[100] The relevant 'rules' are described as the '3%' and 'mixture' rules. The former states that all empty containers that contain not more than 3% of cytotoxic drugs by weight in relation to the total capacity of the container need not be disposed of as hazardous waste. The 'mixture' rule states that if any amount of a listed waste is mixed with any other, the entire mixture is considered to be hazardous. This is to prevent the deliberate dilution of cytotoxic waste to avoid disposal regulations.

Many cytotoxics can be disposed of by chemical destruction. Details of recommended methods are summarised in Part 2 of this handbook. Other important sources of information on chemical destruction of cytotoxic drugs are recommended.[94,101–103]

Table 3.2: *Chemical methods for degradation of antineoplastic drugs*[94,103]

Drug	Method
Bleomycin Etoposide Mitomycin C Teniposide Methotrexate	Oxidation with potassium permanganate or 5.25% sodium hypochlorite solution (bleach) completely degrades and inactivates these drugs
Doxorubicin	Oxidation with 5.25% sodium hypochlorite. Sodium thiosulphate must be added to the solution first
Cisplatin	Complexing with sodium diethyldithiocarbamate

The method recommended for disposal of cytotoxic drugs is incineration. Disposal into waste which might subsequently be tipped into a landfill site must not, under any circumstances, be used for cytotoxic drugs or materials contaminated with them. Several manufacturers recommend a temperature of 1000°C for the complete destruction of cytotoxic drugs.[104] Opinion differs with regard to the need for this, but until adequate research has been carried out, this should be regarded as an ideal to be attained if possible. Perhaps of more importance than the actual temperature is the presence of an after-burner on the incinerator to be used. There is a possible risk of a solution containing a cytotoxic drug being aerosolised when it is passed into the incinerator. This may result in undegraded cytotoxic drug being emitted from the incinerator chimney. In the absence of a suitable incinerator, the services of a specialist waste disposal contractor should be employed.

5 Transport of cytotoxic drugs

Packaging and transport systems for cytotoxic drugs must provide adequate physical, chemical and light protection during storage and transportation, be relatively impervious to the atmosphere, robust and tamper-proof, provide adequate protection to the handler(s), contain any leaked solution and allow easy identification of the contained drugs throughout.

All cytotoxic preparations should be packed in leak-proof containers after preparation. Polythene tubing that can be heat-sealed to give an air/water-tight seal and which can be cut to enclose any size or shape of container is recommended.

For transportation around the hospital, standard delivery containers may be utilised, provided that they fulfil the above criteria. Cytotoxic drugs should not be transported in the same container as other drugs, and the nature of the contained material should be clearly indicated on the outer container.

Transportation to other clinical settings outside the hospital may necessitate more stringent, possibly custom-designed packaging.

PROTECTIVE CLOTHING AND EQUIPMENT

Protective clothing and equipment should be worn at all times when handling cytotoxic drugs. The degree of protection that is required will depend on the perceived exposure risk to the operator/handler, and should be based on local or nationally agreed guidelines, if these are available. No protective clothing or equipment will afford total protection to the operator. Moreover, if used inappropriately, they may inadvertently expose the operator to a greater risk. Safe handling procedures should always be followed, even in the presence of protective equipment.

Since 1995 it has been necessary for all personal protective equipment purchased in the European Union to bear the European CE marking.

Table 3.3 summarises the minimum requirements for the handling of cytotoxic drugs in various situations.

Table 3.3: *Minimum requirements for protection of staff when handling cytotoxic drugs in various situations*

Activity	Protective measures
Preparation Controlled environment	Sterile/non-sterile gown, suit or laboratory overall Gloves of a suitable quality Non-absorbent armlets

Uncontrolled environment	As above, plus:
	  non-absorbent apron or overall
	  eye and/or face protection
	  respiratory protective equipment

Checking	Non-absorbent overall Gloves of a suitable quality
Transport	No special protection is required, provided that drugs are transported in a suitable container and the messenger is aware of the potential hazards
Administration/ handling patient waste	Non-absorbent overall or standard overall with non-absorbent armlets and apron Gloves of a suitable quality Eye or face protection
Dealing with spills	Non-absorbent overall or standard overall with non-absorbent armlets and apron Heavy-duty gloves Eye or face protection Respiratory protective equipment

1 Gowns, cleanroom suits and armlets

In general these should be:

▼ lightweight
▼ low-linting
▼ of a low-permeability, disposable or conventional fabric.

Gowns and suits should have the following:

▼ a solid front with covered fastenings
▼ long sleeves that are cuffed at the wrists.

Most commercially available fabrics for use in aseptic preparation areas are permeable to cytotoxic drugs, and additional protection is required if gowns/suits made of these materials are worn.

Laidlaw et al.[105] investigated the permeability of four disposable protective clothing materials to seven antineoplastic drugs over a 4-hour period. The materials tested were Saranex-laminated Tyvek®, polyethylene-coated Tyvek® and non-porous Tyvek and Kaycel®.

All of the materials evaluated afforded protection from occupational exposure to antineoplastic drugs, whereas laboratory coats and disposable isolation gowns were completely absorbent. Saranex®-laminated Tyvek® and polyethylene-coated Tyvek® afforded almost complete protection from the drugs. Non-porous Tyvek® and Kaycel® did allow some drug permeation, although the maximum permeation over a 4-hour exposure time was 3.3% of the applied drug dose.

Connor[106] tested several different polypropylene-based protective gown materials for permeability against a battery of four cancer drugs (carmustine, cyclophosphamide, doxorubicin and cisplatin). Permeability was assessed using a bacterial mutation assay at exposure times ranging from 5 minutes to 4 hours. Testing was performed at ambient temperature using standard concentrations of each drug.

The spun-bonded polypropylene non-woven materials alone were not a sufficient barrier to the agents tested, allowing permeation within 5 minutes. Composite gown materials of spun-bonded polypropylene coated with polyethylene or other proprietary film, and various constructions of meltblown polypropylene between layers of spun-bonded polypropylene, were found to be more acceptable, allowing only minimal permeation after 4 hours of exposure, and providing complete protection for 30 minutes or more. Two composite gowns, namely the Kimberley-Clark Experimental and Digit-Safety Protective gowns, were completely resistant to the four drugs at all time periods.

The penetration and splash protection of six disposable gown materials against 15 antineoplastic drugs has been investigated by Harrison and Kloos.[107] The materials tested were polypropylene homopolymer, polypropylene/molten polyethylene backing, spun-bonded polypropylene, spun-bonded polyethylene (Tyvek®), spun-bonded polypropylene (polyethylene coating), and ethylene/vinyl acetate copolymer (Saranex®) laminated with Tyvek®. The drugs represented a broad range of commonly used water-based and non-water-based cytotoxic agents. Two endpoints were used to rate each gown/drug pair, namely absorption into the gown material vs. beading on the gown surface (splash protection), and visible detection of the drug solution on the opposite side of the gown (penetration). Observations were recorded at the time of initial contact of a drop of the drug solution with the gown material, and after 1 minute.

The researchers recommended that gowns made of polypropylene homopolymer and spun-bonded polypropylene should not be used during the preparation of cytotoxic drugs. The Saranex®-laminated Tyvek® gown afforded complete permeation and splash protection. The response of the other materials was variable.

As a general recommendation, it is suggested that Saranex®-laminated or polyethylene-coated Tyvek® armlets be worn over standard cleanroom clothing in laminar downflow safety cabinets where the arms of the operator are exposed throughout. These armlets may also be worn when preparing drugs in an isolator cabinet, as some rubber sleeves may not protect the operator from gross contamination.

Where disposable gowns are used, these should be made of Saranex®-coated Tyvek®, polyethylene-coated Tyvek® or another suitable composite material which has been shown to be impermeable to cytotoxic drugs,[106] for maximum operator protection. However, these materials allow little airflow and tend to be uncomfortable to wear for an extended time period. Some of the composite gown materials are more comfortable to wear, but staff should be made aware of the lower degree of protection, and should be advised to remove clothing immediately if it comes into contact with drug solution.

2 Respiratory protective equipment

Standard surgeons' masks are suitable for most procedures that are performed in a 'contained environment', as their main aim is to protect the environment from the operator. However, respiratory protection is needed wherever total enclosure/local exhaust ventilation cannot control exposure.

In the UK, advice on respiratory protective equipment is available from the Health and Safety Executive.[108] In the majority of clinical situations, a disposable filtering half-mask which conforms to BS EN 149:1992[109] will provide protection against solid or liquid particles. The filtration efficiency should be FFP2 or FFP3 in order of increasing efficiency. A full-face mask conforming to EN 136:1998,[110] fitted with high-efficiency solid and liquid particle filters, may be required for large-scale spills or contamination.

In the USA, the National Institute for Occupational Safety and Health (NIOSH) provides extensive information on masks intended for critical applications.

The key factor with regard to respiratory protective equipment is that it fits correctly and is sealed tightly to the wearer's face. Face size and shape, facial hair, spectacles, other accessories (cosmetics, jewellery, etc.) and other protective equipment may affect the fit of the mask.[108] A range of different sizes of disposable masks should be made available in clinical areas.

3 Eye protection

Eye protection which conforms to BS 2092 (1987) (to be replaced by EN 166–168)[111] is required for handling cytotoxics in an 'uncontrolled' environment.

The most suitable form of eye protection for clinical use is safety goggles.[77] These afford the eyes total protection from dust and splashes, as the entire periphery of the goggle is in contact with the face.

Faceshields may be necessary where full-face protection from splashes is required, but they do not protect against dust, mist or gases, as the eyes are not fully enclosed.[77]

4 Aprons

These provide a protective, water-resistant barrier to accidental spills or sprays. They can be ethylene oxide sterilised if necessary. Saranex®-laminated or Tyvek® aprons provide added protection when used in an uncontrolled environment.

5 Gloves

Disposable gloves should be worn at all times when preparing, checking and administering cytotoxic drugs.

The suitability of a wide range of commercially available gloves for cytotoxic handling has been investigated.[112–122] However, there is no consensus about which glove material offers the best protection.

A variety of techniques for determining permeation have been employed, including a spectrophotometric method,[114] radiolabelling,[115,116] mutagenicity testing[117,121,122] and chromatographic analysis.[119] Permeation under static and flexed conditions has also been determined.[120] None of the studies considered the effect of solubility of the drug in the collection medium, yet Ehntholt et al.,[123] in an evaluation of protective glove materials in agricultural pesticide operations, found the collection medium to be a significant determinant of the degree of breakthrough measured.

Several of these studies also determined the inter- and intra-batch variability in glove thickness and the surface characteristics.[114] Thomas and Fenton-May[114] found that glove thickness varied considerably, with a tenfold difference between the extremes in the range. Variation in thickness within the same batch was also considerable for some manufacturers. Kotilainen et al.[124] used scanning electron microscopy to examine the surfaces of both PVC and latex gloves. They found that the surface was extremely irregular, with multiple pits and defects, some up to 10 μ in width.

On the basis of these studies it can be concluded that no glove material is completely impermeable to every cytotoxic agent. Although glove thickness is a major factor affecting drug permeation, the molecular weight of the drug, its lipophilicity, the nature of the solvent in which the cytotoxic drug is dissolved, and glove material composition all affect permeation rates.

When selecting gloves for use with cytotoxic drugs, the user must be assured that the glove material is of a suitable thickness and integrity to maximise protection whilst maintaining manual dexterity. Manufacturers should be asked to supply information on material composition, thickness (both mean and variation), chemical permeation and resistance data and durability. The use of poor-quality, low-cost gloves is neither safe nor cost-effective, as multiple glove changes are required to ensure integrity. Increasing concerns about the risk of allergic reactions to latex and powdered medical gloves led the UK National Health Service Executive to issue a Health Service Circular (HSC 1999/186)[125] recommending that healthcare organisations limit their use of these types of gloves. Although the starch powder is not itself an allergen, the protein residue in latex readily attaches to the starch, which then acts as a carrier, allowing surface or airborne transmission. Powder-free gloves should be used for handling cytotoxic drugs.

The practice of double-gloving should be unnecessary so long as gloves with appropriate qualities are used and the gloves are changed regularly during each work session, or immediately after known contact with a cytotoxic agent, or if punctured.

Industrial thickness gloves (> 0.45 mm thick) made from latex with neoprene, nitrile synthetic rubber or similar materials should be used to clean up large-scale spills.

REFERENCES

1 Ferguson LR (1995) Mutagenic properties of anticancer drugs. In: MJ Waring and B Ponder (eds) *The Genetics of Cancer.* Kluwer Academic Publishers, Lancaster, 177–216.
2 Ferguson LR (1996) The mutagenicity of anticancer drugs. *Mutation Res.* **355**: 1–261.
3 Kaldor JM *et al.* (1988) Quantifying the carcinogenicity of antineoplastic drugs. *Eur J Cancer Clin Oncol.* **24**: 703–11.
4 Hawkins MM *et al.* (1992) Epipodophyllotoxins, alkylating agents, and radiation and risk of secondary leukemia after childhood cancer. *BMJ.* **304**: 951–8.
5 Anon. (1986) OSHA work-practice guidelines for personnel dealing with cytotoxic (antineoplastic) drugs. *Am J Hosp Pharm.* **43**: 1193–204.
6 Anon. (1990) AHSP technical assistance bulletin on handling cytotoxic and hazardous drugs. *Am J Hosp Pharm.* **47**: 1033–49.
7 Osanto S *et al.* (1992) Long-term effects of chemotherapy in patients with testicular cancer. *J Clin Oncol.* **10**: 574–9.
8 Robertson LE *et al.* (1994) Therapy-related leukemia and myelodysplastic syndrome in chronic lymphocytic leukemia. *Leukemia.* **8**: 2047–51.
9 Stevenson WT *et al.* (1995) Evaluation of reproductive capacity in germ-cell tumor patients following treatment with cisplatin, etoposide and bleomycin. *J Clin Oncol.* **13**: 2278–80.
10 Larson RA *et al.* (1996) Myeloid leukemia after hematotoxins. *Environ Health Perspect.* **104 (Supplement 6)**: 1303–7.
11 Valanis B *et al.* (1997) Occupational exposure to antineoplastic agents and self-reported infertility among nurses and pharmacists. *J Occup Environ Med.* **39**: 574–80.
12 Kollmannsberger C *et al.* (1998) Risk of secondary myeloid leukemia and myelodysplastic syndrome following standard-dose chemotherapy or high-dose chemotherapy with stem-cell support in patients with potentially curable malignancies. *J Cancer Res Clin Oncol.* **124**: 207–14.
13 Carrano AV and Natarajan AT (1988) ICPEMC Publication No. 14: considerations for population monitoring using cytogenetic techniques. *Mutation Res.* **204**: 379–406.
14 Kaijser GP *et al.* (1990) The risks of handling cytotoxic drugs. 1. Methods of testing exposure. *Pharm Weekbl Sci Ed.* **12**: 212–27.
15 Levin LI *et al.* (1993) Bladder cancer in a 39-year-old female pharmacist. *J Natl. Cancer Inst.* **85**: 1089–91.
16 Baker ES and Connor TH (1996) Monitoring occupational exposure to cancer chemotherapy drugs. *Am J Health Syst Pharm.* **53**: 2713–23.

17 Bos RP and Sessink PJ (1997) Biomonitoring of occupational exposures to cytostatic anticancer drugs. *Rev Environ Health.* **12**: 43–58.

18 Sessink PJ and Bos RP (1999) Drugs hazardous to healthcare workers: evaluation of methods for monitoring occupational exposure to cytostatic drugs. *Drug Safety* **20**: 347–59.

19 Sessink PJ *et al.* (1994) Environmental contamination and assessment of exposure to antineoplastic agents by determination of cyclophosphamide in urine of exposed pharmacy technicians: is skin absorption an important exposure route? *Arch Environ Health.* **49**: 165–9.

20 Sessink PJ *et al.* (1993) Occupational exposure of animal caretakers to cyclophosphamide. *J Occup Med.* **35**: 47–52.

21 Selevan SG *et al.* (1985) A study of occupational exposure to antineoplastic drugs and fetal losses in nurses. *NEJM.* **313**: 1173–8.

22 Hemminki K *et al.* (1985) Spontaneous abortions and malformations in the offspring of nurses exposed to anaesthetic gases, cytotoxic drugs and other potential hazards in hospitals, based on registered information of outcome. *J Epidemiol Commun Health.* **39**: 141–7.

23 McDonald AD *et al.* (1988) Congenital defects and work in pregnancy. *Br J Ind Med.* **45**: 581–8.

24 Taskinen HK (1990) Effects of parental occupational exposures on spontaneous abortion and congenital malformation. *Scand J Work Environ Health.* **16**: 297–314.

25 Stucker I *et al.* (1990) Risk of spontaneous abortion among nurses handling antineo-plastic drugs. *Scand J Work Environ Health.* **16**: 102–7.

26 Falck K *et al.* (1979) Mutagenicity in urine of nurses handling cytotoxic drugs. *Lancet.* **i**: 1250–1.

27 Andersson RW *et al.* (1982) Risks of handling injectable antineoplastic drugs. *Am J Hosp Pharm.* **39**: 1881–7.

28 Benhamou S *et al.* (1986) Mutagenicity in urine from nurses handling cytotoxic drugs. *Eur J Cancer Clin Oncol.* **22**: 1489–93.

29 Labuhn K *et al.* (1998) Nurses' and pharmacists' exposure to antineoplastic drugs: findings from industrial hygiene scans and urine mutagenicity tests. *Cancer Nurs.* **21**: 79–89.

30 Norppa H *et al.* (1980) Increased sister chromatid exchange frequencies in lympho-cytes of nurses handling cytotoxic drugs. *Scand J Work Environ Health.* **6**: 299–303.

31 Sorsa M *et al.* (1982) Induction of sister chromatid exchanges (SCEs) among nurses handling cytotoxic drugs. In: *Banbury Proceedings. Volume 14.* Cold Spring Harbor Laboratory, New York.

32 Nikula E *et al.* (1984) Chromosomal aberrations in lymphocytes of nurses handling cytotoxic drugs. *Scand J Work Environ Health.* **10**: 71–4.

33 Valanis BG *et al.* (1993) Association of antineoplastic drug handling with acute adverse effects in pharmacy personnel. *Am J Hosp Pharm.* **50**: 455–62.

34 Shortridge LA *et al.* (1995) Menstrual cycles in nurses handling antineoplastic drugs. *Cancer Nurs.* **18**: 439–44.

35 Skov T *et al.* (1990) Risks for physicians handling antineoplastic drugs. *Lancet.* **336**: 1446.

36 Vainio H (1982) Mutagenicity in urine of workers occupationally exposed to mutagens and carcinogens. In: A Aito *et al.* (eds) *Biological Monitoring and Health Surveillance of Workers Exposed to Chemicals.* Hemisphere Publishing, Washington, DC, 324–30.

37 Guinee EP *et al.* (1991) Evaluation of genotoxic risk of handling cytostatic drugs in clinical pharmacy practice. *Pharm Weekbl Sci Ed.* **13**: 78–82.

38 Sessink PJM *et al.* (1992) Detection of contamination with antineoplastic agents in a hospital pharmacy department. *Pharm Weekbl Sci.* **14**: 16–22.

39 McDevitt LL *et al.* (1993) Exposure of hospital pharmacists and nurses to antineoplastic agents. *J Occup Med.* **35**: 57–60.

40 Minoia C *et al.* (1998) Application of high-performance liquid chromatography/ tandem mass spectrometry in the environmental and biological monitoring of healthcare personnel occupationally exposed to cyclophosphamide and ifosfamide. *Rapid Commun Mass Spectrom.* **12**: 1485–93.

41 Sessink PJM *et al.* (1997) Exposure of pharmacy technicians to antineoplastic agents: re-evaluation after additional protective measures. *Arch Environ Health.* **52**: 240–4.

42 Connor TH *et al.* (1999) Surface contamination with antineoplastic agents in six cancer treatment centers in Canada and the United States. *Am J Health Syst Pharm.* **56**: 1427–32.

43 Clark C (1999) Report of a seminar on occupational exposure to cytotoxic drugs. *Pharm J.* **263**: 65–7.

44 Gustavsson B (1997) Evaluation of a technetium assay for monitoring of occupational exposure to cytotoxic drugs. *J Oncol Pharm Pract.* **3**: 16.

45 Personal communication (2000) Professor G Sewell, School of Pharmacy and Pharmacology, University of Bath, Bath.

46 McDairmid MA (1990) Medical surveillance for antineoplastic handlers. *Am J Hosp Pharm.* **47**: 1061–6.

47 Stellman JM and Zoloth SR (1986) Cancer chemotherapeutic agents as occupational hazards: a literature review. *Cancer Invest.* **4**: 127–35.

48 Venitt S *et al.* (1984) Monitoring exposure of nursing and pharmacy personnel to cytotoxic drugs: urinary mutation assays and urinary platinum as markers of absorption. *Lancet.* **i**: 777.

49 Hirst M *et al.* (1984) Occupational exposure to cyclophosphamide. *Lancet.* **i**: 186–8.

50 Ensslin AS (1993) Biological monitoring of cyclophosphamide and ifosfamide in urine of hospital personnel occupationally exposed to cytostatic drugs. *Occup Environ Med.* **51**: 229–33.

51 Jagun O *et al.* (1982) Urinary thioether excretion in nurses handling cytotoxic drugs. *Lancet.* **ii**: 443–4.

52 Knudsen LE and Sorsa M (1993) Human biological monitoring of occupational genotoxic exposures. *Pharmacol Toxicol.* **72 (Supplement 1)**: 86–92.

53 Salama SA *et al.* (1999) Biomonitoring using accessible human cells for exposure and health assessment. *Mutation Res.* **436**: 99–112.

54 Ferguson LR (1995) Occupational health and staff monitoring: a genetic toxicologist's viewpoint. *J Oncol Pharm Pract.* **1**: 49–54.

55 Wild CP (1990) Antibodies to DNA alkylation adducts as analytical tools in chemical carcinogenesis. *Mutation Res.* **233**: 219–33.

56 Qian GS *et al.* (1994) A follow-up study of urinary markers of aflatoxin exposure and liver cancer risk in Shanghai, People's Republic of China. *Cancer Epidemiol Biomarkers Prev.* **3 (Supplement 5)**: 3–10.

57 Hemminki K *et al.* (eds) (1994) *DNA Adducts. Identification and biological significance.* International Agency for Research on Cancer, Lyons, 478.

58 Tucker JD and Preston RJ (1996) Chromosome aberrations, micronuclei, sister chromatid exchanges and cancer risk assessment. *Mutation Res.* **365**: 147–59.

59 Collins M *et al.* (1997) Comet assay in human biomonitoring studies: reliability, validation and applications. *Environ Mol Mutagen.* **30**: 139–46.

60 Albertini RJ and Hayes RB (1997) Somatic cell mutations in cancer epidemiology. In: P Toniolo *et al.* (eds) *Application of Biomarkers in Cancer Epidemiology.* International Agency for Research on Cancer, Lyons, 159–84.

61 Shuker DEG (1999) DNA adducts in mammalian cells as indicators of exposure to carcinogens. In: DB McGregor *et al.* (eds) *The Use of Short- and Medium-Term Tests for Carcinogens and Data on Genetic Effects in Carcinogenic Hazard Evaluation.* International Agency for Research on Cancer, Lyons, 287–308.

62 Bonassi S *et al.* (1999) Analysis of correlated data in human biomonitoring studies. The case of high sister chromatid exchange frequency cells. *Mutation Res.* **438**: 13–21.

63 Groopman JD and Kensler TW (1999) The light at the end of the tunnel for chemical-specific biomarkers: daylight or headlight? *Carcinogenesis.* **20**: 1–11.

64 Bonassi S *et al.* (1995) Are chromosomal aberrations in circulating lymphocytes predictive of future cancer onset in humans? Preliminary results of an Italian cohort study. *Cancer Genet Cytogenet.* **79**: 133–5.

65 Hagmar L *et al.* (1998) Chromosomal aberrations in lymphocytes predict human cancer: a report from the European Study Group on Cytogenetic Biomarkers and Health (ESCH). *Cancer Res.* **58**: 4117–21.

66 Phillips DH *et al.* (eds) (1993) *Post-Labelling Methods for Detection of DNA Adducts.* International Agency for Research on Cancer, Lyons, 392.

67 Kyrtopoulos SA *et al.* (1993) Accumulation of O6-methylguanine in human DNA after therapeutic exposure to methylating agents and its relationship with biological effects. *Environ Health Perspect.* **99**: 143–7.

68 Fuchs J *et al.* (1995) DNA damage in nurses handling antineoplastic agents. *Mutation Res.* **342**: 17–23.

69 Fairbairn DW *et al.* (1995) The comet assay: a comprehensive review. *Mutation Res.* **339**: 37–59.

70 Savage JRK and Tucker JD (1996) The nomenclature system for FISH – painted chromosome aberrations. *Mutation Res.* **366**: 153–61.

71 Ferguson LR *et al.* (1988) The use within New Zealand of cytogenetic approaches to monitoring of hospital pharmacists for exposure to cytotoxic drugs: report of a pilot study in Auckland. *Aust J Hosp Pharm.* **18**: 228–33.

72 Ferguson LR *et al.* (1990) Monitoring of drug absorption by pharmacists and oncology nurses in four New Zealand Hospitals using estimation of cytokinesis-blocked micronuclei. *Aust J Hosp Pharm.* **20**: 212–21.

73 Sorsa M *et al.* (1992) Human cytogenetic damage as a predictor of cancer risk. *IARC Sci Publ.* **116**: 543–54.

74 Bonassi S *et al.* (1994) Multiple regression analysis of cytogenetic human data. *Mutation Res.* **313**: 69–80.

75 Sorsa M *et al.* (1995) Biomonitoring of genotoxic anticancer drugs as a tool for improving work hygiene. *J Oncol Pharm Pract.* (ISOPP IV Symposium issue.)

76 Anon. (1999) *The Control of Substances Hazardous to Health Regulations.* The Stationery Office, London.

77 Health and Safety Executive (HSE) (1998) *Personal Protective Equipment at Work Regulations 1992. Guidance on regulations* (10e). HSE Books, Sudbury.

78 Joint Commission on Accreditation of Healthcare Organisations (JCAHO) (1994) *Accreditation Manual for Hospitals.* JCAHO, Oakbrook Terrace, IL.

79 Daly L (1998) Safe handling of cytotoxic drugs. *Austr Nurs J.* **5**: 21–4.

80 Royal College of Nursing (RCN) (1998) *Clinical Practice Guidelines: the administration of cytotoxic chemotherapy (recommendations and technical report).* Nursing Standard Publications, Harrow.

81 Van Raalte J *et al.* (1990) Visible-light system for detecting doxorubicin contamination on skin and surfaces. *Am J Hosp Pharm.* **47**: 1067–74.

82 Dixon T (1990) Location of cytotoxic drug spillages using ultraviolet light. *Aust J Hosp Pharm.* **20**: 469–70.

83 Wren AE *et al.* (1991) A novel technique for the validation of cytotoxic decontamination procedures. *Int Pharm.* **5**: 119.

84 Floridia L *et al.* (1999) High-performance liquid chromatography of methotrexate for environmental monitoring of surface contamination in hospital departments and assessment of occupational exposure. *J Chromatogr B Biomed Sci Appl.* **726**: 95–103.

85 Floridia L *et al.* (1999) Measurement of surface contamination from nucleoside analogue antineoplastic drugs by high-performance liquid chromatography in occupational hygiene studies of oncologic hospital departments. *J Chromatogr B Biomed Sci Appl.* **724**: 325–34.

86 Nygren O and Lundgren C (1997) Determination of platinum in workroom air and in blood and urine from nursing staff attending patients receiving cisplatin chemotherapy. *Int Arch Occup Environ Health.* **70**: 209–14.

87 Personal communication (1995) M Douch, Quality Assurance Pharmacist, Pharmacy Support Unit, Colchester General Hospital, Colchester.

88 Kleinberg ML and Quinn MJ (1981) Airborne drug levels in a laminar-flow hood. *Am J Hosp Pharm.* **38**: 1301–3.

89 DeWerk Neal A *et al.* (1983) Exposure of hospital workers to airborne antineoplastic agents. *Am J Hosp Pharm.* **40**: 597–601.

90 Solimando DA and Wilson JF (1983) Demonstration of skin fluorescence following exposure to doxorubicin. *Cancer Nurs.* **6**: 313–5.

91 McLedon BF and Bron AJ (1978) Corneal toxicity from vinblastine solution. *Br J Opthalmol.* **62**: 97–9.

92 Harrison BR *et al.* (1996) Quality-assurance testing of staff pharmacists handling cytotoxic agents. *Am J Health Syst Pharm.* **53**: 402–7.

93 Harris J and Dodds LJ (1985) Handling of waste from patients receiving cytotoxic drugs. *Pharm J.* **235**: 289–91.

94 Monteith DK *et al.* (1987) Stability and inactivation of mutagenic drugs and their metabolites in the urine of patients administered antineoplastic therapy. *Environ Mol Mutagen.* **10**: 341–56.

95 Cass Y and Musgrave CF (1992) Guidelines for the safe handling of excreta contaminated by cytotoxic agents. *Am J Hosp Pharm.* **49**: 1957–8.

96 Mader RM *et al.* (1996) Exposure of oncologic nurses to methotrexate in the treatment of osteosarcoma. *Arch Environ Health.* **51**: 310–4.

97 Anon. (1980) *Joint Circular from Department of Environment/Welsh Office. Control of pollution (special waste) regulations.* HMSO, London.

98 Richardson ML and Bowron GM (1985) The fate of pharmaceutical chemicals in the aquatic environment. *J Pharm Pharmacol.* **37**: 1–12.

99 Appleby GE (1988) Disposal of pharmaceutical waste. *Pharm J.* **240**: 100.

100 Gallelli JF (1988) Chemical destruction and disposal of antineoplastic drugs. In: *Proceedings of International Symposium on Oncology Pharmacy Practice,* Rotorua, New Zealand. New Zealand Hospital Pharmacists Association, Wellington, 240–51.

101 Castegnaro M *et al.* (1985) *Laboratory Decontamination and Destruction of Carcinogens in Laboratory Wastes.* International Agency for Research on Cancer and Oxford University Press, Fair Lane, NJ.

102 Armour MA *et al.* (1986) *Potentially Carcinogenic Chemicals: Information and Disposal Guide.* University of Alberta and Terochem Laboratories Ltd, Edmonton.

103 Benvenuto JA *et al.* (1993) Degradation and inactivation of antitumor drugs. *J Pharm Sci.* **82**: 988–91.

104 Garner S *et al.* (1988) Disposal of waste cytotoxics. *Pharm J.* **241 (Hospital Supplement 32)**.

105 Laidlaw JL *et al.* (1985) Permeability of four disposable protective-clothing materials to seven antineoplastic drugs. *Am J Hosp Pharm.* **42**: 2449–54.

106 Connor TH (1993) An evaluation of the permeability of disposable polypropylene-based protective gowns to a battery of cancer chemotherapy drugs. *Appl Occup Environ Hygiene.* **8**: 785–9.

107 Harrison BR and Kloos MD (1999) Penetration and splash protection of six disposable gown materials against 15 antineoplastic drugs. *J Oncol Pharm Pract.* **5**: 61–6.

108 Health and Safety Executive (1998) *The Selection, Use and Maintenance of Respiratory Protective Equipment. A practical guide* (2e). HSE Books, Sudbury.

109 British Standards Institute (1992) Filtering half masks to protect against particles. BS EN 149.

110 British Standards Institute (1998) Respiratory protective devices: full face masks – requirements, testing, marketing. BS EN 136.

111 British Standards Institute (1987) Specification for eye protection for industrial and non-industrial uses. BS 2092 (to be replaced by BS EN 166, 167, 168).

112 Connor TH *et al.* (1984) Permeability of latex and polyvinyl chloride gloves to carmustine. *Am J Hosp Pharm.* **41**: 676–9.

113 Oldcorne MA *et al.* (1987) Handling cytotoxic drugs. *Pharm J.* **238**: 488.

114 Thomas PH and Fenton-May V (1987) Protection offered by various gloves to carmustine exposure. *Pharm J.* **238**: 775–7.

115 Slevin ML *et al.* (1984) The efficiency of protective gloves used in the handling of cytotoxic drugs. *Cancer Chemother Pharmacol.* **12**: 151–3.

116 Stoikes ME *et al.* (1987) Permeability of latex and polyvinyl chloride gloves to fluorouracil and methotrexate. *Am J Hosp Pharm.* **44**: 1341–6.

117 Laidlaw JL *et al.* (1984) Permeability of latex and polyvinyl chloride gloves to 20 antineoplastic drugs. *Am J Hosp Pharm.* **41**: 2618–23.

118 Anon. (1987) Working Party Report – guidelines for the handling of cytotoxic drugs: amendment. *Pharm J.* **238**: 414.

119 Corlett SA *et al.* (1991) Permeation of ifosfamide through gloves and cadaver skin. *Pharm J.* **247**: R39.

120 Colligan SA and Horstman SW (1990) Permeation of cancer chemotherapeutic drugs through glove materials under static and flexed conditions. *Appl Occup Environ Hygiene.* **5**: 848–52.

121 Connor TH (1995) Permeability testing of glove materials for use with cancer chemotherapy drugs. *Oncology.* **52**: 256–9.

122 Connor TH (1999) Permeability of nitrile rubber, latex, polyurethane and neoprene to 18 antineoplastic drugs. *Am J Health Syst Pharm.* **56**: 2450–3.

123 Ehntholt DJ *et al.* (1990) A test method for the evaluation of protective glove materials used in agricultural pesticide operations. *Am Ind Hygiene Assoc J.* **51**: 462–8.

124 Kotilainen HR *et al.* (1989) Latex and vinyl examination gloves. Quality control procedures and implications for healthcare workers. *Arch Intern Med.* **149**: 2749–53.

125 NHS Executive (1999) *Latex Medical Gloves and Powdered Latex Medical Gloves. Reducing the risk of allergic reaction to latex and powdered medical gloves.* HSC 1999/186. Department of Health, London.

4

Aspects of service operation

INTRODUCTION

This chapter deals with some of the key elements of clinical governance, which was introduced into the NHS in 1999. In particular, it provides a framework for education and training to ensure competence of the personnel involved and to underpin the lifelong learning/continuing professional development (CPD) agenda. It also includes a new short section on risk management issues which describes the processes that enable errors to be detected, learned from and subsequently eliminated.

Implicit in this is the need for safe systems of work, which are achieved not only by having competent and appropriately educated staff, but also by having an infrastructure consisting of procedures, worksheets and other documentation. Finally, to help assessment of oneself against standards and as a means of professional self-regulation, this section includes a model audit scheme.

DOCUMENTATION

Adequate and efficient documentation is an essential aspect of a pharmacy-operated cytotoxic service. The design of documentation is clearly of importance in ensuring the maintenance of safe procedures and good records of service operation. Furthermore, the use of pharmacy-based documentation, such as patient treatment records, is a vital support to the pharmacist's professional role in ensuring optimal patient care and minimising the risks of adverse events associated with chemotherapy. The range of documents used, their design, reproduction and updating aspects will vary widely between hospitals. They will be governed by local circumstances such as the scale of operation, the grades of staff involved and the extent to which computers are used.

It may be considered that, for some services, documents can be combined or contain superfluous information. However, in this text all of those aspects that require consideration have been indicated. Local circumstances then dictate whether or not they are included in the user documentation.

Most records are now computerised. However, the basic needs of documentation remain the same whatever the information system that is utilised.

1 Documentation needs

The various aspects of cytotoxic services that require documents for safe, reliable and cost-effective operation are shown in Figure 4.1. The actual document needs are summarised under each of the main categories depicted in the figure.

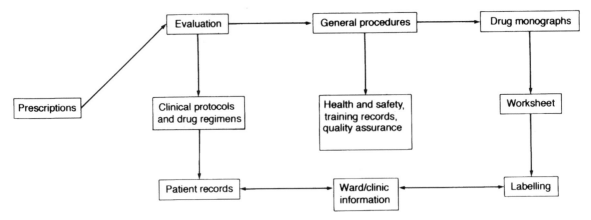

Figure 4.1: *Documentation required for cytotoxic services*

1.1 Prescriptions

There are several options with regard to the ordering of chemotherapy.

- ▼ The patient's prescription may be sent physically or electronically to the pharmacy department.
- ▼ The patient's prescription may be transcribed at ward or clinic level by the visiting pharmacist.
- ▼ A specially designed order form completed by the clinician may be supplied to the pharmacy. This may have a worksheet incorporated in its design.
- ▼ Visual display units or fax machines may be used with terminals at ward, clinic and pharmacy level.

Where a prescription is used, it must fulfil the minimum legal requirements of a prescription for any cytotoxic medicine.

Local hospital or state policy may deem additional information necessary (e.g. patient diagnosis, chemotherapy regimen being used in concise terms, patient details such as surface area, height and weight, and cycle or pulse number, etc.).

An appropriate design must adequately satisfy the requirements of medical, nursing and pharmacy staff, and a degree of compromise may need to be negotiated.

Wherever possible, transcriptions should be avoided because of error potential. Moreover, the prescription itself (or a facsimile) should be available at the time of final release.

1.2 Evaluation

Clinical protocols and drug regimens. Chemotherapy regimens are divided into two main groups:

- ▼ protocols that are part of a formal clinical trial
- ▼ regimens that are based on experience and subject to the clinician's expertise and judgement, many of them being standard first-line treatments.

Clinical trial protocols are often complex and subject to randomisation. For quick reference it may be appropriate to summarise the pharmaceutical aspects in a card or file system which details the following:

- ▼ schedules (induction, consolidation, maintenance, etc.)

▼ drug
▼ dose (per m² or per kg)
▼ how given (route, volume, equipment)
▼ timing (pulses, cycles, etc.)
▼ dosage reductions (when and how appropriate).

For standard treatment regimens, compilations of similar data from reference or clinical sources can also be prepared. However, these are more likely to need updating frequently, and hospital drug information units may be the appropriate means of gathering such information.

Prescription verification. The following checklist covers the key components of prescription verification:

▼ sufficient patient details are provided:
  – full name
  – hospital number
  – date of birth
  – diagnosis
▼ recognition of the regimen/protocol (reference source)
▼ the therapy prescribed is correct and complies with the reference source
▼ drug doses are calculated correctly against surface area/height/weight on prescription
▼ drug doses (single pulses within the cycle, stat doses, etc.) are time and date scheduled according to the protocol
▼ the form of administration (route, diluent, volume, infusion rate) is acceptable and appropriate; for unlicensed drugs/routes of administration, a reference source should be provided by the prescriber, and the appropriate disclaimer documentation signed to accept liability, if required in line with local practice
▼ patient record scrutiny will ensure that treatment progress through the protocol is appropriately timed; cycle delays, dose changes, protocol modifications, etc., should be documented within the pharmacy patient record.

Prescription checking. The checking process should be a separate stage between verification and final release of the product. A procedure based on a checklist such as the following should be implemented:

▼ the drug prepared is as stated on the label and as requested on the prescription
▼ the dose prepared is as stated on the label and as requested on the prescription
▼ diluents used are compatible with the drug
▼ infusion fluids are compatible with both the drug and the diluent used
▼ the stability of the prepared drug is appropriate
▼ the storage conditions on the prepared drug label are appropriate
▼ the label details are correct
▼ all ingredients are checked for batch number and expiry date, and are appropriate for use
▼ the intended route of administration is acceptable and appropriate.

1.3 General procedures

These should be clear, informative and comprehensive, covering all aspects of the pharmacy service. They should be readily accessible, comprehensible to all staff employed in the service and subject to regular review and updating.

Procedures covering the areas listed below are of particular importance:

▼ management structure
▼ receipt and storage of materials
▼ record-keeping
▼ health and safety, including the following:
  – disposal of waste
  – Control of Substances Hazardous to Health (COSHH) requirements
  – handling
  – spillage
  – staff health monitoring
▼ preparation:
  – general
  – checking and labelling
  – packing and distribution
  – computer programs
▼ use of cabinet/isolator, including routine performance tests
▼ changing, including glove policies
▼ cleaning
▼ returned cytotoxics
▼ quality assurance standard operating procedures (SOPs), including the following:
  – settle plates
  – viable counts
  – finger dabs
  – surface sampling – swabs/contact plates
  – particle counting
  – di-octyl-phthalate (DOP aerosol generator or equivalent) filter integrity testing
  – process validation (broth transfers)
  – reading manometers.

For unlicensed products, advice and further information should be sought from the supplier. Such information should be documented for reference and reviewed regularly.

1.4 Worksheets

A general worksheet may be used for all drugs, or specific worksheets may be prepared for particular regimens. Prescription details can be transcribed onto the worksheet or, preferably, the worksheet can be an integral part of the prescription.
  Worksheets should include the following information:

▼ the name of the drug(s)
▼ presentation (physical form, quantity, strength, etc.)
▼ reconstituting solutions/diluents (identification and quantities to be added)
▼ resultant solutions (quantity in volume)
▼ compatible infusion solutions (where appropriate)
▼ storage details
▼ stability
▼ labelling details or sample label
▼ pertinent 'special precautions' (e.g. carmustine vials should be inspected before use for signs of decomposition of the drug).

They should also allow the following information to be recorded:

▼ batch numbers, expiry dates and manufacturer identifiers for all ingredients used
▼ the number of containers used, and the batch number, expiry dates and manufacturer identifiers for containers and compounding equipment which come into contact with the product (e.g. syringes, infusion bags, needles, etc.), or a means of tracing their history
▼ the quantities of solutions to be drawn up or removed
▼ label duplicate
▼ identification of personnel involved in the preparation stages (formulation, assembly of ingredients, reconstitution, etc.)
▼ identification of personnel involved in the checking procedures.

1.5 Labelling

Labels should comply with national regulations and should state the following:

▼ intended route of administration *(particular attention must be paid to identifying clearly preparations intended for intrathecal or regional administration. These must be distinguished from the 'standard' intravenous preparations to reduce the potential for administrative error)*
▼ the name of the drug
▼ quantity of the drug
▼ vehicle containing the drug (infusion solution as appropriate)
▼ final volume
▼ batch number allocated to the product
▼ expiry date
▼ storage conditions that ensure stability, etc.
▼ patient's name and location (ward, etc.)
▼ name and address of the cytotoxic dispensary.

Outer packs for transport should also state clearly details of the contained items and any possible handling hazards.

1.6 Information documents for ward/clinic staff

These should include the elements listed below. The level of detail that is required will depend on local circumstances.

General introduction detailing local policies. These may include the following:

▼ designated areas on ward/clinic for the preparation of cytotoxic agents
▼ personnel (i.e. groups of staff appropriate to undertake reconstitution/ administration)
▼ protective garments that should be worn
▼ equipment that may be used
▼ extravasation policies
▼ disposal of waste.

Drug monographs. These will obviously be much less detailed than those required in pharmacy. They should include the following information:

▼ presentation

▼ reconstitution
▼ compatible solutions
▼ methods of administration
▼ special precautions (operator safety, extravasation, etc.)
▼ stability
▼ accidental spillage (what to do in the event of this).

Arrangements for the supply of cytotoxics from the pharmacy. These include the following:

▼ the procedure for the agreed method of service operation at ward level (e.g. how and when to order)
▼ communication access (personnel to contact, telephone numbers, etc.)
▼ agreed presentations and possible alternatives for each drug.

DOCUMENTATION AND SAFETY IN THE HOME

Although the safety of home chemotherapy has been established over at least a decade, there is a need for continued vigilance, particularly as the number of patients treated in the domiciliary setting continues to increase, and the complexity of infusion regimens and ambulatory pumps is also increasing. The main safety issues focus on the potential risk of exposure of patients' relatives and carers to cytotoxic drugs used in the home or workplace, and the obvious requirement for accurate and reliable infusion delivery by the ambulatory infusion device.

1 Safe handling of cytotoxic drugs in the home

The importance of patient and carer training in the safe handling of cytotoxic drugs has already been stated (*see* Chapter 3) and cannot be overemphasised. The most significant route of cytotoxic contamination appears to be via dermal absorption.[1] It is therefore essential that surface contamination around the home or workplace is avoided. This requires the provision of dedicated refrigerators and sealed, leak-proof polypropylene containers for the storage of prefilled syringes or medication cassettes. A supply of gloves and absorbent preparation mats should be made available to the patient or carer, together with a cytotoxics sharps bin for the safe disposal of cytotoxic waste. Ideally, these consumables should be provided together with the medication[2] (*see* Chapter 3). Arrangements must also be made for the safe disposal of cytotoxic waste, usually through a regular collection service.

The possibility of a cytotoxic drug spillage in the home cannot be overlooked, and patients should be provided with spillage kits designed for such an occurrence. These should contain the following equipment:

▼ protective gloves
▼ goggles
▼ overshoes and gowns to protect the individual dealing with the spillage
▼ booms to contain the spillage
▼ absorbent pads to mop up spilled liquid
▼ prelabelled containers for the safe disposal of contaminated consumables from the spillage kit.

Although written instructions on the use of spillage kits should be included with the kit contents, these are not a substitute for thorough education and training in the use of kits.

Finally, it is always valuable to audit safe handling in the home so that any deficiencies can be identified and rectified. An audit tool with a section applicable to safe handling of cytotoxic drugs in the domiciliary setting has been developed in the UK.[3]

2 Documentation

2.1 Regimen protocols

Comprehensive control documentation is a key element in the provision of safe and effective home chemotherapy. A protocol should be prepared for each regimen used, including the following information:

▼ name and dose of each drug
▼ route of administration (e.g. central venous catheter)
▼ diluent
▼ normal concentration range
▼ infusion rate
▼ duration of infusion
▼ ambulatory device to be used
▼ shelf-life of infusion under storage and in-use conditions (appropriately referenced)
▼ details of any supportive therapy.

Each protocol should be approved by the clinician responsible and also by the oncology pharmacist.

2.2 Programming infusion devices

The programming of infusion devices is a major source of error, and separate protocols for the uses, limitations and programming of each device in use should be prepared. These protocols should also be carefully validated and approved.

For each pump-programming operation, a pump-programming pro forma should be completed detailing all pump settings, which should be signed by the health-care professional making or programming them. These settings should be checked and countersigned by a second individual with proven experience in the use of ambulatory devices, and all pump settings should be checked against the original prescription and the relevant treatment protocol. Any deviations from the protocol must be recorded and approved by the clinician responsible for the patient.

Some of the more recently introduced ambulatory infusion devices (e.g. Graseby Medical 9000 series devices) have the facility to retain a history of each course of treatment administered, and can provide a printout when required. Such printouts are valuable for clinical audit purposes, and after review these should be retained together with completed pump programming pro formas and other documents that are relevant to the patient.

RISK MANAGEMENT

Risk management is an essential component of a quality strategy, and there are few areas of pharmacy practice where risks are greater than those associated with the preparation and subsequent safe administration of injectable cytotoxic drugs.

First, we can identify high-risk factors associated with use of medicines in general. These include the following:

▼ administration of drugs with a low therapeutic index
▼ the intravenous and intrathecal routes
▼ the use of administration devices (e.g. syringe pumps)
▼ certain categories of patient (e.g. intensive treatment unit, neonate, cancer, operations under general anaesthetic)
▼ doses which require calculations, particularly if complex, to be made by junior doctors and nurses
▼ aseptic manipulation of multiple drugs
▼ occupational exposure hazards to those handling the drugs
▼ the use of inadequately trained staff.

It is clear from this fairly simplistic assessment that all of the above apply to injectable cytotoxic drugs, with the possible exception of the last of these, and the overall risk is therefore very high. A further dimension, which is frequently overlooked, is transferred or exported risk. For example, although the pharmacy reconstitution service may prepare injections during normal working hours from Monday to Friday, it may default to a junior doctor with little experience to prepare and administer these drugs at other times. Another instance is labelling, where lack of effective communication could have a fatal outcome. For example, the way in which vinca alkaloids were labelled (IV route only) may have been a factor in some of the fatal events that have followed erroneous administration by the intrathecal route.[4] Certainly these are significant risk factors which need to be examined in a multidisciplinary way.

The use of flow charts can help to identify risks, including those associated with microbiological contamination. The hazard analysis of critical control points (HACCP) concept[5] is utilised in the pharmaceutical industry, and can be used to establish a preventative monitoring system, with each process or step being assessed in terms of the following seven parameters:

▼ analysis and identification of the potential risks (hazard analysis)
▼ identification of the critical control points
▼ definition of limits
▼ in-process controls
▼ the establishment of corrective measures
▼ the confirmatory system (verification)
▼ the documentation system.

The overriding objective is to have safe systems of work by design. As a general principle, errors are reduced by making processes simpler and not the converse, in order to minimise human error. One particular hazard is the transcription of data from one piece of paper to another (e.g. from the patient's prescription to a worksheet). In this case, risks may be managed by having a prescription/order form which incorporates a worksheet or is electronically produced. The prescription verification and checking processes may be made more 'user-friendly' and less prone to error by incorporating (or else having easy access to) treatment protocols and the patient's drug history, and by use of an algorithm to check drug-dose calculations.

Labelling systems can be flawed if, for example, data entries need to overwrite a previous label, where there is a high risk of retaining information pertaining to another patient. The safest system is to have a validated computer program which captures data and minimises human error.

Other components of the risk management process, which also incorporate the UK clinical governance principles,[6] include the following:

▼ operator protection measures
▼ critical incident reporting (no blame culture)
▼ early warning systems (near misses)
▼ complaints procedures (learning from complaints)
▼ capacity model
▼ continuing professional development (CPD) programmes for staff
▼ audit and peer review processes.

QUALITY AUDIT SCHEMES FOR CYTOTOXIC RECONSTITUTION SERVICES

The activities which lead to the provision of a cytotoxic reconstitution service must be safe and effective, and accord with the various standards and guidelines described in this handbook and otherwise promulgated nationally and locally. These standards and guidelines will be continually changing as new ideas emerge and improvements are proposed. It is therefore important that practices are frequently reviewed to ensure that standards are maintained. Even if services are subject to an accreditation process (e.g. by the UK Medicines Control Agency), the principle of self-inspection is commended, and professional audit is now well established in hospital pharmacy. In addition, a systematic critique of process hazards should be undertaken as part of a risk management programme.

The audit process is based on peer review. It is therefore undertaken by colleagues who are well respected and fully conversant with the requirements of a cytotoxic reconstitution service. It is essential that as far as possible the recommendations for change are acted upon and the 'acceptance criteria' are constantly reviewed to reflect current practice. The audit 'cycle' is not complete until change has been implemented and the effects of change have been assessed.

The following audit scheme provides a systematic approach to examining the structure and process aspects of a cytotoxic reconstitution service. The main objectives of the audit process are as follows:

▼ to identify shortcomings and loopholes in procedures and processes
▼ to determine whether procedures are being followed and processes are being carried out effectively by competent staff
▼ to determine whether the facilities, equipment and environment comply with relevant standards

▼ to monitor quality trends and assess the effectiveness of management action to remedy perceived deficiencies

▼ to motivate staff to provide a safe, efficient and cost-effective service.

The audit form (*see* Table 4.1) incorporates a rating scale for level of compliance and also guidance on the means of assessment for each acceptance criterion.

This audit scheme is not proffered as a definitive statement applicable to all situations. Rather, it is intended to be a model which can be adapted to local circumstances. It should also be regarded as one of a number of quality assurance mechanisms that can be applied. For instance, it does not attempt to address the outcomes of the patient's treatment. Information on the development of service standards and an audit system for cytotoxic reconstitution services has also been published by Beaumont and Nicholson.[7]

1 Guidance notes for using quality audit forms

Result ratings

1 Substantial compliance with acceptance criteria.
2 Significant compliance with acceptance criteria.
3 Partial compliance with acceptance criteria.
4 Minimal compliance with acceptance criteria.
5 Non-compliance with acceptance criteria.

Glossary of terms used in connection with the checks required for each criterion

Assess	Requires the auditor(s) to use their professional judgement when attributing a compliance rating.
Data	Generally relates to validation studies and evidence taken from the literature.
Examine	Generally relates to procedures and/or materials which need to be examined for content and validity.
Observe	Generally relates to activities which can be observed by auditor(s) and are representative of normal working practices. In some situations it may be appropriate to undertake this covertly.
Procedure	Relates to written procedures which should be assessed for appropriateness and compliance with official guidelines (e.g. by good manufacturing practice). They should have been recently appraised, signed and, where appropriate, countersigned (e.g. by quality-control staff).
Records	Generally relates to requirements for documentary evidence. These should be inspected at the discretion of the auditor(s).
Test	Applies to situations where the auditor(s) obtain their own evidence by test.

Table 4.1: *Quality audit for cytotoxic reconstitutions*

HOSPITAL: DATE:

No.	Attribute	Acceptance criteria	Check required	Audit result	Comments and action to be taken
001	UK Medicines Act and Section 10 exemptions (UK only)	The activities are carried out under the terms of a manufacturing licence; otherwise, the following conditions are met:			
		1 The preparation is undertaken by, or under the supervision of, a pharmacist	Assess	Yes/No	
		2 The preparation uses 'closed' systems	Assess	Yes/No	
		3 Products have an expiry date of no more than 1 week, or 24 hours if prepared under conditions for short-term use	Records	Yes/No	
002	Capacity model	The facilities, personnel and skill mix enable these activities to be undertaken without compromising safe systems of work at all times	Assess	1 2 3 4 5	
003	Facilities	Facilities are of an appropriate size for the activities undertaken	Assess	1 2 3 4 5	
004		Facilities incorporate appropriate design features in terms of current good manufacturing practice, ergonomics, security, operator protection, work flow, ease of cleaning, etc.	Assess	1 2 3 4 5	
005		Facilities include sufficient shelves, cupboards, benches, etc., for the activities undertaken	Assess	1 2 3 4 5	
006		Walls, floors, ceilings, fixtures and fittings are in good decorative order and maintained to appropriate standards	Assess	1 2 3 4 5	
007		Temperature, humidity control, lighting and noise levels provide comfortable working conditions for staff at all times of year	Assess	1 2 3 4 5	

Table 4.1: *Continued*

No.	Attribute	Acceptance criteria	Check required	Audit result	Comments and action to be taken
	Environmental acceptability (product protection)	(a) Applicable to use of a vertical laminar flow cabinet			
008		Room used complies with EC GMP Grade B air (unmanned) and tested at the designated frequencies	Records	1 2 3 4 5	
009		Cabinet complies with EC GMP Grade A air and tested at the designated frequencies	Records	1 2 3 4 5	
010		The direction of the airflow air is inwards over the whole area of the work aperture (smoke test confirmation)	Records/ test	1 2 3 4 5	
011		The velocity of the downflow air is in accordance with the requirements of relevant standards (e.g. BS 5726 – 0.25–0.50 m/s)	Records	1 2 3 4 5	
012		Safety cabinet/surrounding environment, changing areas, prep rooms and personnel comply with standards for micro-organisms	Records	1 2 3 4 5	
013		Sterile cleanroom garments/ face mask/gloves used for each session	Observe/ procedure	1 2 3 4 5	
014		Cleaning records comply with schedule and the cleaning procedures are appropriate/ validated	Records/ assess	1 2 3 4 5	
015		Manometer readings show adequate differential pressures between rooms, and are recorded daily	Records	1 2 3 4 5	
016		All items are sterile and outer surfaces are swabbed with spore-free 70% (v/v) IMS/IPA before entering the room and again before transfer into the safety cabinet and the process has been validated	Observe/ procedure/ records	1 2 3 4 5	

Table 4.1: *Continued*

No.	Attribute	Acceptance criteria	Check required	Audit result	Comments and action to be taken
		(b) Applicable to use of negative-pressure isolator system			
017		Air in controlled workspace complies with EC GMP Grade A air in the non-operational state and tested at the designated frequencies	Records	1 2 3 4 5	
018		Background environment complies with appropriate standard for air quality according to the design of the isolator and transfer device used at least EC GMP Grade D and tested at the designated frequencies	Records	1 2 3 4 5	
019		Cleaning records comply with schedule (including gaseous sterilisation of the inside of the cabinet when applicable), cleaning procedures are appropriate and the processes have been validated	Records	1 2 3 4 5	
020		Air pressure and filter status within the isolator are monitored continuously. An alarm indicates when these fall outside defined limits	Assess	1 2 3 4 5	
021		Before preparation starts, pressure drops across filters, isolator pressure differentials and airflow rates are checked to confirm that they are within limits and no alarm condition is indicated	Examine	1 2 3 4 5	
022		The transfer device allows transfer of items into the controlled workspace without compromising the Grade A environment, and the process has been validated	Assess/ records	1 2 3 4 5	
023		Dedicated clothing is worn by isolator operators which is appropriate to the background environment. Before preparation starts an appropriate glove-leak test is performed	Assess	1 2 3 4 5	
024		Gloves/garments comply with the limits for perforations specified in BS 4005; 1984 (sterile latex surgeons' gloves)	Examine	1 2 3 4 5	

Table 4.1: *Continued*

No.	Attribute	Acceptance criteria	Check required	Audit result	Comments and action to be taken
025		The procedure for changing gloves prevents a risk to the integrity of the isolator system, and the process has been validated	Assess/ data	1 2 3 4 5	
026		All items are sprayed/ swabbed with spore-free 70% (v/v) IMS/IPA before entering the transfer hatch, and again before entering the controlled workspace	Observe/ procedure/ records	1 2 3 4 5	
027	Environmental acceptability (operator protection)	VLFC complies with KI Discus test or equivalent and tested within 1 year (not applicable for isolators)	Records	1 2 3 4 5	
028		Systems prevent disturbance of air currents during use of cabinet, including opening/ closing of door to room (not applicable for isolators)	Procedure/ assess	1 2 3 4 5	
029		Appropriate types of garments, including gloves, used by staff	Assess	1 2 3 4 5	
030		The glove/sleeve system allows adequate dexterity in use, and gloves are replaced as necessary (isolators only)	Assess	1 2 3 4 5	
031		Luer-lock syringes and large-bore needles are used during manipulations	Observe/ procedure	1 2 3 4 5	
032		Appropriate air-venting of vials occurs to prevent pressure differentials	Observe/ procedure	1 2 3 4 5	
033	Health and safety	All personnel are aware of and comply with the local health and safety policy on handling of cytotoxic materials	Assess	1 2 3 4 5	
034		There is an acceptable procedure for dealing with spillage	Examine	1 2 3 4 5	
035		Appropriate receptacles for contaminated liquids, 'sharps' and other consumables are available	Assess	1 2 3 4 5	
036		An appropriate procedure for disposal of contaminated waste is available	Examine	1 2 3 4 5	

Table 4.1: *Continued*

No.	Attribute	Acceptance criteria	Check required	Audit result	Comments and action to be taken
037		An accident report book is available	Records	1 2 3 4 5	
038		Occupational health arrangements include regular monitoring of all staff who work with cytotoxic drugs, and acknowledging changes in personal circumstances (e.g. becoming pregnant)	Records	1 2 3 4 5	
039	Documentation (general)	All documentation is subject to a system of control which includes regular review, the maintenance of an audit trail and, for computerised systems, a means of restricting access to authorised staff only	Assess	1 2 3 4 5	
040		Satisfactory standard operating procedures have been written/ approved for all items of equipment	Examine	1 2 3 4 5	
041		Worksheets for all different cytotoxic preparations have been written/approved	Examine	1 2 3 4 5	
042		Satisfactory procedures have been written, signed and dated on the following:			
		1 Changing and hand sanitisation prior to entry into preparation area (and this information is displayed)	Examine/ observe	1 2 3 4 5	
		2 Cleaning and maintenance	Examine	1 2 3 4 5	
		3 Environmental and microbiological control	Examine	1 2 3 4 5	
		4 Other routine quality-control testing	Examine	1 2 3 4 5	
		5 Health and safety policy	Examine	1 2 3 4 5	
043	Prescription verification	The prescribed cytotoxic drugs are in accordance with the chemotherapy regimen/protocol, and prescription is explicit with regard to dose, route/rate of administration, time frequency and duration of treatment	Examine	1 2 3 4 5	
044		The prescriptions are signed by authorised medical staff	Examine	1 2 3 4 5	

Table 4.1: *Continued*

No.	Attribute	Acceptance criteria	Check required	Audit result	Comments and action to be taken
045		The prescriptions can be related to current patient data, including diagnosis, age, sex, body weight, height, surface area, haematology and renal function, as appropriate	Examine	1 2 3 4 5	
046		Doses that have been calculated by the prescriber are independently checked	Procedure/ assess	1 2 3 4 5	
047	Compounding	Documentary evidence of correct reconstitution	Records	1 2 3 4 5	
048		Evidence to show that the product is stable and an appropriate shelf-life in the container has been assigned	Data	1 2 3 4 5	
049		Other documentary evidence is completed and satisfactory	Records	1 2 3 4 5	
050		Appropriate segregation techniques are used to prevent compounding errors	Assess	1 2 3 4 5	
051		There is evidence to show that the correct solutions have been incorporated into syringe/bag	Observe	1 2 3 4 5	
052	Presentation	Label has acceptable legibility	Examine/ sample	1 2 3 4 5	
053		Label indicates route of injection and includes appropriate hazard warnings (*note special warnings for vinca alkaloids*)	Examine/ sample	1 2 3 4 5	
054		Label bears unambiguous expression of ingredients/ quantities	Examine/ sample	1 2 3 4 5	
055		Label shows correct expiry date/time	Examine/ sample	1 2 3 4 5	
056		Label shows correct storage conditions	Examine/ sample	1 2 3 4 5	
057		Outer packaging is properly sealed and prevents contents leaking during transit	Examine/ sample	1 2 3 4 5	
058		Contents are clear and free from visible particles	Examine/ sample	1 2 3 4 5	

Table 4.1: *Continued*

No.	Attribute	Acceptance criteria	Check required	Audit result	Comments and action to be taken
059	Personnel	There is an agreed and defined management structure	Assess	1 2 3 4 5	
060		A written training and education manual is available	Examine	1 2 3 4 5	
061		Training records are maintained for all staff	Examine	1 2 3 4 5	
062		Appropriately trained and, where appropriate, supervised pharmacists/pharmacy technicians undertake the manipulations	Assess	1 2 3 4 5	
063		The modus operandi acknowledges the occupational health aspects of the processes involved	Assess	1 2 3 4 5	
064		Staff perform satisfactory process validations to demonstrate initial competence, and subsequently at defined intervals	Records	1 2 3 4 5	
065	Effective use of resources	Notification of pharmacy by ward/clinic allows convenient scheduling	Assess	1 2 3 4 5	
066		Most cost-effective grade(s) of staff are used	Assess	1 2 3 4 5	
067		Choice of units of ingredients minimises wastage	Assess	1 2 3 4 5	
068		The ingredients bear the nearest expiry date of stock	Examine	1 2 3 4 5	
069		The wastage of disposables used is minimal	Observe	1 2 3 4 5	
070	Storage/ distribution and administration	Contents are suitably protected against heat/light, etc.	Examine	1 2 3 4 5	
071		Where products are refrigerated, the refrigerator temperatures are in the appropriate temperature range, and are monitored	Examine/ records	1 2 3 4 5	
072		Syringes/bags are suitably protected and clearly identified for transport to the ward/clinic	Examine	1 2 3 4 5	

Table 4.1: *Continued*

No.	Attribute	Acceptance criteria	Check required	Audit result	Comments and action to be taken
073		Bags can be delivered to the ward/clinic by the intended time of administration	Assess	1 2 3 4 5	
074		Syringes/bags are appropriately stored on the ward if they are not to be used immediately, and do not exceed their expiry date	Assess	1 2 3 4 5	
075	Quality assurance and audit	A comprehensive quality assurance programme underpins all processes	Assess	1 2 3 4 5	
076		There is a programme of regular internal and periodic external audit which includes risk assessment of the processes	Records	1 2 3 4 5	
077		All complaints and errors are logged and investigated promptly and effectively to prevent a recurrence	Records	1 2 3 4 5	

NAME: JOB TITLE: SIGNATURE: DATE:

Auditor(s):

Other staff present:

Copies sent to:

Next audit date:

Essential reference documents:

- Medicines Control Agency (1997) *Rules and Guidance for Pharmaceutical Manufacturers and Distributors*. The Stationery Office, London.
- NHS Quality Control Committee (1995) *The Quality Assurance of Aseptic Preparation Services* (2e). NHS Quality Control Committee, London.
- UK Isolator Group (1994) *A Specification for Isolators for Pharmaceutical Users*. HMSO, London.

EDUCATION AND TRAINING

All staff employed to handle cytotoxic materials should receive education and training appropriate to their level of involvement in the handling, preparation or administration of the drugs.

A training programme should include practical experience, one-to-one teaching, learning exercises which may be tested and information on health and safety. A more advanced programme will also include clinical and theoretical training.

In some countries basic training for technical staff is by competency assessment. In the UK this is known as National Vocational Qualification (NVQ). National

Vocational Qualifications are based on national occupational standards and have two arms:

▼ performance criteria, assessed by observation
▼ underpinning knowledge, assessed by questioning and written assignments.

These standards could be used as a baseline in the assessment of all staff, and would highlight any training needs.

THE TRAINING CHECKLIST

A checklist is a good starting point for a formal or informal training programme. Staff may use the list simply as a guide to the areas that should be covered, or a more extensive programme may be written around the headings in a checklist. Although this training checklist (*see* Table 4.2) is primarily intended for pharmacy staff, it could be adapted for nursing or medical staff who handle cytotoxic drugs.

The aim of the checklist is to enable staff to acquire knowledge of and competence in aseptic procedures, cytotoxic reconstitution, local procedures, current awareness, active information, management, and research and development. These are intended as broad guidelines for training. Local variations will exist depending on circumstances.

The degree of training required in each section depends on the level of involvement of different groups of staff in the provision of chemotherapy. The staff groups are indicated at the top of each column in Table 4.2.

Level 1 Full-time and rotational technicians involved in the provision of a cytotoxic reconstitution service.
Level 2 Pre-registration pharmacists, junior/rotational pharmacists and senior pharmacists from other specialties.
Level 3 Senior pharmacists and technical staff managing a sterile preparation or cytotoxic reconstitution service.

The checklist attempts to differentiate between activities that represent a fundamental part of the individual's job and those where information only is required. In the former, competence must be demonstrated against the standards defined by the manager of the unit. The latter may be covered by directed reading/open learning programmes. Smaller units may require external support to cover some areas.

Table 4.2: *Education and training checklist*

	Level 1	Level 2	Level 3
Aseptic technique			
What it is	A	A	A
Why it is needed	A	A	A
How it is achieved	A	A	A
Test for ensuring and maintaining it	A	A	A
How to detect when it has failed	A	A	A
What to do when it fails	A	A	A
Cytotoxic reconstitution			
What cytotoxics are	A	A	A
Why they are a hazard	A	A	A
How aerosols are generated	A	A	A
How aerosols are prevented	A	A	A
Other possible routes of exposure/contamination	A	A	A
General reconstitution techniques	A	A	A
Special reconstitution techniques	A	A	A
Use of special equipment	A	A	A
Correct documentation	A	A	A
Expiry and storage	A	A	A
Tests for ensuring and maintaining good technique	A	A	A
Local procedures			
For aseptic technique	A	A	A
For cytotoxic reconstitution	A	A	A
Use of equipment			
Special reconstitution devices	A	A	A
Special administration devices	I	I	I
Evaluation of new equipment	A	A	A
Clinical data/pharmaceutical data			
Clinical notes	I	A	A
Laboratory tests	I	A	A
Disease evaluation tests	I	I	A
Clinical/nursing procedures	I	I	A
Administration procedures	I	A	A
Practical pharmacokinetics	I	A	A
Evaluation of information			
Publications	I	A	A
Protocols	I	I	A
Basic statistics	A	A	A
Drug representatives	I	A	A
Promotional material	I	I	A
Verbal communications	A	A	A
Obtaining drug/clinical information			
In-house	A	A	A
Reading list	I	A	A
Library	I	A	A
Oral communications	A	A	A
On-line via drug information centre	I	I	A

Table 4.2: *Continued*

	Level 1	Level 2	Level 3
Data handling			
Protocols	A	A	A
Documentation	A	A	A
Workload statistics	A	I	A
Records	A	I	A
Clinical data	I	I	A
Adverse reaction reporting	I	I	A
Extravasation procedure	I	A	A
Mechanism of action	I	A	A
Overdose	I	A	A
Interactions with other drugs	I	A	A
Kinetics	I	I	A
Disposal	A	A	A
Legal and ethical considerations	A	A	A
Health and safety regulations			
Nationally	A	I	A
Locally	A	A	A
Staff screening	A	I	A
Accident reporting	A	A	A
Accident procedure	A	A	A
Health service background			
National framework for the provision of cytotoxic services	I	I	I
Current awareness	A	A	A
Active information			
Bulletins	I	I	A
Seminars	I	I	A
Lectures	I	I	A
Management			
Education/training of appropriate pharmaceutical, nursing and medical staff	–	–	A
Monitoring of service quality	A	A	A
Work planning	A	A	A
Committee skills	–	–	I
Finance/budgeting	–	–	A
Interviewing	–	–	A
Guidelines for protocol submission, preparation and evaluation	–	–	A
Research and development			
Service development	–	–	A
Technique evaluation	–	–	A
Drug evaluation	–	–	A
Publication	–	–	A

Key: A (activity) = trainee required to demonstrate competence in this area.
I (information) = trainee requires information only.

REFERENCES

1 Sessink P, van der Kerkhaf M, Anzion R *et al.* (1995) Biological and environmental monitoring of occupational exposure to cyclophosphamide in a hospital pharmacy department. *J Oncol Pharm Pract.* **1 (ISOPP IV Symposium Issue)**: 25.

2 Shrubb D and Sewell GJ (1995) Home care, ambulatory chemotherapy, nursing and pharmaceutical issues. *J Oncol Pharm Pract.* **1 (ISOPP IV Symposium Issue)**: 14.

3 Sizer S and Sewell GJ (1996) Check exposure to cytotoxics: development and use of an audit for cytotoxic drug handling in pharmacy, clinical and domiciliary areas. *Pharm Pract.* **6**: 153–6.

4 Jahnke M (1997) Use of the HACCP concept for the risk analysis of pharmaceutical manufacturing processes. *Eur J Parent Sci.* **2**: 113–17.

5 Committee on Safety of Medicines (1990) *Current Problems in Pharmacovigilance No. 30.* Committee on Safety of Medicines, London.

6 Department of Health (1999) *Clinical Governance: quality in the new NHS.* HSC 1999/065. Department of Health, London.

7 Beaumont I and Nicholson M (1995) Cytotoxic reconstitution services – development of service standards and an audit system. *Hosp Pharm.* **2**: 97–9.

5

Administration of chemotherapy

INTRODUCTION

This chapter brings together many of the issues which need to be considered when preparing for or administering chemotherapy. It covers a wide diversity of issues, both practical and theoretical, starting with the physical environment and location. This handbook reflects the growing trend towards outpatient and day-care chemotherapy, as well as the broadening horizons for community and/or home-based chemotherapy.

The physical and pharmacological advantages and disadvantages of this type of therapy, as well as the educational, documentational and safety aspects, are discussed. Finally, the chapter gives some consideration to the advantages and disadvantages of the various alternative routes of administration for chemotherapy which are increasingly entering routine clinical use, and presents a wide variety of issues both in terms of stability in new delivery systems or fluids, and from a practical point of view with regard to preparing and monitoring 'old' drugs in new environments.

NON-HOME ENVIRONMENT

Despite enormous research effort with regard to determining the value of different cytotoxic drugs and combinations in the treatment of malignancies, and the development of protocols for the safe prescription and administration of chemotherapy by most hospitals and oncology departments, relatively little attention has been paid to the environment in which treatment is given. In the UK, only a few of the newest centres have accommodation designed specifically for the administration of chemotherapy. Often this activity is carried out in whatever ward or clinic area the oncology department has occupied for the last few decades, with little concession to the increasing numbers of patients who are receiving chemotherapy, and the increasing complexity of their treatments.

Consideration of the facilities required for the safe administration of chemotherapy in the community and at home, where an increasing number of patients are now being treated, has also been scant. Some of the factors that must be considered when attempting to create a pleasant and safe environment for chemotherapy administration are discussed below.

1 Inpatient chemotherapy

At present, many patients who are receiving routine chemotherapy are admitted to wards that are attempting to cater for a broad cross-section of oncology patients.

This may be inappropriate given the different needs of patients who are receiving active treatment and those receiving palliative care after the exhaustion of active treatment options. It also creates problems for staff who are trying to balance the need to expedite the treatment of short-stay chemotherapy patients, who are in a hurry to get on with their treatment, with the sometimes less urgent – but equally important – physical, spiritual and emotional needs of chronic patients. One solution to this conflict is to have separate nursing teams looking after these two different patient populations.

The physical environment on most medical wards is satisfactory for the administration of chemotherapy, although small bed clusters of two, four or at a maximum six beds, with an appropriate balance of side or single bedrooms within the total ward or unit area, may be more appropriate than traditional open wards for patients whose intravenous therapy requires regular attention during the night, when nursing intervention may disturb neighbouring patients, and whose disease and treatment require a very careful balance between privacy and camaraderie.

Bathroom facilities on wards with large numbers of chemotherapy recipients may also need to be expanded. Many patients will receive large quantities of intravenous fluid, and some will also suffer gastrointestinal upset, resulting in frequent visits to the toilet.

If chemotherapy is being administered on a ward, cytotoxic-drug-contaminated waste will be produced, and proper facilities need to be available for the safe storage of such material prior to disposal. Any storage area should be readily cleaned in the event of any spillage. For this reason, inpatient chemotherapy should only be administered on dedicated oncology wards.

As important as the ward layout is its communication with other key departments, notably pathology and pharmacy. Chemotherapy cannot proceed until blood counts (and often blood biochemistry) have been checked, and until pharmacy-prepared cytotoxic doses are available on the ward. Similarly, patient discharge is dependent on the delivery to the ward of any discharge medication dispensed by pharmacy. Therefore an oncology ward should ideally be situated very close to both pathology and pharmacy departments, and either adequate provision made for portering between ward and departments, or investment made in vacuum-line technology.

In a busy oncology unit, consideration should be given to establishing a satellite pharmacy unit at ward level. If such a unit is planned, this must be done with input from sufficiently experienced pharmacy staff to ensure that it will be of an adequate size and specification to meet the demands that are likely to be placed upon it.

2 Day-patient chemotherapy

An increasing number of patients who would formerly have been treated as inpatients are now receiving chemotherapy in day-case units. This approach has obvious cost advantages to the treatment centre, and is in general preferred by patients. The facilities needed for the administration of prolonged and complex chemotherapy regimens in this way are more akin to those needed on an oncology ward than to those traditionally provided in a medical outpatient clinic. For example, patients need access to beds so that they can lie down if they feel tired or unwell, or are being subjected to procedures such as intrathecal drug therapy which require them to lie down. Beds should be in an area that affords an appropriate degree of privacy. There should be refreshment facilities and ideally a social area with television, etc., to help patients to pass the time and to provide distraction.

Nursing staff also need adequate facilities for storing drugs, dressings and other disposables correctly, and for the preparation of non-cytotoxic drug doses in a clean, calm and quiet environment where interruptions are kept to a minimum in order to reduce the risk of mistakes. Ideally, all medication should be dispensed by the hospital pharmacy.

As with ward areas (*see* page 86) consideration needs to be given to the provision of facilities for the storage of cytotoxic waste, adequate toilet facilities, and the proximity of day-treatment areas to the departments of pharmacy and pathology. In addition, facilities must be available close at hand for dealing with patients who become acutely unwell during treatment and therefore require overnight hospitalisation.

Very few therapies need to be administered as an inpatient stay. This is due to the increasing sophistication of support therapies (e.g. antiemetics). With careful education and selection of patients, even cisplatinum-based therapy can be administered on a day-case basis.

3 Outpatient chemotherapy

Outpatients will continue to be the largest group of chemotherapy recipients in the foreseeable future, and their numbers are increasing rapidly in the UK. Unfortunately, the chemotherapy that they receive is still too often administered in inadequate facilities.

Problems often begin on arrival in the clinic, when patients are kept waiting for long periods to see a doctor, have blood samples taken and processed, have their chemotherapy prepared and administered and, finally, for any take-home medication to be prepared by the pharmacy department.

Such delays are at best unpleasant, but they can be disastrous for patients who are experiencing anticipatory or post-chemotherapy nausea and vomiting. Many reported delays are the result of inadequate resourcing, particularly when patient throughput is increased without a corresponding expansion in the support staff looking after them, but others can be kept to a minimum by good organization.[1]

Almost all of the organisational and operational systems discussed with regard to day-case chemotherapy facilities apply equally well to outpatient treatment. However, the functional links between the chemotherapy clinic and the pharmacy and pathology departments are even more critical, given the need to minimise patient delays. New initiatives such as 'close-banding', where doses are administered using a combination of standard prefilled syringes, can reduce patient waiting times, although this may be incompatible with many national studies which require exact dosing.

HOME ENVIRONMENT

1 Potential benefits of home chemotherapy

Traditionally, a considerable proportion of patients have been admitted to hospital as inpatients or as day-case patients to receive their chemotherapy. This may be socially, geographically or psychologically difficult for either the patient or their carer(s), and despite the best facilities, staff and supportive therapies available in a designated treatment centre, it is the desire of most patients to be able to remain at home and to maintain as normal a lifestyle as possible.[2] Demand for home-based treatment combined with developments in drug administration technology has resulted in the emergence of domiciliary chemotherapy programmes, where the patient is able to receive parenteral chemotherapy in their own home. Home-based chemotherapy not only reduces the stress and inconvenience of attending hospital, but also enables the patient to take an active role in his or her treatment.

Home chemotherapy enables the patient to enjoy greater independence, particularly if the chemotherapy is self-administered. The active involvement of patients in their treatment tends to encourage a more positive attitude to chemotherapy. Drug-related adverse effects may be more readily tolerated if patients are able to remain at home with their families in familiar surroundings.

Families of cancer patients often experience a feeling of helplessness and inadequacy, and home-based treatment provides an opportunity for families and close friends to give assistance and support with treatment. All of these factors can contribute to increased morale of patients and their families.

Psychological studies[3] on both domiciliary and hospitalised patients receiving similar chemotherapy regimens have demonstrated an improved quality of life and a greater sense of well-being in home-based patients. Evidence suggests that quality of life is also schedule dependent, and favours patients who are receiving chemotherapy by continuous infusion.[4] Home treatment also reduces the potential exposure of immunocompromised cancer patients to hospital infections.[2]

A properly managed home chemotherapy programme can reduce the costs associated with hospitalisation and increase treatment availability. In a randomised study of inpatient vs. outpatient continuous infusion chemotherapy for patients with locally advanced head and neck cancer, Vokes et al.[5] estimated a reduction in daily costs of $366 per patient for domiciliary chemotherapy.

2 Limitations of home chemotherapy

In the home setting, professional assistance is not readily available to the patient. Acute drug-related toxicity, equipment failure, extravasation of the drug infusion, thrombus formation, blockage and/or infection of the central venous catheter are difficulties which may cause patients severe distress. Acute toxicity can be kept to a minimum by:

▼ using adequate supportive medication
▼ continuous ambulatory infusions for drug delivery
▼ pharmacodynamic individualisation of the drug dosage.

It is essential that patients are given thorough training in how to react in cases of equipment failure, and that this is supported by written instructions and a

24-hour telephone number to enable home-based patients to contact a member of the oncology team. Most complications can be anticipated, and dealing with them represents an integral part of the patient training programme. With experienced home care oncology teams, complications are rare and catheter infection rates of less than 1% are obtainable.[6] Furthermore, the healthcare team must expect and anticipate either new or alternative manifestations of drug toxicities.

Some patients are incapable of maintaining their treatment at home. This may be because they are unable to understand basic instructions relating to their treatment, or because of a physical disability (e.g. arthritis) that would prevent them from handling the infusion device and other equipment. In some cases, support from family or friends may not be available, and communications with the hospital-based oncology team may be difficult (e.g. the patient may not have access to a telephone). Some patients may prefer the security of a hospital and are unwilling to take on the responsibility of home-based treatment. Careful patient selection is essential, and will exert a profound influence on the outcome of home chemotherapy. In addition, the views of the patient's relatives and carers must be considered.

The economics of home chemotherapy may not always be viewed in a favourable light, largely because healthcare financial systems are inflexible and geared to inpatient treatment. Although home chemotherapy may release hospital beds, costs will increase if these are subsequently occupied by other patients. At best, home-based treatment provides hospital managers with the following choice:

▼ either to reduce the number of oncology beds and save money
▼ or to reoccupy released beds with other patients (not necessarily cancer patients) and reduce the waiting-lists.

In addition, savings made at ward level may be difficult to transfer to the budgets of those departments (e.g. pharmacy), where expenditure is increased as a result of home chemotherapy.

3 Patient selection

Careful patient selection is crucial to the success of a home chemotherapy programme. Before the option of domiciliary treatment is offered, the clinician must establish that the patient is well motivated, physically capable of managing their medication syringes, infusion pump or other equipment, and that they are able to understand the detailed instructions. Normally, patients should have a reasonable performance status (Karnofsky score of at least 60) and should be capable of enjoying a satisfactory quality of life during home treatment. Ideally, support should be available from family and friends who are able to adjust their own routines in order to help to care for the patient. The availability of transport to and from the oncology outpatient clinic must be considered, and although it is possible to offer home chemotherapy to patients who live some distance from their hospital, access to a telephone is essential.

Patients with a wide range of cancers, including leukaemias (during remission) and solid tumours, can be treated in the domiciliary setting.[6-8] In many cases, home patients are receiving palliative treatment for recurrent disease following surgery or radiotherapy, and the disease may be at an advanced stage. Patients in the last stages of disease or with fistulae, internal bleeding, ascites, systemic infection or severe nutritional deficiency are clearly not suitable for home treatment. Similarly, those patients who are unable to cope with the psychological and emotional stress associated with cancer should be offered the professional care that is available in the hospital or hospice system.

4 The home oncology team

The success of home-based chemotherapy is dependent on a team approach to patient care. The team would typically include the following:

▼ consultant oncologist
▼ oncology nurse
▼ oncology pharmacist.

Chemotherapy by continuous infusion using ambulatory pumps may be placed by a surgeon or anaesthetist or, if peripherally inserted, can be placed by trained nurses. If home-based patients are receiving ambulatory chemotherapy, at least one member of the team (usually the pharmacist or nurse) should be available 24 hours a day to deal with any problems that may arise with infusion pumps or the central venous catheter.

The team should also be able to call upon the resources of other departments, such as microbiology and medical electronics (for testing and calibration of infusion pumps). If home chemotherapy is to be based on nurse-administered bolus or short infusion schedules, the team should include a fully trained oncology nurse. It is of course essential that the patient's general practitioner is informed about the treatment. If it becomes necessary to switch from chemotherapy to pain control, the venous access system used for chemotherapy can then be used for the infusion of opiates. In such cases, hospice nurses may become involved in the preparation and administration of opiate or other analgesic/antiemetic infusions.

5 Patient procedures

Although they are based on the experience of a UK home treatment centre,[6,9] the patient procedures described below represent a typical approach that is common to other home oncology centres.

Suitable patients are introduced to the concept of home chemotherapy (and prolonged continuous infusion, if appropriate) by a senior member of the medical team. If a patient decides to accept the option of home-based treatment, they may then be referred to the oncology pharmacist for a more detailed explanation of the treatment. In some centres the patient is invited to view a video presentation, together with the oncology pharmacist, in which healthcare professionals discuss various aspects of home chemotherapy with previously treated patients and their relatives. The video would normally deal with specific issues of interest to the patient, including insertion of the central venous catheter, changing of medication reservoirs, management of the infusion pump or venous access port, and care of the dressing at the site of catheter entry. The video presentation may also include previously treated patients discussing their treatment, their lifestyle, and any difficulties that they encountered with regard to the infusion pump. This often prompts the prospective patient to raise questions about the treatment, and provides an opportunity for any anxieties or fears to be raised. In some institutions the oncology pharmacist is required to take on the role of counsellor – a role that will be developed with each new patient as they attend the oncology outpatient clinic for routine assessment.

Normally the patient is admitted to the oncology ward for insertion of the central venous catheter. This is an aseptic procedure and it is performed under local anaesthetic by an experienced anaesthetist. Prior to discharge from hospital, the patient is trained in the management of their treatment by the oncology pharmacist. The patient is taught how to operate the infusion pump, how to recognise and respond to any warning alarms the pump may have, how to store medication reservoirs and how to change them in the pump when necessary. Instruction is given in the safe disposal of cytotoxic waste and used medication reservoirs. Often potential problems can be anticipated and dealt with before they arise. For example, patients are often concerned about the presence of a small bubble of air in the infusion catheter. This is not clinically significant, and the patient can be reassured before they even experience the problem themselves. Occasionally the patient may forget to close the tap on the catheter before disconnecting the medication reservoir, resulting in venous blood flowing out through the catheter. Difficulties of this nature and the necessary action to take are always discussed with the patient before they leave the hospital. The patient remains on the ward until the pharmacist is satisfied that they are fully competent. This usually takes 24 to 48 hours.

In some cases it may be advisable to train patients' relatives in the relevant techniques so that they are able to offer constructive support to the patient. As a back-up to the training programme, patients also receive concise written instructions and are given telephone numbers which may be used to contact oncology nurses or the oncology pharmacist, 24 hours a day. With the development of peripherally inserted central venous catheters there may be less need to hospitalise patients for catheter insertion. However, it is important to ensure that adequate time is made available for patient training.

On discharge from hospital, the patient is supplied with prefilled syringes or a medication reservoir for ambulatory pump use, or with prefilled syringes for bolus injection. Where drug stability permits, the patient is supplied with sufficient medication for 14 days of treatment (or if the treatment schedule is based on a period of less than 14 days, sufficient medication to complete the course). During breaks in chemotherapy to permit bone-marrow recovery, heparinised saline is supplied to ensure that the subclavian catheter remains patent.

The patient is also given supplies of consumables to take home. These include spare batteries for infusion pumps, protective gloves, sterile wipes for absorbing any minor spillage, and burn-bins for disposing of cytotoxic waste and used syringes/medication reservoirs. To help to protect other members of the patient's household from inadvertent cytotoxic drug contamination, home-based patients should be supplied with a small, locking drug refrigerator (complete with thermometer) for storage of their medication, as well as a spillage clean-up kit to contain and decontaminate accidental drug spillages.

Patients usually attend the oncology outpatient clinic every two weeks where they are seen by the consultant oncologist who monitors the patient's clinical condition. The dressing at the site of catheter entry is changed by the oncology nurse. Outpatient visits also present an opportunity for the oncology pharmacist to deal with any infusion-pump-related problems, or queries concerning adverse effects of the medication. During these fortnightly visits, patients collect further supplies of consumables from the outpatient clinic and further supplies of medication from the hospital pharmacy.

Some patients who are participating in home chemotherapy programmes will be entered into controlled clinical trials, usually of a phase II or phase III nature. Visits to the outpatient clinic provide the clinician with an opportunity to monitor the patient extensively and to determine the quality of life enjoyed by the patient during treatment. If pharmacokinetic studies also form part of the trial, it is preferable for blood samples to be taken by a visiting oncology nurse (or a pharmacist trained in phlebotomy), rather than subject the patient to repeated hospital visits.

6 Preparation of medication for home chemotherapy patients

The introduction of a home chemotherapy programme is likely to affect the workload of the hospital pharmacy department in several areas. Consideration should be given to resource and funding implications before a home chemotherapy programme is implemented.

Unless the number of hospital-based oncology beds is reduced, the introduction of home chemotherapy may result in an increased patient throughput. This would be reflected by increased demands for the preparation of cytotoxic infusions and increased expenditure on the drugs budget. The preparation of prefilled medication reservoirs for ambulatory infusion pumps will require additional staff training.

In the case of home chemotherapy, it must be recognised that even prefilled syringes for bolus medication may be stored in the patient's refrigerator for several weeks before use. Drug infusions delivered by ambulatory pumps are not only stored for long periods (up to 14 days) under refrigerated conditions before use, but are also subjected to temperatures of 35–37°C in the pump reservoir worn under the patient's clothing. It is therefore essential to determine the physical and chemical stability of infusions used in home chemotherapy regimens when under storage (4–8°C) and when in use (35–37°C). Exposure time will vary according to the type of infusion pump used. The prefilled syringes used in the Graseby syringe driver usually contain a maximum of 24 hours' supply of medication, and are changed daily by the patient. If it is proposed to give a full 14 days' supply of medication, stability studies should be performed under storage conditions (4–8°C) over 14 days and under in-use conditions (35–37°C) over 24 hours. In the case of infusion pumps with large-volume cassettes or pouch-type medication reservoirs which contain sufficient infusion for 5 to 14 days' treatment (depending on the regimen), drug stability under in-use conditions (35–37°C) should be determined over the treatment period. Since medication cassettes/pouches are normally connected to the infusion pump within 24 hours of preparation, stability studies under storage conditions (4–8°C) need only be continued over 24 hours. However, if two prefilled medicated cassettes/pouches are supplied to give a total of 14 days' treatment, drug stability would be determined over 7 days under both storage and in-use conditions. It is advisable to monitor the temperature of the drug refrigerator supplied to each patient to ensure that medication is stored at the correct temperature.

Stability data for drug infusions in ambulatory infusion devices (where applicable) are given in the individual drug monographs on pages 263–474.

Provision of several days' or weeks' supply of medication to home patients necessitates a marked deviation from the 'ideal' practice of commencing drug administration within 24 hours of preparation. The chemical and physical stability of the drug infusion must be established and the microbiological aspects of long-term supply must also be considered. It cannot be assumed that cytotoxic infusions are bactericidal,[10] and it is therefore essential that all equipment associated with the aseptic preparation of medication for home patients is carefully monitored, and that all procedures are thoroughly validated. In the UK, recent guidelines issued by the Department of Health[11] preclude the assignment of a shelf-life of more than 7 days to any aseptically dispersed product, irrespective of data that would support a longer expiry period.

This guidance will largely restrict the preparation of medication supplies for home use to those centres that are licensed for the manufacture of aseptic 'specials' by the UK Medicines Control Agency, where longer, more practical shelf-lives are permitted, provided that stability and aseptic procedures have been validated.

COMMUNITY CHEMOTHERAPY

Community or outreach chemotherapy represents the latest and perhaps most logical development of day-case, outpatient and home-based chemotherapy. Either a mobile unit or a specified partially dedicated community facility (e.g. a treatment room in a large general practitioner practice) is established, and staffed or visited on a timetabled basis. The mobile unit or outreach centre is staffed by a combination of primary and secondary healthcare workers, thus giving a much better balance between expertise and 'trusted friend', bridging the healthcare interface and so delivering seamless care to the cancer patient.

The centre actively delivers chemotherapy at predetermined times, but is also available as a 'drop-in' centre to deal with physical or psychological problems on an extended 'full-time' basis.

Outreach centres are co-ordinating cancer centres in that they will screen potential patients, establish care plans and act as a safety and communication bridge for the network. One centre or mobile unit can cover a population of 100 000–150 000, and is thus of such a size that it can be viable whilst still being able to cater for the needs of local patients. The outreach centres suit urban and inner-city areas, whereas mobile centres are suitable for rural communities.

Patients utilising the service can receive either bolus or continuous infusion chemotherapy, and can use one or more of the centres by prior arrangement (e.g. the one nearest to their home and work). They can use any one of the outreach posts or centres in the event of an emergency. This has been facilitated by one-press 'Help'-buttoned autodial mobile telephones, a simple safety procedure with direct 24-hour hospital contact and access backup, and 'smart' cards that contain patients' relevant medical histories.[12]

AMBULATORY INFUSION PUMPS FOR CYTOTOXIC THERAPY

Traditionally, cytotoxic chemotherapy has been administered in single or combined regimens designed to maximise cell-kill whilst minimising toxicity. However, in practice these high-dose, 'pulsed' regimens are not always ideal because of the need to hospitalise patients, and the high incidence of side-effects which can delay further therapy.

Evidence has shown that continuous infusion of a low dose of a cytotoxic drug achieves equivalent or higher tumour concentrations over a longer period than bolus, pulsed therapy,[13] and that clinical benefits, particularly in terms of reduced toxicity[14] and improved quality of life,[4] may be achieved.

In response to the demand for this method of administration there have been rapid advances in pump technology. A wide variety of ambulatory infusion pumps is now available, ranging in complexity from external syringe drivers to implantable, programmable pumps. Some of the more recent introductions offer particularly advanced electronic features, including the ability to print out an infusion history for clinical audit purposes, and programming facilities to emulate circadian drug delivery to exploit the perceived advantages of chronotherapy in cancer treatment.[15]

In many ways the pace of ambulatory infusion device development has increased the difficulties of device selection. Studies that compare the different ambulatory infusion pumps which are available have defined some of the clinical, economic and pharmaceutical parameters of relevance to the selection process.[16,17] Pump selection influences the clinical outcome of ambulatory treatment and also the quality of life experienced by the patient.[18] It is essential that healthcare professionals who are involved in ambulatory care have a detailed knowledge of infusion devices to facilitate appropriate device selection. For this and other reasons (training, spare-parts inventory, etc.) it is preferable that the number of different devices used within an institution is limited and that they are selected by objective evaluation, rather than by individual preference.

The pumps described below represent a selection of those currently and previously available in the UK and USA, which is by no means intended to be comprehensive. Some of the devices described here are no longer available but remain in clinical use.

A larger range of pumps is available worldwide, and the reader is directed to the literature available in their own country for details of additional types of pump which have been used for the administration of cytotoxic chemotherapy.

SYRINGE PUMPS

Models: Perfusor ME; Graseby Medical, MS16A (*see* Figure 5.1) and MS26; Critikon, Syringe Minder 2

Syringe pumps are pocket-sized, usually battery-operated, and are simple in design with only a few alarms (e.g. low battery, end of infusion and occlusion pressure). They use a range of syringes from 1 mL to 35 mL, although individual models may be limited to a narrower range.

The drug reservoir is a prefilled syringe that is firmly clamped onto the pump, which is driven by a small battery-powered motor. A rotating lead screw (or drive shaft) moves the actuator (or drive nut) down the device at a constant rate, pushing the syringe plunger into the syringe barrel. The rate of delivery of the drug is determined by the diameter of the syringe and the speed at which the lead screw rotates.

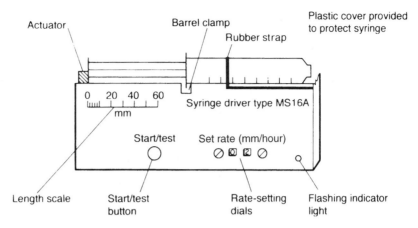

Figure 5.1: *Graseby MS 16A pump*

Syringe pumps have been used successfully for self-administration of cytotoxic agents.[6,19] They can be used with variable flow rates to a high level of accuracy (± 2–5%). Due to the pressure generated, the pump can be used for both intra-arterial and intravenous infusions. Syringe size is a limiting factor, and if large volumes are required it is necessary to replace the syringe reservoir several times during treatment. This can be an advantage in the case of infusions with poor stability, since the infusion is exposed to in-use operating temperatures (33–37°C) for relatively short periods.

To set up the pumps, the administration line is primed either manually, before putting the syringe in the pump, or by a venting mechanism if included in the pump. Priming should be carried out prior to rate setting in pumps that use the mm/hour or mm/day system, since at low infusion rates the dead volume of the tubing could alter the final infusion time by several hours. The syringe is placed into the pump and fixed in position. The actuator should be placed as close to the plunger as possible, so that there is little slack to take up in the lead screw when the pump is started. If the priming procedure or positioning of the actuator is not carried out correctly, then at low infusion rates this could result in no drug being delivered for up to 1 hour, and the patency of the venous access may be compromised.

The infusion rates are calculated in mm/hour for the Graseby MS 16A and Syringe Minder 2 pumps, or in mm/day for the Graseby MS 26 pump. Errors can occur when changing the pump setting if the patient or user does not understand the concept of mm/hour instead of mL/hour, or alternatively if they confuse hours with days. The Syringe Minder 2 pump has preset rates of travel of 1, 2, 3, 4, 5, 6, 8, 10, 11 and 12 mm/hour. The Graseby MS 16A and MS 26 have continuously variable rates which are set as required. The setting of infusion rates is straight-forward for all those syringe drivers that are available in the UK. However, this simplicity also makes them easy to tamper with, which may be a disadvantage in some circumstances.

All of the pumps have a fixed occlusion pressure which causes the pump to alarm or stop. However, due to the need to overcome the build-up of pressure when infusing viscous fluids, the pressure at which the pump will alarm can be high. At low flow rates there is a considerable delay before the alarm is activated. This problem has been overcome in larger infusion pumps by positioning a pressure-sensing device in the extension set rather than in the pump, but this feature is not yet available on the ambulatory pumps.

Patient education and training are required to ensure correct rate setting, mounting of the syringe and priming of the set. Patients and their carers need to be aware of the various alarms and how to deal with the resulting malfunctions. Some knowledge of the mechanism of the syringe pumps is required, and the batteries must be checked regularly.

Despite their lack of sophistication, syringe drivers have several advantages as drug-delivery systems. They are relatively cheap to purchase, and the disposables associated with their use are cheap and readily available from several sources, although only syringes specifically recommended by the pump manufacturer should be used. The simplicity of syringe drivers may make them less intimidating to patients, and the necessity of changing syringes frequently allows the patient to gain confidence in their mastery of the machine rapidly. The low weight and bulk of several of these devices are very popular with patients, who consider this to be a very important feature.[16] A further advantage of the syringe driver to the pharmacist is the large amount of published data on the stability of drugs in plastic syringes. There is a paucity of such information for the dedicated reservoirs of many other ambulatory pumps. The disadvantage of syringe drivers, apart from their susceptibility to tampering already mentioned, is the large number of syringes that have to be filled to provide a course of treatment, normally at least one per day. This can make them considerably more labour-intensive than pumps with larger drug reservoirs.

SPRING-DRIVEN PUMPS

Model: Paragon ambulatory infusion system

This infusion pump employs sophisticated spring-driven technology to provide the driving force for drug delivery.

The Paragon ambulatory infusion system gives precise delivery of parenteral medications that require continuous infusion over periods ranging from 30 minutes to 10 days (e.g. chemotherapy, analgesics, antibiotics and iron-chelating drugs). The system has two fundamental parts, namely a reusable mechanical infuser and a dedicated single-use administration set.

The infuser is a 'capsule' made of durable high-strength plastic. The top part contains a pressure plate governed by a cantilevered stainless-steel spring mechanism. The spring mechanism is designed to equalise the pressure on the administration set throughout the duration of the infusion, thereby resulting in more accurate infusion rates. Into the bottom part of the infuser is placed a single-use administration set. By screwing the two parts of the capsule together, the contents are effectively pressurised to 6 psi. Each medical-grade PVC administration set is calibrated with 0.9% sodium chloride at 32°C (i.e. skin contact temperature), and is designed to run at a fixed flow rate (determined by the presence of an integral precision glass flow controller). A variety of different flow rates is available

(0.5, 1.0, 2.0, 3.0, 4.0, 10, 50, 100 and 200 mL/hour). Stability and compatibility data on a range of drug infusions are available from the UK supplier, Central Homecare Ltd.

The single-use sets are easy to fill via a needle-less two-way valved filling port. In contrast to the filling of elastomeric pumps, there is no back pressure associated with the filling of a Paragon set, because the driving pressure for the system is applied to the set after filling is complete. Because the Paragon infuser can be reused up to 1000 times and only the administration sets are disposed of after use, the system is both economical and environmentally friendly. Also, because of their size and shape, the administration sets are easy to store (either empty or prefilled with drug).

The system is simple to use, making patient training very straightforward. The simple lightweight design of the Paragon ensures silent operation, and no motors or batteries are needed to operate it. Whilst infusing, the patient keeps the Paragon pump inside a bum-bag worn either over the shoulder or round the waist. The correct operating temperature of the system is maintained by ensuring that the administration set is kept in close proximity to the patient's skin. Safety features include an integral 1.2-micron air- and particulate-eliminating filter which helps to provide patient reassurance. In addition, uniquely among mechanical pumps, an optional 'FlowView' indicator provides an indication of the status of the flow rate. This is particularly useful for monitoring very slow infusion rates, as occlusions (either upstream or downstream) are shown in real time by the indicator.

ELASTOMERIC PUMPS

Model: Baxter infusor pump (*see* Figure 5.2)

This group of disposable, single-use pumps employs elastomer technology for drug delivery. The balloon, which acts as both drug reservoir and pump, is made from an inert polyisoprene rubber material. This gives it elastic properties that enable the reservoir, once expanded, to contract to its original shape and size.

The operating principle of the pump is the Hagen–Poiseville law,[20] which states that flow through a tube is a function of pressure difference (*P*), the radius of the lumen (*r*), the length of the tube (*l*) and the viscosity of the liquid (*v*).

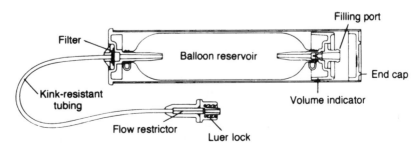

Figure 5.2: *Baxter infusor pump*

The law is represented by the following equation:

$$F = \frac{P \times \pi r^4}{8 \times v \times l}$$

The variable function viscosity will be affected by both vehicle and temperature. The effects of the vehicle are known if glucose or 0.9% sodium chloride solution is used,[21] and temperature fluctuations are kept to a minimum by wearing the infusor close to the skin. High concentrations of drugs occasionally affect viscosity.

An increasing range of infusors is being made available by Baxter. These infuse their contents over periods of up to 7 days.

Infusors are filled by connecting a luer-lock syringe filled with drug solution to the valve assembly in the infusor, and forcing liquid into the elastomer reservoir. This requires significant force and can be tiring, especially if many infusors are to be filled. Once filled, the microbore administration set primes automatically within about 15 minutes.

The patient removes the winged luer cap from the administration set and attaches the infusor to the venous access device. The drug is delivered via a 10-μm filter at a constant rate, which depends on the infusor model and the diluent solution. The duration of infusion can be altered by adjusting the volume filled, and the dose rate can be altered by choice of infusor model and by adjusting the volume filled or the drug concentration. The infusor can be used by the intra-arterial or intravenous route.

Infusors are intended for single use and are not designed to be refilled or resterilised for repeat use. Therefore, although there is no capital cost involved in the pump, since it cannot be reused, revenue costs are high. However, the ongoing introduction of infusor models with longer discharge times may make them competitive with electromechanical pumps that require dedicated disposables. Infusors are lightweight, small, comfortable in use and silent in operation. They are provided with a fabric holder which is pinned inside the patient's clothes.

The infusor has been studied in 18 patients who received 52 treatment courses, representing 247 patient-days of treatment at home rather than in hospital. During this period there was no known failure to infuse and no reported flow rate or administration difficulties. There was one report of a leaking unit.[21]

The infusor has been used to administer a wide range of drug infusions, including antibiotics, analgesics and cytotoxic drugs. There is little published data on the stability or compatibility of these injections in the devices. However, research has been conducted by Baxter Healthcare Ltd on the stability of a variety of drugs in infusors, and data are available from the company. Unfortunately, the parameters by which stability is considered to be satisfactory have not been fully described. This information should therefore be considered for guidance purposes only. Where appropriate it has been included in the relevant drug monographs (*see* pages 263–474).

Patients need to be educated about storage, infusion rates, monitoring the infusion and care of their central line after completion of the infusion. The infusor is popular with patients in comparison with more sophisticated pumps[13] because they do not have to be concerned about battery checks, setting of infusion rates or monitoring for mechanical malfunction of the pump. In addition, because the unit is disposable, they do not have to return equipment to the hospital at the end of treatment.

As well as constant-rate infusors, Baxter now market a variety of infusors with additional flow controls which make them suitable for pulsatile or 'basal-bolus' drug delivery. Although primarily intended for antibiotic administration and patient-controlled analgesia, these devices are likely to be useful to those who are attempting to transfer more complex chemotherapy regimens from the hospital to the domiciliary setting.

PERISTALTIC PUMPS

Models: Pharmacia/Deltec, CADD-1 (*see* Figure 5.3), CADD-PCA, CADD-PLUS

These pumps employ a motorised rotating drum powered by a battery, which rolls over a silicone tube. The drug reservoir is a 50-mL or 100-mL disposable bag enclosed in a rigid plastic shell. These pumps can also be used to deliver the contents of conventional collapsible infusion containers via a special administration set. These devices are programmable, and the infusion rate and drug dose can be varied. The CADD pumps have six alarms comprising internal malfunction, set-up review, pump stoppage, low residual volume in medication cassette, low battery and occlusion. There are a number of lock levels for varying patient involvement in the programming of the dose and rate of infusion. However, when used for chemotherapy, the patient is not normally involved in programming, and

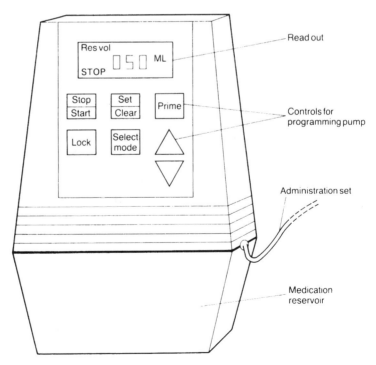

Figure 5.3: *Pharmacia/Deltec CADD-1 pump*

the ability to 'lock' the pump memory against deliberate or accidental alteration is useful. Although these pumps are more sophisticated, they aim to be user-friendly, but still require a significant amount of training to ensure correct usage. With this in mind, the company has prepared training programmes for operators. The pump is robust but rather heavy and, with a 100-mL drug reservoir *in situ*, fairly bulky (19.5 × 9 × 2.8 cm).

The manufacturers of the Pharmacia pump will provide information on the stability of various cytotoxic drugs in Pharmacia cassettes. This information, which is incorporated in the relevant drug monographs, was obtained from unpublished studies conducted at Apotekseolaget AB Central Laboratories and Apotekseolaget AB Karolinska Pharmacy, Stockholm, Sweden.

As well as the CADD constant-rate pump, Pharmacia markets two other pumps which differ only in their programming characteristics. The CADD-PCA delivers a continuous base drug infusion, which may be boosted by the user activating a bolus control, whilst the CADD-PLUS (which is intended for antibiotic administration) can deliver pulsatile infusions. Both of these pumps are also capable of continuous, constant-rate infusion, and may be attractive to the user involved in providing a range of drug administration services, since they offer flexibility of application.

Model: Medfusion Inc., INFU-MED 300 (*see* Figure 5.4)

The INFU-MED 300 is a linear peristaltic pump that delivers drug solutions from soft PVC reservoirs of volume 65, 150 or 250 mL via a silicone tubing administration set which is acted upon by the pump mechanism. In addition, a special 'spike set' makes it possible to use the pump to infuse the contents of conventional collapsible infusion bags. The 65-mL drug reservoir will fit entirely within the pump's rigid plastic cover. Larger reservoirs are carried separately in the pump's fabric carrying pouch. The infusion rate is set by means of an infusion rate-setting dial. This is simple to operate but is also easily tampered with, both accidentally and deliberately.

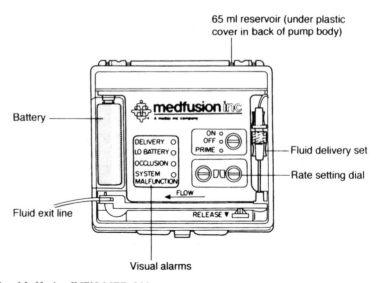

Figure 5.4: *Medfusion INFU-MED 300*

The INFU-MED 300 is simple to use, reasonably compact, and offers a comprehensive range of reservoir sizes, but is neither as small nor as lightweight as certain other devices, and it is therefore less popular with some patients. Although no longer in production and superseded by the Walk Med pumps described below, there are many INFU-MED 300 pumps still in use.

Models: Medfusion Inc., Walk Med 350, 410c, Walk Med 420i/c, Walk Med 430pca, Walk Med 440pic

The Walk Med pumps share their pumping mechanisms and chassis construction with the INFU-MED 300 pump described previously. However, flow control is achieved by programming the pump via an electronic keypad which can be locked in a similar way to that of the Pharmacia pump to prevent unauthorised tampering. Flow parameters are displayed on an LCD display.

The Walk Med 350 is the most basic pump for continuous, steady-rate drug infusion. The other three pumps in the range are all capable of fulfilling this task, and also function as devices for the delivery of patient-controlled analgesia (430pca), intermittent drug infusion (420i/c) or both (440pic), and their flexibility may be attractive to the pharmacist who is involved in operating a range of services. No data are available on the stability of drugs in INFU-MED reservoirs, either from the distributors of the pump or from other published sources. This information will be required before the pump can be accepted for routine use.

Model: Graseby Medical 9000 series (9100, 9200, 9300, 9400, 9500)

The Graseby Medical 9000 series devices are based on a common pump body and a set of five 'smart cards' which slot into the front of the device and give the user a choice of either continuous infusion (9100), intermittent infusion (9200), patient-controlled analgesia (9300), non-zero-order (circadian) programming (9400) or epidural infusion (9500). The facility that enables an infusion history to be downloaded to a computer printer is particularly attractive in the case of cytotoxic drugs. Medication reservoir volumes range from 50 to 250 mL and are enclosed in a rigid plastic case for protection. A spike adapter is also available to allow the use of virtually any collapsible infusion bag with this device. Graseby Medical is able to supply stability data on most of the commonly used cytotoxic drug infusions, including some drug admixtures. Some of this information has been published.[22,23]

Model: Baxter 6060 (formerly Sebratete 6060 Homerun)

The Baxter 6060 ambulatory volumetric infusion pump is a versatile device which can be used to administer ambulatory infusions in a wide range of therapeutic applications. The flow rate is programmable from 0.1 to 400 mL/hour, and two infusion reservoir sizes (100 mL and 200 mL) are available. The reservoirs are held in rigid plastic casing for additional protection.

The device offers advanced programming to provide various delivery profiles (including continuous infusion, intermittent infusion and customisable rate over 25 separate periods). A two-way communication port supports remote programming, infusion history data collection and preventative maintenance.

IMPLANTABLE PUMP SYSTEMS

Implantable pump systems have been developed for drug delivery, offering the patient a more normal lifestyle, since there is no externalised portion of the system to be seen or managed. Additional advantages of the implantable pump system are a reduction in the potential for microbial infections and improved patient compliance with therapy. These advantages are of particular benefit to the ambulatory patient who is receiving long-term therapy. The primary disadvantages of the implantable pump systems are the small volume capacity of the pump reservoirs and the high cost of the pump and surgical implantation of the system.

Implanted in a subcutaneous pocket, the pump can easily be felt through the skin. The silicone injection septum is accessed through the skin using a special Huber-type needle for up to 1000 punctures, depending on the needle size.

Two commercially available implanted pump systems are the Pfizer Infusaid implantable pump and the Medtronic SynchroMed pump.

Model: Pfizer Infusaid implantable pump (*see* Figure 5.5)

The Infusaid pump is made of titanium, is approximately 90 mm in diameter and 28 mm in thickness, weighs slightly more than 200 g, and has a reservoir capacity of approximately 50 mL. The operating mechanism of the pump utilises a non-electronic metal bellows concept. The pump consists of two chambers, separated by flexible metal bellows, and is attached to a silicone rubber catheter that is placed into the delivery site. The outer chamber contains a fluorocarbon charging fluid, and the inner chamber serves as a drug reservoir. When the drug chamber is filled, the charging fluid is compressed. Expansion of the charging fluid exerts a vapour pressure which compresses the drug chamber, forcing drug from the reservoir through the flow restrictor and into the delivery catheter. Because there is no electromechanical component, the energy of the charging fluid is limitless, and does not require replenishment.

The flow rate is controlled by a restricted capillary tube which cannot be changed after implantation. Flow rate is affected by a number of variables, including fluid viscosity, patient temperature and altitude. The Infusaid pump is supplied by the manufacturer with a specific capillary tube to deliver a specific drug at a specific

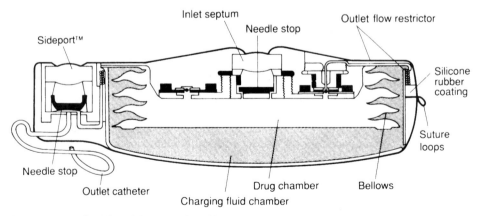

Figure 5.5: *Infusaid Model 400 implantable pump*

flow rate for normal body temperature and at the geographical location of the patient. Increased temperatures (e.g. as experienced by a patient in a hot bath) will increase the flow rate of the pump by approximately 10–13% for each 1°C rise in temperature. Higher altitudes will also cause the pump to flow faster. An infusion pump calibrated for sea level will flow approximately 45% faster at an altitude of 2000 metres. After implantation, slight alterations in flow rate can be achieved by varying the concentration or viscosity of the fluid. Only one model of the Infusaid pump, Model 400, is commercially available, although there is both a single-catheter and a dual-catheter version. The use of the sideport allows direct access to the catheter, bypassing the pump mechanism, for bolus doses if required.

A programmable version of the Infusaid pump, Model 1000, is not yet commercially available but is now being used in clinical trials. The pump uses telemetry via an external programme to change delivery rates after implantation.

Model: Medtronic SynchroMed pump (*see* Figure 5.6)

This pump can be reprogrammed for delivery rate changes (0.1 to 18 mL/day) after implantation using an external programmer. Approximately 70 mm in diameter, 27 mm in thickness, and 200 g in weight, the pump has a usable capacity of 18 mL. The operating mechanism of the SynchroMed pump is a rotary peristaltic system that is powered by an internal lithium battery, improving delivery accuracy and eliminating the dependence on temperature, viscosity and pressure that is characteristic of the Infusaid pump. The typical life of the battery is approximately 3 to 4 years at a flow rate of 0.5 mL/day. Two models of the pump are commercially available, namely Model 8611H and Model 8615. Model 8615 has a sideport access site to bypass the pumping mechanism for bolus doses. The pump can be programmed to deliver continuous, intermittent and complex circadian

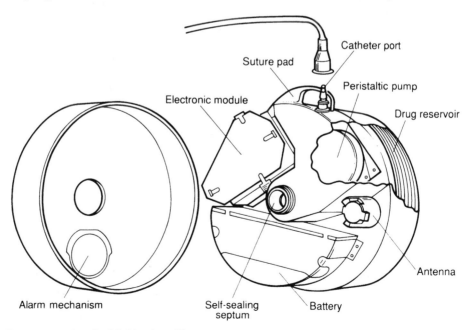

Figure 5.6: *SynchroMed implantable pump*

administrations using the external programmer and a radiotelemetry link via the programming wand.

The use of implantable pumps has been primarily restricted to regional deliveries (e.g. intra-arterial and intrathecal), although the pumps are also being used for systemic applications.[24-26]

CONCLUSION

A summary of the features of the ambulatory pumps discussed above is contained in Table 5.1 (*see* Appendix, page 116).

Ambulatory pumps have made the concept of continuous infusion attainable, with all of the concurrent benefits mentioned previously. All of the pumps provide accurate dosing and are portable. They differ in the number of features that are available, which may include flexible administration rates, variable reservoir sizes and a range of alarms. With all of these devices, not only the capital cost of the pump but also the cost of disposables required must be considered.

For successful home treatment with ambulatory pumps, the patient must feel confident and be proficient in the use of the unit. Patient (or carer) education is an important part of any ambulatory programme,[6] and the level of knowledge required and staff time involved in training and providing a back-up service for each type of pump should be evaluated carefully.

BOLUS AND SHORT-TERM INFUSIONS

Although it is possible to administer home chemotherapy in traditional bolus or short-term infusion schedules, this approach is not always appropriate for domiciliary patients. In the hospital setting it is possible to control the acute toxicity (e.g. nausea and vomiting) associated with conventional chemotherapy schedules. For domiciliary patients, such toxicity is more difficult to control and could be unacceptable, although this may be less of a problem with the introduction of symptomatic treatment such as the $5HT_3$ antagonist antiemetics. Conventional bolus or short-term infusion schedules would normally be administered by a community nurse. Some patients may feel that this restricts their freedom and independence, negating the advantages of home treatment over hospital day-case treatment.

In cases where experience has shown that bolus chemotherapy is well tolerated, it may be possible to offer patients the option of self-medication by using a venous access port (e.g. the Intraport device; *see* Figure 5.7). The catheter is inserted into a central vein (usually the subclavian vein) and the medication port is implanted subcutaneously, usually in the anterior chest wall, with the silastic septum located just beneath the skin. However, for the self-administration of bolus injections some patients find it more convenient if the port is placed subcutaneously in the lower abdomen. The septum is designed for multiple puncture, and when not in use the patency of the system is maintained by flushing with dilute heparinised saline at monthly intervals.[27]

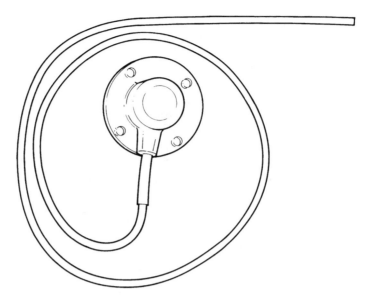

Figure 5.7: *Intraport venous access port*

However, self-medication does raise concerns about compliance and the accuracy that can be achieved in terms of dose, administration rate and dose intervals. An alternative to patient or nurse administration is to use a preprogrammed infusion pump that is capable of delivering intermittent or pulsed infusions. The device can be programmed to deliver a defined volume of drug solution at a preset infusion rate at time intervals specified by the programmer. Examples of ambulatory infusion devices with an intermittent infusion capacity include the CADD-PLUS (Pharmacia/Deltec) (*see* page 99) and the 9000 series (Graseby Medical) (*see* page 101). With the latter device it is possible to print a history of infusions delivered by the pump to audit both pump function and patient compliance.

Self-administration of small-volume subcutaneous injections may be appropriate for low-dose maintenance regimens, provided that drug-related toxicity is minimal and the drug is non-vesicant (e.g. α-interferon). Homecare packs containing medication and the necessary syringes and needles are now available for this purpose. Devices used to aid the subcutaneous administration of insulin to diabetic patients may also be of benefit to leukaemia and cancer patients.

Finally, from the medico–legal viewpoint, bolus or short-term infusions tend to be the licensed or recognised route of administration listed in the manufacturers' data sheets.

PROLONGED CONTINUOUS INFUSION

Among various attempts to improve the therapeutic index of antitumour drugs, one approach involves the replacement of traditional, rapid infusion schedules with prolonged continuous-infusion regimens.[28] Developments in the design, operating capability and operational safety of ambulatory infusion pumps have facilitated continuous-infusion chemotherapy in the domiciliary setting.

The rationale for continuous-infusion chemotherapy is based on the pharmacokinetic characteristics of cytotoxic drugs and on the cytokinetic (growth cycle) profile of tumour cells.[28] Since many cytotoxic drugs exhibit short plasma half-lives, continuous-infusion regimens prolong the exposure of tumour cells to the drug. As tumour cells progress through the cell cycle, a greater proportion of the tumour-cell population is exposed to the drug during the sensitive phase(s) of the cell cycle.

An additional advantage of continuous-infusion regimens in home chemotherapy programmes is that adverse effects associated with peak plasma levels are reduced or eliminated. For example, doxorubicin is less cardiotoxic[29] and fluorouracil is less myelosuppressive[30] in continuous-infusion regimens. There is evidence that nausea and vomiting associated with bolus doses of cisplatinum are significantly reduced when infusional regimens are used.[31] However, other toxicities, such as mucositis and hand–foot syndrome in the case of fluorouracil,[32] may occur more readily with prolonged infusions.

Controlled studies[4,14] indicate that, on balance, drug-related adverse effects are reduced with infusional regimens, and quality of life for the patient is improved.

Continuous infusion is a technique which also lends itself to combined modality treatments. For example, continuous infusion of fluorouracil is now used on an adjuvant or neoadjuvant basis with surgical resection in the treatment of colon cancer. In one reported study,[33] continuous-infusion carboplatin was combined with synchronous radiation therapy. The carboplatin infusion was delivered from an ambulatory pump and, when appropriate, external-beam radiation was administered on an outpatient basis.

ALTERNATIVE ROUTES OF ADMINISTRATION

A brief summary of each alternative administration route for chemotherapy is provided, and the drugs specific to the route are listed.

1 Intravesical

1.1 Advantages

▼ Localised treatment to tumours confined to the bladder with limited systemic absorption, so that systemic toxicity is reduced or eliminated.
▼ High localised drug concentrations in contact with the tumour and surrounding mucosa for prolonged time periods.
▼ Reduced risk of tumour implantation following surgery.

1.2 Disadvantages

▼ Considerable local inflammation and pain.
▼ Inconvenient for patients – there is a retained catheter into the bladder and this is rotated during installation.
▼ Not suitable for drugs that require systemic activation.

1.3 Drugs used in intravesical chemotherapy

A variety of anticancer drugs have been administered via the intravesical route, and the list below represents only the most widely used drugs. Dosage, schedule, diluent volume instilled and residence time in the bladder are also subject to variation between treatment centres. The typical conditions and values are derived from the literature, and in most cases there is no evidence to suggest that these are optimal. The information presented here is intended for guidance only.

Doxorubicin

Dose and volume instilled: 50 mg in 50 mL.[34]

Schedule: Two doses in the first week, then monthly for 1 year and 3-monthly for a further year.[35]

Diluent: Water for injections or 0.9% sodium chloride injection.[36]

Residence time in bladder: 1 hour, with rotation of patient.[34]

UK data sheet recommendation for intravesical use: Yes.[34]

Possible complications: Chemical cystitis, allergic reaction, haematuria, reduced bladder capacity, gastrointestinal effects and fever.[37]

Epirubicin

Dose and volume instilled: 50 mg in 50 mL.[34,38] In cases of chemical cystitis, dose reduction to 30 mg is advised,[37] while for carcinoma *in situ* a dose of 80 mg is recommended.[34]

Schedule: One dose weekly for 8 weeks. For prophylaxis after transurethral resection, one dose weekly for 4 weeks followed by one dose monthly for 11 months is recommended.[34]

Diluent: 0.9% sodium chloride injection.[38]

Residence time in bladder: 1 hour, with rotation of patient.[34]

UK data-sheet recommendation for intravesical use: Yes.[34]

Possible complications: Chemical cystitis, allergic reaction and other adverse effects similar to doxorubicin.[37] Systemic toxicity with epirubicin is rare.[37]

Mitomycin C

Dose and volume instilled: 20–40 mg in 20–40 mL.[39]

Schedule: Weekly or three times a week for a total of 20 doses.[39] One report[40] suggests that in cases of a solitary initial tumour with tumour recurrence at 3 months, or multiple initial tumours with no recurrence at 3 months, a single instillation followed by repeat doses at 3-monthly cystoscopies up to and including 1 year post-diagnosis should be used.

Diluent: Water for injections.[39]

Residence time in bladder: Minimum of 1 hour.[41]

UK data sheet recommendation for intravesical use: Yes.[39]

Possible complications: Chemical cystitis, allergic reactions, leukopenia, thrombo-cytopenia and reduced bladder capacity.[37]

Mitozantrone

Dose and volume instilled: 5–10.5 mg in 30 mL.[42]

Schedule: Once a week for 6 weeks.[42]

Diluent: 0.9% sodium chloride injection.[42]

Residence time in bladder: 2 hours.[42]

UK data-sheet recommendation for intravesical use: Not recommended.[43]

Possible complications: At doses of 9 mg or less, minor bladder irritation.[37] At doses of 10 mg or more, moderate to severe bladder irritation, including urothelial necrosis.[37]

Thiotepa

Dose and volume instilled: 30–60 mg in 60 mL for multiple instillation, or 90 mg in 100 ml for single-dose instillations in adjunctive prophylaxis with surgical resection.[44]

Schedule: Every 2 weeks for a total of 4–8 instillations, starting at least 1 week after tumour resection. Maintenance therapy after the initial dose is given every 4–6 weeks for 1 year or longer.[44]

Diluent: Water for injections.

Residence time in bladder: 2 hours, except for single-dose adjunct to surgical resection, when residence time is 30 minutes with alteration of patient position.[44]

UK data sheet recommendation for intravesical use: Yes.[45]

Possible complications: Leukopenia, thrombocytopenia and irritative voiding symptoms.[37] The risk of drug-related toxicity is increased in patients who have received previous radiotherapy to the bladder.[44]

Bacillus Calmette-Guérin (BCG)

Although it is not a cytotoxic drug, BCG is included here because:

▼ it is widely used in the treatment of superficial bladder cancer
▼ many pharmacies prepare BCG bladder instillations
▼ there may be significant risks to the preparation environment associated with BCG.

Dose and volume instilled: 5×10^8 bacilli (live attenuated vaccine) in 50 mL.[41,45]

Schedule: Once a week for 6 weeks, with repeat courses for recurrent or persistent disease.[41]

Diluent: 0.9% sodium chloride injection.[41,45]

Residence time in bladder: One hour minimum.[41]

UK data sheet recommendation for intravesical use: No information.[46]

Possible complications: Bacterial cystitis (not BCG-related), chemical cystitis, allergic reaction, fever, nausea, malaise, haematuria, prostatitis and epididymitis.[41] There is a potential risk that environmental contamination of pharmacy workstations during the preparation of BCG instillations could result in the contamination of other infusions prepared in the same workstation. One report[47] describes two cases of meningitis resulting from iatrogenic BCG infection in two immunocompromised children receiving intrathecal chemotherapy for leukaemia.

2 Intraperitoneal

2.1 Advantages

▼ Tumours that spread by direct invasion of the omentum or peritoneal lining (e.g. ovarian and colorectal cancers) are sensitive to direct bathing of their often small-volume, poorly vascularised bulk with proportionally high concentrations of drug.
▼ Therapy can be high dose and intermittent or low dose and continuous. The latter is similar to peritoneal dialysis.

2.2 Disadvantages

▼ Difficulties with regard to selection and placement of the catheter are a practical and fairly common problem because the peritoneum is invaded with tumour and 'overgrowth'. Consequent occlusion of the catheter is also a problem. An early manifestation of this problem is the formation of a 'one-way' proteinous/fibrin/tumour flap.
▼ As a function of tumour growth, the peritoneal cavity may fill with proteinous exudate. This ascites may contain malignant cells and/or high concentrations of protein. The high levels of protein can result in protein binding and inactivation of any chemotherapy that is instilled. Furthermore, the dilutional effects are difficult to quantify, and if target concentrations were hoped for these may be difficult to obtain.
▼ Loculation due to previous intraperitoneal therapy, radiation fibrosis or tumour growth/regrowth again means that certain areas, or pockets, receive uniproportional exposure to the therapy.
▼ Peritonitis (either chemical or infective, or both) can develop. It is often painful and can be fatal if allowed to progress to full peritonitis.

2.3 Drugs used in intraperitoneal chemotherapy

These include the following:

▼ bleomycin
▼ carboplatin
▼ cisplatin
▼ 5-fluorouracil
▼ mitomycin C
▼ mitozantrone
▼ paclitaxel.

3 Intrahepatic

3.1 Advantages

▼ This can be achieved via either the portal vein or the hepatic artery. As the liver tissue acts like a sponge, high local concentrations of drug can be achieved. The relative advantage of hepatic infusions over intravenous infusions is described by the following equation:

$$R_d = 1 + \frac{Cl_{TB}}{Q\,(1-E_H)}$$

where R_d is the hepatic advantage
Cl_{TB} is the total body clearance of the drug
Q is arterial blood flow
E_H is the fraction of the drug that is extracted across the liver.

▼ It is estimated and increasingly proved in the literature that liver tissues can be exposed to two- to 400-fold the local drug concentration. It is also practical to have the liver act as a reservoir, spilling drug over into the peripheral circulation and leading to a 'standard' intravenous-type peripheral exposure to the cytotoxic agent.
▼ Metastatic disease in the liver is inevitably fatal and often unresponsive to systemic chemotherapy. Targeted high-dose chemotherapy appears to be highly effective.

3.2 Disadvantages

▼ Complications in catheterising the appropriate veins or arteries.
▼ High pressure in the arterial circulation.
▼ Inflammation, infection and pain in the hepatic tissues.
▼ Hepatic artery thrombosis.
▼ Catheter displacement.
▼ Due to the cellular and vascular architecture of the liver, drug delivery systems such as biodegradable starch microspheres are an attractive method for increasing local drug concentrations.

3.3 Drugs used in intrahepatic chemotherapy

These include the following:

▼ carmustine
▼ cisplatin
▼ 5-fluorouracil
▼ floxuridine
▼ mitomycin C.

4 Isolated limb/breast perfusion

4.1 Advantages

▼ Allows high local drug concentrations to be achieved with minimal systemic exposure.

4.2 Disadvantages

▼ Technically difficult, as it involves isolation of the blood supply to the affected part.
▼ Cannot be done on an outpatient basis.
▼ Very invasive, and may be distressing and uncomfortable for the patient.
▼ Cytotoxic action is limited to the perfused area, and there is no activity against metastatic disease elsewhere. Therefore it is inappropriate for most large tumours.
▼ May require preparation of drugs in unusual perfusion fluids at high (body) temperature and at concentrations for which few stability data are available.
▼ Not suitable for drugs that require systemic activation (e.g. cyclophosphamide).
▼ Not of proven value in any condition, and should be reserved for clinical trials only.

4.3 *Drugs used in isolated limb/breast perfusion chemotherapy*

These include the following:
▼ doxorubicin
▼ mitozantrone.

5 Intrathecal/intraventricular

5.1 *Advantages*

▼ Allows direct access to the CNS of drugs that normally cross the blood–brain barrier in very limited amounts.
▼ Of proven value in leukaemia and certain types of lymphoma, where the CNS provides a sanctuary site for tumour cells during systemic chemotherapy.

5.2 *Disadvantages*

▼ Unpleasant for the patient.
▼ Technically difficult, requiring repeated lumbar punctures or placement of a suitable access device such as an Ommaya reservoir.
▼ Only applicable to a very limited range of non-irritant anticancer agents (e.g. thiotepa, cytarabine, methotrexate and hydrocortisone).
▼ Has been associated with frequent, fatal drug errors in patients receiving concomitant intravenous therapy.[48]
▼ Risks of CNS trauma or infection.
▼ Only formulations known to be suitable for intrathecal use (and preferably licensed for administration by this route) should be used. (Extremes of pH or osmotic strength, or the presence of preservatives may render other formulations unsuitable.)
▼ Of no proven value other than as a prophylactic measure in leukaemia or lymphoma.
▼ Has no place in the treatment of CNS metastases of solid tumours.

5.3 *Drugs used in intrathecal/intraventricular chemotherapy*

These include the following:
▼ cytarabine
▼ methotrexate.

6 Intra-arterial

6.1 *Advantages*

▼ With drugs where the level of extraction by the tissue of the target organ/tumour is high, high tumour exposure with much reduced systemic exposure can be achieved (e.g. fluoropyrimidines administered via the hepatic artery).

6.2 *Disadvantages*

▼ Very high drug levels in the perfused organ may result in excessive local tissue damage.
▼ The drug delivery system needs to work against a high back-pressure. This will activate excess-pressure alarms on some infusion pumps designed for intravenous infusion.

▼ Few drugs have a high enough tissue-extraction ratio to make the procedure worthwhile.
▼ Displacement of the arterial cannula results in excessive bleeding which can be difficult to stop, and which is distressing to the patient.
▼ Not of proven benefit, and should only be used as part of a research protocol.

7 Intrapleural

7.1 Advantages

▼ Potential for delivering active agents to a site of poor systemic penetration, producing an anticancer effect against small-volume disease.
▼ Alleviates symptoms of pleural disease which may occur in up to 80% of patients with certain malignancies (e.g. lung or breast disease).

7.2 Disadvantages

▼ Systemic toxicity, particularly to alkylating agents.
▼ Local inflammation and pain.
▼ Fever (particularly common with bleomycin).
▼ Partial sclerosing of the plural membrane, leading to re-occurrence being loculated and even more difficult to treat.
▼ Highly variable success rates of 20–88%, perhaps reflecting the effect of incomplete drainage prior to instillation leading to dilution of the cytotoxic drug.
▼ Complicated technique.
▼ Cytotoxic instillation is as effective.

7.3 Drugs used in intrapleural chemotherapy

These include the following:

▼ BCG
▼ bleomycin
▼ *Corynebacterium parvum*
▼ doxorubicin
▼ 5-fluorouracil
▼ mitozantrone
▼ mustine
▼ thiotepa.

8 Other local chemotherapies

Users of this handbook should also be aware that a number of cytotoxic drugs have also, on a one-off basis, been instilled into other cavities or directly into organs. These include the following:

▼ intra-ocular – 5-fluorouracil
▼ intrapancreatic – mitomycin C
▼ pericardially – CMF (cyclophosphamide, methotrexate and 5–fluorouracil), bleomycin, thiotepa
▼ topically – carmustine, 5-fluorouracil
▼ subcutaneously – ifosfamide, bleomycin, cytarabine.

REFERENCES

1 Constable SE *et al.* (1995) Reducing the wait for chemotherapy. *UFM Update.* **15**: 10–11.

2 Bacovsky RA (1988) Home parenteral chemotherapy programs. In: *Proceedings of First International Symposium on Oncology Pharmacy Practice.* New Zealand Hospital Pharmacists Association, New Zealand, 294–300.

3 Payne S (1989) *Quality of Life in Women with Advanced Breast Cancer.* PhD Thesis, Department of Psychology, University of Exeter.

4 Coates A *et al.* (1987) Improving the quality of life during chemotherapy for advanced breast cancer. A comparison of intermittent and continuous treatment strategies. *NEJM.* **317**: 1490–5.

5 Vokes EE *et al.* (1989) A randomised study of in-patient versus out-patient continuous infusion chemotherapy for patients with locally advanced head and neck cancer. *Cancer.* **63**: 30–6.

6 Sewell GJ *et al.* (1989) Home-based cancer therapy by continuous infusion. *Pharm J.* **243**: 139–41.

7 Ausman RK *et al.* (1982) Long-term, ambulatory, continuous intravenous infusion of 5-fluorouracil for the treatment of metastatic adenocarcinoma in the liver. *Wisc Med J.* **81**: 25–8.

8 Lokich JJ *et al.* (1982) The delivery of cancer chemotherapy by constant venous infusion: ambulatory management of venous access and portable pump. *Cancer.* **50**: 2731–5.

9 Sewell GJ *et al.* (1987) HOPE for cancer. *J Dist Nurs.* 4–6.

10 Kramer I and Williams DA (1995) Drug stability. *J Oncol Pharm Pract.* **1 (ISOPP IV Symposium Issue)**: 26–7.

11 Department of Health (1995) *Aseptic Dispensing for NHS Patients.* Department of Health, London.

12 Stanley AP (1996) Community chemotherapy: the logical evolution of home-based therapy. *Eur J Cancer.* **35**: 1014–16.

13 Moody DG (1986) External ambulatory infusion devices and the oncology patient. *J Pharm Tech.* **2**: 160–5.

14 Lokich JJ *et al.* (1989) Prospective randomised comparison of continuous infusion fluorouracil with a conventional bolus schedule in metastatic colorectal carcinoma: a mid-Atlantic oncology program study. *J Clin Oncol.* **7**: 425–32.

15 Hrusesky W (1987) The rationale for non-zero-order drug delivery using automatic computer-based drug delivery systems (chronotherapy). *J Biol Resp Modifiers.* **6**: 587–98.

16 Summerhayes M *et al.* (1991) A comparison of two devices for the continuous infusion of cytotoxic drugs in non-hospitalized patients. *Int J Pharm Pract.* **1**: 94–7.

17 Hardy EM, Williamson C and Sewell GJ (1995) An evaluation of six infusion devices for the continuous infusion of cytotoxic drugs in ambulatory patients. *J Oncol Pharm Pract.* **1**: 15–22.

18 Williamson CA, Ridler C and Sewell GJ (1993) A study to determine the quality of life of patients receiving low-dose ambulatory chemotherapy. *Hosp Pharm Pract.* **3**: 197–204.

19 Adams PS *et al.* (1987) Pharmaceutical aspects of home infusion therapy for cancer patients. *Pharm J.* **238**: 476–8.

20 Thomas M *et al.* (1985) Miniaturised continuous delivery systems for injectable solutions: individual patient control and physico-chemical properties. *Proc Guild.* **19**: 3–37.

21 Akahoshi MP *et al.* (1987) Safety and reliability of the Travenol Infusor in administering chemotherapy in the home. *J Pharm Tech.* **3**: 65–8.

22 Sewell GJ and Priston MJ (1995) Stability and compatability studies on cytotoxic and analgesic infusions in a new multi-purpose ambulatory device. *J Oncol Pharm Pract.* **1 (ISOPP Symposium Issue)**: 15.

23 Priston MJ and Sewell GJ (1998) Stability of three cytotoxic drug infusions in the Graseby 9000 ambulatory infusion pump. *J Oncol Pharm Pract.* **4**: 143–9.

24 Kwan JW (1989) High-technology IV infusion devices. *Am J Hosp Pharm.* **46**: 320–35.

25 Kemeny N *et al.* (1987) Intrahepatic or systemic infusion of fluorodeoxyuridine in patients with liver metastases from colorectal carcinoma. *Ann Intern Med.* **107**: 459–65.

26 von Roemeling R *et al.* (1988) Progressive metastatic renal cell carcinoma controlled by continuous 5-fluoro-2-deoxyuridine infusion. *J Urol.* **139**: 259–62.

27 Finley RS (1988) Ambulatory infusion pumps and venous access devices. In: *Proceedings of First International Symposium on Oncology Pharmacy Practice.* New Zealand Hospital Pharmacists Association, New Zealand, 279–93.

28 Lokich JJ (1987) Introduction to the concept and practice of infusion chemotherapy. In: JJ Lokich (ed.) *Cancer Chemotherapy by Infusion.* Precept Press Inc., Chicago, 3–11.

29 Legha SS *et al.* (1982) Reduction of doxorubicin cardiotoxicity by prolonged continuous intravenous infusion. *Ann Intern Med.* **96**: 133–9.

30 Seifert P *et al.* (1975) Comparison of continuously infused 5-fluorouracil with bolus injection in treatment of patients with colorectal adenocarcinoma. *Cancer.* **36**: 123–8.

31 Thigpen JT (1989) A randomised comparison of a rapid prolonged (24hr) infusion of cisplatin therapy for squamous cell carcinoma of the uterine cervix: a gynecologic oncology study. *Gynecol Oncol.* **32**: 198–202.

32 Mortimer J and Anderson I (1989) Managing the toxicities unique to high-dose leukovorin (CF) and fluorouracil (FU). *Proc Am Clin Oncol.* **8**: 98.

33 Allsopp MA and Sewell GJ (1995) A pharmacokinetic–pharmacodynamic study on carboplatin administered in prolonged continuous infusion regimens with synchronous radiotherapy. *J Oncol Pharm Pract.* **1**: 25–32.

34 Association of the British Pharmaceutical Industry (1995) *ABPI Data Sheet Compendium 1995–1996.* DataPharm Publications Ltd, London, 1262.

35 Schulman CC, Denis LJ, Oosterlinck W *et al.* (1983) Early adjuvant adriamycin in superficial bladder carcinoma. *Cancer Chemother Pharmacol.* **11 (Supplement)**: 532.

36 Barbuir PE, Bono AV, Gianno E *et al.* (1984) Intravesical doxorubicin for the prophylaxis of superficial bladder tumours: a multi-centre study. Binor Italian Cooperative Group. *Cancer.* **54**: 756.

37 Thrasher JB and Crawford ED (1992) Complications of intravesical chemotherapy. *Urol Clin North Am.* **19**: 529–39.

38 Cumming JA, Kirk D, Newling DW *et al.* (1990) A multicentre phase II study of intravesical epirubicin in the treatment of superficial bladder tumour. *Eur Urol.* **17**: 20.

39 Association of the British Pharmaceutical Industry (1995) *ABPI Data Sheet Compendium 1995–1996.* DataPharm Publications Ltd, London, 760–1.

40 Hall RR, Parmar MKB, Richards AP *et al.* (1994) Proposal for changes in cystoscopic follow-up of patients with bladder cancer and adjuvant intravesical chemotherapy. *BMJ.* **308**: 257–60.

41 Witjes JA, Meijden APM, Witjes WPJ *et al.* (1993) A randomised prospective study comparing intravesical instillations of mitomycin C, BCG Tice, and BCG-RIVM in pTa – pT1 tumours and primary carcinoma *in situ* of the urinary bladder. *Eur J Cancer.* **29A**: 1672–6.

42 Stewart DJ, Green R, Futter N *et al.* (1990) Phase 1 and pharmacology study of intravesical mitozantrone for recurrent superficial bladder tumours. *J Urol.* **143**: 714.

43 ABPI (1995) *ABPI Data Sheet Compendium 1995–1996.* DataPharm Publications Ltd, London, 808–10.

44 ABPI (1995) *ABPI Data Sheet Compendium 1995–1996.* DataPharm Publications Ltd, London, 818–9.

45 Debruyne FMJ, Van der Meijden PM, Witjes MD *et al.* (1992) Bacillus Calmette-Guerin versus mitomycin intravesical therapy in superficial bladder cancer. *Suppl Urol.* **40**: 11–15.

46 ABPI (1995) *ABPI Data Sheet Compendium 1995–1996.* DataPharm Publications Ltd, London, 560–1.

47 Stone MM, Vannier AM, Storch SK *et al.* (1995) Brief report: meningitis due to iatrogenic BCG injection in two immunocompromised children. *NEJM.* **333**: 561–3.

48 Toft B (2001) *Toft Report: External enquiry into the adverse incident that occurred at Queen's Medical Centre, Nottingham. 4 March, 2001.* Department of Health, London.

APPENDIX

Table 5.1: *Summary of pumps described*

Make/model	Weight**	Dimensions***	Pump mechanism	Reservoir	Battery	Flow rate	Accuracy	Alarm*
Graseby Medical								
MS 16A	275 g	16.5 × 2.3 × 5.3 cm	Syringe pump electric	2 mL–35 mL syringe	9 V	0–99 mm/hour variable	±5%	1,2,3
MS 26	275 g	16.5 × 2.3 × 5.3 cm	Syringe pump electric	2 mL–35 mL syringe	9 V	0–99 mm/day	±5%	1,2,3
Critikon								
Syringe Minder 2	270 g	11.7 × 5 × 1 cm	Syringe pump electric	2 mL–20 mL syringe	9 V	1–12 mm/hour fixed intervals	±3%	1,2,3
Pharmacia/Deltec								
CADD-1	425 g	2.8 × 9 × 16 cm	Peristaltic rotary programmable	50 mL/ 100 mL cassette	9 V	0–299 mL/day	theoretically ±10% in studies ±3%	1,2,3 4,5,6
CADD-PCA	425 g	2.8 × 9 × 16 cm	Peristaltic rotary programmable	50 mL/ 100 mL cassette	9 V	0–20 mL/hour		1,2,3 4,5,6
CADD-PLUS	425 g	2.8 × 9 × 16 cm	Peristaltic rotary programmable	50 mL/ 100 mL cassette	9 V	0–75 mL/day		1,2,3 4,5,6
Baxter								
Single-day infusor	100 g	16.5 × 3 cm diameter	Elastomeric pressure	60 mL	None	2 mL/hour	±5%	None
Multi-day infusor	100 g	16.5 × 3 cm diameter	Elastomeric pressure	60 mL	None	0.5 mL/hour	±5%	None
Seven-day infusor	150 g	25 × 3 cm diameter	Elastomeric pressure	90 mL	None	0.5 mL/hour	±5%	None
Paragon 100 infuser	225 g	10 × 5.8 cm	Mechanical: cantilevered spring	100 mL nominal fill (maximum = 121 mL). Option to part fill	None	0.5–200 mL/hour	±10%	None
Baxter 6060	350 g	11.9 × 9.9 × 5.8 cm	Peristaltic	100 mL/ 250 mL	2 × 9 V	0.1–400 mL/hour	±6%	1,2,3 4,6,7

Table 5.1: *Continued*

Make/model	Weight**	Dimensions***	Pump mechanism	Reservoir	Battery	Flow rate	Accuracy	Alarm*
Medfusion INFU-MED 300	350 g	11.2 × 10.4 × 4.6 cm	Linear peristaltic	65 mL/ 150 mL/ 250 mL collapsible reservoir	9 V	0.1–9.9 mL/hour	±5%	2,3,4
WalkMed 410c	360 g	11.2 × 10.2 × 4.6 cm	Linear peristaltic program-mable	65 mL/ 150 mL/ 250 mL collapsible reservoir	9 V	0.01–30 mL/hour	±5%	2,3, 4,5
WalkMed 420i/c	360 g	11.2 × 10.2 × 4.6 cm	Linear peristaltic program-mable	65 mL/ 150 mL/ 250 mL collapsible reservoir	9 V	0–9.9 mL/hour	±5%	2,3 4,5
WalkMed 430pca	360 g	11.2 × 10.2 × 4.6 cm	Linear peristaltic program-mable	65 mL/ 150 mL/ 250 mL collapsible reservoir	9 V		±5%	2,3 4,5
WalkMed 440pic	360 g	11.2 × 10.4 × 4.6 cm	Linear peristaltic program-mable	65 mL/ 150 mL/ 250 mL collapsible reservoir	9 V		±5%	2,3 4,5
Pfizer Infusaid 400	200 g	9 × 2.8 cm	Non-electronic metal bellows concept	50 mL	None	Flow rate affected by a number of variables		None
Medtronic SynchroMed 8611H	200 g	7 × 2.7 cm	Rotary peristaltic system	18 mL	Lithium	0.1–18 mL/day		None
SynchroMed 8615	200 g	7 × 2.7 cm	Rotary peristaltic system	18 mL	Lithium	0.1–18 mL/day		None
Graseby Medical 9000 series	316 g	16.8 × 10 × 2.7 cm	Peristaltic program-mable	50 mL/ 100 mL/ 175 mL/ 250 mL cassette (also spike for IV bag)	9 V	0–100 mL/hour	±5%	1,2,3, 4,5,7

* Alarms:
  1, end of travel/infusion; 2, low battery; 3, occlusion; 4, internal malfunction; 5, lower residual volume in medication cassette;
  6, start-up review (power up); 7, air in line.
** Includes batteries and smallest reservoir.
*** Includes smallest reservoir (empty) and protective cases for syringe pumps.

Managing complications of chemotherapy administration

INTRODUCTION

Cytotoxic drugs have, without exception, the potential to cause great harm if they are not prescribed, dispensed and administered safely and correctly. Cytotoxic drugs are taken to the very limit of, and often beyond, their toxic threshold. This is in contrast to most other drugs, which have a therapeutic dose set within the maximum and minimum tolerated doses.

It is important that all members of a multidisciplinary healthcare team play a part in safe administration, a process that begins with the writing of a prescription, and is followed by pharmaceutical dispensing, ending with chemotherapy nurses administering. Pharmacy is entrusted with being the gatekeeper of this process. The professional responsibilities of a pharmacist can be defined as the safe and appropriate administration of drugs. To fulfil this function of safe, accurate and appropriate dispensing, a pharmacist needs to have a concise protocol to refer to when dispensing each and every prescription. In broad terms the protocol should cover the following points.

▼ Is the patient fit and able to receive chemotherapy?
▼ Is the chemotherapy that is being prescribed for the patient appropriate, protocolised and pharmaceutically sound?
▼ Is the prescription written in such a way that it can be dispensed safely and without question or doubt?
▼ Has the patient been prescribed appropriate and effective support therapies in order to minimise physical or psychological trauma associated with the chemotherapy?

SUITABILITY OF THE PATIENT FOR CHEMOTHERAPY

In order to carry out all of these functions, a fairly comprehensive clinical knowledge of cytotoxic drugs is required. However, it is beyond the remit of this handbook to consider all of these parameters.

A number of general issues are worth touching on. Checks must be made to confirm that the patient is suitable for the chemotherapy prescribed for them. It is necessary to consider the patient's haematological status (if not dose limiting, haematological suppression is a common toxicity of almost all chemotherapies). An assessment of the patient's general performance or well-being needs to be established, as again it is fairly universal for intravenous chemotherapy to debilitate and fatigue the patient. A number of more drug-specific checks should also be made which are a function of specific drug toxicities. Particularly important are checks on renal function in patients who are destined to receive nephrotoxic agents (e.g. cisplatin) or renally eliminated agents (e.g. methotrexate). Checks of risk factors that predispose ifosfamide recipients to encephalopathy (low serum albumin, poor renal function, presence of a large pelvic mass) should be made, as well as a check of adequate cardiac function in patients scheduled to start anthracycline treatment. In addition, the absence of third-space fluid accumulation in patients due to receive methotrexate should also be confirmed.

SUITABILITY OF THE DOSE

A check must be made on the chemotherapy dose. Chemotherapy is peculiar in that, rather than the dosage being expressed as the number of milligrams or (as in paediatric circles) milligrams per kilogram, the concept of body surface area (BSA) is used to try to individualise the dose to the patient. Here, through a consideration of weight and height and the application of the Du Bois formula (*see* Equation 1) or, more commonly, the Graham and George modification (*see* Equation 2), a BSA is calculated (expressed as metres squared) for the patient. The patient's individualised dose can then be calculated if the number of milligrams per metre squared for the individual doses in the drug regimen is known.

Equation 1

$$BSA\ (cm^2) = weight^{0.425} \times height^{0.725} \times 71.84.$$

Equation 2

$$BSA\ (m^2) = \sqrt{\frac{height(cm) \times weight(kg)}{3600}}.$$

There is much debate as to whether ideal or actual body weight should be used for such calculations, whether body weight including such disease-related symptoms as effusions (particularly those of the peritoneum) should be corrected for, and whether maximum or minimum surface areas should be assigned. It is known that all of the formulae are weak at the periphery of their calculations, but this is particularly true for the Graham and George modification. These peripheries are usually considered to occur where the BSA is less than 1.4 m² and/or greater than 2.1 m². This therefore makes dosing of the paediatric patient on the basis of a body surface area calculation inherently unsafe, and paediatric protocols commonly revert to the use of mg/kg. Other specific formulae for dosing for cytotoxic drugs are now becoming accepted into everyday practice – for example, the dosing of the monoclonal antibody Herceptin, in which a loading dose of 4 mg/kg is followed by weekly infusions of 2 mg/kg. However, the drug for which most research has been undertaken to enable the tailoring of dose to individuals is carboplatin. Here the patient-specific recommendations are based on renal function (Calvert) or the effect on platelet count (Egorin). The latter method distinguishes between previously treated and untreated patients.

Egorin's formula for previously untreated patients is as follows:

$$dose\ (mg/m^2) = 0.091 \times (C/S) \times M + 86.$$

Egorin's formula for previously treated patients is as follows:

$$\text{dose (mg/m}^2) = 0.091 \times (C/S) \times (M-17) + 86$$

where C = creatinine clearance (mL/min), S = body surface area and M = [(pretreated platelet count – desired nadir count)/pretreated platelet count] × 100.

Calvert offered and validated a simpler formula based on renal function and the desired serum exposure, expressed as the area under the serum concentration time curve (AUC).
　　Calvert's original formula is as follows:

$$\text{total dose (mg)} = 4.88 \; (1.22 \times \text{GFR} + 23).$$

　　Calvert's final working formula is as follows:

$$\text{total dose (mg)} = \text{target AUC (GFR} + 25)$$

where GFR = glomular filtration rate and target AUC = 4 to 6 mg/mL for previously treated patients and 6 to 8 mg/mL for previously untreated patients.
　　A third formula by Fish and colleagues has also been proposed, but this formula has found far less clinical acceptance, as some clinicians believe it leads to under-dosing:

$$\text{total dose (mg)} = (a \; \text{GFR} + b) \times K \; 1/\alpha \; (P_0/P_1) \times 1/\alpha$$

where a, b and α are all constants, P_0 = initial platelet count and P_1 = nadir platelet count.

It is thus important that practitioners are clear about how doses in their particular clinical situation are being calculated, while it is obviously better for patients in terms of achieving the best balance between efficiency and toxicity. The more complex the dosage calculation, the greater is the need to be vigilant and interventionist.
　　Therefore in good clinical oncology practice, the dose in mg/m², mg/kg or the total dose in mg should be defined in a treatment protocol outlining the dosage and conditions which make it permissible to administer the chemotherapy.
　　Not only is it important to consider the individual dose per treatment, but for a number of cytotoxic drugs there are cumulative or maximum ceilings which should only be breached with sound clinical reasoning. Probably the most well known of these is vincristine, where the intravenous dose should not exceed 2 mg in any one administration, even though the protocol may specify 1.5 mg/m². Again, this threshold may be deliberately altered in a particular protocol aimed at a more susceptible subgroup of the population. For example, because the elderly are more susceptible to vincristine-induced neuropathy, the maximum dose per course may be 1.0 or 1.5 mg. Furthermore, cardiotoxic thresholds exist for all of the anthracyclines, and whilst it is possible and not fatal to administer beyond these doses, the patient's risk for cardiac complications increases considerably.

Although it is accepted at the time of going to press that pharmacists do not prescribe, it is beholden upon them to intervene in the prescribing process if they consider that the patient has passed either a dose-per-administration ceiling or a cumulative-dose ceiling which is detrimental to their health or the safe administration of the chemotherapy.

SUITABILITY OF THE ADMINISTRATION ROUTE

An important part of the pharmaceutical protocol is to check that the vehicle and schedule of the drug to be administered are suitable. The final generalised check is that the administration route is appropriate. This is particularly important with subcutaneous and intrathecal routes. Although the subcutaneous (or even intramuscular) route is safe and often appropriate for drugs such as cytarabine, methotrexate and bleomycin, it is important to consider the total volume to be injected. Volumes of greater than 1 mL often cause unnecessary pain and suffering to the patient. However, whilst these drugs are safe, there is no indication for the administration of anthracyclines, platinum or taxanes subcutaneously.

Intrathecal injections

Some cancer chemotherapy regimens include specific drugs for injection intrathecally, as part of the treatment protocol, e.g. cytarabine and methotrexate have a valuable and proven role in the treatment and prevention of CNS disease in lymphomas, leukaemias and carmentumorous meningitis. However, some cytotoxic drugs used in the same protocols are extremely toxic to nervous tissue, in particular the vinca alkaloids, but also the anthracyclines, including mitozantrone, which are *always* administered intravenously. The risk of mistake between the different injection routes, for two drugs that are often administered at approximately the same time, has been recognised for many years, and yet incidences of death following mistaken injection into the spine, particularly of the vinca drugs, continue. Following the most recent incident in the UK, a detailed report has been published which identifies all the likely reasons why these mistakes continue in clinical practice, and it provides new guidelines which should minimise the risk in future.[a] The guidelines affect pharmacies and wards. Following these key recommendations is essential for the avoidance of future incidences.

The storage, preparation, dispensing, supply and administration of intrathecal drugs should always be separate from drugs intended for intravenous administration. This includes additional safeguards, such as the dispensing of intrathecal drugs (which in our own institute are treated as though they are 'schedule 1 controlled drugs') in normal working hours and only from the cytotoxic chemotherapy unit by a pharmacist trained in oncology, issued directly to the doctor, normally a consultant or specialist registrar certified and trained to administer intrathecal drugs, and packed, transported and stored as single and separate items. Those drugs intended for administration by any alternative route should never be presented to practitioners, whether medical or nursing, for administration at the same time as intravenous therapies. Although no evidence exists for the co-administration of drugs by alternative routes at the same time, well-established peer-reviewed protocols advocate such practice in this situation if the administration of the IV vincristine dose coincides with the intrathecal therapy – the vincristine should then mandatorily be added to a 50 or 100 mL normal saline minibag and the pharmacist should personally verify that this intravenous injection has been given before issuing the intrathecal drugs. In our institute this is done by the pharmacist going to the ward and exchanging the used IV bag for the intrathecal injection.

There must be recordable and auditable checking procedures, which identify all those involved and their actions. New recommendations on labelling and product formulation require the labels to be distinctive and colour coded (to match the prescription chart), and the route of administration should be printed in the largest font used on the label and in bold type, with all other information in normal type. In routine clinical practice, the vinca product, e.g. vincristine, should be diluted to at least 20 mL*, a maximum concentration of 0.1 mg/mL. Therefore in practice, the issuing of all vincas in 20 mL syringes diluted with normal saline should accommodate the new guidance. For children under the age of 10 years the vincristine can be given undiluted at a concentration of 1.0 mg/mL.* Although the extravasation risk is greater, the volume is still well below that commonly associated with anthracyclines, and the risk–benefit evaluation is overwhelmingly in favour of the larger volume over potentially the wrong route.

On the ward, intrathecal drugs must be stored separately in a secure place, only retrievable by the responsible doctor who has been authorised to undertake intrathecal injection of cytotoxic drugs. Intravenous drugs, i.e. vinca alkaloids, must always be administered before intrathecal chemotherapy. Intrathecal drugs should be prescribed on a separate prescription chart, which is easily identified by colour as different from that used to prescribe intravenous chemotherapy, or on a part of the chart which is colour coded, pre-printed and unique to the prescribing of intrathecal drugs.

It is also recommended that a new design of spinal needle connector that is incompatible with luer mounted syringe fittings be developed for this use, together with a syringe fitting which is only compatible with the new spinal needle fitting. This is currently not available at the time of going to press but if it becomes available during the 'life' of this handbook, its adoption should be *mandatory* and *immediate*.

All the procedures relating to the use of intrathecal injections of chemotherapy must be described in explicit procedures. The criteria for defining those staff permitted to be involved in these procedures, their training, induction, assessment and monitoring of competence, must also be included in a Code of Practice.[b–d]

[a] Toft B (2001) *Toft Report: External enquiry into the adverse incident that occurred at Queen's Medical Centre, Nottingham, 4 March, 2001.* Department of Health, London.
[b] Arico M, Nespoli L, Porta F *et al.* (1990) Severe acute encephalopathy following inadvertent intrathecal doxorubicin administration. *Med Ped Oncol.* 18: 261–3.
[c] Lakhani AK, Zuiable AG, Pollard CM *et al.* (1986) Paraplegia after intrathecal mitozantrone. *Lancet.* 2: 1393.
[d] Fernandez CV, Esau R, Hamilton D *et al.* (1998) Intrathecal vincristine: an analysis of reasons for recurrent fatal chemotherapeutic error with recommendations for prevention. *J Ped Hematol Oncol.* 20: 587–90.

*As this book went to press, new guidance was issued on the safe administration of intrathecal chemotherapy, which requires that only registered, designated personnel should prescribe, dispense, check or administer intrathecal chemotherapy. The guidance also requires formal induction and regular training programmes. Please check the guidance for the full recommendations: NHS Executive (2001) *National Guidance on the Safe Administration of Intrathecal Chemotherapy.* HSC 2001/022.

COMPLICATIONS OF INTRAVENOUS THERAPY

Once they have been safely prescribed and compounded, the final stage before cytotoxic drugs can be effective is their safe administration. This stage is far from straightforward, and requires as much planning and care as the other two steps.

The cytotoxic drugs are by their very nature designed to kill cells in a largely non-discriminatory manner. Furthermore, as chemicals they are far from pleasant. Their inherent natural characteristics mean that their administration is fraught with risk, regardless of the skill of the operator. The remainder of this chapter deals with some of the immediate vascular, cutaneous or dermatological toxicities or complications that are associated with intravenous administration of chemotherapy.

It is often quite difficult to determine the precise role of the cytotoxic drug in these reactions, as all of the latter can be complicated or enhanced by either the underlying malignancy or concurrent medication. Therefore the following points should be borne in mind when attempting to evaluate these reactions:

▼ timing in relation to both the current administration and the overall chemotherapy
▼ the morphology of the reaction
▼ associated clinical and/or laboratory observations
▼ supportive evidence.

ANAPHYLAXIS, HYPERSENSITIVITY OR ALLERGIC REACTIONS

Although these three terms convey a similar clinical picture, they do have individual and specific definitions. However, authors tend to use one particular 'label', and occasionally interchange 'labels' when describing an acute systemic reaction to the drug being administered. As the authors of such reports then often fail to distinguish the precise immunological response that they have observed, the three terms have been pooled together for the purposes of this chapter. Therefore an overview of this problem is presented here.

As a general rule, such reactions occur as a result of over-stimulation of the body's immune system. Their classification is based on the original 1975 text of Gell and Coombs (see Table 6.1 for a summary).

Nearly all cytotoxic drugs could theoretically produce a hypersensitivity reaction, and in fact many of them have done so on an individual patient basis. Only a relatively select group produce significant numbers of reactions (5–15%), and even fewer could be said to have hypersensitivity-related toxicity such that they require premedication test dosing, or discontinuation of therapy if they occur.

Although most cytotoxic drug-induced reactions are thought to be immunologically mediated, and are thus classified as type I IgE-mediated reactions, it is probably more precise to say that we do not know the exact mechanism.

Some cytotoxic drugs appear to cause degranulation of mast cells and/or basophils through a direct action on the cell suface. The consequent release of histamine and other vasoactive substances provides an alternative pathway for management. Some agents activate alternative complement pathways. Such events are not mediated by IgE and are thus more strictly referred to as anaphylactoid reactions.

Table 6.1: *Types of hypersensitivity reactions based on Gell and Coombs classification of hypersensitivity*

Type	Mechanism	Clinical symptoms
Type I IgE-mediated	Antigen interaction with IgE bound to mast cells and basophils causes degranulation. This leads to activation of alternative complement pathways to produce anaphylatoxins and vasoactive substances	Usually rapid onset (less than 30 minutes) on second or subsequent exposures rather than first exposure Hypotension, angioedema, agitation and anxiety, bronchospasm, abdominal cramping Urticaria and rash
Type II Cell destruction (or cytotoxic)	Antibodies react to antigens bound to cells or to tissue-specific components resulting in cell death/destruction (cytotoxicity) by activation of complement and killer cells	Destruction of blood cells (e.g. haemolytic anaemia) Bullous skin eruption
Type II Immune complex-mediated	Deposition of antigen–antibody immune complexes in certain tissues with activation of complement and neutrophils	Fever, chronic urticaria, arthralgia proteinuria, vasculitis, pneumonitis or erythema multiforme
Type IV Cell-mediated	Antigen-specific T-lymphocytes react with antigens and induce the secretion of lymphokines followed by the formation of an inflammatory reaction	Contact dermatitis Chronic granuloma in certain organs

Angioedema and urticaria occasionally result from a stressful situation (e.g. having cancer or chemotherapy), and therefore a neural mechanism exists as an alternative means of vasoactive activation. However, a sensitisation period during which a pre-anaphylaxis state occurs and the patient may report some of the more minor signs and symptoms associated with anaphylaxis or hypersensitivity is by far the commonest during this time. The site of administration may also demonstrate a flare-type reaction.

The signs and symptoms of anaphylaxis are normally fairly rapid in onset, and generally develop as follows:

▼ localised or generalised itching
▼ facial flushing leading to generalised flushing
▼ shortness of breath (sometimes with a wheeze)
▼ uneasiness and agitation
▼ local oedema and then often facial oedema
▼ light-headed dizziness
▼ tightening of the chest
▼ a tachycardic heartbeat
▼ falling blood pressure
▼ 'flu-like' symptoms, often with quite violent shaking.

The recent introduction of docetaxel and paclitaxel has seen a variation of the true anaphylaxis, called *formulation-induced hypersensitivity*, although there is some doubt about this explanation. If untreated, the signs and symptoms as described above for anaphylaxis will result. However, careful prophylactic desensitisation regimens can minimise if not eliminate these types of hypersensitivity reactions. This usually involves giving high doses of steroids before and for varying lengths of time after taxoid infusion. The most commonly used dose is dexamethasone 8 or 20 mg orally, although equally effective intravenous regimens exist. Dexamethasone has a fairly long half-life, and therefore the timing is not critical within ±4 hours. In the case of both doxetaxel and paclitaxel the hypersensitivity is known to be associated with the release of histamine, so immediately prior to administration both H_1- and H_2-type antihistamines should be administered. The author also has experience of using oral sodium cromoglicate, 1 g administered one hour prior to administration, in particularly sensitive patients, in order to stabilise mast cells and thus

Table 6.2: *Summary of reported hypersensitivity reactions to chemotherapy*

Drug	Type of reaction	Frequency
Asparaginase	Type I	25–44%
Amsacrine	Type I	Case reports
Bleomycin	Type I, type III	Case reports
Carboplatin	Type I	5–15%
Cisplatin	Type I	Up to 20% and increases with total exposure
Cyclophosphamide	Type I	Case reports
Cytarabine	Type I and contact skin rashes (type IV?)	Case reports
Dacarbazine	Type I, type III	Case reports
Daunorubicin	Type I	Less than 1–5%
Docetaxel	Type I	Up to 30% unpremeded Less than 5% premeded
Doxorubicin	Type I	Less than 1–5%
Epirubicin	Type I	Less than 1–5%
Etoposide	Type I	3%
Fluorouracil	Type I	Case reports less than 1%
Idarubicin	Type I	Less than 1–5%
Ifosfamide	Type I	Case reports
Melphalan	Type I	2–5%
Methotrexate	Type I, type II, type III	Case reports
Mitomycin	Type I, type III Type IV (intravesical administration)	Case reports up to 10%
Mitozantrone	Type I	Case reports
Mustine	Type I	Case reports
Oxaliplatin	Type I	Case reports
Paclitaxel	Type I	Up to 40% unpremeded 2–5% premeded
Pentostatin	Type I	Case reports
Teniposide	Type I, type II	Case reports up to 13%
Vinblastine	Type I	Case reports

Table 6.3: *Preventative strategies for docetaxel hypersensitivities*

Original oral premed	Rechallenge following hypersensitivity (oral and IV)		Weekly schedule premed	
Minus 24 hours	Minus 24 hours			
8 mg dexamethasone PO	8 mg dexamethasone	PO		
Minus 12 hours	Minus 12 hours		Minus 12 hours	
8 mg dexamethasone PO	8 mg dexamethasone	PO	8 mg dexamethasone	PO
	Minus 45 minutes		Minus 45 minutes	
	8 mg dexamethasone	IV	8 mg dexamethasone	IV
	Minus 30 minutes		Minus 30 minutes	
	4 mg chlorpheniramine	IV	4 mg chlorpheniramine	IV
Plus 12 hours	Plus 12 hours		Plus 12 hours	
8 mg dexamethasone PO	8 mg dexamethasone	PO	8 mg dexamethasone	PO
Plus 24 hours	Plus 24 hours			
8 mg dexamethasone PO	8 mg dexamethasone	PO		
Plus 36 hours	Plus 36 hours			
8 mg dexamethasone PO	8 mg dexamethasone	PO		
Plus 48 hours	Plus 48 hours			
8 mg dexamethasone PO	8 mg dexamethasone	PO		

prevent the hypersensitivity cascade. Table 6.2 summarises these preventative strategies.

Preventative strategies for docetaxel and paclitaxel hypersensitivities are listed in Tables 6.3 and 6.4, respectively.

Both the author and other practitioners have reported the successful use of these regimens in the treatment of hypersenstitive reactions to other cytotoxic drugs, often allowing successful rechallenge with the agent.

CHEMICAL PHLEBITIS AND VENOUS IRRITATION

This consists of reactions which are confined to the venous compartment. There has thus been no misadventure with regards to the actual administration, and such reactions are a function of the chemical properties of the drugs. However, their causative factors and underlying mechanisms are similar to those in extravasation, and include the following:

▼ the pH of the drug
▼ formulation excipients
▼ effect on vascular tone
▼ concentration
▼ temperature
▼ degradation/impurities in the final product.

This is therefore definitely part of the pre-extravasation syndrome, marked by a transient but pronounced inflammation along the line of the vein, which may track for some considerable distance, although some of the factors in the above list can be manipulated in an attempt to prevent or minimise these types of reactions.

Table 6.4: *Preventative strategies for paclitaxel hypersensitivities*

Original oral premed		Simplified IV premed		Rechallenge (oral + IV premed)		Weekly administration premed			
						Cycle 1 and 2		Further cycles	
Minus 12 hours				Minus 12 hours		—		—	
20 mg dexamethasone	PO			20 mg dexamethasone	PO				
Minus 6 hours				Minus 6 hours		—		—	
20 mg dexamethasone	PO			20 mg dexamethasone	PO				
		Minus 45 minutes		Minus 45 minutes		Minus 1 hour		Minus 1 hour	
		10 mg dexamethasone	IV	10 mg dexamethasone	IV	8 mg dexamethasone	IV or PO	4 mg dexamethasone	IV or PO
Minus 30 minutes		Minus 30 minutes		Minus 30 minutes		Minus 30 minutes		Minus 30 minutes	
4 mg chlorpheniramine	IV	4 mg chlorpheniramine	IV	4 mg chlorpheniramine	IV	4 mg chlorpheniramine	IV	4 mg chlorpheniramine	IV
or		or		or		or		or	
50 mg diphenhydramine	IV	50 mg diphenhydramine	IV	50 mg diphenhydramine	IV	50 mg diphenhydramine	IV	50 mg diphenhydramine	IV
Minus 15 minutes		Minus 15 minutes		Minus 15 minutes		Minus 15 minutes		Minus 15 minutes	
300 mg cimetidine	IV	200 mg cimetidine	IV	300 mg cimetidine	IV	300 mg cimetidine	IV	300 mg cimetidine	IV
or		or		or		or		or	
50 mg ranitidine	IV	50 mg ranitidine	IV	50 mg ranitidine	IV	50 mg ranitidine	IV	50 mg ranitidine	IV
or		or		or		or		or	
50 mg nizatidine	IV	50 mg nizatidine	IV	50 mg nizatidine	IV	50 mg nizatidine	IV	50 mg nizatidine	IV

The concentration can vary according to the temperature of the product. Drugs are often stored in the refrigerator in order to give them maximum stability. Unfortunately, they are not then given sufficient time to warm up before administration. As a result, significant thermal gradients exist, causing flare and irritation in the vein, which lead to contraction and/or venous spasm.

Temperatures can be varied (even beyond room temperature of 25°C) by using a thermostatically controlled water bath. In this way it is possible to raise the temperature of the drug to a body temperature of 36.8°C.

Finally, degradation products (e.g. dacarbazine) or formulation impurities (e.g. microscopic 5-fluorouracil crystals) can be predicted from the text in the main monographs for each individual drug. The importance of these reactions covers a wide clinical spectrum ranging from totally insignificant to highly problematic filtration. Protection from light and minimisation of degradation times are both possible strategies for reducing these problems.

Management

The management of these reactions is simple and largely symptomatic, as many of the reactions will subside if left untreated. However, it is vital to ensure that a differential diagnosis of phlebitis or venous irritation has been made, rather than the potentially more devastating extravasation injury. Once this has been established, the following procedure should prove highly effective.

1 Flush the vein with brisk running normal saline.
2 Flush an 8 mg dexamethasone or 100 mg hydrocortisone bolus down the affected vein to reverse the inflammatory effects.
3 Give a 4 mg chlorpheniramine bolus to stabilise any allergic reaction in the vein wall epithelial cells.
4 The use of a warming pad over the vein can bring considerable symptomatic relief.
5 Apply 1% hydrocortisone cream along the line of the affected vein(s) over the next 3 or 4 days.

Rechallenge

As this type of reaction may be the start of some type of vein wall sensitisation and/or part of a pre-extravasation cascade, the practitioner should consider carefully before rechallenging with the causative agent. All practical strategies to prevent or minimise its recurrence should be implemented.

EXTRAVASATION

Extravasation in the context of this handbook is the inappropriate or accidental administration of chemotherapy into the subcutaneous or subdermal tissues rather than into the intended intravenous compartment. The consequences of this action are often pain, erythema, inflammation and discomfort which, if left undiagnosed or inappropriately treated, can lead to necrosis and functional loss of the tissue and limb concerned.

Extravasation injuries can therefore range from apparently insignificant erythematous reactions, through skin sloughing to severe necrosis. Although extravasation is possible with any intravenous injection, it is only considered to be problematic with those compounds that are known to be vesicant or irritant.

1 Occurrence

Although extravasation is a serious consequence of intravenous therapy, evidence exists to demonstrate that appropriately treated extravasation which is dealt with within 24 hours causes no further problems to the patient.[1-4]

However, it is encouraging that the incidence of extravasation, certainly in the oncological population, is remarkably low. Many surveys, including the author's research work in Birmingham, have shown that the general rate of extravasation for intravenous therapy is in the range 20–30%, and in fact some authors have proposed that, if left long enough, any intravenous access will lead to extravasation, and that the time to extravasation will range from 1 to 7 days, but at 7 days 95% of all intravenous access sites will have extravasated (i.e. the cannula will have been displaced from the venous compartment into the surrounding tissues). Although this may be alarming, it must be remembered that other than some local and transient morbidity for the patient, the vast majority of these extravasation injuries are non-complicated. However, in at-risk populations extra care and highly educated administrative personnel mean that the incidence rate falls to below 5%, and is often below 1%.

Extravasation is a condition that is often under-diagnosed, under-treated and unreported. A large number of articles and reviews of extravasation have been published during the past 10 years.[5-11] Their relevance is difficult to assess, as they often refer to isolated incidents that may have been treated in a haphazard manner, without incorporating the knowledge that may be gleaned from a wider view of the literature. However, there are several retrospective reviews and clinical trials that go some way towards providing evidence of the efficacy of various treatments.[12-15] Yet much can be done by means of forethought, planning and improved prevention measures to minimise extravasation.

2 Risk factors associated with extravasation

The following factors contribute to extravasation injury:

▼ error associated with the administration technique (i.e. the human angle)
▼ error associated with the administration device
▼ factors associated with the patient
▼ the inherently physical properties of the drugs concerned.

2.1 Administration

The elimination of human error can be considered to be impossible. In excess of 100 000 doses of chemotherapy and over 1 000 000 intravenous administrations are in progress each day, which inevitably leads to some degree of human error. However, risk associated with these factors should be minimised by the use of good training and educational policy, not only as stand-alone courses but also, importantly, on a continuing educational basis. One of the greatest skills that individuals can bring to the administration of chemotherapy is the fact that it is routine for them. It is neither appropriate nor safe practice to administer chemotherapy on a 'when required' basis. It is a blind process for which no two administrations will be similar, and for that reason it is as much an art as a science.

2.2 The administration device

More rigorous scientific considerations can govern the selection of a suitable cannula. It inherently makes sense and has been demonstrated in a number of studies as well as through the National Extravasation Register that rigid steel cannulas cause more problems than flexible Teflon or silicon cannulas. The selection of device or cannula is also influenced by the competing issues of biology and physics.

Flexible cannulas are supplied in a variety of widths and lengths, and the biology of veins means that the smaller and shorter the cannula, the less the trauma that is associated with the cannulation process. However, the physics of short narrow pipes means that pipes of smaller diameter increase the resistance and decrease the flow of fluid through them. Conversely, the pressure of delivery has to be increased in order to maintain a constant flow.

The insertion of a cannula necessitates the puncture of the vein wall. This wall is relatively fragile, and if the pressure of the blood is greater than that of the fluid entering the vein via the cannula, there is a risk of back-flow into the cannula, or of rupture of the vein around the cannula edge, leading to leakage. Vein walls contain small holes, and therefore the greater the pressure of the incoming fluid, the greater is the likelihood of wall rupture.

A series of professional judgements needs to be made. For example, if the quantity of the necessary chemotherapy to be administered is a 1 mg/10 mL dose of vincristine, then probably a small paediatric cannula is appropriate, whereas a 170 mg/85 mL dose of epirubicin would need a device with a substantially larger diameter.

The science and technology of cannulas have developed rapidly, and there are now a number of high-tech developments, such as the silicon/Teflon IV cannula, and cannula materials that soften once they are exposed to the warmer internal body temperature of 37°C.

The latest and perhaps most exciting of these developments are the periperally inserted catheter (PIC) lines. These allow central venous access via the antecubital fossa into the basilic, subclavian and descending jugular veins, without the need for a long tunnelled section across the chest wall. Although they are easier to insert, they do require a considerably greater degree of care than other long lines, and they are often less acceptable to the patient in terms of cosmetic outcome. As with all long lines, they pose a different but not necessarily lower set of risks or challenges with regard to extravasation.

2.3 Location of cannulation site

Once the appropriate cannulation device has been selected, a site for cannulation needs to be chosen. This must be a site where the cannula can be inserted easily, fastened securely and observed easily, and one which will not come under stress if the patient or administrator moves. Taking these factors into account, the most appropriate site for location of a cannula is considered to be the forearm.

However, this site will not always be available for cannulation. The vessels in the dorsum of the hand are probably the next most appropriate location for cannulation. Such sites as the antecubital fossa should be avoided. As a general rule, joints and creases should be avoided as they often represent a 'small' anatomical space, with nerves and tendons (often with little flesh 'covering') present.

2.4 Factors associated with the patient

Despite these theoretically correct sites for cannula location, a number of other patient-related factors need to be considered. Disease parameters (e.g. lymphoedema in breast disease), or other underlying physiological conditions, (e.g. diabetes) and peripheral circulatory diseases (e.g. Raynard's disease) can all modify this theory. Patients who have received previous radiation therapy at the site of injection may develop severe local reactions to extravasated cytotoxic drugs. This is known as recall injury, and it has been noted in patients who have received doxorubicin.[16]

Cytotoxic drugs also have the potential to cause cutaneous abnormalities in areas that have been damaged previously by radiation, even if the areas are distant from the injection site. Furthermore, areas of previous surgery where the under-lying tissue is likely to be fibrosed and toughened all dramatically increase the risk of extravasation.

Because of the toxic chemical nature of many cytotoxic drugs, and the stress and trauma involved in the cannulation process, together with the fact that chemo-therapy is given over a number of cycles on a three-weekly or even weekly basis, it is thought by many authors that the sites of cannulation should be alternated. A final factor that has to be worked into this complicated equation is the patient's preference. Often patients do not wish to be cannulated in their dominant hand, and in fact there is some evidence to suggest that this is a more complicated, traumatic process in any case, because the underlying muscular structures of the dominant hand or arm are better developed and therefore apply greater pressure to the vascular structures which they surround.

2.5 Factors associated with concurrent medication

Although it is not believed that concurrent medication actually causes extravasa-tion injuries, its presence may exacerbate an injury from other causes, or increase the risk of these injuries occurring. This is currently the theme of a research programme looking at the relative contributions of all the known risk/causative factors, in an attempt to weight and combine them into a single index of risk known as the Joshua Index. The following medicines or groups of medication are believed to have such an influence:

▼ anticoagulants
▼ antiplatelet drugs
▼ antifibrinolytics
▼ vasodilators
▼ vasoconstrictors
▼ hormonal therapies
▼ steroids
▼ diuretics
▼ antihistamines
▼ centrally acting analgesics
▼ topical analgesics
▼ drugs that caused previous hypersensitivity in the particular patient concerned.

2.6 Factors associated with the drugs

Whilst pharmacists may be involved in the education and training of personnel and in the administration of chemotherapy, their influence over this and the choice of cannula and site of cannulation may be limited.

The most important input that pharmacists can have is by consideration of the drugs themselves and by characterising their extravasation risk. It is now well documented that a number of physicochemical factors influence, and usually increase, the extravasation risk associated with individual drugs. These factors include the following:

▼ the ability to bind directly to DNA (most cytotoxic drugs do this)
▼ the ability to kill replicating cells (such drugs also include the cytotoxic and antiviral agents)
▼ the ability to cause tissue or vascular dilatation
▼ the pH, osmolarity and excipients in the formulation of the drug.

These parameters are more specifically defined as pH outside the range 5.5.–8.5 and osmolarity greater than that of plasma (290 mosmol/L) and formulation components such as alcohol, polyethylene glycol and Tweens. Other formulation-related parameters include the concentration and volume of the solutions to be administered.

Unfortunately, the latter two parameters conflict with each other in so far as the smaller the volume, the lower the likelihood of extravasation, but the greater the concentration, the higher the risk of extravasation, or the greater the damage should any extravasation be caused. As the commonest way of decreasing the volume is by increasing the concentration, juggling these two factors again becomes more of an art than a science.

Table 6.5 provides a classification of the cytotoxic drugs that takes into consideration these factors.

Table 6.5: *Classification of cytotoxic drugs according to their potential to cause serious necrosis when extravasated*

Vesicants (Group 1)	Exfoliants (Group 2)	Irritants (Group 3)	Inflammatory agents (Group 4)	Neutrals (Group 5)
Amsacrine	Aclarubicin	Carboplatin	Etoposide	Asparaginase
Carmustine	Cisplatin	Etoposide	phosphate	Bleomycin
Dacarbazine	Daunorubicin	Irinotecan	Fluorouracil	Cladribine
Dactinomycin	liposomal	Teniposide	Methotrexate	Cyclophosphamide
Daunorubicin	Docetaxel		Raltitrexed	Cytarabine
Doxorubicin	Doxorubicin			Fludarabine
Epirubicin	liposomal			Gemcitabine
Idarubicin	Floxuridine			Ifosfamide
Mitomycin	Mitozantrone			Interleukin 2
Mustine	Oxaliplatin			Melphalan
Paclitaxel	Topotecan			Pentostatin
Streptozocin				Thiotepa
Treosulfan				α-Interferons
Vinblastine				
Vincristine				
Vindesine				
Vinorelbine				

DEFINITIONS OF GROUPS

Group 1 – vesicants

Capable of causing pain, inflammation and blistering of the local skin, underlying flesh and structures, leading to tissue death and necrosis.

Group 2 – exfoliants

Capable of causing inflammation and shedding of skin, but less likely to cause tissue death.

Group 3 – irritants

Capable of causing inflammation and irritation, rarely proceeding to breakdown of the tissue.

Group 4 – inflammatory agents

Capable of causing mild to moderate inflammation and flare in local tissues.

Group 5 – neutral

Ostensibly inert or neutral compounds that do not cause inflammation or damage.

In this edition of the handbook we have introduced a more complex classification, in view of the fact that the theoretical risk of extravasation may be greater than that which is seen or has so far been reported in clinical practice. The calculation of risk is based on the factors discussed in general terms in the text. Full details of the exact weighting of the oncology agents with regard to their ability to cause damage following on from extravasation injury, and calculations of risk and classification, can be found on the National Extravasation Information Service website: www.extravasation.org.uk.

PREVENTION OR MINIMISATION OF THE PROBLEMS OF EXTRAVASATION

The position, size and age of the venepuncture site are the factors which have the greatest influence on the likelihood of problems occurring. However, if the following points are borne in mind, the likelihood of extravasation can be significantly reduced.

▼ For slow infusion of high-risk drugs, a central line or PIC line should be used.
▼ To ensure patency of a peripheral intravenous site, it is best to administer cytotoxic drugs through a recently sited cannula. Site the cannula so that it cannot become dislodged, use the forearm and, if possible, avoid sites near joints.

▼ Administer vesicants by slow intravenous push into the side-arm port of a fast-running intravenous infusion of compatible solution.

▼ The most vesicant drug should be administered first.

▼ Assess a peripheral site continually for signs of redness or swelling.

▼ Verify the patency of the intravenous site prior to vesicant infusion and regularly throughout. If there are any doubts, stop and investigate. Resite the cannula if the patency of the cannulation is still not entirely satisfactory.

▼ Ask the patient to report any sensations of burning or pain at the infusion site. Some investigators suggest delaying the administration of antiemetics until after vesicant administration. The sedative and anti-inflammatory effects of antiemetics often mask the early warning signs of extravasation, and may impede the patient's ability to report any sensation at the infusion site.

▼ Never hurry the process. Administer drugs slowly to allow the drug to be diluted by the carrier solution and to enable careful assessment of the intravenous site.

▼ Document carefully the rate of administration, the location and condition of the site, verification of patency, and the patient's responses, when giving any potentially extravasable drugs.

If vein diameter or vein collapse is a problem, then the use of glyceryl trinitrate patches distal to the cannula may be helpful.[17,18]

DIAGNOSIS OF EXTRAVASATION INJURY

It is important when diagnosing extravasation that a misdiagnosis is not made. This is because the treatment is physiologically traumatic to the body and may involve the administration of drugs which, in their own right, could cause or potentiate extravasation.

Early detection of extravasation is crucial. Common misdiagnoses are made because the observer is not differentiating discoloration reactions in the vein, venous shock, flare or phlebitis reactions of the vein wall and/or anaphylaxis. This is complicated further as some cytotoxic drugs are highly coloured agents, and if the vein in question is particularly superficial, then a bright red solution injected into the vein may cause local discoloration.

SYMPTOMS OF EXTRAVASATION

Extravasation should be suspected in the following circumstances.

▼ The patient complains of burning, stinging, pain or any acute change at the injection site. The patient is often the first person to become aware that something is wrong with their intravenous therapy, so instruct them at the beginning of treatment to inform staff about any acute change during treatment. Explain the reason for this in a way which is not frightening but which conveys the need for the patient's input and participation. Give reassurance that, if a leakage of drug does occur, it will probably not cause serious problems if the infusion is promptly stopped and the correct treatment instituted. Patients who are unable to communicate should be particularly closely observed.

▼ Induration, erythema, venous discoloration or swelling is observed at the site (discoloration alone may not indicate extravasation, as doxorubicin, epirubicin and mitozantrone have been reported to cause this condition).

▼ No blood return is obtained. A lack of blood return from the cannula is commonly quoted as a sign that extravasation has occurred. However, it is the most misleading of all signs and has been implicated in a number of serious incidents. This is because although there has been extravasation injury and the cannula has become displaced, the act of trying to draw blood back to test for blood return moves the cannula back into the vein. Thus blood is returned, but there is a hole in the vein wall in the proximity of the cannula tip. Thus when administration recommences, a larger and more significant extravasation injury occurs. Alternatively, the bevel of the needle can puncture the vein wall during venepuncture, allowing drug to escape into the tissue whilst the lumen of the needle may still remain in the blood vessel and allow adequate blood return.

▼ The flow rate is reduced. A reduced rate may be observed when using an infusion pump, so close observation is necessary.

▼ There is increased resistance to the administration. Once possible changes in the position of the body (e.g. bending of wrist or elbow) or cannula support (e.g. the bandaging) have been excluded as possible causes of the increased resistance, then a displaced cannula and thus extravasation are the next most likely causes. This is often one of the first signs of a problem or of pre-extravasation syndrome.

Once the alternative diagnoses have been considered and excluded, and if one or more of these symptoms is present, the practitioner should proceed on the basis of a diagnosis of extravasation.

THE EXTRAVASATION SYNDROME

1 Pre-extravasation syndrome

In general, this is either pre-extravasation syndrome or a type I or type II extravasation injury. The pre-extravasation syndrome (PES) often involves little or no leakage, but particularly severe phlebitis and/or local hypersensitivity together with a number of other local risk factors (e.g. difficult cannulation), and one (but not multiple) patient symptoms, and is probably the easiest to treat by withdrawing intravenous therapy immediately to prevent further deterioration to a full-blown type I or type II extravasation. However, it should be remembered that if the patient has shown susceptibility to pre-extravasation syndrome, further administration should proceed with extreme caution and ideally in the contralateral limb to the site where the problem was diagnosed.

2 Type I extravasations

Type I extravasation injuries raise a bleb or blister and have a defined area of increased firmness around the injury site. Type I injuries are most commonly associated with rapid intravenous bolus-type injections where the pressure applied by the person administering the drugs causes fluid to collect around the injury site. Type I injuries also occur when intravenous infusions are administered through over-pressurised pumps.

3 Type II extravasations

Type II (infiltrating or diffuse) extravasation injuries are characterised by soft, diffuse, 'soggy' tissue-type injuries, where obvious dispersal into the intracellular space has occurred. This type of injury is most commonly associated with the gravity-fed intravenous infusion, or a bolus injection given into the side-arm of a free-flowing intravenous infusion, which has become subtly or partially dislodged.

The treatment of both of these types of injury is the same. However, the success rate at different points in the treatment pathway can be dramatically different.

GENERAL TREATMENT OF EXTRAVASATION

All extravasation injuries should be aspirated (by the removal of or an attempt to remove the offending drug), as this is probably the only viable way of successfully preventing further injury. If the treatment can be delivered quickly, this process is often successful in type I injuries where the blister or bleb can be aspirated, but is notoriously unsuccessful in the diffuse type II tissue infiltrated injuries. During this treatment process, it is important not to remove the offending cannula, and this is the key to locating the affected area. The area around the cannula tip where the injury has occurred should be marked clearly on the skin surface, so that its site and size at first diagnosis can be recalled.

Once the extravasation injury has been characterised with regard to size, volume and type, aspiration is attempted and then traditionally steroids – either hydrocortisone or dexamethasone (there is no evidence to support the use of one steroid over any other) – are administered locally by subcutaneous injection into the area or by central intravenous injection. These drugs may be administered down the original cannula or subcutaneously into the area.

The function of steroids in the treatment of extravasation has no proven basis, and there is at best only limited circumstantial evidence to support their use. The most convincing reason for their inclusion is the idea that the whole process of extravasation involves local tissue trauma. This trauma is made worse by the treatment process, and consequently a local inflammatory cascade is started. The applied steroids suppress or settle this cascade, making further treatment easier, improving its effectiveness and making any such improvement easier to assess.[19–22]

Once these two basic principles have been initiated, treatment can be characterised as one of the following alternatives.

1 'Spread and dilute' using:
 ▼ normal saline
 ▼ hyaluronidase
 ▼ warm, continuous compression and elevation of the limb.

2 'Localise and neutralise' using:
  ▼ antidote (if available)
  ▼ intermittent cold compression.

If these treatments are applied in the wrong situation, the consequences can be catastrophic.[23,24]

Summary

▼ It is vital to act promptly.
▼ There should be clear guidelines for prompt first aid treatment.
▼ The extravasation kit should remain simple to avoid confusion, but should be comprehensive enough to meet fully all reasonable needs.
▼ Comprehensive treatment and expert advice must be available as soon as possible, ideally within 10 minutes of the injury occurring, preferably within 1 hour and definitely within 24 hours. After 24 hours the treatment philosophy is completely different, as it is no longer an active 'curative' treatment, but rather a damage limitation exercise.
▼ There should be clear instructions that are easy to follow.
▼ The emergency treatment should aim to remove as much of the offending drug as is feasible from the subcutaneous tissue, as soon as possible.
▼ The emergency treatment should not cause further tissue damage or, in the event of misdiagnosis, cause damage where extravasation has not occurred.

GENERAL PROCEDURE FOR MANAGEMENT OF EXTRAVASATION

▼ Seek assistance from someone who has more experience of looking at extravasation.
▼ Stop the infusion, disconnect the drip, but *do not remove the cannula*.
▼ Mark the extravasated area with a pen.
▼ Aspirate the extravasated drug, and try also to draw some blood back from the cannula. This may be facilitated by subcutaneous injection of either 0.9% sodium chloride to dilute the drug, or 1500 units of hyaluronidase in 2 mL of water for injection. (Hyaluronidase should *NEVER* be used with vesicant drugs, unless as a specific antidote.)
▼ Remove the cannula.
▼ Give 100 mg hydrocortisone intravenously. This should be administered via a new cannula that is re-sited remotely from the extravasation area.
▼ Give 100 mg hydrocortisone (2 mL) as 0.1–0.2 mL subcutaneous injections at about six to eight points around the circumference of the extravasation site.
▼ Give subcutaneous injections or topical applications of specific antidote where applicable.
▼ Apply 1% hydrocortisone cream to the area.
▼ Cover with sterile gauze and apply heat to disperse the extravasated drug, or cool the area to localise the extravasation.

▼ Measure the area of the extravasation and document the treatment in the patient's notes. Complete a Green Card (*see* page 147). Photographing the area can be very helpful.

▼ Give antihistamine cover (loratadine, 10 mg by mouth, or chlorpheniramine, 4 mg by mouth, once only).

▼ Provide analgesia if required (indomethacin, 25 mg three times a day, or dihydrocodeine, 30 mg four times a day, have proved effective, as have topical non-steroidal creams such as ibugel and oruvail gel).

This general procedure can be refined according to the type of extravasation provision that is required.

SPECIAL NOTES ON GENERAL PROCEDURE FOR MANAGEMENT OF EXTRAVASATION

Aspiration and the washout technique

This is the most logical step in the whole extravasation treatment procedure, in which as much if not all of the offending drug is removed from the subcutaneous tissues. This is attempted using a fine orange or blue, Q- or W-gauge needle which is placed into the centre and then the periphery of the suspected extravasation injury. Further success may be achieved by using the original cannula, if it has not been displaced from the site of the injury. This should be attempted in all cases, but the success rate is highly dependent on the time from diagnosis, and the type of extravasation injury. After the first hour the likelihood of removing the drug is reduced exponentially. Moreover, it is practically impossible to aspirate material from type II extravasation as the drug is dispersed within the extracellular tissues and fluid. However, there is a refinement of this simple and somewhat unpredictable technique in which four to six 'holes' are made, using a sealed round-ended needle, around the circumference and towards the centre of the injury. The subcutaneous tissue is then 'suspended' using 1500–3000 units of hyaluronidase (with or without local anaesthetic – lignocaine 1%, if the area has not been previously anaesthetised) in a volume of approximately 10 mL of water for injection. The subcutaneous tissue containing the extravasated drug is then flushed out using a blunt liposuction catheter and 500 mL of warm 0.9% sodium chloride, injected in 20-mL aliquots through each incision or 'hole' in turn and being allowed to flush out through the other incision.

The role of sodium bicarbonate

Although many reports in the literature discuss the successful use of sodium bicarbonate (indeed one of the authors has used it successfully himself) over the last ten years there has been an increase in the number of reports involving sodium bicarbonate as the causative agent of extravasation injuries. Furthermore, at least 12 of these incidents that were reported via the National Extravasation Reporting Scheme have occurred as a result of using sodium bicarbonate as a treatment agent. Although the overwhelming majority of cases in the literature involved the use of 8.4% sodium bicarbonate, it is the author's opinion that sodium bicarbonate should be taken out of the routine treatment of extravasation and only used by those who are extremely familiar with its potential consequences, and then only in cases of low-pH (0–5) injuries, or where it is believed to be the specific antidote for neutralisation of the injury, and then only at a dilution of 2.1% or 1%. If it has been used in the treatment of an individual extravasation injury, then it should be infiltrated into the 'body' of the injury, not the periphery. It should be introduced very sparingly in 0.3-mL aliquots, and aspiration to remove excess sodium bicarbonate should always be attempted. Note that an 8.4% solution is not only a strong alkaline agent but it is hypertonic as well – hence the need to use diluted sodium bicarbonate. Although 2.1% sodium bicarbonate is not commercially available, it can be produced when required at the scene by a double dilution of the commercial 8.4% ampoules.

Strength of dimethylsulphoxide in the treatment of extravasation injuries

The strength of dimethylsulphoxide (DMSO) that should be used is the subject of much debate. The majority of reports have been successful and used DMSO at strengths in the range of 50–99%. In the UK, 50% DMSO is available as the rimso bladder preparation, but the only source of 95% BP standard is available via the NEXIS website (*see* page 148). The argument is that the higher the concentration, the more rapidly the DMSO is effective. However, it is better to use a lower-strength solution as soon as possible after the injury than to wait for a higher-strength solution to become available.

Pin-cushion technique

The 'pin-cushion' technique involves instilling small volumes (0.2–0.4 mL) of fluid or antidote around and over the area affected by the extravasation injury. Traditionally this is done by marking and measuring the circumference of the injury, and then starting at '12 o'clock' and injecting every 2 hours (i.e. 2 o'clock, 4 o'clock, etc.) on an imaginary clock-face. The injections are administered using a small-gauge orange or blue 8- or 10-gauge needle, and towards the centre of the clock-face. For large extravasation of greater diameter than 2 cm, further injections are made down imaginary radial arms, always moving towards a final injection at the centre of the clock-face. The total volume of fluid, hyaluronidase or antidote is thus determined by the size or spread of the injury. However, in the author's experience it is rare for more than 5 mL to be required. It should also be noted that this procedure causes considerable discomfort for the patient, and if large areas need to be tackled then the use of local anaesthetics or anxiolytics such as diazepam should be considered.

Hydrocortisone vs. dexamethasone in the treatment of extravasation injuries

It is perhaps more appropriate to ask what evidence (if any) there is to support the use of steroids in the treatment of extravasation injuries. In fact there is very little, and the most plausible reason given for their inclusion in treatment protocols is that extravasation represents both localised trauma and irritation to the non-vascular tissues. Such symptoms are best settled by the administration of steroids that are used for their anti-inflammatory properties. Thus there is no beneficial advantage to using either hydrocortisone or dexamethasone. It is more difficult to assess whether intravenous or subcutaneous administration, via the pin-cushion technique or the original cannula (if it is still in the tissue), directly to the affected area or the application of topical steroids plays the largest role in managing the inflammatory reaction. In general, a 'belt-and-braces' approach using all three routes is probably best, but practitioners should weigh the clinical benefit against patient morbidity. The dose most commonly omitted is the intra-venous dose, where the re-siting of a new cannula presents a greater physiological hurdle to the patient.

PROVISION OF AN EMERGENCY POLICY AND EXTRAVASATION KIT

Both the emergency treatment policy and the extravasation kit should be either simple and thus easy to use without the risk of further damage, or else complete and comprehensive but with the consequent necessity for expertise and care.

Whichever option is chosen for the local situation at ward or patient level, it will be necessary to hold the complete set of antidotes and hot and cold facilities at one or several locations within the hospital. A consideration of the following questions may help to decide whether a 'simple' or 'comprehensive' set-up is required.

▼ Does the department or ward routinely (i.e. more than 30% of the time) use group 1 (potentially vesicant) drugs or commonly (i.e. more than 50% of the time) use group 2 (exfoliant or irritant) drugs?
▼ Are the staff specifically trained in the detection and treatment of extravasation?
▼ Does the treatment policy require a special antidote for any of these drugs?
▼ Are potentially hazardous treatments being undertaken 24 hours a day?
▼ Is inpatient or outpatient treatment intended?

If the answer to the first four questions is 'yes', then almost irrespective of the answer to the fifth question a comprehensive set-up is required. The purpose of the fifth question is to help to assess the qualification and education needs of the staff who are most likely to have to perform the procedure. Outpatient areas are often staffed with a lower skill mix, although those administering the treatment are likely to be at least grade F nurses. However, all staff who come into contact with patients who have had or are being administered chemotherapy should be aware of the clinical presentation of extravasation and the need to act promptly in referring to those who are more experienced in the management of the condition. As part of a risk management strategy for extravasation injuries it is 'good practice' to appoint an extravasation co-ordinator for the institute.

Appendix 1 (see page 192) details the contents of a complete/comprehensive extravasation kit as used in the St Chad's Oncology Unit, City Hospital, Dudley Road, Birmingham, UK. The kit also includes two plastic-covered cards containing details of the local emergency policy.

Appendix 2 (see page 192) details the contents of a complete extravasation kit which contains modified emergency cards with details of first-aid treatment and directions indicating where full antidotes can be obtained.

EXTRAVASATION FROM 'LONG LINES'

Although the increased use of long lines has decreased the incidence of extravasation injuries, a word of caution should be given, as they do not represent a universal answer. For whilst the incidence of such injuries may be lower, the severity of the injuries that do occur is far greater. This is probably because detection occurs later, the volumes involved are larger (often up to several hundred millilitres of fluid), and the drug is inevitably from group 1 or 2, and is therefore most capable of causing tissue necrosis. In terms of increasing incidence from lowest to highest the following order is generally true:

▼ PIC
▼ Grosman
▼ Hickman
▼ Portacath.

However, in terms of increasing severity the order is generally as follows:

▼ PIC
▼ Portacath
▼ Hickman
▼ Grosman.

The severity data is rather difficult to interpret but may reflect the length of the superficial tunnel section relative to the length in 'deep tissues'. This division of the long line's length is also the basis of any treatment protocol. The tunnelled subcutaneous section is treated in the same way as any other extravasation described in this chapter. A diagnosis of a subcutaneous section injury is most readily made if 10 mL of 0.9% sodium chloride are injected rapidly down the line. This will usually raise a bleb at the point of damage or leakage from the line, thus allowing targeting of further treatment. Extravasation in the 'deep' implanted section is far more serious, and can only be managed by surgical intervention and washout of the affected tissues.

DOCUMENTATION AND REPORTING OF EXTRAVASATION

It is important that a complete history of an extravasation event is documented, with diagrams and photographs, in the patient's notes. Observation and documentation of the injury should take place on a daily basis for the first few days, and then be extended to weekly observation on a planned follow-up. Figure 6.1 shows an ideal extravasation documentation slip.

In an attempt to collate and analyse data on extravasation events in a large number of patients, a national 'Green Card' scheme for reporting extravasation incidents, their treatment and outcome is co-ordinated through the St Chad's Unit, City Hospital, Dudley Road, Birmingham, UK, and now through the National Extravasation Information Service, via its website (www.extravasation.org.uk).

Extravasation Documentation Form

Patient's name ....

Hospital number ....

Consultant ....

Ward or location ....

Inpatient/day care/outpatient (delete as applicable)

Drug sequence ....

....

....

Needle size and type ....

Approximate volume of extravasation...

Ease of cannulation (please circle)   1   2   3   4   5   6   7   8   9   10
(on a scale of 1 to 10, where 1 is **very easy** and 10 is **extremely difficult**)

Were the drugs being administered via a pump or syringe driver? **Yes/No**
If **Yes**, please indicate model ....

Please indicate the **site** of cannulation and area of extravasation with measurements on the diagrams below.

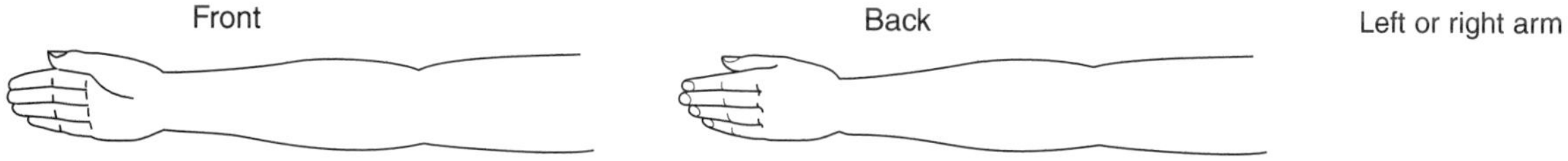

Front   Back   Left or right arm

Time of cannulation ....

Number of attempts at cannulation ....

Other method of administration (please delete as appropriate):
Central or long line/Hickman line/Portacath/drum catheter/Picc line

Other (please specify) ....

Location (please indicate) ....

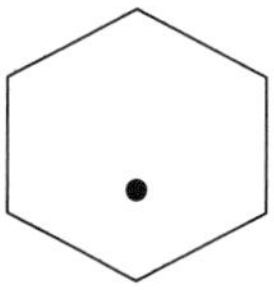

Figure 6.1: *Extravasation documentation form*

Details of extravasation treatment (drug, dose, procedure)

....

....

....

....

Did the patient experience any of the following prior to or after the suspected extravasation?

	Prior to suspected extravasation	After suspected extravasation	Time after extravasation (minutes/hours)
Pain			
Tingling			
Swelling			
Redness/flare			
Itching			
Cold			

Date of extravasation ....

Time of extravasation ....

Acute extravasation treatment started (date and time) ....

....

Patient's statement

....

....

....

Nurse's statement

....

....

....

Event	Done	Date
1-week follow-up visit booked		
1-month follow-up visit booked		
Reported to trust co-ordinator		
Reported to Green Card scheme		

Figure 6.1: *Continued*

Outcome (please tick one of the following)

Resolved following acute treatment	
Resolved using pharmacological treatment only	
Extravasation ulcerated and required skin grafting	
Patient lost to follow-up	

If the extravasation injury ulcerated, was there any functional loss in the affected limb?
Yes/No
If **Yes**, please give details ....
....

If surgery was performed, please give details ....
....

Signature of person administering chemotherapy ....

Date ....

Pictorial record

Acute incident (i.e. within 24 hours)	**1-week follow-up**

1 month or next appointment	**If required – injury at worst point**

If required – injury pre-surgery	**If required – injury post-surgery**

To be copied to trust co-ordinator, and original to be retained in patient's notes

Figure 6.1: *Continued*

1 Aims and objectives of the Green Card scheme

These are as follows:

▼ to obtain accurate statistics on the number of incidents categorised by extra-vasating drug and type of treatment
▼ to collect data on treatment methods and antidotes being used for extravasation incidents
▼ to obtain accurate information on the outcome of incidents
▼ to feed back information on treatments and their effectiveness
▼ to devise and validate a predictive index of risks for extravasation.

2 What do Green Cards ask for?

They ask for the following information:

▼ drug(s) involved
▼ circumstances of detection
▼ extent of the problem
▼ drugs used in the treatment
▼ concurrent medications which may influence vascular tone or integrity
▼ symptoms that occur before and during the acute phase of the injury
▼ concurrent disease, surgery and/or radiotherapy
▼ the patient's ability to respond to or communicate the symptoms of the extra-vasation
▼ procedure for treatment
▼ type of cannulation
▼ location and extent of the extravasation
▼ outcome/follow-up of the extravasation injury.

Green Cards are intended to be user-friendly. The information is strictly confidential, and the reporting centre and patient remain anonymous.

The report cards are available from hospital pharmacy departments or oncology units in the UK. Alternatively, they can be obtained direct from the Extravasation Report Co-ordinator, c/o St Chad's Unit, City Hospital, Dudley Road, Birmingham, B18 7QH, UK, or via the extravasation website.

An example of the current Green Card is shown in Figure 6.2. Users should note that this is the fourth version of the card, and that if previous versions are in circulation at your institute these should be recalled and replaced with the current version.

IN CONFIDENCE REGISTER OF EXTRAVASATION AND ITS TREATMENT FOR THE REPORTING OF EXTRAVASATION FROM ANY THERAPEUTIC COMPOUND

Patient:-   Male*/Female*   Age . . . .   Height (m) . . . .   Weight (kg) . . . .

Ethnic Origin (Please state) . . . .

Drug causing extravasation was . . . .   Dose . . . .

Infused in* . . . . /added to fast running drip of* . . . . / stat*

Given via Cannula/Butterfly (please state size) . . . . over . . . . mins/hr

The above drug formed part of course No. . . . . in the following regime

03000

Drug	Total Dose	Infusion Fluid/Stat	Time	Already Given	Not Yet Given
				Yes/No*	Yes/No*
				Yes/No*	Yes/No*
				Yes/No*	Yes/No*
				Yes/No*	Yes/No*

Is the patient on any of the following therapies:

Anticoagulants e.g. Warfarin   ❏   Antiplatelets e.g. Aspirin   ❏

Antihistamines   ❏   Diuretics   ❏

Hormone Therapy   ❏   Vasodilators e.g. GTN   ❏

Antifibrinolytics e.g. Tranexamic Acid   ❏   Steroids   ❏

Has the patient received I.V antibiotics in the last 3 months | YES* | NO* |

If YES please specify. . . . .

Has the patient had previous :-   Drug Hypersensitivity ❏   Phlebitis ❏

Were the drugs being administered via a pump or syringe driver | YES* | NO* |

If YES please indicate model . . . .

Please indicate SITE of cannulation and area of extravasation with measurements on the diagrams below

       Front   Back   Left* or Right* Arm

Time of cannulation. . . . .   No. of attempts at cannulation. . . . .

Ease of cannulation (please describe) . . . .

Other method of administration :- Central or Long Line*/Hickman Line*/Portacath*/Drum Catheter*/Picc Line*

Other (please specify) . . . . Location (please indicate)

Details of extravasation treatment (Drug, Dose, Procedure) _____

_____

Did the patient experience any of the following prior to or after the suspected extravasation:

	Prior	Post	Time post extravasation
Pain	❏	❏	. . . . hr/mins
Tingling	❏	❏	. . . . hr/mins
Swelling	❏	❏	. . . . hr/mins
Redness/Flare	❏	❏	. . . . hr/mins
Itching	❏	❏	. . . . hr/mins
Cold	❏	❏	. . . . hr/mins

Date of extravasation. . . . . Time of extravasation . . . .

Acute extravasation treatment Started at . . . .

THIS SECTION IS NOT COMPULSORY
Contact name or further details (Dr, Nurse, Pharmacist) Name . . . . Tel No . . . .

Did the patient suffer from any of the following possible contributary factors:

Raynaud's Disease   ❏   Diabetes   ❏   Peripheral Vascular Disease   ❏   Lymphoedema   ❏

Had the patient had either of the following in the last month, to the affected side:

Surgery   ❏   Date . . . .   Radiotherapy   ❏   Date . . . .

Additional comments   _____

_____

Was the patient able to communicate adequately in English | YES* | NO* |

*Please delete or fill in as appropriate   ❏ Please tick all appropriate boxes   Version 4/98

Figure 6.2:   *Example of a Green Card*

3 Developments of the National Extravasation Reporting Scheme

3.1 National EXtravasation Information Service (NEXIS)

The National Extravasation Reporting Scheme (NERS), colloquially known as the 'Green Card scheme', has in the last two years expanded its remit so that it not only collects, collates, analyses and publicises details of extravasation injuries in an anonymous manner and from a national perspective, but now also has a broader educational, research and information role. This role incorporating the NERS has the new name of NEXIS (National EXtravasation Information Service). NEXIS has mainly been achieved through the appointment of a national co-ordinator and director and the development of a website: www.extravasation.org.uk.

The contact details of the director and national co-ordinator are as follows:

Isobel Hawley
National Extravasation Report Co-ordinator
c/o St Chad's Unit
City Hospital
Dudley Road
Birmingham B18 7QH

Andrew Stanley, NEXIS Director
c/o St Chad's Unit
City Hospital
Dudley Road
Birmingham B18 7QH.

3.2 e-reporting

The extravasation website also allows for on-line reporting of extravasation injuries via an electronic Green Card. The electronic card looks identical to the paper version on screen, and it asks for the same information. However, it will e-mail a follow-up request to the reporter automatically at one and three months post incident, using the unique report number to identify the incident back to the reporter. This development is particularly useful if an institute (as part of its clinical governance strategy) has appointed a report/extravasation liaison person (*see* section on legal aspects of administration on page 187).

3.3 Specialist reporting schemes

Other developments include the establishment of specialist schemes to encourage the use of the Green Cards and to use the evidence base that they produce. They are being piloted both by the paediatric oncology pharmacists and nursing groups and by the Scottish Cancer Network. These two projects use the standard Green Cards, but the data is collated by the project co-ordinators before being entered into the national database. It is thus hoped that the 'feedback' will be analysed and available to contributors much more quickly than is currently possible. Details of these two schemes are available from the following contacts or via the National Extravasation Information Service.

National Paediatric Extravasation Scheme
c/o Caroline Osborne
Pharmacy Department

Alder Hey Children's Hospital
Eaton Road
Liverpool L12 2AP

The Scottish Extravasation Scheme
c/o Mark Parsons
Pharmacy Department
Tayside University Hospitals
Ninewells Hospital and Medical School
Dundee DD1 9SY

Rachel Hollis
Nurse Co-ordinator
c/o St James Hospital
Beckett Street
Leeds LS9 7TF.

3.4 European reporting scheme

If the two schemes discussed prove to be valuable, and national co-ordinators and resources can be found, it is intended to expand these initiatives into Europe.

OTHER INTRAVENOUS REACTIONS

Although it is really beyond the scope of this handbook to cover all intravenous reactions, it would also be remiss not to list other reactions that practitioners may encounter with reasonable regularity, and which may aid them in their diagnosis. For more up-to-date information and a more complete overview of these reactions, practitioners are referred to the National Intravenous Training and Information Service (nIVtis) at www.nivtis.org.uk. However, if the following reactions have been reported with cytotoxic drugs, they will be listed under the drug concerned:

▼ recall reactions
▼ urticarial reactions
▼ vasculitis
▼ venous patterning/hyperpigmentation.

INCIDENCE AND SPECIFIC PROCEDURES FOR THE MANAGEMENT OF INTRAVENOUS COMPLICATIONS

Aclarubicin

1 Anaphylaxis/hypersensitivity

Type I hypersensitivity is predicted for aclarubicin in line with that observed for other anthracyclines (see doxorubicin), although no specific reports are available.[25]

2 Chemical phlebitis

No reports found.

3 Venous irritation

No reports found.

4 Extravasation

4.1 Classification of risk

The National Extravasation Reporting Scheme has given aclarubicin a group 2 exfoliant classification. Although aclarubicin is chemically and structurally related to the anthracyclines, its final formulation renders it considerably less acidic than other members of the group, and the extravasation injuries reported seem to be less severe.

4.2 Treatment

Apply dimethylsulphoxide (DMSO) topically to the extravasated area. It should be applied every 2 hours, followed by topical hydrocortisone cream once the affected area has dried, and 30 minutes of cold compression, for the first 24 hours after the injury. Treatment for the next 7–10 days should consist of topical application of DMSO at 6-hourly intervals, alternating with 6-hourly applications of topical hydrocortisone cream, so that a preparation is being applied every 3 hours on an alternate basis. Contact with good skin should be avoided. If blistering occurs, the DMSO should be stopped and further advice sought.

5 Others

Nothing of note.

Amsacrine

1 Anaphylaxis/hypersensitivity

Hypersensitivity is reported with this drug.[25,26]

2 Chemical phlebitis

Concentration-related phlebitis, which consistently occurs in peripheral administrations of this drug, has been reported. This has led to it being more commonly administered centrally.[25,27]

3 Venous irritation

No reports found.

4 Extravasation

4.1 Classification of risk

The National Extravasation Reporting Scheme has given amsacrine a group 1 vesicant classification.

4.2 Treatment

Apply dimethylsulphoxide (DMSO) topically to the extravasated area. This should be applied every 2 hours, followed by hydrocortisone cream and 30 minutes of cold compression, for the first 24 hours. Treatment for the next 14 days should consist of topical application of DMSO at 6-hourly intervals, alternating with 6-hourly applications of topical hydrocortisone cream, so that a preparation is being applied every 3 hours, on an alternate basis. Contact with good skin should be avoided. If blistering occurs, the DMSO treatment should be stopped and further advice sought (sodium bicarbonate may have a role).

5 Others

Nothing of note.

Asparaginase

1 Anaphylaxis/hypersensitivity

This occurs in 6% to 43% of patients. Reactions are more common when the drug is administered intravenously (28.5% of 80 patients showing more mild reactions) and approximately half the frequency when administered intramuscularly (12% of 73 patients showing such reactions). It causes a type I reaction (i.e. the reaction occurs less than 30 minutes after contact) more frequently than any other drug. The risk is reduced by half when asparaginase is administered in combination with 6-mercaptopurine and/or prednisolone.[28]

2 Chemical phlebitis

No reports found.

3 Venous irritation

No reports found.

4 Extravasation

4.1 Classification of risk

The National Extravasation Reporting Scheme has given asparaginase a group 5 neutral classification. It is therefore quite safe and common clinical practice to give this drug by intramuscular injection.

4.2 *Treatment*

If a large volume has extravasated, aspirate as much fluid as possible. Dispersal of the extravasated drug may be facilitated by the use of subcutaneous hyaluronidase (1500 units in 2 mL of water for injection, or 0.9% sodium chloride) injected around the area of the injury. Apply heat and compression to assist natural dispersal of the drug. No further treatment should be required, and the patient should be managed symptomatically.

5 Others

Nothing of note.

Bleomycin

1 Anaphylaxis/hypersensitivity

Rare type I hypersensitivity has been reported.[25]

2 Chemical phlebitis

No reports found.

3 Venous irritation

No reports found.

4 Extravasation

4.1 *Classification of risk*

The National Extravasation Reporting Scheme has given bleomycin a group 5 neutral classification. It is therefore quite safe and common clinical practice to give bleomycin by intramuscular injection, although this can be extremely painful for the patient.

4.2 *Treatment*

If a large volume has extravasated, aspirate as much fluid as possible. Dispersal of the extravasated drug may be facilitated by the use of subcutaneous hyaluronidase (1500 units in 2 mL of water for injection, or 0.9% sodium chloride) injected around the area of the injury. Apply heat and compression to assist natural dispersal of the drug. No further treatment should be required, and the patient should be managed symptomatically.

5 Others

Chemical cellulitis has been reported, as has a radiation recall reaction in previous radiation fields.[29]

Carboplatin

1 Anaphylaxis/hypersensitivity

Platinum compounds will cause anaphylactic reactions, and the reported incidence of such reactions in response to carboplatin is 10–20% when analysed in fairly large series. These can range from type 1–IgE reactions to direct histamine release due to non-immunological mechanisms. Severe reactions are rare but potentially life-threatening for some patients. Severe hypersensitivity can occur after uncomplicated previous multiple courses. It is unique to carboplatin reactions that the reaction often occurs after more than 50% of the infusion bag has been infused, and that eight or more previous cycles may have preceded the cycle during which the reaction occurs. Prevention can be achieved by using dexamethasone as an antiemetic.[28,30,31]

2 Chemical phlebitis

No reports found.

3 Venous irritation

No reports found.

4 Extravasation

4.1 Classification of risk

The National Extravasation Reporting Scheme has given carboplatin a group 3 irritant classification.

4.2 Treatment

With the irritant group, the possibility exists of some local inflammation or necrosis and/or some pain, particularly in sensitive individuals. Aspirate as much fluid as possible, administer 100 mg hydrocortisone via the venflon, give 100 mg subcutaneous hydrocortisone as 0.2-mL injections in a 'pin-cushion' fashion around the circumference of the affected area, apply topical hydrocortisone and cover the area with an ice pack. When the initial inflammatory reaction has subsided, the use of warm compression can aid the dispersal of any residual fluid. There are no specific antidotes for these drugs, and further management should be symptomatic.

5 Others

Nothing of note.

Carmustine

1 Anaphylaxis/hypersensitivity

No reports found.

2 Chemical phlebitis

No reports found.

3 Venous irritation

Local venous irritation is common, and is proportional to the infusion rate and the drug concentration. It is manifested as a 'streaking' of the veins with local flushing, and it has been reported that the effect is due to the residual alcohol concentration.[32]

4 Extravasation

4.1 Classification of risk

The National Extravasation Reporting Scheme has given carmustine a group 1 vesicant classification.

4.2 Treatment

Infiltrate the area with 1–3 mL of 2.1% sodium bicarbonate, leave for 2 minutes and aspirate off again.[33]

5 Others

Topical contact with carmustine may induce local hyperpigmentation.[25]

Cisplatin

1 Anaphylaxis/hypersensitivity

Anaphylactic reactions to systemic platinum compounds are not uncommon, with an incidence rate of 1–20% depending on whether the drug is given alone or in combination therapy.[34] The incidence of type I reactions ranges from 5% as a single agent to 20% when given in combination. Such reactions occur soon after infusion has started and can be life-threatening.[28] There are cases not previously reported of seizure without a rash, wheezing or hypotension.[35] Type II reactions with haemolytic anaemia have been reported in a few cases.[36,37] Hypersensitivity can be prevented by using dexamethasone as an antiemetic.[28] Hypersensitivity is particularly hazardous in patients who are being rechallenged with cisplatin.

2 Chemical phlebitis

One study found that 35 of 271 patients suffered vascular events, with one super-ficial report of phlebitis, after multi-agent cisplatin-based chemotherapy. Two patients experienced other vascular events. However, this did not prevent completion of the schedule of chemotherapy.[38]

3 Venous irritation

No reports found.

4 Extravasation

4.1 Classification of risk

The National Extravasation Reporting Scheme has given cisplatin a group 2 exfoliation classification.

4.2 Treatment

Infiltrate the area with 1–3 mL of 3% sodium thiosulphate, aspirate back, then give 1500 units of hyaluronidase around the area and apply heat and compression. Cisplatin as an intact molecule causes few problems when it extravasates. Problems only arise when it is left untreated, as within 4–6 weeks of the acute event a subcutaneous deposit of platinum is precipitated in the tissues, which will cause pain, inflammation and necrosis.

4.3 Notes

Full-thickness necrosis.[39]

5 Others

Chemical cellulitis has been reported.[25]

Cladribine

1 Anaphylaxis/hypersensitivity

No reports found.

2 Chemical phlebitis

No reports found.

3 Venous irritation

No reports found.

4 Extravasation

4.1 Classification of risk

The National Extravasation Reporting Scheme has given cladribine a group 5 neutral classification.

4.2 Treatment

If a large volume has extravasated, aspirate as much fluid as possible. Dispersal of the extravasated drug may be facilitated by the use of subcutaneous hyaluronidase (1500 units in 2 mL of water for injections, or 0.9% sodium chloride) injected around the area of the injury. Apply heat and compression to assist natural dispersal of the drug. No further treatment should be required. The patient should be managed symptomatically.

5 Others

Nothing of note.

Cyclophosphamide

1 Anaphylaxis/hypersensitivity

Although the incidence of anaphylaxis and hypersensitivity is low, it is important to be aware of the possibility. A case of acute hypersensitivity to intravenous cyclophosphamide occurred when a ninth infusion was administered 16 months after the first one, and a reaction occurred within 20 minutes. Cyclophosphamide has also been associated with a hypersensitivity reaction following hypersensitivity to mustine exposure. There is therefore some concern about cross-sensitivity between the alkylating agents.[40]

2 Chemical phlebitis

No reports found.

3 Venous irritation

No reports found.

4 Extravasation

4.1 Classification of risk

The National Extravasation Reporting Scheme has given cyclophosphamide a group 5 neutral classification.

4.2 Treatment

If a large volume has extravasated, aspirate as much fluid as possible. Dispersal of the extravasated drug may be facilitated by the use of subcutaneous hyaluronidase (1500 units in 2 mL of water for injections, or 0.9% sodium chloride) injected around the area of the injury. Apply heat and compression to assist natural dispersal of the drug. No further treatment should be required, and the patient should be managed symptomatically.

5 Others

Urticaria that is recurrent on re-exposure has been reported.[41]

Cytarabine

1 Anaphylaxis/hypersensitivity

Although cytarabine is a very rare cause of anaphylactic reactions, these are a possibility, as is hypersensitivity. Only four cases have been reported. A report of a 5½-year-old child with acute promyelocytic leukaemia attributed anaphylactic shock mediated by specific IgE antibodies to cytarabine, although some of the patient's symptoms were misleading.[42,43]

2 Chemical phlebitis

No reports found.

3 Venous irritation

No reports found.

4 Extravasation

4.1 Classification of risk

The National Extravasation Reporting Scheme has given cytarabine a group 5 neutral classification. It is therefore quite safe and common clinical practice to give this drug as a subcutaneous injection.

4.2 Treatment

If a large volume has extravasated, aspirate as much fluid as possible. Dispersal of the extravasated drug may be facilitated by the use of subcutaneous hyaluronidase (1500 units in 2 mL of water for injections, or 0.9% sodium chloride) injected around the area of the injury. Apply heat and compression to assist natural dispersal of the drug. No further treatment should be required, and the patient should be managed symptomatically.

5 Others

A case of vasculitis is one of the reported dermatological/vascular complications of cytarabine therapy.[44]

Dacarbazine

1 Anaphylaxis/hypersensitivity

Anaphylaxis is associated with this allergy-induced hepatic toxicity, usually during the second cycle. It is serious but rare. It is not advisable to use the drug as adjuvant therapy.[28] Only one case has been reported, on the second course after discontinuing dacarbazine during the first course because of a reaction.[45]

2 Chemical phlebitis

Dacarbazine is known to cause phlebitis.[26]

3 Venous irritation

Chemical cellulitis and associated venous irritation have been reported.[25]

4 Extravasation

4.1 Classification of risk

The National Extravasation Reporting Scheme has given dacarbazine a group 1 vesicant classification.

4.2 Treatment

Apply dimethylsulphoxide (DMSO) topically to the extravasated area. It should be applied every 2 hours, followed by hydrocortisone cream and 30 minutes of cold compression, for the first 24 hours. Treatment for the next 14 days should consist of topical application of DMSO at 6-hourly intervals, alternating with 6-hourly applications of topical hydrocortisone cream, so that a preparation is being applied every 3 hours on an alternate basis. Contact with good skin should be avoided. If blistering occurs, the DMSO should be stopped and further advice sought (sodium bicarbonate may have a role).

5 Others

Nothing of note.

Dactinomycin

1 Anaphylaxis/hypersensitivity

No reports found.

2 Chemical phlebitis

It has been reported that dactinomycin causes chemical phlebitis.[26]

3 Venous irritation

No reports found.

4 Extravasation

4.1 Classification of risk

The National Extravasation Reporting Scheme has given dactinomycin a group 1 vesicant classification.

4.2 Treatment

Apply dimethylsulphoxide (DMSO) topically to the extravasated area every 2 hours, followed by hydrocortisone cream and 30 minutes of cold compression, for the first 24 hours. Treatment for the next 7–10 days should consist of topical application of DMSO at 6-hourly intervals, alternating with 6-hourly applications of topical hydrocortisone cream, so that a preparation is being applied every 3 hours on an alternate basis. Contact with good skin should be avoided. If blistering occurs, the DMSO should be stopped and further advice sought.

4.3 Notes

The skin and subcutaneous toxicities of dactinomycin can be particularly noxious when the drug is extravasated.[46]

5 Others

Nothing of note.

Daunorubicin

1 Anaphylaxis/hypersensitivity

It has been reported that daunorubicin causes an allergic reaction. Occasional severe and generally type I reactions have been reported,[47] as has cross-reactivity between daunorubicin and doxorubicin.[48]

2 Chemical phlebitis

It has been reported that daunorubicin can cause phlebitis.[26]

3 Venous irritation

No reports found.

4 Extravasation

4.1 Classification of risk

The National Extravasation Reporting Scheme has given daunorubicin a group 1 vesicant classification.

4.2 Treatment

Apply dimethylsulphoxide (DMSO) topically to the extravasated area every 2 hours, followed by hydrocortisone cream and 30 minutes of cold compression, for the first 24 hours. Treatment for the next 7–10 days should consist of topical application of DMSO at 6-hourly intervals, alternating with 6-hourly applications of topical hydrocortisone cream, so that a preparation is being applied every 3 hours on an alternate basis. Contact with good skin should be avoided. If blistering occurs, the DMSO should be stopped and further advice sought (sodium bicarbonate may have a role).

4.3 Notes

Daunorubicin can cause severe tissue necrosis and non-healing skin ulceration when extravasated even in small amounts.[49]

5 Others

Nothing of note.

Daunorubicin liposomal

1 Anaphylaxis/hypersensitivity

No reports found.

2 Chemical phlebitis

No reports found.

3 Venous irritation

No reports found.

4 Extravasation

4.1 Classification of risk

The National Extravasation Reporting Scheme has given daunorubicin liposomal a group 2 exfoliant classification.

4.2 Treatment

With the exfoliant group, the possibility exists of some local inflammation or necrosis and/or some pain, particularly in sensitive individuals. Aspirate as much fluid as possible, give 100 mg of hydrocortisone via the venflon, administer 100 mg subcutaneous hydrocortisone as 0.2-mL injections around the circumference of the affected area, apply topical hydrocortisone and cover the area with an ice pack. Whilst the drug contained within the liposome is obviously a group 1 vesicant, the formulation appears to offer some protection. Furthermore, there is evidence that, if untreated, the liposomes are degraded by the body over a period of 2–3 weeks, resulting in a full-blown daunorubicin extravasation within a further 7–10 days. It is therefore recommended by the National Extravasation Information Service that following this acute treatment (i.e. at 8–12 hours post incident) topical dimethylsulphoxide (DMSO) should be applied over the affected area 2-hourly for the next 24 hours and four times a day there after for a further 10–14 days. This will in fact accelerate the breakdown of the liposomes and hence the liberation of the daunorubicin, but it will destroy the chemical structure of the anthracycline and thus prevent or minimise the extravasation damage. Contact with good skin should be avoided. If blistering occurs, the DMSO should be stopped and further advice sought.

4.3 Notes

This drug is notable for the absence of tissue necrosis. Reported long-term effects include skin discoloration and decreased sensation, both of which resolved in all four patients reported. This corresponded to a 2% incidence with this formulation, which was similar to the extravasation rate reported with the parent drug. Because no serious sequelae have resulted from the extravasation, the recommended route of drug administration is by intravenous drip, although it needs to be monitored.[50]

5 Others

Nothing of note.

Docetaxel

1 Anaphylaxis/hypersensitivity

Anaphylactoid signs and symptoms are a major concern during the administration of docetaxel. They can be life-threatening, and the most severe reactions generally occur within the first 5–10 minutes of the infusion, and within the first or second exposure.[51]

Without the mandatory preventative strategy of histamine blockade and high-dose steroids, hypersensitivity rates of 40–50% are reported.[52] However, with appropriate premedication this can be reduced to a rate of around 2%.[53] The reactions are now believed to occur in response to the taxane compound rather than (as previously thought) to the formulation.[25]

2 Chemical phlebitis

No reports found.

3 Venous irritation

No reports found.

4 Extravasation

4.1 Classification of risk

The National Extravasation Reporting Scheme has given docetaxel a group 2 exfoliant classification.

4.2 Treatment

Infiltrate the area with 1–3 mL of a mixture of 100 mg hydrocortisone and 4 mg chlorpheniramine in 10 mL, as 0.2-mL 'pin-cushion' subcutaneous injections (depending on the size of the area, it may not be necessary to use the whole 3 mL). Large-volume extravasations may need as much as 10 mL. This should be followed by 1500 units of hyaluronidase and warm compression. Warm compression should be alternated with the application of topical mepyramine (Anthisan) or any topical antihistamine cream. The creams should be applied alternately for the following 3 days. In particularly severe cases, 1 g of oral sodium cromoglicate should be administered as soon as possible after the injury, and this can be followed by 200 mg four times a day for the next 3 days.

4.3 Notes

Far fewer cases of extravasation have been reported to docetaxel than to paclitaxel, although the severity of the injuries that do occur is just as devastating.[54] This may reflect differences in formulation between the two products.

5 Others

Nothing of note.

Doxorubicin

1 Anaphylaxis/hypersensitivity

A local hypersensitivity reaction reported in one patient included erythematous streaking of the skin overlying the vein, proximal to the injection site, and pruritus, both of which usually resolve spontaneously within 30 minutes or less. Numerous individual cases of severe and generally type I hypersensitivity have been reported.[55,56] Cross-reactivity between daunorubicin and doxorubicin has also been reported.[48]

2 Chemical phlebitis

It has been reported that a contributing factor to phlebitis in response to doxorubicin is a very acidic formulation.[26]

3 Venous irritation

An urticarial reaction localised to the vein has been reported.[28]

4 Extravasation

4.1 Classification of risk

The National Extravasation Reporting Scheme has given doxorubicin a group 1 vesicant classification.

4.2 Treatment

Apply dimethylsulphoxide (DMSO) topically to the extravasated area every 2 hours, followed by hydrocortisone cream and 30 minutes of cold compression, for the first 24 hours. Treatment for the next 7–10 days should consist of topical application of DMSO at 6-hourly intervals, alternating with 6-hourly applications of topical hydrocortisone cream, so that a preparation is being applied every 3 hours on an alternate basis. Contact with good skin should be avoided. If blistering occurs, the DMSO should be stopped and further advice sought (sodium bicarbonate may have a role).

4.3 Notes

The reported incidence of extravasation injuries ranges from 0.5–6%, even with experienced clinicians. Moreover, when such injuries occur they can cause major wound problems.[49,57,58] Doxorubicin binds to cellular DNA and interferes with wound healing in the tissues in which extravasation has occurred. It has been found up to 5 months after the initial extravasation.[59] The consequences of extravasation include ulceration, which causes significant loss of function, ranging from joint stiffness to loss of tendons. Severe skin problems may also be noted.[60] In one study, 89 of 175 observed patients suffered extravasation, and 25 of 175 injuries necessitated surgery.[26]

5 Others

A recall injury after previous radiation therapy at the site of injection may lead to severe local reactions to extravasated cytotoxic drugs.[16] In a total of 2000 patients, nine instances of cellulitis have been reported, corresponding to an incidence of 0.45%. Localised urticaria in the skin around the injection site and intense colouration of the vein may occur in up to 3% of patients.[61]

Doxorubicin liposomal

1 Anaphylaxis/hypersensitivity

No reports found.

2 Chemical phlebitis

No reports found.

3 Venous irritation

No reports found.

4 Extravasation

4.1 Classification of risk

The National Extravasation Reporting Scheme has given doxorubicin liposomal a group 2 exfoliant classification.

4.2 Treatment

With the exfoliant group, the possibility exists of some local inflammation or necrosis and/or some pain, particularly in sensitive individuals. Aspirate as much fluid as possible, give 100 mg of hydrocortisone via the venflon, administer 100 mg subcutaneous hydrocortisone as 0.2-mL injections around the circumference of the affected area, apply topical hydrocortisone and cover the area with an ice pack. Although the drug contained within the liposome is obviously a group 1 vesicant, the formulation appears to offer some protection. Furthermore, there is evidence that, if untreated, the liposomes are degraded by the body over a period of 2–3 weeks, resulting in a full-blown doxorubicin extravasation within a further 7–10 days. It is therefore recommended by the National Extravasation Information Service that following this acute treatment (i.e. at 8–12 hours post incident) topical dimethyl-sulphoxide (DMSO) should be administered to the affected area 2-hourly for the next 24 hours, and four times a day thereafter for a further 10–14 days. This will in fact accelerate the breakdown of the liposomes and hence the liberation of the daunorubicin, but it will destroy the chemical structure of the anthracycline and thus prevent or minimise the extravasation damage. Contact with good skin should be avoided. If blistering occurs, the DMSO should be stopped and further advice sought.

5 Others

Nothing of note.

Epirubicin

1 Anaphylaxis/hypersensitivity

Type I hypersensitivity has been reported.[62]

2 Chemical phlebitis

It has been reported by the authors that a contributing factor to phlebitis with epirubicin is the acidic nature of the formulation.

3 Venous irritation

This is also reported as a 'formulation' side-effect, although it may in part be due to prepared doses being 'cold'.

4 Extravasation

4.1 Classification of risk

The National Extravasation Reporting Scheme has given epirubicin a group 1 vesicant classification.

4.2 Treatment

Administer dimethylsulphoxide (DMSO) topically to the extravasated area every 2 hours, followed by hydrocortisone cream and 30 minutes of cold compression, for the first 24 hours. Treatment for the next 7–10 days should consist of topical application of DMSO at 6-hourly intervals, alternating with 6-hourly applications of topical hydrocortisone cream, so that a preparation is being applied every 3 hours on an alternate basis. Contact with good skin should be avoided. If blistering occurs, the DMSO should be stopped and further advice sought (sodium bicarbonate may have a role).

5 Others

An urticarial reaction has been reported which progressed to ulceration, following sensitisation to the drug through previous extravasation.[28]

Etoposide

1 Anaphylaxis/hypersensitivity

The incidence of etoposide hypersensitivity is probably 3% or lower, although there are innumerable individual case reports. Usually a high proportion of the reports are to first-time exposure, which suggests that it is unlikely to be a type I,

IgE-mediated reaction. The authors have postulated that it may be due to formulation excipients.[63,64] Common acute vasomotor responses can be overcome by decreasing the rate of infusion.[28]

2 Chemical phlebitis

This has been reported, and is always attributed to formulation excipients or microscopic degradation products. The reaction can be minimised or prevented by dilution into large-volume infusions. It is more common with 250-mL than with 1000-mL infusions.

3 Venous irritation

No reports found.

4 Extravasation

4.1 Classification of risk

The National Extravasation Reporting Scheme has given etoposide a group 3 irritant classification.

4.2 Treatment

With the irritant group, the possibility exists of some local inflammation or necrosis and/or some pain, particularly in sensitive individuals. Aspirate as much fluid as possible, give 100 mg of hydrocortisone via the venflon, administer 100 mg subcutaneous hydrocortisone as 0.2-mL injections around the circumference of the affected area, apply topical hydrocortisone and cover the area with an ice pack. There are no specific antidotes for these drugs, and further management of the patient should be symptomatic.

5 Others

Nothing of note.

Etoposide phosphate

1 Anaphylaxis/hypersensitivity

No reports found.

2 Chemical phlebitis

No reports found.

3 Venous irritation

No reports found.

4 Extravasation

4.1 Classification of risk

The National Extravasation Reporting Scheme has given etoposide phosphate a group 4 inflammatory classification.

4.2 Treatment

With the inflammatory group, the extravasation injury is usually confined to some local inflammation. Aspirate as much fluid as possible, give 100 mg hydrocortisone via the venflon, administer 100 mg subcutaneous hydrocortisone as 0.2-mL injections around the circumference of the affected area, apply topical hydrocortisone and cover the area on an intermittent basis with an ice pack for the first 24 hours. If the local reaction has then settled, apply heat and compression to assist natural dispersal of any residual drug. There are no specific antidotes for these drugs, and further management of the patient should be symptomatic.

5 Others

Nothing of note.

Fluorouracil

1 Anaphylaxis/hypersensitivity

Type I hypersensitivity skin reactions have been reported with infusional treatment,[65] and even more rarely after bolus administration.[66] A further report described a patient developing the reaction after they had previously received topical 5-FU for keratosis. This suggests a sensitivity to 5-FU administered via the topical route.[28]

2 Chemical phlebitis

No reports found.

3 Venous irritation

Irritation (probably related to the alkaline pH of the formulation) has been reported in response to infusional therapy when given peripherally.

4 Extravasation

4.1 Classification of risk

The National Extravasation Reporting Scheme has given fluorouracil a group 4 inflammatory classification.

4.2 Treatment

With the inflammatory group, the extravasation injury is usually confined to some local inflammation. Aspirate as much fluid as possible, give 100 mg hydrocortisone via the venflon, administer 100 mg subcutaneous hydrocortisone as 0.2-mL injections around the circumference of the affected area, apply topical hydrocortisone and cover the area on an intermittent basis with an ice pack for the first 24 hours. If the local reaction has then settled, apply heat and compression to assist natural dispersal of any residual drug. There are no specific antidotes for these drugs, and further management of the patient should be symptomatic.

5 Others

Nothing of note.

Floxuridine

1 Anaphylaxis/hypersensitivity

No reports found.

2 Chemical phlebitis

Several cases of flare or chemical phlebitis have been observed. These were successfully managed in further cycles by greater dilution of the drug.

3 Venous irritation

No reports found.

4 Extravasation

4.1 Classification of risk

The National Extravasation Reporting Scheme has given floxuridine a group 2 exfoliant classification.

4.2 Treatment

Acidic extravasations are some of the most difficult to treat, as the standard practice is to administer either 1% or 2.1% sodium bicarbonate to the area in order to neutralise the acidic drug, followed by heat (i.e. warm compression) to disperse the neutral mixture. This requires that the acid–base titration produces a salt and water, where the neutral salt compound is water-soluble. If the salt is non-soluble in the aqueous-based environment of extracellular fluid, then precipitation of the insoluble salt will cause further problems or damage. However, if the extravasation has been misdiagnosed, or the volume extravasated has been wrongly assessed, the treatment could lead to an alkaline extravasation.

4.3 Notes

As floxuridine is predominantly given intra-arterially, extravasation is rare, due to the use of intra-arterial lines and the rapid mixing afforded by the arterial system. However when extravasation does occur, it is far more serious and the consequences are far more devastating than those associated with venous extravasation.

5 Others

Nothing of note.

Fludarabine

1 Anaphylaxis/hypersensitivity

No reports found.

2 Chemical phlebitis

No reports found.

3 Venous irritation

No reports found.

4 Extravasation

4.1 *Classification of risk*

The National Extravasation Reporting Scheme has given fludarabine a group 5 neutral classification.

4.2 *Treatment*

If a large volume has extravasated, aspirate as much fluid as possible. Dispersal of the extravasated drug may be facilitated by the use of subcutaneous hyaluronidase (1500 units in 2 mL of water for injections, or 0.9% sodium chloride) injected around the area of the injury. Apply heat and compression to assist natural dispersal of the drug. No further treatment should be required, and the patient should be managed symptomatically.

5 Others

Nothing of note.

Gemcitabine

1 Anaphylaxis/hypersensitivity

No reports found.

2 Chemical phlebitis

No reports found.

3 Venous irritation

No reports found.

4 Extravasation

4.1 Classification of risk

The National Extravasation Reporting Scheme has given gemcitabine a group 5 neutral classification.

4.2 Treatment

If a large volume has extravasated, aspirate as much fluid as possible. Dispersal of the extravasated drug may be facilitated by the use of subcutaneous hyaluronidase (1500 units in 2 mL of water for injections, or 0.9% sodium chloride) injected around the area of the injury. Apply heat and compression to assist natural dispersal of the drug. No further treatment should be required, and the patient should be managed symptomatically.

5 Others

Nothing of note.

Idarubicin

1 Anaphylaxis/hypersensitivity

Type I hypersensitivity is predicted for idarubicin in line with that observed for other anthracyclines (see doxorubicin), although no specific reports are available.[25]

2 Chemical phlebitis

No reports found.

3 Venous irritation

No reports found.

4 Extravasation

4.1 Classification of risk

The National Extravasation Reporting Scheme has given idarubicin a group 1 vesicant classification.

4.2 Treatment

Apply dimethylsulphoxide (DMSO) topically to the extravasated area every 2 hours, followed by hydrocortisone cream and 30 minutes of cold compression, for the first 24 hours. Treatment for the next 14 days should consist of topical application of DMSO at 6-hourly intervals, alternating with 6-hourly applications of topical hydrocortisone cream, so that a preparation is being applied every 3 hours on an alternate basis. Contact with good skin should be avoided. If blistering occurs, the DMSO should be stopped and further advice sought (sodium bicarbonate may have a role).

5 Others

Nothing of note.

Ifosfamide

1 Anaphylaxis/hypersensitivity

Type I reactions have been reported when ifosfamide and mesna have been used together. It is of course mandatory to administer these two agents together in order to overcome the chemical cystitis associated with the ifosfamide.[67] However, rechallenge with mesna alone implicated this as the probable allergen. This reactivity was postulated to be an example of a fixed drug eruption, rather than an IgE-mediated one.[68]

2 Chemical phlebitis

No reports found.

3 Venous irritation

No reports found.

4 Extravasation

4.1 Classification of risk

The National Extravasation Reporting Scheme has given ifosfamide a group 5 neutral classification.

4.2 Treatment

If a large volume has extravasated, aspirate as much fluid as possible. Dispersal of the extravasated drug may be facilitated by the use of subcutaneous hyaluronidase (1500 units in 2 mL of water for injections, or 0.9% sodium chloride) injected around the area of the injury. Apply heat and compression to assist natural dispersal of the drug. No further treatment should be required, and the patient should be managed symptomatically.

5 Others

Nothing of note.

Irinotecan

1 Anaphylaxis/hypersensitivity

No reports found.

2 Chemical phlebitis

A couple of causes of mild flare or chemical phlebitis have been observed. These were successfully managed in further cycles by greater dilution of the drug.

3 Venous irritation

No reports found.

4 Extravasation

4.1 Classification of risk

The National Extravasation Reporting Scheme has given irinotecan a group 3 irritant classification.

4.2 Treatment

With the irritant group, the possibility exists of some local inflammation or necrosis and/or some pain, particularly in sensitive individuals. Aspirate as much fluid as possible, give 100 mg hydrocortisone via the venflon, 100 mg subcutaneous hydrocortisone as 0.2-mL injections around the circumference of the affected area, supply topical hydrocortisone and cover the area with an ice pack. There are no specific antidotes for these drugs. Further management should be symptomatic. As irinotecan is known to have an acidic pH, in large-volume extravasations (10 mL or more) the administration of either 1% or 2.1% sodium bicarbonate into the area to neutralise the drug, followed by heat (i.e. warm compression) to disperse the neutral mixture, has been successful. However, this should only be attempted with extreme care (*see* also topotecan).

5 Others

Nothing of note.

Melphalan

1 Anaphylaxis/hypersensitivity

Melphalan caused allergic reactions in 3.9% of 255 patients who were receiving it as a single intravenous drug. The reactions were classical type I, although this drug has also been known to cause a type III reaction.[28]

2 Chemical phlebitis

No reports found.

3 Venous irritation

No reports found.

4 Extravasation

4.1 Classification of risk

The National Extravasation Reporting Scheme has given melphalan a group 5 neutral classification.

4.2 Treatment

If a large volume has extravasated, aspirate as much fluid as possible. Dispersal of the extravasated drug may be facilitated by the use of subcutaneous hyaluronidase (1500 units in 2 mL of water for injections, or 0.9% sodium chloride) injected around the area of the injury. Apply heat and compression to assist natural dispersal of the drug. No further treatment should be required, and the patient should be managed symptomatically.

5 Others

Nothing of note.

Methotrexate

1 Anaphylaxis/hypersensitivity

Occasional reactions have been attributed to this agent. It has caused type I,[69] II and III reactions,[70] although specific tests were not performed to verify the type III reactions.[28]

2 Chemical phlebitis

No reports found.

3 Venous irritation

No reports found.

4 Extravasation

4.1 Classification of risk

The National Extravasation Reporting Scheme has given methotrexate a group 4 inflammatory classification. Despite this classification, it is still safe and common clinical practice to give low-dose, small-volume methotrexate by intramuscular injection.

4.2 Treatment

With the inflammatory group, the extravasation injury is usually confined to some local inflammation. Aspirate as much fluid as possible, give 100 mg hydrocortisone via the venflon, administer 100 mg subcutaneous hydrocortisone as 0.2-mL injections around the circumference of the affected area, apply topical hydrocortisone and cover the area on an intermittent basis with an ice pack for the first 24 hours. If the local reaction has then settled, apply heat and compression to assist natural dispersal of any residual drug. There are no specific antidotes for these drugs. Further management of the patient should be symptomatic.

5 Others

A radiation recall reaction has been reported. This reaction is usually confined to the site of the irradiation.[71,72]

Mitomycin

1 Anaphylaxis/hypersensitivity

An acute hypersensitivity reaction has been reported to cause respiratory distress. In local treatment of superficial bladder cancer, three cases of hypersensitivity were reported causing eosinophilic cystitis.[28]

2 Chemical phlebitis

Mitomycin has been known to cause phlebitis.[26]

3 Venous irritation

No reports found.

4 Extravasation

4.1 Classification of risk

The National Extravasation Reporting Scheme has given mitomycin a group 1 vesicant classification.

4.2 Treatment

Apply dimethylsulphoxide (DMSO) topically to the extravasated area every 2 hours, followed by hydrocortisone cream and 30 minutes of cold compression, for the first 24 hours. Treatment for the next 14 days should consist of topical application of DMSO at 6-hourly intervals, alternating with 6-hourly applications of topical hydrocortisone cream, so that a preparation is being applied every 3 hours on an alternate basis. Contact with good skin should be avoided. If blistering occurs, the DMSO should be stopped and further advice sought.

4.3 Notes

Reports of extravasation injury are scarce. Chronic ulcers may occur at the onset of infusion, which are resistant to conservative treatment and will need surgical intervention. In the event of mitomycin extravasation, surgical excision is often required to prevent serious damage. Of 175 patients with extravasation of cytotoxic drug injuries, four required surgery.[26,73,74]

5 Others

A recall reaction occurred in one patient 3 months after a mitomycin extravasation had been resolved. The patient had been exposed to direct sunlight.[75]

Mitozantrone

1 Anaphylaxis/hypersensitivity

Mitozantrone has caused allergic-type reactions in three reported cases. In one patient, symptoms occurred 7 days after the patient had been given the drug, and in another they occurred immediately after the seventh course and 16 days after the eighth course, consistent with type I and III reactions.[28,76]

2 Chemical phlebitis

No reports found.

3 Venous irritation

No reports found.

4 Extravasation

4.1 Classification of risk

The National Extravasation Reporting Scheme has given mitozantrone a group 2 exfoliant classification.

4.2 Treatment

With the exfoliant group, the possibility exists of some local inflammation or necrosis and/or some pain, particularly in sensitive individuals. Aspirate as much fluid as possible, give 100 mg hydrocortisone via the venflon, administer 100 mg subcutaneous hydrocortisone as 0.2-mL injections around the circumference of the affected area, apply topical hydrocortisone and cover the area with an ice pack.

Dimethylsulphoxide (DMSO) has a beneficial role in these extravasation injuries because of the structural similarities between mitozantrone and the anthracyclines. It is therefore normally applied topically to the affected area four times a day for 5–7 days (it could be alternated with topical hydrocortisone as described previously for the management of doxorubicin extravasation). Contact with good skin should be avoided. If blistering occurs, the DMSO should be stopped and further advice sought.

4.3 Notes

Mitozantrone has rarely caused extravasation. The author has found only six cases of necrosis following extravasation, although multiple skin discoloration and inflammation-only reactions have been reported. Clinical trials of hundreds of patients showed no occurrence of clinically important extravasation. However, there are reports of localised reactions and tissue necrosis.[77] Extravasation causes transient blue discoloration of tissue. Neither cellulitis nor necrosis have been reported previously. In this report, 6 of 600 infusions resulted in extravasation, two of which resulted in complications. Surgery was required to improve movement.[78] In another study only five cases were reported in 8 years of widespread usage, and of these three were probable and two were possible.[79]

5 Others

Nothing of note.

Mustine

1 Anaphylaxis/hypersensitivity

A case of type I reaction to mustine has been reported.[80]

2 Chemical phlebitis

Phlebitis and cellulitis have been reported.

3 Venous irritation

No reports found.

4 Extravasation

4.1 Classification of risk

The National Extravasation Reporting Scheme has given mustine a group 1 vesicant classification.

4.2 Treatment

Infiltrate the area with 1–3 mL of 3% sodium thiosulphate. Introduce a further 100 mg of hydrocortisone to the infiltrated area, and apply cold compression intermittently for 12 hours.

5 Others

Nothing of note.

Oxaliplatin

1 Anaphylaxis/hypersensitivity

Such reactions have only been reported in patients with a history of reactions to platinum compounds. Type I IgE reactions were reported in 0.5% of patients during clinical studies.

2 Chemical phlebitis

No reports found.

3 Venous irritation

No reports found.

4 Extravasation

4.1 Classification of risk

The National Extravasation Reporting Scheme has given oxaliplatin a group 2 (exfoliant) classification.

4.2 Treatment

Oxaliplatin only represents a serious necrotic risk following extravasation if the platinum is allowed to precipitate in the tissues. This will only occur if the cellular environment is allowed to become chloride-'rich'. Therefore, in order to prevent this, following extravasation and standard management the area should be infiltrated with 1500 units of hyaluronidase, and a 500-mL bag of 5% dextrose plus a further 1500 units of hyaluronidase should be placed in the centre of the extravasation area in a 'hypodemclysis' fashion. The area should then be warmed to aid dispersion. The fluid should be left for up to 8 hours or until the 500 mL have dispersed. Caution is needed in diabetic patients.

5 Others

Nothing of note.

Paclitaxel

1 Anaphylaxis/hypersensitivity

Anaphylactoid signs and symptoms are a major concern during administration of paclitaxel. Their occurrence can be life-threatening, and the most severe reactions generally occur within the first 5–10 minutes of the infusion.[81] Without the mandatory preventative strategy of histamine blockade and high-dose steroids, hypersensitivity rates of 40–50% are reported.[82,83] However, with appropriate premedication this can be reduced to a rate of around 2%.[83] After a hypersensitivity reaction, paclitaxel can be safely readministered.[81,84]

2 Chemical phlebitis

In cases where large volumes (> 50 mL) are infused, phlebitis has occurred.[85]

3 Venous irritation

No reports found.

4 Extravasation

4.1 Classification of risk

The National Extravasation Reporting Scheme has given paclitaxel a group 1 vesicant classification.

4.2 Treatment

Infiltrate the area with 1–3 mL of a mixture of 100 mg hydrocortisone and 4 mg chlorpheniramine in a volume of 10 mL, as 0.2-mL 'pin-cushion' subcutaneous injections. Depending on the size of the area, it may not be necessary to use the whole 3 mL. Large-volume extravasations may need as much as 10 mL. This should be followed by 1500 units of hyaluronidase and warm compression. Warm compression should be alternated with the application of topical mepyramine

(Anthisan) or any topical antihistamine cream. The creams should be applied alternately for the following 3 days. In particularly severe cases, 1 g of oral sodium cromoglicate should be administered as soon as possible after the injury, and this can be followed by 200 mg four times a day for the next 3 days.

4.3 Notes

Extravasation can have both short- and long-term effects. Long-term effects are minimal – patients can be left with a permanent thickening of the skin around the infiltration site. For the majority of patients the symptoms that occur after infiltration resolve. Inflammation at injection sites with soft tissue reactions has been reported after paclitaxel extravasation. However, these can progress to fairly severe necrotic injuries if they are not treated promptly. Paclitaxel has a greater risk classification than docetaxel because of the cremophor in its formulation, and prolonged infusions should be avoided.[54,81,86]

5 Others

A recall reaction occurred when a second course of chemotherapy was administered in the left arm and caused a worsening of the symptoms of the extravasated area in the right arm. The author suggested that local exposure to paclitaxel was responsible and that serious consideration should be given to the question of whether to administer further therapy with this agent.[86]

Pentostatin

1 Anaphylaxis/hypersensitivity

Type I hypersensitivity has been reported in at least six individual cases.[87]

2 Chemical phlebitis

No reports found.

3 Venous irritation

No reports found.

4 Extravasation

4.1 Classification of risk

The National Extravasation Reporting Scheme has given pentostatin a group 5 neutral classification.

4.2 Treatment

If a large volume has extravasated, aspirate as much fluid as possible. Dispersal of the extravasated drug may be facilitated by the use of subcutaneous hyaluronidase (1500 units in 2 mL of water for injections, or 0.9% sodium chloride) injected around the area of the injury. Apply heat and compression to assist natural dispersal of the drug. No further treatment should be required, and the patient should be managed symptomatically.

5 Others

Nothing of note.

Raltitrexed

1 Anaphylaxis/hypersensitivity

No reports found.

2 Chemical phlebitis

No reports found.

3 Venous irritation

No reports found.

4 Extravasation

4.1 Classification of risk

The National Extravasation Reporting Scheme has given raltitrexed a group 4 inflammatory classification.

4.2 Treatment

With the inflammatory group, the extravasation injury is usually confined to some local inflammation. Aspirate as much fluid as possible, give 100 mg hydrocortisone via the venflon, administer 100 mg subcutaneous hydrocortisone as 0.2-mL injections around the circumference of the affected area, apply topical hydrocortisone and cover the area on an intermittent basis with an ice pack for the first 24 hours. If the local reaction has then settled, apply heat and compression to assist natural dispersal of any residual drug. There are no specific antidotes for these drugs. Further management should be symptomatic.

5 Others

Nothing of note.

Streptozocin

1 Anaphylaxis/hypersensitivity

No reports found.

2 Chemical phlebitis

Chemical phlebitis has been reported with streptozocin therapy.[88]

3 Venous irritation

Intense perivenous pain, accompanied by a burning sensation and often tracking for a considerable distance along the vein, is a well-documented toxicity of streptozocin administration. This sequela of toxicity is worse following bolus administration. Both dilution of the drug and increasing the infusion time are reported to reduce the symptoms.[89]

4 Extravasation

4.1 Classification of risk

The National Extravasation Reporting Scheme has given streptozocin a group 1 vesicant classification.

4.2 Treatment

Apply dimethylsulphoxide (DMSO) topically to the extravasated area every 2 hours, followed by hydrocortisone cream and 30 minutes of cold compression, for the first 24 hours. Treatment for the next 7–10 days should consist of topical application of DMSO at 6-hourly intervals, alternating with 6-hourly applications of topical hydrocortisone cream, so that a preparation is being applied every 3 hours on an alternate basis. Contact with good skin should be avoided. If blistering occurs, the DMSO should be stopped and further advice sought (sodium bicarbonate may have a role).

5 Others

Nothing of note.

Teniposide

1 Anaphylaxis/hypersensitivity

Hypersensitivity rates of 6% (and up to 13% in neuroblastomas) are reported for this drug. Why neuroblastomas have a rate twice as high as other tumours is not known, although it is not a dose–response phenomenon. Usually a high proportion of these occur in the first exposure, which probably means that they are not type I IgE-mediated reactions. Other suggested causes are the formulation excipients or the reactive metabolites.[90,91]

2 Chemical phlebitis

Phlebitis has been noted with this drug, but authors have been unsure whether this is due to the parent drug, the cremophor or absolute alcohol in the formulation, or its acidic pH.

3 Venous irritation

No reports found.

4 Extravasation

4.1 Classification of risk

The National Extravasation Reporting Scheme has given teniposide a group 3 irritant classification.

4.2 Treatment

With the irritant group the possibility exists of some local inflammation or necrosis and/or some pain, particularly in sensitive individuals. Aspirate as much fluid as possible, give 100 mg hydrocortisone via the venflon, administer 100 mg subcutaneous hydrocortisone as 0.2-mL injections around the circumference of the affected area, apply topical hydrocortisone and cover the area with an ice pack. There are no specific antidotes for these drugs. Further management should be symptomatic.

5 Others

Nothing of note.

Thiotepa

1 Anaphylaxis/hypersensitivity

This agent induces hypersensitivity reactions.[26]

2 Chemical phlebitis

No reports found.

3 Venous irritation

No reports found.

4 Extravasation

4.1 Classification of risk

The National Extravasation Reporting Scheme has given thiotepa a group 5 neutral classification.

4.2 Treatment

If a large volume has extravasated, aspirate as much fluid as possible. Dispersal of the extravasated drug may be facilitated by the use of subcutaneous hyaluronidase (1500 units in 2 mL of water for injections, or 0.9% sodium chloride) injected around the area of the injury. Apply heat and compression to assist natural dispersal of the drug. No further treatment should be required. The patient should be managed symptomatically.

5 Others

Pattern hyperpigmentation, tracing the venous pattern and particularly pronounced in occluded areas, has been reported.[92]

Topotecan

1 Anaphylaxis/hypersensitivity

No reports found.

2 Chemical phlebitis

A couple of cases of mild flare or chemical phlebitis have been observed. These were successfully managed in further cycles by greater dilution of the drug.

3 Venous irritation

No reports found.

4 Extravasation

4.1 Classification of risk

The National Extravasation Reporting Scheme has given topotecan a group 2 exfoliant classification.

4.2 Treatment

Acidic extravasations are among the most difficult to treat, as the standard practice is to administer either 1% or 2.1% sodium bicarbonate to the area in order to neutralise the acidic drug, followed by heat (i.e. warm compression) to disperse the neutral mixture. This requires that the acid–base titration produces a salt and water where the neutral salt compound is water-soluble. If the salt is non-soluble in the aqueous-based environment of extracellular fluid, then precipitation of the insoluble salt will cause further problems or damage. However, if the extravasation has been misdiagnosed, or the volume extravasated has been wrongly assessed, the treatment could lead to an alkaline extravasation.

4.3 Notes

Although extravasation was rarely reported during the development of topotecan, this may reflect its relatively low incidence in this trained population. Of the nine cases seen, all were reported as producing only a mild inflammatory reaction and no specific antidote was applied.

5 Others

Nothing of note.

Treosulfan

1 Anaphylaxis/hypersensitivity

No reports found.

2 Chemical phlebitis

No reports found.

3 Venous irritation

No reports found.

4 Extravasation

4.1 Classification of risk

The National Extravasation Reporting Scheme has given treosulfan a group 1 vesicant classification.

4.2 Treatment

Infiltrate the area with 1–3 mL of 1% or 2.1% sodium bicarbonate, leave for 2 minutes and aspirate off again. With the aim of neutralising the drug, this localised neutralisation should be followed by heat (i.e. warm compression) to disperse the neutral mixture. This requires that the acid–base titration produces a salt and water where the neutral salt compound is water-soluble. If the salt is non-soluble in the aqueous-based environment of extracellular fluid, then precipitation of the insoluble salt will cause further problems or damage. However, if the extravasation has been misdiagnosed, or the volume extravasated has been wrongly assessed, the treatment could lead to an alkaline extravasation.

5 Others

Nothing of note.

Vinblastine

1 Anaphylaxis/hypersensitivity

Although vinblastine alone has not produced confirmed anaphylactic reactions, it has done so in combination with mitomycin. The reaction produced a fulminant dyspnoea, which could be reproduced in at least two patients when rechallenged with the combination.[93,94]

2 Chemical phlebitis

Vinblastine causes the local injury phlebitis.

3 Venous irritation

No reports found.

4 Extravasation

4.1 Classification of risk

The National Extravasation Reporting Scheme has given vinblastine a group 1 vesicant classification.

4.2 Treatment

Infiltrate the area with 1500 units of hyaluronidase, as 0.2-mL injections, over and around the circumference of the affected area. Apply heat and compression for the first 24 hours. For the next 7 days apply a topical non-steroidal anti-inflammatory cream to the affected area four times a day.

5 Others

Nothing of note.

Vincristine

1 Anaphylaxis/hypersensitivity

A child with acute basophilic leukaemia developed an acute reaction immediately after the first dose of intravenous vincristine. This reaction has only been reported once before.[95]

2 Chemical phlebitis

No reports found.

3 Venous irritation

No reports found.

4 Extravasation

4.1 Classification of risk

The National Extravasation Reporting Scheme has given vincristine a group 1 vesicant classification.

4.2 Treatment

Infiltrate the area with 1500 units of hyaluronidase, as 0.2-mL injections, over and around the circumference of the affected area. Apply heat and compression for the first 24 hours. For the next 7 days apply a topical non-steroidal anti-inflammatory cream to the affected area four times a day.

4.3 Incidence

In an observation of 175 patients with extravasation, three cases caused by vincristine required surgery.[26]

5 Others

Nothing of note.

Vindesine

1 Anaphylaxis/hypersensitivity

Although vindesine alone has not produced confirmed anaphylactic reactions, it has done so in combination with mitomycin. The reaction produced a fulminant dyspnoea, which could be reproduced in at least two patients when rechallenged with the combination.[93,94]

2 Chemical phlebitis

No reports found.

3 Venous irritation

No reports found.

4 Extravasation

4.1 Classification of risk

The National Extravasation Reporting Scheme has given vindesine a group 1 vesicant classification.

4.2 Treatment

Infiltrate the area with 1500 units of hyaluronidase, as 0.2-mL injections, over and around the circumference of the affected area. Apply heat and compression for the first 24 hours. For the next 7 days apply a topical non-steroidal anti-inflammatory cream to the affected area four times a day.

5 Others

Nothing of note.

Vinorelbine

1 Anaphylaxis/hypersensitivity

Although vinorelbine alone has not produced confirmed anaphylactic reactions, it has done so in combination with mitomycin. The reaction produced a fulminant dyspnoea, which could be reproduced in at least two patients when rechallenged with the combination.[93,94]

2 Chemical phlebitis

Chemical phlebitis has been reported, although it is often difficult to distinguish it from venous irritation at a clinical level.

3 Venous irritation

This has been reported in up to 12% of patients. The effect appears to be cumulative. It is reported to be less problematic when given as a slow bolus (6–10 minutes) rather than as a short infusion (20–30 minutes).[96]

4 Extravasation

4.1 Classification of risk

The National Extravasation Reporting Scheme has given vinorelbine a group 1 vesicant classification.

4.2 Treatment

Infiltrate the area with 1500 units of hyaluronidase, as 0.2-mL injections, over and around the circumference of the affected area. Apply heat and compression for the first 24 hours. For the next 7 days apply a topical non-steroidal anti-inflammatory cream to the affected area four times a day.

5 Others

Nothing of note.

Interferon

1 Anaphylaxis/hypersensitivity

No reports found.

2 Chemical phlebitis

No reports found.

3 Venous irritation

No reports found.

4 Extravasation

4.1 Classification of risk

The National Extravasation Reporting Scheme has given α-interferon a group 5 neutral classification.

4.2 Treatment

If a large volume has extravasated, aspirate as much fluid as possible. Dispersal of the extravasated drug may be facilitated by the use of subcutaneous hyaluronidase (1500 units in 2 mL of water for injection, or 0.9% sodium chloride) injected around the area of the injury. Apply heat and compression to assist natural dispersal of the drug. No further treatment should be required. The patient should be managed symptomatically.

5 Others

Nothing of note.

Interleukin 2

1 Anaphylaxis/hypersensitivity

No reports found.

2 Chemical phlebitis

No reports found.

3 Venous irritation

Skin flare erythema and rash occasionally progress to exfoliation. This may be due to poor subcutaneous administration or a local manifestation of capillary leak syndrome.[97]

4 Extravasation

4.1 Classification of risk

The National Extravasation Reporting Scheme has given interleukin 2 a group 5 neutral classification.

4.2 Treatment

If a large volume has extravasated, aspirate as much fluid as possible. Dispersal of the extravasated drug may be facilitated by the use of subcutaneous hyaluronidase (1500 units in 2 mL of water for injection, or 0.9% sodium chloride) injected around the area of the injury. Apply heat and compression to assist natural dispersal of the drug. No further treatment should be required. The patient should be managed symptomatically.

5 Others

Nothing of note.

LEGAL ASPECTS OF ADMINISTRATION

Finally, some consideration should be given to the legal aspects of administration. This is most easily summarised with the 'four C's' as follows:

▼ competency
▼ consent
▼ controls
▼ checks

Both the institution and the individual (whether they be a nurse, doctor or pharmacist) have a duty of care to the patient and therefore must feel competent both in their own right as a member of the oncology team, and as a member of the institute, to deliver chemotherapy. This competence requires assessment, documentation and regular reappraisal so that the individual or institute is not left exposed to unnecessary risk.

As we have seen previously in this chapter, the two most devastating outcomes of mis-administration, namely extravasation and anaphylaxis, are not wholly under the control of the operator, *and in the vast majority of cases they will be due to intrinsic properties of the drugs.*

However, the intravenous process does include an operator element, and neglect in this area could be a negligence of their duty of care, just as the administration of chemotherapy to known or suspected hypersensitive individuals would also represent a failure to deliver treatment with due care and attention.

Although it is important not to increase the anxiety associated with the administration of chemotherapy, the patient is often the best and most accurate source for diagnosis of impending mishap, and therefore before intravenous cannulation and administration are attempted the patient should be informed about and consent to the process. This may consist of written consent to the whole course of chemotherapy. However, if this is the case, then what the patient is expected to experience and/or to report needs to be reiterated with verbal consent prior to each individual cycle, in order to avoid any allegation of assault. This should therefore take the form of some brief outline of what is to happen, what constitutes a successful outcome, and signs and symptoms of early mishap to report.

The institution and individual should put in place controls and checking procedures, in order to minimise and facilitate early detection of extravasation and any mishap in the administration process. This will include access to a documented extravasation and anaphylaxis policy, as well as the individual concerned developing some type of 'look and feel' routine which they can adhere to during the administration of chemotherapy. Furthermore, as part of its clinical governance strategy the institute should appoint an intravenous therapy/report/extravasation liaison person, who can co-ordinate procedures for training and competence of staff, administration and emergency procedures, and the reporting and follow-up of any mishap.

Only the person who is administering chemotherapy can exercise the honesty to acknowledge that a mishap has or may have occurred.

REFERENCES

1 Hecker JF (1990) Survival of intravenous chemotherapy infusion sites. *Br J Cancer.* **62**: 660–2.

2 Bareford D (1985) Treatment of extravasation of vincristine with hydrocortisone and hyaluronidase. *BMJ.* **291**: 1242.

3 Rudolph R (1978) Ulcers of the hand and wrist caused by doxorubicin hydrochloride. *Orthop Rev.* **7**: 93–5.

4 Tsavaris NB *et al.* (1990) Conservative approach to the treatment of chemotherapy-induced extravasation. *J Dermatol Surg Oncol.* **16**: 519–22.

5 Ignoffo RJ and Friedman MA (1980) Therapy of local toxicities caused by extravasation of cancer chemotherapeutic drugs. *Cancer Treat Rev.* **7**: 17–27.

6 Banerjee A *et al.* (1987) Cancer chemotherapy agent-induced perivenous extravasation injuries. *Postgrad Med J.* **63**: 5–9.

7 Rudolph R and Larson DL (1987) Etiology and treatment of chemotherapeutic agent extravasation injuries: a review. *J Clin Oncol.* **5**: 1116–26.

8 Dorr RT (1981) Extravasation of vesicant antineoplastics. *Ariz Med.* **28**: 271–5.

9 Cullen ML (1982) Current interventions for doxorubicin extravasations. *Oncol Nurs Forum.* **9**: 52–3.

10 Linder RM *et al.* (1983) Management of extensive doxorubicin hydrochloride extravasation injuries. *J Hand Surg.* **8**: 32–8.

11 Cohen MH (1979) Amelioration of adriamycin skin necrosis: an experimental study. *Cancer Treat Rep.* **63**: 1003–4.

12 Hart LL and Middleton RK (eds) (1989) Treatment of doxorubicin extravasations. *Drug Intell Clin Pharm.* **23**: 386–7.

13 Larson DL (1985) What is the appropriate management of tissue extravasation by antitumor agents? *Plast Reconstr Surg.* **75**: 397–405.

14 Coleman JJ *et al.* (1983) Treatment of adriamycin-induced skin ulcers: a prospective controlled study. *J Surg Oncol.* **22**: 129–35.

15 Olver IN *et al.* (1988) A prospective study of topical dimethyl sulfoxide for treating anthracycline extravasation. *J Clin Oncol.* **6**: 1732–5.

16 Donaldson SS *et al.* (1974) Adriamycin activity: a recall phenomenon after radiation therapy. *Ann Intern Med.* **81**: 407–8.

17 Khawaja HT *et al.* (1988) Effect of transdermal glyceryl trinitrate on the survival of peripheral intravenous infusions: a double-blind prospective clinical study. *Br J Surg.* **75**: 1212–15.

18 Wright A *et al.* (1985) Use of transdermal glyceryl trinitrate to reduce failure of intravenous infusion due to phlebitis and extravasation. *Lancet.* **ii**: 1148–50.

19 Cox K *et al.* (1988) The management of cytotoxic drug extravasation: guidelines drawn up by a working party for the Clinical Oncological Society of Australia. *Med J Aust.* **148**: 185–9.

20 Hirsh JD and Conlon PF (1983) Implementing guidelines for managing extravasation of antineoplastics. *Am J Hosp Pharm.* **40**: 1516–19.

21 Schneider SM and Distelhorst CW (1989) Chemotherapy-induced emergencies. *Semin Oncol.* **16**: 572–8.

22 Harwood KV and Aisner J (1984) Treatment of chemotherapy extravasation: current status. *Cancer Treat Rep.* **68**: 939–45.

23 McNeece J and Lightly J (1986) *Cytotoxic Extravasation Manual.* Pharmacy Department, Leeds General Infirmary, Leeds.

24 Smith R (1985) Prevention and treatment of extravasation. *Br J Parenter Ther.* **6**: 114–18.

25 Perry M (1996) Dermatological toxicity and hypersensitivity reactions. *Chemother Source Book.* **2**: 595–634.

26 Wiezba K and Hanano M (1987) Cytostatics and immunosuppressive drugs. *Side Effects of Drugs Annual.* **11**: 384–409.

27 Dollery C (1998) *Ther Drugs.* **2**.

28 O'Brien ME and Souberbielle BE (1992) Allergic reactions to cytotoxic drugs – an update. *Ann Oncol.* **3**: 605–10.

29 Cohen I, Master M, O'Keefe E *et al.* (1973) Cutaneous toxicity of bleomycin therapy. *Arch Dermatol.* **107**: 553–5.

30 Sood AK, Gelder MS, Huang S-W *et al.* (1995) Anaphylaxis to carboplatin following multiple previous uncomplicated courses. *Gynecol Oncol.* **57**: 131–2.

31 Markman M, Kennedy A, Webster K *et al.* (1999) Clinical features of hypersensitivity reactions to carboplatin. *J Clin Oncol.* **17**: 1141–5.

32 Layton P, Greenburg H and Stetson P (1984) BCNU solubility and toxicity in the treatment of malignant astrocytomas. *J Neurosurg.* **60**: 1134–7.

33 Colvin M, Hartner J and Summerfield M (1980) Stability of carmustine in the presence of sodium bicarbonate. *Am J Hosp Pharm.* **37**: 677–8.

34 Saunders MP, Denton CP, O'Brien MER *et al.* (1992) Hypersensitivity reactions to cisplatin and carboplatin – a report on six cases. *Ann Oncol.* **3**: 574–6.

35 Zweizig S, Roman LD and Muderspach LI (1994) A case report. Death from anaphylaxis to cisplatin. *Gynecol Oncol.* **53**: 121–2.

36 Getaz E, Berkley S, Fitzpatrick J *et al.* (1980) Cisplatin-induced haemolysis. *NEJM.* **302**: 334–5.

37 Levi J, Avony R and Dalley D (1981) Haemolytic anaemia after cisplatin treatment. *BMJ.* **282**: 2003–4.

38 Czaykowski PM, Moore MJ and Tannock IF (1998) High risk of vascular events in patients with urothelial transitional-cell carcinoma treated with cisplatin-based chemotherapy. *J Urol.* **160**: 2021–4.

39 Leyden M and Sullivan J (1983) Full-thickness skin necrosis due to inadvertent interstitial infusion of cisplatin. *Cancer Treat Rep.* **67**: 199.

40 Ross W and Chabner B (1977) Allergic reactions to cyclophosphamide in a mechlorethamine-sensitive patient. *Cancer Treat Rep.* **61**: 495–6.

41 Lakin J and Cahill R (1976) Generalised urticaria to cyclophosphamide: type I hypersensitivity to an immunosuppressive agent. *J Allergy Clin Immunol.* **58**: 160–71.

42 Berkowitz FE, Wehde S, Ngwenya ET *et al.* (1987) Anaphylactic shock due to cytarabine in a leukemic child. *Am J Dis Child.* **141**: 1000–1.

43 Slater J (1999) Cytarabine anaphylaxis. *Am J Dis Child.* **142**: 483.

44 Hippe E, Jonnson V, Schroder H *et al.* (1988) Ara-C vasculitis. *Eur J Haematol.* **41**: 96.

45 Abhyanker S, Rao SP, Pollio L *et al.* (1988) Anaphylactic shock due to dacarbazine. *Am J Dis Child.* **142**: 918.

46 Coppes MJ, Jorgenson K and Arlette JP (1997) Cutaneous toxicity following administration of dactinomycin. *Med Pediatr Oncol.* **29**: 226–7.

47 Freeman AL (1970) Clinical note: allergic reaction to daunorubicin. *Cancer Chem Rep.* **54**: 475–6.

48 Crowther D, Powles R, Bateman C *et al.* (1973) Management of adult acute myelogenous leukaemia. *BMJ.* **1**: 131–7.

49 Lawrence J, Walsh D, Zapotowski A *et al.* (1989) Topical dimethylsulfoxide may prevent tissue damage from anthracycline extravasation. *Cancer Chemother Pharmacol.* **23**: 316–8.

50 Cabriales D, Bresnahan J, Testa D *et al.* (1998) Extravasation of liposomal daunorubicin in patients with AIDS – associated Kaposi's sarcoma: a report of four cases. *Oncol Nurse Forum.* **28**: 67–70.

51 Vervei J, Clavel M and Chevalier B (1995) Paclitaxel (Taxol) and docetaxel (Taxotere) are not simply two of a kind. *Ann Oncol.* **5**: 495–505.

52 Burris H, Irvin R, Kutlin J *et al.* (1993) Phase I clinical trial of Taxotere administered as either a 2-hour or 6-hour intravenous infusion. *J Clin Oncol.* **11**: 950–8.

53 Schrijvus D, Wanders J, Dirix L *et al.* (1993) Coping with toxicities of docetaxel (Taxotere). *Ann Oncol.* **4**: 610–11.

54 Bertelli G, Cafferata M, Ardizzoni *et al.* (1997) Skin ulceration potential of paclitaxel in a mouse skin model *in vivo*. *Cancer.* **79**: 2266–9.

55 Solimando D and Wilson J (1984) Doxorubicin-induced hypersensitivity reactions. *Drug Intell Clin Pharm.* **18**: 808–11.

56 Collins J (1984) Hypersensitivity reactions to doxorubicin. *Drug Intell Clin Pharm.* **18**: 402–3.

57 Linder RM, Upton J and Osteen R (1983) Management of extensive doxorubicin hydrochloride extravasation injuries. *J Hand Surgery.* **8**: 32–8.

58 Lebredo L, Barrie R and Woltering EA (1992) DMSO protects against adriamycin-induced tissue necrosis. *Cancer Chemother Pharmacol.* **23**: 316–8.

59 Gault D and Challands J (1997) Extravasation of drugs. *Anaesth Rev.* **13**: 223–41.

60 Laughlin RA, Landeen JM and Habai MB (1979) The management of inadvertent subcutaneous adriamycin infiltration. *Am J Surg.* **137**: 408–13.

61 Vogelzany M (1979) 'Adriamycin flare': a skin reaction resembling extravasation. *Cancer Treat Rep.* **63**: 2067–9.

62 Cassidy J and Rantain E (1989) Hypersensitivity reaction to epirubicin. *Med Oncol Tumor Pharm.* **6**: 297–8.

63 Hudson M, Weinstein H, Donabon S *et al.* (1993) Acute hypersensitivity reactions to etoposide in a VEPA regimen for Hodgkins disease. *J Clin Oncol.* **49**: 1084–94.

64 de Souza P, Friedlander M, Wilde C *et al.* (1994) Hypersensitivity reactions to etoposides. A report of three cases and review of the literature. *Am J Clin Oncol.* **17**: 387–9.

65 Smidhar K (1986) Allergic reaction to 5-fluorouracil infusion. *Cancer.* **58**: 862–4.

66 Santos A and Medina F (1986) Anaphylactic reactions following IV administration of fluorouracil. *Cancer Treat Rep.* **70**: 1346.

67 Case D, Anderson J, Ervin T *et al.* (1988) Phase II trial of ifosfamide and mesna in previously treated patients with non-Hodgkins lymphoma: cancer and leukaemia group B study. *Med Pediatr Oncol.* **16**: 182–6.

68 Zonzits E, Aberer W and Tappeiner G (1992) Drug eruptions from mesna. *Arch Dermatol.* **128**: 80–2.

69 Vega A, Cabanas R, Coutrevas J *et al.* (1994) Anaphylaxis to methotrexate: a possible IgE-mediated mechanism. *J Allergy Clin Immunol.* **94**: 268–70.

70 Sostman H, Matthay R, Putman C *et al.* (1976) Methotrexate-induced pneumonitis. *Medicine.* **55**: 371–88.

71 Korossy K and Hood A (1981) Methotrexate reactivation of sunburn reaction. *Arch Dermatol.* **117**: 310–11.

72 Kim Y, Aye M, Fayos J *et al.* (1977) Radiation necrosis of the scalp: a complication of cranial irradiation and methotrexate. *Radiology.* **124**: 813–4.

73 Khanna AK, Khanna A, Asthana AK *et al*. (1985) Mitomycin C extravasation ulcers. *J Surg Oncol*. **28**: 108–10.

74 Alberts D and Dorr R (1991) Case report: topical DMSO for mitomycin C-induced skin ulceration. *Oncol Nurs Forum*. **18**: 693–5.

75 Bertelli G (1995) Prevention and management of extravasation of cytotoxic drugs. *Drug Safety*. **12**: 245–55.

76 Taylor W, Cantrell B, Roberts J *et al*. (1986) Allergic reaction to mitozantrone. *Lancet*. **1**: 1439.

77 Levin M, Caravone D and Geiser C (1996) Mitoxantrone extravasation and tissue necrosis. *Am J Health Syst Pharm*. **53**: 1192.

78 Holland JF (1986) Local tissue as a result of extravasation of mitozantrone. *BMJ*. **292**: 802.

79 Ketelbey JW (1989) Cytotoxic drug extravasation. *Med J Austr*. **150**: 52.

80 Wilson K and Alexander S (1981) Hypersensitivity to mechlorethamine. *Ann Intern Med*. **94**: 823.

81 Lubejko BG and Sartorius SE (1993) Nursing considerations on paclitaxel (Taxol) administration. *Semin Oncol*. **20**: 26–30.

82 Onetto N, Canetta R, Winograd B *et al*. (1993) Overview of taxol safety. *Monogr Natl Cancer Inst*. **15**: 131–9.

83 Weiss R, Donehower R, Weirnik P *et al*. (1990) Hypersensitivity reactions from taxol. *J Clin Oncol*. **8**: 1263–8.

84 Peereboom D, Donohourer R, Eisenhauer E *et al*. (1993) Successful retreatment with taxol after major hypersensitivity reactions. *J Clin Oncol*. **11**: 885–90.

85 Rowinsky EK, Eisenhauer EA, Chaudhry V *et al*. (1993) Clinical toxicities encountered with paclitaxel (Taxol). *Semin Oncol*. **20 (Supplement 1)**: 1–15.

86 Hidlago M, Benito J, Colomer R *et al*. (1993) Recall reaction of a severe local peripheral neuropathy after Paclitaxel extravasation. *J Natl Cancer Inst*. **88**: 1320.

87 O'Dwyer P, King S, Eisenhauer E *et al*. (1988) Hypersensitivity reactions to deoxycoformycin. *Cancer Chemother Pharmacol*. **23**: 173–5.

88 US Government (1998) *The Physician's Desk Reference*.

89 DuPriest R, Huntington M, Massey W *et al*. (1975) Streptozocin therapy in 22 cancer patients. *Cancer*. **35**: 358–76.

90 O'Dwyrer P, King S, Fortner C *et al*. (1986) Hypersensitivity reactions to teniposide (vm-26): an analysis. *J Clin Oncol*. **4**: 1262–9.

91 Hayes F, Abiomowitch M and Green A (1985) Allergic reactions to teniposide in patients with neuroblastoma and lymphoid malignancies. *Cancer Treat Rep*. **69**: 439–41.

92 Horn T, Beveridge R, Egorin M *et al*. (1989) Observations and proposed mechanism of N, N', N″-triethylenethiophosphoramide (thioTEPA)-induced hyperpigmentation. *Arch Dermatol*. **125**: 524–7.

93 Dyke R (1984) Acute bronchospasm after a vinca alkaloid in patients previously treated with mitomycin. *NEJM*. **310**: 389.

94 Rivera M, Kris M, Gralla R *et al*. (1995) Syndrome of acute dyspnea related to combined mitomycin plus vinca alkaloid chemotherapy. *Am J Clin Oncol*. **18**: 245–50.

95 Bernini JC, Timmons CF and Saunders E (1995) Anaphylactoid reaction and coagulopathy secondary to vincristine-mediated degranulation. *Cancer*. **1**: 110–4.

96 Rittenburg C, Gralla R and Rehmeyer T (1995) Assessing and managing venous irritation associated with vinorelbine tartrate. *Oncol Nurse Forum*. **22**: 707–10.

97 Thompson J, Lee D, Lindgreen L *et al.* (1989) Influence of schedule of interleukin 2 administration on therapy with interleukin 2 and lymphokine-activated killer cells. *Cancer Res.* **49**: 235–40.

Note: Some of the facts mentioned in the individual drug citations have been extracted from the ABPI database. Readers should refer to the current issues for any modifications.

APPENDIX 1

Contents of a 'comprehensive' extravasation box:

▼ dimethylsulphoxide solution (50–100%)
▼ hyaluronidase (1500 units injection)
▼ hydrocortisone (100 mg injection, and 1% cream)
▼ sodium bicarbonate (8.4% injection*)
▼ sodium chloride (0.9% injection)
▼ sodium thiosulphate (50% injection*)
▼ terfenadine (60 mg tablets)
▼ water for injections (2 mL and 10 mL)
▼ a selection of needles, syringes, alcohol wipes, cotton-wool balls and sterile gauze
▼ directions to the nearest cold pack and heat pad.

* Overlabelled with directions for dilution.
Two examples of the overlabels are given below.

SODIUM BICARBONATE 8.4%
DO NOT USE UNDILUTED
5 mL of this solution should be added to 5 mL of water for injection, and then 5 mL of this new solution should be added to a further 5 mL of water for injection. This will then give a 2.1% sodium bicarbonate solution.

SODIUM THIOSULPHATE 50%
DO NOT USE UNDILUTED
Dilute 1.2 mL of 50% sodium thiosulphate to 20 mL with water for injection. This will then give a 3% sodium thiosulphate solution.

APPENDIX 2

Contents of a 'simple' extravasation box:

▼ hyaluronidase (1500 units)
▼ hydrocortisone (100 mg injection, and 1% cream)
▼ sodium chloride (0.9% injection)
▼ water for injections (2 mL)

▼ a selection of needles, syringes, alcohol wipes, cotton-wool balls and sterile gauze
▼ directions to the nearest cold pack and heat pad.

Note: Any of these specific antidotes or hot and cold sources can be ordered and purchased from the National Extravasation Service website: www.extravasation. org.uk.

7

Monitoring and treatment of adverse effects in cancer chemotherapy

INTRODUCTION

Despite significant efforts over the last 20 years to develop antineoplastic compounds with fewer adverse effects, the toxicity of cancer chemotherapy remains one of the main obstacles to its effective use. Most of the currently available drugs have been selected on the basis of their activity against proliferating cells. Unfortunately, this cytotoxic activity is not highly selective and does not discriminate between malignant cells and normal cells undergoing rapid division. As a result, cytotoxic drugs probably have the narrowest therapeutic index of any class of drug in common use.

The adverse effects that occur most frequently with this group of drugs in the days and weeks immediately following treatment include suppression of bone-marrow activity, anorexia, nausea and vomiting, mucositis and alopecia. Patients will require supportive care, both in the hospital and in the community, to help them to overcome these problems. Organ toxicities such as pulmonary toxicity, neurotoxicity and cardiotoxicity are more drug specific, and unlike most of the acute adverse effects, they may not be reversible. Long-term effects may not be apparent until months or years after treatment. These problems include infertility due to suppression of ovarian and testicular function, and occasionally the induction of a secondary malignancy in patients who have previously been successfully treated. In addition, cytotoxic drugs can give rise to a whole spectrum of rare, unpredictable or idiosyncratic reactions. The use of cytotoxic drugs in combination, in an attempt to increase their activity, adds to the toxicity of treatment, despite efforts being made to combine agents with different dose-limiting toxicities.

Reductions in dose or delays in treatment as a result of toxicity may compromise the success of potentially curative therapy, but for the majority of patients chemotherapy is given to palliate the disease, and sometimes to prolong life. This has a considerable bearing on the degree of toxicity that is considered to be 'acceptable' to the patient.

Managing the toxicity of chemotherapy involves a number of approaches. Treatment must be individually tailored to each patient and appropriate measures taken to avoid or minimise predictable toxicity. Adverse effects which do arise despite these measures must be treated and accurately documented. In order to contribute effectively to patient care, the pharmacist must have a detailed knowledge of the drugs prescribed and must be able to anticipate potential adverse effects, in order to monitor prescribing and advise on appropriate supportive therapy.

INDIVIDUALISING THERAPY

Although each cytotoxic drug varies in its particular spectrum of toxicity, some general precautions can be taken to minimise the risk of predictable adverse effects occurring. Appropriate investigations must be performed before treatment commences to ensure that the patient is fit for chemotherapy. In particular, their haematological, renal and hepatic function should be investigated. In general, patients with a white cell count below $3000/mm^3$ or a platelet count below $100\,000/mm^3$ should not be given myelosuppressive cytotoxic drugs.

Unlike most classes of drug, where a standard dose range can be safely recommended for the majority of patients, the dose of cytotoxic drugs must be individually calculated for each patient on the basis of their weight or, more commonly, on the basis of body surface area (*see* page 120). Doses may then require further adjustment in the presence of renal or hepatic impairment to ensure that delayed excretion does not result in increased toxicity.

Methotrexate serum concentrations are measured following high-dose therapy to help to determine the dose and duration of folinic acid necessary for adequate rescue. The concept of individualising treatment based on serum drug concentrations is being explored with other agents, largely to optimise the efficacy of treatment.

MANAGEMENT OF ADVERSE EFFECTS

Significant progress has been made in reducing the mortality and morbidity of cancer chemotherapy through the improved management of adverse effects. Ondansetron and granisetron, the $5HT_3$-receptor antagonists, have been significant additions to the armoury of available antiemetics. Reduced mortality in the febrile neutropenic patient has been achieved by the prompt use of combinations of antibiotics, usually an aminoglycoside and an anti-pseudomonal penicillin, to provide broad-spectrum cover. The availability of antifungal and antiviral agents has also been invaluable. Furthermore, the value of broad-spectrum oral antibiotics plus or minus oral antifungals is now the subject of well-designed double-blind randomised controlled studies to assess their value as prophylactic cover for the neutropenic patient at the time of predicted chemotherapy-induced nadir. Despite these advances, successful treatment of chemotherapy-related toxicity is expensive, and involves prolonged hospitalisation and a reduction in the patient's quality of life. Thus patient management must focus on the *prevention* of toxicity.

1 Extravasation

Extravasation of many cytotoxic drugs can have disastrous consequences. The long-term outcome may be permanent tissue damage, despite the best efforts being made to rescue the situation. In the absence of adequate treatment, the approach to this problem relies heavily on safe techniques for administration of cytotoxic drugs (*see* Chapter 6).

2 Nausea and vomiting

Occasionally, cytotoxic regimens or single agents such as vincristine or fluorouracil do not require antiemetic drugs to be given routinely, but for any cytotoxic drug that causes severe or moderate emesis, antiemetics should always be prescribed prophylactically and not used on an 'as required' basis after vomiting has begun. Although the availability of new, effective antiemetics and better use of existing agents has improved the control of acute nausea and vomiting, delayed emesis remains a significant problem, particularly for patients who have received cisplatin. Antiemetics should be taken regularly by all patients following treatment with cisplatin. Dexamethasone is probably the most effective agent available at the present time for the management of delayed emesis, and it should be the basis of therapy, but further research is required in this area. More detailed information can be found by referring to the reference list on page 254.

3 Infection

A number of measures can be taken to minimise the risk of infection developing. Good oral hygiene is important, as the mouth is a major source of infection, particularly in neutropenic patients. Patients should be instructed to brush their teeth regularly with a soft toothbrush, and to use regular antiseptic mouthwashes following toothbrushing and after every meal. Prophylactic antifungal therapy may also be appropriate.

Focal sepsis is a particular problem with intravenous catheter sites, and is more prevalent with the increased use of central venous catheters. Ideally, lines should only be handled by trained staff, using strict aseptic techniques and following agreed procedures for handling.

The haematopoietic growth factors G-CSF and GM-CSF shorten the duration of neutropenia following chemotherapy, thus reducing the likelihood or severity of infection. They are also being exploited to allow increased intensity of treatment where bone-marrow suppression is the dose-limiting toxicity, in the hope of improving response rates and survival.

Also available now is the sulfhydryl free-radical scavenger amifostine which is licensed for the reduction of risk of infection related to neutropenia in patients undergoing treatment with cisplatin and cyclophosphamide, and for the reduction of nephrotoxicity due to cisplatin, and to protect against xerostomia during radiotherapy.

4 Alopecia

In an effort to avoid alopecia, scalp-cooling techniques have been developed using ice caps and more sophisticated refrigeration systems. The procedure itself is unpleasant and can only be used with agents with a short elimination half-life, such as doxorubicin, which has a half-life of 30 minutes. The results of studies conducted over the last 15 years remain equivocal. Hair loss may be avoided when doxorubicin is used as a single agent, but is less effective when doxorubicin is used in combination with other drugs that are capable of causing alopecia, or when it is used at doses above 40 mg/m^2. In the absence of reliable methods of avoiding alopecia, patients should be prepared for hair loss and given practical advice on

Table 7.1: *An example of the classification for patient toxicity and response used in a monitoring chart*

	Toxicity grading (based on WHO ratings)				
	0	*1*	*2*	*3*	*4*
Alopecia	No change	Minimal hair loss	Moderate, patchy alopecia	Complete alopecia but reversible	Non-reversible alopecia
Nausea/ vomiting	None	Nausea	Transient vomiting	Vomiting requiring treatment	Intractable vomiting
Diarrhoea	None	Transient < 2 days	Tolerable but > 2 days	Intolerable, requiring therapy	Haemorrhagic dehydration
Oral	No change	Soreness, erythema	Erythema, ulcers: can eat solids	Ulcers: requires liquid diet	Alimentation not possible
Neurotoxicity	None	Paraesthesiae and/or decreased tendon reflexes	Severe paraesthesiae and/or mild weakness	Intolerable paraesthesiae and/or marked motor loss	Paralysis
Skin	No change	Erythema	Dry desquamation, vesiculation, pruritus	Moist desquamation, ulceration	Exfoliative dermatitis: necrosis requiring surgical intervention
Performance status	Capable of normal activity. No restrictions	Incapable of strenuous activity; capable of light work. Ambulatory	Ambulatory. Capable of all self-care. Unable to work. Up and about for > 50% of waking hours	Limited self-care. Confined to bed/chair for > 50% of waking hours	Completely disabled. No self-care. Totally confined to bed/chair

Source: Birmingham Oncology Treatment Chart, St Chad's Unit, City Hospital, Dudley Road, Birmingham.

coping with this – for example, when to expect loss of hair, how rapidly this will occur, and advice on obtaining a wig.

MONITORING TOXICITY

Safe administration of chemotherapy relies on clear and accurate documentation of all treatment given. The total cumulative dose administered should be recorded for drugs such as doxorubicin where this is critical. Both the response to and the toxicity of therapy should be carefully documented. A detailed assessment of response is normally made after a predetermined number of treatment cycles, and toxicity is generally assessed following every cycle. The occurrence of toxicity may result in a dose reduction, delay or some other modification to treatment in subsequent cycles. A number of international rating scales are available for rating predictable, acute reactions arising from chemotherapy, including that of the World Health Organization (WHO) and the National Cancer Institute (NCI). Standardising the assessment of treatment-related toxicity in this way allows comparisons to be made between published reports of clinical trials. One example is shown in Table 7.1.

CLINICAL MONITORING

Prescriptions for cancer chemotherapy are often complex, involving combinations of both parenteral and oral cytotoxic drugs, intravenous fluids and other supportive therapies. In order to monitor and check prescribing, the pharmacist must recognise and anticipate a whole range of potential problems. Table 7.2 presents a framework for monitoring the prescribing of cytotoxic drugs to help to ensure that the treatment received by patients is optimal.

The following drug tables highlight the main acute toxicities of specific cytotoxic drugs which can occur in the initial weeks following treatment. They do *not* include all documented adverse effects of the drugs, but they attempt to provide a guide to the clinical monitoring of chemotherapy. For example, allergic or hypersensitivity reactions have occurred with many cytotoxic drugs. For more comprehensive information the reader should refer to original reference sources (see below). A rating scale has been used to indicate the incidence and severity of adverse effects (*see* Table 7.3). However, these effects may be dependent on the dose and method of administration, and will also be influenced by patient factors such as the presence of any pre-existing disease. In addition, the toxicity of treatment will be compounded if these agents are used in combination. Thus for some toxicities there may be an additional plus sign in parentheses, to indicate that a significant number of reports or circumstances exist which perhaps warrant a more severe classification.

Table 7.2:   *A checklist for prescription monitoring in cancer chemotherapy*

Patient details
▼ Diagnosis
▼ Age
▼ Weight, height, body surface area
▼ Haematological function
▼ Renal function
▼ Liver function
▼ Underlying disease
▼ Allergy
▼ Previous treatment
▼ Previous reaction to treatment (i.e. toxicity from previous cycles requiring dose modification of subsequent cycles)
▼ Total exposure to drugs with cumulative toxicity (e.g. doxorubicin)

Protocol
▼ Is treatment prescribed according to established regimen or clinical trial protocol?
▼ Is the drug name clear and unambiguous?
▼ Dose
▼ Timing, scheduling number of days' therapy
▼ Have all drugs in the regime been prescribed?
▼ Recommended dose modifications for organ dysfunction or previous toxicity
▼ Stop date indicated for oral therapy

Administration
▼ Appropriate route of administration
▼ Suitable venous access
▼ Appropriate infusion fluid and dilution
▼ Appropriate rate of administration
▼ Appropriate scheduling with regard to time of day, and day of week

Interactions
▼ With other prescribed therapy
▼ Pharmaceutical interactions with concurrent intravenous therapy or infusion fluids

Supportive care – ensure that appropriate adjuvant therapy prescribed, such as:
▼ antiemetics
▼ mouth care
▼ eye care
▼ hydration
▼ allopurinol
▼ prophylactic antibiotics/antifungals/antivirals
▼ growth factors
▼ antidotes; folinic acid, mesna.

Table 7.3: *Toxicity rating scale and abbreviations used in the following tables*

+	Occasional or mild
++	Common or moderately severe
+++	Invariable or dose limiting
FBC	Full blood count
ECG	Electrocardiogram
LFT	Liver function tests
WBC	White blood cell
SIADH	Syndrome of inappropriate antidiuretic hormone secretion
CNS	Central nervous system

CHEMOTHERAPEUTIC AGENTS

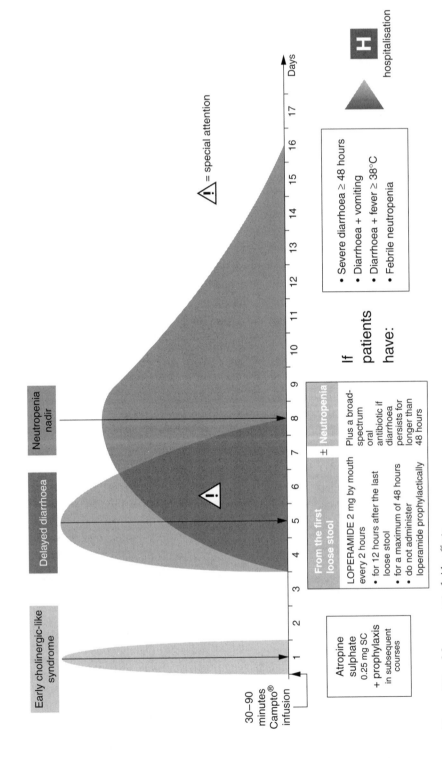

Figure 7.1: *Management of side-effects*

Aclarubicin

	Toxicity grading	Comment	Clinical monitoring/ intervention
Gastrointestinal tract			
Nausea/vomiting	++	Severe at doses greater than 120 mg/m²	Prophylactic antiemetics
Other	+++	Mucositis Oral ulceration Diarrhoea	Good mouth care
Haematological			
Myelosuppression	+++	WBC nadir days 14–21, recovery days 21–28	Pretreatment FBC
Thrombocytopenia		Nadir days 7–14, recovery days 14–28	–
Cutaneous			
Alopecia	+	–	–
Tissue necrosis (on extravasation)	Group 2	–	–
Cardiovascular	++ +	Acute cardiotoxicity Congestive heart failure	ECG monitoring Caution in patients with impaired cardiac function or previously treated with anthracyclines
Pulmonary	–	–	–
CNS	–	–	–
Renal/bladder	–	–	–
Hepatic	++	–	Monitor hepatic function and consider dose reduction in presence of hepatic impairment
Other	–	–	–

Aldesleukin (IL-2)

	Toxicity grading	Comment	Clinical monitoring/ intervention
Gastrointestinal tract			
Nausea/vomiting	++	–	Prophylactic antiemetics
Other	++	Diarrhoea	Antidiarrhoeals
		Mucositis	Prophylactic mouth care
Haematological			
Myelosuppression	+	Anaemia Thrombocytopenia	Pretreatment FBC
Cutaneous			
Alopecia	–	–	–
Tissue necrosis (on extravasation)	Group 5	–	–
Other	++	Erythematous rash	Prophylactic antihistamine
	–	Skin desquamation	Water-based lotion
Cardiovascular	+++	Hypotension/ arrhythmias Peripheral and pulmonary oedema Weight gain/dyspnoea Capillary leak syndrome	Monitor thoughout treatment
Pulmonary	–	–	–
CNS	++	Confusion Disorientation	–
Renal/bladder	+++	Nephrotoxic transient increase in serum creatinine Potentially fatal decreases in glomerular filtration rates	Monitor renal function
Hepatic	++	Liver enzyme disturbances	Monitor hepatic function
Other	++	Flu-like symptoms: fever, chills, malaise, nasal congestion	Prophylactic paracetamol

α-Interferon

	Toxicity grading	Comment	Clinical monitoring/ intervention
Gastrointestinal tract			
Nausea/vomiting	+	Usualy accompanied by diarrhoea	–
Other	++	Anorexia	Regular monitoring of patient's weight
Haematological			
Myelosuppression	++	Nadir day 14 Recovery day 21	Pretreatment FBC Monitor with regular FBCs
Cutaneous			
Alopecia	+	Mild to moderate	–
Tissue necrosis (on extravasation)	Group 5	–	–
Cardiovascular	+	Dose-related transient hypotension, arrhythmias, palpitations	Monitor cardiac function in at-risk patients
Pulmonary	–	–	–
CNS	++	Depression, confusion, dizziness, vertigo At high does, convulsions, coma, paraesthesiae, neuropathy	–
Renal/bladder	–	–	–
Hepatic	–	–	–
Other	–	Flu-like symptoms: fever, chills, headaches, malaise Pain/reaction at injection site Elevated serum glucose levels	Administer injection in the evening Prophylactic paracetamol Rotate site of injection

Amsacrine

	Toxicity grading	Comment	Clinical monitoring/ intervention
Gastrointestinal tract			
Nausea/vomiting	++	–	Prophylactic antiemetics
Other	++	Mucositis	Prophylactic mouth care
Haematological			
Myelosuppression	+++	Prolonged Nadir days 10–16 Recovery days 21–25	Pretreatment FBC
Cutaneous			
Alopecia	++	–	–
Tissue necrosis (on extravasation)	Group 1	–	–
Other	–	Irritant to intact skin	–
Cardiovascular	++	Rare but potentially serious ventricular arrhythmias and congestive heart failure	Pretreatment ECG Caution in patients previously treated with anthracyclines Avoid in hypokalaemia
Pulmonary	–	–	–
CNS	–	–	–
Renal/bladder	–	–	–
Hepatic	–	Cholestasis	Monitor hepatic function and consider reduction in presence of hepatic impairment
Other	–	–	–

Asparaginase

	Toxicity grading	*Comment*	*Clinical monitoring/ intervention*
Gastrointestinal tract			
Nausea/vomiting	+	Usually acute in onset and short-lived	–
Haematological			
Myelosuppression	+	Nadir day 14 Recovery day 21	Pretreatment FBC
Coagulation	+	Depressed clotting factors	Monitor prothrombin time
Cutaneous			
Alopecia	–	–	–
Tissue necrosis (on extravasation)	Group 5	–	–
Cardiovascular	–	–	–
Pulmonary	–	–	–
CNS	++	Encephalopathy	Monitor renal status
Renal/bladder	+	Mild decrease in renal function	Monitor renal function
Hepatic	+++	Liver enzyme abnormalities common Severe hepatotoxicity rare	Consider dose reduction in hepatic impairment
Other	+++	Hypersensitivity	Consider intradermal test dose of 50 IU in 0.1–0.2 mL Observe for 3 hours Facilities for management of anaphylaxis should be available
	+++	Pyrexia and rigors	
	+	Hyperglycaemia	Monitor urine glucose
	+	Pancreatitis	Monitor amylase

Bleomycin

	Toxicity grading	Comment	Clinical monitoring/ intervention
Gastrointestinal tract			
Nausea/vomiting	+	Onset 3–6 hours	–
Other	+	Mucositis	–
Haematological			
Myelosuppression	–	Uncommon	–
Cutaneous			
Alopecia	–	–	–
Tissue necrosis (on extravasation)	Group 5	–	–
Other	++	Hyperpigmentation of mucous membranes, skin and nails	–
Cardiovascular	–	–	–
Pulmonary	+++	Pneumonitis Fibrosis Postoperative respiratory failure	Monitor pulmonary function Regular chest X-rays Avoid cumulative doses greater than 500 IU Treatment with corticosteroids may be considered
CNS	–	–	Caution in patients undergoing surgery following treatment with bleomycin
Renal/bladder	++	–	Monitor renal function Consider dose reduction in renal impairment
Hepatic	–	–	–
Other	++	Fever	Prophylactic paracetamol or concomitant hydrocortisone

Carboplatin

	Toxicity grading	Comment	Clinical monitoring/intervention
Gastrointestinal tract			
Nausea/vomiting	++	Onset 2–6 hours Duration 6–12 hours	Prophylactic antiemetics
Haematological			
Myelosuppression	++	Nadir days 7–10 Recovery day 21	Pretreatment FBC
Thrombocytopenia	+++	Nadir days 10–21 Recovery days 28–35	
Cutaneous			
Alopecia	+	Rare	–
Tissue necrosis (on extravasation)	Group 3	–	–
Cardiovascular	–	–	–
Pulmonary	–	–	–
CNS	+	Peripheral neuropathies Ototoxicity	– –
Renal/bladder	++	Nephrotoxicity mainly at high doses	Hydration with high doses Monitor renal function Consider dose modification on basis of renal function
Hepatic	–	–	–
Other	+	Electrolyte disturbance	Monitor biochemistry Supplement as required

Carmustine

	Toxicity grading	Comment	Clinical monitoring/ intervention
Gastrointestinal tract			
Nausea/vomiting	++	Dose related Onset 2–4 hours Duration 4–6 hours	Prophylactic antiemetics
Haematological			
Myelosuppression	++	Delayed	Pretreatment FBC
Thrombocytopenia	+++	Nadir 4–6 weeks	Treatment interval > 6 weeks
Cutaneous			
Alopecia	+	Rare	–
Tissue necrosis (on extravasation)	Group 1	–	–
Cardiovascular	–	–	–
Pulmonary	–	Acute pulmonary infiltrate and/or fibrosis Also delayed-onset pulmonary toxicity	–
CNS	+	Rare	–
Renal/bladder	–	–	–
Hepatic	–	Reversible elevation of LFTs	–
Other	++	Pain on injection	Administer slowly by infusion

Cisplatin

	Toxicity grading	Comment	Clinical monitoring/ intervention
Gastrointestinal tract			
Nausea/vomiting	+++	Onset 1–2 hours Duration 12–48 hours	Prophylactic antiemetics
Other	++	Diarrhoea Sudden onset	Anti-diarrhoeal prophylaxis for future cycles
Haematological			
Myelosuppression	+	Nadir days 14–23 Recovery days 21–35	
Cutaneous			
Alopecia	–	–	–
Tissue necrosis (on extravasation)	Group 2	–	–
Cardiovascular	–	–	–
Pulmonary	–	–	–
CNS	+++	Peripheral neuropathy Ototoxicity	Regular neurological examinations Audiometry
Renal/bladder	+++	Renal toxicity	Adequate pre- and post-treatment hydration; to maintain diuresis, mannitol may be given Monitor renal function prior to each cycle and adjust dose accordingly
Hepatic	–	–	–
Other	+++ ++ +	Electrolyte imbalance: hypomagnesaemia hypocalcaemia hypersensitivity	Rarely symptomatic Monitor and supplement as appropriate

Cladribine

	Toxicity grading	Comment	Clinical monitoring/ intervention
Gastrointestinal tract			
Nausea/vomiting	+	Mild to moderate duration	Prophylactic antiemetics
Haematological			
Myelosuppression	+++	WBC nadir days 7–14 Recovery days 28–30	Pretreatment FBC
Cutaneous			
Alopecia	+	–	–
Tissue necrosis (on extravasation)	Group 5	–	–
Other	++	Rash occurs in approximately 50% of patients	–
Cardiovascular	–	–	–
Pulmonary	–	–	–
CNS	–	–	–
Renal/bladder	+	Rare but not unreported	–
Hepatic	+	Rare but not unreported	–
Other	++	Fever due to tumour lysis	–

Cyclophosphamide

	Toxicity grading	Comment	Clinical monitoring/ intervention
Gastrointestinal tract			
Nausea/vomiting	++	Onset 4–12 hours Duration 4–10 hours	Prophylactic antiemetics
Other	++	Mucositis	Prophylactic mouth care
Haematological			
Myelosuppression	+++	Nadir days 10–14 Recovery days 21–28	Pretreatment FBC
Cutaneous			
Alopecia	+++	Complete with IV therapy Partial with oral therapy	–
Tissue necrosis (on extravasation)	Group 5	–	–
Cardiovascular	+	Cardiac toxicity reported with high doses	–
Pulmonary	+	Interstitial pneumonitis Pulmonary fibrosis	–
CNS	–	–	–
Renal/bladder	+++	Haemorrhagic cystitis Tubular damage	Less problematic than ifosfamide Ensure adequate hydration Consider mesna at doses greater than 1.5 g/m^2 Monitor renal function
Hepatic	–	–	–
Other	+	SIADH	–

Cytarabine

	Toxicity grading	Comment	Clinical monitoring/ intervention
Gastrointestinal tract			
Nausea/vomiting	++	Dose related Onset 6–12 hours Duration 3–8 hours	Prophylactic antiemetics
Other	++	Mucositis Diarrhoea	Prophylactic mouth care
Haematological			
Myelosuppression	+++	Nadir days 14–18 Recovery days 21–28 Thrombocytopenia Rapid recovery	Pretreatment FBC
Cutaneous			
Alopecia	+	+	–
Tissue necrosis (on extravasation)	Group 5	–	–
Cardiovascular	–	–	–
Pulmonary	++	Respiratory distress Pulmonary oedema	–
CNS	++	Toxicity at high dose, including dysarthria, ataxia	May be alleviated by pyridoxine
Renal/bladder	–	–	Reduce dose in renal impairment
Hepatic	+	Rare hepatic dysfunction	Monitor hepatic function and modify dose as necessary
Other	++	Ocular toxicity, including conjunctivitis and photophobia 'Cytarabine syndrome': fever, myalgia, bone pain, conjunctivitis, chest pain, malaise	Prophylactic steroid eye drops with high-dose therapy Corticosteroids

Dacarbazine

	Toxicity grading	Comment	Clinical monitoring/ intervention
Gastrointestinal tract			
Nausea/vomiting	+++	Onset 1–3 hours Duration 1–12 hours	Prophylactic antiemetics
Haematological			
Myelosuppression	++	Nadir days 10–14 Recovery days 21–28	Pretreatment FBC
Cutaneous			
Alopecia	+	Rare	–
Tissue necrosis (on extravasation)	Group 1	–	–
Cardiovascular	–	–	–
Pulmonary	–	–	–
CNS	–	–	–
Renal/bladder	–	–	–
Hepatic	+	Rare hepatotoxicity	–
Other	+	Rare flu-like syndrome, myalgia, fever, malaise starting within 7 days of treatment	–

Dactinomycin

	Toxicity grading	Comment	Clinical monitoring/ intervention
Gastrointestinal tract			
Nausea/vomiting	++	Onset 2–6 hours	Prophylactic antiemetics
Other	++	Mucositis	Prophylactic mouth care
Haematological			
Myelosuppression	++	Nadir days 10–14 Recovery days 21–28	Pretreatment FBC
Cutaneous			
Alopecia	+	–	–
Tissue necrosis (on extravasation)	Group 1	–	–
Cardiovascular	–	–	–
Pulmonary	–	–	–
CNS	–	–	–
Renal/bladder	–	–	–
Hepatic	–	–	Monitor liver function Consider dose reduction in hepatic impairment
Other	–	–	–

Daunorubicin

	Toxicity grading	Comment	Clinical monitoring/ intervention
Gastrointestinal tract			
Nausea/vomiting	++	Onset 2–6 hours	Prophylactic antiemetics
Other	++	Mucositis	Prophylactic mouth care
Haematological			
Myelosuppression	+++	Nadir days 9–14 Recovery days 21–28	Pretreatment FBC
Cutaneous			
Alopecia	++	–	–
Tissue necrosis (on extravasation)	Group 1	–	–
Cardiovascular	+++	Cardiomyopathy	Monitor cardiac function Maximum cumulative dose 600 mg/m^2
Pulmonary	–	–	–
CNS	–	–	–
Renal/bladder	–	–	–
Hepatic	–	–	Monitor hepatic function Consider dose reduction for hepatic impairment
Other	–	–	–

Daunorubicin liposomal

	Toxicity grading	Comment	Clinical monitoring/ intervention
Gastrointestinal tract			
Nausea/vomiting	+	–	Prophylactic antiemetics
Other	+	Mucositis is notably reduced	Prophylactic mouth care
Haematological			
Myelosuppression	+++	WBC nadir days 7–14 Recovery day 28	Pretreatment FBC
Cutaneous			
Alopecia	+	–	–
Tissue necrosis (on extravasation)	Group 2	Potential for more severe injuries as liposomes break down	–
Cardiovascular	+	Markedly reduced compared to non-liposomal formulation	–
Pulmonary	–	–	–
CNS	–	–	–
Renal/bladder	–	–	–
Hepatic	–	–	–
Other	++	Low-grade fever with or without fatigue	–

Docetaxel

	Toxicity grading	Comment	Clinical monitoring/ intervention
Gastrointestinal tract			
Nausea/vomiting	++	–	Prophylactic antiemetics
Other	++	Stomatitis and mucositis	Prophylactic mouth care
Haematological			
Myelosuppression	+++	Nadir days 7–9 Recovery days 14–16	Pretreatment FBC
Cutaneous			
Alopecia	++	Completely reversible	–
Tissue necrosis (on extravasation)	Group 2	–	–
Other	–	Skin erythema particularly of palms and soles, often associated with oedema leading to desquamation. Reversible, resolving within 21 days	–
Cardiovascular	–	–	–
Pulmonary	–	Associated with hypersensitivity reactions and fluid retention	
CNS	+++	Paraesthesiae and dysaesthesiae are fairly common but rarely severe. Some loss of deep tendon reflex, which is irreversible	–
Renal/bladder	–	–	–
Hepatic	++	Increased alkaline phosphatase and transaminases	Monitor hepatic function
Other			
Hypersensitivity	+++	–	Reactions are dramatically reduced by the use of high-dose steroid (dexamethasone), 20 mg at 12 hours and 6 hours pre-infusion and immediately pretreatment with H_1 and H_2 antihistamines

Docetaxel *Continued*

	Toxicity grading	Comment	Clinical monitoring/ intervention
Fluid retention	+++	Occurs in 61% of untreated patients and 43% of patients treated with hypersensitivity schedule; cumulative in incidence and severity	Pretreatment according to hyper-sensitivity schedule, slowly reversible

Doxorubicin

	Toxicity grading	Comment	Clinical monitoring/ intervention
Gastrointestinal tract			
Nausea/vomiting	++	Onset 4–6 hours Duration 6 hours	Prophylactic antiemetics
Other	+++	Mucositis	Prophylactic mouth care
Haematological			
Myelosuppression	+++	Nadir days 10–14 Recovery days 21–28	Pretreatment FBC
Cutaneous			
Alopecia	+++	–	–
Tissue necrosis (on extravasation)	Group 1	–	–
Cardiovascular	+++	Dose-limiting toxicity Cardiomyopathy arrhythmias	ECG monitoring Caution in patients with impaired cardiac function or previously treated with anthracyclines Maximum cumulative dose 450–550 mg/m^2
Pulmonary	–	–	–
CNS	–	–	–
Renal/bladder	–	–	–
Hepatic	++	Increased bilirubin Rare hepatocellular necrosis	Monitor hepatic function and modify dose as required
Other	–	Hyperpigmentation of skin, mucous membranes, nails	–

Doxorubicin liposomal

	Toxicity grading	Comment	Clinical monitoring/ intervention
Gastrointestinal tract			
Nausea/vomiting	++	Onset 4–6 hours Duration 6 hours	Prophylactic antiemetics
Stomatitis	++(+)	–	Consider extension of dose interval, good mouth care
Diarrhoea	+	–	Prophylactic antidiarrhoeals
Haematological			
Myelosuppression	++	Predominantly leucopenia	Pretreatment FBC
Anaemia	++	–	Pretreatment FBC, transfusion as required
Cutaneous			
Alopecia	++	–	–
Tissue necrosis (on extravasation)	Group 2	–	–
Other	++(+)	Pulmar–plantar erythrodysaesthesia	Treat symptomatically, reduce dose or discontinue further treatment
Cardiovascular	+++	Dose-limiting cardiomyopathy	Pretreatment ECG or MUGA scan*; monitor closely at cumulative doses greater than 450 mg/m²
Pulmonary	–	–	–
CNS	–	–	–
Renal/bladder	–	–	–
Hepatic	+(+)	–	Monitor hepatic function and modify dose as required
Other		Chills/fever/rigor	Stop infusion and only
Infusion-associated reactions	+(+)		restart following steroid and antihistamine cover

*multiple-gated arteriography

Edrecolomab (Panorex)

	Toxicity grading	Comment	Clinical monitoring/ intervention
Gastrointestinal tract			
Nausea/vomiting	++	–	Prophylactic antiemetics
Other	++	Diarrhoea	Antidiarrhoeals
	++	Abdominal cramping	–
Haematological			
Myelosuppression	–	–	–
Cutaneous			
Alopecia	–	–	–
Tissue necrosis (on extravasation)	Group 5	–	–
Cardiovascular	–	–	–
Pulmonary	–	–	–
CNS	–	–	–
Renal/bladder	–	–	–
Hepatic	–	–	–
Other	++(+)	Chills/fever/rigor, usually within the first 2 hours, frequently occurring with nausea, urticaria, headache, hypotension, flushing and/or tumour pain	Stop infusion and treat presenting symptoms Restart at half previous rate and titrate against effect Premedication with paracetamol and chlorpheniramine is advisable

Epirubicin

	Toxicity grading	Comment	Clinical monitoring/ intervention
Gastrointestinal tract			
Nausea/vomiting	++	Onset 4–6 hours Duration 6 hours	Prophylactic antiemetics
Other	+++	Mucositis	Prophylactic mouth care
Haematological			
Myelosuppression	+++	Nadir days 10–14 Recovery days 21–28	Pretreatment FBC
Cutaneous			
Alopecia	+++	–	–
Tissue necrosis (on extravasation)	Group 1	–	–
Cardiovascular	+++	Dose-limiting toxicity Cardiomyopathy arrhythmias	ECG monitoring Caution in patients with impaired cardiac function or previously treated with anthracyclines Maximum cumulative dose 900 mg/m^2
Pulmonary	–	–	–
CNS	–	–	–
Renal/bladder	–	–	–
Hepatic	++	Increased bilirubin Rare hepatocellular necrosis	Monitor hepatic function and modify dose as required
Other	–	Hyperpigmentation of skin, mucous membranes, nails	–

Etoposide

	Toxicity grading	Comment	Clinical monitoring/ intervention
Gastrointestinal tract			
Nausea/vomiting	++	Onset 3–8 hours Duration 12 hours	Prophylactic antiemetics
Other	++	Mucositis	Prophylactic mouth care
Haematological			
Myelosuppression	+++	Nadir days 14–16 Recovery days 21–28	Pretreatment FBC
Cutaneous			
Alopecia	++	–	–
Tissue necrosis (on extravasation)	Group 3	–	–
Cardiovascular	+	Hypotension on rapid infusion	Administer over 1 hour
Pulmonary	–	–	–
CNS	–	–	–
Renal/bladder	–	–	Monitor renal function Consider dose modification in patients with renal impairment
Hepatic	–	–	Monitor hepatic function Consider dose modification in patients with hepatic impairment
Other	–	–	–

Etoposide phosphate

	Toxicity grading	Comment	Clinical monitoring/ intervention
Gastrointestinal tract			
Nausea/vomiting	++	Slightly more prolonged than etoposide	Prophylactic antiemetics
Mucositis	++		Prophylactic mouth care
Haematological			
Myelosuppression	+++	Nadir days 18–23	Pretreatment FBC
Thrombocytopenia	+	Recovery days 28–35	
Anaemia	++		
Cutaneous			
Alopecia	+++	–	–
Tissue necrosis (on extravasation)	Group 4	–	–
Cardiovascular	–	–	–
Pulmonary	+	Spontaneous apnoea	Full resumption of function following discontinuation of infusion
CNS	–	–	–
Renal/bladder	+	Potential for accumulation in cases of functional impairment	Monitor renal function Consider dose modification in patients with renal impairment
Hepatic	–	Potential for accumulation in case of functional impairment	–
Other	–	–	–

Floxuridine

	Toxicity grading	Comment	Clinical monitoring/ intervention
Gastrointestinal tract			
Nausea/vomiting	++	Onset 3–6 hours	Prophylactic antiemetics
Other	++(+)	Secretory diarrhoea	Stop medication and treat with antidiarrhoeals, restart only with caution
	++	Mucositis	Prophylactic mouth care
Haematological			
Myelosuppression	+++	Nadir days 10–18 Recovery days 21–25	Pretreatment FBC
Thrombocytopenia	+	–	Pretreatment FBC
Anaemia	+	–	Pretreatment FBC
Cutaneous			
Alopecia	+	–	–
Tissue necrosis (on extravasation)	Group 2	–	–
Other	+	Rash	–
Cardiovascular	–	–	–
Pulmonary	–	–	–
CNS	+	Blurred vision and vertigo	Discontinuation of drug
		Convulsions	Discontinuation of drug
		CNS toxicity can have both an acute and a chronic component, and patients are at greater risk with infusional therapy	
Renal/bladder	–	–	–
Hepatic	+(+)	Hepatic dysfunction has been noted, but may be due to concurrent disease	Pretreatment LFT
Other	–	–	–

Fludarabine

	Toxicity grading	Comment	Clinical monitoring/ intervention
Gastrointestinal tract			
Nausea/vomiting	+	Transient but occurring in up to 30% of patients	Prophylactic antiemetics
Other	+	Diarrhoea	Prophylactic mouth care
Haematological			
Myelosuppression	+++	Nadir days 10–17 Recovery days 21–28	Pretreatment FBC
Cutaneous			
Alopecia	–	–	–
Tissue necrosis (on extravasation)	Group 5	–	–
Cardiovascular	–	–	–
Pulmonary	+++	Interstitial pneumonitis due to cumulative dose	Steroids
CNS	+++	–	–
Renal/bladder	–	–	–
Hepatic	++	Elevation of hepatic transaminase and creatinine	Monitor hepatic function
Other	–	–	–

Fluorouracil

	Toxicity grading	Comment	Clinical monitoring/ intervention
Gastrointestinal tract			
Nausea/vomiting	+	Onset 3–6 hours Dose limiting	Prophylactic antiemetics
Other	+++	Diarrhoea	Treatment may need to be stopped; may need prophylactic antidiarrhoeals
		Stomatitis	Possible benefit from sucralfate or prophylactic allopurinol suspension
Haematological			
Myelosuppression	+	Nadir day 14 Recovery days 21–25	Schedule dependent
Cutaneous			
Alopecia	+	–	–
Tissue necrosis (on extravasation)	Group 4	5FU 'burns' can cause problems with venous access	–
Cardiovascular	++	Rare vascular toxicity including angina/ cardiac spasm Myocardial infarction	Monitor cardiac function Caution in patients with cardiac disease
Pulmonary	–	–	–
CNS	+	Rare CNS dysfunction, ataxia, confusion, headaches	–
Renal/bladder	–	–	–
Hepatic	–	–	–
Other	–	–	–

Gemcitabine

	Toxicity grading	Comment	Clinical monitoring/ intervention
Gastrointestinal tract			
Nausea/vomiting	+	Partially schedule dependent	Prophylactic antiemetics
Haematological			
Myelosuppression	++	Dose limiting, but not cumulative WBC nadir days 8–12	Pretreatment FBC
Cutaneous			
Alopecia	+	–	–
Tissue necrosis (on extravasation)	Group 5	–	–
Other	++	Rash Generalised onset within 48–72 hours Presents as an erythematous maculopapular rash of neck and extremities	Response to steroids
Cardiovascular	–	–	–
Pulmonary	–	–	–
CNS	–	–	–
Renal/bladder	–	–	–
Hepatic	–	–	–
Other	–	–	–

Idarubicin

	Toxicity grading	Comment	Clinical monitoring/ intervention
Gastrointestinal tract			
Nausea/vomiting	++	–	Prophylactic antiemetics
Other	++	Mucositis	Prophylactic mouth care
Haematological			
Myelosuppression	+++	–	Pretreatment FBC
Cutaneous			
Alopecia	+++	–	–
Tissue necrosis (on extravasation)	Group 1	–	–
Cardiovascular	+++	Cardiomyopathy	Monitor cardiac function Caution in patients with cardiac disease or previously treated with anthracyclines
Pulmonary	–	–	–
CNS	–	–	–
Renal/bladder	–	–	Monitor renal function Consider dose reduction for renal impairment
Hepatic	–	–	Monitor hepatic function Consider dose reduction for hepatic impairment
Other	–	–	–

Ifosfamide

	Toxicity grading	Comment	Clinical monitoring/ intervention
Gastrointestinal tract			
Nausea/vomiting	+++	Onset 1–2 hours Duration 12–24 hours	Prophylactic antiemetics
Haematological			
Myelosuppression	+++	Nadir days 5–10 Recovery days 14–21	Pretreatment FBC
Cutaneous			
Alopecia	+++	Usually complete Onset 1–3 weeks	–
Tissue necrosis (on extravasation)	Group 5	–	–
Cardiovascular	–	–	–
Pulmonary	–	–	–
CNS	+++	Encephalopathy Neurotoxicity Confusion/lethargy	Assess risk factors: renal function, albumin, presence or absence of pelvic disease
Renal/bladder	+++	Haemorrhagic cystitis Urothelial toxicity Tubular damage	Prophylactic mesna required Ensure adequate hydration Monitor renal function Consider dose reduction in presence of renal impairment
Hepatic	–	–	–
Other	–	–	–

Irinotecan

	Toxicity grading	Comment	Clinical monitoring/ intervention
Gastrointestinal tract			
Nausea/vomiting	++	Onset 2–6 hours	Prophylactic antiemetics
Delayed diarrhoea	+++	Onset 24 hours post treatment. Particularly life-threatening if concurrent with neutropenia	Loperamide 2 mg every 2 hours continuing for at least 12 hours after last liquid stool. Hydration, electrolytes and possible hospital period
Haematological			
Myelosuppression	+++	WBC nadir days 5–12 Recovery by day 22	Pretreatment FBC
Thrombocytopenia	+	Nadir day 14	
Anaemia	++		
Cutaneous			
Alopecia	++	–	–
Tissue necrosis (on extravasation)	Group 3	–	–
Cardiovascular	–	–	–
Pulmonary	–	–	–
CNS	–	–	–
Renal/bladder	+(+)	Transient elevation of serum creatinine	Pretreatment biochemical profile, and dose modification if persistent
Hepatic	+(+)	Elevation of transaminase and/or alkaline phosphatase	Pretreatment LFT, and dose modification if persistent
Other			
Acute cholinergic syndrome	+++	Acute early diarrhoea plus sweating ± abdominal cramping ± lachrymation ± salivation	Atropine sulphate 0.25 mg subcutaneously

Melphalan

	Toxicity grading	Comment	Clinical monitoring/ intervention
Gastrointestinal tract			
Nausea/vomiting	++	Onset 6–12 hours	Prophylactic antiemetics
Haematological			
Myelosuppression	++	Delayed Nadir days 10–18 Recovery 6–7 weeks	Pretreatment FBC
Cutaneous			
Alopecia	–	Uncommon	–
Tissue necrosis (on extravasation)	Group 5	–	–
Cardiovascular	–	–	–
Pulmonary	+	Rare pulmonary fibrosis	–
CNS	–	–	–
Renal/bladder	–	–	Monitor renal function Consider dose reduction for renal impairment
Hepatic	–	–	–
Other	–	–	–

Methotrexate

	Toxicity grading	Comment	Clinical monitoring/ intervention
Gastrointestinal tract			
Nausea/vomiting	++	Dose related	Prophylactic antiemetics with doses > 100 mg/m²
Other	+++	Stomatitis	Ensure folinic acid rescue starts at 24 hours post chemotherapy with doses of > 100 mg/m²
Haematological			
Myelosuppression	++	Dose related Nadir day 10 Recovery day 21	Pretreatment FBC
Cutaneous			
Alopecia	–	–	–
Tissue necrosis (on extravasation)	Group 4	–	–
Cardiovascular	–	–	–
Pulmonary	–	–	–
CNS	–	–	–
Renal/bladder	+++	Electrolyte disturbance Tubular damage and destruction	Monitor renal function Maintain diuresis Maintain urinary pH at > 7.5 with doses > 1 g/m² Monitor methotrexate plasma concentration and adjust folinic acid dose accordingly
Hepatic	–	–	–
Other	–	Conjunctivitis Sore, itching eyes	Symptomatic treatment with hypromellose 0.3% eyedrops

Mitomycin

	Toxicity grading	Comment	Clinical monitoring/intervention
Gastrointestinal tract			
Nausea/vomiting	+	Onset 1–4 hours	Prophylactic antiemetics
Haematological			
Myelosuppression	++	Nadir 3–4 weeks Recovery 6–8 weeks	Pretreatment FBC
Cutaneous			
Alopecia	–	–	–
Tissue necrosis (on extravasation)	Group 1	–	–
Cardiovascular	–	–	–
Pulmonary	+	Pulmonary fibrosis	–
CNS	–	–	–
Renal/bladder	–	Renal toxicity	Monitor renal function
Hepatic	–	–	–
Other	–	–	–

Mitozantrone

	Toxicity grading	Comment	Clinical monitoring/ intervention
Gastrointestinal tract			
Nausea/vomiting	+	–	Prophylactic antiemetics
Other	+	Mucositis	–
Haematological			
Myelosuppression	+	Nadir day 14 Recovery day 21	Pretreatment FBC
Cutaneous			
Alopecia	++	–	–
Tissue necrosis (on extravasation)	Group 2	–	–
Cardiovascular	++	Cardiomyopathy	Monitor cardiac function if cumulative dose is > 160 mg/m², in presence of cardiac disease or previous anthracycline therapy
Pulmonary	–	–	–
CNS	–	–	–
Renal/bladder	–	–	–
Hepatic	+	–	Particular problem in patients with bilirubin > 35–40 umol/L Monitor hepatic function
Other	–	–	–

Mustine

	Toxicity grading	Comment	Clinical monitoring/ intervention
Gastrointestinal tract			
Nausea/vomiting	+++	Onset 0.5–2 hours	Prophylactic antiemetics
Haematological			
Myelosuppression	+++	Nadir days 9–14 Recovery days 16–28	Pretreatment FBC
Cutaneous			
Alopecia	++	–	–
Tissue necrosis (on extravasation)	Group 1	–	–
Cardiovascular	–	–	–
Pulmonary	–	Fibrotic changes rare	–
CNS	–	–	–
Renal/bladder	–	–	–
Hepatic	–	–	–
Other	–	–	–

Oxaliplatin

	Toxicity grading	Comment	Clinical monitoring/ intervention
Gastrointestinal tract			
Nausea/vomiting	++(+)	Onset 1–6 hours Duration 24–48 hours	Prophylactic antiemetics
Haematological			
Myelosuppression	+(+)	–	Pretreatment FBC
Thrombocytopenia	+(+)	–	–
Cutaneous			
Alopecia	–	–	–
Tissue necrosis (on extravasation)	Group 2	–	–
Cardiovascular	–	–	–
Pulmonary	–	–	–
CNS	+++	Peripheral neuropathy, often showing resultion within 2–4 weeks of stopping therapy	Regular neurological examination
Renal/bladder	–	–	–
Hepatic	–	–	–
Other			
Raynaud's-type syndrome	+	Presenting as cold extremities, particularly the lips and ear lobes; probably a dysaesthesia due to the neurological toxicity	–

Paclitaxel

	Toxicity grading	Comment	Clinical monitoring/ intervention
Gastrointestinal tract			
Nausea/vomiting	++	Schedule-related onset 30 minutes to 3 hours	Prophylactic antiemetics
Other	+	Mucositis	Good mouth care
Haematological			
Myelosuppression	+++	Nadir days 9–11 Recovery day 15	Pretreatment FBC
Cutaneous			
Alopecia	+++	Complete but reversible	–
Tissue necrosis (on extravasation)	Group 1	–	–
Cardiovascular	++	Commonly bradycardic, particularly problematic in patients with other risk factors	–
Pulmonary		Only in association with hypersensitivity reaction, burning sensation on soles of feet	–
CNS	+++	Peripheral neuro-pathies, loss of deep tendon reflexes, fairly rapidly reversible	–
Renal/bladder	–	–	–
Hepatic	–	–	–
Other	+++	Hypersensitivity, probably due to the cremophor vehicle rather than to paclitaxel	Reactions are dramatically reduced, if not eliminated, by the use of high-dose steroid dexamethasone 20 mg at 12 hours and 6 hours prior to infusion, and immediate pretreatment with H_1 and H_2 antihistamines

Pentostatin

	Toxicity grading	Comment	Clinical monitoring/ intervention
Gastrointestinal tract			
Nausea/vomiting	++	–	Prophylactic antiemetics
Haematological			
Myelosuppression	+++	Nadir days 12–17 Recovery days 21–28	Pretreatment FBC
Cutaneous			
Alopecia	–	–	–
Tissue necrosis (on extravasation)	Group 5	–	–
Other	+	Skin rash in patients with hairy-cell leukaemia	Topical hydrocortisone
	++	Dry skin	Emollient creams
Cardiovascular	–	–	–
Pulmonary	–	–	–
CNS	++	Dose-dependent lethargy and fatigue Rarely coma and seizures	–
Renal/bladder	+++	Tubular toxicity leading to increased tubular creatinine and acute renal failure	Monitor renal function Dose reduced in mild to moderate failure
Hepatic	–	–	–
Other	+	Keratoconjunctivitis of the eye	Responds to steroid eyedrops

Raltitrexed

	Toxicity grading	Comment	Clinical monitoring/ intervention
Gastrointestinal tract			
Nausea/vomiting	+++	Often only of moderate intensity	Prophylactic antiemetics
Other	+++	Mild to moderate diarrhoea	Prophylactic antidiarrhoeals
Haematological			
Myelosuppression	++	–	Pretreatment FBC
Anaemia	+++	–	Pretreatment FBC and transfusion as required
Cutaneous			
Alopecia	–	–	–
Tissue necrosis (on extravasation)	Group 4	–	–
Other	++	Erythematous or pruritic rash	–
Cardiovascular	–	–	–
Pulmonary	–	–	–
CNS	–	–	–
Renal/bladder	–	–	–
Hepatic	+++	Elevation of lower transaminases	Monitor hepatic function
Other	+++	Asthma, malaise and flu-like symptoms, may be dose limiting	–

Rituximab

	Toxicity grading	Comment	Clinical monitoring/ intervention
Gastrointestinal tract			
Nausea/vomiting	+	–	–
Haematological			
Myelosuppression	+	Very rare; less than 2% of all grades	Periodic FBC
Cutaneous			
Alopecia	–	–	–
Tissue necrosis (on extravasation)	Group 5	–	–
Pain at infusion site	+	–	–
Cardiovascular	–	–	–
Pulmonary	+	Rare episodes of bronchoconstriction	Can be successfully treated with bronchodilators
CNS	–	–	–
Renal/bladder	–	–	–
Hepatic	–	–	–
Other			
Infusion-related syndrome	++(+)	Chills/fever/rigor, usually within the first 2 hours, frequently occurring with nausea, urticaria, headache, hypotension, flushing and/or tumour pain	Stop infusion and treat presenting symptoms Restart at half previous rate and titrate against effect Premedication with paracetamol and chlorpheniramine is advisable

Streptozocin

	Toxicity grading	Comment	Clinical monitoring/ intervention
Gastrointestinal tract			
Nausea/vomiting	+++	Onset 2–6 hours Duration 12–24 hours	Prophylactic antiemetics
Diarrhoea	+	–	–
Haematological			
Myelosuppression	+	Usually mild, but has been reported as occasionally very severe (fatal), affecting both white cells and platelets; appears to be schedule dependent	Pretreatment FBC
Cutaneous			
Alopecia	+	–	–
Tissue necrosis (on extravasation)	Group 1	–	–
Cardiovascular	–	–	–
Pulmonary	–	–	–
CNS	–	–	–
Renal/bladder	+++	Dose related, cumulative and may be fatal, causing azotemia, anuria, hypophosphataemia, glycosuria and renal tubular acidosis	Pretreatment renal function. Check urine during and after administration for proteinuria. Post-treatment hydration
Hepatic	+(+)	Elevation of SGOT and LDH; also hypoalbuminaemia	Pretreatment LFT
Other	–	–	–

Teniposide

	Toxicity grading	Comment	Clinical monitoring/ intervention
Gastrointestinal tract			
Nausea/vomiting	++	–	Prophylactic antiemetics
Mucositis	++	–	Prophylactic mouth care
Haematological			
Myelosuppression	++(+)	Nadir days 3–14 Recovery day 21 Duration approximately 7 days	Pretreatment FBC
Cutaneous			
Alopecia	+	–	–
Tissue necrosis (on extravasation)	Group 3	–	–
Skin rashes	+++	Although severe, only seen in patients receiving more than 1 mg/m^2	–
Cardiovascular	++	Rare but potentially severe – hypotension is well documented but appears to be related to the rate of administration	–
Pulmonary	–	–	–
CNS	–	–	–
Renal/bladder	–	–	–
Hepatic	–	–	–
Other	–	–	–

Thiotepa

	Toxicity grading	Comment	Clinical monitoring/ intervention
Gastrointestinal tract			
Nausea/vomiting	+	–	Antiemetics as required
Haematological			
Myelosuppression	++	Nadir day 14 Recovery 4 weeks	Pretreatment FBC
Thrombocytopenia	+++	–	–
Cutaneous			
Alopecia	–	Rare	–
Tissue necrosis (on extravasation)	Group 5	–	–
Cardiovascular	–	–	–
Pulmonary	–	–	–
CNS	–	–	–
Renal/bladder	–	–	–
Hepatic	–	–	–
Other	–	–	–

Topotecan

	Toxicity grading	Comment	Clinical monitoring/ intervention
Gastrointestinal tract			
Nausea/vomiting	+	Schedule dependent, possibly cumulative, far less frequent at grade 3 or 4	Prophylactic antiemetics
Haematological			
Myelosuppression	+++	Nadir days 11–12 Onset day 9 Duration 7 days Recovery day 21	Pretreatment FBC, with appropriate transfusion, dose reduction or the use of GCSF if dose limiting
Thrombocytopenia	++	Onset day 14 Duration 5 days	–
Anaemia	+	–	–
Cutaneous			
Alopecia	++	Approx 1:2.5 partial to completely reversible	–
Tissue necrosis (on extravasation)	Group 2	–	Care and observation whilst administering the drug
Cardiovascular	–	–	–
Pulmonary	–	–	–
CNS	–	–	–
Renal/bladder	–	Not directly toxic to kidneys but, due to renal excretion, will need dose modification for patients with creatinine clearance rates of between 20 and 39 mL/min	Pretreatment creatinine clearance
Hepatic	–	–	–
Other	+	Fatigue and asthenia	–

Trastuzumab

	Toxicity grading	Comment	Clinical monitoring/ intervention
Gastrointestinal tract			
Nausea/vomiting	+	–	
Diarrhoea	+(+)	–	Prophylactic antidiarrhoeal
Haematological			
Myelosuppression	+	Less than 1% of all patients	–
Cutaneous			
Alopecia	–	–	–
Tissue necrosis (on extravasation)	Group 5	–	–
Cardiovascular	++(+)	Congestive heart failure, particularly left ventricular function	Thorough baseline investigation, including ECG and MUGA scan
Pulmonary	+	–	Possible exacerbation of asthma, monitis and sinusitis
CNS	–	–	–
Renal/bladder	–	–	–
Hepatic	++	–	Pretreatment LFT
Other			
Infusion-related syndrome	+(+)	Chills/fever/rigor usually within the first 2 hours, frequently occurring with nausea, urticaria, headache, hypotension, flushing and/or tumour pain	Stop infusion and treat presenting symptoms Restart at half previous rate and titrate against effect Premedication with paracetamol and chlorpheniramine is advisable

Treosulfan

	Toxicity grading	Comment	Clinical monitoring/ intervention
Gastrointestinal tract			
Nausea/vomiting	++	Onset 0–4 hours Duration 4–12 hours	Prophylactic antiemetics
Haematological			
Myelosuppression	+++	Onset days 12–14 Nadir days 14–16 Recovery day 28	Pretreatment FBC
Cutaneous			
Alopecia	+++	–	–
Tissue necrosis (on extravasation)	Group 1	–	–
Other	+	Erythematous rash with some skin pigmentation	–
Cardiovascular	–	–	–
Pulmonary	–	–	–
CNS	–	–	–
Renal/bladder	–	–	–
Hepatic	–	–	–
Other	–	–	–

Vinblastine

	Toxicity grading	Comment	Clinical monitoring/ intervention
Gastrointestinal tract			
Nausea/vomiting	+	Onset 4–8 hours	Antiemetics as required
Other	++	Constipation	Consider prophylactic laxatives
	+	Stomatitis	Prophylactic mouth care
Haematological			
Myelosuppression	++	Nadir day 10 Recovery days 14–21	Pretreatment FBC
Cutaneous			
Alopecia	+	–	–
Tissue necrosis (on extravasation)	Group 1	–	–
Cardiovascular	–	–	–
Pulmonary	–	–	–
CNS	++	Neuropathy	–
Renal/bladder	–	–	–
Hepatic	–	–	Monitor hepatic function Consider dose reduction for hepatic impairment
Other	+	SIADH	–

Vincristine

	Toxicity grading	Comment	Clinical monitoring/ intervention
Gastrointestinal tract			
Nausea/vomiting	+	Onset 4–8 hours	Antiemetics as required
Other	++	Constipation	Consider prophylactic laxatives
	+	Stomatitis	Prophylactic mouth care
Haematological			
Myelosuppression	+	Nadir day 10 Recovery day 21	Pretreatment FBC
Cutaneous			
Alopecia	+	–	–
Tissue necrosis (on extravasation)	Group 1	–	–
Cardiovascular	–	–	–
Pulmonary	–	–	–
CNS	+++	Neuropathy	–
Renal/bladder	–	–	–
Hepatic	–	–	Monitor hepatic function Consider dose reduction for hepatic/biliary impairment
Other	–	SIADH	–

Vindesine

	Toxicity grading	Comment	Clinical monitoring/ intervention
Gastrointestinal tract			
Nausea/vomiting	+	Onset 4–8 hours	Antiemetics as required
Other	+	Constipation	Consider prophylactic laxatives
Haematological			
Myelosuppression	++	Nadir days 3–5 Recovery days 7–10	Pretreatment FBC
Cutaneous			
Alopecia	++	–	–
Tissue necrosis (on extravasation)	Group 1	–	–
Cardiovascular	–	–	–
Pulmonary	–	–	–
CNS	++	Neuropathy	–
Renal/bladder	–	–	–
Hepatic	–	–	Monitor hepatic function Consider dose reduction for hepatic/biliary impairment
Other	–	–	–

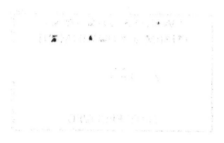

Vinorelbine

	Toxicity grading	Comment	Clinical monitoring/ intervention
Gastrointestinal tract			
Nausea/vomiting	+(+)	Mainly grade I or II	Pretreatment antiemetics
Constipation	++	Autonomic intestinal paresis	Retreat only when bowel function recovers
Haematological			
Myelosuppression	+++	WBC nadir days 5–7 up to day 12 Recovery day 21	Pretreatment FBC
Cutaneous			
Alopecia	+	–	–
Tissue necrosis (on extravasation)	Group 1	–	–
Cardiovascular	–	–	–
Pulmonary	–	–	–
CNS	++	Dose dependent but reversible	Mainly loss of deep tendon reflex, appropriate pretreatment neurological examination
Renal/bladder	–	–	–
Hepatic	–	–	Dose reduction by one-third has been clearly successful in breast cancer patients with greater than 75% liver involvement
Other			
Jaw pain	+	Possibly neurological in origin	–

SOURCES OF INFORMATION

ABPI (1991) *ABPI Data Sheet Compendium 1991–1992*. DataPharm Publications Ltd, London.

Borison HL and McCarthy LE (1983) Neuropharmacology of chemotherapy-induced emesis. *Drugs.* **25 (Supplement 1)**: 8–17.

Cain M and Tenni P (1992) *Drug Therapy in Cancer: a practical guide for health professionals*. Society of Hospital Pharmacists of Australia, Sydney.

Chabner BA and Myers CE (1989) Clinical pharmacology of cancer chemotherapy. In: VT DeVita *et al*. (eds) *Cancer: principles and practice of oncology* (3e). Lippincott, New York.

Dollery C (ed.) (1991) *Therapeutic Drugs*. Churchill Livingstone, Edinburgh.

Fahey M *et al*. (1984) Prescription monitoring and the oncology patient. *Pharm J.* **233**: 483–5.

Middleton J *et al*. (1985) Failure of scalp hypothermia to prevent hair loss when cyclophosphamide is added to doxorubicin and vincristine. *Cancer Treat Rep.* **69**: 373–5.

Perry MC and Yarbro JW (1984) *Toxicity of Chemotherapy*. Grune & Stratton, Orlando, FL.

Priestman TJ (1989) *Cancer Chemotherapy: an introduction* (3e). Springer-Verlag, London.

Reynold JEF (ed.) (1982) *The Extra Pharmacopoeia* (29e). Pharmaceutical Press, London.

Souhami R and Tobias J (1986) *Cancer and its Management*. Blackwell Scientific Publications, Oxford.

Stanley AP (1992) Management of symptoms associated with cancer treatment. I. *Pharm J.* **249**: 50–3.

Stanley AP (1992) Management of symptoms associated with cancer treatment. II. *Pharm J.* **249**: 90–2.

Tierney AJ (1987) Preventing chemotherapy-induced alopecia in cancer patients: is scalp cooling worthwhile? *J Adv Nurs.* **12**: 303–10.

Triozzi A and Laszlo J (1987) Optimum management of nausea and vomiting in cancer chemotherapy. *Drugs.* **34**: 136–49.

World Health Organization (1989) *WHO Handbook for Reporting Results of Cancer Treatment*. World Health Organization, Geneva.

Storage of cytotoxic drugs after reconstitution or repackaging: a statement regarding extended shelf-life

Many parenteral cytotoxic drugs require reconstitution. In a centralised service, cytotoxic injections will normally be drawn up into a syringe or into an infusion container ready for administration. Manufacturers are currently required by licensing authorities to indicate on the data sheet and package insert that reconstituted drugs, with or without preservative, should be stored in a refrigerator (unless dictated by the chemical nature of the drug) and must be used within a specified period, usually not more than 24 hours. This is to ensure that, although the drug may be stable, any micro-organisms introduced during the reconstitution procedures (assumed to be on the ward) will have insufficient opportunity to multiply and reach hazardous numbers before the injection is administered.

This recommendation or directive will therefore not usually relate to considerations of chemical stability. Consequently, provided that any manipulations undertaken to prepare the drug for administration are performed under aseptic conditions, ensuring that an adequate level of sterility assurance is maintained, the shelf-life of such reconstituted or repackaged injections can be extended at the discretion of the responsible hospital pharmacist.

It is essential that good aseptic techniques are employed and adequate quality assurance programmes are maintained. The shelf-life of such injectable drugs can then be governed by chemical stability considerations together with local practice and procedures. This allows far greater flexibility, and provides opportunities for greater efficiency in operating centralised cytotoxic services.

Guidance in each monograph with regard to storage after reconstitution assumes that subsequent manipulations are undertaken under appropriate aseptic conditions. The monographs have been prepared from reviews of the literature, guidance from the respective manufacturer and the authors' own studies and experience. However, responsibility for the final preparation must rest with the pharmacist responsible for the cytotoxic services.

Introduction to drug monographs: compendium of intravenous drugs used in cancer chemotherapy

These monographs describe injectable cytotoxic drugs, biologicals and adjuvant drugs used in cancer chemotherapy. Wherever possible, information has been referenced to specific sources. Data and information from the particular manufacturer may originate from a variety of sources, including UK data sheets, package inserts and personal communications held on file by the author of each monograph. Since the content of data sheets changes frequently, the reader is referred to the current product data sheet for the latest information.

Each monograph has a common structure for ease of reference and uniformity. The purpose of each section is described below. The major aim in producing the monographs is to provide the user with all of the available information for each injection with regard to stability, in the context of a cytotoxic service operated by a pharmacy department.

1 General details

Under the heading *Approved names*, the first name(s) refers to International Non-Propriety Name (INNM) titles, followed by alternatives in common use.

As well as nomenclature, this section includes names of manufacturers and suppliers in the UK.

2 Chemistry

This section provides a summary of the chemical properties of the drug that are relevant to the injection form (structure, solubility, etc.).

3 Stability profile

A summary of the chemical stability of each drug is given, including chemical and physical parameters that influence stability after reconstitution and repackaging. Degradation pathways, when known, are included as background information. Important practical aspects, including container compatibility, and reported incompatibilities with other drugs, are noted. Although useful for reference purposes, much of the data relates to short-term physical compatibility of admixtures in the laboratory, and is not necessarily applicable to the clinical setting. A summary of the stability of the reconstituted injection follows.

In view of the increasing use of ambulatory administration of cytotoxic drugs, a separate subsection has been included for these specialised devices.

4 Clinical use

A brief summary of dosage regimens commonly used is included for guidance purposes only.

5 Preparation of injection

Details of how the injection is prepared for bolus injection and infusion, as relevant, are included, together with handling precautions and details concerning treatment of extravasation. With regard to injections prepared for different routes of administration, the pharmacist responsible for these services should ensure that everything possible is done to distinguish *intrathecal* injections, in particular, from those intended for other routes.

6 Destruction of drug or contaminated articles

The recommended methods for inactivating each cytotoxic drug are summarised under the headings *Incineration*, *Chemical* and *Contact with skin*. The incineration conditions indicate the minimum temperatures recommended, usually by the manufacturer (*see* Chapter 6 for further details on safe handling).

NOTE: While the authors of each monograph have taken every care to provide accurate and complete information, as far as it is possible to do so, the authors or publishers cannot accept any liability for the information contained therein.

ACLARUBICIN

1 General details

Approved names: Aclarubicin, Aclacinomycin A.

Proprietary name: Aclarubicin Medac Injection.

Manufacturer or supplier: Medac GmbH, Fehlandstraße 3, 20354 Hamburg, Germany.

Presentation and formulation details: Sterile, pyrogen-free, yellow or orange-yellow, freeze-dried powder in vials containing aclarubicin hydrochloride equivalent to 20 mg aclarubicin.[1]

Storage and shelf-life of unopened container: Three years, protected from light. Store at room temperature.[1]

2 Chemistry

Type: Aclarubicin is a cytotoxic antibiotic of the anthracycline group (Class II).

Molecular structure: methyl (1R,2R,4S)-4-(O-{2,6-dideoxy-4-O-[(2R,6S)-tetrahydro-6-methyl-5-oxopyran-2-yl]-α-L-*lyxo*-hexapyranosyl}-(1→4)-2,3,6-trideoxy-3-dimethylamino-L-*lyxo*-hexopyranosyloxy)-2-ethyl-1,2,3,4,6,11-hexahydro-2,5,7-trihydroxy-6,11-dioxonaphthacen-1-carboxylate hydrochloride.[2]

Molecular weight: 848.3

Solubility: Aclarubicin is freely soluble in water.[2] Its solubility is pH dependent. In buffered solution at pH 6 its solubility is approximately 400 mg/mL, whereas at pH 7.4 it is only 0.05 mg/mL.[3]

3 Stability profile

3.1 Physical and chemical stability

According to the manufacturer, reconstituted aqueous and saline solutions stored below 4°C should be used within 24 hours of preparation, or within 6 hours at room temperature when protected from light.[1] A review of the literature suggests that aclarubicin may be stable for longer periods.[4,5] However, very few data have been published. In addition, Krämer and Wenchel[4] quote 'in-house data', the full details of which have not been published. For these reasons further studies are needed to assess the long-term stability of aclarubicin. The stability of aclarubicin hydrochloride in aqueous solution depends on a number of factors, the most important of which are pH, temperature and the type of solvent used for reconstitution. Aclarubicin is also light sensitive, and may be adsorbed on to glass and certain plastics in the same way as other anthracyclines.

Effect of pH: Aclarubicin is most stable at pH 5–6. At pH values greater than 7 the hydrochloride is insoluble and/or slightly soluble degradation products are formed.[6] Aclarubicin is not stable at pH values less than 4.[3] Poochikian *et al.*[5] studied the stability of aclarubicin (128 μg/mL) in glass at ambient temperature (21°C) in 5% glucose (pH 4.5), 0.9% sodium chloride (pH 6.2), lactated Ringer's solution (pH 6.3) and Normosol-R (pH 7.4). The results showed that aclarubicin was more stable in 0.9% sodium chloride ($t_{90\%}$ = 108 hours) than in 5% glucose ($t_{90\%}$ = 88 hours), lactated Ringer's solution ($t_{90\%}$ = 72 hours) or Normosol-R ($t_{90\%}$ = 32 hours). These data indicate that the stability of aclarubicin is highly dependent on the pH of the medium.

In acidic solution the rate of degradation of the anthracyclines is strongly dependent on structural modifications in the amino sugar moiety.[7] As aclarubicin contains a trisaccharide, its rate of degradation is likely to be different to those of doxorubicin, daunorubicin and epirubicin, which all contain monosaccharides. However, there are no published data available to confirm this hypothesis.

In alkaline solution, the rate of degradation of the anthracyclines is affected by structural modifications in the aglycone portion of the molecule.[8] As aclarubicin possesses a unique aglycone, aklavinone, its stability in alkaline media cannot be predicted from existing data for other anthracylines. In addition, its poor solubility in alkaline solution may preclude stability determination under these conditions.

Effect of light: Data on the photodegradation of doxorubicin, daunorubicin and epirubicin have been published,[9,10] but there are no data available for aclarubicin. The rates of photodegradation of doxorubicin, daunorubicin and epirubicin have been reported to be similar, and may be substantial at concentrations less than 100 μg/mL if solutions are exposed to light for sufficient periods of time.[10] Exposure of very dilute solutions of aclarubicin to light promotes degradation.[1] At higher concentrations, such as those used for cancer chemotherapy (at least 500 μg/mL), no special precautions are necessary to protect freshly prepared solutions of doxorubicin, daunorubicin and epirubicin from light.[10] According to the manufacturer of aclarubicin, all reconstituted solutions should be protected from light.[1]

Effect of temperature: At ambient temperature (21°C), Poochikian *et al.*[5] observed that aclarubicin was chemically stable (less than 10% degradation) in 5% glucose, 0.9% sodium chloride, lactated Ringer's solution and Normosol-R for at least 48 hours. At 5°C, aclarubicin (2 mg/mL) has also been reported to be stable in 0.9% sodium chloride, water for injections and 5% glucose for at least 14 days when protected from light.[6]

Container compatibility: Aclarubicin appears to be compatible with polypropylene, PVC, EVA and glass.[4-6] Doxorubicin, daunorubicin and epirubicin are adsorbed on to glass but not on to siliconised glass or polypropylene.[11] Therefore aclarubicin may behave in a similar manner. In clinical practice, when aclarubicin is used at concentrations of approximately 500 µg/mL, adsorptive losses during storage and delivery are expected to be negligible.

Compatibility with other drugs: The manufacturer recommends that no other drugs are mixed with aclarubicin.[1]

3.2 Stability in clinical practice

Aclarubicin hydrochloride (2 mg/mL) appears to be chemically stable for at least 14 days in 0.9% sodium chloride, water for injections and 5% glucose at 5°C when protected from light.[6] However, the manufacturer recommends that reconstituted solutions should be used within 24 hours if stored at 4°C or within 6 hours if stored at room temperature and protected from light. If 5% glucose or 0.9% sodium chloride are used to dilute aclarubicin, their pH should be between 5 and 6.[1]

3.3 Stability in specialised delivery systems

No data are available.

4 Clinical use

Type of cytotoxic: Cytotoxic antibiotic interacting with DNA to interfere with nucleic acid synthesis.

Main indications: Remission induction in patients with acute non-lymphocytic leukaemia (ANLL) who are resistant or refractory to first-line chemotherapy. Aclarubicin may be used in combination regimens with other cytotoxic agents, but the dosage may need to be reduced.[1]

Dosage and administration: The dosage is usually calculated on the basis of body surface area. The manufacturer gives the following recommendations:

▼ In adults, including the elderly, the usual initial dosage is 175–300 mg/m² over 3 to 7 consecutive days – for example, 80–100 mg/m² daily for 3 days or 25 mg/m² daily for 7 days.[1] The maintenance dosage should be treatments of 25–100 mg/m² given as a single infusion every 3 to 4 weeks.[1]
▼ In children, experience suggests that aclarubicin is well tolerated at the standard dosage level.[1]

However, the dosage schedules should take into account the haematological status of the patient and the dosages of other cytotoxic drugs when used in combination. Aclarubicin should be used with caution in patients with impaired hepatic, renal or cardiac function. The total cumulative dosage administered should be decided according to the cardiological status of the patient. Most patients have received a maximum of 400 mg/m². However, larger doses have been used in some patients without ill consequence.[1]

5 Preparation of injection

Reconstitution: The contents of the 20-mg vial should be reconstituted with 10 mL of water for injections or 0.9% sodium chloride. After addition of the diluent and gentle shaking, the contents of the vial will dissolve to produce a solution of 2 mg/mL.[1] The pH of the reconstituted solution is 5.0 to 6.5.[3] To prepare an infusion solution, the required volume of reconstituted solution should be diluted with 200–500 mL of 0.9% sodium chloride or, if necessary, 5% glucose (with a pH value of between 5 and 6). The final concentration should be in the range 0.2–0.5 mg/mL.[1]

Bolus administration: In Phase I–II trials, aclarubicin has been administered by bolus injection.[12–14] However, the manufacturer recommends that aclarubicin is administered by intravenous infusion over a period of 30–60 minutes.[1]

Intravenous infusion: In Phase I–II trials aclarubicin has been given by short-term infusion using various schedules (20 mg daily for 7–14 days,[15] 0.33 to 0.70 mg/kg daily for 7–20 days[16] and 60 mg/m² daily for 5 days[17]). In another study, short-term infusion (10–30 mg/m² daily for 10–30 days) was compared with bolus injection (15 mg/m² daily for 10 days).[18]

Extravasation: Group 2 classification (exfoliant). Irritant (may cause inflammation and induration on extravasation, but is unlikely to cause tissue necrosis)[19–22] (*see* Chapter 6).

6 Destruction of drug or contaminated articles

Incineration: 1000°C.[1]

Chemical: 10% sodium hypochlorite (1% available chlorine)/24 hours.[6]

Contact with skin: Wash well with water, or with soap and water. If the eyes are contaminated, immediate irrigation with 0.9% sodium chloride is necessary.[1]

References

1 Association of the British Pharmaceutical Industry (1999) *ABPI Data Sheet Compendium 1999–2000*. DataPharm Publications Ltd, London.
2 Mori S *et al.* (1980) Physicochemical properties and stability of aclacinomycin A hydrochloride. *Jpn J Antibiot*. **33**: 618–22.
3 Medac GmbH (1995) Personal communication.
4 Krämer I and Wenchel HM (1991) Viability of micro-organisms in antineoplastic drug solutions. *Eur J Hosp Pharm*. **1**: 14–19.
5 Poochikian GK *et al.* (1981) Stability of anthracycline antitumour agents in four infusion fluids. *Am J Hosp Pharm*. **38**: 483–6.
6 Medac GmbH (1995) Chemical and pharmaceutical documentation. Unpublished information.

7 Beijnen JH *et al.* (1985) Aspects of the chemical stability of daunorubicin and seven other anthracyclines in acidic solution. *Pharm Weekbl (Sci Edn).* **7**: 109–16.

8 Beijnen JH *et al.* (1986) Aspects of the degradation kinetics of doxorubicin in aqueous solution. *Int J Pharm.* **32**: 123–31.

9 Tavoloni N *et al.* (1980) Photolytic degradation of adriamycin. Communications. *J Pharm Pharmacol.* **32**: 860–2.

10 Wood MJ *et al.* (1990) Photodegradation of doxorubicin, daunorubicin and epirubicin measured by high-performance liquid chromatography. *J Clin Pharm Ther.* **15**: 291–300.

11 Bosanquet AG (1986) Stability of solutions of antineoplastic agents during preparation and storage for *in vitro* assays. II. Assay methods, adriamycin and the other antitumour antibiotics. *Cancer Chemother Pharmacol.* **17**: 1–10.

12 Machover D *et al.* (1984) Phase I–II study of aclarubicin for treatment of acute myeloid leukaemia. *Cancer Treat Rep.* **68**: 881–6.

13 Mitrou PS *et al.* (1985) Aclarubicin (aclacinomycin A) in the treatment of relapsing acute leukaemias. *Eur J Cancer Clin Oncol.* **21**: 919–23.

14 Mitrou PS (1987) Aclarubicin in single agent and combined chemotherapy of acute myeloid leukaemias. *Eur J Haematol.* **38 (Supplement 47)**: 59–65.

15 Takahashi I *et al.* (1980) Treatment of refractory acute leukaemia with aclacinomycin A. *Acta Med Okayama.* **34**: 349–54.

16 Suzuki H *et al.* (1980) Phase I and preliminary phase II studies on aclacinomycin A in patients with acute leukaemia. *Jpn J Clin Oncol.* **10**: 111–17.

17 Rowe JM *et al.* (1988) Aclacinomycin A and etoposide (VP-16-213): an effective regimen in previously treated patients with refractory acute myelogenous leukaemia. *Blood.* **71**: 992–6.

18 Maral C *et al.* (1983) Aclacinomycin A: present status of experimental and clinical studies. *Drugs Exptl Clin Res.* **ix**: 375–82.

19 Warrell RP Jnr *et al.* (1982) Phase I–II evaluation of a new anthracycline antibiotic, aclacinomycin A, in adults with refractory leukaemia. *Cancer Treat Rep.* **66**: 1619–23.

20 Majima H (1980) Preliminary clinical study of aclacinomycin A. In: *Rec Results Cancer Res.* **70**: 75–81.

21 Spehn J *et al.* (1983) Aclacinomycin A in thyroid cancer. In: *Proceedings of the Thirteenth International Congress on Chemotherapy,* Vienna, Aug–Sept 1983, 211/63–211/66.

22 Bedikian AY *et al.* (1983) Phase II evaluation of aclacinomycin A (ACM-A, NSC208734) in patients with metastatic colorectal cancer. *Am J Clin Oncol.* **6**: 187–90.

Prepared by Jayne Wood

AMSACRINE

1 General details

Approved names: Amsacrine, AMSA, m-AMSA.

Proprietary name: Amsidine Concentrate for Intravenous Infusion.

Manufacturer or supplier: Goldshield Pharmaceuticals Ltd.

Presentation and formulation details: Orange/red solution of amsacrine in 2-mL ampoules containing 1.5 mL injection, 50 mg/mL amsacrine (75 mg/vial). The diluent vial contains 13.5 mL of 0.0353 M/L lactic acid solution. Amsacrine is dissolved in anhydrous N,N-dimethylacetamide (DMA). The diluent vial contains lactic acid in order to form the lactate salt of amsacrine when the drug is added to the diluent, under the acid conditions that prevail. The presence of DMA also prevents the formation of the gelatinous material that is normally seen in aqueous amsacrine lactate solutions.

Storage and shelf-life of unopened container: Three years at ambient temperature not exceeding 25°C, protected from light.

2 Chemistry

Type: Acridine-like DNA intercalating agent.

Molecular structure: 4'-(acridine-9-ylamino)methanesulphon-*m*-anisidine.

Molecular weight: 393.5.

Solubility: in water = 0.3 mg/mL

in DMA = 100 mg/mL.

3 Stability profile

3.1 Physical and chemical stability

Amsacrine is relatively stable in an aqueous vehicle, provided that reconstitution takes place in the presence of lactate ions, and the pH remains acidic. It is stable for 48 hours after dilution in 5% glucose.[1] As the drug is incompatible with chloride or sulphate ions, saline must be avoided as a diluent. The hydrochloride salt of amsacrine is poorly water soluble.

Degradation pathways: 9(10H)-acridone, 9-chloroacridine and 4-aminomethane-sulphon-*m*-amsidine are formed as degradation products.

Physical stability is not significantly affected by normal temperature ranges. The drug is light-sensitive. After dilution in 5% glucose at a final concentration of 150 μg/mL, amsacrine is stable during exposure to diffuse daylight or fluorescent light over a 48-hour period.[1] Since amsacrine solutions are relatively insoluble in water, DMA is included in the drug diluent to prevent precipitation when the drug is reconstituted.

It has been reported that DMA may increase extraction of components of rubber or certain plastic material.[2] Consequently, it is recommended that only glass syringes should be employed to transfer the drug concentrate to the diluent vial and from vial to infusion. However, this study only examined leaching from PVC infusion containers and administration sets. Most plastic syringes are composed of polypropylene barrels with rubber plungers, so this study is not relevant. The company points out that studies using the amsacrine/DMA solution in polypropylene syringes were not conclusive in demonstrating elution of these substances. However, contamination with such chemicals may affect the stability and toxicity profile of amsacrine, and glass syringes should be used for the initial steps in the preparation of the infusion. However, once diluted in 500 mL of 5% glucose, DMA is sufficiently dilute not to interact with plastic infusion containers, sets or lines.[3] One other problem that can arise is due to the effect of DMA on the physical performance characteristics of syringes. Experience indicates that amsacrine concentrate does not affect the physical performance of polypropylene syringes.

Compatibility information: No further information is available.

3.2 Stability in clinical practice

The reconstituted drug is stable in the diluent provided for 48 hours at room temperature and ambient lighting. It should be protected from exposure to strong daylight. Amsacrine is also stable after dilution in 5% glucose for 8 hours,[4] although there is evidence to indicate that such solutions are stable for 48 hours.[3,5]

Amsacrine must not be diluted in saline infusions.[4] If diluted in 5% glucose at a concentration of 150 μg/mL, it is not degraded during exposure to diffuse daylight or fluorescent light over a 48-hour period.[3] It has also been reported that amsacrine was not absorbed by PVC or polybutadiene-containing administration sets.[3]

3.3 Stability in specialised delivery systems

No data are available.

4 Clinical use

Type of cytotoxic: Inhibitor of DNA.

Main indications: Acute leukaemia.

Dosage: Induction of remission – 90 mg/m²/day for 5 consecutive days. In patients with impaired hepatic or renal function, reduce the dose by 20–30% (60–75 mg/m²/day). For maintenance use 150 mg/m² as a single dose, or 50 mg/m²/day for 3 days, repeated every 3–4 weeks.[4]

5 Preparation of injection

Dilution: Transfer 1.5 mL of amsacrine solution in DMA (in the ampoule) to the diluent vial, preferably using a glass syringe. The resulting solution contains 5 mg/mL of amsacrine.

Bolus administration: Not recommended.

Intravenous infusion: Add the required volume of diluted amsacrine to 500 mL of 5% glucose infusion. Infuse over 60–90 minutes. Problems of phlebitis are more likely to occur with higher concentrations, and the data sheet recommends dilution of 75 mg amsacrine in 500 mL 5% glucose solution.[4]

Extravasation: Group 1 classification (vesicant). This is very damaging, and there is no known antidote. Apply an ice-pack to the affected area (*see* Chapter 6).

6 Destruction of drug or contaminated articles

Incineration: >260°C.

Chemical: 10% sodium hypochlorite/24 hours (not recommended by the manufacturer).

Contact with skin: Wash with soap and water.

References

1 D'Arcy PF (1983) Reactions and interactions in handling anticancer drugs. *Drug Intell Clin Pharm.* **17**: 532–8.
2 Vishnuvajjala RB and Cradock JC (1984) Compatibility of plastic infusion devices with diluted N-methyl-formamide and N,N-dimethylacetamide. *Am J Hosp Pharm.* **41**: 1160–3.
3 Cartwright-Shamoon JM *et al.* (1988) Examination of sorption and photo-degradation of amsacrine in intravenous burette administration sets. *Int J Pharm.* **42**: 41–6.
4 Goldshield Pharmaceuticals Ltd (1999) *Datasheet and Package Insert.* Goldshield Pharmaceuticals Ltd, Croydon.
5 Trissel LA (2001) *Handbook on Injectable Drugs* (11e). American Society of Hospital Pharmacists, Bethesda, MD.

Prepared by Michael Allwood

ASPARAGINASE

1 General details

Approved names: Crisantaspase, Erwinia L-asparaginase.

Proprietary name: Erwinase.

Manufacturer or supplier: Ipsen Ltd.

Presentation and formulation details: White, freeze-dried powder in 2-mL rubber-capped vials containing 10 000 IU asparaginase. Each pack contains 20 vials.

Inactive ingredients are glucose 5.0 mg, sodium chloride 0.6 mg. 1 IU crisantaspase releases 1 μmol ammonia/minute from L-asparagine.

Storage and shelf-life of unopened container: Three years at 2–8°C.[1]

2 Chemistry

Type: Bacterial enzyme protein from *Erwinia chrysanthemi*.

Molecular weight: 130 000.

Activity: 700 IU/mg.

Solubility in water: Highly soluble.[2]

3 Stability profile

3.1 Physical and chemical stability

Stable in solution for at least 20 days at 37°C. Denaturation of the protein and loss of enzyme activity occur outside the physiological pH range (6–7.5).[3]

Degradation pathways: No information available.

Physical: Polymerisation of the reconstituted enzyme solution occurs after 15 minutes. Gelatinous fibres are produced. Enzyme activity is retained. Polymerisation is accelerated by contact with the rubber closure of the vial.[3]

Container compatibility: Stable in glass containers and glass or polypropylene syringes.[4] Avoid contact with rubber. No data on stability in plastic syringes, but most syringes contain a rubber plunger.

Compatibility with other drugs: The manufacturer recommends that asparaginase should not be mixed with other drugs.

3.2 Stability in clinical practice

Solutions should be administered as soon as possible after reconstitution, since gelatinous fibres form after 15 minutes. The supplier recommends a maximum shelf-life of 8 hours after reconstitution in glass or polypropylene syringes.[1] However, the effect is not progressive and does not affect the potency of the solution. Sterile solutions transferred to glass syringes retain potency for at least 20 days at 37°C.[4]

3.3 Stability in specialised delivery systems

No data available.

4 Clinical use

Type of cytotoxic: Therapeutic enzyme – not a true cytotoxic agent.

Main indications: Used in combination with other agents in treatment of acute lymphatic leukaemia and some other neoplastic conditions.

Dosage: 200 IU/kg body weight (6000 IU/m² body surface area) by intramuscular injection three times per week for 3 weeks.[1] Also refer to current MRC protocols.

5 Preparation of injection

Reconstitution: The contents of the vial should be reconstituted with 1–2 mL of 0.9% sodium chloride injection and dissolved with gentle mixing to avoid contact with the rubber stopper.

Administration: The intramuscular route is preferred, as it is associated with less risk of anaphylaxis. The solution may also be given by subcutaneous injection. Intravenous injection or infusion is rarely indicated, but may be used if necessary.

Intravenous infusion: Administration by infusion is not usually necessary. Asparaginase is stable for at least 7 days in solution in 0.9% sodium chloride and 5% glucose.[2] Enzyme activity may be adversely affected if the pH of the solution is outside the normal physiological range.[3]

Extravasation: Group 5 classification (neutral). Administration is usually by intravenous, intramuscular or subcutaneous injection. No harmful local effects will result from extravasation of solutions given intravenously (*see* Chapter 6).

6 Destruction of drug or contaminated articles

Incineration: Non-cytotoxic, no special precautions required.[1]

Chemical: Strong acids or alkalis denature the protein.

Contact with skin: Wash with water.

References

1 Ipsen Ltd (2000) *Summary of Product Characteristics – Erwinia.* Ipsen Ltd, Maidenhead.
2 Wade HE (1986) *Development of Erwinase (Erwinia asparaginase).* Lecture to symposium on Erwinia asparaginase in the treatment of leukaemia, Frankfurt, Germany, 21 November 1986.
3 Speywood Pharmaceuticals Ltd (1988) Personal communication.
4 Speywood Pharmaceuticals Ltd (1991) Personal communication.

Prepared by Michael Allwood

BLEOMYCIN

1 General details

Approved names: Bleomycin, bleomycin sulphate.

Proprietary name: Bleo-Kyowa.

Manufacturer or supplier: Faulding Pharmaceuticals plc., Kyowa Hakko UK Ltd.

Presentation and formulation details: Cream-coloured freeze-dried powder of bleomycin sulphate equivalent to 15 000 IU bleomycin in a clear glass ampoule. Contains no excipients.

Storage and shelf-life of unopened container: Store at room temperature and protect from light.[1] Shelf-life is 3 years.

2 Chemistry

Type: Anti-tumour antibiotic.

Molecular structure: Glycopeptide. The drug consists of at least ten components, the main ones being bleomycin A_2 and bleomycin B_2.[2]

Solubility in water: Very soluble.

3 Stability profile

3.1 Physical and chemical stability

Bleomycin is reported to be stable at room temperature in 0.9% sodium chloride, protected from light, for 28 days (data on file at company), equally stable at 2–8°C and less stable in 5% glucose.[2,3]

Degradation pathways: No information available.

Physical: Stable in pH range 4–10.[4] Light may cause bleomycin to break down.[1]

Container compatibility: Early studies suggested that bleomycin binds to PVC containers.[5,6] Subsequent work indicated that sorption does not occur, but adducts are formed in 5% glucose.[7] The stability of bleomycin in the following systems has been investigated by the manufacturer:

▼ 0.9% saline in an infusion bag (bleomycin 15 000 IU/100 mL)
▼ 5% glucose in an infusion bag (bleomycin 15 000 IU/100 mL)
▼ 0.9% saline in polypropylene syringes (bleomycin 60 000 IU/100 mL).

The stabilities of bleomycin A_2 and B_2 were evaluated after 28 days of storage at room temperature in the dark. Bleomycin was found to be relatively stable in 0.9% sodium chloride, with only 4% loss in infusion bags and 6% loss in plastic syringes. In contrast, a 54% loss occurred from the glucose solution in the infusion bag. It can be concluded that bleomycin is relatively stable in PVC containers and plastic syringes, provided that the diluent is 0.9% saline.

Compatibility with other drugs: Bleomycin is reported to be physically compatible with a range of other drugs in situations such as brief mixing in a syringe or in a simulated 'Y'-site injection.[4,8–16] It has been found to be incompatible with a number of drugs, including aminophylline, ascorbic acid, dexamethasone, diazepam, hydrocortisone sodium succinate, penicillin G, terbutaline, and any agents that contain sulphydryl groups.[4] Methotrexate and mitomycin, whilst appearing to be compatible in 'Y'-site studies, are not compatible in any stored mixture.[8]

3.2 Stability in clinical practice

The solution, after reconstitution in 0.9% sodium chloride, is stable for at least 7 days, if protected from light and stored in the refrigerator. After further dilution in 0.9% sodium chloride, in PVC containers, it is similarly stable. Bleomycin, 2000 IU/mL, in 0.9% sodium chloride, stored in PVC bags at 2–8°C is stable for 42 days.[17] Drug diluted in 5% glucose or glucose/saline appears to be unstable, and such diluents should be avoided.

3.3 Stability in specialised delivery systems

Bleomycin, 109 IU/mL, diluted in 0.9% sodium chloride and stored in Intermate or Infusor devices, is stable for at least 48 hours at room temperature.[18]

4 Clinical use

Type of cytotoxic: Anti-tumour antibiotic.

Main indications: Squamous-cell carcinoma, Hodgkin's disease and lymphomas, testicular teratoma, and malignant effusions of serous cavities.

Dosage: As a single agent, 15 000–30 000 IU twice or three times weekly up to a total of 100 000–500 000 IU, depending on the age and condition of the patient. Lower doses are used in combined therapy. For malignant effusions, a solution containing 60 000 IU in 100 mL 0.9% sodium chloride is employed.

5 Preparation of injection

Dilution: Dissolve dose in up to 5 mL water for injection or 0.9% sodium chloride (1% lignocaine may be used if pain occurs at the injection site – intramuscular use only).

Bolus administration: Inject slowly or via fast-running drip.

Intravenous infusion: Dilute in up to 200 mL 0.9% sodium chloride and administer slowly.

Extravasation: Group 5 classification (neutral) (*see* Chapter 6).

6 Destruction of drug or contaminated articles

Incineration: 1000°C.

Chemical: 10% hypochlorite/24 hours.

Contact with skin: Wash with soap and water.

References

1 ABPI (1999–2000) *ABPI Data Sheet Compendium 1999–2000.* DataPharm Publications Ltd, London, 697–9.

2 McEvoy GK (ed.) (1985) *American Hospital Formulary Service Drug Information.* American Society of Hospital Pharmacists, Bethesda, MD.

3 Anon. (1981) *Outline Guide for the Use of Cancer Chemotherapeutic Agents.* MD Anderson Hospital and Tumor Institute, University of Texas Cancer Center, Houston, TX.

4 Dorr RT *et al.* (1982) Bleomycin compatibility with selected intravenous medications. *J Med.* **13**: 121–30.

5 Benvenuto JA *et al.* (1981) Stability and compatibility of antitumor agents in glass and plastic containers. *Am J Hosp Pharm.* **38**: 1914–18.

6 Adams J *et al.* (1982) Instability of bleomycin in plastic containers. *Am J Hosp Pharm.* **39**: 1636.

7 Koberda M *et al.* (1990) Stability of bleomycin sulphate reconstituted in 5% dextrose or 0.9% sodium chloride injection stored in glass vials or PVC containers. *Am J Hosp Pharm.* **47**: 2528–9.

8 Cohen MH *et al.* (1985) Drug precipitation within IV tubing: a potential hazard of chemotherapy administration. *Cancer Treat Rep.* **69**: 1325–6.

9 Trissel LA and Martinez JF (1994) Physical compatibility of allopurinol sodium with selected drugs during simulated Y-site administration. *Am J Hosp Pharm.* **51**: 1792–9.

10 Trissel LA and Martinez JF (1994) Physical compatibility of filgrastim with selected drugs during simulated Y-site administration. *Am J Hosp Pharm.* **51**: 1907–13.

11 Trissel LA *et al.* (1991) Visual compatibility of fludarabine phosphate with antineoplastic drugs, anti-infectives, and other selected drugs during simulated Y-site injection. *Am J Hosp Pharm.* **48**: 2186–9.

12 Trissel LA and Martinez JF (1993) Melphalan physical compatibility with selected drugs during simulated Y-site administration. *Am J Hosp Pharm.* **50**: 2359–63.

13 Trissel LA *et al.* (1991) Visual compatibility of ondansetron hydrochloride with other selected drugs during simulated Y-site injection. *Am J Hosp Pharm.* **48**: 988–92.

14 Trissel LA and Bready BB (1992) Turbidimetric assessment of the compatibility of Taxol with selected other drugs during simulated Y-site injection. *Am J Hosp Pharm.* **49**: 1716–19.

15 Trissel LA and Martinez JF (1994) Physical compatibility of piperacillin sodium plus tazobactam sodium with selected drugs during simulated Y-site administration. *Am J Hosp Pharm.* **51**: 672–8.

16 Trissel LA and Martinez JF (1994) Visual, turbidimetric, and particle-content assessment of compatibility of vinorelbine tartrate with selected drugs during simulated Y-site injection. *Am J Hosp Pharm.* **51**: 495–9.

17 Faulding Pharmaceuticals plc (2000) Personal communication.

18 Baxter Healthcare Ltd (2000) Personal communication.

Prepared by Richard Needle

CARBOPLATIN

1 General details

Approved names: Carboplatin, JM-8.

Proprietary name: Paraplatin, Carboplatin.

Manufacturer or supplier: Bristol-Myers Squibb Pharmaceuticals Ltd, Faulding Pharmaceuticals plc.

Presentation and formulation details: Supplied in vials containing 50, 150 and 450 mg of carboplatin, as a 10 mg/mL solution in water for injections.[1] The solution has a pH of 5–7.[2]

Storage and shelf-life of unopened container: Stable for 18–24 months (depending on manufacturer) when stored below 25°C and protected from light.[1]

2 Chemistry

Type: Platinum-containing complex.

Molecular structure: *cis*-diamine (1,1-cyclobutanedicarboxylato) platinum.

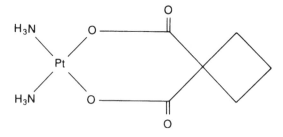

Molecular weight: 371.24.[3]
Solubility: 14 mg/mL.[3]

3 Stability profile

3.1 Physical and chemical stability

Carboplatin is relatively stable in aqueous solutions and its stability does not appear to be concentration dependent.[4,5] Degradation is accelerated by chloride and hydroxyl ions.[6] The $t_{95\%}$ (time to 5% loss) values for carboplatin in 0.9% sodium chloride and water for injections at 25°C are 29.2 hours and 52.7 hours, respectively.[6] The dilution of carboplatin in 0.9% sodium chloride is not recommended due to the increased rates of decomposition which have been seen, possibly resulting in the production of the more potent and toxic cisplatin.[4,5,11]

Degradation pathways: Carboplatin degrades by two simultaneous pathways, which are summarised in Figure 1[6] and can be described as follows:

▼ hydrolytic reactions which give activated platinum species.
▼ nucleophilic substitution with chloride or other nucleophiles.

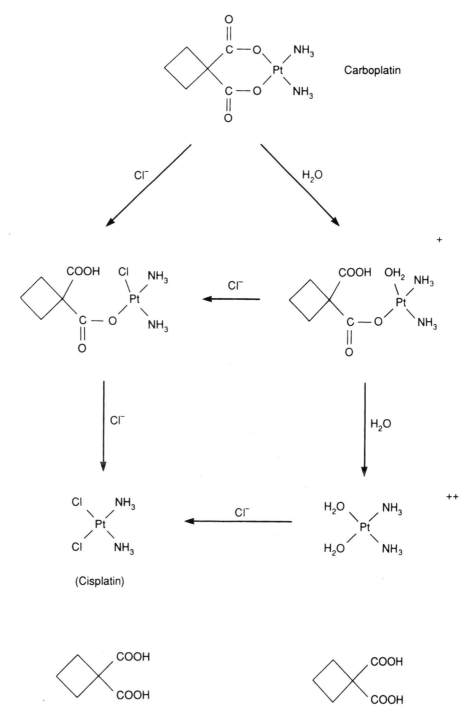

Figure 1: *Degradation pathways for carboplatin in chloride-containing solutions*

One degradation product is cisplatin.[4–6] The range of degradation products (some are intermediates) can include the following:

▼ monosubstitution with Cl⁻
▼ disubstitution with Cl⁻ (cisplatin)
▼ monosubstitution with water
▼ substitution with water and chloride ions.

Effect of pH: The pH of maximum stability has been reported to be in the range 4–6.5.[2,6] Degradation rate increases rapidly above pH 6.5.

Effect of temperature: see Table 1.[6,24]

Table 1: *The effect of temperature on the stability of carboplatin in different infusions*

Temperature (°C)	Concentration (mg/mL)	$t_{95\%}$ (hours) in:		
		0.9% Sodium chloride	Water for injections	5% Glucose
4	3.7	24.0	32.0	40
21	3.7	22.0	32.0	44
25	1.0	29.2	52.7	–
37	3.7	9.0	14.0	16

Carboplatin is stable when frozen at –25°C for 7 days.[5]

Effect of light: Light can affect the stability of carboplatin.[1,8] In studies, carboplatin solutions of 3.2 mg/mL and 0.8 mg/mL were exposed to various intensities of light compared to dark. Accelerated degradation was seen, with 10% of carboplatin degraded in 1–10 hours, depending on the light exposure.[9] It is concluded that under clinical conditions protection from light is necessary.

Container compatibility: Carboplatin is compatible with glass,[4,10] PVC,[11] plastic syringes,[12] polypropylene[10,13] and polyethylene.[10]
   Carboplatin reacts with aluminium, resulting in precipitation and loss of potency. Therefore care should be taken to avoid using aluminium-containing equipment when making and administering carboplatin solutions.[1,2]

Compatibility with other drugs: Mixing of carboplatin with any solution containing chloride ions can lead to accelerated degradation, and should be avoided if possible. Physical compatibility of carboplatin with etoposide,[2,14–16] cisplatin[2] and ifosfamide[2,14] has been reported.
   In the presence of a citrate buffer, a solution of 0.1 mg/mL carboplatin and 1 mg/mL fluorouracil in 5% glucose showed less than 3% loss of either drug after 48 hours at room temperature.[17] Fluorouracil is incompatible with carboplatin in the absence of a buffer.[2] Carboplatin is incompatible with bicarbonate[16] and mesna.[2,16]
   Carboplatin 2 mg/mL is physically compatible with paclitaxel 0.3 and 1.2 mg/mL for 7 days at 4°C and for 24 hours at 23°C and 32°C in 5% glucose.[18]

3.2 Stability in clinical practice

If diluted in water for injections or 5% glucose as directed, carboplatin is stable for at least 8 hours at room temperature or 24 hours when refrigerated.[1] Carboplatin solutions should be protected from light. Carboplatin 0.1 and 1 mg/mL in 5% glucose,

0.9% sodium chloride or a range of other infusion solutions is reported to be stable for 24 hours at 25°C. However, approximately 5% loss was seen in 0.9% sodium chloride, with the possibility of some cisplatin production. The stability of carboplatin 1 mg/mL in 0.9% sodium chloride at 25°C is supported by evidence of less than 1% degradation over 24 hours in normal light.[19] Despite this, the National Cancer Institute in the USA does not recommend using chloride-containing solutions with carboplatin.

Carboplatin 10 mg/mL stored in plastic syringes is stable for at least 5 days at 4°C, with no loss recorded over that period.[12] Lockich and Anderson report that carboplatin solutions of unspecified concentration showed less than 10% degradation for up to 7 days at room temperature (20–25°C).[14]

Carboplatin 0.5–4 mg/mL was tested over a 21-day period at 4°C and 25°C in PVC bags protected from light. All solutions were stable for 7 days at room temperature and for 21 days at 4°C with less than 1% loss.[7]

Carboplatin 10 mg/mL at room temperature and 4°C is stable in water for 7 days, and for 24–48 hours in 0.9% sodium chloride.[16] Carboplatin 2.4 mg/mL in 5% glucose is stable for 9 days in a PVC bag at room temperature if protected from light.[11]

3.3 Stability in specialised delivery systems

Carboplatin 1 mg/mL is stable for 14 days at 37°C and 4°C in water for injections stored in PVC reservoirs.[20] Carboplatin 10 mg/mL is reported to be stable with no degradation for 8 days at 25°C in polypropylene syringes for the Intelliject pump.[13] However, Sewell et al. found that 3.1% decomposition occurred at 37°C.[12] Carboplatin 1 mg/mL in 5% glucose was stable for 28 days at 4, 22 and 35°C in PVC infusion containers.[21] Carboplatin solutions of 6 and 10 mg/mL are physically stable for 14 days at 37°C in Deltec infusion containers.[22]

Carboplatin 0.5–10 mg/mL in 5% glucose infusion and stored in Intermate or infusor devices at 2–8°C is stable for 91 days, followed by 7 days at room temperature.[23]

4 Clinical use

Type of cytotoxic: The exact mechanism of action remains uncertain, but the drug has biochemical properties similar to those of alkylating agents.

Main indications: Carboplatin is used in the treatment of ovarian carcinoma of epithelial origin and small-cell lung cancer.[1] It is also used to treat other tumour types, including testicular[3] and bladder cancers.

Dosage and administration: Carboplatin is administered intravenously. The recommended dosage in previously untreated adult patients with normal kidney function is 400 mg/m² as a single intravenous dose over 15–60 minutes.[1] the Calvert equation may be used to calculate the dose of carboplatin in patients with or without renal impairment:[23,24]

$$\text{Dose (mg)} = \text{target AUC} \times (\text{GFR} + 25)$$

where AUC = desired area under the plasma concentration curve and GFR = glomerular filtration rate.

Recommended AUC values are 4–6 mg/mL for previously treated and 6–8 mg/mL for previously untreated patients. Target AUC values of 5 and 7 mg/mL are recommended for single-agent carboplatin in these respective patient groups.

Carboplatin should not be readministered until 4 weeks after the previous course. Dose reductions of 20–25% are recommended in patients with risk factors such as prior myelosuppressive treatment. Carboplatin is not recommended for patients with severe pre-existing renal impairment (creatinine clearance ≤20 mL/min).[1]

5 Preparation of injection

Bolus administration: Solution may be administered by slow intravenous injection over at least 15 minutes by infusion pump.

Intravenous infusion: Dilute 5% glucose or 0.9% sodium chloride to as low as 0.5 mg/mL.[1,2]

Extravasation: Group 3 classification (irritant) (*see* Chapter 6).

6 Destruction of drug or contaminated articles

Incineration: 1000°C.

Chemical: Dilute in large volumes of water, and allow to stand for 48 hours.

Contact with skin: Wash with copious amounts of water. If there is contact with eyes, wash with water or 0.9% sodium chloride and seek medical advice.

References

1 ABPI (1999) *ABPI Data Sheet Compendium 1999–2000.* DataPharm Publications Ltd, London, 240–1, 393–4.
2 Trissel LA (2001) *Handbook on Injectable Drugs* (11e). American Society of Health-System Pharmacists, Bethesda, MD.
3 Dorr RT and Von Hoff DD (1994) *Cancer Chemotherapy Handbook* (2e). Appleton & Lange, Norwalk, CT.
4 Cheung Y *et al.* (1987) Stability of cisplatin, iproplatin, carboplatin and tetraplatin in commonly used intravenous solutions. *Am J Hosp Pharm.* **44**: 124–30.
5 Bosanquet AG (1989) Stability of solutions of antineoplastic agents during preparation and storage for *in vitro* assays. *Cancer Chemother Pharmacol.* **23**: 197–207.
6 Allsopp MA *et al.* (1991) The degradation of carboplatin in aqueous solutions containing chloride or other selected nucleophiles. *Int J Pharm.* **69**: 197–210.
7 Amador FD *et al.* (1998) Stability of carboplatin in polyvinyl chloride bags. *Am J Health Syst Pharm.* **55**: 602–4.
8 Carballar R *et al.* (1997) Stability study of carboplatin in aqueous solution and under illumination by high-performance liquid chromatography. *Biomed Chromatogr.* **11**: 119–20.
9 Torres F *et al.* (1996) Stability of carboplatin in 5% glucose solution exposed to light. *Int J Pharm.* **129**: 275–7.
10 Prat J *et al.* (1994) Stability of carboplatin in 5% glucose solution in glass, polyethylene and polypropylene containers. *J Pharm Biomed Anal.* **12**: 81–4.
11 Benaji B *et al.* (1994) Stability and compatibility of cisplatin and carboplatin with PVC infusion bags. *J Clin Pharm Ther.* **19**: 95–100.
12 Sewell GJ *et al.* (1987) The stability of carboplatin in ambulatory continuous infusion regimens. *J Clin Ther.* **12**: 427–32.

13 Valiere C *et al.* (1996) Stability and compatibility study of a carboplatin solution in syringes for continuous ambulatory infusion. *Int J Pharm.* **138**: 125–8.

14 Lokich J and Anderson N (1995) Infusional cancer chemotherapy: historical evolution and future development at the cancer center of Boston. *Cancer Invest.* **13**: 202–26.

15 Salamone FR and Muller RJ (1990) Intravenous admixture compatibility of cancer chemotherapeutic agents. *Hosp Pharm.* **25**: 567–70.

16 Williams DA and Lokich J (1992) A review of the stability and compatibility of antineoplastic drugs for multiple-drug infusions. *Cancer Chemother Pharmacol.* **31**: 171–81.

17 Sewell GJ *et al.* (1994) Stability studies on admixtures of 5-fluorouracil with carboplatin and 5-fluorouracil with heparin administration in continuous infusion regimens. *J Clin Pharm Ther.* **19**: 127–33.

18 Zhang Y *et al.* (1997) Compatibility and stability of paclitaxel combined with cisplatin and with carboplatin in infusion solutions. *Ann Pharmacother.* **31**: 1465–70.

19 Perrone RK *et al.* (1989) Extent of cisplatin formation in carboplatin admixtures. *Am J Hosp Pharm.* **46**: 258–9.

20 Northcott M *et al.* (1991) The stability of carboplatin, diamorphine, 5-fluorouracil and mitozantrone infusions in an ambulatory pump under storage and prolonged 'in-use' conditions. *J Clin Pharm Ther.* **16**: 123–9.

21 Rochard E *et al.* (1994) Stability and compatibility study of carboplatin with three portable infusion pump reservoirs. *Int J Pharm.* **101**: 257–62.

22 Hadfield JA *et al.* (1993) The suitability of carboplatin solutions for 14-day continuous infusion by ambulatory pump: an HPLC-dynamic FAB study. *J Pharm Biomed Anal.* **11**: 723–7.

23 Baxter Healthcare Ltd. (2000) Personal communication.

24 Calvert AH *et al.* (1989) Carboplatin dosage: prospective evaluation of a simple formula based on renal function. *J Clin Oncol.* **7**: 1748–56.

Prepared by Paula Myers

CARMUSTINE

1 General details

Approved names: Carmustine, BCNU.

Proprietary name: Bicnu.

Manufacturer or supplier: Bristol-Myers Squibb Pharmaceuticals Ltd.

Presentation and formulation details: White, freeze-dried flaky powder in 30-mL-capacity vial, containing 100 mg carmustine, with diluent vial containing 3 mL absolute alcohol.

Storage and shelf-life of unopened container: Three years at 2–8°C; protect from light.

2 Chemistry

Type: Nitrosourea.

Molecular structure: N,N'-*bis*(2-chloroethyl)-1-nitrosourea.

$$CICH_2CH_2N \overset{\overset{\displaystyle NO}{\displaystyle |}}{-} \overset{\overset{\displaystyle O}{\displaystyle \parallel}}{C} - NHCH_2CH_2Cl$$

Molecular weight: 214.04.

Melting point: 27°C (Merck Index quotes 30–32°C).

Solubility: 4 mg/mL in water; 150 mg/mL in 95% ethanol.

3 Stability profile

3.1 Physical and chemical stability

Carmustine is relatively unstable after reconstitution. Its stability depends on a number of factors. The most important chemical factor is pH.

Degradation pathways (in aqueous solution):[1] BCNU degrades to:

2-chloroethylamine hydrochloride + acetaldehyde + nitrogen + carbon dioxide.
($Cl.CH_2CH_2NH_3HCl + CH_3CHO + N_2 + CO_2$).

Carmustine has a very low melting point (27°C according to the manufacturer,[2] although another source quotes 30–32°C).[3] The drug, if melted, liquifies to become an oily film in the base of the vial. The physical change may also be associated with decomposition and such vials must be discarded. There is slow decomposition at room temperature. One report suggests 3% degradation in 36 days.[4]

The manufacturer indicates that the reconstituted injection decomposes by zero-order kinetics.[2] Thus at ambient temperature this report anticipated losses of 6% in 3 hours, whilst at 4°C losses of 4% in 24 hours are to be expected (the pH of the reconstituted injection is 5.6–6.0).

Studies[5,6] indicate that carmustine is most stable in aqueous buffered solutions between pH 3.5 and 5.0. In more acid conditions, there is a small increase in degradation rate, whilst at pH values above 4.8 degradation rates increase rapidly.

For example, at pH 5.0 (buffer) $t_{95\%}$ = 5 hours (24°C) or 60 hours (4°C), but at pH 7.3 (buffer) $t_{95\%}$ = 40 minutes (22°C) or 9 hours (4°C). Degradation may also be accelerated by buffering agents, especially phosphates.[1] The pH will rise during degradation in unbuffered medium, causing an acceleration in degradation rate with time. It has been suggested that, because of the importance of pH, diluted solutions will be more stable in 5% glucose than in 0.9% sodium chloride.[6]

Effect of light: Fredriksson *et al.*[6] have shown that carmustine is relatively light-sensitive. Under artificial laboratory conditions using a light cabinet, the reaction rates at various light intensities were reported. Samples were placed in covered Petri dishes, not accurately reflecting degradation rates in practice. The authors reported a value for $t_{90\%}$ of 2.9 hours at an intensity of 1000 lux (a relatively high light intensity). The light-induced degradation rate is reduced in a bulk solution packed in a glass or plastic infusion container. Degradation may also occur during passage of the infusion through the administration set. Unfortunately, the data from this report cannot be used to predict the outcome of light exposure in practice, but they do indicate the need to protect the drug from light exposure during storage after reconstitution and dilution into infusions. In contrast, information summarised from the manufacturer suggests that the drug is stable for 8 hours at 25°C when exposed to fluorescent light.[2]

Effect of freezing: One report suggests that carmustine is stable in infusions when in the frozen state,[6] but further studies will be necessary to confirm this observation, since the evidence is somewhat conflicting.[7]

Container compatibility: Benvenuto *et al.*[8] indicated that infusions of carmustine in 5% glucose may be less stable in PVC than in glass containers. Some sorption to plastic containers (PVC Viaflex) was indicated. Losses of the order of 10% after 0.5–1 hour and 35% after 4 hours were evident (drug concentration = 1.25 mg/mL in 5% glucose at pH 4.4). However, these tests were performed in 50-mL bags; in 500-mL bags, the surface area to volume ratio is lower, so absorption rates may be reduced.

More recent studies[5] suggest that carmustine interacts with PVC, EVA and polyurethane administration sets, although no sorption to polyethylene was apparent. Tests under simulated infusion conditions from glass bottles suggest that if 500 mL of drug (0.20 mg/mL) are infused over 1 hour, about 4.6% (4.6 mg) of the dose is lost by sorption, but over 2 hours 6.5% (6.5 mg) will be lost.

However, all of these tests were performed at a drug concentration of about 0.2 mg/mL. No studies on the effect of drug concentration were reported. It is likely that the losses may be substantially reduced (as a proportion of the total dose) at higher drug concentrations.

The evidence therefore indicates that carmustine binds to some plastics, especially PVC, but the full clinical implications with regard to dose delivery from an infusion have yet to be fully quantified. In practice, it may be relatively unimportant.

Compatibility with other drugs: Carmustine (1.5 µg/mL) has been reported to be physically compatible with teniposide (100 µg/mL),[9] filgrastim (30 µg/mL)[10] and vinorelbine (1 µg/mL).[11]

3.2 Stability in clinical practice

After reconstitution in the vial the injection can be stored for up to 48 hours in the refrigerator. After dilution in up to 500 mL 0.9% sodium chloride or 5% glucose in glass or polyethylene containers, the resulting infusion may be stored for up to 48 hours in the refrigerator.[2] If diluted in an infusion in a PVC container, it should not be stored, but must be used as soon as possible.

Carmustine is unstable after addition to any infusion containing sodium bicarbonate (due to alkaline pH).

3.3 Stability in specialised delivery systems

No data available.

4 Clinical use

Type of cytotoxic: Nitrosourea, alkylating agent.

Main indications: Brain tumours, in combination therapy for multiple myeloma, Hodgkin's disease and other lymphomas.

Dosage: 200 mg/m² every 6 weeks as a single agent, but adjusted if necessary according to the haematological response. Lower doses are used in combination with other chemotherapeutic agents.

5 Preparation of injection

Dilution: To each vial add 3 mL diluent (absolute ethanol), dissolve the contents and then dilute with 27 mL water for injections. The resulting solution contains 3.3 mg in 1 mL of 10% ethanol. Dissolution may be faster if the vial and diluent are allowed to equilibrate at room temperature.

Bolus administration: Not recommended, but if it is essential, inject very slowly via the bolus site of a fast-running drip infusion.

Intravenous infusion: Dilute in 5% glucose (up to 500 mL), preferably in a glass or polyethylene (e.g. Polyfusor) container, and administer over 1–2 hours as a slow infusion. Protect the contents from light by covering the infusion with a light-protecting overwrap if infused over 2 hours or exposed to sunlight. Do not store in a PVC container, but use immediately after preparation. Non-PVC-containing sets are recommended.

Extravasation: Group 1 classification (vesicant) (*see* Chapter 6).

6 Destruction of drug or contaminated articles

Incineration: 1000°C.[2]

Chemical: 8.4% sodium bicarbonate solution for 24–48 hours.

Contact with skin: Wash with copious amounts of water. In cases of local irritancy apply sodium bicarbonate solution.

References

1 Montgomery JA *et al.* (1967) The modes of decomposition of 1,3-*bis* (2-chloro-ethyl)-1-nitrosourea and related compounds. *J Med Chem.* **10**: 668–74.
2 ABPI (1999) *ABPI Data Sheet Compendium 1999–2000.* DataPharm Publications Ltd, London, 238.

3 Trissel LA (2000) *Handbook on Injectable Drugs* (11e). American Society of Hospital Pharmacists, Bethesda, MD.
4 Kleinman LM *et al.* (1976) Investigational drug information. *Drug Intell Clin Pharm.* **10**: 48–9.
5 Lasker PA and Ayres JW (1977) Degradation of carmustine in aqueous media. *J Pharm Sci.* **66**: 1073–6.
6 Fredriksson K *et al.* (1986) Stability of carmustine – kinetics and compatibility during administration. *Acta Pharm Suec.* **23**: 115–24.
7 Bosanquet AG (1985) Stability of solutions of antineoplastic agents during preparation and storage for *in vitro* assays. General considerations and nitrosoureas and alkylating agents. *Cancer Chemother Pharmacol.* **14**: 83–95.
8 Benvenuto JA *et al.* (1981) Stability and compatibility of antitumour agents in glass and plastic containers. *Am J Hosp Pharm.* **38**: 1914–18.
9 Trissel LA and Martinez JF (1994) Screening for Y-site physical incompatibilities. *Hosp Pharm.* **29**: 1010–17.
10 Trissel LA and Martinez JF (1994) Compatibility of filgrastim with selected drugs during simulated Y-site administration. *Am J Hosp Pharm.* **51**: 1907–13.
11 Trissel LA and Martinez JF (1994) Visual, turbidimetric and particle content assessment of compatibility of vinorelbine tartrate with selected drugs during simulated Y-site injection. *Am J Hosp Pharm.* **51**: 495–9.

Prepared by Michael Allwood

CISPLATIN

1 General details

Approved names: Cisplatin, *cis*-platinum, *cis*-DDP, DDP.

Proprietary name: Cisplatin.

Manufacturer or supplier: Pharmacia & Upjohn Ltd, Faulding Pharmaceuticals plc.

Presentation and formulation details: Supplied as a yellowish-white freeze-dried powder in vials containing 10 and 50 mg of cisplatin with sodium chloride and mannitol (P&U); supplied as 10, 50 and 100 mL vials, each mL of solution containing 1 mg cisplatin, 9 mg sodium chloride and 1 mg of mannitol in water for injections (Faulding).[1] The solution has a pH of 3.7–6.[2]

Storage and shelf-life of unopened containers: Both the powder and the solution should be stored at room temperature (15–25°C) and protected from light.[1] Intact vials of the dry product are stable for 2 years when stored under these conditions.

2 Chemistry

Type: Platinum-containing complex.

Molecular structure: Planar molecule, with the platinum atom surrounded by two chloride atoms and two ammonia molecules in the *cis* position.

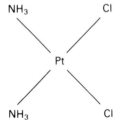

Molecular weight: 300.[3]

Solubility: 1 mg/mL in water.[3]

3 Stability profile

3.1 Physical and chemical stability

Cisplatin is unstable in an aqueous vehicle unless chloride ions are present in sufficient concentration.[4] Losses of 30–35% occur within 4 hours, or of 70–80% within 24 hours at room temperature in water.[2] Cisplatin becomes stable at sodium chloride concentrations of 0.3% or more,[5] with losses of only 2–3% over a 72-hour period at room temperature or under refrigeration.[2] An equilibrium is reached between cisplatin and chloride ions. In 0.9% sodium chloride, approximately 97% of cisplatin is still present at equilibrium.[2,6,7] This degree of degradation does not compromise therapeutic efficacy or toxicity profiles.

Degradation pathways: Cisplatin undergoes hydrolytic reactions in aqueous media at room temperature[8] (*see* Figure 2). The chloride ligand is displaced by water[4] such

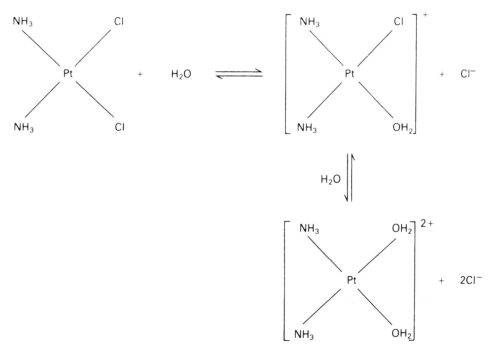

Figure 2: *Degradation pathways proposed for cisplatin*

that one or both chloride ions are displaced, forming mono- or diaqua- species, depending on the chloride ion concentration in solution.[2,7] The reaction is reversible. When enough liberated chloride ions accumulate in solution, the reaction reaches equilibrium and no further degradation occurs.[4]

Effect of light: Cisplatin is relatively sensitive to daylight, but reports have suggested that the drug is not adversely affected by normal room lighting after dilution in 0.9% sodium chloride.[6] However, more recent studies confirm previous reports of cisplatin decomposition after exposure to typical laboratory light,[2,9] with as much as 12% decomposition occurring within 25 hours.[2] This is confirmed by the manufacturer, who recommends that cisplatin solutions be protected from light or used within 6 hours if exposed to light.[1]

Effect of pH: The pH of maximum stability for cisplatin is 3.5–5.5.[2] Alkaline solutions, especially bicarbonate should be avoided because they adversely affect the stability of cisplatin, increasing hydrolysis[2] and in some cases causing precipitation.[6]

Effect of temperature: Cooling of cisplatin solutions may lead to precipitation, due to its limited solubility. Precipitation may be reversed by warming solutions to redissolve the cisplatin.[2] Precipitation of cisplatin was not observed when solutions in 0.9% sodium chloride at concentrations of ≤0.5 mg/mL were refrigerated for up to 72 hours, or when solutions of 0.6 mg/mL were refrigerated for up to 48 hours.[7] At a concentration of 1 mg/mL precipitation occurred within 1 hour. Cisplatin at 0.05–0.2 mg/mL in 5% glucose and 0.45% sodium chloride was stable for 4 days at 4°C plus an additional 48 hours at 25°C.[10]

Container compatibility: Cisplatin appears to be stable in glass,[4] PVC,[4,10] polyethylene[4] and polypropylene containers.[4] Cisplatin reacts with aluminium, and care should be taken to avoid contact of cisplatin solutions with equipment containing aluminium. Stainless steel is compatible.[2,11]

Compatibility with other drugs: Cisplatin at 0.05–0.2 mg/mL is compatible with magnesium sulphate at 1 mg/mL and mannitol at 18.75 mg/mL in 5% glucose and 0.45% sodium chloride for 4 days at 4°C plus 48 hours at room temperature.[10] However, it has been reported that advance mixing of cisplatin and mannitol can result in the formation of cisplatin–mannitol complexes after 2–3 days,[2,12] and therefore if mannitol is required it should be added immediately before administration. Cisplatin at 0.2 mg/mL and etoposide at 0.2 and 0.4 mg/mL in 0.9% sodium chloride or 5% glucose and 0.45% sodium chloride are stable when protected from light for 24 hours at room temperature, with less than 10% loss of either drug.[2,13] Cisplatin at 0.2 mg/mL and paclitaxel at 0.3 mg/mL is stable for 24 hours in polyolefin bags at 4, 24 and 32°C, but at a paclitaxel concentration of 1.2 mg/mL unacceptable losses of cisplatin were observed within 24 hours.[14] Cisplatin has been reported to be stable with fluorouracil.[15] However, studies have shown unacceptable stability, and the two drugs are regarded as incompatible.[2,16] Cisplatin has also been reported to be physically compatible with cytarabine,[15] cyclophosphamide, ifosfamide and ondansetron.[2]

3.2 Stability in clinical practice

Reconstituted or diluted cisplatin injections are stable if diluted in 0.9% sodium chloride for 20 hours at 25°C, but will precipitate on refrigeration.[1] Reconstituted solutions should be protected from light.[1,2,7] To avoid precipitation, only solutions of <0.6 mg/mL should be refrigerated and are stable at 4°C for 48 hours.[7] Solutions of <0.2 mg/mL are stable for 4 days at 4°C.[11] If precipitation does occur, the solution must be discarded.[17] However, infusions may be frozen at −15°C for up to 30 days and thawed at room temperature for 48 hours before use.[2]

Cisplatin at 0.6 mg/mL in 0.9% sodium chloride and in 5% glucose showed less than 4% loss after storage for 9 days at room temperature, when protected from light in PVC containers.[18] Cisplatin at 1 mg/mL in 0.9% sodium chloride is reported to be stable for 14 days at room temperature when protected from light.[18] Other investigators have confirmed a 14-day stability at room temperature for unspecified concentrations of cisplatin, with less then 10% losses reported.[19] Cisplatin at 0.16 mg/mL is stable for 14 days in 0.9% sodium chloride at 4, 20 and 30°C when protected from light.[4]

Cisplatin (Faulding) at 0.15 mg/mL in 0.9% sodium chloride in glass or PVC (Viaflex) containers stored at 4°C or 20°C and protected from light showed less than 5% loss after 14 days.[20] However, refrigeration is not recommended. Cisplatin (Faulding) at 50 µg/mL in 0.9% sodium chloride infusion, with magnesium sulphate at 1 g/L and potassium chloride at 20 mmol/L, in PVC (Viaflex) containers stored at 23°C and protected from light showed less than 5% loss after 7 days. However, solutions that were exposed to fluorescent light showed less than 5% loss after 24 hours, but losses were 10% after 48 hours.[21] In similar solutions of cisplatin containing mannitol at 15 g/L in place of magnesium sulphate, losses of cisplatin were less than 10% after 5 days.[20]

The stability of cisplatin solutions (at 1 and 1.6 mg/mL) in plastic infusion bags was studied for 14 days at 25, 37, and 60°C. No evidence of any decomposition was seen. However, some precipitation occurred in the 1.6 mg/mL solution at temperatures below 37°C.[21]

3.3 Stability in specialised delivery systems

Cisplatin at 1 mg/ml in 0.9% sodium chloride in the medication cassette (CADD-1 pump, Deltec, Pharmacia) stored at 25°C has been reported to be stable for 7 days, although 10% loss was recorded after 14 days.[22] Cisplatin is reported to be stable for 14 days at room temperature (20–25°C) if protected from light for use as prolonged infusions.[19]

4 Clinical use

Type of cytotoxic: The exact mechanism remains uncertain, but it exhibits biochemical properties similar to those of alkylating agents.

Main indications: Cisplatin is used for many indications either as a single agent or in combination chemotherapy. Its uses include the treatment of testicular, ovarian, cervical, lung and bladder tumours.[1]

Dose and administration: Cisplatin is used in many different dosage regimens. Schedules commonly used as a single agent include 50–120 mg/m^2 by infusion every 3–4 weeks, or 15–20 mg/m^2 by infusion daily for 5 consecutive days every 3 weeks. In combination chemotherapy the dosage may be adjusted to 20 mg/m^2 and upwards every 3 weeks.[1]

5 Preparation of injection

Reconstitution: Cisplatin powder should be dissolved in water for injections to give a 1 mg/mL solution. The manufacturer recommends that cisplatin solution should to be added to 2 L of 0.9% sodium chloride solution or a glucose/sodium chloride solution. The resulting infusion bag should be protected from light and stored at room temperature. In practice, volumes of less than 2 L are usually used for the administration of cisplatin.

Bolus administration: Must not be used.

Intravenous infusion: The manufacturers recommend that cisplatin solution be infused over 6–8 hours. Pre- and post-hydration are essential to induce diuresis during and after the cisplatin infusion in order to ensure adequate renal clearance of the drug. The manufacturer recommends 8–12 hours of pre-hydration and 24 hours of post-hydration. However, in practice a shorter period of hydration may sometimes be used.

Extravasation: Group 2 classification (exfoliant) (*see* Chapter 6).

6 Destruction of drug or contaminated articles

Incineration: 800°C.

Chemical: Dilute in large volume of water, allow to stand for 48 hours.

Contact with skin: Wash with copious amounts of water.[1]

References

1 ABPI (1999) *ABPI Data Sheet Compendium 1999–2000*. DataPharm Publications Ltd, London.

2 Trissel LA (1998) *Handbook on Injectable Drugs* (10e). American Society of Health-System Pharmacists, Bethesda, MD.

3 Dorr RT and Von Hoff DD (1994) *Cancer Chemotherapy Handbook* (2e). Appleton & Lange, Norwalk, CT.

4 Cubells MP *et al.* (1993) Stability of cisplatin in sodium chloride 0.9% intravenous solution related to the container's material. *Pharm World Sci.* **15**: 34–6.

5 Cheung YH *et al.* (1987) Stability of cisplatin, iproplatin, carboplatin and tetraplatin in commonly used intravenous solutions. *Am J Hosp Pharm.* **44**: 124–30.

6 Hincal AA *et al.* (1979) Cisplatin stability in aqueous parenteral vehicles. *J Parent Drug Assoc.* **33**: 107–16.

7 Green RF *et al.* (1979) Stability of cisplatin in aqueous solution. *Am J Hosp Pharm.* **36**: 38–43.

8 LeRoy AF (1979) Some quantitative data on *cis*-dichlorodiamineplatinum(II) species in solution. *Cancer Treat Rep.* **63**: 231–3.

9 Macka M *et al.* (1994) Decomposition of cisplatin in aqueous solutions containing chlorides by ultrasonic energy and light. *J Pharm Sci.* **83**: 815–18.

10 La Follette JM *et al.* (1985) Stability of cisplatin admixtures in polyvinyl chloride bags. *Am J Hosp Pharm.* **42**: 2652.

11 Bohart RD and Ogawa G (1979) An observation on the stability of *cis*-dichlorodiamineplatinum(II): a caution regarding its administration. *Cancer Treat Rep.* **63**: 2117–18.

12 Dorr RT (1979) Incompatibilities with parenteral anticancer drugs. *Am J Intrav Ther.* **6**: 42–52.

13 Stewart CF and Hampton EM (1989) Stability of cisplatin and etoposide in intravenous admixtures. *Am J Hosp Pharm.* **46**: 1400–4.

14 Zhang Y *et al.* (1997) Compatibility and stability of paclitaxel combined with cisplatin and with carboplatin in infusion solutions. *Ann Pharmacother.* **31**: 1465–70.

15 Salamone FR (1990) Intravenous admixture compatibility of cancer chemotherapeutic agents. *Hosp Pharm.* **25**: 567–70.

16 Stewart CF and Fleming RA (1990) Compatibility of cisplatin and fluorouracil on 0.9% sodium chloride injection. *Am J Hosp Pharm.* **47**: 1373–7.

17 Williams DA and Lokich J (1992) A review of the stability and compatibility of antineoplastic drugs for multiple-drug infusions. *Cancer Chemother Pharmacol.* **31**: 171–81.

18 Benaji B *et al.* (1994) Stability and compatibility of cisplatin and carboplatin with PVC infusion bags. *J Clin Pharm Ther.* **19**: 95–100.

19 Lokich J and Anderson N (1995) Infusional cancer chemotherapy: historical evolution and future development at the Cancer Center of Boston. *Cancer Invest.* **13**: 202–26.

20 Faulding Pharmaceuticals plc (2000) Personal communication.

21 Hrubisko M *et al.* (1992) Suitability of cisplatin solutions for 14-day continuous infusion by ambulatory pump. *Cancer Chemother Pharmacol.* **29**: 252–5.

22 Pharmacia Deltec Inc. (1991) Personal communication.

Prepared by Paula Myers

CLADRIBINE

1 General details

Approved name: Cladribine.

Proprietary name: Leustat.

Manufacturer or supplier: Janssen-Cilag Ltd.

Presentation and formulation details: 20-mL glass vials containing 10 mL solution. Each mL contains 1.0 mg cladribine and 9 mg (0.15 mEq) sodium chloride. The solution has a pH of 5.5–8.0. Phosphoric acid and/or dibasic sodium phosphate may be added to adjust the pH.[1]

Storage and shelf-life of unopened containers: Shelf-life is 24 months if stored at room temperature[1] protected from light. Freezing does not adversely affect stability. If freezing occurs, thaw naturally to room temperature. Do not use heat or microwave.

2 Chemistry

Type: Purine nucleoside analogue.

Molecular structure: 72-chloro-6-amino-9-(2-deoxy-β-D-erythropentofuranosyl) purine.

Molecular formula:

Molecular weight: 285.7.

Solubility: A stable white to off-white crystalline powder that is sparingly soluble in water. Dissolves more easily in 0.9% sodium chloride at 60–65°C. The pH of the injection is 5.5–8.0.[1]

3 Stability profile

3.1 Physical and chemical stability

Cladribine injection (1.0 mg/mL) stored at 2–8°C is stable for at least 18 months.[1] The drug solution has been found to lose less than 5% of activity in 7 days at 37°C. When diluted to a concentration of 0.15–0.3 mg/mL in 0.9% sodium chloride containing 0.9% benzyl alcohol as the preservative, the solution is chemically stable for at least 14 days.

3.2 Stability in clinical practice

Infusions of cladribine are chemically and physically stable for at least 24 hours at room temperature under normal room fluorescent light in PVC (Viaflex) infusion containers.[1] After dilution in 500 mL 0.9% sodium chloride infusion in PVC bags, cladribine is stable for 96 hours when stored at 2–8°C followed by up to 48 hours at room temperature.[2]

3.3 Stability in specialised delivery systems

Cladribine infusions have demonstrated acceptable chemical and physical stability for at least 7 days in Deltec (Pharmacia) medication cassettes.[3]

4 Clinical use

Type of cytotoxic: Antimetabolite.

Main indications: Active hairy-cell leukaemia. It also has activity in other haematological malignancies, especially advanced refractory chronic lymphocytic leukaemia and low-grade lymphocytic lymphoma.

Dosage and administration: 3.6 mg/m^2/day, repeated daily for 7 days. Its safety and efficacy have not been established in children, although clinical trials have employed doses of 3–10.7 mg/m^2/day for 5 consecutive days.

5 Preparation of injection

Reconstitution: Cladribine must be diluted in 0.9% sodium chloride prior to administration. The dose required is added to 500 mL 0.9% sodium chloride. The use of 5% glucose as a diluent is not recommended because of the poor stability of cladribine.[1]

Bolus administration: Must not be used.

Intravenous infusion: Continuous infusion over 24 hours. This procedure is repeated daily for 7 days.

Extravasation: Group 5 classification (neutral) (*see* Chapter 6).

6 Destruction of drug or contaminated articles

Incineration: No specific information available.

Chemical: No specific information available.

Contact with skin: No specific information available.

References

1 ABPI (1995) *ABPI Data Sheet Compendium 1995–1996.* DataPharm Publications Ltd, London.
2 Janssen Cilag (Switzerland) (1999) Personal communication.
3 Micromedex (1995) *Drug Evaluation Monograph.* Vol. 84. Englewood, CO.

Prepared by Yaacov Cass

CYCLOPHOSPHAMIDE

1 General details

Approved names: Cyclophosphamide, cyclophospham.

Proprietary names: Endoxana, Cyclophosphamide.

Manufacturer or supplier: ASTA Medica Ltd, Pharmacia and Upjohn Ltd.

Presentation and formulation details: Sterile, white powder in vials containing 107 mg, 214 mg, 535 mg or 1069 mg of cyclophosphamide BP, equivalent to 100 mg, 200 mg, 500 mg or 1000 mg, respectively, of anhydrous cyclophosphamide. Sodium chloride is also present to render the solution isotonic after reconstitution with the recommended amount of water for injections.[1,2]

Storage and shelf-life of unopened container: Five years if below 25°C and protected from light.[1,2]

2 Chemistry

Type: A cytotoxic which is converted in the body to an active alkylating agent with properties similar to those of mustine.[3]

2.1. Cyclophosphamide (Pharmacia and Upjohn Ltd)

Molecular structure: Contains 2-[*bis*(2-chloroethyl)amino]-perhydro-1,3,2 oxazaphosphorine-2-oxide monohydrate.

Molecular weight: 279.1.

Melting point: 49.5–53°C.[3]

2.2 Endoxana (ASTA Medica Ltd)

Molecular structure: Contains the anhydrous salt 2-[*bis*(2-chloroethyl)amino]-tetrahydro-2H-1,3,2 oxazaphosphorine-2-oxide, $C_7H_{15}N_2O_2PCl_2$.

Molecular weight: 261.08.

Melting point: 41–45°C.[4]

Solubility: Cyclophosphamide is soluble 1 in 25 parts of water and 0.9% sodium chloride.[3,5]

3 Stability profile

3.1. Physical and chemical stability

The manufacturer states that cyclophosphamide in 0.9% sodium chloride is chemically stable for 6 days at room temperature, and in 5% glucose is chemically stable for 48 hours at room temperature (25°C). However, as there is no preservative contained in the formulation, the above solution should be used within 8 hours unless prepared under strict aseptic conditions.[1] A review of the literature reveals that cyclophosphamide may be chemically stable for longer periods if stored at 4°C.

The loss of cyclophosphamide monohydrate from aqueous solution results from hydrolysis, loss of a chloride ion, or both.[6-9] Degradation follows first-order kinetics and is accompanied by a slight downward shift in pH which does not appear to affect the kinetics of drug loss. An increase in temperature accelerates the rate of breakdown, as can the presence of benzyl alcohol.[10]

Effect of pH: Hirata *et al.*[6] showed that the rate constant for drug loss at 75°C was independent of pH (pH 2–10). Outside these limits acidic and basic catalysis was observed. In solutions of pH between 2 and 14, cyclophosphamide degrades via a bicyclic compound and a number of secondary intermediates, to give N-(2-hydroxyethyl)-N′-(3-hydroxypropyl) ethylene-diamine.[7,11,12] Under more acidic conditions (pH ≤ 1) cyclophosphamide degrades via a different mechanism to yield *bis* (2-chloroethyl) amine and 3-aminopropan-1-ol.[6,12]

Effect of light: There are no published data which have systematically compared photodegradation of cyclophosphamide with degradation in identical solutions stored in the dark. Two studies have examined degradation in solutions of cyclophosphamide which were not protected from light. Gallelli[13] observed that cyclophosphamide at 4 mg/mL in 0.9% sodium chloride, stored in glass vials, exhibited 3.5% decomposition over a period of 24 hours at room temperature. Benvenuto *et al.*[14] observed that solutions of cyclophosphamide, 6.6 mg/mL in 5% glucose in both PVC and glass, were stable for 24 hours at room temperature. From these data it is difficult to draw conclusions about the effect of light on the stability of cyclophosphamide.

Effect of temperature: If heated above 32°C, cyclophosphamide may decompose to a damp-looking gel which should not be used.[1] The use of heat to speed up dissolution of cyclophosphamide is not recommended, as decomposition may result. [15]

Brooke *et al.*[10] observed a 2% loss of potency in a solution of cyclophosphamide at 20 mg/mL in glass vials after 4 days of storage at room temperature (24–27°C), and an 8% loss after 17 weeks at 4°C. The rate constants for drug loss recorded in that study were not significantly different for solutions reconstituted with water for injections, 5% glucose or glucose/saline admixtures.

Kirk *et al.*[16] studied the stability of cyclophosphamide in glass ampoules, polypropylene syringes and PVC infusion containers. In PVC infusion bags (Viaflex, Baxter), polypropylene syringes (Becton Dickinson, Plastipak) and glass ampoules, cyclophosphamide showed no appreciable degradation after 4 weeks at 4°C. After 19 weeks at 4°C, 5.7% and 8% degradation was observed in solutions stored in syringes and minibags, respectively.

Fleming *et al.*[17] studied the stability of admixtures of cyclophosphamide at 300 µg/mL with ondansetron at 50 µg/mL and cyclophosphamide at 2 mg/mL with ondansetron at 400 µg/mL in 5% glucose and 0.9% sodium chloride in PVC bags under fluorescent light at 4°C and at 25°C. The results showed that in both sodium chloride and glucose solutions cyclophosphamide at 300 µg/mL with ondansetron at 50 µg/mL was stable for 4 days at 25°C and for 8 days at 4°C. Similarly, admixtures of cyclophosphamide at 2 mg/mL with ondansetron at

400 μg/mL were stable in both sodium chloride and glucose solutions for 4 days at 25°C and for 8 days at 4°C.

Martel et al.[18] studied the stability of cyclophosphamide at 20 mg/mL in glass vials in water for injections when protected from light and stored at 4, 23 and 33°C. The results showed that it was stable (less than 10% degradation) at all three temperatures studied for a period of 12 months.

Beijnen et al.[19] studied the stability of two formulations of cyclophosphamide (Endoxan and Cycloblastine) at 20 mg/mL and 1 mg/mL in water for injections, 0.9% sodium chloride and 5% glucose in glass and PVC under normal cycles of fluorescent light/dark at 4, 20–22 and 37°C. The results showed that cyclophosphamide at 20 mg/mL was stable (less than 5% degradation) in water for injections at 4°C for 7 days in the dark. At higher temperatures, 10% degradation occurred after 7 days at ambient temperature, and 50% loss occurred after 7 days of storage at 37°C. Similar data were found in admixtures with 5% glucose and 0.9% sodium chloride and an initial drug concentration of 1 mg/mL. There were no significant differences in the chemical stability of dry-filled or lyophilised formulations.

The effect of freezing cyclophosphamide was also investigated by Kirk et al.[16] The results showed that in syringes, PVC minibags or glass ampoules no appreciable degradation occurred after 4 weeks of storage at –20°C. After 19 weeks, 4% and 8% degradation was observed in syringes and infusion bags, respectively. However, two problems were encountered with freezing cyclophosphamide. First, at higher concentrations (20 mg/mL) precipitation occurred during thawing. Although dissolution occurred after vigorous shaking, the possibility of injecting particles into the patient arises. Secondly, during freezing the integrity of polypropylene syringes was compromised by a marked contraction of the plungers, allowing seepage of fluid past the plunger and on to the inner surface of the barrel. Although this probably represents a negligible drug loss, the potential risk of microbial contamination is unacceptable. Therefore, freezing of cyclophosphamide in plastic syringes is not recommended.

The effect of thawing cyclophosphamide in a microwave has also been investigated.[16] The results indicated that during microwave thawing an uneven distribution of energy may occur and lead to overheating and consequent degradation. For this reason, thawing solutions in a microwave is not recommended.

Container compatibility: Cyclophosphamide is compatible with glass, PVC and polypropylene.[16] It is not adsorbed on to either PVC or polypropylene. Adsorption on to glass has not been documented. The type of container used for storage (glass or PVC) has no influence on the overall chemical stability of Endoxan and Cycloblastine at 20 mg/mL in the dark. However, in dilute solutions (1 mg/mL in 0.9% sodium chloride) exposed to normal fluorescent light in a day–night cycle after 7 days at ambient temperature, cyclophosphamide was stable in PVC (less than 5% degradation) but showed 10% degradation in glass. In PVC minibags containing 0.9% sodum chloride, cyclophosphamide at 1 mg/mL shows less than 5% degradation when stored at 7 days at ambient temperature in the dark. When exposed to normal fluorescent light at ambient temperature, solutions containing 1 mg/mL showed approximately 5% degradation in both glass and PVC. In clinical practice, when cyclophosphamide is used at concentrations of approximately 20 mg/mL, adsorptive losses during storage are likely to be negligible.[16]

Compatibility with other drugs: Cyclophosphamide is compatible with and may be infused in 5% glucose, 0.9% sodium chloride or mixtures of glucose and saline.[20] The manufacturers recommend that no other drugs are mixed with cyclophosphamide.

3.2. Stability in clinical practice

Cyclophosphamide is compatible with glass, PVC and polypropylene containers, and appears to be chemically stable for at least 28 days at 4°C. Solutions of cyclophosphamide should not be frozen.[16]

3.3. Stability in specialised delivery systems

Cyclophosphamide (2–20 mg/mL) is stable for 48 days in 0.9% sodium chloride at 25°C followed by 24 hours at 33°C in the Baxter infusor and Intermate device.[21] At a concentration of 20 mg/mL in water for injections it is also stable in the CADD pump for 14 days at 4°C and 24 hours at 35°C.[21]

4 Clinical use

Type of cytotoxic: Alkylating agent.

Main indications: As a single agent and in combination chemotherapy cyclophosphamide has been successfully used to induce and maintain regressions in a wide range of neoplastic diseases, including leukaemias, lymphomas, soft-tissue and osteogenic sarcomas, paediatric malignances and adult solid tumours – in particular breast and lung carcinoma.[2]

Dosage and administration: The dose, route and frequency of administration should be determined by the tumour type, tumour stage, general condition of the patient and whether other chemotherapy or radiation is to be administered concurrently. The following sample regimens may serve as guides.

▼ Low dose: 80–240 mg/m² (2–6 mg/kg) as a single dose intravenously each week or in divided doses orally.
▼ Medium dose: 400–600 mg/m² (10–15 mg/kg) as a single dose intravenously each week.
▼ High dose: 800–1600 mg/m² (20–40 mg/kg) as a single dose intravenously at intervals of 10–20 days.
▼ Higher doses should be used only at the discretion of a physician who is experienced in cytotoxic chemotherapy.

It is recommended that the dose of cyclophosphamide should be reduced when it is given in combination with other antineoplastic agents or radiotherapy, and in patients with bone-marrow depression. Cyclophosphamide should also be used with caution in patients with renal and/or hepatic failure.[2]

Cyclophosphamide is metabolised to the compound acrolein, which is toxic to the bladder. During treatment with conventional doses, a large urine output (a minimum of 100 mL/hour) should be maintained in order to avoid haemorrhagic cystitis. At higher doses a urine output of 100 mL/hour should be maintained for 24 hours after administration.[1] In addition, with single doses of cyclophosphamide over 10 mg/kg, intravenous or oral mesna should be given concurrently.[1]

5 Preparation of injection

Reconstitution: The contents of a vial are reconstituted with water for injections (5 mL per 100 mg of anhydrous cyclophosphamide). After addition of the diluent and vigorous shaking, the contents of the vial will dissolve to produce a solution of 20 mg/mL. Formation of a solution may be delayed because of the slow dissolution rate of cyclophosphamide in aqueous media. The pH of an aqueous solution is between 4.0 and 6.0.[2] Water for injections preserved with benzyl alcohol should not be used for preparation.[10, 22]

Bolus administration: Cyclophosphamide is usually given directly into a vein, over 2 to 3 minutes, or directly into the tubing of a fast-running intravenous infusion. Cyclophosphamide injection may also be given intraperitoneally or intrapleurally, but these routes offer no therapeutic advantage over the intravenous route.[1] Cyclophosphamide has been given intra-arterially and by local perfusion.[1]

Intravenous infusion: High doses of cyclophosphamide may be added to an infusion of 5% glucose, 0.9% sodium chloride or glucose/saline and infused over 1 to 2 hours. Both prolonged intermittent and continuous infusion of cyclophosphamide have been studied.[23-27] In a phase I study of a 72-hour continuous infusion, patients received from 300 mg/m²/day to 750 mg/m²/day.[25] Another study employed a 5-day continuous infusion at a rate of 400 mg/m²/day.[23] Protracted infusion of cyclophosphamide has been reported by Lokich *et al.*[27] at doses of 50–100 mg/m²/day for periods of 28 days or more.

Extravasation: Group 5 classification (neutral) (*see* Chapter 6).

6 Destruction of drug or contaminated articles

Incineration: 900°C.[4,28]

Chemical: 0.2 M potassium hydroxide in methanol solution for 1 hour or 5% sodium hypochlorite solution for 24 hours.[4,28]

Contact with skin: Wash well with water, or with soap and water. If the eyes are contaminated, immediate irrigation with 0.9% sodium chloride should be performed.[1,2]

References

1 ABPI (1999) *ABPI Data Sheet Compendium 1999–2000.* Datapharm Publications Ltd, London, 88–9.
2 ABPI (1999) *ABPI Data Sheet Compendium 1999–2000.* Datapharm Publications Ltd, London, 1175–6.
3 Reynolds JEF (ed.) (1996) *The Extra Pharmacopoeia* (31e). Pharmaceutical Press, London.
4 ASTA Medica Ltd (1999) Personal communication.
5 Dorr RT and Fritz WL (1980) *Cancer Chemotherapy Handbook.* Elsevier, Amsterdam.
6 Hirata M *et al.* (1967) Studies on cyclophosphamide. Part 1. Chemical determination and degradation kinetics in aqueous media. *Shionogi Kenkyusho Nempo.* **17**: 107–13.
7 Friedman OM (1967) Recent biological and chemical studies of cyclophosphamide (NSC 26271). *Cancer Chemother Rep.* **51**: 327–33.

8 Arnold H and Klose H (1961) Die hydrolyse hexacyclisher N-lostphosphamidester in gepufferten system. *Arzneimittel-Forsch.* **11**: 159–63.

9 Friedman OM (1965) Studies on the hydrolysis of cyclophosphamide. I. Identification of N-(2-hydroxyethyl)-N'-(3-hydroxypropyl) ethylenediamine as the main product. *J Am Chem Soc.* **87**: 4978–9.

10 Brooke D *et al.* (1973) Chemical stability of cyclophosphamide in parenteral solutions. *Am J Hosp Pharm.* **30**: 134–7.

11 Chakrabarti JK and Friedman OM (1973) Studies on the hydrolysis of cyclophosphamide. II. Isolation and characterization of intermediate hydrolytic products. *J Heterocyc Chem.* **10**: 55–8.

12 Zon G *et al.* (1977) High resolution nuclear magnetic resonance investigations of the chemical stability of cyclophosphamide and related phosphoramidic compounds. *J Am Chem Soc.* **99**: 5785–95.

13 Gallelli JF (1967) Stability studies of drugs used in intravenous solutions. Part 1. *Am J Hosp Pharm.* **24**: 425–33.

14 Benvenuto JA *et al.* (1981) Stability and compatibility of antitumour agents in glass and plastic containers. *Am J Hosp Pharm.* **38**: 1914–18.

15 Brooke D *et al.* (1975) Effect of briefly heating cyclophosphamide solutions. *Am J Hosp Pharm.* **32**: 44–5.

16 Kirk B *et al.* (1984) Chemical stability of cyclophosphamide injection. The effect of low temperature storage and microwave thawing. *Br J Parent Ther.* 90–7.

17 Fleming RA *et al.* (1995) Stability of ondansetron hydrochloride and cyclophosphamide in injectable solutions. *Am J Health Syst Pharm.* **52**: 514–6.

18 Martel P *et al.* (1997) Stability of the principal cytostatic agents during storage at unusual temperatures. *Int J Pharm.* **149**: 37–42.

19 Beijnen JH *et al.* (1992) Chemical stability of two sterile parenteral formulations of cyclophosphamide (Endoxan) after reconstitution and dilution in commonly used infusion fluids. *J Parent Sci Technol.* **46**: 111–6.

20 Trissel LA (2000) *Handbook of Injectable Drugs* (11e). American Society of Hospital Pharmacists, Bethesda, MD.

21 Baxter Healthcare Ltd (2000) Personal communication.

22 D'Arcy PF (1983) Handling anticancer drugs. *Drug Intell Clin Pharm.* **17**: 532–8.

23 Tchekmedyian NS *et al.* (1986) Phase I clinical and pharmacokinetic study of cyclophosphamide administered by 5-day continuous intravenous infusion. *Cancer Chemother Rep.* **18**: 33–8.

24 Solidoro A *et al.* (1981) Intermittent continuous IV infusion of high-dose cyclophosphamide for remission induction in acute lymphocytic leukaemia. *Cancer Treat Rep.* **65**: 213–18.

25 Bedikian AY and Bodey GP (1983) Phase I study of cyclophosphamide (NSC 26271) by 72-hour continuous intravenous infusion. *Am J Clin Oncol.* **6**: 365–8.

26 Smith DB *et al.* (1986) A phase II study of cyclophosphamide as a 24-hour infusion in advanced non-small-cell lung cancer. *Eur J Cancer Clin Oncol.* **22**: 435–7.

27 Lokich JJ and Botha A (1984) Phase I study of continuous infusion cyclophosphamide for protracted duration: a preliminary report. *Cancer Drug Deliv.* **1**: 329–32.

28 Pharmacia and Upjohn Ltd (1999) Personal communication.

Prepared by Jayne Wood

CYTARABINE

1 General details

Approved names: Cytarabine, arabinosylcytosine, ara-C, cytosine arabinoside.

Proprietary names: Cytosar, Cytarabine Injection Solution.

Manufacturer or supplier: Pharmacia and Upjohn Ltd, Faulding Pharmaceuticals plc.

Presentation and formulation details:

▼ Cytarabine Injection Solution is available as an isotonic solution in vials containing 20 mg/mL presented as 100 mg in 5 mL, 500 mg in 25 mL and 1 g in 25 mL. Cytarabine Injection Solution 20 mg/mL is suitable for subcutaneous, intravenous or intrathecal use.[1]

▼ Cytarabine Injection Solution is also available as a hypertonic solution containing 100 mg/mL presented as 100 mg in 1 mL, 500 mg in 5mL, 1 g in 10 mL and 2 g in 20 mL. Cytarabine Injection Solution at 100 mg/mL may be given by the subcutaneous or intravenous route, but it is not recommended for intrathecal use, due to the slight hypertonicity of the formulation.[1]

▼ Cytosar is supplied as an off-white, sterile, freeze-dried cake of 100 mg or 500 mg cytarabine in a vial. Cytosar is supplied as a single vial with diluent (water for injections) or as 10 vials without diluent.[2] It may be given by the subcutaneous or intravenous route, but is not recommended for intrathecal use.

Storage and shelf-life of unopened container: Vials of Cytarabine Injection Solution (Faulding Pharmaceuticals plc) are stable for 3 years at room temperature if presented in conventional glass and onco-tain vials and for 2 years if presented in shell-glass vials.[1] Vials of Cytosar are stable for 5 years if stored at room temperature.[2]

2 Chemistry

Type: A pyrimidine nucleoside analogue.[2]

Molecular structure: 4-amino-1-β-D-arabinofuranosylpyrimidin-2-(1H)-one.

Molecular weight: 243.2.

Solubility: Cytarabine is soluble 1 in 10 parts of water.[3]

3 Stability Profile

3.1. *Physical and chemical stability*

The manufacturer states that ampoules of cytarabine injection solution should be discarded within 24 hours of opening. When diluted with 0.9% sodium chloride or 5% glucose, infusion solutions of cytarabine are stable for at least 24 hours at 2–8°C.[1] After reconstitution the manufacturers recommend that Cytosar should be discarded immediately and not stored.[2] A review of the literature reveals that Cytarabine Injection Solution may be chemically stable for longer periods.

Effect of pH: In aqueous buffered solution cytarabine is broken down by hydrolytic deamination to uracil arabinoside.[4] Cytarabine is most stable in the neutral pH region, and has been calculated to retain 90% potency for 6.5 months in 0.06 M phosphate buffer, pH 6.9, at 25°C. The rate of degradation of cytarabine in alkaline solution is approximately 10 times as high as that in acidic solution.[5]

Effect of light: At a concentration of 5 mg/mL in Elliots B and Lactate Ringer solution, cytarabine exhibited no change in concentration over 7 days under fluorescent light, at room temperature and 30°C. In 0.9% sodium chloride, no decomposition occurred after 24 hours, but a 3% loss at room temperature and a 6% loss at 30°C was observed over 7 days.[6] Benvenuto *et al.*[7] studied the stability of cytarabine (2 mg/mL) in glass and PVC bags (Viaflex, Baxter) in 5% glucose, stored at room temperature and exposed to normal daylight. The results showed that cytarabine was stable for 24 hours. These data indicate that photodegradation of cytarabine is not significant.

Effect of temperature: Gannon and Sesin[8] studied the stability of cytarabine in glass and polypropylene syringes at 25°C and 5°C. The results showed that cytarabine (20 mg/mL) was more stable at 5°C in glass than in plastic. The maximum decrease in potency over the 7-day period of study in any of the containers was 2.9%. However, in that study cytarabine concentration was measured using an ultraviolet spectrophotometric assay. High-performance liquid chromatography (HPLC) is a more accurate, specific and reliable method of quantitation of drug concentration. The authors of that study indicated that further research was warranted using HPLC to confirm the overall stability of cytarabine.

Munson *et al.*[9] studied the stability of cytarabine in 5% glucose and glucose/saline in glass and PVC containers, with added sodium bicarbonate, at 8 and 22°C. Stability in water for injections in plastic syringes (Pharmaseal) was also studied at 22, 8 and –10°C. The results showed that in plastic syringes, cytarabine at 20 mg/mL and 50 mg/mL was chemically stable for 1 week at all temperatures studied. The addition of sodium bicarbonate at 50 mEq/L to solutions had no effect on the chemical stability of cytarabine for at least 1 week either at 22°C or at 8°C.[9] Weir and Ireland[10] observed that cytarabine (100 mg in 5 mL, 500 mg in 10 mL and 1 g in 20 mL) in polypropylene syringes was chemically stable for at least 30 days at 4°C and 21°C.

Kirk *et al.*[11] noted that freezing cyclophosphamide in polypropylene syringes resulted in contraction of the plunger and seepage of the drug past the barrel. Although this probably represents a negligible drug loss, the potential risk of microbial contamination is unacceptable. For this reason, freezing of cytarabine in polypropylene syringes is not recommended.

Stewart *et al.*[12] studied the stability of admixtures of cytarabine and ondansetron in 5% glucose in PVC infusion bags at 23°C under fluorescent light. The results showed that cytarabine (200 µg/mL) with ondansetron (30 µg/mL) and cytarabine (40 mg/mL) with ondansetron (300 µg/mL) were stable for 48 hours.

Container compatibility: Cytarabine is compatible with glass, PVC and poly-propylene.[8,9] Adsorption of cytarabine on to glass has not been documented. In clinical practice, when cytarabine is used at concentrations between 500 µg/mL and 20 mg/mL, adsorptive losses during storage and delivery are likely to be negligible.

Compatibility with other drugs: Compatibility depends on several factors, including the drug concentration, diluent, pH and temperature. Cytarabine appears to be physically incompatible with 5-fluorouracil and heparin sodium, gentamicin, hydrocortisone sodium succinate, methylprednisolone and benzylpenicillin.[1,13] The manufacturers recommend that no other drugs should be mixed with cytarabine.

3.2. Stability in clinical practice

Cytarabine is compatible with glass, PVC and polypropylene.[8,9] Cytarabine appears to be chemically stable for at least 1 week in two-piece syringes (Pharmaseal[9] and Becton Dickinson Plastipak[10]) and possibly 1 month,[14] when reconstituted with water for injections, 5% glucose and/or sodium chloride and stored at 2–8°C. It is important to note that bacterially contaminated intrathecal injections could pose very grave risks. Consequently, such solutions should be administered as soon as possible after reconstitution.[15]

3.3. Stability in specialised delivery systems

Cytarabine (20 mg/mL) is stable in 0.9% sodium chloride in the CADD pump for 14 days at 4°C.[16] Cytarabine (25 and 1.25 mg/mL in 0.9% sodium chloride and 5% dextrose) is stable in 80-mL EVA reservoirs (RES80 A, Celsa Laboratories, Chasseneuil, France) for 28 days at 4 and 22°C and for 7 days at 35°C.[16] Cytarabine (5 mg/mL) is stable when diluted in 5% glucose and stored in Baxter infusors and Intermate devices for 7 days at 25°C followed by 24 hours at 33°C.[17] Cytarabine (1 mg/mL in Elliots B solution) showed no appreciable drug decomposition when stored for up to 15 days in an Infusaid Model 400 implantable pump at 37°C.[18]

4 Clinical use

Type of cytotoxic: Antimetabolite which interacts with DNA to prevent cell division.

Main indications: Induction of clinical remission and/or maintenance therapy in patients with acute myeloid leukaemia, acute non-lymphoblastic leukaemias, acute lymphoblastic leukaemias, blast crises of chronic myeloid leukaemia and diffuse histiocytic lymphomas (non-Hodgkin's lymphomas of high malignancy).[1]

Dosage and administration:

Remission induction – continuous dosing: For remission induction the usual dose is 2 mg/kg daily for 10 days. If after 10 days neither a therapeutic response nor toxicity has been observed, the dose may be increased to 4 mg/kg. Alternatively, 0.5–1 mg/kg may be given as an infusion of up to 24 hours' duration for 10 days, and then an infusion at a rate of 2 mg/kg/day until toxicity is observed.[1,2]

Remission induction – intermittent dosing: administer 3–5 mg/kg daily for 5 consecutive days. This course may be repeated every 2–9 days until either a therapeutic response or toxicity occurs.[1,2]

Maintenance therapy:

▼ Leukaemias: 1–1.5 mg/kg once or twice weekly.
▼ CNS leukaemias: 10–30 mg/m² three times weekly, intrathecally.

5 Preparation of injection

Reconstitution: The contents of the vial (Cytosar) may be reconstituted with water for injections, 0.9% sodium chloride or 5% glucose. When reconstituted with the accompanying diluent (water for injections) gentle shaking of the vial will produce a solution containing 20 mg/mL (100-mg vial) or 50 mg/mL (500-mg vial) of cytarabine.

Bolus administration: Cytarabine Injection Solution at 20 mg/mL may be administered by intravenous, intrathecal or subcutaneous injection. For intrathecal injection it is recommended that 5–8 mL of cerebrospinal fluid (CSF) should be drawn up, mixed with the injection solution in the syringe and slowly re-injected.[1] Intrathecal use of Cytarabine Injection Solution at 100 mg/mL is contraindicated due to slight hypertonicity of the formulation.[1] Cytarabine (Cytosar) may be administered by intravenous or subcutaneous injection.[2]

Intravenous infusion: Continuous infusions of cytarabine have ranged from 8–12 hours to 120–168 hours.[1,19] Kreis *et al.*[20] investigated a low-dose infusion given over 21 days. Slevin *et al.*[21] compared intravenous and subcutaneous infusions. The results in that study showed that subcutaneous infusion was well tolerated without any local discomfort or excoriation. Continuous infusions (compared to bolus doses) show more pronounced gastrointestinal side-effects.[1]

Intrathecal administration: If the intended route of administration is intrathecal, please refer to Chapter 6 with regard to the prescribing, dispensing, labelling and issuing of this drug.

Extravasation: Group 5 classification (neutral) (*see* Chapter 6).

6 Destruction of drugs or contaminated articles

Incineration: 1000°C.[10,22]

Chemical: Hydrochloric acid for 24 hours.[10,22]

Contact with skin: Wash well with water, or with soap and water. If the eyes are contaminated, immediate irrigation with 0.9% sodium chloride should be performed.[10,22]

References

1 ABPI (1999) *ABPI Data Sheet Compendium 1999–2000*. DataPharm Publications Ltd, London, 396–8.
2 ABPI (1999) *ABPI Data Sheet Compendium 1999–2000*. DataPharm Publications Ltd, London, 1177–8.

3 Reynolds JEF (ed.) (1996) *The Extra Pharmacopoeia* (31e). Pharmaceutical Press, London.

4 Notari RE (1967) A mechanism for the hydrolytic deamination of cytosine arabinoside in aqueous buffer. *J Pharm Sci.* **56**: 804–9.

5 Notari RE *et al.* (1972) Arabinosylcytosine stability in aqueous solutions: pH profile and shelf-life predictions. *J Pharm Sci.* **61**: 1189–96.

6 Cradock JC *et al.* (1978) Evaluation of some pharmaceutical aspects of intrathecal methotrexate sodium, cytarabine and hydrocortisone sodium succinate. *Am J Hosp Pharm.* **35**: 402–6.

7 Benvenuto JA *et al.* (1981) Stability and compatibility of antitumour agents in glass and plastic containers. *Am J Hosp Pharm.* **38**: 1914–18.

8 Gannon PM and Sesin GP (1983) Stability of cytarabine following repackaging in plastic syringes and glass containers. *Am J Int Ther Clin Nutr.* **10**: 11–16.

9 Munson JW *et al.* (1982) Cytosine arabinoside stability in intravenous admixtures with sodium bicarbonate and in plastic syringes. *Drug Intell Clin Pharm.* **16**: 765–7.

10 Weir PJ and Ireland DS (1990) Chemical stability of cytarabine and vinblastine injection. *Br J Pharm Pract.* **12**: 53–6.

11 Kirk B *et al.* (1984) Chemical stability of cyclophosphamide injection: the effect of low-temperature storage and microwave thawing. *Br J Parent Ther.* 90–7.

12 Stewart JT *et al.* (1996) Stability of ondansetron hydrochloride and five antineoplastic medications. *Am J Health-Syst Pharm.* **53**: 1297–300.

13 Trissel LA (1996) *Handbook of Injectable Drugs* (9e). American Society of Hospital Pharmacists, Bethesda, MD.

14 Faulding Pharmaceuticals plc (1999) Personal communication.

15 Sarubbi FA *et al.* (1978) Nosocomial meningitis and bacteraemia due to contaminated amphotericin B. *JAMA.* **35**: 402–6.

16 Rochard EB *et al.* (1992) Stability of fluorouracil, cytarabine or doxorubicin hydrochloride in ethylene vinylacetate portable infusion-pump reservoirs. *Am J Hosp Pharm.* **49**: 619–23.

17 Baxter Healthcare Ltd (2000) Personal communication.

18 Keller JH and Ensminger WD (1982) Stability of cancer chemotherapy agents in a totally implanted pump drug delivery system. *Am J Hosp Pharm.* **39**: 1321–3.

19 Spriggs DR *et al.* (1985) Continuous infusion of high-dose cytarabine: a phase I and pharmacological study. *Cancer Res.* **45**: 3932–6.

20 Kreis W *et al.* (1985) Pharmacokinetics of low dose 1-β-D arabinofuranosylcytosine given by continuous IV infusion over 21 days. *Cancer Res.* **45**: 6498–501.

21 Slevin ML *et al.* (1983) Subcutaneous infusion of cytosine arabinoside – a practical alternative to intravenous infusion. *Cancer Chemother Pharmacol.* **10**: 112–4.

22 Pharmacia and Upjohn Ltd (1999) Personal communication.

Prepared by Jayne Wood

DACARBAZINE

1 General details

Approved name: Dacarbazine.

Proprietary name: DTIC-Dome, Dacarbazine.

Manufacturer or supplier: Medac GmbH, Faulding Pharmaceuticals plc.

Presentation and formulation details: A colourless or ivory-coloured powder in amber glass vials containing 100 mg or 200 mg dacarbazine as the citrate salt. The 100-mg vial containss 100 mg citric acid and 50 mg mannitol. The 200-mg vial contains 100 mg citric acid and 37.5 mg mannitol. The vials do not contain any preservatives.[1]

Storage and shelf-life of unopened container: Three years stored at 2–8°C and protected from light.[1]

2 Chemistry

Type: Triazene, alkylating agent.

Molecular structure: 5-(3,3-dimethyl-1-triazenyl)-1H-imidazole-4-carboxamide.

Molecular weight: 182.2.

Solubility: 1 mg/mL in water and 60 mg/mL in 10% citric acid.

3 Stability profile

3.1 Physical and chemical stability

Although the manufacturer recommends that reconstituted solutions should be stored at room temperature in normal light and used within 8 hours (or 72 hours if stored at 4°C), it has been reported that solutions are stable for at least 24 hours at room temperature, and for 96 hours under refrigeration when protected from light.[2]

Effect of light: Dacarbazine is very light sensitive.[3,4] Exposure to sunlight causes rapid degradation.[3] However, exposure to artificial fluorescent light or diffuse daylight is far less detrimental. A detailed study at 4 mg/mL in 0.9% sodium chloride showed that approximately 4–6% losses were recorded over 24 hours during administration under conditions of normal room light (diffuse daylight and fluorescent light), whilst solutions that were exposed to strong daylight showed losses of 12% in 30 minutes.[2,3] Photodegradation is indicated by a colour change from yellow to pink.[2,5]

The breakdown products of dacarbazine when exposed to light are thought to contribute to its infusion-related adverse effects, including pain on administration, although this has not been confirmed.[4] Lighting the room with only a red photographic lamp was reported to decrease the incidence of these adverse effects.

Degradation pathways: Horton and Stevens[5] have investigated the degradation route of dacarbazine in solutions of different pH, either exposed to daylight or maintained in the dark (*see* Figure 3). The principal degradation products are 5-diazoimidazole-4-carboxamide (DIAZO-IC: II), 2-azahypoxanthine (III), a metastable intermediate carbene moiety (IV) and 4-carbamoylimidazolium-5-olate (V). The primary degradation product of photolysis is DIAZO-IC. Further degradation then occurs to conjugated polymers, which give rise to the pink coloration.

Container compatibility: Dacarbazine is compatible with PVC containers and administration sets, and with Amberset (Avon Medical Ltd).[3] No loss or degradation was evident when dacarbazine was stored in PVC infusion bags and administered through PVC infusion sets over 1 hour at a concentration of 1.2 mg/mL at room temperature while protected from light.[6] There is no further information on the compatibility of dacarbazine with other delivery systems, such as plastic syringes.[7]

Compatibility with other drugs: A white precipitate formed immediately when dacarbazine (25 mg/mL) in 0.9% sodium chloride was flushed with heparin sodium (100 U/mL).[1,8] A precipitate did not form with dacarbazine at 10 mg/mL.[2,8] Dacarbazine forms an immediate precipitate with hydrocortisone sodium succinate,[1,2] but not with hydrocortisone sodium phosphate or lignocaine 1–2%.[2]

Dacarbazine at 4 mg/mL has been shown to be compatible at a Y-site with amifostine (10 mg/mL), filgrastim (30 µg/mL), fludarabine (1 mg/mL), ondansetron (1 mg/mL), paclitaxel (1.2 mg/mL), sargramostim (10 µg/mL), teniposide (0.1 mg/mL), thiotepa (1 mg/mL) and vinorelbine tartrate (1 mg/mL) for 4 hours at room temperature.[2] Dacarbazine (4 mg/mL) is also compatible with melphalan (0.1 mg/mL) for 3 hours at 22°C, and at a concentration of 1.7 mg/mL is compatible with granisetron (1 mg/mL) for 4 hours at 22°C.[2]

Dacarbazine is also reported to be compatible with bleomycin, carmustine, cyclophosphamide, cytarabine, dactinomycin, doxorubicin, fluorouracil, mercaptopurine, methotrexate and vinblastine, although no specific details are available.[9]

3.2 Stability in clinical practice

After reconstitution with water for injections the resulting 10 mg/mL solution is stable for 96 hours at 4°C if protected from light, or for 24 hours at normal room temperature.[1,2] When further diluted in 5% glucose or 0.9% sodium chloride, dacarbazine is stable for 8 hours at room temperature,[2] or for 24 hours at 2–8°C.[1,2]

Dacarbazine for Injection BP (Faulding), 100 mg reconstituted in water for injections in amber glass vials to a nominal concentration of 10 mg/mL and stored at 4°C and protected from light, showed less than 5% loss after 4 days of storage.[10]

Dacarbazine is very sensitive to UV light, and all unnecessary exposure to daylight should be avoided. During administration the infusion container should be protected from light. The use of a UV-light-protecting administration set should be recommended for administration in daylight conditions.[3]

3.3 Stability in specialised delivery systems

No information available.[7]

4 Clinical use

Type of cytotoxic: Alkylating agent.

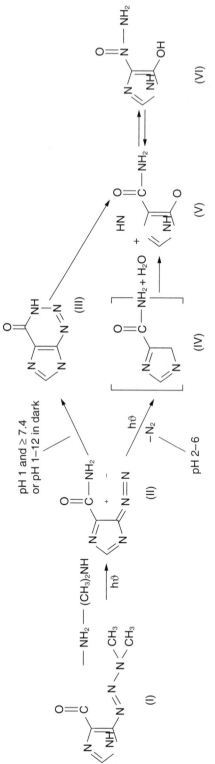

Figure 3: *The degradation route of dacarbazine (DTIC) in solutions of different pH, either exposed to daylight or maintained in the dark*

Main indications: As a single agent in metastatic malignant melanoma, sarcoma and Hodgkin's disease, or in combination with other drugs for carcinoma of the colon, ovary, breast, lung, testicular teratoma and some solid tumours in children.[1]

Dosage and administration: 2–4.5 mg/kg/day for 10 days repeated every 28 days;[1] 250 mg/m²/day for 5 days repeated every 21 days.[1] Other dosage regimens have been used.

5 Preparation of injection

Reconstitution: The 100-mg vial is reconstituted with 9.9 mL of water for injections, and the 200-mg vial with 19.7 mL. Both give a final concentration of 10 mg/mL and a pH of 3.0 and 4.0, respectively.[1]

Bolus administration: Inject IV slowly over 1–2 minutes.[1]

Intravenous infusion: Dilute in 125–250 mL 0.9% sodium chloride or 5% glucose and infuse over 15–30 minutes.[1]

Extravasation: Group 1 classification (vesicant) (*see* Chapter 6).

6 Destruction of drug or contaminated articles

Incineration: 500°C.[7]

Chemical: 10% sulphuric acid for 24 hours.[2]

Contact with skin: Wash with water.[7]

References

1 ABPI (1999) *ABPI Data Sheet Compendium 1999–2000.* DataPharm Publications Ltd, London, 168–9, 358–9, 283–4.

2 Trissel LA (2000) *Handbook on Injectable Drugs* (11e). American Society of Health-System Pharmacists, Bethesda, MD.

3 Kirk B (1987) The evaluation of a light-protecting giving set. *Intens Ther Clin Monitor.* **8**: 78–86.

4 Baird GM and Willoughby MLN (1978) Photodegradation of dacarbazine. *Lancet.* **ii**: 681.

5 Horton JK and Stevens MFG (1981) A new light on the photo-decomposition of the antitumour drug DTIC. *J Pharm Pharmacol.* **33**: 808–11.

6 Dine T *et al.* (1994) Stability and compatibility studies of four cytostatic agents (fluorouracil, dacarbazine, cyclophosphamide and ifosfamide) with PVC infusion bags. *Pharm Sci Commun.* **4**: 97–101.

7 Bayer Ltd (1999) Personal communication.

8 Nelson RW *et al.* (1987) Visual incompatibility of dacarbazine and heparin. *Am J Hosp Pharm.* **44**: 2028.

9 Salamone FR and Muller RJ (1990) Intravenous admixture compatibility of cancer chemotherapeutic agents. *Hosp Pharm.* **25**: 567–70.

10 Faulding Pharmaceuticals plc (2000) Personal communication.

Prepared by Paula Myers

DACTINOMYCIN

1 General details

Approved names: Dactinomycin, actinomycin D.

Proprietary name: Cosmegen Lyovac.

Manufacturer or supplier: Merck, Sharpe & Dohme Ltd.

Presentation and formulation details: Yellow lyophilised powder in vial containing 500 µg dactinomycin. Each vial contains 20 mg mannitol.

Storage and shelf-life of unopened container: Five years when stored in a cool, dry place and protected from light.

2 Chemistry

Type: Antibiotic.

Molecular structure: Actinomycin (thr-val-pro-sar-meval).

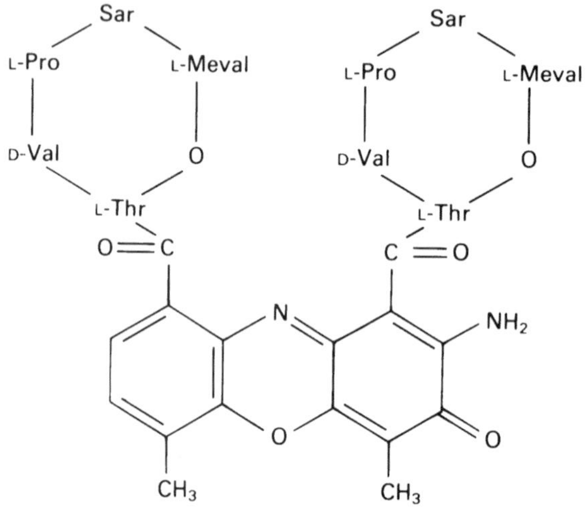

Sar
L-Pro   L-Meval
D-Val   O
L-Thr
O=C

Sar
L-Pro   L-Meval
D-Val   O
L-Thr
C=O

N   NH₂

O   O

CH₃   CH₃

Molecular weight: 1255.5.

Solubility: Soluble in water.

3 Stability profile

3.1 Physical and chemical stability

Degradation in aqueous solution is pH dependent. The pH of reconstituted drug is 5.5–7.0 and it is most stable between pH 5 and 7. One report indicates approximately 2–3% degradation in 6 days at 25°C at these pH values (30 µg/mL).[1] At pH 9.0, 80% loss was noted under the same conditions.[1]

Degradation pathways: Alkaline conditions – ring opening of the acridine-like centre.[2]

Physical: Degradation is reduced at lower temperatures. In aqueous solution, degradation at 2–6°C is negligible over a 6-day period.[1]

Container compatibility: Syringes – no information available. Dactinomycin is reported to be compatible with glass and PVC containers for infusions.[3]

No information is available on the compatibility of administration sets, but it should be noted that dactinomycin is compatible with PVC.[2]

There is evidence of dactinomycin binding to certain types of in-line filters.[4] For example, when 500 µg were diluted in 500 mL of infusion fluid, a total of 67 µg (approximately 13%) were subsequently bound to the in-line cellulose acetate membrane filter. Binding to polycarbonate filters has also been reported.[4] When dactinomycin at 500 µg/mL[5] was injected through a 0.2-µm nylon filter (Utipor, Pall), 87% of the drug was delivered.[6]

Compatibility with other drugs and excipients: No further information available. Incompatible with benzyl alcohol and other preservatives; avoid preserved diluents for reconstitution.

3.2 Stability in clinical practice

The drug is relatively stable after reconstitution in water for injections, and may be stored at 2–6°C for 7 days. The drug is also reasonably stable after further dilution in 0.9% sodium chloride or 5% glucose, showing less than 10% degradation after 24 hours at ambient temperature.[3] It should be protected from daylight during storage. The reconstituted drug is also stable when frozen.[7]

3.3 Stability in specialised delivery systems

No data available.

4 Clinical use

Type of cytotoxic: Cytotoxic antibiotic.

Main indications: Wilms' tumour, rhabdomyosarcoma, and carcinoma of the testis or uterus.

Dosage: Adults, up to 400–600 µg/m^2/day for up to 5 days; children, 15 µg/kg for up to 5 days.

5 Preparation of injection

Reconstitution: Add 1.1 mL of water for injections and shake to dissolve.

Bolus administration: Inject into the tubing of a fast-running infusion of 5% glucose or 0.9% sodium chloride.

Intravenous infusion: Add to up to 500 mL of 0.9% sodium chloride or 5% glucose. The infusion may be stored for 24 hours at 2–6°C.

Stability in plastic syringes: No information available.

Extravasation: Group 1 classification (vesicant) (*see* Chapter 6).

6 Destruction of drug or contaminated articles

Incineration: 1000°C.

Chemical: 5% trisodium phosphate (2 parts to 1 part of dactinomycin solution), or 20% sodium hydroxide for 24 hours.

Contact with skin: Wash in water or sodium phosphate solution.

References

1 Crevar GE and Slotnick IJ (1964) A note on the stability of actinomycin D. *J Pharm Pharmacol.* **16**: 429.

2 Johnson AW (1960) The chemistry of actinomycin D and related compounds. *Ann NY Acad Sci.* **89**: 336–41.

3 Benvenuto JA *et al.* (1981) Stability and compatibility of antitumor agents in glass and plastic containers. *Am J Hosp Pharm.* **38**: 1914–18.

4 Rusmin S *et al.* (1977) Effect of inline filtration on the potency of drugs administered intravenously. *Am J Hosp Pharm.* **34**: 1071–4.

5 ABPI (1999) *ABPI Data Sheet Compendium 1999–2000.* DataPharm Publications Ltd, London, 876–7.

6 Ennis CE *et al.* (1983) *In vitro* study of inline filtration of medication commonly administered to paediatric patients. *J Parent Ent Nutr.* **7**: 156–8.

7 Bosanquet AG (1986) Stability of solutions of antineoplastic agents during preparation and storage for *in vitro* assays. II. Assay methods, adriamycin and other antitumour antibiotics. *Cancer Chemother Pharmacol.* **17**: 1–10.

Prepared by Michael Allwood

DAUNORUBICIN

1 General details

Approved name: Daunorubicin.

Proprietary name: Cerubidin.

Manufacturer or supplier: Rhône-Poulenc Rorer UK Ltd.

Presentation and formulation details: Sterile, pyrogen-free, orange-red, microcrystal-line powder in vials of 20 mg of daunorubicin as the hydrochloride, with mannitol as a stabilising agent.[1]

Storage and shelf-life of unopened container: Three years if stored at room temperature and protected from sunlight.[1]

2 Chemistry

Type: A cytotoxic antibiotic consisting of an amino-sugar moiety linked through a glycosidic bond to the C7 of a tetracyclic aglycone, daunosamine.[2]

Molecular structure: (1S,3S)-3-acetyl-1,2,3,4,6,11-hexahydro-3,5,12-trihydroxy-10-methoxy-6,11-dioxonapthacen-1-yl 3-amino-2,3,6-trideoxy-α-L-*lyxo*-pyranoside hydrochloride; (8S-*cis*)-8-acetyl-10-[(3-amino-2,3,6-trideoxy-α-L-*lyxo*-hexapyranosyl)] oxy-7,8,9,10-tetrahydro-6,8,11-trihydroxy-1-methoxy-5,12-naphthacenedione hydrochloride.

Molecular weight: 564.0.

Solubility: Daunorubicin is soluble in water for injections, 5% glucose and 0.9% sodium chloride.[2]

3 Stability profile

3.1. *Physical and chemical stability*

The manufacturer states that the reconstituted solution is stable for up to 24 hours at 2–8°C when protected from strong daylight. The literature reveals that daunorubicin may be chemically stable for longer periods, although few data have been published.[3-5] The stability of daunorubicin depends on a number of factors. Degradation in aqueous solution is pH dependent. Daunorubicin is also light sensitive and is adsorbed on to glass and certain plastics.

Effect of pH: Daunorubicin becomes progressively more stable as the pH of the drug fluid admixture becomes more acidic (pH 7.4–4.5).[4] Maximum stability is observed at about pH 5.[6] Decomposition of daunorubicin has been studied by Beijnen *et al.*[7,8] Acidic hydrolysis of daunorubicin (pH below 3.5) yields a red-coloured, water-insoluble aglycone (daunorubicinone) and a water-soluble amino sugar (daunosamine). At pH values above 3.5, two major degradation products are formed, both of which are aglycones, namely 7,8-dehydro-9,10-desacetyldaunorubicinone and 7,8-9,10-bisanhydrodaunorubicinone.[6,8] On addition to strongly alkaline solution, a colour change from red to a deep blue-purple is observed and rapid degradation of daunorubicin occurs. Analysis of the decomposition of daunorubicin at pH 8.0 showed the formation of seven possible degradation products.[9]

Effect of light: Results from a study in which the rates of photodegradation of doxorubicin, daunorubicin and epirubicin were compared indicated that the rate of photodegradation of all three analogues was similar.[10] This suggests that the rate of photodegradation of daunorubicin may be significant at concentrations of less than 100 μg/mL if solutions are exposed to light for sufficient time. However, at higher concentrations, such as those used for cancer chemotherapy (at least 500 μg/mL), no special precautions appear to be necessary to protect freshly prepared solutions of daunorubicin from light.[10]

Effect of temperature: Poochikian *et al.*[4] observed that daunorubicin (20 μg/ml) was stable for 72 hours in 5% glucose and 0.9% sodium chloride in glass containers at 21°C. In that study the solutions were not protected from light and, at the low concentrations used, photodegradation may represent a considerable proportion of the overall degradation. Conversely, in a well-controlled study where the solutions were protected from light, Beijnen *et al.*[5] reported that daunorubicin was stable in polypropylene tubes for 28 days in 5% glucose (pH 4.7), 3.3% glucose with 0.3% sodium chloride (pH 4.4) and 0.9% sodium chloride (pH 7.0) at 25°C. Daunorubicin has also been reported to be stable for 7 days at room temperature.[3] Wood *et al.*[11] observed that daunorubicin was stable in 5% glucose (pH 4.36) and 0.9% sodium chloride (pH 5.20 and 6.47) in PVC minibags for at least 43 days at 25, 4 and 20°C. Repeated freezing and thawing of solutions stored at –20°C did not cause degradation. In the same study, daunorubicin was also reported to be stable for at least 43 days when reconstituted with water for injections and stored in polypropylene syringes at 4°C. Dine *et al.*[12] reported that daunorubicin (16 μg/mL in 5% glucose and 0.9% sodium chloride) was stable in PVC infusion bags (Macopharma Laboratories) for 7 days at 4°C when protected from light.

Container compatibility: Daunorubicin is compatible with polypropylene, PVC and glass.[11,13] Daunorubicin adsorbs on to glass but not on to siliconised glass or polypropylene.[14] In clinical practice, when daunorubicin is used at concentrations of at least 500 μg/mL, adsorptive losses during storage and delivery are negligible.[11,13]

Compatibility with other drugs: Daunorubicin is incompatible with dexamethasone sodium phosphate and heparin sodium.[1] The manufacturer recommends that no other drugs are mixed with daunorubicin.

3.2. Stability in clinical practice

Daunorubicin is compatible with polypropylene, PVC and glass.[11,13] Daunorubicin appears to be chemically stable for at least 28 days in PVC minibags (100 mg/mL) in 5% glucose and 0.9% sodium chloride at 4°C and –20°C, and for at least 28 days in polypropylene syringes (2 mg/mL) at 4°C.[11]

3.3. Stability in specialised delivery systems.

No data are available.

4 Clinical use

Type of cytotoxic: Cytotoxic antibiotic that interacts with DNA to interfere with nucleic acid synthesis. Cytotoxic effects are most marked on cells in the S phase.

Main indications: In the treatment of acute leukaemia, daunorubicin is particularly effective in inducing remissions in acute myelogenous and lymphocytic leukaemias.[1] Daunorubicin should not be used in patients recently exposed to or with existing chicken-pox or herpes zoster.[1]

Dosage and administration:

▼ *Remission induction (adults):* For remission induction a dose of 40–60 mg/m^2 on alternate days is given for a course of up to three injections.
▼ *Acute myelogenous leukaemia (adults):* The recommended dose is 45 mg/m^2/day.
▼ *Acute lymphoblastic leukaemia (adults):* The recommended dose is 45 mg/m^2/day.
▼ *Children:* In children over 2 years the dose is the same as for adults. In children under 2 years or with surface area less than 0.5 m^2 the dose is 1 mg/m^2/day.
▼ *Elderly:* Daunorubicin should be used with care in patients with inadequate bone-marrow reserves due to old age. A reduction of up to 50% of the dosage is recommended.

The number of injections required varies from one patient to another, and must be determined in each case by response and tolerance. The dosage should be reduced in patients with impaired hepatic or renal function. A 25% reduction is recommended in patients with serum bilirubin concentrations in the range 20–50 μmol/L or a serum creatinine concentration in the range 105–265 μmol/L. A 50% dosage reduction is recommended in patients with serum bilirubin levels above 50 μmol/L or a serum creatinine level above 265 μmol/L.

When administered with other cytotoxic agents with overlapping toxicity, the dosage should be appropriately reduced. A cumulative dose of 600 mg/m^2 in adults, 300 mg/m^2 in children over 2 years or 10 mg/kg in children under 2 years should not be exceeded, as above this level the risk of irreversible congestive cardiac failure increases greatly.[1] The cumulative dose should be limited to 400 mg/m^2 when radiation to the mediastinum has been previously administered.[1] Cardiotoxicity may be more frequent in children and the elderly.

5 Preparation of injection

Reconstitution: The contents of the 20-mg vial are reconstituted with 4 mL of water for injections. After addition of the diluent and gentle shaking, the contents of the vial will dissolve to produce a solution of 5 mg/mL.[1]

Bolus administration: Administration is only by the intravenous route. The manufacturer recommends that the calculated dose should be further diluted with 0.9% sodium chloride to give a final concentration of 1 mg/mL. This solution should be injected over a 20-minute period into the side-arm of a freely running intravenous infusion of 0.9% sodium chloride. This technique minimises the risk of thrombosis or perivenous extravasation, which can lead to severe cellulitis or vesication.[1]

Intravenous infusion: Although daunorubicin has been used as a continuous infusion in a phase I trial in previously treated patients with leukaemia, no phase II evaluation was undertaken because of the somewhat limited antileukaemic activity in patients who had previously received other anthracycline therapy.[15] In a study where fractionated daunorubicin was given to 16 patients with acute myeloid leukaemia, a good response rate was obtained, together with a low incidence of side-effects. In addition, no significant cardiotoxicity was observed, despite total doses of up to 1363 mg/m² of daunorubicin.[16]

Extravasation: Group 1 classification (vesicant) (*see* Chapter 6).

6 Destruction of drug or contaminated articles

Incineration: 700°C.[17]

Chemical: 10% sodium hypochlorite (1% available chlorine) for 24 hours.[17]

Contact with skin: Wash well with water, soap and water, or sodium bicarbonate solution. If the eyes are contaminated, immediate irrigation with 0.9% sodium chloride should be performed.[17]

References

1 ABPI (1999) *ABPI Datasheet Compendium 1999–2000.* DataPharm Publications Ltd, London, 1281–2.

2 Reynolds JEF (ed.) (1996) *The Extra Pharmacopoeia* (31e). Pharmaceutical Press, London.

3 Trissel LA (2000) *Handbook of Injectable Drugs* (11e). American Society of Hospital Pharmacists, Bethesda, MD.

4 Poochikian GK *et al.* (1981) Stability of anthracycline antitumour agents in four infusion fluids. *Am J Hosp Pharm.* **38**: 483–6.

5 Beijnen JH *et al.* (1985) Stability of anthracycline antitumour agents in infusion fluids. *J Parent Sci Technol.* **39**: 220–2.

6 Beijnen JH *et al.* (1986) Aspects of the degradation kinetics of daunorubicin in aqueous solution. *Int J Pharm.* **31**: 75–82.

7 Beijnen JH *et al.* (1985) Aspects of the chemical stability of daunorubicin and seven other anthracyclines in acidic solution. *Pharm Weekbl (Sci Edn).* **7**: 109–16.

8 Beijnen JH *et al.* (1986) Aspects of the degradation kinetics of doxorubicin in aqueous solution. *Int J Pharm.* **32**: 123–31.

9 Beijnen JH *et al.* (1987) Structure elucidation and characterization of daunorubicin degradation products. *Int J Pharm.* **34**: 247–57.

10 Wood MJ *et al.* (1990) Photodegradation of doxorubicin, daunorubicin and epirubicin measured by high-performance liquid chromatography. *J Clin Pharm Ther.* **15**: 291–300.

11 Wood MJ *et al.* (1990) Stability of doxorubicin, daunorubicin and epirubicin in plastic syringes and minibags. *J Clin Pharm Ther.* **15**: 279–89.

12 Dine T *et al.* (1992) Stability and compatibility of four anthracyclines: doxorubicin, daunorubicin, epirubicin and pirarubicin with PVC infusion bags. *Pharm Weekbl (Sci Edn).* **14**: 365–9.

13 Wood MJ (1989) *Investigations into the stability of doxorubicin, daunorubicin and epirubicin in infusion fluids.* MPhil Thesis. University of Aston, Birmingham.

14 Bosanquet AG (1986) Stability of solutions of antineoplastic agents during preparation and storage for *in vitro* assays. II. Assay methods, adriamycin and the other antitumour antibiotics. *Cancer Chemother Pharmacol.* **17**: 1–10.

15 Legha SS *et al.* (1987) Anthracyclines. In: JJ Lokich (ed.) *Cancer Chemotherapy by Infusion.* MTP Press Ltd, Lancaster.

16 Donohue SM and Boughton BJ (1989) Fractionated anthracycline therapy in acute myeloblastic leukaemia in adults. *Cancer Chemother Pharmacol.* **23**: 401–2.

17 Rhône-Poulenc Rorer UK Ltd (1997) Personal communication.

Prepared by Jayne Wood

DAUNORUBICIN LIPOSOMAL

1 General details

Approved name: Liposomal daunorubicin.

Proprietary/other name: Daunoxome.

Manufacturer or supplier: Nexstar Ltd.

Presentation and formulation details: Daunoxome is a translucent, red emulsion supplied in single-dose vials. Each vial contains 50 mg of daunorubicin encapsulated in liposomes composed of cholesterol (180 mg) and the phospholipid distearoyl-phosphatidylcholine (DSPC) (15 mg). The average diameter of the liposomes is 45 nm. The lipid to drug ratio is 18:1 (total lipid:daunorubicin base), equivalent to a 10:5:1 molar composition of DSPC:cholesterol:daunorubicin. The liposomes encapsulating daunorubicin are suspended as a medium of 2.125 mg sucrose and 94 mg glycine with 7 mg calcium chloride dehydrate.[1] The liposome emulsion ranges from red and clear to slightly opalescent in appearance.

Storage and shelf-life of unopened container: 40 weeks at 2–8°C. Do not freeze. Protect from light.

2 Chemistry

Type: Cytotoxic anthracycline antibiotic.

Molecular structure: As for daunorubicin, but enclosed in a carrier system consisting of a unilamellar liposome.

Molecular formula: see monograph for daunorubicin.

Molecular weight: A particle suspension.

pH of suspension: 4.5–6.5.

3 Stability profile

3.1 Physical and chemical stability

Solutions diluted in 5% glucose are physically stable for up to 6 hours.[1]

Compatibility with other drugs: No interaction with other drugs has been recorded. Daunorubicin liposomal has been safely administered with zidovudine, dideoxy-cytidine and GCSF. The product is reported to be incompatible with heparin or dexamethasone.[1]

3.2 Stability in clinical practice

The manufacturer indicates that the diluted injection in 5% glucose should be administered within 6 hours of preparation.[1] Daunoxome must not be diluted using 0.9% sodium chloride or any other electrolyte solution.[1]

3.3 Stability in specialised delivery systems

No data available.

4 Clinical use

Type of cytotoxic: Cytotoxic antibiotic that interacts with DNA to interfere with nucleic acid synthesis. Cytotoxic effects are most marked on cells in the S phase. Daunoxome is a liposomal preparation formulated to maximise the selectivity of daunorubicin for solid tumours *in situ*.

While in the circulation the daunoxome formulation helps to protect the entrapped daunorubicin from chemical and enzymatic degradation, minimises protein binding and generally decreases uptake by normal (non-reticuloendothelial system) tissues. The specific mechanism by which daunoxome is able to deliver daunorubicin in solid tumours *in situ* is not known. However, it is believed to be a function of increased permeability of the tumour neovasculature to particulates in the size range of daunoxome. Thus by decreasing non-specific binding to normal tissues and plasma proteins, selective binding to normal tissues and plasma proteins and selective extravasation in the tumour, neovasculature pharmacokinetics are shifted in favour of an accumulation of Daunoxome in tumour tissue. Once within the tumour environment, Daunoxome vesicles enter the tumour cells intact. Daunorubicin is then released over time directly into the cells, where it is able to exert its antineoplastic activity.

Main indications: Advanced HIV-associated Kaposi's sarcoma where conventional chemotherapy has failed. Phase IV clinical trials are currently in progress.

Dosage and administration: The recommended dose is 40 mg/m² every 2 weeks.[1] Dilute in 5% glucose to a concentration in the range of 0.2–1 mg daunorubicin/mL and administer intravenously over 30–60 minutes.

Children and the elderly: Safe use in these two groups has not been established.

5 Preparation of injection

Reconstitution: Should be diluted in 5% glucose to a concentration of 0.2–1 mg/mg daunorubicin/mL.

Intravenous infusion: Administer by intravenous injection or infusion for 30–60 minutes. Do not use 0.9% sodium chloride or any other infusion. An in-line filter is not recommended for the intravenous infusion of Daunoxome. However, if such a filter is used, the mean pore diameter of the filter should not be less than 5 μm.[2]

Extravasation: Group 2 classification (exfoliant). In contrast to conventional daunorubicin, no local tissue necrosis has been observed with Daunoxome (*see* Chapter 6).[1]

6 Destruction of drug or contaminated articles

Incineration: No specific information available.

Chemical: No specific information available.

Contact with skin: No specific information available.

References

1 ABPI (1999) *ABPI Data Sheet Compendium 1999–2000*. DataPharm Publications Ltd, London, 950–1.
2 Vestar Ltd (1995) Personal communication.

Prepared by Yaacov Cass

DOCETAXEL

1 General details

Approved name: Docetaxel.

Proprietary name: Taxotere.

Synonyms: RP 56976, NSC 628503.

Marketing authorisation holder: Rhône-Poulenc Rorer SA, 20 Avenue Raymond Aron, 92165, Antony Cedex, France.

Manufacturer or supplier: Rhône-Poulenc Rorer UK Ltd.

Presentation and formulation details: Taxotere concentrate for infusion is a clear, yellow to brown-yellow solution containing 40 mg/mL docetaxel (anhydrous) and 1 mL polysorbate 80. Each vial contains either a nominal 20 mg or 80 mg docetaxel, with an overage of approximately 7% of docetaxel. The 'Solvent for Taxotere' vial contains 1.83 mL of 13% (w/w) ethanol in water for each 20 mg of docetaxel. Addition of the entire content of the solvent vial to the docetaxel vial provides a solution containing 10 mg/mL docetaxel.[1]

Storage and shelf-life of unopened container: Docetaxel vials should be stored at between 2 and 25°C and protected from bright light. The shelf-life under these conditions is 15 months for docetaxel (80 mg) and 12 months for docetaxel (20 mg).[1]

2 Chemistry

Type: Taxoid obtained by semisynthesis from a non-cytotoxic precursor, 10-deacetyl-baccatin III, extracted from the needles of the European yew tree, *Taxus baccata*. It is an analogue of paclitaxel.

Mechanism of action: Promotes assembly of microtubules (necessary for mitosis) and prevents their disassembly, 'freezing' the cell skeleton and leading to inhibition of mitosis and cell death.

Molecular structure: (2R,3S)-N-carboxy-3-phenylisoserine, N-tert-butylester, 13-ester with 5β, 20 epoxy-1,2α,4,7β,10β,13α-hexahydroxytax-11-en-9-one 4-acetate 2 benzoate, trihydrate. The molecular structure of docetaxel differs from that of paclitaxel in two ways. First, a hydroxy group replaces an acetyl group on the 10-position of the baccatin III, and secondly, an $OC(CH_3)_3$ moiety replaces a benzamide phenyl group in the 3' position on the C13 side-chain.

Molecular weight: 807.9.

Solubility: Almost insoluble in water, but soluble in polysorbate 80.

3 Stability profile

3.1 Physical and chemical stability

Docetaxel injection, after adding the solvent, is stable for 8 hours at 2°C and 25°C.[2]

Container compatibility: Docetaxel after dilution for infusion causes leaching of diethylhexyl phthalate (DEHP) from PVC bags,[3] resulting in significant leaching after 8 hours of storage.[4] Docetaxel infusions should therefore be prepared in glass or polyolefin containers and non-PVC administration sets.[5]

Compatibility with other drugs: Docetaxel injection has been reported to be physically compatible with a wide range of drugs during simulated Y-site co-administration.[5,6]

3.2 Stability in clinical practice

Docetaxel infusion in 0.9% sodium chloride or 5% glucose should be administered within 4 hours of preparation.[1]

3.3 Stability in specialised delivery systems

No information available.

4 Clinical use

Type of cytotoxic: A cytostatic agent with a molecular action on the dynamic equilibrium of tubulin in the microtubular apparatus of the cell.

Main indications: Monotherapy of advanced or metastatic breast cancer. Patients who are resistant to or have recurrent disease after a cytotoxic therapy, or who have relapsed during an adjuvant cytotoxic therapy. The cytotoxic therapy should have included an anthracycline.

Recommended dose: 100 mg/m² as a 1-hour intravenous infusion every 3 weeks.

Dosage reductions: Reduce to 75 mg/m² in cases of mild liver impairment, febrile neutropenia, neutrophil count less than 500/mm³ for more than 1 week, severe or cumulative cutaneous reactions or severe peripheral neuropathy. If symptoms persist, reduce to 55 mg/m², or discontinue.

Contraindications: Increased serum bilirubin and/or ALT and AST values more than 3.5 times the upper limit of normal (ULN), with alkaline phosphatase more than six times the ULN.

Other tumour types: Clinical trials are ongoing in non-small-cell lung cancer, ovarian, head and neck and other tumour types, where docetaxel has shown promising activity in preclinical and Phase I trials.

5 Preparation of injection

Docetaxel 80 mg: The labelled strength is 80 mg docetaxel per vial, and the labelled volume is 2 mL. Practically, 80-mg docetaxel vials contain 2.3 mL of the 40 mg/mL solution, equivalent to 94.4 mg docetaxel. The solvent vial has a labelled volume of 6 mL, but has been correspondingly overfilled to contain 7.33 mL ± 5%. These overfill volumes have been established and validated during the development of docetaxel to compensate for liquid loss during preparation of the premix solution due to foaming, adhesion to the walls of the vial and 'dead volumes'. This overfill ensures that there is a minimum extractable premix volume of 8 mL containing 10 mg/mL docetaxel.

Docetaxel 20 mg: The labelled strength is 20 mg docetaxel per vial, and the labelled volume is 0.5 mL. Practically, 20-mg docetaxel vials contain 0.59 mL of the 40 mg/mL solution, equivalent to 23.6 mg docetaxel. The solvent vial has a labelled volume of 1.5 mL, but has been correspondingly overfilled to contain 1.83 mL ± 5%. This overfill ensures that there is a minimum extractable premix volume of 2 mL containing 10 mg/mL docetaxel.[1,2]

Preparation of premix solution: Remove the required number of boxes containing docetaxel concentrate vials and their corresponding solvent vials from the refrigerator, and allow to stand for 5 minutes at room temperature. Using a syringe fitted with a needle, aseptically withdraw the entire contents of the solvent vial and inject them into the corresponding docetaxel concentrate vial. Remove the syringe and needle and shake the mixture manually for 15 seconds. Allow to stand for 5 minutes at room temperature, and then check that the solution is homogeneous and clear. Foaming is common, due to the polysorbate 80, and may persist for up to 5 minutes. The premix solution is stable for 8 hours in the refrigerator or at room temperature.[2]

Bolus administration: Must not be used.

Infusion: More than one premix vial may be necessary to obtain the required dose for the patient. Based on the required dose expressed in mg, use graduated syringes fitted with a needle to withdraw the necessary premix volume containing 10 mg/mL docetaxel (e.g. a dose of 140 mg would require 14 mL of premix solution). Inject the premix solution into a standard PVC infusion bag containing 250 mL of 5% glucose or 0.9% sodium chloride solution. If a dose greater than 240 mg of docetaxel is required, use a larger volume of the infusion vehicle so that a concentration of 0.9% mg/mL docetaxel is not exceeded.[2]

The docetaxel infusion solution should be administered intravenously by a 1-hour infusion at room temperature and normal lighting conditions.

Extravasation: Group 2 classification (exfoliant) (*see* Chapter 6).

6 Destruction of drug or contaminated articles

Incineration: 1000°C.

Chemical: None recommended. All other waste, including contaminated packaging or cleaning materials and protective gloves, must be placed with clinical waste for incineration.

Contact with skin: Wash with copious amounts of water.

Contact with eyes: Irrigate the eyes with copious amounts of water or saline, and seek an ophthalmic opinion.

References

1 ABPI (1999) *ABPI Data Sheet Compendium 1999–2000*. DataPharm Publications Ltd, London, 1296–8.
2 Lam YW *et al.* (1997) Pharmacokinetics and pharmacodynamics of the taxanes. *J Oncol Pharm Pract*. **3**: 76–93.
3 Pearson SD and Trissel LA (1993) Leaching of DEHP from polyvinyl chloride containers by selected drugs and formulation components. *Am J Hosp Pharm*. **50**: 1405–9.
4 Mazzio DJ *et al.* (1997) Compatibility of docetaxel and paclitaxel in intravenous solutions with polyvinyl chloride materials. *Am J Health-Syst Pharm*. **54**: 455–9.
5 Trissel LA (2001) *Handbook of Injectable Drugs* (11e). American Society of Health-Systems Pharmacists, Bethesda, MD.
6 Trissel LA *et al.* (1999) Compatibility of docetaxel with selected drugs during simulated Y-site administration. *Int J Pharm Compound*. **3**: 241–4.

Prepared by Andrew Stanley and Yaacov Cass

DOXORUBICIN

1 General details

Approved name: Doxorubicin, Doxorubicin Hydrochloride.

Proprietary name: Doxorubicin Rapid Dissolution, Doxorubicin Solution for Injection, Doxorubicin Hydrochloride for Injection.

Manufacturer or supplier: Pharmacia and Upjohn Ltd, Faulding Pharmaceuticals plc.

Presentation and formulation details:

▼ Doxorubicin Rapid Dissolution: Sterile, orange-red, freeze-dried powder in vials containing 10 mg and 50 mg of doxorubicin hydrochloride with lactose and hydroxybenzoate. The purpose of inclusion of hydroxybenzoate 0.02% (which is a subpreservative concentration) is to prevent gel formation, which used to occur occasionally on reconstitution of adriamycin. Adriamycin has been replaced by Doxorubicin Rapid Dissolution.[1]

▼ Doxorubicin Hydrochloride for Injection: Sterile, freeze-dried powder in vials containing 10 mg and 50 mg of doxorubicin hydrochloride.[2]

▼ Doxorubicin Solution for Injection: Sterile, red, mobile solution in vials of 10 mg, 20 mg, 50 mg and 200 mg, each containing doxorubicin hydrochloride as a 2 mg/mL solution in 0.9% sodium chloride injection. The solution is adjusted to pH 3 with 0.5 M hydrochloric acid.[1]

Storage and shelf-life of unopened container:

▼ Doxorubicin Rapid Dissolution: 4 years at room temperature and protected from light.[3]

▼ Doxorubicin Hydrochloride for Injection (Faulding): 3 years at room temperature and protected from light.[2]

▼ Doxorubicin Solution for Injection: If stored in the refrigerator (2–8°C), 2 years. Once removed from the refrigerator the shelf-life is 48 hours.[3]

2 Chemistry

Type: A cytotoxic antibiotic consisting of an amino-sugar daunosamine, linked through a glycosidic bond to the C7 of a tetracyclic aglycone, doxorubicinone.[4]

Molecular structure: 8-hydroxyacetyl (8S,10S)-10-[(3-amino-2,3,6-trideoxy-α-L-*lyxo* pyranosyl)oxy]-6,8,11-trihydroxy-1-methoxy-7,8,9,10-tetrahydro-naphthacene-5,12-dione hydrochloride.

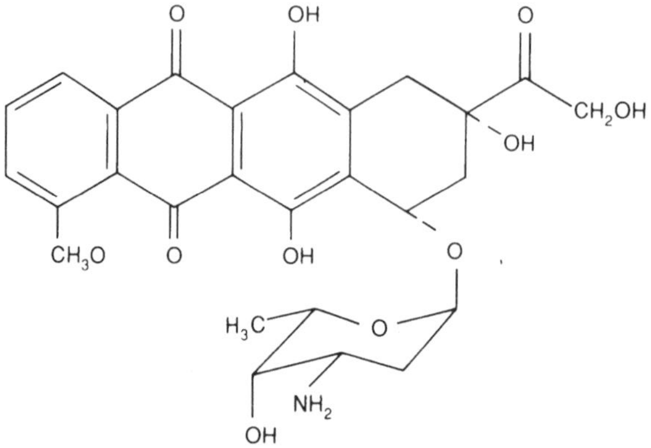

Molecular weight: 580.0.

Solubility: Doxorubicin is soluble in water for injections, 5% glucose and 0.9% sodium chloride.[4]

3 Stability profile

3.1. Physical and chemical stability

The manufacturer states that reconstituted solutions of Doxorubicin Rapid Dissolution are chemically stable for up to 48 hours at room temperature in normal artificial light.[1] Doxorubicin Solution for Injection, which has a pH of 3, is stable for 18 months at 2–8°C and for 48 hours at room temperature.[3] A review of the literature reveals that doxorubicin appears to be chemically stable for long periods,[5–12] but the data are limited and contradictory, and require critical assessment. The stability of doxorubicin depends on a number of factors, the most important of which are temperature, pH and the type of solvent used for reconstitution.[13,14] Doxorubicin is also light sensitive and is adsorbed on to glass and certain plastics.

Effect of pH: Doxorubicin becomes more stable as the pH of the drug infusion fluid admixture becomes more acidic (pH 7.4–4.5).[6] Maximum stability is observed at about pH 4.[15] Decomposition in acidic solution has been studied by several authors.[16,17] Acidic hydrolysis of doxorubicin (pH below 4) yields a red-coloured, water-insoluble aglycone (doxorubicinone) and a water-soluble amino sugar (daunosamine). On addition of doxorubicin to strongly alkaline solution, a colour change from red to deep blue-purple is observed and rapid degradation of doxorubicin occurs. Abdeen *et al.*[18] acidified and extracted a solution of doxorubicin in 2 M sodium hydroxide and isolated at least five compounds, which were not identified. Analysis of degradation mixtures at pH 8.0 by Beijnen *et al.*[15] showed one major degradation product, namely 7,8-dehydro-9,10 desacetyl-daunorubicinone.

Effect of light: The large differences in stability which have been reported by different groups for virtually identical experiments[6,19] may be partially explained by poor control of photodegradation. Photodegradation of doxorubicin may be substantial at concentrations below 100 µg/mL, if solutions are exposed to light for sufficient time.[19,20] However, at higher concentrations, such as those used for cancer chemotherapy (at least 500 µg/mL), no special precautions appear to be necessary to protect freshly prepared solutions of doxorubicin from light.[19,20]

Effect of temperature: In a well-controlled study, Beijnen *et al.*[9] reported that doxorubicin was stable in 5% glucose (pH 4.7) and 3.3% glucose with 0.3% sodium chloride (pH 4.4), in polypropylene tubes, for 28 days at 25°C in the dark. However, in 0.9% sodium chloride (pH 7.0) significant degradation occurred after 6 days at the same temperature. Wood *et al.*[21] reported that doxorubicin was stable in 0.9% sodium chloride (pH 6.47) in PVC minibags stored in the dark for 20 days at 25°C. In 5% glucose (pH 4.36) and 0.9% sodium chloride (pH 5.20 and pH 6.47), doxorubicin was stable in PVC minibags for at least 43 days at 4°C. In the same study, doxorubicin was also observed to be stable for 43 days when reconstituted with water for injections and stored in polypropylene syringes at 4°C.[21]

Martel *et al.*[22] studied the stability of doxorubicin at 2 mg/mL in glass vials in water for injections at 4, 23 and 33°C while protected from the light. Results showed that doxorubicin was stable (less than 10% degradation) for 12 months at all three temperatures studied.

Stewart et al.[23] studied the stability of mixtures of doxorubicin and ondansetron in 5% glucose in PVC infusion bags at 23°C. Their results showed that doxorubicin at 100 μg/mL with ondansetron at 30 μg/mL or 300 μg/mL or doxorubicin at 2 mg/mL with ondansetron at 30 μg/mL or 300 μg/mL were stable for 48 hours.

Dine et al.[24] reported that doxorubicin (16 μg/mL in 5% glucose and 0.9% sodium chloride) was stable in PVC infusion bags (Macopharma Laboratories) for 7 days at 4°C when protected from light. Walker et al.[25] reported that doxorubicin at 2 mg/mL in 0.9% sodium chloride in glass vials and plastic syringes (Monoject and Terumo) and also at 1 mg/mL in 0.9% sodium chloride in plastic syringes (Monoject) was stable when stored at 4 and 23°C while exposed to light for 124 days. Leaching of plasticisers from the syringes was not detected during the study period. Hoffman et al.[5] observed that solutions of doxorubicin (2 mg/mL) in water for injections were stable for 6 months at 4°C. Those authors indicated that filtration through a 0.22-μm filter would ensure sterility without loss of drug.

Stewart et al.[26] reported that a mixture of doxorubicin (800 μg/mL) with vincristine (28 μg/mL) and ondansetron (960 μg/mL) in 0.9% sodium chloride in PVC bags was stable (less than 10% degradation) for 24 hours at 4°C followed by 120 hours at 30°C. Those authors also reported that a mixture of doxorubicin (800 μg/mL) with dacarbazine (8 mg/mL) and ondansetron (640 μg/mL) in 5% glucose in PVC bags was stable (less than 10% degradation) for 8 hours, and a mixture of doxorubicin (1.5 mg/mL) with dacarbazine (20 mg/mL) and ondansetron (640 μg/mL) in 5% glucose in PVC bags was stable for 24 hours at 30°C for up to 7 days at 4°C followed by 24 hours at 30°C.

Several authors have published data on the effects of freezing doxorubicin. Hoffman et al.[5] observed that aqueous solutions of doxorubicin (2 mg/mL) could be frozen and stored for 1 month at −20°C without significant degradation, but indicated that doxorubicin reconstituted with sodium chloride should not be frozen. Conversely, doxorubicin has been reported to be stable in 0.9% sodium chloride for 30 days[8] and 2 weeks,[12] respectively, at −20°C. Wood et al.[21] reported that doxorubicin was stable in 5% glucose (pH 4.36) and 0.9% sodium chloride (pH 5.20 and pH 6.47) in PVC minibags for at least 43 days at −20°C.

The effects of thawing doxorubicin by microwave radiation have also been investigated.[8,12] Karlsen et al.[8] observed that the concentration of doxorubicin in PVC minibags declined significantly after four rethawings in a microwave oven. Keusters et al.[12] compared the effects of freezing and thawing doxorubicin at room temperature with thawing in the microwave. Their results showed that doxorubicin was stable for 2 weeks at −20°C when thawed by either method. After re-freezing and subsequent re-thawing, a small but significant decrease in concentration was observed in solutions thawed by both methods. Alternatively, Hoffman et al.[5] observed that aqueous solutions of doxorubicin could be frozen and thawed at room temperature seven times without significant loss of potency. Wood et al.[21] also observed that repeated freezing and thawing of solutions of doxorubicin in PVC minibags at room temperature did not lead to significant degradation.

Uneven distribution of energy can occur during microwave thawing, which may overheat solutions and lead to degradation.[27] For this reason, thawing in a microwave oven is not recommended. If frozen, doxorubicin should be thawed at room temperature.

Container compatibility: Doxorubicin is compatible with polypropylene, PVC and glass.[21,28] It has been reported to be more stable in plastic (PVC) than in glass.[7] Doxorubicin adsorbs on to glass and polyethylene but not on to siliconised glass or polypropylene.[10,28] Solutions which contain concentrations of 2 mg/mL do not adsorb on to membrane filters, but with more dilute solutions, especially when associated with small volumes, more than 95% of doxorubicin is adsorbed on to cellulose ester membranes, and about 40% binds to polytetrafluoroethylene (PTFE) membranes.[29,30] In clinical practice, when doxorubicin is used at concentrations of at least 500 µg/mL, adsorption during storage and delivery is negligible.[21,28]

Compatibility with other drugs: Doxorubicin is incompatible with heparin, dexamethasone sodium phosphate, hydrocortisone sodium succinate and diazepam, as precipitation occurs. The manufacturers recommend that no other drugs are mixed with doxorubicin. Combinations of doxorubicin and fluorouracil or aminophylline result in a colour change from red to blue-purple, which indicates the onset of rapid degradation of doxorubicin.[31]

A combination of doxorubicin (1.4 mg/mL, 1.88 mg/mL and 2.37 mg/mL) and vincristine (3.3 µg/mL and 5.3 µg/mL) in 0.9% sodium chloride, and in a mixture of 2.5% glucose with 0.45% sodium chloride, appears to be stable for at least 7 days in polysiloxane bags at 25, 30 or 37°C.[32] Mixtures of doxorubicin and vinblastine (500 µg/mL with 75 µg/mL and 1.5 mg/mL with 150 µg/mL, respectively) in 0.9% sodium chloride appear to be relatively stable (less than 10% degradation) for at least 5 days at 25°C when exposed to light, and at 32°C and 8°C when protected from light and stored in Cormed PVC reservoir bags and PVC monoject syringes.[33] Doxorubicin (1.67 mg/mL) and vincristine (36 µg/mL) in 0.9% sodium chloride are stable (less than 5% degradation) in the Pharmacia/Deltec and in the Baxter infusor for 7 days at 4°C and then for 4 days at 35°C.[34] A combination of vincristine (1–4 µg/mL), doxorubicin (25–100 µg/mL) and etoposide (125–500 µg/mL) in 0.9% sodium chloride was compatible (no colour change or precipitation) and stable (less than 10% degradation) for up to 72 hours in polyolefin-lined intravenous bags at 23–25°C, provided that the etoposide concentration did not exceed 250 µg/mL. Vincristine at 1.6 µg/mL, doxorubicin at 40 µg/mL and etoposide at 200 µg/mL were compatible and stable for up to 72 hours in the dark at 31–33°C.[35]

3.2. Stability in clinical practice

Doxorubicin is compatible with polypropylene, PVC and glass.[21,28] Doxorubicin appears to be chemically stable in PVC minibags (100 µg/mL) for at least 28 days in 5% glucose or 0.9% sodium chloride when stored at 4°C and –20°C, and in polypropylene syringes (2 mg/mL) for at least 28 days at 4°C.[21]

3.2. Stability in specialised delivery systems

Both of the commercially available preparations of doxorubicin (at 2 mg/mL in 0.9% sodium chloride) are stable in portable pump reservoirs (Pharmacia Deltec Medication Cassette 602100A) for up to 14 days at 3 and 23°C, and for an additional 28 days at 30°C.[36] Doxorubicin (500 µg/mL and 1.25 mg/mL) is stable in 0.9% sodium chloride and 5% dextrose solution in EVA reservoirs (RES80 A, Celsa Laboratories, Chasseneuil, France) for 14 days at 4 and 22°C and for 7 days at 35°C.[37] Doxorubicin (from 200 µg/mL to 1 mg/mL) is stable in 0.9% sodium chloride for 96 days at 2–8°C followed by 9 days at 25°C in the Baxter infusor and Intermate device.[38] Doxorubicin (from 1 mg/mL to 2 mg/mL) is stable in 0.9% sodium chloride for 42 days at 2–8°C followed by 5 days at 25°C in the Baxter Infusor and Intermate device.[38] Doxorubicin (from 200 µg/mL to 5 mg/mL) is stable in 0.9% sodium chloride for 34 days at 2–8°C followed by 9 days at 25°C in the Baxter infusor and Intermate device.[38]

At a concentration of 2 mg/mL, doxorubicin is also stable in the CADD pump for 14 days at 4°C.[38] Doxorubicin (at 1.5 mg/mL) and vinblastine (at 150 µg/mL) and doxorubicin (at 500 µg/mL) and vinblastine (at 75 µg/mL) are stable for 10 days in a Cormed ML6-46 reservoir pump.[39] Doxorubicin (concentration range 400–600 µg/mL) admixed with cyclophosphamide (concentration range 6–8 mg/mL) is stable for 7 days in a Cormed ML6-46 reservoir pump.[39] Doxorubicin (3 mg/mL and 5 mg/mL in 0.9% sodium chloride) is stable for 2 weeks in the reservoir of a Medtronic DAD implantable infusion pump at 37°C.[40] Doxorubicin (at 1.67 mg/mL) and vincristine (at 36 µg/mL) in 0.9% sodium chloride is stable (less than 5% degradation) in the Pharmacia/Deltec and in the Baxter infusor for 7 days at 4°C and then 4 days at 35°C.[34] Doxorubicin (800 µg/mL) with ondansetron (640 µg/mL) and dacarbazine (8 mg/mL) in 5% glucose was stable in the Baxter infusor for 24 hours at 30°C or up to 7 days at 4°C followed by 24 hours at 30°C.[26] Doxorubicin (1.5 mg/mL) with ondansetron (640 µg/mL) and dacarbazine (20 mg/mL) in 5% glucose was also stable in the Baxter infusor for 24 hours at 30°C or up to 7 days at 4°C followed by 24 hours at 30°C.[26] Doxorubicin (400 µg/mL) with ondansetron (480 µg/mL) and vincristine (14 µg/mL) in 0.9% sodium chloride was stable in the Baxter infusor for up to 5 days at 4°C followed by 24 hours at 30°C.[26] Mixtures of doxorubicin and vinblastine (500 µg/mL with 75 µg/mL and 1.5 mg/mL with 150 µg/mL, respectively) in 0.9% sodium chloride appear to be relatively stable for at least 5 days at 25°C exposed to light, and at 32°C and 8°C when protected from light and stored in Cormed PVC reservoir bags and PVC monoject syringes.[33]

4 Clinical use

Type of cytotoxic: Cytotoxic antibiotic interacting with DNA to interfere with nucleic acid synthesis. Cytotoxic effects are most marked on cells in the S phase.

Main indications: Successfully used to produce regression in acute leukaemia, lymphomas, soft-tissue and osteogenic sarcomas, paediatric malignancies and adult solid tumours, in particular breast and lung carcinomas. Doxorubicin is frequently used in combination regimens with other cytotoxic drugs.[1]

Dosage: This is usually calculated on the basis of body surface area. For single-agent therapy, 60–75 mg/m² is given every 3 weeks. When administered in combination with other anti-tumour agents which possess overlapping toxicity, the dosage may need to be reduced to 30–40 mg/m² every 3 weeks. The total dose for the cycle may be divided over three successive days (20–25 mg/m² on each day). Administration of doxorubicin in a weekly regimen (20 mg/m²) has also been shown to be as effective as the 3-weekly regimen, and also leads to a reduction in cardiotoxicity. The dosage may need to be reduced in patients who have had prior treatment with other cytotoxic drugs, and in children and the elderly. If hepatic function is impaired, the doxorubicin dosage should be reduced to 50% if serum bilirubin concentrations are between 1.2 and 3 mg/100 mL, and to 25% if serum bilirubin concentrations are higher than 3 mg/100 mL. A cumulative dose of 450–550 mg/m² should only be exceeded with extreme caution, as above this level the risk of irreversible congestive cardiac failure increases greatly.[1,2]

5 Preparation of injection

Doxorubicin rapid dissolution: The contents of the 10-mg vial are reconstituted with 5 mL of water for injections or 0.9% sodium chloride, and those of the 50-mg vial are reconstituted with 25 mL of the same solvent. After addition of the diluent and gentle shaking without inversion, the contents of the vial will dissolve within 30 seconds to produce a solution of concentration 2 mg/mL.[1]

Bolus administration: Administration is most frequently by the intravenous route. The manufacturer recommends that the reconstituted solution should be given over 2 to 3 minutes via the tubing of a freely running intravenous infusion of 0.9% sodium chloride, 5% glucose or sodium chloride with glucose. This technique minimises the risk of thrombosis or perivenous extravasation, which can lead to severe cellulitis or vesication. Doxorubicin may also be administered by the intra-arterial or intravesical route. Intra-arterial administration is potentially extremely hazardous, and should only be attempted by those who are fully conversant with the technique.[1,2]

Intravenous infusion: Although the optimum schedule of continuous infusion of doxorubicin has not been established, most current investigations can be grouped into two broad categories. Most experience has been acquired with a schedule consisting of short-term infusions given over 1 to 4 days, with cycles repeated every 3 to 4 weeks. The most thoroughly investigated short-term infusion has been the 96-hour cycle, which generally takes 5 days to complete. In more recent studies, patients have received infusions for several months or longer.

Based on the marked decrease in the cardiac toxicity seen with short-term infusions of doxorubicin, a number of investigators have recently initiated studies with low-dose doxorubicin given as a continous infusion on a more protracted basis.[41-44] With a daily dose of 1–2 mg/m^2, the maximum total daily dose has ranged between 3 and 5 mg/m^2 for periods of several weeks to several months in responding patients. Some investigators have used higher daily doses for 2-week cycles of therapy, followed by 2 weeks without chemotherapy to allow recovery from side-effects.[45]

Extravasation: Group 1 classification (vesicant) (*see* Chapter 6).

6 Destruction of drug or contaminated articles

Incineration: 700°C.[3]

Chemical: 10% sodium hypochlorite (1% available chlorine) for 24 hours.[1]

Contact with skin: Wash well with water, soap and water, or sodium bicarbonate solution. If the eyes are contaminated, immediate irrigation with 0.9% sodium chloride solution should be performed.[1]

References

1 ABPI (1999) *ABPI Data Sheet Compendium 1999–2000.* DataPharm Publications Ltd, London, 1190–2.

2 ABPI (1999) *ABPI Data Sheet Compendium 1999–2000*. DataPharm Publications Ltd, London, 404–5.

3 Pharmacia and Upjohn Ltd (1999) Personal communcation.

4 Reynolds JEF (ed.) (1996) *The Extra Pharmacopoeia* (31e). Pharmaceutical Press, London.

5 Hoffman DM *et al.* (1979) Stability of refrigerated and frozen solutions of doxorubicin hydrochloride. *Am J Hosp Pharm.* **36**: 1536–8.

6 Poochikian GK *et al.* (1981) Stability of anthracycline antitumour agents in four infusion fluids. *Am J Hosp Pharm.* **38**: 483–6.

7 Benvenuto JA *et al.* (1981) Stability and compatibility of antitumour agents in glass and plastic containers. *Am J Hosp Pharm.* **38**: 1914–8.

8 Karlsen J *et al.* (1983) Stability of cytotoxic intravenous solutions subjected to freeze–thaw treatment. *Nor Pharm Acta.* **45**: 61–7.

9 Beijnen JH *et al.* (1985) Stability of anthracycline antitumour agents in infusion fluids. *J Parent Sci Technol.* **39**: 220–2.

10 Bosanquet AG (1986) Stability of solutions of antineoplastic agents during preparation and storage for *in vitro* assays. II. Assay methods, adriamycin and the other antitumour antibiotics. *Cancer Chemother Pharmacol.* **17**: 1–10.

11 Bouma J *et al.* (1986) Anthracycline antitumour agents: a review of physicochemical, analytical and stability properties. *Pharm Weekbl (Sci Edn).* **8**: 109–35.

12 Keusters L *et al.* (1986) Stability of solutions of doxorubicin and epirubicin in plastic minibags for intravesical use after storage at –20°C and thawing by microwave radiation. *Pharm Weekbl (Sci Edn).* **8**: 194–7.

13 Gupta PK *et al.* (1988) Investigation of the stability of doxorubicin hydrochloride using factorial design. *Drug Dev Indust Pharm.* **14**: 1657–71.

14 Janssen MJH *et al.* (1985) Doxorubicin decomposition on storage: effect of pH, type of buffer and liposome encapsulation. *Int J Pharm.* **23**: 1–11.

15 Beijnen JH *et al.* (1986) Aspects of the degradation kinetics of doxorubicin in aqueous solution. *Int J Pharm.* **32**: 123–31.

16 Wasserman K and Bundgaard H (1983) Kinetics of the acid-catalysed hydrolysis of doxorubicin. *Int J Pharm.* **14**: 73–8.

17 Beijnen JH *et al.* (1985) Aspects of the stability of doxorubicin and seven other anthracyclines in acidic solution. *Pharm Weekbl (Sci Edn).* **7**: 109–16.

18 Abdeen Z *et al.* (1985) Degradation of adriamycin in aqueous sodium hydroxide: Formation of a ring-A oxabicyclononenone. *J Chem Res.* 254–5.

19 Tavoloni N *et al.* (1980) Photolytic degradation of adriamycin. Communications. *J Pharm Pharmacol.* **32**: 860–2.

20 Wood MJ *et al.* (1990) Photodegradation of doxorubicin, daunorubicin and epirubicin measured by high-performance liquid chromatography. *J Clin Pharm Ther.* **15**: 291–300.

21 Wood MJ *et al.* (1990) Stability of doxorubicin, daunorubicin and epirubicin in plastic syringes and minibags. *J Clin Pharm Ther.* **15**: 279–89.

22 Martel P *et al.* (1997) Stability of the principal cytostatics during storage at unusual temperatures. *Int J Pharm.* **149**: 37–42.

23 Stewart JT *et al.* (1996) Stability of ondansetron hydrochloride and five antineoplastic medications. *Am J Health-Syst Pharm.* **53**: 1297–300.

24 Dine T *et al.* (1992) Stability and compatibility of four anthracyclines, doxorubicin, daunorubicin, epirubicin and pirarubicin, with PVC infusion bags. *Pharm Weekbl (Sci Edn).* **14**: 365–9.

25 Walker S *et al.* (1991) Doxorubicin stability in syringes and glass vials and evaluation of chemical contamination. *Can J Hosp Pharm.* **44**: 71–8.

26 Stewart JT *et al.* (1997) Stability of ondansetron hydrochloride, doxorubicin hydrochloride and dacarbazine or vincristine sulphate in elastomeric portable infusion devices and polyvinyl chloride bags. *Am J Health-Syst Pharm.* **54**: 915–20.

27 Williamson M and Luce JK (1987) Microwave thawing of doxorubicin hydrochloride admixtures not recommended. *Am J Hosp Pharm.* **44**: 505, 510.

28 Wood MJ (1989) *Investigations into the stability of doxorubicin, daunorubicin and epirubicin in infusion fluids.* MPhil Thesis. University of Aston, Birmingham.

29 Pavlik EJ *et al.* (1982) Sensitivity of anticancer agents *in vitro*, standardizing the cytotoxic response and characterizing the sensitivities of a reference cell line. *Gynecol Oncol.* **14**: 243–61.

30 Pavlik EJ *et al.* (1984) Stability of doxorubicin in relation to chemosensitivity determinations: loss of lethality and retention of antiproliferative activity. *Cancer Invest.* **2**: 449–58.

31 Trissel LA (2001) *Handbook of Injectable Drugs* (11e). American Society of Hospital Pharmacists, Bethesda, MD.

32 Beijnen JH *et al.* (1986) Stability of intravenous admixtures of doxorubicin and vincristine. *Am J Hosp Pharm.* **43**: 3022–7.

33 Gaj E and Sesin P (1984) Compatibility of doxorubicin hydrochloride and vinblastine sulphate. The stability of a solution stored in Cormed reservoir bags or monoject plastic syringes. *Am J Int Ther Clin Nutr.* **11**: 8–20.

34 Nyhammar EK *et al.* (1996) Stability of doxorubicin hydrochloride and vincristine sulphate in two portable infusion-pump reservoirs. *Am J Health-Syst Pharm.* **53**: 1171–3.

35 Wolfe LJ *et al.* (1999) Compatibility and stability of vincristine sulphate, doxorubicin hydrochloride and etoposide in 0.9% sodium chloride injection. *Am J Health-Syst Pharm.* **56**: 985–9.

36 Stiles ML and Allen LV Jr (1991) Stability of doxorubicin hydrochloride in portable pump reservoirs. *Am J Hosp Pharm.* **48**: 1976–7.

37 Rochard EB *et al.* (1992) Stability of fluorouracil, cytarabine or doxorubicin hydrochloride in ethylene vinylacetate portable infusion-pump reservoirs. *Am J Hosp Pharm.* **49**: 619–23.

38 Baxter Healthcare Ltd (2000) Personal communication.

39 Lokich JJ *et al.* (1986) Doxorubicin/vinblastine and doxorubicin/cyclophosphamide combination chemotherapy by continuous infusion. *Cancer.* **58**: 1020–3.

40 Vogelsang NJ *et al.* (1985) Phase I trial of an implanted, battery-powered, programmable drug delivery system for continuous doxorubicin administration. *J Clin Oncol.* **3**: 407–14.

41 Garnick MB *et al.* (1983) Clinical evaluation of long-term continuous-infusion doxorubicin. *Cancer Treat Rep.* **67**: 133–42.

42 Bowen J *et al.* (1981) Phase-I study of adriamycin by 5-day continuous intravenous infusion. *Proc Am Assoc Cancer Res.* **22**: 354 (C-84).

43 Lokich JJ *et al.* (1983) Constant infusion schedule for adriamycin: a phase I–II clinical trial of a 30-day schedule by ambulatory pump delivery system. *J Clin Oncol.* **1**: 24–8.

44 Vogelsang NJ *et al.* (1984) Continuous doxorubicin infusion using an implanted lithium battery-powered drug administration device system (DADS, Medtronic, Inc.). *Proc Am Soc Clin Oncol.* **3**: 263 (C-1030).

45 Legha SS *et al.* (1987) Anthracyclines. In: JJ Lokich (ed.) *Cancer Chemotherapy by Infusion.* MTP Press Ltd, Lancaster.

Prepared by Jayne Wood

DOXORUBICIN LIPOSOMAL

1 General details

Approved name: Liposomal doxorubicin.

Proprietary name: Caelyx.

Manufacturer or supplier: Schering-Plough Ltd.

Presentation and formulation details: Liposomal doxorubicin consists of doxorubicin hydrochloride encapsulated in liposomes.[1] The product is a STEALTH® liposome formulation. Doxorubicin hydrochloride (HCl) is encapsulated in liposomes with surface-bound methoxypolyethylene glycol (MPEG).[1] This process is known as pegylation, and it protects the liposomes from immune detection and removal by the reticuloendothelial system (RES), thereby increasing the half-life of the drug in the bloodstream and allowing maximum tumour uptake. The STEALTH® liposome carriers are composed of N-(carbonyl-methoxypolyethylene glycol 2000)-1,2-distearoyl-sn-glycero-3-phosphoethanolamine sodium salt (MPEG-DSPE), fully hydrogenated soy phosphatidylcholine (HSPC) and cholesterol.[1] Other ingredients include ammonium sulphate, sucrose, histidine, water for injections, hydrochloric acid and/or sodium hydroxide. More than 90% of the drug is encapsulated in liposomes designed to provide a prolonged circulation time in the bloodstream, the half-life being approximately 55 hours.[2] The mean particle size is approximately 100 nm.

The product is a sterile, translucent, red suspension in 10-mL glass, single-use vials. Each vial contains 20 mg doxorubicin HCl at a concentration of 2 mg/mL.[1]

Storage and shelf-life of unopened container: Unopened vials have a shelf-life of 18 months if stored at 2–8°C. Avoid freezing.[1]

2 Chemistry

Type: Cytotoxic anthracycline antibiotic.

Molecular structure: As for doxorubicin, but encapsulated in liposomes.

Molecular formula: see monograph for doxorubicin.

Molecular weight: A particulate suspension.

pH of suspension: 6.5.

3 Stability profile

3.1 Physical and chemical stability

Doxorubicin liposomal diluted in 5% glucose is physically stable for 24 hours if stored at 2–8°C.[1]

Compatibility with other drugs: The manufacturer recommends that doxorubicin liposomal should not be allowed to mix with any other drugs.[1,3] However, the physical compatibility of doxorubicin liposomal during simulated Y-site administration with a wide range of drugs has been studied.[4]

3.2 Stability in clinical practice

Liposomal doxorubicin must only be diluted in 5% glucose,[1,3] and can be stored for up to 24 hours at 2–8°C.[1]

3.3 Stability in specialised delivery systems

No information available.

4 Clinical use

Type of cytotoxic: Doxorubicin encapsulated in liposomes coated with bio-compatible polymers has been shown in animal models to be less toxic and to distribute more selectively to tumours, compared with the same dose of conventional doxorubicin. These liposomes are also claimed to evade rapid detection and uptake by cells of the reticuloendothelial system, unlike conventional liposomes, which are rapidly cleared from the bloodstream. The treatment rationale for the use of doxorubicin encapsulated in STEALTH® liposomes is to protect liposomes from detection by the RES and to increase the circulation time of the drug in the bloodstream, thereby increasing the drug concentration in the tumour. For example, the concentration of doxorubicin in the liposomal form used in Kaposi's sarcoma (KS) lesions was a median of 19 (range 3–53) times higher than in normal skin 48 hours after administration.[2,5]

It should be noted that doxorubicin liposomal (Caelyx) displays unique pharma-cokinetic properties and must not be used interchangeably with other formulations of doxorubicin hydrochloride.

Main indication: AIDS-related Kaposi's sarcoma.

Dosage and administration: Doxorubicin liposomal should be administered intravenously at 20 mg/m² every 2 to 3 weeks in the treatment of AIDS-related Kaposi's sarcoma. Intervals between doses of less than 10 days should be avoided in order to prevent drug accumulation and increased toxicity. Patients should be treated for 2 to 3 months to achieve a therapeutic response. Treatment should be continued as necessary to maintain a therapeutic response.

5 Preparation of injection

Bolus administration: Must be avoided. Liposomal doxorubicin must not be given by the intramuscular or subcutaneous route.

Intravenous infusion: Liposomal doxorubicin must be diluted before administration. It is diluted in 250 mL of 5% glucose and administered by intravenous infusion over 30 minutes, using either a peripheral vein or a central venous line. It is recommended that the infusion line be connected through the side port of an intravenous infusion of 5% glucose in order to achieve further dilution and thereby minimise the risk of thrombosis and extravasation. An in-line filter must not be used.

Extravasation: Group 2 classification (exfoliant). (Animal studies indicate that administration of doxorubicin as a liposomal formulation reduces the potential for extravasation injury, compared with doxorubicin.) (*See* Chapter 6.)

6 Destruction of drug or contaminated articles

Incineration: 700°C.

Chemical: 10% sodium hypochlorite (recommended for doxorubicin).

Contact with skin: Wash immediately and thoroughly with soap and water.

References

1 ABPI (1999) *ABPI Data Sheet Compendium 1999–2000.* DataPharm Publications Ltd, London, 1473–4.
2 Hillery AM (1998) Liposomal drug delivery – clinical applications. *Pharm J.* **261**: 712–15.
3 Sequus Pharmaceuticals Inc. (Alza International) (1999) Personal communication.
4 Trissel LA *et al.* (1997) Compatibility of doxorubicin hydrochloride liposomal injection with selected drugs during simulated Y-site administration. *Am J Health-Syst Pharm.* **54**: 2708–13.
5 Gabison A *et al.* (1994) Clinical studies of liposome-encapsulated anthracyclines. *Acta Oncol.* **7**: 779–86.

Prepared by Yaacov Cass

EPIRUBICIN

1 General details

Approved name: Epirubicin.

Proprietary name: Pharmorubicin Rapid Dissolution, Pharmorubicin Solution for Injection.

Manufacturer or supplier: Pharmacia and Upjohn Ltd.

Presentation and formulation details:

▼ Pharmorubicin Rapid Dissolution: Sterile, pyrogen-free, red, freeze-dried powder in vials containing 10 mg, 20 mg or 50 mg of epirubicin hydrochloride with lactose and hydroxybenzoate. The inclusion of hydroxybenzoate 0.04% (which is a subpreservative concentration) is to prevent gel formation, which used to occur occasionally on reconstitution of Pharmorubicin.[1]

▼ Pharmorubicin Solution for Injection: Sterile, red, mobile solution in vials containing 10 mg, 50 mg or 200 mg of epirubicin hydrochloride as a 2 mg/mL solution in 0.9% sodium chloride.[2]

Storage and shelf-life of unopened container:

▼ Pharmorubicin Rapid Dissolution: 3 years when protected from sunlight at room temperature.[3]

▼ Pharmorubicin Solution for Injection: If stored at 2-8°C the shelf-life is 2 years.[2] Once removed from the refrigerator the shelf-life is 48 hours. Use within 24 hours of first penetration of the rubber stopper.[2]

2 Chemistry

Type: A cytotoxic antibiotic consisting of an amino sugar, acosamine, linked through a glycosidic bond to the C7 of a tetracyclic aglycone, doxorubicinone.

Molecular structure: (8S,10S)-10-(3-amino-2,3,6-trideoxy-α-L-*arabino*-hexopyrano-syloxy)-8-glycolloyl-7,8,9,10-tetrahydro-6,8,11-trihydroxy-1-methoxy-naphthacene-5,12-dione hydrochloride.

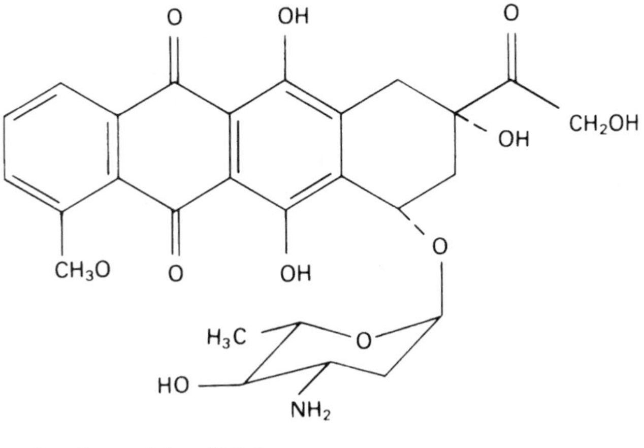

Molecular weight: 580.0.

Solubility: Epirubicin is soluble in water for injections, 5% glucose and 0.9% sodium chloride.[4]

3 Stability profile

3.1 *Physical and chemical stability*

The manufacturer states that reconstituted solutions of Pharmorubicin Rapid Dissolution are chemically stable for up to 48 hours at 2–8°C or 24 hours at room temperature.[1] Pharmorubicin Solution for Injection is stable for 2 years at 2–8°C and for 48 hours at room temperature.[3] The literature indicates that epirubicin may be chemically stable for longer periods, although few data have been published.[5,6] The stability of epirubicin depends on a number of factors. Degradation in aqueous solution is pH dependent. Epirubicin is also light sensitive and is adsorbed on to glass and certain plastics.

Effect of pH: Acidic hydrolysis of epirubicin (pH below 4) yields a red-coloured, water-insoluble aglycone (doxorubicinone) and a water-soluble amino sugar (acosamine). At pH values above 4, the degradation pathway of epirubicin has not been elucidated. However, on addition to strongly alkaline solution a colour change from red to deep blue-purple is observed and rapid degradation occurs. Data on the degradation of epirubicin in alkaline solution have been published which indicate that at pH 8.0 the main degradation product is 7,8,-dehydro-9, 10-desacetyldaunorubicinone.[7]

Effect of light: Data on the kinetics of degradation of doxorubicin in fluorescent light have been published,[8] but until recently there were no data available for epirubicin. Results from a study in which the rates of photodegradation of doxorubicin, daunorubicin and epirubicin were compared indicated that the rate of photodegradation of epirubicin was similar to that of doxorubicin. This suggests that photodegradation of epirubicin may be significant at concentrations below 100 µg/mL if solutions are exposed to light for sufficient time.[9] However, at higher concentrations, such as those used for cancer chemotherapy (at least 500 µg/mL), no special precautions are necessary to protect freshly prepared solutions of epirubicin from light.[9] This hypothesis is supported by the results of Pujol *et al.*,[10] who studied the stability of epirubicin at 2 mg/mL in 0.9% sodium chloride in polypropylene syringes at 25°C and 4°C, both protected from light and exposed to room light. The results showed that epirubicin was stable for at least 14 days at room temperature and for 180 days at 4°C. As no differences in stability were found for solutions stored under room light or stored in the dark, those authors also indicated that no special precautions are necessary to protect epirubicin solutions (at 2 mg/mL) from light.

Effect of temperature: In a well-controlled study, Beijnen *et al.*[7] reported that epirubicin was stable, in polypropylene tubes, in 5% glucose (pH 4.7) and 3.3% glucose with 0.3% sodium chloride (pH 4.4) for 28 days at 25°C, when stored in the dark. However, in 0.9% sodium chloride (pH 7.0) significant degradation occurred after 8 days at the same temperature.[7] Martel *et al.*[11] studied the stability of epirubicin at 2 mg/mL in glass vials at 4, 23 and 33°C when protected from light. Their results showed that epirubicin was stable for 12 months (less than 10% degradation) at all three temperatures studied. Wood *et al.*[12] reported that epirubicin was stable for at least 43 days in PVC minibags in 5% glucose (pH 4.36) and 0.9% sodium chloride (pH 5.20) at 25 and 4°C. When dissolved in 0.9% sodium chloride (pH 6.47), epirubicin was stable for 24 days at 25°C and at least 43 days at 4°C. In the same study, epirubicin was reported to be stable for at least 43 days, when reconstituted with water for injections and stored in polypropylene syringes at 4°C.

Adams et al.[13] reported that epirubicin (at 0.5 mg/mL and 1 mg/mL in 0.9% sodium chloride) was stable in plastic syringes (Braun Omnifix) for 28 days at 4 and 20°C. Dine et al.[14] reported that epirubicin (at 20 µg/mL in 5% glucose and 0.9% sodium chloride was stable in PVC infusion bags (Macopharma Laboratories) for 7 days at 4°C when protected from light. De Vroe et al.[15] investigated the stability of epirubicin during storage and simulated continuous infusion. Sorption to administration sets was also studied. The results showed that epirubicin (at 50 µg/mL) was stable in PVC, glass and high-density polyethylene (HDPE) in 0.9% sodium chloride (pH 5.5) and 5% glucose (pH 4.26) for periods of 24 and 25 days, respectively, at 4°C. No sorption on to infusion containers or administration sets was observed during simulated infusion. Infusion through an end-line filter (Pall ELD-96 LL) resulted in a negligible loss of potency.

Two studies have investigated the effects of freezing epirubicin. In the first, epirubicin was reported to be stable for 4 weeks when frozen at –20°C in PVC minibags containing 0.9% sodium chloride.[6] In the second, epirubicin was observed to be stable for at least 43 days in PVC minibags in 5% glucose (pH 4.36) and 0.9% sodium chloride (pH 5.20 and 6.47) at –20°C.[12] Repeated freezing and re-thawing of these minibags at ambient temperature did not cause degradation.

Container compatibility: Epirubicin is compatible with polypropylene, PVC and glass.[12,15,16] Epirubicin adsorbs on to glass and polyethylene, but not on to siliconised glass or polypropylene.[12,16] However, in clinical practice, when epirubicin is used at concentrations of at least 500 µg/mL, adsorptive losses during storage and delivery are negligible.[12,15,16]

Compatibility with other drugs: Prolonged contact with any solution of alkaline pH should be avoided. Epirubicin should not be mixed with heparin, as a precipitate may form.[1,2] The manufacturers recommend that epirubicin should not be mixed with any other drugs.

3.2. Stability in clinical practice

Epirubicin is compatible with polypropylene, PVC and glass.[12,15,16] Epirubicin appears to be chemically stable in PVC minibags (100 µg/mL) for at least 28 days in 5% glucose and 0.9% sodium chloride at 4 and –20°C, and in polypropylene syringes (2 mg/mL) for at least 28 days at 4°C.[12] After reconstitution with water for injections, vials of epirubicin (2 mg/mL) are stable for at least 14 days at 4°C.[10,16]

3.3. Stability in specialised delivery systems

Epirubicin (at 200 µg/mL to 1 mg/mL) in sodium chloride is stable for 91 days in the Baxter infusor and Intermate devices at 2–8°C, followed by up to 7 days at 33°C.[17]

4 Clinical use

Type of cytotoxic: Cytotoxic antibiotic that interacts with DNA to interfere with nucleic acid synthesis.

Main indications: Epirubicin as a single agent has produced regression in a wide range of neoplastic conditions, including breast, ovarian, gastric, lung and colorectal carcinomas, lymphomas, leukaemias and multiple myeloma. Intravesical epirubicin has been found to be beneficial in the treatment of papillary transitional-cell carcinoma of the bladder, and in the prophylaxis of recurrences after transurethral resection. Epirubicin may be used in combination with other cytotoxic agents.[1,2]

Dosage and administration:
Conventional doses: dosage is usually calculated on the basis of body surface area. For single-agent intravenous therapy the dose range most commonly used is 60–90 mg/m^2 every 3 weeks. The total dose for the cycle may be divided over two successive days. When epirubicin is used in combination therapy with other cytotoxic drugs, the dosage should be reduced. The dosage should also be reduced in cases of hepatic impairment.[1] In moderate hepatic impairment (bilirubin concentration 1.4–3 mg/100 mL) the dosage should be reduced by 50%, and in severe impairment (bilirubin concentration above 3 mg/100 mL) the dosage should be reduced by 75%.

High doses: use epirubicin as a single agent in previously untreated small-cell lung cancer at high doses (120 mg/m^2) on day 1 every 3 weeks. For previously untreated non-small-cell lung cancer (squamous, large-cell and adenocarcinoma), use 135 mg/m^2 on day 1 or 45 mg/m^2 on days 1, 2 and 3, every 3 weeks.

Epirubicin can be used intravesically to treat papillary transitional-cell carcinoma of the bladder and carcinoma *in situ*. However, it should not be used to treat invasive bladder tumours which have penetrated the bladder wall, where systemic therapy or surgery is more appropriate. Epirubicin has also been used successfully intravesically as a prophylactic agent after transurethral resection of superficial tumours in order to prevent recurrences.

For therapy of papillary transitional-cell carcinoma of the bladder, weekly instillations of 50 mg in 50 mL of normal saline or water for injections are given for 8 weeks. If local toxicity occurs (chemical cystitis), a dose reduction to 30 mg in 50 mL is advised. For carcinoma *in situ* the dose may be increased to 80 mg in 50 mL (depending on patient tolerance). For prophylaxis, weekly administration of 50 mg in 50 mL for 4 weeks is followed by monthly instillations for 11 months at the same dosage. The solution should be retained intravesically for 1 hour. During the instillation, the pelvis of the patient should be rotated occasionally, and they should be instructed to void at the end of the instillation time.[1]

A cumulative dose of 900–1000 mg/m^2 should only be exceeded with extreme caution, as above this level the risk of irreversible congestive cardiac failure increases greatly. A lower cumulative dose of epirubicin is recommended for patients with prior or concomitant mediastinal radiation or therapy with related anthracycline compounds (e.g. doxorubicin or daunorubicin) or anthracene derivatives.[1,2]

5 Preparation of injection

Reconstitution: The contents of the 10-mg vial are reconstituted with 5 mL of water for injections or 0.9% sodium chloride, those of the 20-mg vial with 10 mL, and those of the 50-mg vial with 25 mL of either of the same solvents. After addition of the diluent and gentle shaking of the contents, without inversion of the vial, the contents will dissolve within 30 seconds to produce a solution of 2 mg/mL.[1]

Bolus administration: Injection is only by the intravenous route. Epirubicin should not be injected intramuscularly or intrathecally. The reconstituted solution is given over 3 to 5 minutes via the tubing of a freely running intravenous infusion of 0.9% sodium chloride. This technique minimises the risk of thrombosis or perivenous extravasation, which can lead to severe cellulitis or vesication.[1,2] Administration of epirubicin by intra-arterial, intrapleural and intraperitoneal routes has been investigated in clinical trials.[18-20]

Intravenous infusion: Continuous-infusion schedules of epirubicin have been investigated in America. At New York University epirubicin has been given as a 6-hour infusion.[21] At the MD Anderson Hospital in Houston, TX, a 48-hour infusion of doxorubicin (60–70 mg/m^2) has been compared with a 48-hour infusion of epirubicin (90–105 mg/m^2).[22]

Extravasation: Group 1 classification (vesicant) (*see* Chapter 6).

6 Destruction of drug or contaminated articles

Incineration: 700°C.[3]

Chemical: 10% sodium hypochlorite (1% available chlorine) for 24 hours.[1,2]

Contact with skin: Wash well with water, soap and water, or sodium bicarbonate solution. If the eyes are contaminated, immediate irrigation with 0.9% sodium chloride solution should be performed. [1,2]

References

1 ABPI (1999) *ABPI Data Sheet Compendium 1999–2000.* DataPharm Publications Ltd, London, 1224–5.

2 ABPI (1999) *ABPI Data Sheet Compendium 1999–2000.* DataPharm Publications Ltd, London, 1225–6.

3 Pharmacia and Upjohn Ltd (1999) Personal communication.

4 Reynolds JEF (ed.) (1996) *The Extra Pharmacopoeia* (31e). Pharmaceutical Press, London, 569–70.

5 Beijnen JH *et al.* (1985) Stability of anthracycline antitumour agents in infusion fluids. *J Parent Sci Technol.* **39**: 220–22.

6 Keusters L *et al.* (1986) Stability of solutions of doxorubicin and epirubicin in plastic minibags for intravesical use after storage at –20°C and thawing by microwave radiation. *Pharm Weekbl (Sci Edn).* **8**: 194–7.

7 Beijnen JH *et al.* (1986) Aspects of the degradation kinetics of doxorubicin in aqueous solution. *Int J Pharm.* **32**: 123–31.

8 Tavoloni N *et al.* (1980) Photolytic degradation of adriamycin. *J Pharm Pharmacol.* **32**: 860–2.

9 Wood MJ *et al.* (1990) Photodegradation of doxorubicin, daunorubicin and epirubicin measured by high-performance liquid chromatography. *J Clin Pharm Ther.* **15**: 291–300.

10 Pujol M *et al.* (1997) Stability of epirubicin in NaCl 0.9% injection. *Ann Pharmacother.* **31**: 992–5.

11 Martel P *et al.* (1997) Stability of the principal cytostatic agents during storage at unusual temperatures. *Int J Pharm.* **149**: 37–42.

12 Wood MJ *et al.* (1990) Stability of doxorubicin, daunorubicin and epirubicin in plastic syringes and minibags. *J Clin Pharm Ther.* **15**: 279–89.

13 Adams PS *et al.* (1987) Pharmaceutical aspects of home infusion therapy for cancer patients. *Pharm J.* **238**: 476–8.

14 Dine T *et al.* (1992) Stability and compatibility of four anthracyclines: doxorubicin, daunorubicin, epirubicin and pirarubicin with PVC infusion bags. *Pharm Weekbl (Sci Edn).* **14**: 365–9.

15 De Vroe C *et al.* (1990) A study on the stability of three antineoplastic drugs and on their sorption by IV delivery systems and endline filters. *Int J Pharm.* **65**: 49–56.

16 Wood MJ (1989) *Investigations into the stability of doxorubicin, daunorubicin and epirubicin in infusion fluids.* MPhil Thesis. University of Aston, Birmingham.

17 Baxter Healthcare Ltd (2000) Personal communication.

18 Ferrazzi E *et al.* (1982) Preliminary phase II experience with 4'epidoxorubicin. In: FM Muggia, CW Young and SK Carter (eds) *Anthracycline Antibiotics in Cancer Therapy.* Martinus Nijhoff, The Hague.

19 Strocchi E *et al.* (1983) 4'epidoxorubicin in locoregional therapy: pharmacokinetic study after intrahepatic arterial and intraperitoneal administration. In: *Proceedings of the Fourth National Cancer Institute – European Organisation for Research and Treatment of Cancer Symposium*, Brussels, 14–17 Dec, Abst 18.

20 Friedman MA and Ignoffo RJ (1984) Intra-arterial use of adriamycin. In: M Ogawa, FM Muggia and M Rozencweig (eds) *Adriamycin: Its Expanding Role in Cancer Treatment.* Excerpta Medica, Tokyo.

21 Muggia FM and Green MD (1984) Special modes of administration. In: G Bonnadonna (ed.) *Advances in Anthracycline Chemotherapy: Epirubicin.* Masson, Milan.

22 Bodey GP *et al.* (1983) Clinical trials with 4'epidoxorubicin. In: *Proceedings of the 13th International Congress on Chemotherapy.* Vienna, Aug–Sept, 215/23–215/26.

Prepared by Jayne Wood

ETOPOSIDE

1 General details

Approved name: Etoposide.

Proprietary name: Vepesid.

Manufacturer or supplier: Bristol-Myers Squibb Pharmaceuticals Ltd.

Presentation and formulation details: Glass vials containing 100 mg etoposide in 5 mL solution (20 mg/mL). Each vial also contains polyethylene glycol 300, ethyl alcohol, polysorbate 80, benzyl alcohol and citric acid.

Storage and shelf-life of unopened container: Five years from the date of manufacture when stored at room temperature and protected from light.[1]

2 Chemistry

Type: Semisynthetic podophyllotoxin derivative.

Molecular structure: 4-*o*-demethyl-1-1 *o*-(4,6-*o*-ethylidene-β-D-glucopyranosyl)-epi-podophyllotoxin.

Molecular weight: 588.6.

Solubility: Highly insoluble in water, but soluble in organic solvents.[1] In dilutions with 0.9% sodium chloride, the concentration of etoposide should not exceed 0.25 mg/mL.[2] However, in other reports it is suggested that concentrations up to 0.4 mg/mL are acceptable in clinical practice.[3,4] Occasional precipitation of drug has been reported in infusions where the etoposide concentration exceeded

0.4 mg/mL.[4] Etoposide precipitation is unpredictable, and depends not only on drug concentration but also on other physical factors.[5]

3 Stability profile

3.1 Physical and chemical stability

Etoposide degrades by hydrolytic cleavage of the glucopyranosyl moiety, or by epimerisation to the *cis*-lactone.

Effect of pH: Maximum stability is found at pH 5.0.[6] The aglycone may hydrolyse in acid, while base-catalysed epimerisation occurs in alkali.[6]

Effect of light: Etoposide should be protected from light during storage,[2] and from strong daylight during administration.

Container compatibility: According to the manufacturers,[1] glass or PVC containers are suitable for etoposide infusion. However, significant leaching of DEHP plasticiser occurs from a PVC medication reservoir into an infusion containing etoposide (0.4 mg/mL).[7] DEHP concentrations in 100 mL volume infusion after 24 hours at 37°C and 8°C exceeded 100 µg/mL and 20 µg/mL, respectively.[7] For this reason, EVA or glass containers should be used for etoposide administration.

Dilute infusions of etoposide are compatible with polypropylene syringes,[8] but undiluted Vepesid injection has been implicated in the formation of hairline cracks in infusion devices constructed of plastics produced from the monomers acrylonitride, butadiene and styrene.[9] The effect on these plastics (known collectively as ABS plastic) has been attributed to the action of polyethylene glycol (PEG) 300, a solubilising agent in the formulation. Caution should be exercised in the use of any plastic infusion device with undiluted etoposide injection.

Etoposide injection is incompatible with cellulose acetate membrane filters, but is compatible with nylon or fluripore-type membranes.[10] Etoposide infusion is also compatible with the Pall ELD 96 pyrogen retentive 'set-saver' filter.[11]

Compatibility with other drugs: The manufacturer does not recommend mixing etoposide with any other drug.[2] A combination of vincristine (up to 2 µg/mL), doxorubicin hydrochloride (up to 50 µg/mL) and etoposide (Vepesid) diluted in 0.9% sodium chloride and stored in polyolefin-lined bags (Excel 250-mL capacity container) was compatible and stable for at least 72 hours when stored at room temperature, provided that the concentration of etoposide did not exceed 0.25 mg/mL.[12] Combinations containing vincristine sulphate 1.6 µg/mL, doxorubicin hydrochloride 40 µg/mL and etoposide 0.2 mg/mL were also stable for 72 hours when stored at 31–33°C.[13] The physical compatibility of etoposide with a wide range of drugs has been summarised by Trissel.[12]

3.2 Stability in clinical practice

Etoposide infusions (0.4 mg/mL) in 5% glucose and in 0.9% sodium chloride are chemically stable for at least 4 days at room temperature.[5] As in an earlier report,[3] the stability of etoposide was not influenced by the type of container material (glass or PVC) or by normal room fluorescent lighting. However, one report has suggested that etoposide may be daylight-sensitive and is unstable beyond 6 hours in unprotected solutions.[4]

Polypropylene syringes containing etoposide infusion (1 mg/mL in water for injections) prepared for continuous infusion were chemically stable at 4 and 20°C for 28 days.[8] However, etoposide precipitated during administration and clinical use of concentrated infusions cannot be recommended.

Etoposide injection diluted with water to 10 mg/mL for oral use and filled into 5-mL plastic *oral* syringes (Burron Medical, model 0–5C) was stable for 22 days at ambient temperature (22°C) irrespective of the lighting conditions employed.[14]

3.3 Stability in specialised delivery systems

Etoposide at 0.4 mg/mL diluted in 0.9% sodium chloride and stored in Graseby 9000 series PVC Medication Cassettes is physically and chemically stable for 14 days at 8°C and 7 days at 37°C.[7] However, substantial extraction of DEHP occurs amounting to 35 µg/mL after 14 days of storage at 8°C or 100 µg/mL after 7 days at 37°C.[15]

4 Clinical use

Type of cytotoxic: Mitotic inhibitor that arrests the cell cycle in the G_2 phase.

Main indications: Small-cell carcinoma of the lung. Resistant non-seminomatous testicular carcinoma.

Dosage by injection: 60–120 mg/m² by intravenous infusion daily, for 5 consecutive days repeated every 3 to 4 weeks. Alternatively, 100 mg/m²/day on days 1, 2, 3 and 5, every 3 to 4 weeks.

Oral: Twice the intravenous dose should be given on 5 consecutive days, every 3 to 4 weeks, myelosuppression permitting.

5 Preparation of the injection

Dilution: The injection should be diluted in 0.9% sodium chloride solution to give a maximum concentration of 0.25 mg/mL etoposide in the infusion.

Bolus administration: Not recommended.

Intravenous infusion: The dose should be given by infusion over not less than 30 minutes.

Extravasation: Group 3 classification (irritant) (*see* Chapter 6).

6 Destruction of drug or contaminated articles

Incineration: 1000°C.

Chemical: 10% sodium hypochlorite solution (1% available chlorine) for 24 hours.

Contact with skin: Accidental exposure to etoposide may cause skin reactions. A soap and water wash should be employed.

References

1 ABPI (1999) *ABPI Data Sheet Compendium 1999–2000.* DataPharm Publications Ltd, London, 246–7.

2 Reynolds JEF (ed.) (1982) *The Extra Pharmacopoeia* (29e). Pharmaceutical Press, London.

3 Phillips NC and Lauper RD (1983) Review of etoposide. *Clin Pharm.* **2**: 112–19.

4 Arnold AM (1979) Podophyllotoxin derivative VP16-213. *Cancer Chemother Pharmacol.* **3**: 71–80.

5 Beijnen JH *et al.* (1991) Chemical and physical stability of etoposide and teniposide in commonly used infusion fluids. *J Parent Sci Technol.* **45**: 108–12.

6 Lidenberg WJM *et al.* (1985) Analysis and degradation kinetics of etoposide (VP16-213) in aqueous solution. *Pharm Weekbl Sci Ed.* **1**: 291.

7 Sewell GJ and Priston MJ (1995) Stability and compatibility studies on a range of drug infusions in a new, multipurpose ambulatory pump. Presentation at National Quality Control Symposium (Aseptic Preparation Services), Coventry, UK, 27–28 September 1995.

8 Adams PS *et al.* (1987) Pharmaceutical aspects of home infusion therapy for cancer patients. *Pharm J.* **238**: 476–8.

9 Schwinghammer TL and Reilly M (1988) Cracking of ABS plastic devices used to infuse undiluted etoposide injection (letter). *Am J Hosp Pharm.* **45**: 1277.

10 Forrest SC (1984) Vepesid injection (letter). *Pharm J.* **232**: 88.

11 Pall Biomedical, Portsmouth, UK (1995) Personal communication.

12 Trissel LA (2001) *Handbook of Injectable Drugs* (11e). American Society of Health-Systems Pharmacists, Bethesda, MD.

13 Wolfe JL *et al.* (1999) Compatibility and stability of vincristine sulphate, doxorubicin hydrochloride and etoposide in 0.9% sodium chloride injection. *Am J Health-Syst Pharm.* **56**: 985–9.

14 McLeod HL and Relling MV (1992) Stability of etoposide solution for oral use. *Am J Hosp Pharm.* **49**: 2784–5.

15 Priston MJ and Sewell GJ (1998) Stability of three cytotoxic drug infusions in the Graseby 9000 ambulatory infusion pump. *J Oncol Pharm Pract.* **4**: 143–9.

Prepared by Graham Sewell

ETOPOSIDE PHOSPHATE

1 General details

Approved name: Etoposide phosphate.

Proprietary name: Etopophos Injection.

Manufacturer or supplier: Bristol-Myers Squibb Pharmaceuticals Ltd.

Presentation and formulation details: Glass vials containing 113.6 mg etoposide phosphate, equivalent to 100 mg etoposide, as a lyophilised powder for reconstitution. Each vial also contains 300 mg dextran 40 and 32.7 mg sodium citrate.[1]

Storage and shelf-life of unopened container: 18 months if stored at 2–8°C and protected from light.[1]

2 Chemistry

Type: Dephosphorylated etoposide, a semisynthetic podophyllotoxin derivative.

Molecular structure: 4′-demethylepipodophyllotoxin 9-[4,6-0-(R)-ethylidene-beta-D-glucopyranoside] 4′-(dihydrogen phosphate).

Molecular weight: 760.7.

Solubility: Solubility in water is greater than 100 mg/mL.[2]

pH: Solutions reconstituted in water for injections have a pH of approximately 2.9.[2]

3 Stability profile

3.1 Physical and chemical stability

Etoposide degrades by hydrolytic cleavage of the glucopyranosyl moiety to form etoposide, or by epimerisation of the *cis*-lactone.

Effect of pH: Maximum stability is found at pH 5.[3] The aglycone may hydrolyse in acid conditions, while base-catalysed epimerisation occurs in alkali.[3]

Effect of light: Etoposide should be protected from light during storage and from strong daylight during administration.[1,4]

Container compatibility: Etoposide phosphate injection is compatible with glass, PVC and plastic syringes, and there are no known interactions with acrylic or other polymers.[5]

Compatibility with other drugs: Etoposide phosphate has been reported to be physically compatible with a large number of drugs.[6]

3.2 Stability in clinical practice

The manufacturer indicates that Etopophos Injection, following reconstitution in water for injections, 5% glucose or 0.9% sodium chloride to a concentration of 10–20 mg/mL etoposide equivalent, is chemically and physically stable for 48 hours at 37°C, 96 hours at 25°C and 7 days at 2–8°C.[7] Following dilution in 5% glucose or 0.9% sodium chloride to concentrations as low as 0.1 mg/mL, it is also chemically and physically stable for 48 hours at 37°C, 96 hours at 25°C and 7 days at 2–8°C.[3] Etopophos infusions can be stored at 2–8°C after preparation.[7]

It has recently been reported that Etopophos, reconstituted and diluted in 5% glucose or 0.9% sodium chloride to concentrations in the range 0.1–10 mg/mL etoposide equivalent in PVC bags is stable for at least 7 days at 31°C, and 31 days at 23°C or 4°C.[5] It is similarly stable after reconstitution in water for injections to concentrations in the range 10–20 mg/mL, and when stored in plastic syringes (Plastipak, BD) it was stable for the same time period.[5]

3.3 Stability in specialised delivery systems

Etoposide phosphate solutions containing 1.5 mg/mL in PVC reservoirs (Pharmacia Deltec) and stored at 20 or 37°C were stable for at least 7 days.[8]

4 Clinical use

Type of cytotoxic: Etoposide phosphate is converted to etoposide *in vivo*. Etoposide is a mitotic inhibitor that arrests the cell cycle in the G_2 phase.

Main indications: Small-cell carcinoma of the lung and resistant non-seminomatous testicular carcinoma.

Dosage: Recommended dosage is 60–120 mg/m² (etoposide equivalent) daily for 5 consecutive days, repeated not more frequently than at 21-day intervals.[1] When used in combination therapy, the dosage should be reduced to the lower end of the dosage range.

5 Preparation of injection

Reconstitution: The contents are reconstituted with 5 or 10 mL of water for injections, 5% glucose or 0.9% sodium chloride, yielding a solution containing 20 or 10 mg/mL etoposide equivalent (22.7 mg/mL or 11.4 mg/mL etoposide phosphate). The solution can be diluted in 5% glucose or 0.9% sodium chloride infusion to 0.1 mg/mL etoposide equivalent (0.14 mg/mL etoposide phosphate).[1]

Bolus administration: The reconstituted solution may be injected undiluted.

Intravenous infusion: Infuse over not less than 5 minutes.

Extravasation: Group 4 classification (inflammatory) (*see* Chapter 6).

6 Destruction of drug or contaminated articles

Incineration: 1000°C.

Chemical: 10% sodium hypochlorite (1% available chlorine) for 24 hours.

Contact with skin: Accidental exposure may cause skin reactions. A soap and water wash should be employed.

References

1 ABPI (1999) *ABPI Data Sheet Compendium 1999–2000.* DataPharm Publications Ltd, London, 250–1.
2 Trissel LA (2001) *Handbook of Injectable Drugs.* (11e). American Society of Health-Systems Pharmacists, Bethesda, MD.
3 Lidenberg WJM *et al.* (1995) Analysis and degradation kinetics of etoposide (VP 16-213) in aqueous solution. *Pharm Weekbl (Sci Edn).* **1**: 291–8.
4 Beijnen JH *et al.* (1991) Chemical and physical stability of etoposide and teniposide in commonly used infusion fluids. *J Parent Sci Technol.* **45**: 108–12.
5 Zhang Y and Trissel LA (1999) Physical and chemical stability of etoposide phosphate solutions. *J Am Pharm Assoc.* **39**: 146–50.
6 Trissel LA *et al.* (1999) Compatibility of etoposide phosphate with selected drugs during simulated Y-site injection. *J Am Pharm Assoc.* **39**: 141–5.
7 Bristol Myers Squibb Ltd (2000) Personal communication.
8 Webster LK *et al.* (1995) Conversion of etoposide phosphate to etoposide under ambulatory infusion conditions. *J Oncol Pharm Pract.* **1**: 33–6.

Prepared by Andrew Stanley

FLOXURIDINE*

1 General details

Approved name: Floxuridine.

Proprietary name: FUDR.

Manufacturer or supplier: Hoffman La Roche.

Presentation and formulation details: White powder in vials containing 500 mg floxuridine.

Storage and shelf-life of unopened container: Three years if stored at 15–30°C.

2 Chemistry

Type: Nucleoside consisting of the pyrimidine base fluorouracil and the sugar deoxyribose.

Molecular structure: 5-fluoro-2′-deoxyuridine-5′-phosphate (FUDR monophosphate).

Molecular weight: 246.2.

Solubility: Freely soluble in water and soluble in ethanol.

3 Stability profile

3.1 Physical and chemical stability

The manufacturer indicates that floxuridine is relatively stable in aqueous solutions. After reconstitution, the solution has a pH of 4.0–5.5. The pH for optimum stability is between 4 and 7.[1]

Compatibility with other drugs: Floxuridine has been shown to be compatible and chemically stable for limited periods with a range of drugs, including carboplatin,[2] cisplatin,[3] etoposide[2] and fluorouracil.[4]

3.2 Stability in clinical practice

Reconstituted solution should be stored at 2–8°C and used within 14 days.[5] Floxuridine diluted in 0.9% sodium chloride to contain 1–50 mg/mL, and stored in plastic syringes at 30°C, is stable for 21 days.[6]

*Not licensed in the UK.

3.3 Stability in specialised delivery systems

Floxuridine diluted in 0.9% sodium chloride to contain 2.5–12.5 mg/mL and stored in the reservoirs of an implantable pump (Infusaid Model 400 pump) under simulated clinical conditions (37°C) was reported to be stable for 12 days.[7] A similar study using solutions containing 10 mg/mL floxuridine stored in the reservoir of the Fresenius VIP 30 pump indicated that floxuridine was stable for 6 weeks.[8]

Note: Not licensed in the UK (approved in the USA).

4 Clinical use

Type of cytotoxic: Antimetabolite that is metabolised to fluorouracil after administration.

Main indications: Primarily used intra-arterially to treat hepatic metastases from colorectal or gastrointestinal carcinoma.[1]

Dosage: The usual dosage of floxuridine by continuous infusion is 0.1–0.6 mg/kg/day. Higher dosages (0.4–0.6 mg/kg daily) are usually used for hepatic artery infusion, since the liver metabolises the drug and thus reduces the risk of systemic toxicity.[1]

Floxuridine has been administered intravenously in the treatment of solid tumours. A dose of 0.5–1 mg/kg for 6–15 days, or until toxicity occurs, has been used. By single intravenous injection the usual dosage is 30 mg/kg/day for 5 days, followed by 15 mg/kg every other day for up to 11 days, or until toxicity occurs.[1]

5 Preparation of injection

Reconstitution: Floxuridine should be reconstituted with 5 mL of water for injection to provide a solution containing 100 mg/mL. Reconstituted vials are stable for 2 weeks at 2–8°C.[1,5]

The desired dose is diluted in 0.9% sodium chloride or 5% glucose in the required volume.

Extravasation: Group 2 classification (exfoliant) (*see* Chapter 6).

6 Destruction of drug or contaminated articles

Incineration: No specific information available.

Chemical: No specific information available.

Contact with skin: No specific information available.

References

1 McEvoy GK (1999) *Drug Information – American Hospital Formulary Service.* American Society of Health-Systems Pharmacists, Bethesda, MD.
2 Williams DA (1990) Stability and compatibility of antineoplastic drugs. In: JJ Lokich (ed.) *Cancer Chemotherapy by Infusion* (2e). Precept Press, Chicago, IL.
3 Lokich JJ *et al.* (1988) Combined floxuridine and cisplatin in a 14-day infusion. *Cancer.* **62**: 233–7.

4 Lokich JJ *et al.* (1988) Combined 5-fluorouracil and floxuridine administered as a 14-day infusion. *Cancer.* **62**: 825–7.

5 Trissel LA (2001) *Handbook of Injectable Drugs* (11e). American Society of Health-Systems Pharmacists, Bethesda, MD.

6 Stiles ML *et al.* (1996) Stability of deferoxamine mesylate, floxuridine, fluorouracil, hydromorphone, lorazepam and midazolam hydrochloride in polypropylene infusion-pump syringes. *Am J Health-Syst Pharm.* **53**: 1583–8.

7 Keller JH and Ensminger WD (1982) Stability of cancer chemotherapeutic agents in a totally implanted drug delivery system. *Am J Hosp Pharm.* **39**: 1321–3.

8 Sadjak A and Winersteiger R (1995) Compatibility of morphine, baclofen, floxuridine and fluorouracil in an implantable medication pump. *Arzneim Forsch.* **45**: 93–9.

Prepared by Yaacov Cass

FLUDARABINE

1 General details

Approved names: Fludarabine, fludarabine phosphate, 2-fluoro-adenine-arabinoside-5-phosphate, 2-fluoro-ARA-AMP.

Proprietary name: Fludara.

Manufacturer or supplier: Schering Health Care Ltd.

Presentation and formulation details: 5-mL vials each containing fludarabine phosphate 50 mg (equivalent to fludarabine 39.05 mg) as a sterile lyophilised cake. Vials also contain mannitol and sodium hydroxide to adjust pH.[1,2]

Storage and shelf-life of unopened container: When stored at room temperature below 30°C the vials have a shelf-life of 24 months.[2]

2 Chemistry

Type: Fluorinated purine derivative.

Molecular structure: 2-Fluoro-9-(5-*O*-phosphono-β-D-arabinofuranosyl)-9*H*-purin-6-amine.[3]

Molecular weight: 401.2.

Solubility: 9 mg/mL in water.

3 Stability profile

3.1 Physical and chemical stability

Effect of pH: Chemically stable in solution between pH 4.5 and 8, with an optimum pH of 7.6.[1] The final product has a pH range of 7.2–8.2.[2]

Effect of temperature: At a concentration of 25 mg/mL in distilled water, stored at room temperature (22–25°C) in normal laboratory light, fludarabine phosphate exhibited less than 2% decomposition over 16 days.[3]

When diluted to a concentration of 1 mg/mL in 5% glucose or in 0.9% sodium chloride, less than 3% decomposition occurred over 16 days at room temperature (22–25°C) under normal laboratory light.[3]

When diluted to a concentration of 0.04 mg/mL in 5% glucose or 9.0% sodium chloride in glass bottles or PVC bags, little or no loss occurred over 48 hours at room temperature (22–25°C) while exposed to normal laboratory light, or under refrigeration (2–8°C).[1,3]

Compatibility with other drugs: The compatibility of fludarabine with a wide range of drugs has been reported.[4,5]

3.2 Stability in clinical practice

Although the manufacturer recommends that the contents of the vial should be used within 8 hours of being reconstituted,[2] solutions are stable, exhibiting less than 2% decomposition over 16 days when stored at room temperature and exposed to normal laboratory light.[1] At 1 mg/mL in 5% glucose or 0.9% sodium chloride, solutions are stable for 16 days at room temperature under normal laboratory light.[3]

3.3 Stability in specialised delivery systems

No information available.

4 Clinical use

Type of cytotoxic: Antimetabolite.

Dosage: 25 mg/m^2 daily for 5 consecutive days, repeated every 28 days. The cycle may be repeated up to six times.[2]

5 Preparation of injection

Reconstitution: Add 2 mL of water for injections to the contents of a vial and mix gently for 10–15 seconds.[2]

Bolus administration: Dilute further to 10 mL with 0.9% sodium chloride.[2]

Intravenous infusion: Dilute in 100–125 mL of 0.9% sodium chloride for infusion over 30 minutes.[2]

Extravasation: Group 5 classification (neutral) (*see* Chapter 6).

6 Destruction of drug or contaminated articles

Incineration: Preferred method of disposal; no specific temperature.[6]

Chemical: No chemical destruction method is recommended.[6]

Contact with skin: Wash skin thoroughly with soap and water. In the event of contact with the eyes, wash with copious amounts of water.[2]

References

1 Trissel LA (2000) *Handbook on Injectable Drugs* (10e). American Society of Hospital Pharmacists, Bethesda, MD.

2 ABPI (1999) *ABPI Data Sheet Compendium 1999–2000.* DataPharm Publications Ltd, London.

3 Anon. (1994) *NCI Investigational Drugs: pharmaceutical data.* National Cancer Institute, Bethesda, MD.

4 Williams DA and Lokich JJ (1992) A review of the stability and compatibility of anti-neoplastic drugs for multiple drug infusion. *Cancer Chemother Pharmacol.* **31**: 178–81.

5 Trissel LA *et al.* (1991) Visual compatibility of fludarabine phosphate with anti-neoplastic drugs, anti-infectives, and other selected drugs during simulated Y-site injection. *Am J Hosp Pharm.* **48**: 2186–9.

6 Schering Health Care Ltd (1999) Personal communication.

Prepared by Paula Myers

FLUOROURACIL

1 General details

Approved name: Fluorouracil, 5-fluorouracil.

Proprietary name: Fluorouracil.

Manufacturer or supplier: Cambridge Laboratories Ltd, Faulding Pharmaceuticals plc.

Presentation and formulation details: Solutions contain 25 or 50 mg/mL fluorouracil in 10-, 20- or 100-mL vials or Onco-tain containers.[1] Injections also contain sodium hydroxide to adjust pH to 8.9.[1]

Storage and shelf-life of unopened container: The shelf-life is 2 years when stored at room temperature and protected from light.

2 Chemistry

Type: Fluorinated pyrimidine.

Molecular structure: 5-fluoro-2,4(1H,3H)pyrimidine-dione.

Molecular weight: 130.1.

Solubility: 12.5 mg/mL in water and 6 mg/mL in ethanol.

3 Stability profile

3.1 Physical and chemical stability

Fluorouracil breakdown occurs by two routes. Thermal and photochemical decomposition causes the opening of the pyrimidine ring between N3 and C4 and N1 and C5 to produce urea. Alkaline hydrolysis leads to the production of barbituric acid and uracil, which is further degraded to urea. The rate of alkaline hydrolysis increases rapidly above pH 9.0, so the injection is formulated within the pH range 8.6–9.0. Although the drug is stable at acid pH, solubility is reduced.

The injection should be protected from strong daylight and temperatures above 25°C.

Container compatibility: There is no evidence to indicate that fluorouracil is incompatible with plastic syringes, PVC and EVA containers or the reservoirs of ambulatory delivery devices.[1–6] However, some containers allow moisture loss during storage which will lead to increased drug concentration. Because of its limited aqueous solubility, solutions containing 50 mg/mL fluorouracil may be subject to precipitation during storage.

Compatibility with other drugs: Fluorouracil has been shown to be compatible with bleomycin,[7] cyclophosphamide and methotrexate,[8] etoposide,[9] floxuridine,[10] ifosfamide,[9] heparin[11] and metoclopramide,[12] although early studies had indicated that fluorouracil could be mixed with calcium folinate.[13,14] More recent work has indicated that a crystalline deposit forms in stored mixtures in less than 4 days[15,16] and, as a consequence, calcium folinate should not be mixed with fluorouracil.

Compatibility studies of mixing with other drugs briefly in a syringe, or in a simulated Y-site injection, have indicated compatibility with a number of drugs.[17–24] Compatibility with ondansetron appears to be concentration dependent.[25,26] Incompatibility is likely to be seen with acidic drugs, or drugs that are unstable in an alkaline environment, and has been demonstrated with carboplatin,[9] cisplatin,[27] cytarabine,[28] diazepam,[29] doxorubicin,[29] droperidol,[17] epirubicin,[30] filgrastim,[31] gallium nitrate,[32] vinorelbine[33] and heparin.[34]

3.2 Stability in clinical practice

Fluorouracil at 5–10 mg/mL, diluted in 0.9% sodium chloride or 5% glucose in PVC bags, and stored at 5°C, is stable for at least 16 weeks or 42 days at room temperature.[2,3] Likewise, solutions containing 10–25 mg/mL fluorouracil, diluted in water for injections or 0.9% sodium chloride stored at room temperatures between 5 and 25°C in EVA bags, are stable for at least 28 days.[4] Fluorouracil solutions at 25 mg/mL, stored at 5 or 25°C in plastic syringes (Plastipak, Becton Dickinson) are stable for 28 days,[6] while solutions containing 50 mg/mL are equally stable provided that storage is at room temperature,[34] or are stable for 21 days if stored at 30°C.[35] There is a risk of precipitation if solutions containing concentrations greater than 25 mg/mL fluorouracil are refrigerated for extended periods. Refrigeration of such solutions should therefore be avoided.

More dilute solutions containing 1 mg/mL fluorouracil diluted in 5% glucose or 1–4 mg/mL fluorouracil diluted in 0.9% sodium chloride, stored in PVC bags at 20–21°C either in the dark or exposed to fluorescent light, are stable for 7 days.[34]

3.3 Stability in specialised delivery systems

Fluorouracil at 50 mg/mL (undiluted), tested in the reservoirs of four different ambulatory pumps (CADD-1 Model 5100, Cormed II Model 10500, Medfusion Infumed 200 and Pancretec Provider IV, Model 2000), during simulated infusion at 10 mL/day over 7 days at 25 and 37°C, was reported to be chemically stable, with minimal evidence of leaching plasticiser (DEHP).[36] However, visual evidence of precipitation was reported in all of the devices, indicating the dangers associated with extended storage of high-concentration fluorouracil, which may be caused by a combination of factors, including variations in pH, storage conditions and temperature, commercial source of drug and diluent and the container. Moisture loss during storage would increase drug concentration, enhancing the risk of precipitation. Similar effects were observed with solutions in EVA reservoirs.[37] However, solutions containing 45 mg/mL fluorouracil diluted in 0.9% sodium chloride and stored in EVA at 25°C were stable for 3 days with no visual evidence of precipitation.[35] Therefore 50 mg/mL solutions of fluorouracil should be used with caution, especially in reservoirs which permit moisture transmission, such as PVC and EVA.

Fluorouracil stability has been confirmed in Intermate and Infusor devices as follows:[38]

▼ 1–5 mg/mL fluorouracil in 0.9% sodium chloride – 14 days at 2–8°C followed by 7 days at 33°C.
▼ 5–42 mg/mL fluorouracil in 0.9% sodium chloride – 14 days at 2–8°C followed by 3 days at room temperature and 7 days at 33°C.
▼ 42–50 mg/mL fluorouracil in 0.9% sodium chloride or undiluted – 14 days at room temperature followed by 4 days at 33°C.

In the CADD-1 infusion reservoir, filled with solutions containing 25 or 50 mg/mL fluorouracil and stored at 10–22°C for 18 days, followed by simulated delivery at a rate of 6 mL/hour for 16 days at 32°C, no losses were reported. There was some tendency for concentrations to rise and therefore to prevent precipitation – it is suggested that a small (5–10 mL) overage of the diluent should be included for solutions containing 50 mg/mL nominal concentration.[34] In a similar test in the Medex reservoir within the Walk Med devices, fluorouracil was stable for 14 days at 5–8°C followed by a delivery period of up to 11 days at 32°C. Again a small overage is recommended to prevent precipitation of solutions containing 50 mg/mL fluorouracil.[34]

In the Medex infusion reservoir, solutions containing 25 mg/mL fluorouracil stored at 5°C or 25°C, with or without occlusive overwraps, were stable for at least 6 months. Reservoirs with the overwrap were stable for up to 12 months.[34]

4 Clinical use

Type of cytotoxic: Antimetabolite.

Main indications: Palliative treatment of a variety of carcinomas, both alone and in combination.

Dosage: Up to 15 mg/kg intravenously once weekly; maximum daily dose is usually 1 g. Fluorouracil may be used as an induction once daily for 5–7 days or in a 3- to 4-week cycle as part of combination therapy. It is also commonly used in conjunction with calcium folinate for colorectal cancer. A dosage of 5–7.5 mg/kg by continuous intra-arterial infusion over 24 hours has also been used.

5 Preparation of injection

Dilution: May be administered undiluted or diluted as an infusion.

Bolus administration: Administer injection slowly (over not less than 3–5 minutes) directly into the vein or via a fast-running drip.

Intravenous infusion: Dilute in 300–500 mL 5% glucose or 0.9% sodium chloride and administer either over 30–60 minutes, or over 4–24 hours if convenient.

Extravasation: Group 4 classification (inflammatory) (*see* Chapter 6).

6 Destruction of drug or contaminated articles

Incineration: 700°C.

Chemical: 10% sodium hypochlorite for 24 hours.

Contact with skin: Wash thoroughly with soap and water.

References

1 ABPI (1999) *ABPI Data Sheet Compendium 1999–2000*. DataPharm Publications Ltd, London, 271–2, 407–9.

2 Quebbeman EJ *et al.* (1984) Stability of fluorouracil in plastic containers used for continuous infusion at home. *Am J Hosp Pharm.* **41**: 1153–6.

3 Vincke AE *et al.* (1989) Extended stability of 5-fluorouracil and methotrexate solutions in PVC containers. *Int J Pharm.* **54**: 181–9.

4 Rochard EB *et al.* (1992) Stability of fluorouracil, cytarabine or doxorubicin hydrochloride in ethylene vinylacetate portable infusion-pump reservoirs. *Am J Hosp Pharm.* **49**: 619–23.

5 Sesin GP *et al.* (1982) Stability study of 5-fluorouracil following repackaging in plastic disposable syringes and multidose vials. *Am J Intraven Ther Clin Nutr.* **9**: 23–5, 29–30.

6 Sewell GJ (1988) Cancer chemotherapy by infusion: drug stability and compatibility considerations. *Proceedings of the First International Symposium on Oncological Pharmacy Practice*, Rotorua, New Zealand.

7 Dorr RT *et al.* (1982) Bleomycin compatibility with selected intravenous medications. *J Med.* **13**: 121–30.

8 Lokich JJ *et al.* (1989) Cyclophosphamide, methotrexate and 5-fluorouracil in a three-drug admixture. *Cancer.* **63**: 822–4.

9 Williams DA and Lokich JJ (1992) A review of the stability and compatibility of antineoplastic drugs for multiple-drug infusions. *Cancer Chemother Pharmacol.* **31**: 171–81.

10 Anderson N *et al.* (1989) Combined 5-fluorouracil and floxuridine administered as a 14-day infusion. *Cancer.* **63**: 825–7.

11 Barberi-Heyob M *et al.* (1995) Addition of heparin in 5-fluorouracil solution for portal vein infusion has no influence on its stability under clinically relevant conditions. *Anti-Cancer Drugs.* **6**: 163–4.

12 Wang DP *et al.* (1995) Stability of a fluorouracil–metoclopramide hydrochloride mixture. *Am J Health-Syst Pharm.* **52**: 98–9.

13 Anderson N *et al.* (1989) A Phase 1 clinical trial of combined fluoropyrimidines with leucovorin in a 14-day infusion. *Cancer.* **63**: 233–7.

14 Milano G *et al.* (1993) Long-term stability of 5-fluorouracil and folinic acid admixtures. *Eur J Cancer.* **29A**: 129–32.

15 Adralan B and Flores MR (1993) A new complication of permanent indwelling central venous catheters using high-dose fluorouracil and leucovorin. *J Clin Oncol.* **11**: 384.

16 Trissel LA *et al.* (1995) Incompatibility of fluorouracil with leucovorin calcium or levoleucovorin calcium. *Am J Health-Syst Pharm.* **52**: 710–15.

17 Cohen MH *et al.* (1985) Drug precipitation within IV tubing: a potential hazard of chemotherapy administration. *Cancer Treat Rep.* **69**: 1325–6.

18 Trissel LA and Martinez JF (1994) Physical compatibility of allopurinol sodium with selected drugs during simulated Y-site administration. *Am J Hosp Pharm.* **51**: 1792–9.

19 Trissel LA *et al.* (1991) Visual compatibility of fludarabine phosphate with antineoplastic drugs, anti-infectives, and other selected drugs during simulated Y-site injection. *Am J Hosp Pharm.* **48**: 2186–9.

20 Allen LV and Stiles ML (1981) Compatibility of various admixtures with secondary additives at Y-injection sites of intravenous administration sets. Part 2. *Am J Hosp Pharm.* **38**: 380–1.

21 Woloschuck DMM *et al.* (1991) Stability and compatibility of fluorouracil and mannitol during simulated Y-site administration. *Am J Hosp Pharm.* **48**: 2158–60.

22 Trissel LA and Martinez JF (1993) Melphalan physical compatibility with selected drugs during simulated Y-site administration. *Am J Hosp Pharm.* **50**: 2359–63.

23 Trissel LA and Bready BB (1992) Turbidimetric assessment of the compatibility of taxol with selected other drugs during simulated Y-site injection. *Am J Hosp Pharm.* **49**: 1716–19.

24 Trissel LA and Martinez JF (1994) Physical compatibility of piperacillin sodium plus tazobactam sodium with selected drugs during simulated Y-site administration. *Am J Hosp Pharm.* **51**: 672–8.

25 Trissel LA *et al.* (1991) Visual compatibility of ondansetron hydrochloride with other selected drugs during simulated Y-site injection. *Am J Hosp Pharm.* **48**: 988–92.

26 Leak RF and Woodford JD (1989) Pharmaceutical development of ondansetron injection. *Eur J Cancer Clin Oncol.* **25 (Supplement 1)**: S66–69.

27 Stewart CF and Fleming RA (1990) Compatibility of cisplatin and fluorouracil in 0.9% sodium chloride injection. *Am J Hosp Pharm.* **47**: 1373–7.

28 McRae MP and King JC (1976) Compatibility of antineoplastic, antibiotic and corticosteroid drugs in intravenous admixtures. *Am J Hosp Pharm.* **33**: 1010–13.

29 Dorr RT (1979) Incompatibilities with parenteral and anticancer drugs. *Am J Intraven Ther Clin Nutr.* **6**: 42, 45, 46, 52.

30 Adams PS *et al.* (1987) Pharmaceutical aspects of home infusion therapy for cancer patients. *Pharm J.* **238**: 476–8.

31 Trissel LA and Martinez JF (1994) Physical compatibility of filgrastim with selected drugs during simulated Y-site administration. *Am J Hosp Pharm.* **51**: 1907–13.

32 Lober CA and Dollard PA (1993) Visual compatibility of gallium nitrate with selected drugs during simulated Y-site injection. *Am J Hosp Pharm.* **50**: 1208–10.

33 Trissel LA and Martinez JF (1994) Visual, turbidimetric, and particle-content assessment of compatibility of vinorelbine tartrate with selected drugs during simulated Y-site injection. *Am J Hosp Pharm.* **51**: 495–9.

34 Faulding Pharmacueticals plc (2000) Personal communication.

35 Baud-Camus F *et al.* (1996) Stability of fluorouracil in polypropylene syringes and EVA infusion-pump reservoirs. *Am J Health-Syst Pharm.* **53**: 1461.

36 Stiles ML *et al.* (1989) Stability of fluorouracil administered through four portable infusion pumps. *Am J Hosp Pharm.* **46**: 2036–40.

37 Martel P *et al.* (1996) Long-term stability of 5-fluorouracil stored in PVC bags and ambulatory pump reservoirs. *J Pharm Biomed Anal.* **14**: 395–9.

38 Baxter Healthcare Ltd (2000) Personal communication.

Prepared by Richard Needle

GEMCITABINE

1 General details

Approved name: Gemcitabine hydrochloride.

Proprietary name: Gemzar.

Manufacturer or supplier: Eli Lilly Ltd.

Presentation and formulation details: White to off-white lyophilised powder in glass vials containing gemcitabine hydrochloride equivalent to 200 mg or 1000 mg of gemcitabine. The vials also contain mannitol and sodium acetate.[1]

Storage and shelf-life of unopened container: The shelf-life is 2 years when stored at room temperature (15–25°C) and protected from light.[2]

2 Chemistry

Type: Pyrimidine analogue.

Molecular structure: 2'-deoxy-2',2'-difluorocytidine monohydrochloride.

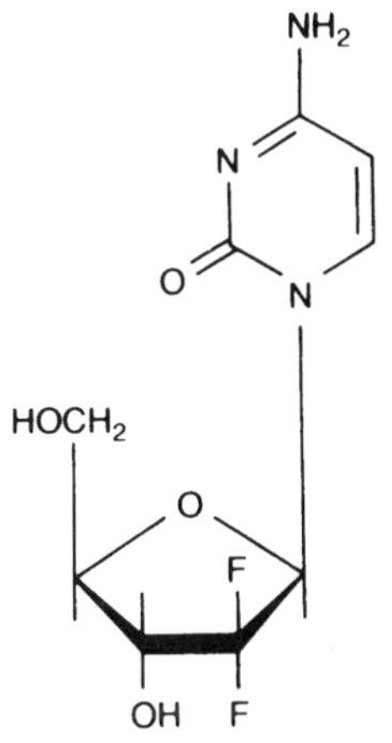

NH$_2$

N

O

N

HOCH$_2$

O

F

OH   F

Molecular weight: 299.7.

Characteristics and solubility: A powder reconstitution produces a clear colourless to straw-coloured solution. Because of drug solubility limitations, doses of 2500 mg/m^2 and greater must be diluted in at least 1000 mL of 0.9% sodium chloride.

3 Stability profile

3.1 Physical and chemical stability

The lyophilised product is stable for 24 months when stored at room temperature (15–25°C).[2]

Container compatibility: Gemcitabine injection diluted in 0.9% sodium chloride is compatible with glass, PVC and polypropylene containers, and with plastic syringes.[2]

Compatibility with other drugs: No further information available.

3.2 Stability in clinical practice

The stability of solutions of gemcitabine has been investigated up to 48 hours when reconstituted with 0.9% sodium chloride. There was no significant decomposition of gemcitabine.[2] Solutions should not be refrigerated, as crystallisation will occur.[2]

Gemcitabine diluted in 0.9% sodium chloride or 5% glucose PVC minibags to concentrations of 0.1 mg/mL or 10 mg/mL, and stored at 4°C or 23°C, was physically and chemically stable for 35 days.[3] Solutions containing 38 mg/mL gemcitabine in water for injections or 0.9% sodium chloride stored either in the original vials or in plastic syringes at 23°C were also stable for 35 days. Such solutions must not be stored at 4°C because crystallisation may occur.[3]

3.3 Stability in specialised delivery systems

Gemcitabine diluted in 0.9% sodium chloride to a concentration of 3–40 mg/mL in Infusor or Intermate devices and stored at room temperature is stable for 7 days.[4]

4 Clinical use

Type of cytotoxic: Pyrimidine antimetabolite which inhibits DNA replication and repair. Gemcitabine appears to be cell-cycle-specific for S-phase, causing cells to accumulate at the G_1-S-phase boundary.

Main indications: Palliative treatment of adult patients with locally advanced or metastatic non-small-cell lung cancer.

Dosage: The recommended dose is 1000 mg/m² given by 30-minute intravenous infusion. This dose should be repeated once weekly for 3 weeks, followed by a 1-week rest period. The 4-week cycle is then repeated.

5 Preparation of injection

Reconstitution: Add at least 5 mL of 0.9% sodium chloride to the 200-mg vial or at least 25 mL to the 1-g vial. Shake to dissolve. The appropriate amount of drug may be administered as prepared or further diluted with 0.9% sodium chloride. Due to solubility considerations, the maximum concentration on reconstitution is 40 mg/mL. Solutions of reconstituted gemcitabine must be kept at room temperature (15–25°C).[2] Crystallisation may occur if refrigerated.

Extravasation: Group 5 classification (neutral) (*see* Chapter 6).

6 Destruction of drug or contaminated articles

Incineration: 700°C.

Chemical: 0.5 M sulphuric acid and 0.1 M potassium permanganate solution for 2 hours.

Contact with skin: Wash thoroughly with soap and copious amounts of water.

References

1 ABPI (1999) *ABPI Data Sheet Compendium 1999–2000.* DataPharm Publications Ltd, London, 741–2.

2 Eli Lilly and Co. Ltd (2000) Personal communication.
3 Xu G *et al*. (1999) Physical and chemical stability of gemcitabine hydrochloride solutions. *J Am Pharm Assoc*. **39**: 509–13.
4 Baxter Healthcare Ltd (2000) Personal communication.

Prepared by Michael Allwood

IDARUBICIN

1 General details

Approved name: Idarubicin.

Proprietary name: Zavedos.

Manufacturer or supplier: Pharmacia and Upjohn Ltd.

Presentation and formulation details: Sterile, pyrogen-free, orange-red, freeze-dried powder in vials containing 5 mg and 10 mg of idarubicin hydrochloride, with 50 mg and 100 mg of lactose, respectively.[1] (Idarubicin capsules (5 mg, 10 mg and 25 mg) are available for the treatment of patients in whom intravenous therapy cannot be employed.[2])

Storage and shelf-life of unopened container: Three years at room temperature if protected from sunlight.[3]

2 Chemistry

Type: A cytotoxic antibiotic consisting of an amino sugar (daunosamine) linked through a glycosidic bond to the C7 of a tetracyclic aglycone (4-demethoxy-daunorubicinone).

Molecular structure: (7S,9S)-9-Acetyl-7-(3-amino-2,3,6-trideoxy-α-L-*lyxo*-hexopyranosyloxy)-7,8,9,10-tetrahydro-6,9,11-trihydroxynaphthacene-5,12-dione hydrochloride.

Molecular weight: 533.97.

Solubility: Idarubicin is sparingly soluble in water for injections, 5% glucose and 0.9% sodium chloride.[4]

3 Stability profile

3.1. *Physical and chemical stability*

The manufacturer states that the reconstituted solution is chemically stable for at least 48 hours at 2–8°C and 24 hours at room temperature.[1] Very few data on the long-term stability of idarubicin are available. The stability of the anthracyclines is dependent on a number of factors, including the pH of the medium. They are also light-sensitive and are adsorbed on to glass and certain plastics.

Effect of pH: Acidic hydrolysis of idarubicin is expected to yield a red-coloured, water-insoluble aglycone (4-demethoxydaunorubicinone) and a water-soluble amino sugar (daunosamine). The rate of cleavage of the glycosidic bond in acidic media is strongly dependent on structural modifications in the amino-sugar moiety.[5] As daunorubicin and idarubicin both possess daunosamine as the sugar moiety, the rate of degradation of these analogues in acidic solution is expected to be similar. There are no published data to confirm this hypothesis. In alkaline solution the rate of degradation of the anthracyclines is affected by structural modifications in the aglycone portion of the molecule.[5] As idarubicin possesses a unique aglycone, 4-demethoxydaunorubicinone, its stability in alkaline media cannot be predicted from existing data for the other anthracyclines. The manufacturers recommend that prolonged contact of idarubicin with any solution of alkaline pH should be avoided, as it will result in degradation.[1]

Effect of light: Data on the photodegradation of doxorubicin, daunorubicin and epirubicin have been published.[6,7] The rates of photodegradation of these three analogues have been reported to be similar, and they may be substantial at concentrations below 100 µg/mL if solutions are exposed to light for sufficient time.[7] Similarly, dilute solutions of idarubicin (10 µg/mL) are light-sensitive, undergoing some degradation with exposure to light over periods longer than 6 hours.[8] At higher concentrations, such as those used for cancer chemotherapy (at least 500 µg/mL), no special precautions are necessary to protect freshly prepared solutions of doxorubicin, daunorubicin and epirubicin from light.[6] The manufacturers suggest that idarubicin is treated in a similar fashion to these other anthracyclines, and that no precautions are necessary to protect freshly prepared solutions of idarubicin from light.[3]

Effect of temperature: A review of the literature reveals one well-controlled study in which Beijnen *et al.*[9] reported that idarubicin was stable in polypropylene tubes in 5% glucose (pH 4.7), 3.3% glucose with 0.3% sodium chloride (pH 4.4), lactated Ringer's solution (pH 6.8) and 0.9% sodium chloride (pH 7.0) for 28 days when stored in the dark at 25°C.

Haze formation: Idarubicin solutions in 0.9% sodium chloride exhibit a low-level haze that is visible under high-intensity light and measurable with a turbidimeter. Dilution of the drug from concentrations of 500 µg/mL to 1 mg/mL increases this haze until a maximum is reached at about 50 µg/mL. This haze appears to be normal for idarubicin in solution, and is not an incompatibility.[10]

Container compatibility: Idarubicin is compatible with polypropylene, PVC and glass.[3] Doxorubicin, daunorubicin and epirubicin are adsorbed on to glass but not on to siliconised glass or polypropylene.[11,12] Therefore idarubicin may behave in a similar manner. In clinical practice, when idarubicin is used at concentrations of at least 500 µg/mL, adsorptive losses during storage and delivery are expected to be negligible.

Compatibility with other drugs: Prolonged contact with any solution of alkaline pH should be avoided, as it will result in degradation.[1] Idarubicin has been observed to be physically incompatible with acyclovir, ceftazidime, clindamycin, dexamethasone, etoposide, frusemide, gentamicin, hydrocortisone, imipenem–cilastin, lorazepam, methotrexate, mezlocillin, sodium bicarbonate, vancomycin and vincristine.[13] Idarubicin should not be mixed with heparin, as a precipitate may form.[1] The manufacturer recommends that no other drugs should be mixed with idarubicin.[1]

3.2. Stability in clinical practice

Idarubicin (100 µg/mL) appears to be chemically stable for at least 28 days in 5% glucose, glucose/saline admixtures and 0.9% sodium chloride at 25°C.[9] After reconstitution, vials of idarubicin should be refrigerated.[3]

3.3. Stability in specialised delivery systems

No data are available.

4 Clinical use

Type of cytotoxic: Cytotoxic antibiotic that interacts with DNA to interfere with nucleic acid synthesis.

Main indications: Remission induction in untreated adults with acute non-lymphocytic leukaemia, or for remission induction in relapsed or refractory patients. Idarubicin is also indicated in acute lymphocytic leukaemia as second-line treatment in adults and children. It may be used in combination regimens with other cytotoxic agents.[1]

Dosage: This is usually calculated on the basis of body surface area. The manufacturer gives the following recommendations for the intravenous preparation.

▼ Acute non-lymphocytic leukaemia: In adults the suggested dosage schedule is 12 mg/m^2 intravenously daily for 3 days in combination with cytarabine. Another dosage schedule in which idarubicin has been used as a single agent and in combination is 8 mg/m^2 intravenously daily for 5 days.

▼ Acute lymphocytic leukaemia: As a single agent the suggested dose is 12 mg/m^2 intravenously daily for 3 days in adults and 10 mg/m^2 intravenously daily for 3 days in children.

On the basis of the recommended intravenous dosage schedules, the total cumulative dose administered over two courses can be expected to reach 60–80mg/m^2. Although a cumulative dosage limit cannot yet be defined, a specific cardiological evaluation in cancer patients showed no significant modifications of cardiac function in patients treated with intravenous idarubicin at a mean cumulative dosage of 93 mg/m^2.[1]

▼ Oral idarubicin: In acute non-lymphocytic leukaemia patients in whom oral idarubicin is used the dose is 30 mg/m^2 daily for 3 days as a single agent, or 15–30 mg/m^2 orally daily for three days in combination with other anti-leukaemic agents. In advanced breast cancer the recommended dosage schedule as a single agent is 45 mg/m^2 orally given either on a single day or divided over three consecutive days to be repeated every 3 or 4 weeks based on haematological recovery. A maximum cumulative dose of 400 mg/m^2 for oral idarubicin is recommended.[2]

However, all of the above dosage schedules should take into account the haematological status of the patient and the dosages of other cytotoxic drugs when used in combination. Idarubicin therapy should not be started in patients with severe renal and liver impairment or in patients with uncontrolled infections. In a number of phase III trials treatment was not given if bilirubin levels exceeded 2 mg/100 mL. With other anthracyclines a 50% dosage reduction is generally employed if bilirubin levels are in the range 1.2–2.0 mg/100 mL. [1]

5 Preparation of injection

Reconstitution: The contents of the 5-mg vial should be dissolved in 5 mL of water for injections and those of the 10-mg vial in 10 mL of the same solvent. After addition of the diluent and gentle shaking, the contents of the vial will dissolve to produce a solution of 1 mg/mL. [1]

Bolus administration: Administration is only by the intravenous route. The reconstituted solution should be given, over 5 to 10 minutes, into the side-arm of a freely running intravenous infusion of 0.9% sodium chloride. This technique minimises the risk of thrombosis or perivenous extravasation, which can lead to severe cellulitis or necrosis. [1]

Intravenous infusion: The doses and duration of infusions of idarubicin that have been used in clinical trials range from 8 mg/m^2 to 16 mg/m^2 over 4, 24 or 72 hours.[3,14–16]

Extravasation: Group 1 classification (vesicant) (*see* Chapter 6).

6 Destruction of drug or contaminated articles

Incineration: 700°C. [3]

Chemical: 10% sodium hypochlorite (1% available chlorine) solution for 24 hours.[1]

Contact with skin: Wash well with water, or with soap and water. If the eyes are contaminated, immediate irrigation with 0.9% sodium chloride should be performed.[1]

References

1 ABPI (1999) *ABPI Data Sheet Compendium 1999–2000.* DataPharm Publications Ltd, London, 1249.
2 ABPI (1999) *ABPI Data Sheet Compendium 1999–2000.* DataPharm Publications Ltd, London, 1249–50.
3 Pharmacia and Upjohn Ltd (1999) Personal communication.
4 Cagnasso MG (ed.) (1992) *Idarubicin: summary of preclinical studies up to March 1980.* Farmitalia Carlo Erba Ltd, Milan.
5 Beijnen JH *et al.* (1986) Aspects of the degradation kinetics of doxorubicin in aqueous solution. *Int J Pharm.* **32**: 123–31.
6 Tavoloni N *et al.* (1980) Photolytic degradation of adriamycin. *J Pharm Pharmacol.* **32**: 860–2.
7 Wood MJ *et al.* (1990) Photodegradation of doxorubicin, daunorubicin and epirubicin measured by high-performance liquid chromatography. *J Clin Pharm Ther.* **15**: 291–300.

8 Trissel LA (2001) *Handbook of Injectable Drugs* (11e). American Society of Hospital Pharmacists, Bethesda, MD.

9 Beijnen JH *et al.* (1985) Stability of anthracycline antitumour agents in infusion fluids. *J Parent Sci Technol.* **39:** 220–2.

10 Trissel LA (1993) Idarubicin hydrochloride turbidity versus incompatibility. *Am J Hosp Pharm.* **50:** 1134, 1137.

11 Bosanquet AG (1986) Stability of solutions of antineoplastic agents during preparation and storage for *in vitro* assays. II. Assay methods, adriamycin and the other antitumour antibiotics. *Cancer Chemother Pharmacol.* **17:** 1–10.

12 Wood MJ (1989) *Investigations into the stability of doxorubicin, daunorubicin and epirubicin in infusion fluids.* MPhil Thesis. University of Aston, Birmingham.

13 Turowski RC and Durthaler JM (1991) Visual compatibility of idarubicin hydrochloride with selected drugs during simulated Y-site injection. *Am J Hosp Pharm.* **48:** 2181–4.

14 Speth PAJ *et al.* (1986) Plasma and human leukaemic cell pharmacokinetics of oral and intravenous 4-demethoxy-daunomycin. *Clin Pharm Ther.* **40:** 643–9.

15 Speth PAJ *et al.* (1989) Idarubicin vs. daunorubicin: pre-clinical and clinical pharmacokinetic studies. *Semin Oncol.* **16 (Supplement 2):** 2–9.

16 Vogler WR *et al.* (1988) A Phase III trial comparing daunorubicin or idarubicin combined with cytosine arabinoside in acute myelogenous leukaemia (AML). Abstract of two symposia. In: *Twelfth Congress of the International Society of Haematology,* Milan, Italy. Aug–Sept, 1988.

Prepared by Jayne Wood

IFOSFAMIDE

1 General details

Approved name: Ifosfamide, iphosphamide, isophosphamide.

Proprietary name: Mitoxana.

Manufacturer or supplier: ASTA Medica Ltd.

Presentation and formulation details: White freeze-dried powder in glass vials containing 1 g or 2 g ifosfamide. Contains no excipients.

Storage and shelf-life of unopened container: Vials should be stored below 25°C, and protected from light.[1] The intact vials are stable for at least 5 years at 22–25°C.[2]

2 Chemistry

Type: Nitrogen mustard.

Molecular structure: N,3-(2-chloroethyl)tetrahydro-2H-1,2,3 oxaphosphorin-2-amine.

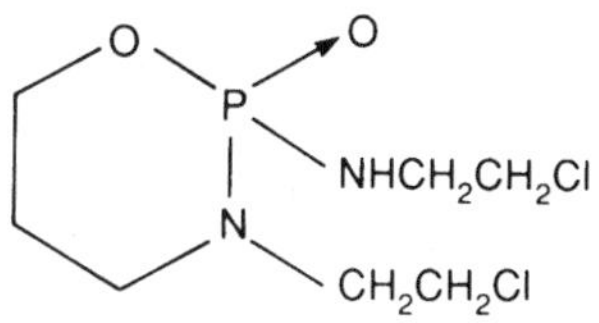

$$O \diagdown \quad O$$

P

NHCH$_2$CH$_2$Cl

N

CH$_2$CH$_2$Cl

Molecular weight: 261.1.

Solubility: In water, 1 in 10; in methylene chloride, up to 1 g/mL; in carbon disulphide, 15 mg/mL. Readily soluble in ethanol.

3 Stability profile

3.1 Physical and chemical stability

Ifosfamide is relatively stable after reconstitution.

Effect of pH: No information available.

Effect of light: Infusions should be protected from light during storage. Light protection during administration is not necessary.

Container compatibility: Compatible with glass, PVC and polypropylene containers.[3]

Compatibility with other drugs: Compatible with mesna (*see* Mesna monograph on page 470 for details). No further information is available.

Reconstitution of ifosfamide with water for injections containing benzyl alcohol (0.9%) results in the formation of two separate liquid phases.[4] Ifosfamide should therefore be reconstituted with unpreserved water for injections.

3.2 Stability in clinical practice

Reconstituted solutions of ifosfamide are chemically stable for 7 days at room temperature or 6 weeks if refrigerated.[2,3] The manufacturer indicates that ifosfamide at 40 mg/mL in water for injections, 0.9% sodium chloride, 4% glucose/0.18% sodium chloride or 5% glucose is chemically stable for 7 days at room temperature.[1]

Ifosfamide at 50 mg/mL in polypropylene syringes is stable for 7 days at 4°C or 20°C.[5] The chemical stability of combinations containing ifosfamide and mesna at concentrations recommended by the manufacturer in 0.9% sodium chloride for 28 days at 28°C or 7 days at room temperature has been confirmed.[1] Solutions diluted in 5% glucose are only stable for 24 hours at room temperature.[1]

Dilution of the reconstituted solution to ifosfamide concentrations of 16 and 0.6 mg/mL in the following intravenous infusion solutions resulted in <5% decomposition over 7 days at room temperature, and no decomposition over 6 weeks under refrigeration:[2]

5% glucose in Ringer's injection, lactated
5% glucose in 0.9% sodium chloride
glucose in water
Ringer's injection, lactated
0.45% sodium chloride
0.9% sodium chloride
1/6 M sodium lactate.

Ifosfamide infusion at 50 mg/mL in 10-mL polypropylene syringes showed no drug loss over 7 days at 4 and 20°C.[5] Combinations of ifosfamide (50 mg/mL) and mesna (40 mg/mL) in 10-mL syringes are also stable for 28 days at 4 and 20°C.[5] Ifosfamide (50 mg/mL) and combinations of ifosfamide with mesna (each at 50 mg/mL) showed no drug loss at 37°C over 24 hours.[6] In a further study,[7] ifosfamide in aqueous solution (either alone or mixed with mesna) was found to be stable for 9 days when stored in a dark environment at 27°C.

3.3 Stability in specialised delivery systems

Ifosfamide at 20, 40 or 80 mg/mL in 0.9% sodium chloride, or at 80 mg/mL in water for injections, was reported to be stable for 8 days at 35°C stored in 100-mL PVC medication cassettes (Pharmacia device).[8] Ifosfamide in combination with mesna (each at 50 mg/mL) was stable for 24 hours at 37°C in Graseby 9000 Medication Cassettes.[6] Further study showed that ifosfamide at 20 mg/mL in combination with mesna at 20 mg/mL, diluted in water for injections and stored in the Graseby 9000 Medication Cassettes, was physically and chemically stable for 14 days at 8°C or 7 days at 37°C.[9]

4 Clinical use

Type of cytotoxic: Alkylating agent of the nitrogen-mustard type, activated by hepatic microsomal enzymes to produce antitumour metabolites.

Main indications: Tumours of the lung, ovary, cervix, breast and testis and soft-tissue sarcoma. Ifosfamide also produces a response in osteosarcoma, malignant lymphoma, carcinoma of the pancreas, head and neck tumours and acute leukaemias (except acute myelocytic leukaemia).

Dosage: Ifosfamide should not be used without the concurrent administration of mesna (*see* Mesna monograph on page 470).

The usual dose for each course is 8–10 g/m², equally fractionated as single daily doses over 5 days, or alternatively 5–6 g/m² (maximum of 10 g) administered as a

24-hour infusion. Courses are normally repeated at intervals of 2 to 4 weeks for intermittent therapy, or 3 to 4 weeks for 24-hour infusions. The white-cell count should not be less than $4 \times 10^3/mm^3$ and the platelet count should not be less than $100 \times 10^3/mm^3$ before starting each course. Usually four courses are given, but up to seven (six by 24-hour infusion) have been administered.

5 Preparation of injection

Reconstitution: The injection should be reconstituted to give a solution of approximately 8% (80 mg/mL) using:

▼ 12.5 mL water for injections with 1 g ifosfamide
▼ 25 mL water for injections with 2 g ifosfamide.

Bolus administration: Dilute to less than 4% and inject into the vein with the patient supine, or inject directly into a fast-running infusion.

Intravenous infusion: Infuse in 5% glucose, glucose–saline or 0.9% sodium chloride infusion over 30–120 minutes, or infuse over 24 hours in 3×1 L glucose–saline or 0.9% sodium chloride. Increased doses of mesna are recommended in children and in patients with urothelial damage from previous therapies (*see* Mesna monograph on page 470).

Extravasation: Group 5 classification (neutral) (*see* Chapter 6).

6 Destruction of drug or contaminated waste

Incineration: 1000°C.

Chemical: 2 N sodium hydroxide in dimethyl formamide for 24 hours.

Contact with skin: Wash with water.

References

1 ABPI (1999) *ABPI Data Sheet Compendium 1999–2000.* DataPharm Publications Ltd, London, 104–5.
2 Trissel LA *et al.* (1979) Investigational drug information: ifosfamide and semustine. *Drug Intell Clin Pharm.* **13**: 340–3.
3 Trissel LA *et al.* (1985) *Investigational Drugs Pharmaceutical Data.* National Cancer Institute, Bethesda, MD.
4 Behme RJ *et al.* (1988) Incompatibility of ifosfamide with benzyl-alcohol-preserved bacteriostatic water for injections. *Am J Hosp Pharm.* **45**: 627–8.
5 Adams PS *et al.* (1987) Pharmaceutical aspects of home infusion therapy for cancer patients. *Pharm J.* **238**: 476–8.
6 Sewell GJ, Priston MJ, Allsopp M *et al.* (1994) Stability of drug infusions in ambulatory infusion devices. *Aust J Hosp Pharm.* **24**: 102.
7 Radford JA *et al.* (1990) The stability of ifosfamide in aqueous solution and its suitability for continuous 7-day infusion by ambulatory pump. *Cancer Chemother Pharmacol.* **26**: 144–6.

8 Munoz M *et al.* (1992) Stability of ifosfamide in 0.9% sodium chloride solution in water for injection in a portable IV pump cassette. *Am J Hosp Pharm.* **49**: 1137–9.

9 Priston MJ and Sewell GJ (1998) Stability of three cytotoxic drug infusions in the Graseby 9000 ambulatory infusion pump. *J Oncol Pharm Pract.* **4**: 43–9.

Prepared by Graham Sewell

IRINOTECAN

1 General details

Approved name: Irinotecan, camptothecin-11.

Proprietary name: Campto.

Manufacturer or supplier: Rhône-Poulenc Rorer (France).

Presentation and formulation details: Irinotecan is a pale yellow concentrated solution containing 40 mg irinotecan/mL in 2-mL or 5-mL vials.[1] The formulation also contains sorbitol 45 mg/mL and lactic acid 0.9 mg/mL.[2]

Storage and shelf-life of unopened container: 24 months if stored at room temperature (15–25°C).

2 Chemistry

Type: Synthetic derivative of camptothecin, a plant alkaloid obtained from the Chinese tree *Camptotheca acuminata*.[2]

Molecular structure: 7-ethyl-10 [4-(1-piperidino)-1-piperidino] carbonyloxycamptothecin.

Molecular weight: 677.2.

Solubility: Only slightly soluble in water, but freely soluble in acetic acid. The pH of an aqueous solution is 3.5–4.5.[1]

3 Stability profile

3.1 Physical and chemical stability

Irinotecan appears to be relatively stable in aqueous solution.

Effect of light: Irinotecan is light-sensitive, exposure to light leading to the formation of a precipitate.[3]

Container compatibility: Infusions containing irinotecan are compatible with PVC infusion containers, with no evidence of extraction of plasticisers during 4 days of storage at 4–8°C.[1,4]

Compatibility with other drugs: Irinotecan is incompatible with gemcitabine.[5]

3.2 Stability in clinical practice

Irinotecan reconstituted and diluted in 0.9% sodium chloride or 5% glucose to solutions containing between 0.12 and 1.1 mg/mL is stable (less than 10% loss) for 12 hours at room temperature or 48 hours at 2–8°C.[2] Solutions for storage at 2–8°C should be diluted in 5% glucose, as precipitation may occur if they are diluted and stored in 0.9% sodium chloride.[2]

Irinotecan should be protected from exposure to daylight during infusion, although infusions are stable under conditions of ambient fluorescent light.[2]

3.3 Stability in specialised delivery systems

No data available.

4 Clinical use

Type of cytotoxic: DNA topoisomerase-1-inhibitor.

Main indications: Irinotecan is indicated in second-line treatment of metastatic colorectal cancer following the failure of primary chemotherapy.

Dosage: The recommended initial dose is 350 mg/m² administered as an intravenous infusion over not less than 30–90 minutes. This dose should be administered at 3-weekly intervals.[1]

If the patient experiences severe asymptomatic neutropenia (neutrophil count < 500/mm³), or febrile neutropenia (temperature 38°C and neutrophil count 1000/mm³), the dose to be administered during later courses should be reduced to 300 mg/m².[1,3]

5 Preparation of injection

Reconstitution: Irinotecan should be reconstituted in water for injections. Add the appropriate volume (2 mL or 5 mL, respectively) to the vial and shake to dissolve, to give a solution containing 40 mg irinotecan/mL.[1]

Dilution: The reconstituted dilution should be added to 250 mL of 0.9% sodium chloride or 5% glucose.

Bolus administration: Not recommended.

Intravenous infusion: Infuse into a peripheral or central vein over 30–90 minutes.[1]

Extravasation: Group 3 classification (exfoliant) (*see* Chapter 6).

6 Destruction of drug or contaminated articles

Incineration: No specific information available.

Chemical: No specific information available.

Contact with skin: Wash immediately with soap and water. If undiluted solution comes into contact with mucous membrane, rinse immediately with copious water.

References

1 ABPI (1999) *ABPI Data Sheet Compendium 1999–2000*. DataPharm Publications Ltd, London, 1279–81.

2 Trissel LA (2001) *Handbook of Injectable Drugs* (11e). American Society of Health-Systems Pharmacists, Bethesda, MD.

3 Akimoto K *et al.* (1996) Photodegradation reactions of CPT-11, a derivative of camptothecin. Part II. Photodegradation behaviour of CPT-11 in aqueous solution. *Drug Stability*. **1**: 141–6.

4 Micromedex Inc. (1995) Irinotecan. In: *Drug Evaluation Monographs 1994–95*. Micromedex Inc., Englewood, CO.

5 Trissel LA *et al.* (1999) Compatibility of gemcitabine hydrochloride with 107 selected drugs during simulated Y-site injection. *J Am Pharm Assoc*. **39**: 514–8.

Prepared by Yaacov Cass

MELPHALAN

1 General details

Approved names: Melphalan, phenylalanine mustard, L-sarcolysine.

Proprietary name: Alkeran.

Manufacturer or supplier: Glaxo Wellcome.

Presentation and formulation details: 50 mg sterile anhydrous melphalan BP (as the hydrochloride) in 20-mL vial; includes 20 mg povidone K12.[1] A 10-mL buffer solution with 60% (v/v) propylene glycol, sodium citrate and ethanol is provided.[1]

Storage and shelf-life of unopened container: The shelf-life is 3 years if stored below 30°C and protected from light.

2 Chemistry

Type: Alkylating agent related to nitrogen mustard.

Molecular structure: 4-[*bis*(2-chloroethyl)amino]-L-phenylalanine.

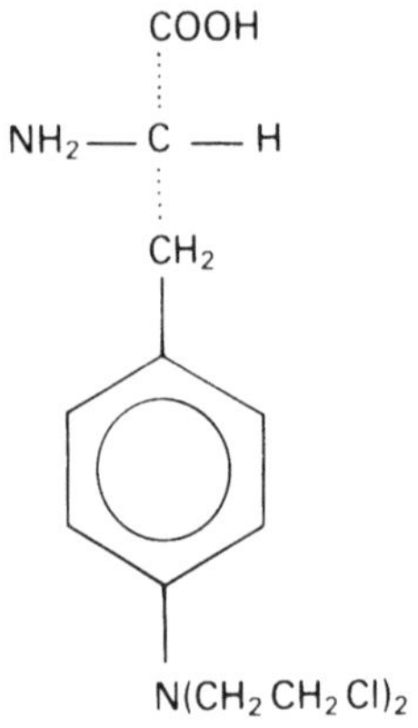

Molecular weight: 305.2 (base); 345.9 (hydrochloride).

Solubility: Practically insoluble in water but soluble in ethanol.

3 Stability profile

3.1 Physical and chemical stability

The reconstituted drug is relatively unstable. The rate of degradation is influenced by temperature, aqueous vehicle and pH.[2] The degradation products are also less water-soluble than melphalan, and a precipitate may form on standing, especially in the reconstituted vial.[3] The reconstituted injection retains 90% of its initial potency for approximately 19 hours.

Effect of pH: The drug is most stable at pH 3.0. Stability is slightly reduced at pH 5–7, but substantially reduced at pH 9.0. Data from Tabibi and Cradock[3] have quantified this effect as shown opposite.

pH (buffer)	$t_{1/2}$ (hours)
3.0	5.3
5.0	4.9
7.0	4.8
9.0	3.9

The addition of reconstituted injection to infusions will tend to acidify such solutions. The pH values of infusions after adding melphalan injection (final concentration 40 µg/mL) are as follows:[2]

Infusion fluid	pH
5% glucose	4.1
0.9% sodium chloride	4.2
Ringer's lactate	5.9

Effect of chloride ions: Studies have shown that chloride reduces the rate of hydrolysis of melphalan.[2,4-6] For example, $t_{90\%}$ of melphalan in 5% glucose is 1.5 hours and in 0.9% sodium chloride it is 4.5 hours at 20°C. Hydrophobic interaction of melphalan with propylene glycol also contributes to greater stability.[6]

Studies[2] provide some evidence of the significant influence of storage temperature on rates of degradation. Increasing the temperature from 15°C to 20°C raised the degradation rate by approximately 25% in various infusion fluids. Unfortunately, no studies were conducted under refrigerated storage conditions, but the manufacturer suggests that the drug may precipitate on refrigeration.

Effect of light: No information available.

Degradation pathways: Melphalan is degraded to monohydroxymelphalan (II), and then to dihydroxymelphalan (III).[3] The kinetics can be described as pseudo-first-order (*see* Figure 4).[2,5]

Degradation products are said to be much less cytotoxic.[7]

Container compatibility: Melphalan is compatible with plastic containers, administration sets and plastic syringes.[7]

Compatibility with other drugs: Physical compatibility of melphalan at 0.1 mg/mL was investigated with a wide range of drugs during simulated Y-site administration. The results indicate that melphalan at 0.1 mg/mL is compatible with most drugs, although it is incompatible with amphotericin B and chlorpromazine.[8]

3.2 Stability in clinical practice

Reconstituted vials must be used or further diluted within 30 minutes.[1] They can be further diluted in 0.9% sodium chloride and infused over 2 hours. The diluted drug should not be stored for longer than 2 hours at ambient temperature (refrigeration may cause precipitation). Melphalan is not absorbed by in-line filters.[9] It is also suggested that solutions of melphalan can be stored frozen in 0.9% sodium chloride for 6 months without undergoing significant degradation.[10] Melphalan at 0.2 mg/mL in 0.9% sodium chloride infusion in PVC bags was stable (not more than 10% degradation) for up to 72 hours at –20°C, 6 hours at 4°C and 3 hours at room temperature (not greater than 26°C).[10] No precipitation was

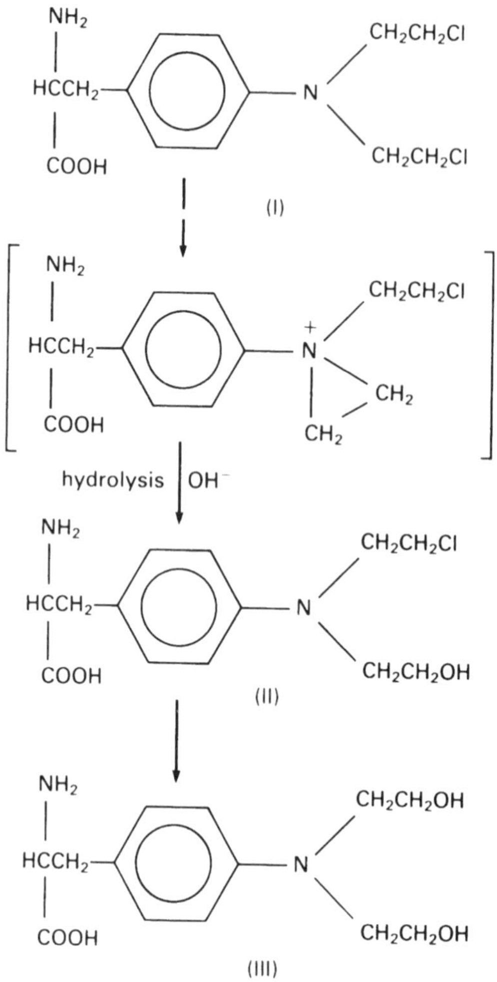

Figure 4: *Degradation of melphalan; first-step hydrolysis*

observed during storage at 4°C.[10] It was also reported that stability was greater in 3% sodium chloride, extending to 48 hours at 4°C and 6 hours at room temperature.[10] Solutions containing 2 mg/mL melphalan showed similar stability.[10]

No special precautions are required to protect the injection from normal lighting conditions. However, exposure to strong daylight should be avoided.

3.3 Stability in specialised delivery systems

No data available.

4 Clinical use

Type of cytotoxic: Alkylating agent.

Main indications: Localised malignant melanomas; localised soft-tissue sarcoma of the extremities.

Dosage: Between 8 and 30 mg/m² should be administered intravenously every 2 to 6 weeks, or alternatively regional perfusion of between 0.6 and 1.5 mg/kg (depending on the site) through the part of the body that is affected by the tumour.

5 Preparation of injection

Reconstitution: Add the contents of the diluent vial to the freeze-dried powder and immediately shake vigorously until dissolved. The resulting solution contains 5 mg/mL anhydrous melphalan. Refrigeration of the solution should be avoided.[1]

Bolus administration: Inject within 30 minutes of preparation into the tubing of a fast-running infusion.

Intravenous infusion: Dilute only in 0.9% sodium chloride, and infuse slowly over 2 hours.[9] Consult the relevant literature for details and alternative methods of tissue perfusion.

Extravasation: Group 5 classification (neutral) (*see* Chapter 6).

6 Destruction of drug or contaminated articles

Incineration: 500°C.

Chemical: 5% sodium thiosulphate in sodium hydroxide solution for 24 hours.

Contact with skin: Wash with water.

References

1 ABPI (1999) *ABPI Data Sheet Compendium 1999–2000.* DataPharm Publications Ltd, London, 460–1.
2 Flora KP *et al.* (1979) Application of a simple HPLC method for the determination of melphalan in the presence of its hydrolysis products. *J Chromatogr.* **177**: 91–7.
3 Tabibi SE and Cradock JC (1984) Stability of melphalan in infusion fluids. *Am J Hosp Pharm.* **41**: 1380–2.
4 Trissel LA (1992) *Handbook of Injectable Drugs* (8e). American Society of Hospital Pharmacists, Bethesda, MD.
5 Chang SY *et al.* (1978) Hydrolysis and protein binding of melphalan. *J Pharm Sci.* **67**: 682–4.
6 Chang SY *et al.* (1979) The stability of melphalan in the presence of chloride ions. *J Pharm Pharmacol.* **31**: 853–4.
7 Calmic Medical Division. Unpublished data.
8 Tissel LA and Martinez JF (1993) Physical compatibility of melphalan with selected drugs during simulated Y-site administration. *Am J Hosp Pharm.* **50**: 2359–63.
9 Bosanquet AG (1985) Stability of solutions of melphalan during preparation and storage for *in vitro* chemosensitivity assays. *J Pharm Sci.* **74**: 348–51.
10 Pinguet F *et al.* (1994) Effect of sodium chloride concentration and temperature on melphalan stability during storage and use. *Am J Hosp Pharm.* **51**: 2701–4.

Prepared by Michael Allwood

METHOTREXATE

1 General details

Approved name: Methotrexate.

Proprietary name: Methotrexate Injection.

Manufacturer or supplier: Wyeth Laboratories Ltd, Faulding Pharmaceuticals plc.

Presentation and formulation details:

Methotrexate Injection (Wyeth): A clear, yellowish solution for injection or infusion containing methotrexate sodium equivalent to 25 mg/mL, 50 mg/2 mL, 100 mg/ 4 mL, 200 mg/8 mL, 500 mg/20 mL, 1 g/40 mL, 5 g/200 mL of methotrexate per vial, together with sodium hydroxide. All formulations are preservative-free.

Methotrexate Injection (Faulding): A clear, yellowish solution of methotrexate in water for injections with sodium hydroxide to adjust pH to between 8 and 9. The lower strengths are made isotonic with sodium chloride. The 1 g in 10 mL and 5 g in 50 mL presentations do not contain sodium chloride and are slightly hypertonic. It is available in the following strengths and packs: 5 mg/2 mL, 50 mg/2 mL, 500 mg/ 20 mL, 1 g/10 mL, 5 g/50 mL. All solutions are preservative-free.

Storage and shelf-life of unopened containers: Methotrexate preparations (Wyeth) should be stored at controlled room temperature (15–30°C) and protected from direct sunlight. All preparations have a shelf-life of 2 years from the date of manufacture.

Methotrexate Injection (Faulding) should be stored below 25°C, and it should be protected from light and freezing. All preparations have a shelf-life of 2 years from the date of manufacture.

2 Chemistry

Type: 4-amino-N-methyl analogue of folic acid.

Molecular structure:

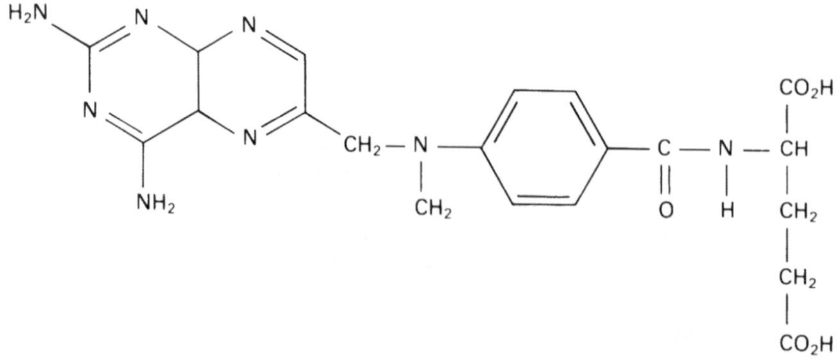

Molecular weight: 454.44.

Solubility: Practically insoluble in water. Dissolves in solutions of mineral acids and in dilute solutions of alkali hydroxides and carbonates.[1]

3 Stability profile

3.1 *Physical and chemical stability*

Methotrexate is relatively stable in aqueous solution provided that the recommended storage conditions are observed. The compound is susceptible to both hydrolytic and photolytic degradation. The rate of hydrolytic degradation increases with rising pH, with minimum degradation occurring at pH 6.6–8.2.[2]

Degradation pathways: The major hydrolytic degradation compound is N-methyl-pteroylglutamic acid (methopterin). The major photolytic degradation compounds are *p*-aminobenzoylglutamic acid and 2-amino-4-hydroxypteridine-6-carboxylic acid.[3]

Effect of light: The drug is light-sensitive and forms a yellow precipitate on prolonged exposure to direct sunlight. Polypropylene and styrene acrylonitrile syringes provide better light protection than glass ampoules when the drug is stored under controlled light conditions at 25°C.[4] In all cases, no precipitate was observed over a 7-day storage period. Samples stored in the dark showed no evidence of precipitation.[4]

McElnay *et al.*[5] studied the photodegradation of methotrexate 0.1% (w/v) in 0.9% (w/v) sodium chloride in three burette administration systems (a standard set, a 'light-protective' Amberset and a 'low-adsorption' Sureset (Avon Medical)). Storage under normal lighting conditions (diffuse daylight/fluorescent-tube room lighting) led to little change in drug concentration over the first 24 hours of storage, although a decrease in concentration (maximum 12%) was noted in both the standard sets and Suresets by 48 hours. A much more rapid decrease in methotrexate concentration was demonstrated when the drug solution was exposed to sunlight. An 11% decline in methotrexate concentration occurred in the standard sets in 7 hours (Suresets were not investigated). The use of Ambersets, or wrapping the standard sets in tinfoil, prevented photodegradation over this period. Storage in the administration tubing of all three sets under normal lighting conditions resulted in more than 10% degradation within 12 hours in the standard sets and Suresets, and within 48 hours in the light-protected Suresets and Ambersets. All of these results were obtained for a static system, and it is difficult to extrapolate them to the dynamic situation of an intravenous administration.

Trissel[6] describes some more recent work by researchers in France on the stability of methotrexate sodium 1 mg/mL (R. Bellon) in 0.9% sodium chloride stored in EVA and PVC containers. The drug was evaluated for stability in translucent containers (Perfupack, Baxter) and five opaque containers (green PVC Opafuseur (Bruneau), white EVA Perfu-opaque (Baxter), orange PVC PF170 (Cair), white PVC V86 (Codan) and white EVA Perfecran (Fandre)), when exposed to sunlight for 28 days. Photodegradation was detected in the solution stored in the translucent Perfupack using HPLC. Losses were in the range 18.5–27% after 24 hours of exposure to sunlight at this concentration. The losses in a 5 mg/mL solution were less (about 5% in 24 hours). At 1 mg/mL, losses of 4% or less occurred over 24 hours in the opaque containers.

Effect of pH: Methotrexate is a bicarboxylic acid with a pK_a in the range 4.8–5.7.[7] Thus, it is essentially ionised at physiological pH. At pH values between 2.6 and 6.6, the drug is converted to the bicarboxylic acid, which is relatively insoluble in aqueous solution and will precipitate. Commercially available injection is stabilised to approximately pH 8.4. However, dilution in acidic solutions may result in precipitation of the drug. For this reason, dilutions in 5% glucose should be checked carefully for evidence of precipitation.

Container compatibility: At a pH value of 8.4, methotrexate injection is largely ionised and is therefore unlikely to exhibit sorption phenomena.

McElnay et al.[5] found the sorption of methotrexate, 0.1% (w/v) in 0.9% (w/v) sodium chloride, stored in 'low-sorption' Suresets and standard or Ambersets (Avon Medical) to be negligible, but they were unable to explain the greater than 10% loss of drug when methotrexate was stored in light-protected polybutadiene and PVC tubing for 48 hours at room temperature. Beitz et al.[8] undertook a comparative stability study of a range of cytotoxic drug solutions in low-density polyethylene (LDPE) containers, glass bottles and polyvinyl chloride (PVC) infusion bags. The main purpose of the study was to collect data on the compatibility of cytotoxic drug solutions with polyethylene containers. PVC bags were included in the investigation to compare the absorption properties of PVC with LDPE.

Methotrexate at a concentration used in therapeutic regimens (0.36 mg/mL) was stored in 250 mL LDPE containers (Ecoflac, B. Braun), glass bottles (B. Braun) and PVC bags (Viaflex, Baxter) containing 0.9% saline or 5% glucose at 4°C. Stability (95–105% of the initial concentration) and compatibility were measured over a 72-hour period using a stability-indicating HPLC assay.

The drug remained stable over the storage period in all three containers, with no evidence of degradation peaks and no turbidity, visible changes in colour or precipitation. There was no evidence of adsorption of the drug on to LDPE or PVC. No other studies have shown significant sorption on to PVC containers. The sorption of methotrexate in 5% glucose to the latex reservoir of Baxter infusors was also found to be negligible.[9]

Methotrexate 50 mg in 100 mL 0.9% (w/v) sodium chloride was not absorbed by a 0.2-μm endotoxin-retentive and end-line filter (Pall Intravenous Set Saver, Pall Biomedical Ltd) when infused at a rate of 80 mL/hour.[10]

Although extraction into solution is possible, especially with plastic syringes, the extent and rate of leaching are likely to be low at room temperature.[11,12] It should be noted, however, that 2-mercaptobenzothiazole (a mercaptan present in the rubber plunger) is soluble in alkali and alkali carbonate solutions,[13] and may leach into the alkaline methotrexate injection on prolonged storage in plastic syringes. Mercaptans may cause problems as analytical or toxicological contaminants.

More recently, Jacolot et al.[14] studied the physicochemical stability of and compatibility between a 2.5 mg/mL methotrexate solution (Lederle) and plastic syringes (Becton Dickinson) over a 7-day period at 4 and 25°C, protected from light. The compatibility study consisted of the titration of reducing substances, thin-layer chromatography (TLC) of extracted additives, assay of extracted ions by atomic absorption spectrometry (AAS), resistivity measurement, dynamometric test and UV, visible and infra-red absorption spectrophotometry.

Methotrexate (2.5 mg/mL) was stable and compatible over 7 days when stored at 4 and 25°C in the tested syringes. No pH variation (8.1 ± 0.17) or loss of organoleptic character modification was observed after 7 days of storage. This is reflected in other studies on the stability of methotrexate in syringes. Determination of reducing substances and characterisation of additives were compatible with the

European Pharmacopoeia guidelines. There was no evidence of ionised compound extraction from the syringes using AAS. The UV and visible absorption spectra showed the absence of extractable components from plastic syringes in the methotrexate solutions, and although infra-red absorption spectra detected a silicone-oil layer coating the syringes, there appeared to be no significant absorption of methotrexate.

Compatibility with other drugs: D'Arcy[15] found methotrexate to be chemically and physically incompatible with cytarabine, fluorouracil and prednisolone sodium phosphate. However, two other studies have shown the drug to be compatible and stable with cytarabine and fluorouracil under defined storage conditions. In the first study,[16] the stability of cytarabine, methotrexate sodium and hydrocortisone sodium succinate admixtures was investigated. Two admixtures, namely cytarabine 50 mg, methotrexate 12 mg (as the sodium salt) and hydrocortisone 25 mg (as the sodium succinate salt), and cytarabine 30 mg, methotrexate 12 mg (as the sodium salt) and hydrocortisone 15 mg (as the sodium succinate salt) were prepared in one of four diluents (Elliott's B solution, 0.9% sodium chloride, 5% glucose and lactated Ringer's solution). The drugs were reconstituted according to the manufacturers' instructions with the infusion fluid under test. After reconstitution, the drug solutions were mixed in the desired proportions and diluted to 12 mL with the respective infusion fluid. Each admixture was filtered through a 0.45-μm membrane filter, placed in a 12-mL disposable syringe (the type of plastic was not identified) and kept at 25±0.1°C in a water bath. Cytarabine and methotrexate were stable in the fluids studied for 24 hours at 25°C. Alteration in stability related to vehicles or drug concentration combinations was not evident, and the stability of each of the drugs did not appear to be affected by the presence of the other two drugs. Hydrocortisone sodium succinate was found to be less stable in Elliott's B solution, with only 94.1% of the drug remaining in the first admixture, and 86% remaining in the second after 24 hours. Alkaline catalysis may explain the increased degradation of the drug in Elliott's B solution, which has a higher pH than the other vehicles. No precipitation was observed in either group of admixtures during 8 hours at 25°C, although storage for several days resulted in some precipitation. The nature of the precipitate was not identified.

At the concentrations studied, cytarabine, methotrexate and hydrocortisone sodium succinate may be mixed in 0.9% sodium chloride, 5% glucose or lactated Ringer's solution and stored in plastic disposable syringes for up to 24 hours at 25°C. Admixtures in Elliott's B solution should be used within 10 hours. A more recent study by Zhang *et al.*[17] investigated the individual physical and chemical stabilities of each of the three drugs in Elliott's B solution in 30-mL glass vials and 20-mL plastic syringes (Becton-Dickinson). Methotrexate at 2 mg/mL was physically and chemically compatible with Elliott's B solution over 48 hours at 4 and 23°C.

The second study[18] investigated the compatibility and stability of cyclophosphamide, methotrexate and 5-fluorouracil in a three-drug admixture. Cyclophosphamide (100 mg), methotrexate (1.5 mg) and 5-fluorouracil (500 mg) were reconstituted in a total volume of 60 mL of 0.9% sodium chloride. The solution was maintained at room temperature in PVC plastic reservoir bags (Lifecare 1500 System, Abbott). No significant loss of 5-fluorouracil or methotrexate was observed up to 14 days after reconstitution of the three-drug admixture. However, a 9.3% loss of cyclophosphamide was observed, accompanied by the appearance of a degradation product in the HPLC chromatogram after 7 days. Control admixtures indicated that the cyclo-phosphamide and methotrexate were chemically incompatible and that there was a pH change in this admixture from 6.6 to 4.6. At this pH methotrexate stability is compromised.

Based on this information, it may be possible to administer cyclophosphamide, methotrexate and 5-fluorouracil as a three-drug admixture in an infusion pump, in the proportions reported, for up to 7 days. However, solutions should be checked carefully for precipitation, and such admixtures should not be used in implantable infusion pumps. Stewart et al.[19] studied the stability of methotrexate sodium with ondansetron hydrochloride at high and low concentrations, which represented the range of concentrations likely to be used in clinical practice. Ondansetron and methotrexate were mixed with 5% glucose injection in 50 mL PVC infusion bags to give a final nominal concentration of ondansetron 0.03 or 0.3 mg/mL and methotrexate 0.5 or 6 mg/mL. Control solutions of each drug alone at each concentration were also prepared in 5% glucose injection in PVC infusion bags. All solutions were stored at 21.8–23.4°C and 23–48% relative humidity under continuous fluorescent light. The admixtures were physically and chemically stable over the 48-hour period studied. The authors concluded that the investigation supports Y-site administration or mixing of ondansetron with methotrexate over the range of concentrations and under the conditions studied.

In addition, Trissel[6] lists a wide range of compatibility information. Although useful for reference purposes, much of the data relate to short-term physical compatibility of admixtures in the laboratory setting and are not applicable clinically.

3.2 Stability in clinical practice

Although the manufacturers do not recommend reuse of the methotrexate injection after opening, its relative stability in aqueous solution would suggest that, provided the injection is manipulated under aseptic conditions and is stored in the original container at 4–8°C in the absence of light once opened, chemical and physical stability will be preserved. In general, a shelf-life of 1 month at 4°C after opening would seem to be satisfactory.

Infusions: Information on the stability of the drug when diluted in the recommended solutions for infusion is variable. The manufacturers are limited by the terms of their product licences to recommending a maximum shelf-life of 24 hours at 25°C. However, a number of reports suggest that methotrexate is stable over a wide range of concentrations when stored in Viaflex (Baxter) containers for longer than 24 hours.[20-24] In particular, research conducted by Baxter Laboratories[21] indicated that, at a concentration of 1–10 mg/mL in 5% glucose and 1.25–12.5 mg/mL in 0.9% sodium chloride infusions, methotrexate is stable (<10% degradation) for up to 1 month at 4°C, and 5 days at 25°C when stored in both Baxter infusors and Viaflex minibags. More recent data[22] indicate that solutions of methotrexate with concentrations in the range 1.25–12.5 mg/mL reconstituted with 0.9% sodium chloride are chemically stable for at least 15 days in the Baxter infusor when stored at 4°C. However, due to a lack of stability data at 33°C, the company advise that methotrexate should be delivered using the half-day infusor only.

Further studies[23] on the stability of methotrexate at 1.25–12.5 mg/mL in 0.9% sodium chloride, stored in both glass and PVC containers (Viaflex, Baxter), have shown that the drug is physically and chemically stable for up to 15 weeks at 4°C followed by 1 week of storage at room temperature.

Although there is some evidence that methotrexate infusion solutions prepared in Viaflex (Baxter) minibags can be frozen to –20°C and stored for at least 3 months without a significant reduction in methotrexate concentration or change in pH,[24] microwave ovens should not be used to thaw solutions prior to use without careful validation of the thawing process.

Infusion solutions should be protected from light at all times.

Syringe storage: Methotrexate injection at a concentration of 50 mg/mL or less, stored in sealed Monoject (Sherwood Medical) or Plastipak (Becton-Dickinson) plastic disposable syringes in the absence of light and at a temperature not exceeding 25°C, is stable (<10% degradation) for a period of up to 8 months.[4] Storage in Sabre (Gillette) and Steriseal (NI Ltd) syringes should not exceed 70 days.[4]

3.3 Stability in specialised delivery systems

Methotrexate over the concentration range 0.33–10.0 mg/mL in 0.9% (w/v) sodium chloride stored in an implantable infusion pump (Model 400, Shiley Infusaid Inc.) at 37°C was found to be stable for up to 12 days.[25] The solutions were filtered through a 5-µm filter prior to addition to the pump.

Methotrexate (Lederle) at a concentration of 25 mg/mL in 0.9% sodium chloride stored in a medication cassette reservoir (Pharmacia/Deltec) exhibited no evidence of degradation over 7 days of storage at 25°C and 14 days of storage at 5°C.[26]

4 Clinical use

Type of cytotoxic: Antimetabolite.

Main indications: Meningeal leukaemia, choriocarcinoma, non-Hodgkin's lymphomas, solid tumours, severe psoriasis, and rheumatoid arthritis that is unresponsive to conventional therapy.

Dosage and administration: Methotrexate injection may be given by the intramuscular, intravenous (bolus injection or infusion), intrathecal, intra-arterial or intraventricular routes. Subcutaneous administration of methotrexate has been evaluated.[27] Methotrexate administered by this route is well tolerated and well absorbed. Intra-tumour administration using implantable catheters and subcutaneous refillable pumps has also been investigated.[25]

Dosages vary considerably depending on the condition being treated, and are based on the patient's body weight or surface area,[28,29] except in the case of intrathecal or intraventricular administration, when a maximum dose of 15 mg is recommended.

It must be noted that all preparations of methotrexate (Wyeth) are suitable for intrathecal use, although it is recommended that only the low-volume preparations are used, in order to avoid possible confusion. Methotrexate injection (Faulding) at 500 mg/20 mL, 1 g/10 mL and 5 g/50 mL is not suitable for intrathecal use. The 1 g/10 mL and 5 g/50 mL solutions are hypertonic.

High doses may cause the precipitation of methotrexate and its metabolites in the renal tubules. A high fluid throughput and alkalinisation of the urine to pH 6.5–7.0 by the oral or intravenous administration of sodium bicarbonate (e.g. 5 × 625 mg tablets every 3 hours) or acetazolamide (500 mg orally four times a day) is recommended as a preventive measure.[29]

Doses exceeding 100 mg are usually given by intravenous infusion over a period not exceeding 24 hours. Lower doses may be given by rapid intravenous bolus injection over 2 to 3 minutes, or by infusion. The concentration of the final injection is not critical.

Intrathecal administration: If the intended route of administration is intrathecal, please refer to Chapter 6 with regard to the prescribing, dispensing, labelling and issuing of this drug.

5 Preparation of injection

Dilution: The drug may be diluted in 0.9% sodium chloride, 5% glucose, glucose–saline, compound sodium chloride, compound sodium lactate infusions or Elliott's B solution.

Extravasation: Irritant, but does not cause tissue damage (*see* Chapter 6).

6 Destruction of drug or contaminated articles

Incineration: 1000°C.[30]

Chemical: None recommended.

Contact with skin: Wash with water and soothe any transient stinging with a bland cream. Irrigate eyes with copious amounts of water or saline. If significant quantities are inhaled or injected, calcium folinate cover should be considered.

References

1 Reynolds JEF (ed.) (1999) *The Extra Pharmacopoeia* (32e). The Pharmaceutical Press, London.
2 Hansen J *et al.* (1983) Kinetics of degradation of methotrexate in aqueous solution. *Int J Pharm.* **16**: 141–52.
3 Chatterji DC and Gallelli JF (1978) Thermal and photolytic decomposition of methotrexate in aqueous solution. *J Pharm Sci.* **67**: 526–31.
4 Wright MP and Newton JM (1988) Stability of methotrexate injection in prefilled plastic disposable syringes. *Int J Pharm.* **45**: 237–44.
5 McElnay JC *et al.* (1988) Stability of methotrexate and vinblastine in burette administration sets. *Int J Pharm.* **47**: 239–47.
6 Lorillon P *et al.* (1992) Photosensibilité du 5-fluorouracile et du methotrexate dans des perfuseurs translucides ou opaques. *J Pharm Clin.* **11**: 285–95.
7 Bleyer WA (1978) The clinical pharmacology of methotrexate. New applications of an old drug. *Cancer.* **41**: 36–50.
8 Beitz C *et al.* (1999) Compatibility of plastics with cytotoxic drug solutions – comparison of polyethylene with other container materials. *Int J Pharm.* **185**: 113–21.
9 Bertocchio F *et al.* (1986) Study of the viability of an infusion system. *J Pharm Clin.* **5**: 331–9.
10 Stevens RF and Wilkins KM (1989) Use of cytotoxic drugs with an end-line filter: a study of four drugs commonly administered to paediatric patients. *J Clin Pharm Ther.* **14**: 475–9.

11 Sherwood Medical Industries Ltd (1984) Personal communication.

12 Gillette UK Ltd (1984) Personal communication.

13 Merck & Co. Inc. (1983) *The Merck Index* (10e). Merck & Co. Inc., Rathway, NJ.

14 Jacolot A *et al.* (1996) Stability and compatibility of 2.5 mg/mL methotrexate solution in plastic syringes over 7 days. *Int J Pharm.* 128: 283–6.

15 D'Arcy PF (1983) Reactions and interactions in handling anticancer drugs. *Drug Intell Clin Pharm.* **17**: 532–8.

16 Cheung Y *et al.* (1984) Stability of cytarabine, methotrexate sodium and hydrocortisone sodium succinate admixtures. *Am J Hosp Pharm.* **41**: 1802–6.

17 Zhang Y *et al.* (1996) Physical and chemical stability of methotrexate sodium, cytarabine and hydrocortisone sodium succinate in Elliott's B solution. *Hosp Pharm.* **31**: 965–70.

18 Lokich J *et al.* (1989) Cyclophosphamide, methotrexate and 5-fluorouracil in a three-drug admixture. Phase I trial of 14-day continuous ambulatory infusion. *Cancer.* **63**: 822–4.

19 Stewart JT *et al.* (1996) Stability of ondansetron hydrochloride and five antineoplastic medications. *Am J Health-Syst Pharm.* **53**: 1297–300.

20 Roach M (1979) Methotrexate infusions. *Pharm J.* **223**: 557.

21 Trissel LA (2001) *Handbook of Injectable Drugs* (11e). American Society of Health-Systems Pharmacists, Bethesda, MD.

22 Baxter Healthcare Ltd (1992) Personal communication.

23 Vincke BJ *et al.* (1989) Extended stability of 5-fluorouracil and methotrexate solutions in PVC containers. *Int J Pharm.* **54**: 181–9.

24 Dyvik O *et al.* (1986) Methotrexate in infusion solutions: a stability test for the hospital pharmacy. *J Clin Hosp Pharm.* **11**: 343–8.

25 Nierenberg D *et al.* (1991) Continuous intratumoral infusion of methotrexate for recurrent glioblastoma: a pilot study. *Neurosurgery.* **28**: 752–61.

26 Landersjo L and Nyhammar E (1989) *Stability and Compatibility of Methotrexate in Medication Cassettes.* Apoteksbolaget AB, Stockholm, Sweden.

27 Balis FM *et al.* (1988) Pharmacokinetics of subcutaneous methotrexate. *J Clin Oncol.* **6**: 1882–6.

28 Wyeth Laboratories Ltd (1995) *Methotrexate Injection 25 mg/mL (Wyeth): summary of product characteristics.* Authorised 18 July 1995; revised (partially) January 1999. Wyeth Laboratories Ltd, Maidenhead.

29 Faulding Pharmaceuticals plc (1985 and 1987) *Methotrexate Injection (Faulding): summary of product characteristics.* Authorised 21 August 1985 and 13 March 1987; revised (partially) 17 March 1998. Faulding Pharmaceuticals plc, Warwick.

30 Bristol Myers Pharmaceuticals Ltd (1985) Personal communication.

Prepared by Patricia Wright

MITOMYCIN

1 General details

Approved names: Mitomycin C, mitomycin X.

Proprietary name: Mitomycin C Kyowa.

Manufacturer or supplier: Faulding Pharmaceuticals plc, Kyowa Hakko UK Ltd.

Presentation and formulation details: Purple lyophilised powder in vials containing 2 mg, 10 mg or 20 mg.[1,2] Vials contain 24 mg sodium chloride/1 mg mitomycin.

Storage and shelf-life of unopened container: 3–4 years at ambient temperature and protected from light.[2]

2 Chemistry

Molecular structure: 1 S-(1,8,8a,8b)-6-amino-8-(aminocarbonyl)oxy-methyl-1,1,2,-8, 8a,8b-hexahydro-methoxy-5-methyl-azirino 2′,3′,4,7, pyrrolo-1,2-indole-4,7-dione.

Molecular weight: 349.

Solubility: Sparingly soluble in water.

3 Stability profile

3.1 Physical and chemical stability

Mitomycin C is relatively unstable in aqueous solution, showing losses of approximately 10% in 7 days at 25°C.[3] In phosphate buffer at pH 7.4, losses of less than 5% in 7 days were reported.[3] Stability is pH dependent and is greatest between pH 7 and 8.[2] Mitomycin is significantly less stable in acid conditions. A degradation rate constant of 5×10^{-6}/second at pH 4.9 and 20°C was reported.[2]

Degradation pathways: In alkali the 7-amino group is replaced by a hydroxyl group, while the remainder of the mitosane skeleton remains intact.[4]

In acid the methoxy group is cleaved to form a 9-9α-unsaturated bond.[4] In addition, the 1,2-fused aziridine ring is opened to give two isomeric compounds 1 and 2, with a hydroxyl group at position 1 and an amino group at position 2.

The degradation rate is related to temperature after reconstitution. The reconstituted drug is significantly more stable at 2–6°C compared with ambient conditions. However, solubility is substantially reduced in the refrigerator, and solutions containing 0.5 mg/mL in water for injections may precipitate at 2–6°C. The reconstituted drug should be protected from daylight, although light-induced degradation would not normally be a significant factor during bolus administration.

Effect of light: Mitomycin is not sensitive to fluorescent (artificial) light.[3]

Container compatibility: Studies suggest that stability is not greatly influenced by the nature of the container in which the drug is diluted (glass bottles, PVC containers) when the dilution vehicle is 0.9% sodium chloride infusion,[5] or in syringes (diluted in water).[6] However, the studies would suggest that mitomycin does not adsorb significantly to standard administration sets.[3]

Compatibility with other drugs: Mitomycin at 10–50 µg/mL in 0.9% sodium chloride may be mixed with bleomycin 20–30 IU if used immediately, but compatibility depends on concentration.[4] Some degradation of bleomycin was reported, but mitomycin stability was not assessed. Trissel reported studies which suggest that mitomycin may be physically compatible with a number of other drugs.[7,8]

3.2 Stability in clinical practice

Current guidelines from the UK supplier recommend that reconstituted vials are stable for 12 hours if stored at room temperature. Refrigeration may cause precipitation, and is therefore not recommended. The drug may be further diluted, preferably in 0.9% sodium chloride. In 5% glucose, the diluted infusion should be used immediately, although it may be stored for not more than 12 hours in 0.9% sodium chloride. Few studies have been reported on stability after dilution in infusion fluids. One report indicates that degradation is more rapid in 5% glucose than in 0.9% sodium chloride.[9] The studies suggest an initial rapid fall (about 10–15%) in content after dilution. However, these studies have not been repeated and remain controversial.

The stability of mitomycin was also studied in 0.9% sodium chloride and 5% glucose, with or without buffering, stored in PVC containers.[9] The drug, at a concentration of 50 µg/mL, was unstable in both (unbuffered) vehicles. There was about 75% degradation in 5% glucose after 12 hours of storage at room temperature. In contrast, if vehicles were phosphate-buffered to pH 7.8, mitomycin appeared to be stable for more than 120 days at 5°C. However, these results have been questioned.[10] In a further study, unbuffered solutions in 0.9% sodium chloride were reported to be stable when stored at −30°C for at least 28 days.[11] Sorption to PVC containers does not occur.[3,12] However, mitomycin at 0.5 mg/mL in water for injections, stored at 2–6°C, may precipitate.

Mitomycin reconstituted to a concentration of 0.5 mg/mL with water for injection and packed in 1-mL polypropylene syringes exhibited less than 10% loss after storage at 25°C for 11 days, or 42 days after storage at 5°C.[6]

The most recent study indicates that solutions of mitomycin C dissolved in water for injections to give concentrations of 0.6 mg/mL stored in PVC (Urotainer™) bags protected from light were stable (less than 10% degradation) for 4 days at ambient temperature, or at least 7 days at 4°C. Higher concentrations showed evidence of precipitation, especially at 4°C.[11] Solutions containing 0.6 mg/mL mitomycin C in 0.9% sodium chloride were stable for 4 days at 4°C.[11]

3.3 Stability in specialised delivery systems

No data available.

4 Clinical use

Type of cytotoxic: Antitumour antibiotic.

Main indications: Bladder, rectal and skin cancer.

Dosage: 4–10 mg (0.06–0.15 mg/kg) at 1- to 6-weekly intervals. Up to 40–80 mg (2 mg/kg) cumulative doses have been given in some treatments.

5 Preparation of injection

Reconstitution: solutions are formed rapidly.
2-mg vial + 5 mL of water for injections or 20% glucose = 0.4 mg/mL.
10-mg vial + 10 mL of water for injections or 20% glucose = 1 mg/mL.
20-mg vial + 20 mL of water for injections or 20% glucose = 1 mg/mL.
May be stored for up to 12 hours at room temperature (do not refrigerate).[1,2]

Bolus administration: Inject slowly into a vein or slow-running drip at a rate of approximately 1 mL/minute, or more rapidly into a fast-running drip of 0.9% sodium chloride or 5% glucose. The stability of reconstituted drug in plastic syringes is not known.

Intravenous infusion: Dilute with 0.9% sodium chloride (use within 12 hours) or 5% glucose (use immediately) and infuse over 1 hour. Extended storage for 4–7 days may be acceptable provided that the mitomycin C concentration does not exceed 0.6 mg/mL.[1]

Extravasation: Group 1 classification (vesicant). Very damaging (*see* Chapter 6).

6 Destruction of drug or contaminated articles

Incineration: 1000°C.

Chemical: 2–5% of hydrochloric acid or sodium hydroxide for 12 hours.

Contact with skin: Very irritant. Neutralise with several washes of sodium bicarbonate solution (8.4%) followed by soap and water; avoid hand creams.

References

1 ABPI (1999) *ABPI Data Sheet Compendium 1999–2000*. DataPharm Publications Ltd, London, 419–22.

2 ABPI (1999) *ABPI Data Sheet Compendium 1999–2000*. DataPharm Publications Ltd, London, 698–9.

3 Beijnen JH *et al*. (1990) Chemical stability of the anti-tumor drug mitomycin C in solutions for intravesical installation. *J Parent Sci Technol*. **44**: 332–5.

4 Beijnen JH and Underberg WJM (1985) Degradation of mitomycin C in acidic conditions. *Int J Pharm*. **24**: 219–29.

5 Benvenuto JA *et al*. (1981) Stability and compatibility of antitumour agents in glass and plastic containers. *Am J Hosp Pharm*. **38**: 1914–18.

6 Gupta MP *et al*. (1998) Stability of mitomycin aqueous solutions when stored in tuberculin syringes. *Int J Pharm Comp*. **1**: 282–3.

7 Trissel LA (2001) *Handbook of Injectable Drugs* (11e). American Society of Health-Systems Pharmacists, Bethesda, MD.

8 Dorr RT *et al*. (1982) Bleomycin compatibility with selected intravenous medications. *J Med*. **13**: 121–30.

9 Quebberman EJ *et al*. (1985) Stability of mitomycin admixtures. *Am J Hosp Pharm*. **42**: 1750–4.

10 Keller JH (1986) Stability of mitomycin admixtures. *Am J Hosp Pharm*. **43**: 59–64.

11 Stole LML *et al*. (1986) Stability after freezing and thawing of solutions of mitomycin C in plastic minibags for intravesical use. *Pharm Weekbl (Sci Edn)* **8**: 286–8.

12 Quebberman EJ and Hoffman NE (1986) Stability of mitomycin admixtures. *Am J Hosp Pharm*. **43**: 64.

Prepared by Michael Allwood

MITOZANTRONE

1 General details

Approved name: Mitozantrone.

Proprietary name: Novantrone.

Manufacturer or supplier: Wyeth Laboratories Ltd.

Presentation and formulation details: Vials containing mitozantrone dihydrochloride solution, equivalent to 2 mg/mL mitozantrone. Solutions of 20 mg in 10 mL, 25 mg in 12.5 mL and 30 mg in 15 mL are available. Each vial also contains sodium chloride 0.8% (w/v), sodium metabisulphate 0.01% (w/v) and sodium acetate/acetic acid buffer to approximately pH 3.[1]

Storage and shelf-life of unopened container: Store at controlled room temperature at 15–25°C. Stable for 2 years from the date of manufacture.

2 Chemistry

Type: Anthracenedione.

Molecular structure: 1,4-dihydroxy-5,8-*bis*-2-(2-hydroxyethyl) aminoethylamine-9,10-anthraquinone dihydrochloride.

$OH \quad O \quad NHCH_2CH_2NHCH_2CH_2OH$

$OH \quad O \quad NHCH_2CH_2NHCH_2CH_2OH$

Molecular weight: 517.4.

Solubility: Water soluble.

3 Stability profile

3.1 Physical and chemical stability

Mitozantrone degrades by oxidation of the phenylenediamine moiety to the corresponding quinoneimine, which then hydrolyses to the quinone.[2]

Effect of pH: Stability is optimal in acidic conditions.

Effect of light: Vials of mitozantrone may precipitate during refrigerated storage. Exposure of vials to sunlight for 1 month has little effect on the potency or appearance of the product.

Container compatibility: Mitozantrone is adsorbed on to glass but not on to polypropylene or PVC.[3,4]

Compatibility with other drugs: Unstable in alkaline infusions. The injection should not be mixed with infusions containing heparin, as precipitation may occur.[1] Trissel[5] reported that hydrocortisone sodium phosphate or succinate may be compatible, but this may depend on the container.

3.2 Stability in clinical practice

Dilution to 5 mg/L in 0.9% sodium chloride or 5% glucose infusions produced solutions that were physically and chemically compatible, exhibiting no decomposition over 48 hours.[5] The Data Sheet[1] states that dilutions retain potency for 24 hours at room temperature. Polypropylene syringes containing mitozantrone diluted to 2 mg in 10 mL with water for injections (for use in continuous infusion schedules) were found to be stable for 14 days at 4 and 20°C[6] and for 24 hours at 37°C.[3] Studies on mitozantrone given as an intraperitoneal infusion demonstrated drug degradation in peritoneal fluid, and concluded that the intraperitoneal route cannot be recommended for mitozantrone.[7]

3.3 Stability in specialised delivery systems

Mitozantrone infusions (0.2 mg/mL in water for injections) in PVC medication reservoirs (for use with an ambulatory infusion pump) were chemically and physically stable for 14 days at 4°C and under 'in-use' conditions at 37°C.[8] Intermate and Infusor devices containing mitozantrone 0.1–0.5 mg/mL in 0.9% sodium chloride are stable for 48 hours at room temperature followed by up to 5 days at 33°C, and solutions containing 0.2 mg/mL mitozantrone are stable for 8 days at ambient temperature.[9]

Infusions containing 0.5 mg/mL mitozantrone in 0.9% sodium chloride have also been reported to be stable in the CADD Medication Cassette (Pharmacia Deltec) for 10 days at 25°C or 14 days at 5°C.[10]

4 Clinical use

Type of cytotoxic: Antibiotic antitumour agent.

Indications: Advanced breast cancer, non-Hodgkin's lymphoma, adult acute non-lymphocytic leukaemia in relapse, paediatric leukaemia, hepatoma.

Dosage: As a single agent, 14 mg/m² (12 mg/m² in patients with low bone-marrow reserves).

5 Preparation of injection

Dilute the required volume of mitozantrone solution to at least 50 mL in either 0.9% sodium chloride, 5% glucose or 0.18% sodium chloride and 4% glucose.

Bolus administration: Not recommended (mitozantrone must be diluted before administration).

Intravenous infusion: Mitozantrone infusion should be administered over not less than 3 minutes via the tubing of a freely running intravenous infusion of the above fluids.

Extravasation: Group 2 classification (exfoliant) (*see* Chapter 6).

6 Destruction of drug or contaminated articles

Incineration: 800°C.

Chemical: 40% sodium hypochlorite solution (4% available chlorine) for 24 hours.

Contact with skin: Wash with water.

References

1 ABPI (1999) *ABPI Data Sheet Compendium 1999–2000.* DataPharm Publications, London, 1746–7.

2 Reynolds DL *et al.* (1981) Clinical analysis of the antineoplastic agent 1,4-dihydroxy-5,8-*bis*-2(2-hydroxyethyl) aminoethyl-amino 9,10-anthracenedione dihydrochloride (NSC 301739) in plasma. *J Chromatogr.* **222**: 225–40.

3 Sewell GJ *et al.* (1988) Pharmaceutical aspects of domiciliary continuous infusion chemotherapy. *Br J Cancer.* **58**: 536.

4 Priston MJ and Sewell GJ (1994) Improved LC assay for the determination of mitozantrone in plasma: analytical considerations. *J Pharm Biomed Anal.* **12**: 1153–62.

5 Trissel LA *et al.* (1985) *Investigational Drugs, Pharmaceutical Data.* Pharmaceutical aspects of home infusion therapy for cancer patients. National Cancer Institute, Bethesda, MD.

6 Adams PS *et al.* (1987) Pharmaceutical aspects of home infusion therapy for cancer patients. *Pharm J.* **328**: 476–8.

7 Sewell GJ and Priston MJ (1994) Pharmacokinetic and stability studies on mitozantrone injected into the peritoneal cavity. *Aust J Hosp Pharm.* **24**: 99–100.

8 Northcott M *et al.* (1991) The stability of carboplatin, diamorphine, 5-fluorouracil and mitozantrone infusions in an ambulatory pump under storage and prolonged 'in-use' conditions. *J Clin Pharm Ther.* **16**: 123–9.

9 Baxter Healthcare Ltd (2000) Personal communication.

10 Pharmacia Deltec (1991) Personal communication.

Prepared by Graham Sewell

MUSTINE

1 General details

Approved names: Chlormethine, mustine hydrochloride, mustagen, mechlorethamine hydrochloride, nitrogen mustard.

Proprietary name: (Mustine Hydrochloride for Injection BP).

Manufacturer or supplier: Knoll Pharmaceuticals Ltd.

Presentation and formulation details: White lyophilised powder in 20-mL vials, containing 10 mg mustine hydrochloride with no excipients.

Storage and shelf-life of unopened container: Two years when stored at 2–15°C.

2 Chemistry

Molecular structure: 2-chloro-N-(2-chloroethyl)-N-methylethanamine hydrochloride.

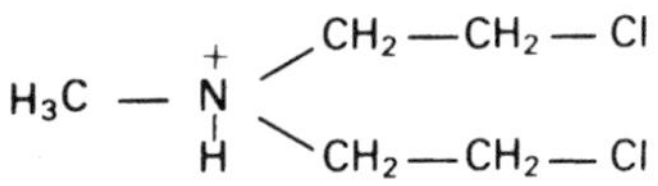

Molecular weight: 192.5 (hydrochloride).

Solubility: Very soluble in water.

3 Stability profile

3.1 Physical and chemical stability

Degradation pathways: The degradation route of mustine hydrochloride (II) in dilute aqueous solution is shown below.

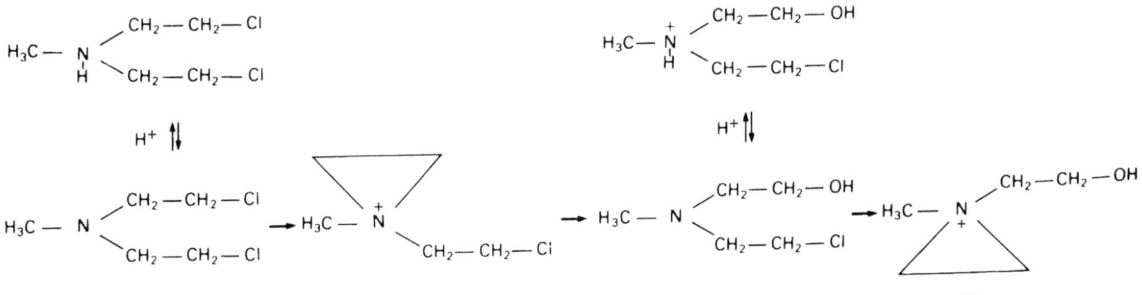

In aqueous solution mustine appears to lose alkylating activity relatively slowly. Alkylating activity arises from mustine together with compounds II and III in the degradation pathway. However, certain of these degradation products are either more carcinogenic than mustine, or may be more neurotoxic.[1,2] Kirk[1] has reviewed the conflicting reports in the literature concerning the rate of degradation of mustine in aqueous solution. It is pointed out that almost all studies were conducted using a test for alkylating activity which was not fully stability-indicating. Certain of the products of degradation have alkylating activity *in vitro*. However, an analysis of previous studies indicates that degradation is very pH dependent,[3] with the compound degrading rapidly in neutral or alkaline conditions. An unbuffered solution of mustine has a pH of 3–5 and will be more stable. The study by Kirk[2] showed that solutions of mustine after reconstitution in 0.9% sodium chloride or water for injections (1 mg/mL) at room temperature degrade by 8–10% in 6 hours, or by 3–6% at 4°C. Solutions diluted in 0.9% sodium chloride (18–36 μg/mL) exhibited 15% loss over 6 hours at room temperature, whilst in 5% glucose about 11% loss was recorded.

Stability after reconstitution is decreased as the temperature is raised. Mustine is stable in the frozen state (–20°C) for 4 weeks, showing about 5% loss.[1,4]

Mustine does not appear to be unduly sensitive to light.

Container compatibility: Kirk[1] has shown that mustine does not appear to interact with styrene acrylonitrile syringes (Gillette) or PVC infusion containers.

Compatibility with other drugs: Mustine is incompatible with methohexital sodium.[5] No further information is available.

3.2 Stability in clinical practice

Reconstituted mustine injection (1 mg/mL) should be used within 4 hours at room temperature or 6 hours if stored in the refrigerator.[4] Mustine injection diluted in 500 mL of 0.9% sodium chloride should be administered within 2 hours, and dilutions in 500 mL of 5% glucose should be used within 4 hours.[1]

3.3 Stability in specialised delivery systems

No data available.

4 Clinical use

Type of cytotoxic: Alkylating agent.

Main indications: Hodgkin's disease (with other agents).

Dosage: Single dose of 0.4 mg/kg body weight or a course of four daily doses of 0.1 mg/kg body weight.

5 Preparation of injection

Reconstitution: To each vial add 10 mL of water for injections or 0.9% sodium chloride. The resulting solution contains 1 mg/mL.

Bolus administration: Inject intravenously slowly (over 2 minutes) into the bolus site of a fast-running drip of 5% glucose or 0.9% sodium chloride (60 drops/minute).

Intravenous infusion: Add the required volume of reconstituted injection to 500 mL of 0.9% sodium chloride and infuse slowly over 1 to 2 hours.

Extravasation: Group 1 classification (vesicant). Very damaging (*see* Chapter 6).

6 Destruction of drug or contaminated articles

Incineration: 800°C.

Chemical:

Sodium hydroxide (SG1.5)	1 part	
IMS	4 parts	for 48 hours.
Water	3 parts	

(Prepare 24 hours before use.)

Contact with skin: Wash immediately with large amounts of water. Can be neutralised with sodium thiosulphate or sodium bicarbonate.

References

1 Kirk B (1986) Stability of reconstituted mustine injection BP during storage. *Br J Parent Ther.* **7**: 86–92.

2 Kirk B (1987) A study of the stability of aqueous solutions of mustine hydrochloride using colorimetric and HPLC assay techniques. *Proc Guild.* **23**: 47–52.

3 Friedman OM and Boger E (1961) Colorimetric estimation of nitrogen mustards in aqueous media. *Anal Chem.* **33**: 907–10.

4 ABPI (1999) *ABPI Data Sheet Compendium 1999–2000.* DataPharm Publications Ltd, London, 687–8.

5 Trissel LA (2001) *Handbook of Injectable Drugs* (11e). American Society of Hospital Pharmacists, Bethesda, MD.

Prepared by Michael Allwood

OXALIPLATIN

1 General details

Approved name: Oxaliplatin.

Proprietary name: Eloxatin.

Manufacturer or supplier: Sanofi Winthrop Ltd.

Presentation and formulation details: White freeze-dried powder in glass vials containing 50 mg or 100 mg oxaliplatin for reconstitution. Each vial also contains lactose monohydrate.

Storage and shelf-life of unopened container: Three years when stored at room temperature.[1]

2 Chemistry

Type: Platinum-containing complex.

Molecular structure: Cis-[oxalato(trans - - 1,2-diaminocyclohexane) platinum.

Molecular weight: 397.3.

Solubility: Solubility in water 6 mg/mL.

3 Stability profile

3.1 Physical and chemical stability

No information available.

Container compatibility: Contact with aluminium must be avoided.

Compatibility with other drugs: Incompatible with 5-fluorouracil, folinic acid and all chloride-containing drugs or solutions.[1]

3.2 Stability in clinical practice

Oxaliplatin is stable after reconstitution, as well as after dilution for at least 48 hours at either 2–8°C or 30°C.[1]

3.3 Stability in specialised delivery systems

No data available.

4 Clinical use

Type of cytotoxic: The exact mechanism of action remains uncertain, but the drug has biochemical properties similar to those of alkylating agents.

Main indications: Metastatic colorectal cancer.

Dosage: 85 mg/m² repeated every 2 weeks, in combination with 5-fluorouracil and folinic acid. No adjustment is necessary in mild renal impairment. Oxaliplatin is always administered before 5-fluorouracil.

5 Preparation of injection

Reconstitution: Reconstitute by adding 10 mL (50-mg vial) or 20 mL (100-mg vial) of water for injections or 5% glucose, to provide a solution containing 5 mg/mL oxaliplatin.[1]

Bolus administration: Not recommended (oxaliplatin must be diluted before administration).

Intravenous infusion: The required dose, after reconstitution, must be diluted in 250–500 mL 5% glucose infusion and infused over 2–6 hours through either a peripheral or central venous line.[1]

Extravasation: Group 2 classification (exfoliant) (*see* Chapter 6).

6 Destruction of drug or contaminated articles

Incineration: 800°C.

Chemical: No information available.

Contact with skin: Wash with copious amounts of water.

References

1 Sanofi Winthrop Ltd (1999) *Product Information Sheet*. Sanofi Winthrop Ltd, Guildford.

Prepared by Michael Allwood

PACLITAXEL

1 General details

Approved name: Paclitaxel.

Proprietary name: Taxol.

Manufacturer or supplier: Bristol-Myers Squibb Pharmaceuticals Ltd.

Presentation and formulation details: Vials containing 30 mg or 100 mg paclitaxel at a concentration of 6 mg/mL. The injection is a clear straw-coloured solution. The vehicle consists of a mixture of polyoxyethylated castor oil (Cremophor EL) and dehydrated alcohol USP in equal proportions.

Storage and shelf-life of unopened container: Vials should be stored at 15–25°C and have a shelf-life of 2 years.[1]

2 Chemistry

Type: Paclitaxel is a taxane diterpenoid, or taxoid compound.

Molecular structure: 5β,20-Epoxy-1,2α,4,7β,10β,13α-hexahydroxytax-11-en-9-one 4,10-diacetane 2-benzoate 13-ester with (2R,3S)-N-benzoyl-3-phenylisoserine.

Molecular weight: 853.9.

Solubility: Insoluble in water; soluble in polyethoxylated castor oil and ethanol.

3 Stability profile

3.1 Physical and chemical stability

Paclitaxel is stable until its expiry date if kept under the recommended storage conditions. It must be diluted prior to use. Solutions are stable for at least 27 hours at room temperature.[1] The stability of paclitaxel has been determined in several studies.

The first stability study of paclitaxel concentrate diluted in infusion solutions indicated that no loss of potency occurred over a 24-hour period when a 0.03 mg/mL concentration was passed through a 0.22-μm filter and stored at room temperature.[2]

Waugh et al.[3] determined the stability of paclitaxel in various containers and infusion solutions. Paclitaxel was diluted in 0.9% sodium chloride and 5% glucose to clinically useful concentrations and stored in PVC infusion bags, polyolefin plastic containers and glass bottles. Solutions were kept at room temperature and filtered through a 0.2-μm membrane. The authors concluded that paclitaxel was visually and chemically stable for at least 24 hours under these conditions, a conclusion that has subsequently been confirmed by other studies.[4,5]

Chin et al.[6] have shown that paclitaxel solutions are stable for 48 hours at room temperature under normal fluorescent light. Xu et al.[7] have established that paclitaxel solutions remain stable for 3 days at temperatures up to 32°C.

Paclitaxel has also been shown to maintain its potency for a period of 3 years when frozen at –15°C. Potency was confirmed following thawing every 3 months. However, some turbidity was observed in the formulation.[8]

Paclitaxel solutions may develop haziness on standing. This has been attributed to the surfactant vehicle, as no paclitaxel precipitation or loss of potency has been observed.[3,9] A similar haze develops if the solution is stored at –15°C or refrigerated (at 2–8°C). This again redissolves on warming without loss of potency.[8]

Container compatibility: Paclitaxel solution is incompatible wth PVC bags and intravenous tubing. Because paclitaxel is not water soluble, it is formulated as a concentrated solution containing polyethoxylated castor oil and ethanol. The polyethoxylated castor oil can result in leaching of diethylphthalate (DEHP) plasticisers from PVC equipment, and therefore the preparation, storage and administration of diluted paclitaxel should be conducted using non-PVC equipment. Suitable containers for use with paclitaxel include glass bottles, semi-rigid polyolefin plastic bags and polypropylene containers.

Allwood[10] noted that the use of PVC infusion containers and administration sets to administer paclitaxel infusion is discouraged because of the risk of DEHP extraction from PVC, and glass containers are recommended. However, the author commented that PVC infusion containers have the advantage of ease and familiarity of handling, and recently investigated likely exposure to DEHP by patients receiving paclitaxel. Total exposure levels were determined using tests simulating clinical practice based on Data Sheet recommendations. A paclitaxel vehicle was used which has been shown to behave identically to paclitaxel injections in terms of DEHP extraction. The vehicle was diluted in 500 mL 5% glucose in Viaflex at concentrations equivalent to 0.6 mg/mL and 1.2 mg/mL paclitaxel. Infusion commenced immediately after drug preparation. The total volume of infusion was collected and analysed for DEHP concentration using HPLC. The results indicated that, in these conditions, patients may receive from 10 mg to 30 mg DEHP from doses of 300 mg and 600 mg paclitaxel, respectively.[11] These figures compared favourably with studies which have shown that the level of DEHP contained in stored blood may be as much as 50 mg/L and that patients may receive up to 128 mg DEHP per transfusion. The author noted that the likelihood of chronic exposure to DEHP is negligible in patients receiving paclitaxel on four to six occasions.[11]

Taxol injection diluted in 5% glucose or 0.9% sodium chloride to concentrations of 0.3 to 1.2 mg/mL paclitaxel is compatible with polyolefin containers.[6] EVA containers have also been tested, and although paclitaxel was chemically stable for up to 72 hours at room temperature or 32°C, there was some evidence of leaching into the drug solution from the container within 24 hours.[12]

3.2 Stability in clinical practice

The manufacturer indicates that Taxol, diluted to a concentration of 0.3–1.2 mg/mL paclitaxel in 5% glucose or 0.9% sodium chloride, in glass infusion containers, is stable for 27 hours at room temperature.[1] Diluted solutions must not be refrigerated. Solutions diluted to the same concentrations in polyolefin containers are stable for 48 hours at room temperature under normal fluorescent lighting,[6] while similar solutions in EVA containers have been reported to be chemically stable for 72 hours at 25 or 32°C, although some leaching of unknown material from the container was noted after 24 hours.[12]

3.3 Stability in specialised delivery systems

No information available.

4 Clinical use

Type of cytotoxic: Paclitaxel is a cytostatic agent with a molecular action on the dynamic equilibrium of tubulin in the microtubular apparatus of the cell.

Main indications: Treatment of metastatic ovarian cancer where standard platinum therapy has failed, and treatment of metastatic breast cancer where standard anthracycline-containing therapy has failed or is inappropriate.

Dosage: All patients must be premedicated with corticosteroids, antihistamines and H_2 antagonists prior to paclitaxel administration. The recommended dose of paclitaxel is 175 mg/m² given as a 3-hour intravenous infusion, with a 3-week interval between courses. Subsequent doses should be reviewed according to patient tolerance.[11] Paclitaxel should not be readministered until the neutrophil count is at least 1.5×10^9/L and the platelet count is at least 100×10^9/L. Patients who experience severe neutropenia (neutrophil count $< 0.5 \times 10^9$/L for 7 days or more) or severe peripheral neuropathy should receive a dose reduction of 20% for subsequent courses.[1]

5 Preparation of injection

Bolus administration: Paclitaxel is administered by intravenous infusion only.

Intravenous infusion: Paclitaxel must be diluted prior to infusion to reach a final concentration of 0.3–1.2 mg/mL.[11] Recommended diluents are 0.9% sodium chloride, 5% glucose, 0.18% sodium chloride and 4% glucose, and 5% glucose in Ringer's solution. Paclitaxel should be administered using non-PVC-containing equipment, through an in-line filter with a microporous membrane not exceeding 0.22 μm. PVC containers must not be used. Paclitaxel should be administered under the supervision of a physician who is experienced in the administration of chemotherapeutic agents.

Extravasation: Group 1 classification (vesicant) (*see* Chapter 6).

6 Destruction of drug or contaminated articles

Disposal: Excess and waste materials should be placed in double-sealed polythene bags and incinerated at a temperature above 1000°C. Liquid waste should be flushed with copious amounts of water.

Contact with skin or eyes: Wash immediately with copious amounts of water, and seek medical attention as soon as possible.

References

1 ABPI (1999) *Data Sheet Compendium 1999–2000*. DataPharm Publications Ltd, London, 255–6.
2 Trissel LA *et al.* (1987) *NCI Investigational Drugs*: *taxol, pharmaceutical data*. National Cancer Institute, Bethesda, MD.
3 Waugh WN *et al.* (1992) Stability, compatibility and plasticizer extraction of Taxol (NC-125973) injection diluted in infusion solutions and stored in various containers. *Am J Hosp Pharm.* **48**: 1520–4.
4 National Cancer Institute (1991) *National Cancer Institute Clinical Brochure (revised)*. *Taxol NSC-125973*. National Cancer Institute, Bethesda, MD.
5 Bristol-Myers Squibb Pharmaceuticals Ltd. Personal communication.
6 Chin A *et al.* (1994) Paclitaxel stability and compatibility in polyolefin containers. *Ann Pharmacother.* **28**: 35–6.
7 Xu QA *et al.* (1994) *Stability of Paclitaxel in 5% Dextrose Injection and 0.9% Sodium Chloride Injection at Various Temperatures*. American Society of Hospital Pharmacists Annual Meeting, Reno, Nevada, USA. June 1994.
8 Bristol-Myers Squibb Pharmaceuticals Ltd (1996) Personal communication.
9 Pearson SD and Trissel LA (1993) Leaching of diethylphthalate from polyvinyl chloride containers by selected drugs and formulation components. *Am J Hosp Pharm.* **50**: 1405–9.
10 Allwood MC (1994) Taxol and PVC. *Pharm J.* **252**: 556.
11 Allwood MC and Martin H (1996) The extraction of diethylphthalate (DEHP) from polyvinyl chloride components of intravenous infusion containers and administration sets by paclitaxel injection. *Int J Pharm.* **127**: 65–71.
12 Xu QA *et al.* (1998) Compatibility of paclitaxel in 5% glucose and 0.9% sodium chloride injections with EVA minibags. *Austr J Hosp Pharm.* **28**: 156–9.

Prepared by Andrew Stanley

PENTOSTATIN

1 General details

Approved names: Co-vidarabine, deoxycoformycin, 2-deoxycoformycin, pentostatin.

Proprietary name: Nipent.

Manufacturer or supplier: Wyeth Laboratories.

Presentation and formulation details: Vials containing a lyophilised white powder containing 10 mg pentostatin. Each vial also contains 50 mg mannitol and sodium hydroxide or hydrochloric acid to maintain the pH at 7.0–8.2.[1]

Storage and shelf-life: If stored at 2–8°C, stable for 5 years.[2] Other information suggests that the intact vials are stable for 3 years at room temperature.[3]

2 Chemistry

Type: Purine derivative.

Molecular structure: (R)-3-(2-deoxy-β-D-*erythro*-pentofuramosyl)-3,6,7,8-tetrahydro-imidazo[4,5[d][1,3]diazepin-9-ol.

Molecular weight: 268.3.

Solubility: Greater than 30 mg/mL in water.

3 Stability profile

3.1 Physical and chemical stability

Data on the stability and compatibility of pentostatin with diluents and other drugs are limited. Hydrolytic degradation is important.

Effect of pH: Pentostatin is more stable under alkaline than acidic conditions. The pH of maximum stability is in the range 6.5–11.5. Solutions in water for injections have a pH of approximately 7–8.5.[3]

Effect of ionic strength: At pH 6–8, hydrolysis is independent of the ionic strength of the solution.[3]

Container compatibility: It has been reported that pentostatin diluted in 5% glucose or 0.9% sodium chloride does not interact with PVC infusion containers or administration sets at concentrations in the range 0.18–0.33 mg/mL, as evidenced by both visual and chemical analysis.[1,3]

Compatibility with other drugs: Pentostatin has been investigated for its compatibility under simulated Y-site conditions with a variety of other drugs. Fludarabine phosphate (1 mg/mL), ondansetron hydrochloride (1 mg/mL), paclitaxel (1.2 mg/mL) and sargramostim (10 µg/mL) were all physically compatible with pentostatin (0.4 mg/mL) for 4 hours at 22°C under normal fluorescent light. Melphalan hydrochloride (0.1 mg/mL) showed no sign of incompatibility, increased turbidity or particle content when mixed in a Y-site with pentostatin (0.4 mg/mL) for 3 hours at 22°C under fluorescent light.[3]

3.2 Stability in clinical practice

Although the manufacturer recommends that the reconstituted solution should be stored at 2–8°C and used within 8 hours,[1] pentostatin solutions of 2 mg/mL in water[3] and 0.9% sodium chloride[2,4] are stable for 72 hours at room temperature, exhibiting only a 2–4% loss.

Solutions of 20 µg/mL in 0.9% sodium chloride[2-4] or lactated Ringer's solution[2,3] are reported to be stable for 48 hours at room temperature (22–25°C), exhibiting only 0–4% decomposition.

Solutions in 5% glucose are less stable, as pentostatin stability is compromised at pH values below 5.[4] At concentrations of 20 µg/mL in 5% glucose, approximately 2% decomposition occurs over 24 hours at room temperature, and as much as 8–10% loss has been reported to occur within 48 hours.[2,3] Degradation in 5% glucose was even more marked (10% after 11 hours at 23°C) when a 2 µg/mL solution was studied.[4] If longer storage in 5% glucose is required, buffering to a neutral pH would result in up to 10% decomposition after 72 hours.[4]

Pentostatin solutions at a concentration of 20 µg/mL in 5% glucose or 0.9% sodium chloride are stable, with no potency loss, after 96 hours at 5°C.[3]

3.3 Stability in specialised delivery systems

No information available.

4 Clinical use

Type of cytotoxic: The exact mechanism of action remains uncertain, but the drug has biochemical properties similar to those of alkylating agents.

Main indications: Hairy-cell leukaemia, B-cell chronic lymphocytic leukaemia, prolymphocytic leukaemia, adult T-cell leukaemia/lymphoma and cutaneous T-cell lymphoma.[5]

Dosage: In hairy-cell leukaemia, 4 mg/m² every alternate week, continuing for at least two doses after remission, or for a maximum of 12 months.[1] A range of other dose schedules have been used in other conditions.[5]

5 Preparation of injection

Reconstitution: Each 10-mg vial of powder should be dissolved in 5 mL of water for injections.[1]

Bolus administration: Undiluted.

Intravenous infusion: Dilute in 25–50 mL of 5% glucose or 0.9% sodium chloride and infuse over 20–30 minutes.[1]

Extravasation: Group 5 classification (neutral), although no extravasation injuries have been reported in clinical studies.[1] (*See* Chapter 6.)

6 Destruction of drug or contaminated articles

Incineration: No recommendation is made with regard to incineration temperature, although this is the preferred method of disposal.[6]

Chemical: The manufacturer recommends that 5% sodium hypochlorite solution should be used to treat spills and wastes prior to disposal.[6]

Contact with skin or eyes: Contact with eyes would be expected to produce irritation; the extent of percutaneous absorption is unknown. Contaminated skin or eyes should be washed with copious amounts of water.[6]

References

1 ABPI (1999) *ABPI Data Sheet Compendium 1998–1999*. DataPharm Publications Ltd, London, 1744–5.
2 National Cancer Institute (1994) *NCI Investigational Drugs: pharmaceutical data*. National Cancer Institute, Bethesda, MD.
3 Trissel LA (1998) *Handbook of Injectable Drugs* (10e). American Society of Health-System Pharmacists, Bethesda, MD.
4 Al-Razzak LA *et al.* (1990) Chemical stability of pentostatin (NSC-218321), a cytotoxic and immunosuppressant agent. *Pharm Res.* **7**: 452–60.
5 Brogden RN and Sorkin EM (1993) Pentostatin. A review of its pharmacodynamic and pharmacokinetic properties and therapeutic potential in lymphoproliferative disorders. *Drugs.* **46**: 652–77.
6 Wyeth Laboratories (1999) Personal communication.

Prepared by Paula Myers

RALTITREXED

1 General details

Approved name: Raltitrexed.

Proprietary name: Tomudex.

Manufacturer or supplier: Astra Zeneca Ltd.

Presentation and formulation details: Sterile lyophilised powder for intravenous injection containing 2 mg raltitrexed packed in 5-mL glass vials. Inactive ingredients are dibasic sodium phosphate heptahydrate, mannitol and sodium hydroxide.[1]

Storage and shelf-life of unopened container: The expiry time of raltitrexed is 18 months when stored below 25°C and protected from light.[1]

2 Chemistry

Type: A folate analogue belonging to a family of antimetabolites with potent direct and specific inhibitory activity against the enzyme thymidylate synthase (TS).

Molecular structure: N-(5-[N-(3,4-dihydro-2-methyl-4-oxoquinazolin-6-ylmethyl)-N-methylamino]-2-thenoyl)-L-glutamic acid.

Molecular weight: 458.49.

Solubility: Raltitrexed exhibits pH-dependent solubility. At pH values higher than 5.5 the solubility of the compound increases rapidly to greater than 100 mg/mL in water.

3 Stability profile

3.1 Physical and chemical stability

Prior to reconstitution, raltitrexed is both chemically and physically stable when stored at 2–8°C and protected from light.[1] It is known that it degrades by two mechanisms, namely hydrolysis and oxidation. For this reason, the product is prepared as a freeze-dried powder in nitrogen-filled vials. Information on the kinetics of the chemical stability of raltitrexed after reconstitution is not available.

Container compatibility: There is no evidence of sorption to PVC or polyethylene infusion containers during storage for 24 hours at 25°C.[2]

3.2 Stability in clinical practice

Raltitrexed reconstituted in 5% glucose or 0.9% sodium chloride to provide a concentration of 0.5 mg/mL, and further diluted in up to 250 mL of the same infusion fluid, is stable for 24 hours at temperatures not exceeding 25°C.[1]

3.3 Stability in specialised delivery systems

No information available.

4 Clinical use

Type of cytotoxic: Antimetabolite.

Main indications: Palliative treatment of advanced colorectal cancer.

Dosage and administration: The recommended adult dose is $3 \, mg/m^2$ given as a single intravenous infusion. Dose escalation is not recommended, since higher doses have been associated with an increased incidence of life-threatening toxicity.[1]

5 Preparation of injection

Reconstitution: The contents of the vial, containing 2 mg raltitrexed, should be reconstituted with 4 mL of water for injections to produce a solution containing 0.5 mg/mL. Reconstituted solutions can be stored at 2–8°C for up to 24 hours.[1]

Bolus administration: Not recommended.

Intravenous infusion: The appropriate dose is diluted in 50–250 mL of either 0.9% sodium chloride or 5% glucose and administered by intravenous infusion over a period of 15 minutes.

Extravasation: Group 5 classification (inflammatory). There is no clinical experience of extravasation, and perivascular tolerance studies in animals revealed no significant irritant reaction.[1] (*See* Chapter 6.)

6 Destruction of drug or contaminated articles

Incineration: 1000°C recommended.

Chemical: No data available.

Contact with skin: Remove and destroy contaminated clothing, and wash skin immediately with water. If the eyes are contaminated, irrigate with eyewash or clean water, holding the eyelids apart, for at least 10 minutes.[1]

References

1 ABPI (1999) *ABPI Data Sheet Compendium 1999–2000.* DataPharm Publications Ltd, London, 1813–4.
2 Astra Zeneca UK Ltd (1996) Personal communication.

Prepared by Andrew Stanley

STREPTOZOCIN*

1 General details

Approved name: Streptozocin.

Proprietary name: Zanosar.

Manufacturer or supplier: In the UK, supplied on a 'named patient' basis through IDIS Ltd.

Presentation and formulation details: Pale yellow, freeze-dried powder containing 1 g streptozocin. Contains sodium hydroxide to adjust pH. Each vial also contains 220 mg citric acid. Contains no preservatives.

Storage and shelf-life of unopened container: Two years stored at 2–8°C, protected from light.

2 Chemistry

Type: Nitrosourea.

Molecular structure: 2-deoxy-2-(methyl-nitrosoamino)carbonylamino-β-D-gluco-pyranose.

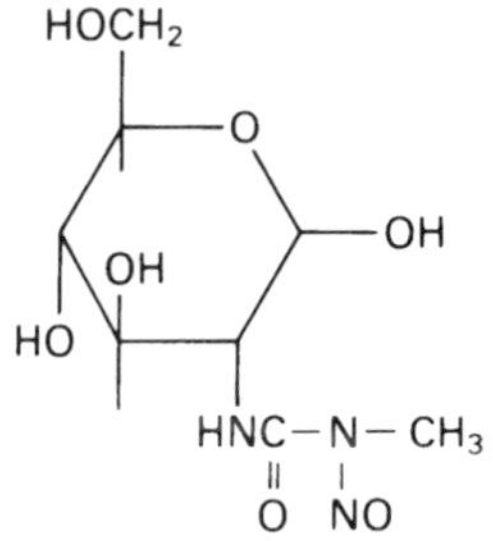

HOCH₂

—O

OH

—OH

HO

HNC—N—CH₃
‖ |
O NO

Molecular weight: 265.2.

Solubility: Soluble in water, 0.9% sodium chloride and ethanol.

3 Stability profile

3.1 Physical and chemical stability

Effect of temperature: Streptozocin was reconstituted in 1 L of 20% glucose. The final concentration of the solution was 1 mg/mL. The study indicated less than 10% degradation after 72 hours at both 5°C and 22–24°C.[1]

The injection was stable for more than 60 hours at 4 and 25°C when reconstituted with water for injections or 0.9% sodium chloride.[1]

1 g vials were reconstituted with 9.5 mL of 0.9% sodium chloride irrigation, 20% glucose and deionised water. The vials were stored at 3 and 24°C. The pH fell slightly after 48 hours at 24°C, consistent with initial degradation of streptozocin. All solutions were clear, pale yellow at reconstitution, and no colour changes were discernible over 48 hours. No particulates or cloudiness were observed in the vials.[1]

*Not licensed in the UK.

Effect of light: A significant loss of potency was observed after 340 days and 740 days of exposure to light.[1]

The freeze-dried product, when stored under conditions of minimal light exposure, did not show significant potency reduction.[1]

Container compatibility: Vials containing 1 g of streptozocin were reconstituted with 9.5 mL of 5% glucose or 0.9% sodium chloride. Aliquots of 10 mL were transferred to 1-L plastic IV bags (Abbott). Samples were assayed for DEHP over a 48-hour period. No leaching of DEHP from the plastic into the streptozocin solution was observed.[1]

Compatibility with other drugs: Streptozocin has been shown to be compatible with some drugs.[2]

2.2 Stability in clinical practice

The reconstituted solution is stable for 48 hours at room temperature and for 96 hours if refrigerated.[2]

2.3 Stability in specialised delivery systems

No information available.

4 Clinical use

Type of cytotoxic: Antimetabolite.

Main indications: Metastatic islet-cell tumours of the pancreas.

5 Preparation of injection

Reconstitution: Reconstitute each 1-g vial with 9.5 mL of 0.9% sodium chloride or 5% glucose to yield a solution containing 100 mg/mL streptozocin.[2]

Bolus administration: Bolus is not recommended because it is extremely uncomfortable for the patient.[2]

Intravenous infusion: In 250–500 mL 0.9% sodium chloride or 5% glucose, over 30–60 minutes.

Extravasation: Group 1 classification (vesicant). No specific recommendations for management (*see* Chapter 6).

6 Destruction of drug or contaminated articles

Incineration: No specific information.

Chemical: No specific information.

Contact with the skin: No specific information.

References

1 Upjohn (UK) Ltd (1990) Personal communication.
2 Trissel LA (2001) *Handbook of Injectable Drugs* (11e). American Society of Health-Systems Pharmacists, Bethesda, MD.

Prepared by Andrew Stanley

TENIPOSIDE

1 General details

Approved names: Teniposide, VM26, PTG thenylidene-ligan-P.

Proprietary name: Vumon.

Manufacturer or supplier: Bristol-Myers Squibb, USA.

Presentation and formulation details: 5-mL ampoules containing teniposide 10 mg/mL. Also contains benzyl alcohol, N,N-dimethylacetamide, polyoxyethylated caster oil (Cremophor EL), dehydrated alcohol (43% v/v) and maleic acid to adjust pH.

The ampoule contents must be diluted before use.

Storage and shelf-life of unopened container: Store at 2–8°C. The stability of the contents of the ampoules appears to be unaffected by exposure to fluorescent light or freezing.[1]

2 Chemistry

Type: Podophyllotoxin derivative.

Molecular structure: Epipodophyllotoxin, 4-dimethyl-9-(4,6-O-2-thenylidene-β-*D*-glucopyranoside).

Molecular weight: 656.

3 Stability profile

3.1 Physical and chemical stability

Teniposide is very poorly soluble in water and therefore liable to precipitate after dilution of the injection. Even at the lowest recommended concentrations (0.1–0.2 mg/mL) precipitation of teniposide may occur in an unpredictable manner which can be initiated by several factors, including excessive agitation and contact with incompatible surfaces.[2] Teniposide is relatively chemically stable, with approximately 5% loss over 4 days either protected from light or exposed to fluorescent light.[3]

Container compatibility: Teniposide shows no evidence of sorption on to plastic containers. However, DEHP leaching has been observed when teniposide injection was diluted in 0.9% sodium chloride or 5% glucose to concentrations as low as 0.1 mg/mL stored in PVC bags.[4,5]

Compatibility with other drugs: Physical compatibility of teniposide was investigated with a wide range of drugs during simulated Y-site administration.[6] The results indicate that teniposide at 0.1 mg/mL is compatible with many drugs, the exceptions being idarubicin and heparin.[7]

3.2 Stability in clinical practice

Once diluted in 0.9% sodium chloride or 5% glucose, teniposide should be administered within 4 hours for concentrations higher than 0.2 mg/mL, or within 24 hours for lower concentrations to avoid the risk of precipitation.[2] Infusions should not be refrigerated.[2] Contact with PVC containers and administration sets causes DEHP extraction as well as softening and cracking of plastic components. Therefore the use of non-PVC containers and sets is preferable.

4 Clinical use

Type of cytotoxic: Mitotic inhibitor.

Main indications: Teniposide is used in the treatment of the following diseases, usually in combination with other cytotoxics: malignant lymphomas, Hodgkin's disease, acute lymphoblastic leukaemia, brain tumours, bladder cancer, neuroblastoma and other solid tumours in children.

Dosage and administration: As monotherapy, the total dose per course is 300 mg/m^2 given over 3–5 days, repeated every 3 weeks. When used in combination therapy the dose should be appropriately reduced.[8]

5 Preparation of injection

Reconstitution: Not applicable; teniposide is provided in ampoules in solution.

Bolus administration: Not recommended.

Intravenous infusion: Dilute with the desired volume of 5% glucose or 0.9% sodium chloride to a concentration between 0.1 and 1 mg/mL.[8] Avoid violent agitation during mixing, and infuse over at least 30–60 minutes.[1]

Extravasation: Group 3 classification (irritant). Avoid extravasation, which can cause local tissue irritation and phlebitis. No specific management is recommended (*see* Chapter 6).

6 Destruction of drug or contaminated articles

Incineration: No specific information available.

Chemical: No specific information available.

Contact with skin: No specific information available.

References

1 Trissel LA (2001) *Handbook of Injectable Drugs* (11e). American Society of Health-Systems Pharmacists, Bethesda, MD.
2 Beijnen JH *et al.* (1991) Chemical and physical stability of etoposide and teniposide in commonly used infusion fluids. *J Parent Sci Technol.* **45**: 108–12.
3 Strong DK and Morris LA (1990) Precipitation of teniposide during infusion. *Am J Hosp Pharm.* **47**: 512, 518–9.
4 Pearson SD and Trissel LA (1993) Leaching of diethylhexyl phthalate from polyvinyl chloride containers by selected drugs and formulation components. *Am J Hosp Pharm.* **50**: 1405–9.
5 Faouzi MA *et al.* (1994) Leaching of diethylhexyl phthalate from PVC bags into intravenous teniposide solution. *Int J Pharm.* **105**: 89–93.
6 Trissel LA and Martinez JF (1994) Screening teniposide for Y-site physical incompatibilities. *Hosp Pharm.* **29**: 1012–4, 1017.
7 Bogardus JB *et al.* (1990) Precipitation of teniposide during infusion. *Am J Hosp Pharm.* **48**: 518.
8 Bristol-Myers Squibb SpA., Latina, Italy (1996) Vumon Product Information.

Prepared by Paula Myers

THIOTEPA

1 General details

Approved names: Thiotepa, thiophosphoramide, TESPA, TSPA.

Proprietary name: Thiotepa.

Manufacturer or supplier: Wyeth Laboratories Ltd.

Presentation and formulation details: Lyophilised powder in vials containing 15 mg thiotepa (15 mg nominal; 15.6 mg with overage).[1]

Storage and shelf-life of unopened container: The injection has a shelf-life of 18 months when stored between 2 and 8°C.

2 Chemistry

Type: Alkylating agent.

Molecular structure: 1,1'1"-phosphinothioyldinetris-aziridine.

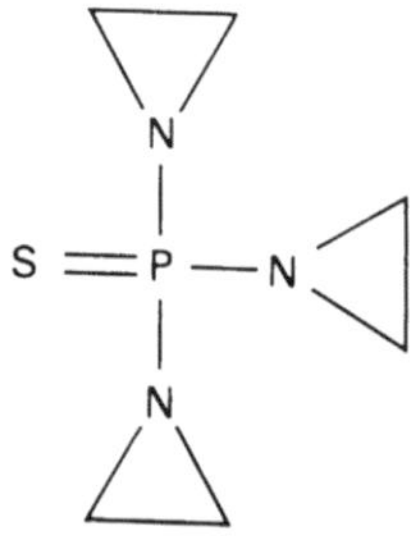

Molecular weight: 189.2.

Solubility: Soluble in water, in ethanol, in chloroform and in ether.

3 Stability profile

3.1 Physical and chemical stability

The stability of thiotepa in aqueous solution is pH dependent; it is least stable in acid solutions. The acid-catalysed reaction of thiotepa in the presence of chloride ions yields a series of chloroethyl derivatives (I–III) according to the following scheme:[2]

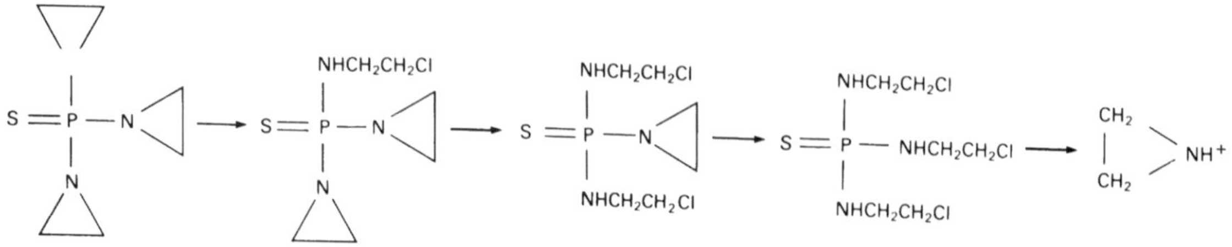

In strong acid solutions and in aqueous solutions at elevated temperatures, thiotepa undergoes P-N cleavage and/or ring-opening to give the azaridinium ion (IV).[3] Thiotepa will also polymerise to form insoluble polymeric derivatives.

At 37°C in buffer at pH 4.2 the rate constant for loss of thiotepa was 9.8×10^{-3}/minute, giving a $t_{90\%}$ of 10 minutes. At pH 7 degradation was much slower; no breakdown could be detected after 2 hours at 37°C but longer-term data were not available.[4]

Any polymerisation reaction is likely to be catalysed by light, reducing the stability of thiotepa.

Container compatibility: Thiotepa is compatible with PVC and polyolefin infusion containers.[5]

Compatibility with other drugs: Thiotepa is incompatible in solutions with mitozantrone. When mitozantrone and thiotepa were mixed in 5% glucose in a 10-mL syringe and the solution was stored at room temperature and protected from light, 10% of the mitozantrone degraded within the first 24 hours, and over 50% after 7 days.[6]

3.2 Stability in clinical practice

The manufacturer indicates that the powder, reconstituted in water for injections to a concentration of 10 mg/mL, is stable for a maximum of 24 hours at 2–8°C.[1] If a precipitate forms (caused by polymerisation), the reconstituted injection must be discarded. Stability after reconstitution and dilution depends on the concentration and the diluent used, since thiotepa is less stable at low concentrations and in chloride-containing solutions. Thiotepa at 0.5 mg/mL in 5% glucose is stable for 8 hours at temperatures not exceeding 23°C. Solutions containing 5 mg/mL thiotepa in 5% glucose are stable for 3 days at 23°C or 14 days at 4°C.[7] In 0.9% sodium chloride, solutions containing 1–3 mg/mL thiotepa are stable for 24 hours at 25°C and at least 48 hours at 8°C, while solutions containing 0.5 mg/mL are stable for no more than 8 hours.[8]

When administered as a bladder irrigation it is recommended that up to 60 mg thiotepa in 60 ml sterile water are instilled and that the solution is retained in the bladder for up to 2 hours.[8] However, thiotepa is unstable in acidic urine at 37°C. At pH 5.5, $t_{90\%}$ is 70 minutes, and at pH 4.0, $t_{90\%}$ is 3.3 minutes, with only 2.1% of the initial dose of thiotepa remaining after 2 hours.[3]

3.3 Stability in specialised delivery systems

No data available.

4 Clinical use

Type of cytotoxic: Thiotepa is a polyfunctional alkylating agent. It releases ethylenimine radicals which disrupt the bonds of DNA.

Main indications: Adenocarcinoma of the breast and of the ovary. Controlling intra-cavity effusions secondary to diffuse or localised neoplastic disease of various serosal cavities. Treatment of superficial papillary carcinoma of the bladder. Thiotepa has been effective against lymphosarcoma and Hodgkin's disease, but is now largely superseded by other treatments. It has also been used for the post-operative management of pterygium.[9,10]

Both thiotepa and its active metabolite, tepa, efficiently cross the blood–brain barrier. A phase II evaluation of thiotepa in paediatric CNS malignancies has been reported.[11]

Dosage and administration: By rapid intravenous infusion, 0.3–0.4 mg/kg at 1- to 4-week intervals. By intracavity instillation, 10–65 mg in 20–60 mL of sterile water. By intravesical administration, up to 60 mg in 30–60 mL of sterile water.

5 Preparation of injection

Reconstitution: Reconstitution of the 15-mg vial with 1.5 mL of water for injections gives a solution containing 10.4 mg/mL (approximately 14.7 mg from each vial). Since this solution is hypotonic, 0.9% sodium chloride may be the preferred diluent.

Bolus administration: The reconstituted injection is usually administered as a rapid intravenous injection. It may also be administered as a bolus injection by intra-arterial, intramuscular and intrathecal routes, or used for intracavity instillation.[1]

Intravenous infusion: Not recommended.

Bladder instillation: For bladder instillation the patient is dehydrated for 8 to 12 hours. The solution is instilled into the bladder and retained there for 2 hours.

Extravasation: Group 5 classification (neutral) (*see* Chapter 6).

6 Destruction of drug or contaminated articles

Incineration: 800°C.

Chemical: Dilute in large quantities of boiling water.

Contact with skin: Wash off with water.

References

1 ABPI (1999) *Data Sheet Compendium 1999–2000.* DataPharm Publications Ltd, London, 1759–60.

2 Maxwell J *et al.* (1974) Behaviour of an aziridine alkylating agent in acid solution. *Biochem Pharmacol.* **23**: 168–70.

3 Zon G *et al.* (1976) Observations of 1,1′,1″ phosphinothioylidinetris-aziridine (thiotepa) in acidic and saline media. A ¹H-NMR study. *Biochem Pharmacol.* **25**: 989–92.

4 Cohen GE *et al.* (1984) Effects of pH and temperature on the stability and decomposition of N,N′N″ triethylenethio-phosphoramide in urine and buffer. *Cancer Res.* **44**: 4312–16.

5 Xu QA *et al.* (1996) Stability of thiotepa (lyophilized) in 5% glucose injection at 4 and 32°C. *Am J Health-Syst Pharm.* **53**: 2728–30.

6 Cacek T and Weber R (1991) Visual and chemical stability of mitoxantrone mixed individually with vincristine, etoposide, thiotepa, metoclopramide and cytarabine in plastic syringes. *American Society of Hospital Pharmacists Midyear Clin Meeting.* **25**: 470E.

7 Murray KM *et al.* (1997) Stability of thiotepa (lyophilized) in 0.9% sodium chloride injection. *Am J Health-Syst Pharm.* **54**: 2588–91.

8 Uyas HM *et al.* (1987) Drug stability guidelines for a continuous infusion chemo-therapy programme. *Hosp Pharm.* **22**: 685–7.

9 Erlich D (1977) The management of pterygium. *Ophthal Surg.* **8**: 23–30.

10 Olander K (1978) Management of pterygium: should thiotepa be used? *Ann Ophthalmol.* **10**: 853–6.

11 Steinberg SM *et al.* (1993) A phase II evaluation of thiotepa in pediatric central nervous system malignancies. *Cancer.* **72**: 271–5.

Prepared by Gerard Lee

TOPOTECAN

1 General details

Approved names: Topotecan, hycamptamine.

Proprietary name: Hycamtin.

Manufacturer or supplier: SmithKline Beecham Pharmaceuticals plc.

Presentation and formulation details: Vials of pale yellow lyophilised powder containing 4 mg topotecan as the hydrochloride salt, 65 mg mannitol and 75 mg tartaric acid.[1]

Storage and shelf-life of unopened container: Store at room temperature; shelf-life is 2 years.[1]

2 Chemistry

Type: Topoisomerase 1 inhibitor, water-soluble derivative of the alkaloid campto-thecin.

Molecular structure: (S)-10-[(dimethylamino)methyl]-4-ethyl-4,9-dihydroxy-1H-pyrano [3′,4′:6,7]indolizino[1,2-b]-quinoline-3,14-(4H,12H)-dione.

Molecular weight: 421.45.

3 Stability profile

3.1 Physical and chemical stability

Topotecan is relatively stable in aqueous solutions after reconstitution. However, it can undergo reversible hydrolysis, resulting in the opening of the lactone ring and formation of an inactive hydroxyl carboxylate form.[1] This hydrolytic reaction, which is probably the only significant degradation reaction of topotecan dissolved in its recommended diluents, requires an alkaline environment. In solutions of pH less than 4 the lactone is exclusively present, whereas when the pH rises above 10, the hydroxyl carboxylate form predominates.[2] It has been reported that stability increases approximately threefold for each 0.5-pH-unit fall below pH 4

($t_{98\%}$ = 0.2 years) to a pH of 2 ($t_{98\%}$ = 19.2 years).[3] For this reason, commercially available topotecan injection is buffered with tartaric acid and pH adjusted, using hydrochloric acid or sodium hydroxide, to a pH between 2.5 and 3.5.[4]

According to the manufacturer, topotecan solutions containing 10, 20 and 500 µg/mL in 0.9% sodium chloride and 10 and 500 µg/mL in 5% glucose exhibit less than 3% loss when stored for up to 4 days at room temperature in glass flasks or PVC infusion bags.[5,6]

Effect of light: Topotecan diluted in water, 0.9% sodium chloride or 5% glucose stored in ambient light declined by 5% after 7 days,[4] suggesting that topotecan is relatively stable in artificial light conditions.

Container compatibility: Topotecan at 25–50 µg/mL, is compatible with PVC, polyolefin and glass infusion containers.[1]

Compatibility with other drugs: No data available. However, topotecan is compatible with 0.9% benzyl alcohol, an antimicrobial preservative.[1]

3.2 Stability in clinical practice

Topotecan at 1 mg/mL, after reconstitution in water for injections, if stored at 5, 25 or 30°C is stable for 28 days.[7] Topotecan at 25–50 µg/mL , in 0.9% sodium chloride or 5% glucose, stored in PVC, polyolefin or glass infusion containers at 5°C or 23–24°C, is stable for at least 7 days and 24 hours respectively.[4] Further studies indicate that solutions containing 10–500 µg/mL topotecan diluted in 0.9% sodium chloride or 5% glucose in PVC bags are stable for 4 days at room temperature or for 7 days at 5°C.[8]

3.3 Stability in specialised delivery systems

Topotecan solutions containing 10–50 µg/mL diluted in 0.9% sodium chloride or 5% glucose and stored in LV2 polyisoprene (Baxter) reservoirs are stable at 2–8°C for 28 days followed by a further 5 days at 37°C.[4] Solutions containing 100–500 µg/mL topotecan in water for injections (with benzyl alcohol) and stored in Deltec (Pharmacia) cassettes at 5°C or room temperature are stable for 21 days.[9]

4 Clinical use

Type of cytotoxic: Inhibits DNA replication by making reversible breaks in DNA, permitting torsional relaxation of the molecule during transcription.[10]

Main indications: Topotecan has been investigated in a variety of malignant conditions, including cancers of the lung,[11,12] bowel,[13] ovary[14–16] and breast.[17]

Dosage: Repeated daily dosing of 1.5 mg/m²/day (range 1.25–2 mg/m²/day) for 5 days, repeated at not less than 3-weekly intervals.[1] A minimum of four courses is recommended.[1]

5 Preparation of injection

Reconstitution: Each 5-mg vial of powder should be dissolved in 5 mL of water for injections.

Bolus administration: Not recommended.

Intravenous infusion: The appropriate quantity of reconstituted injection solution should be further diluted in 0.9% sodium chloride or 5% glucose to a concentration of 25–50 µg/mL, prior to infusion over a period of not less than 30 minutes.[1]

Extravasation: Group 2 classification (exfoliant) (*see* Chapter 6).

6 Destruction of drug or contaminated articles

Incineration: High-temperature incineration (minimum of 800°C).

Chemical: No specific recommendations.

Contact with skin: Wash with copious amounts of water.

References

1 ABPI (1999) *Data Sheet Compendium 1999–2000.* DataPharm Publications Ltd, London, 1600–1.

2 Fassberg J and Stella VJ (1992) A kinetic and mechanistic study of the hydrolysis of camptothecin and some analogues. *J Pharm Sci.* **81**: 676–84.

3 Underberg WJM *et al.* (1990) Equilibrium kinetics of the new experimental antitumour compound SK&F 104864A in aqueous solution. *J Pharm Biomed Anal.* **8**: 681–3.

4 Kramer 1 and Thiesen J (1999) Stability of topotecan infusion solutions in polyvinylchloride bags and elastomeric portable infusion devices. *J Oncol Pharm Pract.* **5**: 75–82.

5 SmithKline Beecham. Personal communication.

6 National Cancer Institute (1988, 1990) *NCI Investigational Drugs: pharmaceutical data.* National Cancer Institute, Bethesda, MD.

7 Patel K *et al.* (1998) Microbial inhibitory properties and stability of topotecan hydrochloride injection. *Am J Health-Syst Pharm.* **55**: 1584–7.

8 Craig SB *et al.* (1997) Stability and compatibility of topotecan hydrochloride for injection with common infusions and containers. *J Pharm Biomed Anal.* **16**: 199–205.

9 SmithKline Beecham Pharmaceuticals plc (2000) Personal communication.

10 Anon. (1995) Topoisomerase 1 inhibitors: a novel class of antineoplastic drugs. *Drugs Ther Perspect.* **5**: 7–9.

11 Perez-Soler R *et al.* (1995) Phase II study of topotecan in patients with squamous-cell carcinoma of the lung previously untreated with chemotherapy. *Eur J Cancer.* **31A (Supplement 5)**: S224.

12 Perez-Soler R *et al.* (1995) Phase II study of topotecan in patients with small-cell lung cancer (SCLC) refractory to etoposide. *Proc Am Soc Clin Oncol.* **14**: 355.

13 Creemer GJ *et al.* (1995) Phase II study with topotecan (T) administered as a 21-day continuous infusion to patients with colorectal cancer. *Eur J Cancer.* **31A (Supplement 5)**: S146.

14 Armstrong D *et al.* (1995) A phase II trial of topotecan as salvage therapy in epithelial ovarian cancer. *Proc Am Soc Clin Oncol.* **14**: 275.

15 Ten Bokkel Huinink W *et al.* (1997) Topotecan versus paclitaxel for the treatment of recurrent epithelial ovarian cancer. *J Clin Oncol.* **15**: 2183–93.

16 Swisher EM *et al.* (1997) Topotecan in platinum- and paclitaxel-resistant ovarian cancer. *Gynecol Oncol.* **66**: 480–6.

17 Chang, AY *et al.* (1995) Clinical and laboratory studies of topotecan in breast cancer. *Proc Am Soc Clin Oncol.* **14**: 105.

Prepared by Andrew Stanley

TREOSULFAN

1 General details

Approved name: Treosulfan.

Proprietary names: Treosulfan Injection.

Manufacturer or supplier: Medac Gesellschaft für Klinische Spezialpräparate GmbH (Germany).

Presentation and formulation details: White crystalline powder in vials containing 1 g and 5 g treosulfan. No excipients are used in the formulation.

Storage and shelf-life of unopened container: Five years at room temperature.

2 Chemistry

Type: Bifunctional alkylating agent.

Molecular structure: (2S,3S)-threitol-1,4-bismethane sulphonate.

$$H_3C-SO_2-O-CH_2-\overset{\overset{\displaystyle OH}{|}}{\underset{\underset{\displaystyle H}{|}}{C}}-\overset{\overset{\displaystyle H}{|}}{\underset{\underset{\displaystyle OH}{|}}{C}}-CH_2-O-SO_2-CH_3$$

Molecular weight: 278.3.

Melting point: 101.5–105°C.

Solubility: 6% in water; 5.8% in 0.9% sodium chloride; 5.5% in 5% glucose; 2.5% in 50% glucose.

3 Stability profile

3.1 *Physical and chemical stability*

Treosulfan is relatively stable after reconstitution and further dilution (0.9% sodium chloride or 5% glucose). The reconstituted drug is stable for 5 days at room temperature and ambient light.[1]

Degradation pathway: In alkaline media, treosulfan degrades to methanesulphonic acid and diepoxybutane. The transformation of treosulfan into epoxides is highly pH dependent. The transformation reaction to L-diepoxybutane via the corresponding monoepoxide has been demonstrated *in vitro*.[2] At pH values lower than 6.0, practically no transformation of treosulfan occurs.

Effect of pH: Acidic media do not influence the stability of treosulfan. In alkaline media, treosulfan degrades to methanesulphonic acid and diepoxybutane.

Effect of light: Treosulfan is not light-sensitive.

Effect of temperature: Samples of treosulfan were stored in sealed ampoules in heating cabinets at 60°C. Deterioration of 1% was found after storage for 3 months.[3]

Container compatibility: Contact with intravenous infusion administration sets (McGaw V 1428 Metriset, Transcodan administration set, Avon A 100 blood administration set) does not seem to affect a treosulfan solution. The content of treosulfan remains unaltered after 4 hours. There is no increase in the content of acidic degradation products.[4] Contact with ethylvinylacetate infusion bags does not affect the reconstituted treosulfan solution after storage for 5 days under ambient light.[5]

Compatibility with other drugs: No information available.

3.2 Stability in clinical practice

After reconstitution with water for injections, the resulting 50 mg/mL solution is chemically stable in the vial and may be stored for 5 days at room temperature (ambient light).[1,3] The solution can be further diluted in 5% glucose or 0.9% sodium chloride infusions and the resulting solution is stable for the same period of time.

3.3 Stability in specialised delivery systems

No information available.

4 Clinical use

Type of cytotoxic: Treosulfan is a bifunctional alkylating agent which has been shown to possess antineoplastic activity in the animal tumour screen and in clinical trials.

Mechanism of action: The activity of treosulfan is due to the formation of epoxide compounds *in vivo.*[6]

Main indications: For the treatment of all types of ovarian cancer, either supplementary to surgery or palliatively. Some uncontrolled studies have suggested activity in a wider range of neoplasms. Because of a lack of cross-resistance reported between treosulfan and other cytotoxic agents, treosulfan may be useful in any neoplasm that is refractory to conventional therapy.

Dosage and administration: Injection of 5–15 g intravenously every 1 to 3 weeks, depending on blood count and concurrent chemotherapy. Single injections of up to 15 g have been given with no serious adverse effects. Doses of up to 3 g have been given intraperitoneally.

    Treatment should not be given if the white-blood-cell count is less than 3000/μL, or if the thrombocyte count is less than 100 000/μL. A repeat blood count should be performed after an interval of 1 week, when treatment may be restarted if haematological parameters are satisfactory. Lower doses of treosulfan should be used if other cytotoxic drugs or radiotherapy are being given concurrently. Treatment should be initiated as soon as possible after diagnosis.

5 Preparation of injection

Reconstitution: The contents of each infusion bottle should be dissolved in 20 mL (1 g) or 100 mL (5 g) of water for injections, respectively. A transfer needle may be used for this purpose.

    To avoid solubility problems during the dissolution of treosulfan the following stages should be adopted.

1 Solvent, water for injections, is warmed to a maximum temperature of 30°C.
2 Treosulfan is carefully removed from the inner surface of the infusion bottle by shaking. This procedure is very important, because moistening of powder that sticks to the surface results in caking. In cases where caking does occur the bottle must be shaken vigorously until the cake has dissolved.
3 One side of either a double-sided cannula or an adapter is put into the rubber stopper of the water bottle or bag. The treosulfan bottle is then put on the other end of the cannula or the adapter, with the bottom on top. The whole construction is turned around and the water allowed to run into the lower bottle while the bottle is shaken gently.

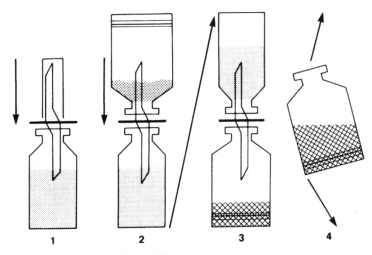

Figure 5: *Steps in dissolution of treosulfan*

If the above procedures are followed, the whole dissolution procedure should take no longer than 2 minutes.

Bolus administration: Doses of up to 5 g of treosulfan may be given as a bolus injection. Larger doses should be administered as an intravenous infusion at a rate of 5 g every 15–30 minutes.

Infusion: Solutions originally reconstituted with water for injections may be further diluted with either 5% glucose or 0.9% sodium chloride infusion.

Extravasation: Group 1 classification (vesicant). Care should be taken during administration of the injection to avoid extravasation into tissues, as this will cause local pain and tissue damage. If extravasation does occur, the injection should be discontinued immediately and any remaining portion of the dose should be introduced into another vein (*see* Chapter 6).

6 Destruction of drug or contaminated articles

Incineration: 1000°C.

Chemical: No information available.

Contact with skin: Wash with cold water.

Contact with eyes: If the eyes are contaminated, irrigate immediately with 0.9% sodium chloride.

References

1 Medac GmbH Hamburg (1994) Stability after reconstitution and storage in glass containers. Data on stability of treosulfan in various injection fluids. Unpublished information.
2 Feit PW and Rastrup-Andersen N (1970) Studies on epoxide formation from (2S,3S)-threitol 1,4-bismethanesulfonate. The preparation and biological activity of (2S,3S)-1,2-epoxy-3,4-butanediol 4-methanesulfonate. *J Am Chem.* **13**: 1173–5.
3 Medac GmbH Hamburg (1995) Stability studies at higher temperatures. Unpublished information.
4 Medac GmbH Hamburg (1996) Solubility and compatibility of treosulfan substance in various intravenous infusions. Compatibility of treosulfan substance with administration sets for intravenous infusions. Unpublished information.
5 Medac GmbH Hamburg (1996) Stability after reconstitution and storage in ethylvinylacetate-infusion bags. Unpublished information.
6 ABPI (1999) *ABPI Data Sheet Compendium 1999–2000.* DataPharm Publications Ltd, London, 824–5.

Prepared by Andrew Stanley

VINBLASTINE

1 General details

Approved names: Vinblastine, vincaleukoblastine.

Proprietary name: Velbe (Lilly).

Manufacturer or supplier: Eli Lilly & Co. Ltd, Faulding plc.

Presentation and formulation details: Lyophilised powder containing 10 mg vinblastine sulphate. This is supplied with 10 mL of aqueous diluent containing 90 mg sodium chloride and 0.2 ml benzyl alcohol (Lilly, Lederle, Faulding), or as a solution of 10 mg/mL lyophilised powder (Faulding).

Storage and shelf-life of unopened container: The injection has a shelf-life of 3 years when stored between 0 and 6°C. The solution shelf-life is 24 months at 2–8°C.[1,2]

2 Chemistry

Type: Vinca alkaloid.

Molecular structure: Vincaleukoblastine.

Molecular weight: 811 (vinblastine sulphate: 909).

Solubility: The base is insoluble in water and soluble in ethanol and chloroform. The sulphate salt is soluble 1 in 10 in water, 1 in 1200 in ethanol, and 1 in 50 in chloroform. pK_a: 5.4, 7.4.

3 Stability profile

3.1 Physical and chemical stability

Degradation pathways: Aqueous solutions of vinblastine are less stable at lower pH values; 4-desacetylvinblastine is the primary degradation product at pH 2.[3]

More recent studies indicate that the hydrolytic decomposition pathways for vinblastine are more complex. Below pH 1.5 and above pH 10.5, desacetylvinblastine has been confirmed as the major degradation product. However, between pH 2.5 and 7.0, the amount of desacetylvinblastine found was negligible, and at least three other degradation products were detected.[4] Studies on 1 mg/mL solutions of vinblastine sulphate at pH 4.5–5.0 identified up to six breakdown products. The major ones were tentatively identified as 19'-oxo-vinblastine and an isomer of vinblastine, but none of the decomposition products were positively categorised. From the data at 25, 37 and 55°C, $t_{90\%}$ values were estimated to be 16.6 days at 37°C, 150 days at 25°C and 10.7 years at 5°C.[5]

When exposed to direct incandescent light, decomposition is accelerated. At 25°C the $t_{90\%}$ is approximately 7 days, and at 30°C solutions of vinblastine sulphate had lost 10% of their potency after slightly more than 1 day.[6] The major degradation products were different to those identified in thermal degradation studies, but the same pattern of products was identified in both cases.

Vinblastine base is practically insoluble in water and can precipitate from solutions of vinblastine sulphate above pH 6.

Container compatibility: No loss of potency was detected in solutions of vinblastine sulphate (10 mg/mL) stored for 30 days in polypropylene syringes at 4°C or room temperature.[7] There was no significant loss of potency when vinblastine sulphate solution (10 mg in 50 mL) in 5% glucose or 0.9% sodium chloride was filtered through a 0.22-μm cellulose ester membrane filter.[8]

No losses of vinblastine (2.5 mg/10 mL) could be detected to nylon, polysulphone or cellulose ester filters when using a syringe pump driver to deliver the drug. However, there was significant adsorption to the Pall ELD 96 activated nylon filter. A 30–40% loss of potency was detected during the first 30 minutes of infusion with the concentration only returning to its initial value after 2 to 3 hours.[9]

Losses of 24% occurred over 24 hours at 37°C from a 1 mg/mL solution of vinblastine sulphate in bacteriostatic 0.9% saline in an Infusaid implantable pump. Over 12 days losses totalled 48%. Similar solutions in glass vials exhibited no losses after 24 hours and a 20% loss after 12 days at 37°C.[10]

Vinblastine has been shown to be adsorbed on to PVC tubing and cellulose proprionate burette chambers. Up to 48% loss was found from a 3 μg/mL solution stored for 48 hours in PVC tubing, and up to 20% loss of potency was found in similar solutions stored in cellulose proprionate burette chambers for 48 hours.[11] These results were obtained for a static system, and it is difficult to extrapolate them to the dynamic situation of an intravenous administration. The adsorption losses did not occur in polybutadiene tubing or methacrylate butadiene styrene burettes.[11]

Studies suggest that under normal conditions of administration no significant losses of vinblastine are likely when diluted in PVC bags and infused through PVC administration sets. These studies included infusions in 0.9% sodium chloride or 5% glucose containing either 40 μg/mL at a rate of approximately 2 mL/minute,[12] or 250 μg/mL, using a syringe pump at 0.875 mL/hour.[9]

Compatibility with other drugs: Trissel reports studies which suggest that vinblastine may be compatible with a number of drugs.[13] Vinblastine is incompatible with frusemide, for example if allowed to mix in the same administration line.[2]

3.2 Stability in clinical practice

The reconstituted injection is chemically stable for at least 28 days at 4°C and at 25°C,[5] provided that it is protected from light. When stored at 37°C in the dark, the shelf-life of the reconstituted injection is 14 days. In direct incandescent light, the injection is chemically stable for 7 days at room temperature.[6]

No degradation was detected in vinblastine solution at 20 μg/mL in 0.9% sodium chloride, 5% glucose and in Ringer's lactate, stored in polypropylene tubes in the dark, after 21 days at 4°C. At 25°C there was 2–3% degradation of vinblastine in the three infusion solutions after 21 days.[14]

3.3 Stability in specialised delivery systems

Vinblastine at 0.015–0.5 mg/mL, diluted in 0.9% sodium chloride and stored in Infusor or Intermate devices, is stable for 21 days at 2–8°C followed by up to 5 days at 33°C.[15]

4 Clinical use

Type of cytotoxic: Vinblastine arrests mitosis at metaphase and inhibits RNA synthesis.

Main indications: Vinblastine is used in combination with other chemotherapeutic agents for the treatment of metastatic testicular carcinoma, Hodgkin's and non-Hodgkin's lymphoma, neuroblastoma, histiocytosis X, mycosis fungoides, Kaposi's sarcoma, advanced breast carcinoma and choriocarcinoma.

Dosage: Usually 4–8 mg/m² weekly. Weekly injections starting at 3.7 mg/m² and rising by increments of 1.85 mg/m² up to a maximum of 18.5 mg/m², or until the white cell count has fallen to 3000/mm³.[16]

5 Preparation of injection

Reconstitution: Reconstitution of the 10-mg vial with 10 mL of sterile diluent gives a 1 mg/mL solution.

Bolus administration: Intravenously, directly into a vein or into the tubing of a running infusion, over a 1-minute period.

Intravenous infusion: Vinblastine has been given as a continuous 5-day infusion (1.4–2.0 mg/m²/day).[17] Infusions should be administered through a central line. **Extra Warning:** Since death will almost certainly result from inadvertent intrathecal administration, syringes or other containers of vinblastine in a form prepared for administration should be labelled **for intravenous use only – fatal if given by other routes**. The drug should be diluted to at least 20 mL, a maximum concentration of 0.1 mg/mL, and packed and transported as a single item (*see* Chapter 6 for further guidance).*

Constant ambulatory intravenous infusion has been investigated using a tunnelled subclavian catheter and the Cor-med ML6 infusion pump[18] and the Travenol

*As this book went to press, new guidance was issued on the safe administration of intrathecal chemotherapy, which requires that only registered, designated personnel should prescribe, dispense, check or administer intrathecal chemotherapy. The guidance also requires formal induction and regular training programmes. Please check the guidance for the full recommendations: NHS Executive (2001) *National Guidance on the Safe Administration of Intrathecal Chemotherapy.* HSC 2001/022.

infusor system.[19] However, there are insufficient data to allow reliable conclusions to be drawn from this work.

Extravasation: Group 1 classification (vesicant) (*see* Chapter 6).

6 Destruction of drug or contaminated articles

Incineration: 1000°C.

Chemical: 10% sodium hypochlorite for 24 hours.

Contact with skin: Wash with copious amounts of water.

References

1 ABPI (1999) *ABPI Data Sheet Compendium 1999–2000*. DataPharm Publications Ltd, London, 764–5.
2 ABPI (1999) *ABPI Data Sheet Compendium 1999–2000*. DataPharm Publications Ltd, London, 429–30.
3 Burns JH (1972) *Analytical Profiles of Drug Substances. Vol. 1.* Academic Press, Orlando, FL.
4 Vendrig DEMM *et al.* (1988) Degradation kinetics of vinblastine sulphate in aqueous solutions. *Int J Pharm.* **43**: 131–8.
5 Black J *et al.* (1988) Studies on the stability of vinblastine sulphate in aqueous solution. *J Pharm Sci.* **77**: 630.
6 Black J *et al.* (1988) Stability of vinblastine sulphate when exposed to light. *Drug Intell Clin Pharm.* **22**: 634.
7 Weir PJ *et al.* (1990) The chemical stability of cytarabine and vinblastine injections. *Br J Pharm Pract.* **12**: 53–4.
8 Butler LD *et al.* (1980) Effect of in-line filtration on the potency of low-dose drugs. *Am J Hosp Pharm.* **37**: 935.
9 Francomb MM *et al.* (1994) Adsorption of vincristine, vinblastine, doxorubicin and mitozantrone to in-line intravenous filters. *Int J Pharm.* **103**: 87–92.
10 Keller JH and Ensminger WD (1982) Stability of cancer chemotherapeutic agents in totally implanted drug delivery systems. *Am J Hosp Pharm.* **39**: 1321.
11 McElany JC *et al.* (1988) Stability of methotrexate and vinblastine in burette administration sets. *Int J Pharm.* **47**: 239–47.
12 Dyne T *et al.* (1991) Stability and compatibility studies of vinblastine, vincristine, vindesine and vinorelbine with PVC infusion bags. *Int J Pharm.* **77**: 279–85.
13 Trissel LA (2001) *Handbook of Injectable Drugs* (11e). American Society of Health-Systems Pharmacists, Bethesda, MD.
14 Beijnen JH *et al.* (1989) Stability of vinca alkaloid anticancer drugs in three commonly used infusion fluids. *J Parent Sci Technol.* **43**: 84–7.
15 Baxter Healthcare Ltd (2000) Personal communication.
16 Anon. (1986) *Physicians Desk Reference* (40e). Medical Economics Company, Oradell, NJ.
17 Yap HY *et al.* (1980) Vinblastine given as a continuous five-day infusion in the treatment of refractory advanced breast cancer. *Cancer Treat Rep.* **64**: 279.
18 Lokich J *et al.* (1982) The delivery of cancer chemotherapy by constant venous infusion. *Cancer.* **50**: 2731.
19 Akokoshi MP *et al.* (1987) Safety and reliability of the Travenol Infusor. *J Pharm Technol.* **March/April**: 65.

Prepared by Gerard Lee

VINCRISTINE

1 General details

Approved names: Vincristine, leurocristine.

Proprietary name: Oncovin (Lilly).

Manufacturer or supplier: Faulding DBL Ltd, Eli Lilly & Co. Ltd.

Presentation and formulation details: Solution containing 1 mg/mL vincristine sulphate in 1-mL, 2-mL or 5-mL vials, preservative-free (Faulding),[1] or containing antimicrobial preservatives (methylhydroxybenzoate 1.8 mg/mL and propyl-hydroxybenzoate 0.2 mg/mL) (Eli Lilly),[2] and in prefilled syringes (1 mg in 1 mL, 2 mg in 2 mL) (Faulding).[1]

Storage and shelf-life of unopened containers: When stored at 2–8°C, the solution has a shelf-life of 2 years in vials or 18 months in syringes.[2]

2 Chemistry

Type: Vinca alkaloid.

Molecular structure: 22-oxo-vincaleukoblastine (sulphate salt).

Molecular weight: 825.1 (vincristine sulphate: 923).

Solubility: Sulphate salt: 1 in 2 in water, 1 in 600 in ethanol, 1 in 30 in chloroform.

pK_a: 5.0, 7.4.

3 Stability profile

3.1 Physical and chemical stability

When vincristine sulphate was incubated at 37°C in 0.2 M glycine buffer containing 1% bovine serum albumin, five degradation products could be detected.[3] The major breakdown product was confirmed as 4-deacetyl vincristine, and the remaining degradants were postulated to be an isomer of vincristine and of the 4-deacetyl derivative, 4-deacetyl-3-deoxy vincristine and N-formyl-leurosine. The degradation products represented 14%, 44% and 56% of the parent vincristine after incubation at 37°C for 72 hours at pH 4.0, 7.4, and 8.8, respectively.

Studies on the degradation kinetics of vincristine sulphate at 80°C, pH 2–11, indicate that vincristine is most stable at pH 4.8 and that its stability is comparable to that of vinblastine.[4] A half-life of 136 hours is given for vincristine in solutions at pH 4.8 and 80°C, with an activation energy of 70–80 kJ/mole, but the data are not easily extrapolated to temperatures of 25°C and below.

The reconstituted injection has a pH of 3.5–5.5. Precipitation can occur at alkaline pH values.

Container compatibility: Vincristine 2 mg in 250 mL (40 µg/mL) of 0.9% sodium chloride or 5% glucose in PVC bags infused at a rate of approximately 2 mL/minute showed no evidence of loss due to sorption,[5] suggesting that vincristine can be added to PVC containers and infused through PVC sets, at least if the minimum concentration is not less that 40 µg/mL.

After filtration through a 0.22-µm cellulose ester filter, 6.5% of a 1 mg/50 mL solution in 5% glucose and 12% of a 1 mg/50 mL solution in 0.9% sodium chloride was bound to the filter.[6] Vincristine sulphate, 1.5 mg in 3 mL, when injected as a bolus through a 0.22-µm nylon filter, and after flushing the filter with 10 mL of normal saline, showed losses of 10% of the vincristine to the filter.[7]

No losses of vincristine (0.25 mg/10 mL) could be detected to nylon, polysulphone or cellulose ester filters when using a syringe pump driver to deliver the drug. However, significant absorption to the Pall ELD 96 filter was found. A 30–40% loss of potency could be seen in the first 30 minutes of the infusion, with the concentration only returning to its initial value after 2 to 3 hours.[8]

Compatibility with other drugs: Vincristine has been shown to be physically compatible with a wide range of other drugs.[9] In particular, various combinations containing up to 4 µg/mL vincristine with doxorubicin (up to 100 µg/mL) and etoposide (not exceeding 200 µg/mL) diluted in 0.9% sodium chloride.[10]

3.2 Stability in clinical practice

Vincristine solution at 1 mg/mL in plastic syringes (Plastipak, Becton Dickinson) is stable for 28 days at 2–8°C.[11] It is also stable in plastic syringes after dilution in 0.9% sodium chloride to concentrations containing 0.1–0.2 mg/mL for 28 days at 2–8°C.[11]

Combinations containing relatively low concentrations of vincristine (1–2 µg/mL), doxorubicin (25–50 µg/mL) and etoposide (up to 200 µg/mL) diluted in 0.9% sodium chloride and stored in polyolefin containers at 23–25°C, with or without exposure to normal lighting, were stable for periods of up to 72 hours.[10] Higher concentrations of etoposide caused precipitation.

No degradation was detected in vincristine solution at 20 µg/mL in 0.9% sodium chloride, 5% glucose and Ringer's lactate when stored at 4°C for 21 days in polypropylene tubes in the dark.[12] At 25°C there was a 5% loss of vincristine in 5% glucose after 21 days, but losses in the other two infusion solutions were insignificant.

There was no evidence of physical or chemical incompatibility between vincristine and mitozantrone mixed together in 5% glucose solution contained in 10-mL plastic syringes and stored, protected from light, at room temperature for 7 days.[2,13] Admixtures of doxorubicin and vincristine (1.88–2.37 mg/mL and 0.033–0.053 mg/mL, respectively) are stable for at least 7 days at 37°C in 0.9% sodium chloride, or 0.45% sodium chloride and 2.5% glucose.[14]

Vincristine was reported to be stable after dilution in 0.9% sodium chloride to contain 0.5, 1, 2 or 3 mg/mL vincristine, in volumes of 25 or 50 mL, stored in PVC minibags or 20 mL in 30 mL capacity polypropylene syringes, at 4°C for 7 days followed by 2 days at 23°C.[15]

3.3 Stability in specialised delivery systems

Solutions of vincristine containing 0.04–0.2 mg/mL in 0.9% sodium chloride and stored in the Infusor or Intermate devices are stable for 29 days at 2–8°C followed by 2 days at room temperature or 10 days at 2–8°C.[16] A solution containing 0.2 mg/mL in 0.9% sodium chloride is stable for up to 51 days at 2–8°C followed by 2 days at room temperature.[15] However, due to the lack of stability data at 33°C, only half-day infusors should be used.[14] A mixture containing vincristine sulphate at 0.036 mg/mL and doxorubicin hydrochloride at 1.67 mg/mL in 0.9% sodium chloride infusion, stored in either Deltec system (Pharmacia Upjohn Ltd) or Infusor (Baxter Healthcare Ltd) reservoirs, has been shown to be stable for 7 days at 4°C followed by 4 days at 35°C.[17]

4 Clinical use

Type of cytotoxic: Vincristine blocks mitosis with metaphase arrest by binding to tubulin and inhibiting the assembly of microtubules. It is M-phase specific.

Main indications: Vincristine is used, principally in combination chemotherapy regimens, against Hodgkin's and non-Hodgkin's lymphomas, acute lymphocytic leukaemia, lymphosarcoma, reticulum-cell sarcoma, rhabdomyosarcoma, neuroblastoma, Wilms' tumour, advanced breast carcinoma and small-cell lung carcinoma. It has modest to moderate activity in many other malignancies.[18]

Dosage: 1.4 mg/m² weekly, up to a maximum of 2 mg/week. In children weighing less than 10 kg, 0.05 mg/kg weekly is used. Due to the narrow therapeutic range, the dose should be individually adjusted.

5 Preparation of injection

Reconstitution: Add 1 mL of diluent to a 1-mg vial, 2 mL to a 2-mg vial and 5 mL to a 5-mg vial to give a 1 mg/mL solution.

Bolus administration: Vincristine is for intravenous administration only. It is recommended that the undiluted solution is administered by bolus intravenous injection, or into the tubing of a running intravenous infusion. As the drug is a vesicant, care must be taken to avoid extravasation during administration.

Intravenous infusion: Vincristine has been administered by continuous infusion,[18,19] with reported higher blood concentrations and increased tumour response at a dose of 0.5 mg/m² daily for 5 days in 3-week cycles.[19,20]

Extra Warning: Since death will almost certainly result from inadvertent intrathecal administration, syringes or other containers of vincristine in a form prepared for administration should be labelled **for intravenous use only – fatal if given by other routes**. The drug should be diluted to at least 20 mL, a maximum concentration of 0.1 mg/mL, and packed and transported as a single item (*see* Chapter 6 for further guidance).*

Extravasation: Group 1 classification (vesicant) (*see* Chapter 6).

6 Destruction of drugs or contaminated articles

Incineration: 1000°C.

Chemical: 5% sodium hypochlorite for 24 hours.

Contact with skin: Wash with copious amounts of water.

References

1 ABPI (1999) *ABPI Data Sheet Compendium 1999–2000.* DataPharm Publications Ltd, London, 430–1.

2 ABPI (1999) *ABPI Data Sheet Compendium 1999–2000.* DataPharm Publications Ltd, London, 758–60.

3 Sethi VS and Thimmaiah KN (1985) Structural studies on the degradation products of vincristine dihydrogen sulphate. *Cancer Res.* **45**: 5386–9.

4 Dyne T *et al.* (1991) Stability and compatibility studies of vinblastine, vincristine, vindesine and vinorelbine with PVC infusion bags. *Int J Pharm.* **77**: 279–85.

5 Vendrig DEMM *et al.* (1989) Degradation kinetics of vincristine sulphate and vindesine sulphate in aqueous solutions. *Int J Pharm.* **50**: 189–96.

6 Butler LD *et al.* (1980) Effect of in-line filtration on the potency of low-dose drugs. *Am J Hosp Pharm.* **37**: 935–41.

7 Ennis CE *et al.* (1983) *In vitro* study of in-line filtration of medications commonly administered to paediatric cancer patients. *J Parent Enter Nutr.* **7**: 156–8.

8 Francomb MM *et al.* (1994) Adsorption of vincristine, vinblastine, doxorubicin and mitozantrone to in-line intravenous filters. *Int J Pharm.* **103**: 87–92.

9 Trissel LA (2001) *Handbook of Injectable Drugs* (11e). American Society of Hospital Pharmacists, Bethesda, MD.

10 Wolfe JL *et al.* (1999) Compatibility and stability of vincristine sulfate, doxorubicin hydrochloride and etoposide in 0.9% sodium chloride injection. *Am J Health-Syst Pharm.* **56**: 985–9.

*As this book went to press, new guidance was issued on the safe administration of intrathecal chemotherapy, which requires that only registered, designated personnel should prescribe, dispense, check or administer intrathecal chemotherapy. The guidance also requires formal induction and regular training programmes. Please check the guidance for the full recommendations: NHS Executive (2001) *National Guidance on the Safe Administration of Intrathecal Chemotherapy.* HSC 2001/022.

11 Faulding Pharmaceuticals plc (2000) Personal communication.

12 Beijnen JH *et al.* (1989) Stability of vinca alkaloid anticancer drugs in three commonly used infusion fluids. *J Parent Sci Technol.* **43**: 84–7.

13 Cacek T and Weber R (1990) Visual and chemical stability of mitoxantrone mixed individually with vincristine, etoposide, thiotepa, metoclopramide and cytarabine in plastic syringes. *American Society of Hospital Pharmacists Midyear Clin Meeting.* **25**: P-47OE.

14 Beijnen JH *et al.* (1986) Stability of intravenous admixtures of doxorubicin and vincristine. *Am J Hosp Pharm.* **43**: 3022–7.

15 Trissel LA *et al.* (2001) The stability of diluted vincristine sulfate used as a deterrent to inadvertent intrathecal injection. *Hospital Pharmacy.* **36**: 740–5.

16 Baxter Healthcare Ltd (2000) Personal communication.

17 Nyhammar EJ *et al.* (1996) Stability of doxorubicin hydrochloride and vincristine sulfate in two portable infusion-pump reservoirs. *Am J Health-Syst Pharm.* **53**: 1171–3.

18 Smith BD (1987) Antitumour update: vinca alkaloids and epipodophyllotoxins. *Hosp Formul.* **22**: 363–73.

19 Jackson DV *et al.* (1984) Intravenous vincristine infusion. *Cancer.* **48**: 2559–664.

20 Jackson DV *et al.* (1981) Pharmacokinetics of vincristine infusion. *Cancer Treat Rep.* **65**: 1043–8.

Prepared by Gerard Lee

VINDESINE

1 General details

Approved names: Vindesine, desacetyl vinblastine amide.

Proprietary name: Eldisine.

Manufacturer or supplier: Eli Lilly & Co. Ltd.

Presentation and formulation details: Lyophilised powder consisting of 5 mg vindesine sulphate with 25 mg mannitol. Supplied with 5 mL of sterile diluent containing 0.9% sodium chloride and 2% benzyl alcohol adjusted to pH 4.2–4.5 with hydrochloric acid or sodium hydroxide.[1]

Storage and shelf-life of unopened container: When stored at 2–6°C, the injection has a shelf-life of 3 years.

2 Chemistry

Type: Vinca alkaloid and synthetic derivative of vinblastine.

Molecular structure: 3-(aminocarbonyl)-O-deacetyl-3-de(methoxy-carbonyl)-vinca-leukoblastine.

Molecular weight: 753.9 (vindesine sulphate: 852).

Solubility: The sulphate salt is freely soluble in water.

pK_a: 5.4, 7.4.

3 Stability profile

3.1 Physical and chemical stability

In studies on the stability of vindesine in buffered serum albumin solution, Thimmaiah *et al.* have found that, when vindesine sulphate (500 mg in 10 mL) is incubated at 37°C in 0.2 M glycine buffer containing 1% bovine serum albumin, two degradation products can be detected.[2] These were tentatively identified as an eneamine/ether derivative of vindesine (I) and 3'4'-epoxyvindesine-N-oxide (II) (*see* Figure 6).

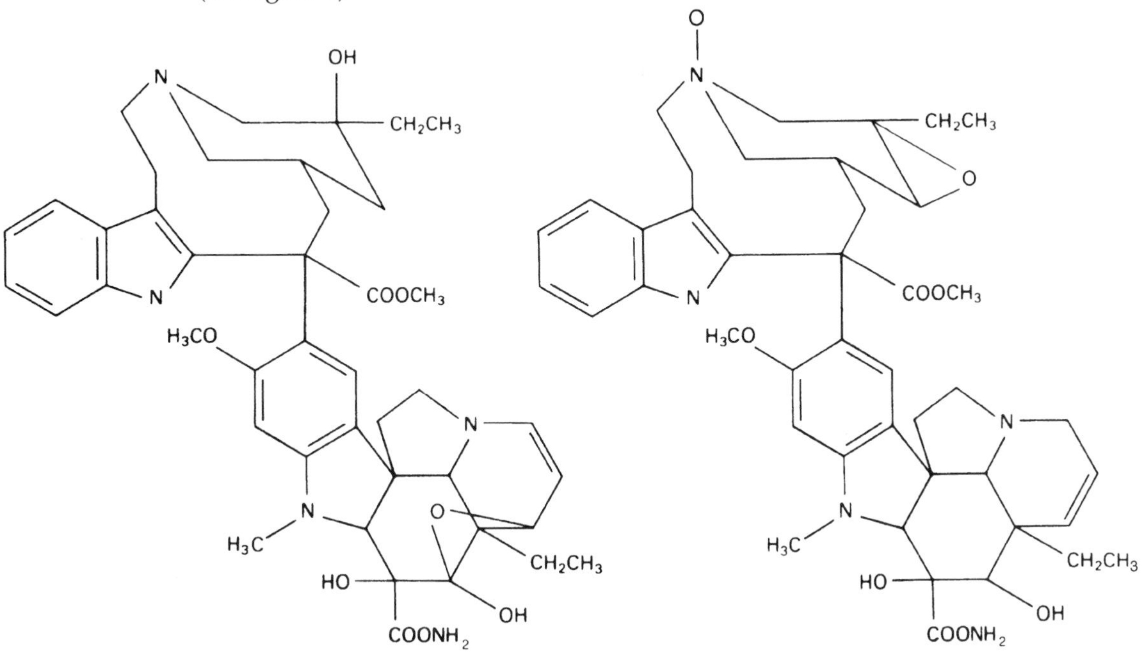

Figure 6: *Two major degradation products of vindesine incubated at 37°C in 0.2 M glycine buffer*

The degradation products were formed to the extent of about 11, 34 and 39% of the parent vindesine after 72 hours of incubation at 37°C at pH 4.0, 7.4 and 8.8, respectively.

Investigations of the degradation kinetics of vindesine sulphate at 80°C in the pH range 2–11 indicate that it is most stable at pH 1.9, and that it is more stable than vinblastine and vincristine in aqueous solution.[3] A half-life of 690 hours is quoted for vindesine at 80°C and pH 1.9 with an activation energy of 124 kJ/mole, but the data are not easily extrapolated to temperatures of 25°C and below.

Studies of the cell-killing efficiency of vindesine solutions used in the human tumour clonogenic assay indicate a deterioration of cytotoxic activity for solutions stored in glass at low concentrations.[4] The lethal efficacy of 60 µg/mL solutions decreased to almost zero when tested after 1, 2 and 3 weeks of storage. A 225 µg/mL solution retained its lethal activity throughout the 3-week period. The original reconstituted injection (1 mg/mL), stored in glass under the same conditions, retained its cytotoxic activity when diluted to the test concentrations. This would indicate that the loss of efficacy at low concentrations is not due to chemical inactivation, but is more likely to be a result of sorptive losses to the glass vial.

The reconstituted injection has a pH of 4.2–4.5. Precipitation can occur at alkaline pH values.

Container compatibility: No incompatibilities have been reported with PVC containers and plastic syringes. There is evidence of sorptive losses of 60 µg/mL solutions in borosilicate glass vials.[4]

Compatibility with other drugs: No further information available.

3.2 Stability in clinical practice

The reconstituted injection is chemically stable for at least 30 days when stored at 4°C.[1] No degradation was detected in vindesine solution at 20 µg/mL in 0.9% sodium chloride, 5% glucose or Ringer's lactate when stored for 21 days at 4°C and 25°C in polypropylene tubes in the dark.[5]

3.3 Stability in specialised delivery systems

No data available.

4 Clinical use

Type of cytotoxic: Vindesine causes metaphase arrest by binding to tubulin, a substructure of the microtubular spindle apparatus. This leads to inhibition of tubulin polymerisation, which interrupts mitosis and leads to cell death.[6] A complete review of the antineoplastic activity of vindesine has been provided by Cersosima *et al.*[6]

Main indications: Acute lymphoblastic leukaemia, chronic myelogenous leukaemia in blast crisis, malignant melanoma and advanced breast carcinoma.

Dosage: 3–4 mg/m² weekly as a bolus injection, or by 4-hour[7] or 48-hour infusion.[8] Further details of dosage regimens have been provided by Cersosima *et al.*[6]

5 Preparation of injection

Reconstitution: Reconstitute the 5-mg vial with 5 mL of sterile diluent to give a 1 mg/mL solution.

Bolus administration: Inject reconstituted preparation into the tubing of a fast-running intravenous drip.

Intravenous infusion: Prepare in 5% glucose or 0.9% sodium chloride. Multi-electrolyte infusion solutions, such as lactated Ringer's solution, are not recommended because of the possibility of precipitation, but this is not a problem for concentrations lower than 20 µg/mL.[5]

Extra Warning: Since death will almost certainly result from inadvertent intrathecal administration, syringes or other containers of vindesine in a form prepared for administration should be labelled **for intravenous use only – fatal if given by other routes**. The drug should be diluted to at least 20 mL, a maximum concentration of 0.1 mg/mL, and packed and transported as a single item (*see* Chapter 6 for further guidance).*

*As this book went to press, new guidance was issued on the safe administration of intrathecal chemotherapy, which requires that only registered, designated personnel should prescribe, dispense, check or administer intrathecal chemotherapy. The guidance also requires formal induction and regular training programmes. Please check the guidance for the full recommendations: NHS Executive (2001) *National Guidance on the Safe Administration of Intrathecal Chemotherapy.* HSC 2001/022.

Extravasation: Group 1 classification (vesicant). Administration of 1000 units of hyaluronidase in 20 mL saline may aid recovery (*see* Chapter 6).

6 Destruction of drug or contaminated articles

Incineration: 1000°C.

Chemical: 10% sodium hypochlorite for 24 hours.

Contact with skin: Wash with copious amounts of water.

References

1 ABPI (1999) *ABPI Data Sheet Compendium 1999–2000.* DataPharm Publications Ltd, London, 737–9.
2 Thimmaiah KN *et al.* (1990) Chemical characterisation of the *in-vitro* degradation products of vindesine sulphate. *Microchem J.* **42**: 115–20.
3 Vendrig DEMM *et al.* (1989) Degradation kinetics of vincristine sulphate and vindesine sulphate in aqueous solution. *Int J Pharm.* **50**: 189–96.
4 Yang L-Y and Drewinko B (1985) Cytotoxic efficacy of reconstituted and stored anti-tumour agents. *Cancer Res.* **45**: 1511–15.
5 Beijnen JH *et al.* (1988) Stability of vinca alkaloid anticancer drugs in three commonly used infusion fluids. *J Parent Sci Technol.* **43**: 84–7.
6 Cersosima RJ *et al.* (1983) Pharmacology, clinical efficacy and adverse effects of vindesine sulphate, a new vinca alkaloid. *Pharmacotherapy* **3**: 259–68.
7 Ettinger LJ *et al.* (1982) Vindesine – phase II study in childhood malignancies: a report for cancer and leukaemia group. *Med Pediatr Oncol.* **10**: 35–44.
8 Mathe G *et al.* (1981) Phase II clinical trials with hematogical malignancies. *Anticancer Res.* **1**: 1–10.

Prepared by Gerard Lee

VINORELBINE

1 General details

Approved name: Vinorelbine.

Proprietary name: Navelbine.

Manufacturer or supplier: Pierre Fabre Ltd.

Presentation and formulation details: A sterile white/yellow solution supplied in 1, 4 and 5 mL glass vials containing 10 mg/mL vinorelbine tartrate.[1]

Storage and shelf-life of unopened container: Vinorelbine should be stored in a refrigerator (2–8°C) and protected from light. Under these conditions the product is stable for 3 years.[1]

2 Chemistry

Type: 5′ Nor vinca alkaloid.

Molecular structure:

Molecular weight: 1378 (base: 778 + 2 tartric acid mioitie: 300).

Solubility: Soluble in water and alcohol.

3 Stability profile

3.1 Physical and chemical stability

After dilution the product can be refrigerated (2–8°C) for up to 24 hours prior to use. Studies have examined the chemical stability of vinorelbine once prepared for use with 0.9% sodium chloride or 5% glucose. Vinorelbine was found to be chemically stable when stored at room temperature and under normal light conditions for 30 days.[2]

Container compatibility: Vinorelbine after dilution in 0.9% sodium chloride or 5% glucose and storage in glass vials or PVC infusion bags at room temperature and normal light conditions for 30 days showed no evidence of interaction with the containers.[2]

Compatibility with other drugs: No information available.

3.2 Stability in clinical practice

Vinorelbine diluted in 0.9% sodium chloride and stored at 2–8°C is stable for not less than 24 hours.[1]

3.3 Stability in specialised delivery systems

No information available.

4 Clinical use

Type of cytotoxic: Vinorelbine is a cytostatic antineoplastic drug of the vinca alkaloid family with a molecular action on the dynamic equilibrium of tubulin in the microtubular apparatus of the cell.[1]

Main indications: As a single agent or in combination for the first-line treatment of stage III or IV non-small-cell lung cancer. Treatment of advanced breast cancer stage III and IV that is relapsing after or refractory to an anthracycline-containing regimen.

Dosage: Vinorelbine is usually given at a dose of 25–30 mg/m² weekly. In combination with other chemotherapy agents, a dose of 25–30 mg/m² on days 1 and 8 every 21 or 28 days may be used.

5 Preparation of injection

Syringes or other containers of vinorelbine in a form prepared for administration should be labelled **for intravenous use only**.

Bolus administration: Vinorelbine may be administered intravenously by slow bolus (5–10 minutes) after dilution in 20–50 mL 0.9% sodium chloride.[1] Rittenberg *et al.*[3] showed that a significantly lower incidence of venous irritation was associated with the slow bolus injection (over 5–10 minutes) compared with short infusion (over 20–30 minutes).

Intravenous infusion: Vinorelbine diluted in 125 mL 0.9% sodium chloride or 5% glucose should be infused over 20–30 minutes.[1]

Extra Warning: Since death will almost certainly result from inadvertent intrathecal administration, syringes or other containers of vinorelbine in a form prepared for administration should be labelled **for intravenous use only – fatal if given by other routes**. The drug should be diluted, packed and transported as a single item (*see* Chapter 6 for further guidance).*

Extravasation: Group 1 classification (vesicant). Extravasation should be managed in the same manner as with other vinca alkaloids (*see* Chapter 6).

---

*As this book went to press, new guidance was issued on the safe administration of intrathecal chemotherapy, which requires that only registered, designated personnel should prescribe, dispense, check or administer intrathecal chemotherapy. The guidance also requires formal induction and regular training programmes. Please check the guidance for the full recommendations: NHS Executive (2001) *National Guidance on the Safe Administration of Intrathecal Chemotherapy.* HSC 2001/022.

6 Destruction of drug or contaminated articles[4]

Incineration: 1000°C.

Chemical: 5% sodium hypochlorite for 2 hours.

Environmental precautions: Recover as much of the product as possible. If accidentally spilled, wash the area with a 12% solution of domestic bleach.

Contact with skin: Rinse copiously with water.

References

1 ABPI (1999) *ABPI Data Sheet Compendium 1999–2000*. DataPharm Publications Ltd, London, 1257–8.
2 Bauer M (1990) Navelbine compatibility with PVC perfusion bottles and neutral glass bottles. In: *Pierre Fabre Research Centre Dossier*. Pierre Fabre Research Centre, Paris.
3 Rittenberg CN *et al.* (1995) Assessing and managing venous irritation with vinorelbine tartrate (Navelbine). *Oncol Nurse Forum.* **22**: 707–10.
4 Pierre Fabre Ltd (1997) *Navelbine (vinorelbine INN) Material Safety Data Sheet.* Pierre Fabre Ltd, Winchester.

Prepared by Andrew Stanley

ALDESLEUKIN (IL-2)

1 General details

Approved name: Aldesleukin.

Proprietary name: Proleukin.

Manufacturer or supplier: Chiron (UK) Ltd.

Presentation and formulation details: Aldesleukin is a sterile white lyophilised powder for parenteral use containing 1.2 mg (18×10^6 IU/mg) aldesleukin, a recombinant human interleukin-2 (rIL-2), supplied in glass vials (5 mL).

When reconstituted with 1.2 mL of water for injections BP, each vial delivers 1 mL solution containing 18×10^6 IU (1 mg) aldesleukin, 50 mg mannitol and 0.2 mg sodium dodecyl sulphate, buffered with sodium phosphate to a pH of 7.5 (range 7.2–7.8).

Storage and shelf-life of unopened container: Unopened vials expire 2 years from the date of manufacture when stored at 2–8°C.

2 Chemistry

Aldesleukin is produced by recombinant DNA technology using an *Escherichia coli* strain which contains a genetically engineered modification of the human IL-2 gene. This modified recombinant human IL-2 differs from native IL-2 in the following ways.

▼ The molecule is not glycosylated because it is derived from *Escherichia coli*.
▼ The molecule has no N-terminal alanine.
▼ The molecule has serine substituted for cysteine at amino acid position 125.

The two amino-acid changes result in a more homogeneous IL-2 product. The biological activities of aldesleukin and native human IL-2, a naturally occurring lymphokine, are similar in that both regulate the immune response. The administration of aldesleukin has been shown to reduce both tumour growth and spread. The exact mechanism by which aldesleukin-mediated immunostimulation leads to anti-tumour activity is not yet known.

Molecular structure:

Des-alanyl-1, serine-125 human interleukin-2; recombinant interleukin-2

10
Pro-Thr-Ser-Ser-Ser-Thr-Lys-Lys-Thr-Gln-Leu-Gln-Leu-Glu-His-Leu-

20   30
Leu-Leu-Asp-Leu-Gln-Met-Ile-Leu-Asn-Gly-Ile-Asn-Asn-Tyr-Lys-Asn-

40
Pro-Lys-Leu-Thr-Arg-Met-Leu-Thr-Phe-Lys-Phe-Tyr-Met-Pro-Lys-Lys-

50   60
Ala-Thr-Glu-Leu-Lys-His-Leu-Gln-Cys-Leu-Glu-Glu-Glu-Leu-Lys-Pro-

70   80
Leu-Glu-Glu-Val-Leu-Asn-Leu-Ala-Gln-Ser-Lys-Asn-Phe-His-Leu-Arg-

90
Pro-Arg-Asp-Leu-Ile-Ser-Asn-Ile-Asn-Val-Ile-Val-Leu-Glu-Leu-Lys-

100   110
Gly-Ser-Glu-Thr-Thr-Phe-Met-Cys-Glu-Tyr-Ala-Asp-Glu-Thr-Ala-Thr-

120
Ile-Val-Glu-Phe-Leu-Asn-Arg-Trp-Ile-Thr-Phe-Ser-Gln-Ser-Ile-Ile-

Ser-Thr-Leu-Thr

Molecular weight: Approximately 15 600.

Solubility: Aldesleukin is freely soluble in water.

3 Stability profile

3.1 Physical and chemical stability

Store vials of lyophilised aldesleukin (rIL-2) in a refrigerator at 2–8°C. Reconstituted or diluted aldesleukin may be stored at refrigerated and room temperature (2–30°C).

As rIL-2 is not glycosylated it is less water soluble (more lipophilic) compared with endogenous IL-2. The more lipophilic properties of rIL-2 make it necessary to use sodium dodecyl sulphate (SDS) during the production and formulation of aldesleukin. SDS is a surface-active compound which reversibly binds to rIL-2 and brings the lipophilic molecule into solution. In a solution of reconstituted IL-2 there is an equilibrium between rIL-2-bound SDS and free SDS. The ability of SDS to keep rIL-2 in solution is dependent on the concentrations of SDS and rIL-2. The addition of human serum albumin (HSA) is not needed when the reconstituted IL-2 is further diluted (with 5% glucose) to rIL-2 concentrations of 100–1000 µg/mL, because the SDS concentration is high enough to keep the rIL-2 in solution within this concentration range.

It is also not advisable to use HSA, because its addition to rIL-2 at these high concentrations will result in the binding of HSA to SDS, which disturbs the sensitive equilibrium between the free SDS and the rIL-2-bound SDS. This can result in the precipitation of rIL-2.

However, when the solution is further diluted to concentrations below 100 µg/mL, the addition of HSA (0.1%) is necessary to prevent precipitation of rIL-2.

Human serum albumin should be added and mixed with 5% glucose injection prior to the addition of IL-2. It is added to protect against loss of bioactivity.

Container compatibility: IL-2 should be administered using infusion bags or syringes composed of one of the following materials: polypropylene syringes (e.g. Becton-Dickinson Plastipak or Sherwood Monoject), polyvinylchloride bags (e.g. Viaflex), polyolefine bags (e.g. PAB-Excel) or glass bottles.

Extension sets composed of polyethylene or standard administration sets can be used.

In-line filters should not be used when administering interleukin.

Effect of light: No information is available.

Effect of pH: Stable at pH values in the range 7.2–7.8. With time interleukin undergoes hydrolysis outside this range.

Compatibility with other drugs: Reconstitution and dilution procedures other than those recommended may result in incomplete delivery of bioactivity and/or the formation of biologically inactive protein.

The use of bacteriostatic water for injections, or of 0.9% sodium chloride should be avoided because of increased aggregation. Interleukin should not be mixed with other drugs.

3.2 Stability in clinical practice

Due to the unstable nature of IL-2, it must be used within 24 hours of preparation and stored refrigerated (at 2–8°C) until use.[1]

4 Clinical use

Main indications: Used in the treatment of metastatic renal-cell carcinoma, but excluding those patients in whom *all* of the following three prognostic factors are present:

▼ a performance status of ECOG 1 or greater
▼ more than one organ with metastatic disease sites
▼ a period of less than 24 months between the initial diagnosis of primary tumour and the date when the patient is evaluated for IL-2 treatment.

Dosage: Full details of dosage recommendations for each of the licensed indications are provided in the manufacturer's data sheet.[1] Aldesleukin has also been extensively investigated in renal-cell carcinoma, melanoma and colorectal tumours using subcutaneous administration schedules to try to minimise the side-effects of the rIL-2.[2]

5 Preparation of injection

Reconstitution: Each vial of IL-2 for injection should be reconstituted with 1.2 mL of water for injections. The diluent should be directed against the side of the vial to avoid excess foaming, and the contents should be swirled gently until they have completely dissolved. Do not shake the solution. The resulting solution should be a clear colourless liquid. When reconstituted as directed, it contains 18×10^6 IU (1 mg)/mL aldesleukin.

Extravasation: Group 5 classification (neutral). However, IL-2 may cause local capillary leak syndrome and/or local tissue reaction (*see* Chapter 6).

6 Destruction of drug or contaminated articles

Disposal: Excess IL-2 solution may be disposed of into a drain with copious amounts of water. All other waste, including contaminated packaging or cleaning materials and used protective clothing, must be placed with clinical waste for incineration. When dealing with broken vials, disposable gloves, eye protection and a dust mask should be worn.

Contact with skin: Remove contaminated clothing and wash skin thoroughly with soap and water. If the eyes are contaminated, irrigate with water and obtain medical advice.

References

1 Eurocetus (UK) Ltd (1999) *UK Data Sheet January 1992.* Eurocetus (UK) Ltd, Hounslow.
2 Eurocetus (UK) Ltd (1996) Personal communication.

Prepared by Andrew Stanley

EDRECOLOMAB

1 General details

Approved name: Edrecolomab (monoclonal antibody 17-1A).

Proprietary name: Panorex.

Manufacturer or supplier: Glaxo Wellcome GmbH & Co.

Presentation and formulation details: Clear colourless or slightly yellow solution in sterile vials containing 10 mL of solution, with 10 mg/mL edrocolomab. A 0.22-μm low-protein-binding single-use filter is also included in the package.

Storage and shelf-life of unopened container: The product has a shelf-life of 2 years when stored at 2–8°C.[1] The temperature of the product must not be allowed to exceed 25°C, and the product must not be stored above 10°C for more than 72 hours.[2]

2 Chemistry

Type: Edrecolomab is a mouse-derived monoclonal lgG2a antibody that recognises human tumour-associated antigen C017-1A.[3]

Molecular weight: Approximately 150 000.

Solubility: Edrecolomab is freely soluble in isotonic aqueous solutions.[1] Precipitation of protein may occur when edrecolomab is diluted with hypotonic solutions such as distilled water, or with solutions of pH lower than 5.0.[1]

3 Stability profile

3.1 Physical and chemical stability

Although edrecolomab should be stored in a refrigerator at 2–8°C, solutions must not be allowed to freeze, or shaken vigorously, as protein aggregates may form.

Container compatibility: Edrecolomab diluted in 0.9% sodium chloride is compatible with glass, polyethylene or PVC containers.[4]

Compatibility with other drugs: No information available.

3.2 Stability in clinical practice

After dilution, the injection should be administered within 4–6 hours.[1]

3.3 Stability in specialised delivery systems

No information available.

4 Clinical use

Type of cytotoxic agent: Edrecolomab is a mouse-derived monoclonal lgG2a antibody. It binds specifically to human tumour-associated antigen C01 7-1 A, which is expressed on the cell surface of a wide variety of tumours and normal epithelial tissue. Edrecolomab is thought to destroy tumour cells by activating an array of endogenous cytotoxic mechanisms, including antibody-dependent cell-mediated cytotoxicity and possibly antibody-dependent complement-mediated cytotoxicity. Edrecolomab may induce antitumour activity indirectly by inducing a host anti-idiotypic antibody response.[3]

Main indications: Postoperative adjuvant therapy of colorectal cancer, Duke's stage C.[1,3]

Dosage: The first dose of 500 mg should be administered at any time from 7 to 42 days postoperatively (preferably between 7 and 14 days). Starting 28 days after the first dose, four additional single doses of 100 mg are administered at 28-day intervals.[3] The total maximum cumulative dose is 900 mg.

5 Preparation of injection

Reconstitution: The solution for injection should appear clear and colourless or slightly yellow and should be examined for particulate matter or discoloration. The vial contents are drawn up gently, avoiding foaming, into a syringe. The contents of the syringe must then be filtered through the 0.22-µm low-protein-binding filter (included in the package) into 200–250 mL of 0.9% sodium chloride (sufficient for up to 500 mg of edrecolomab) and mixed by careful agitation. If the infusate is observed to be cloudy, it should be discarded and a fresh solution prepared.[1]

Bolus administration: Not recommended.

Intravenous infusion: The infusion should be delivered over at least 2 hours.[4]

Extravasation: Group 5 classification (neutral). No recommendations available (*see* Chapter 6).

6 Destruction of drug or contaminated articles.

Disposal: Excess edrecolomab solution may be disposed of into a drain with copious amounts of water. All other waste, including contaminated packaging or cleaning materials and used protective clothing, must be placed with clinical waste for incineration.

Contact with skin: Remove contaminated clothing and wash skin thoroughly with soap and water. If the eyes are contaminated, irrigate with water and obtain medical advice.

References

1 Glaxo Wellcome Centocor (1996) *Panorex: Package insert*. Glaxo Wellcome GmbH & Co.
2 Glaxo Wellcome (1999) Personal communication.
3 Adkins JC and Spencer CM (1998) Edrecolomab (monoclonal antibody 17-1A). *Drugs.* **56**: 619–26.
4 Edrecolomab, Micromedex Inc. Volume 98. 31 December 1998. Englewood, CO.

Prepared by Alexander Tabachnik and Yaacov Cass

INTERFERON α-2a

1 General details

Approved name: Interferon α-2a(rbe).

Proprietary name: Roferon-A solution for injection, Roferon-A in pre-filled syringes.

Manufacturer or supplier: Roche Products Ltd.

Presentation and formulation details: Roferon-A solution for injection in vials containing 3, 4, 5, 6, 9 or 18 million international units (MIU) in 1 mL, or 18 MIU in 3 mL.

Roferon-A is also available in pre-filled syringes containing 3, 4, 5, 6 or 9 MIU in 0.5 mL.[1,2]

Roferon-A also contains ammonium acetate, sodium chloride, 1% benzyl alcohol (as preservative), polysorbate 80, acetic acid, sodium hydroxide and water for injections BP. The sodium concentration is 0.123 mmol/L and the solutions are human serum albumin free.[2]

Storage and shelf-life of unopened container: Unopened vials of interferon α-2a(rbe) solution or pre-filled syringes have an expiry date 2 years after the date of manufacture when stored between 2 and 8°C.

2 Chemistry

Interferon α-2a(rbe) is a recombinant interferon. It is a highly purified, sterile non-glycosylated protein containing 165 amino acids with two disulphide bridges (between residues 1 and 98 and residues 29 and 138).[3] It is produced by recombinant DNA technology using a genetically engineered *Escherichia coli* strain containing DNA that codes for the human protein. It differs from other recombinant interferons in that amino acid 23 is a lysine group and amino acid 34 is a histidine group.

Interferon α-2a(rbe) has been shown to possess many of the activities of 'natural' human α-interferon. It has antiviral, antiproliferative and immunomodulatory actions.[4]

Molecular weight: Approximately 19 000.

Solubility: Interferon α-2a(rbe) is freely soluble in water.

Molecular structure: see page 444.

3 Stability profile

3.1 Physical and chemical stability

Reconstituted vials should not be used after storage for more than 24 hours in a refrigerator (2–8°C) or 2 hours at room temperature. Reconstituted vials of 3 MIU and 18 MIU interferon α-2a(rbe) in 1 mL of water for injections, frozen immediately after reconstitution to –20°C, have shown no physical degradation or loss of chemical activity on thawing after 1 month.[5] Interferon α-2a(rbe) is sensitive to heat, light and atmospheric oxygen.

Compatibility with other drugs: Data for interferon α-2a(rbe) and other compounds are not available. Therefore the manufacturer recommends that it should not be mixed with other drugs.

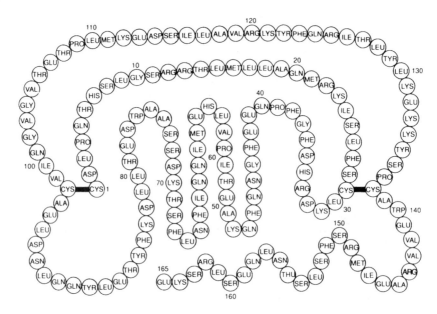

3.2 Stability in clinical practice

The interferon α-2a(rbe) solution for injection is chemically and bacterially stable for 30 days after opening if it is stored at between 2 and 8°C and protected from light.[1]

4 Clinical use

Type of cytotoxic agent: Activator of natural killer cells.

Main indications: Interferon α-2a(rbe) is licensed for use as a single agent in the treatment of hairy-cell leukaemia, chronic phase Philadelphia chromosome-positive chronic myelogenous leukaemia and cutaneous T-cell lymphoma. It is also indicated for recurrent or metastatic renal-cell carcinoma and AIDS-related Kaposi's sarcoma in patients without a history of opportunistic infection. In addition, it is licensed for the treatment of chronic active hepatitis B and chronic hepatitis C.[1]

Dosage: The following can be administered by subcutaneous or intramuscular injection.

▼ Hairy-cell leukaemia: induction dose of 3 MIU daily for 16–24 weeks, followed by maintenance therapy of 3 MIU three times per week.

▼ Chronic myelogenous leukaemia: induction dose of 3 MIU daily escalated to 9 MIU daily over 84 days. Maintenance therapy at 9 MIU daily (optimal) to 9 MIU three times weekly (minimum), for a maximum of 18 months, or until there is a complete haematological response. In complete haematological responders continue therapy in order to achieve a cytogenetic response.

▼ Cutaneous T-cell lymphoma: induction dose of 3 MIU daily escalated to 18 MIU daily over 84 days. Maintenance therapy at the maximum tolerable dose (maximum 18 MIU) three times weekly.

▼ Renal-cell carcinoma: induction dose of 3 MIU daily escalated to 36 MIU daily over 84 days. Maintenance therapy at 18–36 MIU three times weekly (doses over 18 MIU to be given by intramuscular injection only).

▼ AIDS-related Kaposi's sarcoma: induction dose of 3 MIU daily escalated to 36 MIU daily over 84 days. Maintenance therapy at the maximum tolerable dose (up to 36 MIU) three times weekly.

▼ Chronic hepatitis B: 2.5–5.0 MIU/m² three times weekly for 4–6 months, with dose escalation permissible if markers of viral replication do not decrease after 1 month of treatment.

▼ Chronic hepatitis C: 6 MIU three times weekly for 3 months, followed by 3 MIU three times weekly for a further 3 months in responding patients (those showing normalisation of ALT).

▼ Follicular non-Hodgkin's lymphoma: interferon α-2a(rbe) should be administered concomitantly with a conventional chemotherapy regimen (such as the combination of cyclophosphamide, prednisone, vincristine and doxorubicin) according to a schedule such as 6 MIU/m² given subcutaneously or intramuscularly from day 22 to day 26 of each 28-day cycle.

5 Preparation of injection

Bolus administration: 2–15 MIU/m² by subcutaneous injection.

Intravenous infusion: Not recommended due to poor drug stability.

Extravasation: Group 5 classification (neutral) (*see* Chapter 6).

6 Destruction of drug or contaminated articles

Disposal: Excess interferon α-2a(rbe) solution may be disposed of into a drain with copious amounts of water. All other waste, including contaminated packaging or cleaning materials and used protective clothing, must be placed with clinical waste for incineration.[6] When dealing with broken vials, disposable gloves, eye protection and a face mask should be worn.[6]

Contact with skin: Remove contaminated clothing and wash skin thoroughly with soap and water. If the eyes are contaminated, irrigate with water and obtain medical advice.[6]

References

1 (1992) American Product Information Sheet *Am J Hosp Pharm.* **49**: 550–2.

2 ABPI (1999) *ABPI Data Sheet Compendium 1999–2000.* DataPharm Publications Ltd, London, 1359–63.

3 Wetzel R (1981) Assignment of the disulphide bonds of leukocyte interferon. *Nature.* **189**: 606–7.

4 Baron S *et al.* (1991) The interferons: mechanisms of action and clinical applications. *JAMA.* **266**: 1375–83.

5 Roche Products Ltd (1995) Personal communication.

6 Roche Products Ltd (1991) *Interferon alfa-2a(rbe). COSHH Safety Data Sheet.* Roche Products Ltd, Welwyn Garden City.

Prepared by Andrew Stanley

INTERFERON α-2b

1 General details

Approved name: Interferon α-2b(rbe).

Proprietary name: Intron A.

Manufacturer or supplier: Schering-Plough Ltd.

Presentation and formulation details: Intron A is available as a multi-dose injection pen containing 15 (6 doses of 3 MIU), 25 (6 doses of 5 MIU) or 50 MIU (6 doses of 10 MIU) (total deliverable doses of 18, 30 and 60 MIU, respectively).

The powder contains glycine, mono- and dibasic sodium phosphate, human albumin and water for injections. The solution and multi-dose pen also contain sodium edetate, sodium chloride, m-cresol, polysorbate 80 and water for injections.[1]

Storage and shelf-life of unopened container: Store in the refrigerator. The shelf-life of the powder is 3 years, that of the solution is 18 months and that of the multi-dose pen is 12 months.[1]

2 Chemistry

Type: Interferon α-2b(rbe) is a recombinant interferon. It is a highly purified, sterile, non-glycosylated single-chain protein containing 165 amino acids with two disulphide bridges between residues 1 and 98, and 29 and 138.[2] It is produced by recombinant DNA technology using a genetically engineered *Escherichia coli* strain containing DNA that codes for the human protein. It differs from other recombinant interferons in that amino acid 23 is an arginine group and amino acid 34 is a histidine group.

Molecular structure:

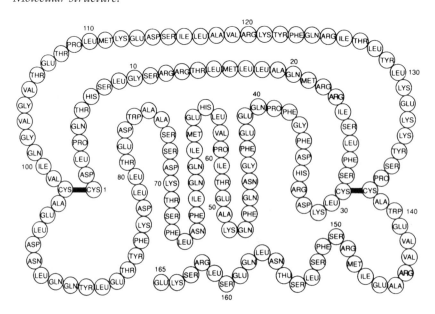

Molecular weight: Approximately 20 000.

Solubility: Interferon α-2b(rbe) is freely soluble, and concentrations up to 10 MIU/mL are all isotonic when diluted with 1 mL of water for injections. Up to 60 MIU will dissolve in 1 mL of water for injections.[2]

3 Stability profile

Interferon α-2b(rbe) degrades by cleavage of disulphide bridges. The liberated sulphydryl groups form oligomers (dimers and trimers) with other monomers. It is believed that only one disulphide bridge is required for biological activity.

3.1 *Physical and chemical stability*

Interferon α-2b(rbe) lyophilised powder is not photosensitive,[2] and is generally unstable after reconstitution. Solutions of interferon α-2b(rbe) should be stored in the refrigerator at 2–8°C.

Effect of pH: Interferon α-2b(rbe) is most stable in the pH range 6.9–7.5.[2]

Container compatibility: No adsorption has been found to occur on to the surface of polypropylene syringes. At low concentrations (less than 0.1 MIU/mL) interferon may bind to PVC. However this is believed to be a non-significant interaction.[1]

Compatibility with other drugs: Interferon α-2b(rbe) powder should only be reconstituted with water for injections. However, it is known to be compatible with 0.9% sodium chloride, Ringer's solution and lactated Ringer's (Hartmann's) solution, although it is incompatible with glucose solutions.

3.2 *Stability in clinical practice*

Qualitative gradient-elution HPLC studies[3] on the degradation of aqueous solutions of interferon α-2b(rbe) lyophilised powder at a concentration of 430 000 IU/mL have shown significant degradation over 5 days of storage at 4°C, with measurable degradation products appearing after 48 hours. At 37°C, degradation product peaks were observed after 4 hours.

However, interferon α-2b(rbe) has been shown to be stable for infusion over a 24-hour period[2] if the following criteria are strictly adhered to:

▼ temperature is not greater than 25°C
▼ concentration of interferon α-2b is higher than 1 MIU/mL
▼ infusion container is glass or PVC (Viaflex).

The stability of interferon α-2b(rbe) can be summarised as shown in the following table:[2–6]

Presentation	Temperature (°C)	Stability period
Lyophilised powder in vials	2–8	3 years
Lyophilised powder in vials	15–25	28 days
Reconstituted solutions in vial or syringe	2–8	28 days
Reconstituted solutions in vial	15–25	14 days
Reconstituted solutions in syringe	15–25	24 hours
Reconstituted solution frozen (including four freeze–thaw cycles)	−20	56 days
Reconstituted solution frozen	−80	1 year
Reconstituted solution 100 million units in 50 mL (2 million units/mL) in water for injections in a bladder Urotainer	4	21 days
Multi-dose pen	2–8	12 months
Solution in vial	2–8	2 years
Solution in vial	15–25	4 weeks

4 Clinical use

Type of cytotoxic agent: Activator of natural killer cells.

Indications: Interferon α-2b(rbe) is licensed within the UK for use in the treatment of chronic myelogenous leukaemia, multiple myeloma (maintenance therapy), low-grade non-Hodgkin's lymphoma (adjunctive with chemotherapy), hairy-cell leukaemia, AIDS-related Kaposi's sarcoma (in patients without a history of opportunistic infection), genital warts (condylomata acuminata), chronic active hepatitis B and chronic hepatitis C.[1] Non-licensed indications (for which there are large research programmes) include malignant melanoma, renal-cell carcinoma and superficial bladder cancer.

Dosage:

▼ Chronic myelogenous leukaemia: the recommended daily dose is 4 to 5 MIU administered subcutaneously daily. When the white-blood-cell count is controlled, the dosage may be administered three times a week (on alternate days).
▼ Multiple myeloma: maintenance therapy – in patients who are in plateau phase following induction chemotherapy. May be administered as monotherapy subcutaneously at a dose of 3 MIU/m² three times a week (on alternate days).
▼ Non-Hodgkin's lymphoma: adjunctive with chemotherapy. May be administered subcutaneously at a dose of 5 MIU three times per week (on alternate days) for a duration of 18 months.
▼ Hairy-cell leukaemia: the recommended dose is 2 MIU/m², administered three times a week (every other day). The normalisation of one or more haematological variables begins with 1 month of therapy. Improvement in all three haematological variables (granulocyte count, platelet count and haemoglobin level) may require treatment for 6 months or more.

▼ AIDS-related Kaposi's sarcoma: the optimal dosage is not yet known. Efficacy has been demonstrated at a dose of 30 MIU/m^2 three to five times a week, subcutaneously or intramuscularly. Lower doses (i.e. 10 to 12 MIU/m^2/day) have also been used without apparent loss of efficacy.

▼ Condylomata acuminata: the lesion or lesions to be injected should be cleaned first with a sterile alcohol pad. The intralesional injection should be made at the base of the lesion using a fine needle (30-gauge). Inject 0.1 mL of reconstituted solution containing 1 MIU into the lesion three times per week on alternate days for 3 weeks. As many as five lesions can be treated at one time. The maximum total dose administered each week should not exceed 15 MIU.

▼ Chronic active hepatitis B: the optimal schedule of treatment has not yet been established. The dosage is usually in the range of 2.5 to 5 MIU/m^2 of body surface area administered subcutaneously three times a week for a period of 4 to 6 months.

▼ Chronic hepatitis C/non-A, non-B: the recommended dose is 3 MIU administered subcutaneously three times a week for up to 18 months.

5 Preparation of injection

Intron A lyophilised powder should be reconstituted with 1 mL of water for injections (or for condylomata acuminata with sufficient to produce a concentration of 1 MIU/0.1 mL). The vials should be swirled gently. Vigorous shaking should be avoided. Intron A ready-made solution is supplied at a concentration of 10 MIU.

Bolus administration: 2–30 MIU/m^2 injected subcutaneously.
The multi-dose pen should be removed from the refrigerator 30 minutes before each use to allow warming to room temperature. A fresh needle should be used for each injection, and the device should not be used for more than 2 weeks after first opening the container. The device should not be stored at room temperature for more than 48 hours.[1]

Intravenous infusion: Not recommended due to poor drug stability, unless interferon α-2b(rbe) is being used as part of a high-dose protocol, when adherence to the infusion stability criteria and conditions should be observed.

Extravasation: Group 5 classification (neutral). No recommendations available (*see* Chapter 6).

6 Destruction of drug or contaminated articles

Disposal: Excess interferon α-2b(rbe) solution may be disposed of into a drain with copious amounts of water. All other waste, including contaminated packaging or cleaning materials and used protective clothing, must be placed with clinical waste for incineration. When dealing with broken vials, disposable gloves, eye protection and a dust mask should be worn.

Contact with skin: Remove contaminated clothing and wash skin thoroughly with soap and water. If the eyes are contaminated, irrigate with water and obtain medical advice.

References

1 ABPI (1999) *Data Sheet Compendium 1999–2000*. DataPharm Publications Ltd, London, 1481–8.
2 Schering Corporation (1995) Personal communication.
3 Palmer AJ *et al.* (1988) Qualitative studies on interferon alfa-2b in prolonged continuous infusion regimes using gradient-elution high-performance liquid chromatography. *J Clin Pharm Ther.* **13**: 225–31.
4 Merigan TC *et al.* (1978) Preliminary observations on the effect of human leukocyte interferon in non-Hodgkin's lymphoma. *NEJM.* **199**: 1449–54.
5 Swada T *et al.* (1979) Preliminary report on the clinical use of human leukocyte interferon in neuroblastoma. *Cancer Treat Rep.* **63**: 2111.
6 Schepart B *et al.* (1995) Long-term stability of interferon alfa-2b diluted to 2 million units/mL. *Am J Health-Syst Pharm.* **52**: 2128–30.

Prepared by Andrew Stanley

RITUXIMAB

1 General details

Approved name: Rituximab.

Proprietary name: MabThera.

Manufacturer or supplier: Roche Products Ltd.

Presentation and formulation details: A sterile solution supplied in a single-use preservative-free clear glass vial with butyl rubber stopper containing rituximab 100 mg/mL as a 10-mL or 50-mL vial. Inactive excipients include sodium citrate, polysorbate 80, sodium chloride, sodium hydroxide and hydrochloric acid.

Storage and shelf-life of unopened container: Rituximab should be stored at 2–8°C and protected from direct sunlight. Under these conditions it has a shelf-life of 24 months.[1]

2 Chemistry

Type: Chimeric mouse/human anti-CD20 antibody.

Structure: Ig G1 kappa antibody containing murine light- and heavy-chain variable regions and human gamma-1 heavy-chain and kappa light-chain constant 4'-(dihydrogen phosphate).

Solubility: Soluble in water.

3 Stability profile

When rituximab is diluted as directed, it is chemically stable at room temperature for 12 hours. If necessary, it may initially be stored at 2–8°C and is chemically stable for 24 hours.[1]

No incompatibilities between rituximab and polyvinyl chloride or polyethylene bags or infusion sets have been observed.[1]

4 Clinical use

Indications: Treatment of patients with stage III–IV follicular lymphoma who are chemoresistant or who are in their second or subsequent relapse after chemotherapy.[1]

Dosage and administration: 375 mg/m² as an intravenous infusion once weekly for 4 weeks.

5 Preparation of injection

At all stages of preparation the product must be handled gently to avoid foaming.

Bolus administration: Not recommended.

Intravenous infusion: Withdraw the appropriate amount of Rituximab from the vial and add an infusion bag containing 0.9% sodium chloride or 5% glucose to give a final concentration of 1–4 mg/mL. The infusion bag should be inverted gently to mix the solution in order to avoid foaming.[1] For the first infusion, the initial rate for infusion is 50 mg/hour, and after the first 30 minutes it can be escalated by 50 mg/hour increments every 30 minutes to a maximum of 400 mg/hour. For subsequent infusions the initial rate of infusion can be 100 mg/hour, increasing by 100 mg/hour increments at 30-minute intervals to a maximum of 400 mg/hour.

Extravasation: Group 5 classification (neutral). No recommendations available.

6 Destruction of drug or contaminated articles

Disposal: Incinerate as special waste.[2]

Contact with skin: Wash with soap and water for at least 15 minutes. In the event of redness or itching, obtain medical advice.[2]

References

1 ABPI (1999) *ABPI Data Sheet Compendium* 1999–2000. DataPharm Publications Ltd, London, 1331–2.
2 Roche Products Ltd (1998) *MabThera Safety Data Sheet*. Roche Products Ltd, Welwyn Garden City.

Prepared by Andrew Stanley

AMIFOSTINE

1 General details

Approved name: Amifostine.

Proprietary names: Ethyol.

Manufacturer or supplier: Schering-Plough Ltd.

Presentation and formulation details: Amifostine is supplied as a sterile lyophilised powder. Each vial contains 500 mg of amifostine anhydrous and 500 mg of mannitol.[1,2]

Storage and shelf-life of unopened container: Shelf-life is 2 years stored at room temperature.[2]

2 Chemistry

Type: Amifostine is a pro-drug that is non-reactive with the electrophilic groups of chemotherapeutic agents.

Molecular structure: 5-2 (3-aminopropylamino)-ethylphosphoric acid.

$$NH_2-CH_2-CH_2-CH_2-NH(CH_2)_2\ S-\overset{\displaystyle OH}{\underset{\displaystyle OH}{P}}\!\!=\!\!O$$

Molecular weight: 214.2.

Solubility: Amifostine is soluble in water, 0.9% sodium chloride and phosphate buffer at pH 7.0.[1]

3 Stability profile

3.1 Physical and chemical stability

Solutions containing amifostine 500 mg/10 mL and 0.9% sodium chloride are stable for 8 hours at room temperature (15–25°C), or for 24 hours under refrigeration (2–8°C).[1,3]

Effect of pH: The pH of the reconstituted solution is in the range 6–8.

Effect of light: No information available.

Container compatibility: Amifostine has been shown to be compatible with glass and PVC infusion containers.[1]

3.2 Stability in clinical practice

Amifostine at 50 mg/mL is stable in 0.9% sodium chloride for 8 hours at 15–25°C, and for 24 hours at 2–8°C.[1,3]

4 Clinical use

Type of pharmaceutical: Amifostine is dephosphorylated by the enzyme alkaline phosphatase to the active free thiol S[(aminopropyl) amino] ethanethiol.

Dephosphorylation occurs more rapidly in normal tissue than in bulky tumour masses, as tumour masses are relatively hypovascular and the interstitial pH of tumours is relatively acidic and thereby kinetically unfavourable to the capillary-associated alkaline phosphatase. The dephosphorylated metabolite readily enters non-cancerous cells by facilitated diffusion, providing protection against oxygen-based radicals and electrophilic reactive drugs (e.g. alkylating agents and aquated organoplatinum anticancer drugs) by donating H^+ from its nucleophilic-free sulphydryl group, thus deactivating reactive cytotoxic agents.[4]

Main indications: Amifostine is licensed for the reduction of neutropenic-related risk of infection due to combined cyclophosphamide–cisplatinum therapy in patients with advanced FIGO stage III or IV ovarian carcinoma.[2]

Dosage: 910 mg/m². Similar doses are used for the reduction of nephotoxicity associated with cisplatin.[2]

5 Preparation of injection

Reconstitution: The contents of the vial are dissolved in 9.7 mL of 0.9% sodium chloride and gently shaken to produce a solution containing 50 mg/mL amifostine.

Bolus administration: Not recommended.

Intravenous infusion: The required volume of reconstituted solution is added to 100–200 mL of 0.9% sodium chloride and infused over not less than 15 minutes.[2]

References

1 Schering-Plough UK (1996) Personal communication.
2 ABPI (1999) *ABPI DataSheet Compendium 1999–2000.* Datapharm Publications Ltd, London, 1480–1.
3 Schering-Plough Ltd (1995) *Investigators' Brochure – Ethyol.* Schering-Plough Ltd, Welwyn Garden City.
4 Schering-Plough Ltd (1994) *Ethyol (Amifostine) for the Prevention of Chemotherapy-Induced Toxicity. Product Monograph.* Schering-Plough Ltd, Welwyn Garden City.

Prepared by Andrew Stanley

CALCIUM FOLINATE

1 General details

Approved names: Calcium folinate, Calcium leucovorin.

Proprietary names: Lederfolin, Refolinon, Rescufolin, Wellcovorin.

Manufacturer or supplier: Wyeth Laboratories Ltd, Pharmacia, Nordic, Faulding Pharmaceuticals plc.

Presentation and formulation details: Lyophilised powder for reconstitution in glass vials, or solution in water for injections in ampoules or vials. Solutions also contain sodium chloride, and pH is adjusted to 6.5–8.5 (depending on the manufacturer) using sodium hydroxide or hydrochloric acid.[1,2]

Storage and shelf-life of unopened container: Lyophilised powder for reconstitution has a shelf-life of 3 years when stored at 15–30°C. Solution has a shelf-life of 18 months or 2 years when stored at 2–8°C and protected from light.

2 Chemistry

Molecular structure: Calcium *N*-[4-(2-amino-5-formyl-5,6,7,8-tetrahydro-4-hydroxypteridin-6-ylmethylamino)benzoyl]-L(+)glutamate.

Molecular weight: 511.5.

Solubility: Very soluble in water and practically insoluble in alcohol.

3 Stability profile

3.1 Physical and chemical stability

Calcium folinate degradation occurs by two routes, namely hydrolysis or a conversion reaction. The main products of hydrolysis are 5-formyl tetrahydropteridin-6-carboxylic acid and *N*-(*p*-aminobenzoyl) glutamic acid, which undergoes further hydrolysis to *p*-aminobenzoic acid and glutamic acid. The conversion reaction involves the exchange of the formyl group from the N^5 nitrogen of the pteridinyl moiety to the N^{10} nitrogen of the *p*-aminobenzoylglutamic acid group to produce N^{10} formylfolic acid.[3] Hydrolysis occurs at acid pH values, particularly below pH 5.

Compatibility with infusion fluids: Calcium folinate is compatible with sodium chloride, glucose and compound sodium lactate infusion fluids. and is stable in both glass and PVC containers.[3,4]

Compatibility with other drugs: Calcium folinate has been shown to be compatible with cisplatin with or without floxuridine,[5] and with floxuridine alone.[6,7] Studies had indicated that calcium folinate could be mixed with fluorouracil.[7,8] However, a crystalline precipitate may form in stored mixtures in less than 4 days[9,10] and, as a consequence, manufacturers state that calcium folinate should not be mixed with fluorouracil.

Compatibility studies of mixing with other drugs briefly in a syringe, or in a simulated Y-site injection, have indicated compatibility with a number of drugs.[11–14] Incompatibility was observed with droperidol[11] and foscarnet.[15]

3.2 Stability in clinical practice

If stored at room temperature or refrigerated, and protected from light, calcium folinate has been shown to be stable for 96 hours at a concentration of 1.0–1.5 mg/mL in 0.9% sodium chloride or 5% glucose. Lower concentrations appear to be less stable and are therefore not suitable for extended expiry.[3]

The extended stability data that have been reported for mixtures with fluoropyrimidines should be treated with caution since the discovery of crystalline deposits in mixtures with fluorouracil. Mixtures for immediate intravenous infusion may be compatible, but are not recommended by the manufacturers.

3.3 Stability in specialised delivery systems

No data available.

4 Clinical use

Type of pharmaceutical: An essential coenzyme. It is the calcium salt of a formyl derivative of tetrahydrofolic acid, the metabolite and active form of folic acid.

Main indications: These are as follows:

▼ to reduce the toxicity and counteract the action of folate antagonists such as methotrexate in cytotoxic therapy (calcium folinate rescue)
▼ to enhance the effects of fluorouracil cytotoxic therapy.

Dosage:

▼ For calcium folinate rescue, normal dosage is for up to 150 mg to be given in divided doses over 24–28 hours, starting 8–24 hours after the methotrexate dose.
▼ For enhancing the effect of fluorouracil, doses of 20–200 mg/m² are given prior to doses of fluorouracil.

5 Preparation of injection

Reconstitution: Calcium folinate should be reconstituted with water for injections.

Bolus administration: Doses of 15–30 mg may be administered as an intravenous or intramuscular injection.

Intravenous infusion: Calcium folate may be diluted in 0.9% sodium chloride, 5% glucose or compound sodium lactate infusions, and administered over not less than 3–5 minutes because of the calcium content.

6 Destruction of drug or contaminated articles

Calcium folinate is non-hazardous and can be handled and disposed of as a non-cytotoxic pharmaceutical.

References

1 ABPI (1999) *ABPI Data Sheet Compendium 1999–2000*. DataPharm Publications Ltd, London, 392–3.
2 ABPI (1999) *ABPI Data Sheet Compendium 1999–2000*. DataPharm Publications Ltd, London, 1723–5.
3 Lecompte D *et al.* (1991) Stability study of reconstituted and diluted solutions of calcium folinate. *Pharm Ind.* **1**: 90–4.
4 Benvenuto JA *et al.* (1981) Stability and compatibility of antitumour agents in glass and plastic containers. *Am J Hosp Pharm.* **38**: 1914–18.
5 Williams DA and Lokich J (1992) A review of the stability and compatibility of antineoplastic drugs for multiple-drug infusions. *Cancer Chemother Pharmacol.* **31**: 171–81.
6 Smith JA *et al.* (1989) Stability of floxuridine and leucovorin calcium admixtures for intraperitoneal administration. *Am J Hosp Pharm.* **46**: 985–9.
7 Anderson N *et al.* (1989) A phase 1 clinical trial of combined fluoropyrimidines with leucovorin in a 14-day infusion. *Cancer.* **63**: 233–7.
8 Milano G *et al.* (1993) Long-term stability of 5-fluorouracil and folinic acid admixtures. *Eur J Cancer.* **29A**: 129–32.
9 Adralan B and Flores MR (1993) A new complication of permanent indwelling central venous catheters using high-dose fluorouracil and leucovorin. *J Clin Oncol.* **11**: 384.
10 Trissel LA *et al.* (1995) Incompatibility of fluorouracil with leucovorin calcium or levoleucovorin calcium. *Am J Health-Syst Pharm.* **52**: 710–15.
11 Cohen MH *et al.* (1985) Drug precipitation within IV tubing: a potential hazard of chemotherapy administration. *Cancer Treat Rep.* **69**: 1325–6.
12 Trissel LA and Martinez JF (1994) Physical compatibility of filgrastim with selected drugs during simulated Y-site administration. *Am J Hosp Pharm.* **51**: 1907–13.
13 Trissel LA and Martinez JF (1994) Physical compatibility of piperacillin sodium plus tazobactam sodium with selected drugs during simulated Y-site administration. *Am J Hosp Pharm.* **51**: 672–8.
14 Min DI *et al.* (1992) Visual compatibility of tacrolimus with commonly used drugs during simulated Y-site injection. *Am J Hosp Pharm.* **49**: 2964–6.
15 Lor E and Takagi J (1990) Visible compatibility of foscarnet with other injectable drugs. *Am J Hosp Pharm.* **47**: 157–9.

Prepared by Richard Needle

CALCIUM LEVOFOLINATE

1 General details

Approved names: Calcium levofolinate, levoleucovorin.

Proprietary names: Isovorin.

Manufacturer or supplier: Wyeth Laboratories Ltd.

Presentation and formulation details: Solution in water for injections, also containing sodium chloride, hydrochloric acid and sodium hydroxide.[1]

2 Chemistry

Molecular structure: pure L-isomer of calcium folinate.

Molecular weight: 511.5.

Solubility: Very soluble in water.

3 Stability profile

3.1 Physical and chemical stability

It is anticipated that calcium levofolinate has a similar stability profile to calcium folinate.

Compatibility with infusion fluids: Calcium levofolinate is compatible with 0.9% sodium chloride, 5% glucose and compound sodium lactate infusions, and is compatible with glass, PVC, elastomeric and polypropylene containers.[2]

Compatibility with other drugs: It is anticipated that calcium levofolinate has an identical compatibility profile to calcium folinate.

3.2 Stability in clinical practice

The commercially available solution of concentration 10 mg/mL in a PVC minibag or a syringe protected from light has been shown to be stable for 98 days in a refrigerator followed by 3 days at room temperature. The 10 mg/mL solution, when stored in an elastomeric container and protected from light, is stable for 98 days in a refrigerator followed by 7 days at body temperature (33°C), or 14 days at room temperature followed by 7 days at body temperature.[2]

   When diluted to 5 mg/mL in 0.9% sodium chloride or 5% glucose, the stability profile has been shown to be equal to that of the 10 mg/mL solution.[2]

When diluted to 0.2 mg/mL in 0.9% sodium chloride, calcium levofolinate is stable in a PVC bag or syringe, when protected from light, for 61 days in a refrigerator or for 21 days at room temperature.[2]

When diluted to 0.2 mg/mL in 5% glucose and protected from light in a PVC minibag or a syringe, it is stable for 33 days in a refrigerator.[2]

4 Clinical use

Type of pharmaceutical: An essential coenzyme. It is the calcium salt of the pharmacologically active L-isomer of 5-formyltetrahydrofolic acid, the metabolite and active form of folic acid.

Main indications: These are as follows:

▼ to reduce the toxicity and counteract the action of folate antagonists such as methotrexate in cytotoxic therapy (calcium folinate rescue)
▼ to enhance the effects of fluorouracil cytotoxic therapy.

Dosage:

▼ For calcium levofolinate rescue the normal dosage is 7.5 mg administered by intramuscular injection or intravenous injection or infusion every 6 hours for 10 doses, starting 24 hours after the beginning of the methotrexate dose.
▼ For enhancing the effect of fluorouracil, doses of between 10 and 100 mg/m^2 are given prior to doses of fluorouracil.

5 Preparation of injection

Bolus administration: The commercially available injection may be administered as an intramuscular or intravenous bolus.

Intravenous infusion: May be diluted in sodium chloride, glucose or compound sodium lactate solution. Not more than 160 mg calcium levofolinate should be administered per minute because of the calcium content.

6 Destruction of drug or contaminated articles

Calcium levofolinate is non-hazardous and can be handled and disposed of as a non-cytotoxic pharmaceutical.

References

1 ABPI (1999) *ABPI Data Sheet Compendium 1999–2000.* DataPharm Publications Ltd, London, 1732–3.
2 Wyeth Laboratories (1999) Personal communication.

Prepared by Richard Needle

DEXRAZOXONE

1 General details

Approved name: Dexrazoxone.

Proprietary names: Zinecard, ADR-529, ICRF-187.

Manufacturer or supplier: Pharmacia, Upjohn.

Presentation and formulation details: Sterile white to off-white lyophilised powder in vials containing either 250 mg or 500 mg dexrazoxone, pH-adjusted with hydrochloric acid.

   Each vial is supplied with a vial of diluent containing M/6 sodium lactate injection USP in vials of 25 mL (accompanying 250 mg vials) and 50 mL (accompanying 500-mg vials), where each mL of diluent contains 18.6 mg anhydrous sodium lactate in water for injections, the pH being adjusted with sodium hydroxide and/or hydrochloric acid.[1]

Storage and shelf-life of unopened container: Two years if stored at 15–30°C.

2 Chemistry

Type: Dexrazoxone is a cyclic derivative of edetic acid (EDTA).[2]

Molecular structure: 4,4'-(1-methyl-1,2-ethanediyl) *bis* [2,6-piperazinedione].

Molecular weight: 268.28.

Solubility: Dexrazoxone is only sparingly soluble in water.

3 Stability profile

3.1 Physical and chemical stability

The reconstituted solution at a concentration of 10 mg/10 mL is reported to be stable for 6 hours when stored at 2–8°C.[3,4]

Effect of pH: No information is available. However, the molecule is likely to be sensitive to extremes of pH.

Effects of temperature: Dexrazoxone shows significant degradation at temperatures above 8°C, with a maximum stability of 6 hours at 15–30°C.[3]

3.2 Stability in clinical practice

The reconstituted solution may be diluted with either 0.9% sodium chloride or 5% glucose to a concentration of 1.4–5.0 mg/mL and should be refrigerated if it is not to be used immediately, with a maximum shelf life after reconstitution of 6 hours, at temperatures up to 30°C.

4 Clinical use

Main indications: Reduction of the incidence and severity of cardiomyopathy associated with doxorubicin administration in women with metastatic breast cancer who have received a cumulative dose of 300 mg/m² doxorubicin, and who would benefit from continuation of doxorubicin therapy.[1-3]

Dosage: Dexrazoxone is used at a ratio of 10:1 with doxorubicin (e.g. 500 mg/m² dexrazoxone to 50 mg/m² doxorubicin). Dexrazoxone should be administered not more than 30 minutes after initiating doxorubicin therapy.

5 Preparation of injection

Reconstitution: Reconstitute the contents of each vial with the diluent supplied to provide a solution containing 10 mg/mL dexrazoxone.

Bolus injection: May be administered by slow intravenous injection.

Intravenous infusion: May be further diluted and administered by intravenous infusion.

6 Destruction of drug or contaminated articles

Incineration: 1000°C.

Chemical: Dexrazoxone may be inactivated by adding sodium hypochlorite solution (at the same strength as household bleach) until the dexrazoxone solution is decolorised.[4]

Contact with skin and eyes: Dexrazoxone is an irritant to mucous membranes. The affected areas should be washed with copious amounts of water, and a medical opinion obtained.[4]

References

1 Pharmacia Upjohn (1995) *US Data Sheet.* Pharmacia Upjohn, Kalamazoo.
2 Anon. (1995) New drug counters doxorubicin cardiotoxicity not for use at start of chemotherapy. *Am J Health-Syst Pharm.* **52**: 2076.
3 Pharmacia Upjohn (1996) *Zinecard – Cardioprotective Agent Product Monograph.* Pharmacia Upjohn, Milton Keynes.
4 Pharmacia Upjohn (1995) Personal communication.

Prepared by Andrew Stanley

FILGRASTIM

1 General details

Approved name: Filgrastim.

Proprietary name: Neupogen.

Manufacturer or supplier: Amgen Ltd.

Presentation and formulation details: Filgrastim is a sterile clear colourless liquid, formulated in an aqueous sodium acetate buffer, pH 4, containing 4% mannitol and 0.004% polysorbate 80.

Filgrastim contains 30 MU (300 μg/mL). Neupogen 30 contains 30 MU of filgrastim in a 1-mL pre-filled syringe. Neupogen 48 contains 48 MU of filgrastim in a 1.6-mL pre-filled syringe.

Storage and shelf-life of unopened container: Filgrastim should be stored at 2–8°C. It should not be frozen. The pack is provided with an indicator to detect possible freezing. Vials that have been frozen (the indicator shows red) should not be used. A single brief period (up to 7 days) of exposure to elevated temperatures (up to 37°C) does not affect stability. Unopened vials or pre-filled syringes of filgrastim have a shelf-life of 2 years from the date of manufacture.[1]

2 Chemistry

Type: Non-glycosylated recombinant methionyl human granulocyte-colony-stimulating factor (r-metHuG-CSF), produced by recombinant DNA technology using an *Escherichia coli* strain.

Molecular structure: The amino-acid composition of the mature r-metHuG-CSF sequence is as follows:

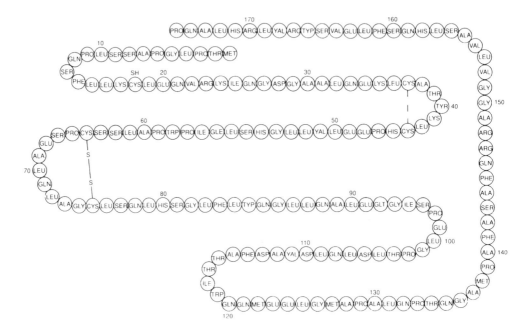

The solution contains filgrastim (r-metHuG-CSF) as a hydrophobic protein composed of 175 amino acids. The recombinant protein differs from natural human G-CSF by virtue of an additional amino-terminal methionine residue and the absence of O-glycosylation. There are no potential sites of N-glycosylation on the natural human G-CSF or recombinant G-CSF molecules.

Molecular weight: Approximately 18–22 000.

Solubility: Filgrastim is soluble in aqueous solutions.

3 Stability profile

3.1 *Physical and chemical stability*

pH and physical stability: The pH of filgrastim is 4.0. Low pH and low salt concentration, together with additives, enhance filgrastim stability by preventing protein aggregation. The product should not be vigorously shaken when diluting, in order to avoid the formation of protein aggregates which might induce undesirable effects in the patient (e.g. formation of antibodies).

Stability on dilution: Diluted filgrastim solutions should not be prepared more than 24 hours before administration, and should be stored at between 2 and 8°C. Solutions of filgrastim at concentrations of 15 µg/mL or higher are stable at room temperature for up to 1 week.[2]

Container compatibility: Filgrastim diluted in 5% glucose or in 5% glucose plus human albumin is compatible with a variety of plastics. These include PVC, polyolefin (a copolymer of polypropylene and polyethylene) and polypropylene.[2] If filgrastim is to be used as an infusion with the administration set composed of unknown material, human serum albumin (HSA) should always be added as a protective protein to the diluent to a concentration of at least 2 mg/mL. It is not necessary to protect filgrastim from light when the drug is being prepared for administration, but it is recommended that filgrastim is stored within the dispensing pack.[2]

Drug compatibility: The compatibility of filgrastim with other products and solutions has not been evaluated. Therefore filgrastim should not be given together with any other drugs in the same infusion set, and also it should not be diluted in any other solution containing sodium chloride.

3.2 *Stability in clinical practice*

Undiluted filgrastim in tuberculin syringes (Becton-Dickinson)[2] is stable for up to 24 hours at controlled room temperature (25°C and not exceeding 37°C) or for up to 7 days in the refrigerator at 2–8°C. Filgrastim does not contain any preservatives. The manufacturer recommends that, in order to reduce the possibility of bacterial proliferation, filgrastim in syringes should be stored at 2–8°C and used within 24 hours of preparation.[1]

Filgrastim may be diluted in 5% glucose intravenous solution. Very dilute solutions of filgrastim may be adsorbed on to glass and plastic materials. Therefore dilution to a final concentration of less than 0.2 MU (2 µg/mL) is not recommended.[2]

For solutions diluted to concentrations below 1.5 MU (15 µg/mL), human serum albumia (HSA) should be added to a final concentration of 2 mg/mL (i.e. in a final injection volume of 20 mL). Total doses of filgrastim of less than 30 MU (300 μg) should be given with 0.2 mL of 20% HSA.[2]

4 Clinical use

Indications: Filgrastim is indicated for reducing both the duration of neutropenia and the incidence of febrile neutropenia in patients treated with established cytotoxic chemotherapy for non-myeloid malignancy. This allows the clinician to optimise cytotoxic chemotherapy and to reduce the incidence of febrile neutropenia and its clinical sequelae. The indication includes the reduction in duration of neutropenia and its clinical sequelae after myeloablative therapy which is followed by bone-marrow transplantation.

In patients with severe congenital, cyclic or idiopathic neutropenia (with an absolute neutrophil count (ANC) of $\leq 0.5 \times 10^9$/L), or a history of severe or recurrent infections, long-term treatment with filgrastim is indicated to increase the ANC and reduce the incidence and duration of infection-related events.

Filgrastim mobilises peripheral blood progenitor cells (PBPCs) (as a single mobilising agent, or following myelosuppressive chemotherapy) for autologous PBPC transplant. The infusion of filgrastim-mobilised PBPCs accelerates haematopoietic recovery, reducing the need for platelet transfusions after myelosuppressive chemotherapy.

Filgrastim is also indicated in patients with advanced HIV infection and neutropenia (ANC $<1 \times 10^9$/L), allowing scheduled dosing of myelosuppressive medication.

Dosage:

▼ Established cytotoxic chemotherapy (adults): when filgrastim is administered as an adjunct to standard dose chemotherapy, the recommended dose is 5 μg/kg/day. Individual patients may require dose escalation if the time taken to respond or the magnitude of the neutrophil response is unacceptable after 5 to 7 days of filgrastim therapy. A maximum tolerated dose has not yet been identified. Patients have received doses as high as 115 μg/kg/day, with no toxic effects attributable to filgrastim.

▼ Myeloablative therapy followed by bone-marrow transplantation: filgrastim administration should not commence during the initial 24 hours after bone-marrow infusion. The initial dosage of 10 μg/kg/day is reduced to 5 μg/kg/day once the neutrophil nadir has passed and the ANC has exceeded 1.0×10^9/L for three consecutive days.

▼ Mobilisation of PBPCs: as a single agent, 10 μg/kg/day subcutaneously for six consecutive days is the recommended dose for achieving effective mobilisation of PBPCs. Alternatively, in conjunction with myelosuppressive chemotherapy, 5 μg/kg/day is given subcutaneously daily from the first day post-chemotherapy until the expected neutrophil nadir has passed and the neutrophil count has recovered to the normal range. For patients who have not had extensive chemotherapy, a single apheresis is often sufficient. In other circumstances, additional leukaphereses are recommended.

▼ Severe chronic neutropenia (children or adults): for the treatment of congenital neutropenia, the initial recommended dose is 12 μg/kg/day subcutaneously, but a lower dosage of 5 μg/kg/day subcutaneously is used for idiopathic or cyclic neutropenia. Treatment is continued until an ANC of $>1.5 \times 10^9$/L can be maintained. Then the minimum doses required to maintain this level are ascertained and administered.

▼ Advanced HIV infection: for the treatment of neutropenia, an initial dose of 1–4 µg/kg/day subcutaneously is recommended until a normal neutrophil count (ANC of $\geq 2.0 \times 10^9$/L) is reached and can be maintained. Subsequent maintenance doses of 300 µg/day subcutaneously are recommended. Further dose adjustment (and possibly long-term administration) may be necessary to maintain the ANC at $\geq 2.0 \times 10^9$/L.

Filgrastim can be administered either as a bolus subcutaneous injection or as a short (30-minute) or continuous IV or subcutaneous infusion.[1]

Timing of administration: Filgrastim administration should be initiated at least 24 hours after the last dose of chemotherapy and should be discontinued at least 24 hours before the next chemotherapy dose. This is because filgrastim stimulates neutrophil precursor-cell proliferation and, since many antineoplastic agents target rapidly proliferating cells, co-administration of filgrastim and antineoplastic therapy may theoretically lead to abolition of neutrophil precursors. Filgrastim administration should be continued throughout the expected chemotherapy-induced nadir until the patient achieves an ANC of $\geq 10\,000$ cells/mL.[1]

Patients who are receiving dose-intensified chemotherapy should be continued on filgrastim until two consecutive ANCs register more than 10 000 cells/mL. The time needed to achieve this ANC level will vary depending on the chemotherapy regimen, the patient's underlying disease, the prior treatment history and the dose of filgrastim.[1]

5 Preparation of injection

Reconstitution: Not applicable.

Extravasation: Group 5 classification (neutral). No recommendations available (*see* Chapter 6).

6 Destruction of drug or contaminated articles

Disposal: Excess filgrastim solution may be disposed of into a drain with copious amounts of water. All other waste, including contaminated packaging or cleaning materials and used protective clothing, must be placed with clinical waste for incineration. When dealing with broken vials, disposable gloves, eye protection and a face mask should be worn.

Contact with skin: This is not thought to be a serious problem. A general procedure should be adopted of removing contaminated clothing and washing the skin thoroughly with soap and water. If the eyes are contaminated, irrigate with water and obtain medical advice.

References

1 ABPI (1999) *ABPI Data Sheet Compendium 1999–2000.* DataPharm Publications Ltd, London, 84–6.
2 Amgen (UK) Ltd (1996) Personal communication.

Prepared by Andrew Stanley

LENOGRASTIM

1 General details

Approved name: Lenograstim.

Proprietary name: Granocyte.

Manufacturer or supplier: Chugai Pharma UK Ltd.

Presentation and formulation details: Lenograstim is presented as single-use vials of lyophilised product with an ampoule of solvent containing water for injections.

Composition of the lyophilisate:[1]

Lenograstim	33.6 MIU	13.4 MIU
	263 µg	105 µg
Human albumin	1 mg	1 mg
Mannitol	50 mg	50 mg
Polysorbate-20	0.1 mg	0.1 mg
Disodium phosphate		
Sodium dihydrogen phosphate	pH 6.5	pH 6.5

The reconstituted product is formulated in an aqueous phosphate buffer at pH 6.5 and contains 5% mannitol, 0.1% human albumin and 0.01% polysorbate-20.[1]

Shelf-life of unopened container: 2 years.[1]

2 Chemistry

Type: Lenograstim, human G-CSF, is a recombinant glycoprotein identical to the naturally produced human granulocyte-colony-stimulating factor isolated from CHU-2, a human cell line.

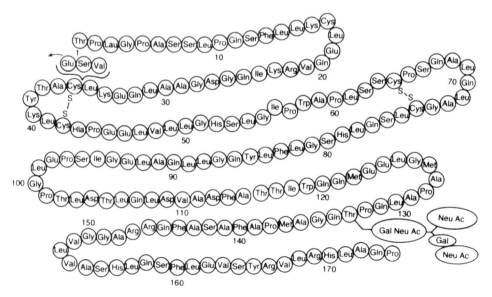

Molecular weight: Approximately 19 000.

Solubility: Soluble in aqueous solutions.

3 Stability profile

3.1 Physical and chemical stability

pH and physical stability: Lenograstim is formulated in a buffer, and after reconstitution the pH of the solution is 6.5. Protein aggregates may form when the solution is shaken vigorously. Therefore during reconstitution and when in solution lenograstim should not be shaken vigorously.[1,2]

Stability on reconstitution: Reconstituted lenograstim is stable in vials for up to 7 days at room temperature.[2]

Stability on dilution: Lenograstim should not be reconstituted and diluted more than 24 hours before administration. Diluted solutions should be stored in a refrigerator at 2–8°C.[1,2]

Container compatibility: When diluted in a saline solution, lenograstim is compatible with the polyvinyl chloride giving sets.[1]

If the material of the giving set is not known, the human albumin in the formulation acts as a protective protein to stabilise lenograstim against adsorption on to plastics.[1,2]

Compatibility with other drugs: The compatibility of lenograstim has been tested with intravenous fluids at room temperature for 24 hours. Lenograstim is compatible with 0.9% sodium chloride, 5% glucose and compound sodium lactate solutions for up to 24 hours.[1,2]

Compatibility with admixtures of other drugs has not been evaluated. Therefore lenograstim should not be given together with any other drugs in the same infusion set.[1,2]

3.2 Stability in clinical practice

Lenograstim should be stored in a refrigerator at 2–8°C. However, the stability of lenograstim is unaffected by exposure to temperatures of up to 30°C for a period of 14 days. After a single exposure within these limits, lenograstim may be returned to refrigeration and the original expiry date considered to apply.[2]

Lenograstim has been tested after storage for 6 months at 30°C. After this period the product was within the quality specification and therefore would be acceptable for use. The effect of this period of exposure on ultimate shelf-life is not defined. For periods of exposure longer than 2 weeks at room temperature, but less than 6 months, lenograstim should be returned to refrigeration and used within 6 months of the date of first exposure.[2]

Lenograstim reconstituted with 1 mL of water for injections is stable in polypropylene syringes for up to 14 days after storage at 30°C for 24 hours, and then at 5°C.

Lenograstim should be diluted in 0.9% sodium chloride for intravenous infusion.[1] The maximum dilution which should be performed is one vial into 100 mL of fluid (0.32 MIU/mL; 2.5 µg/mL).

Since human albumin solution is included in the formulation, it does not need to be added when dilution is performed.

4 Clinical use

Main indications: Lenograstim is indicated for reducing the duration of neutropenia and associated complications in patients with non-myeloid malignancy who have undergone bone-marrow transplantation or treatment with established cytotoxic chemotherapy regimens. By earlier recovery of neutrophil counts, the risk and severity of infection may be reduced and the cytotoxic chemotherapy schedule may be maintained in a higher proportion of patients.[1]

Dosage: The recommended dose of lenograstim is 150 µg/m²/day (19.2 MIU/m²/day). The 33.6-MIU vial of lenograstim is sufficient to treat patients with a body surface area (BSA) of up to 1.8 m², while the 13.4-MIU vial is sufficient to treat patients with a BSA of up to 0.7 m².

▼ Chemotherapy-induced neutropenia: lenograstim should be administered daily at the recommended dose as a subcutaneous injection starting on the day after completion of chemotherapy. Daily administration of lenograstim should continue until the expected nadir has passed and the neutrophil count has returned to a stable level compatible with treatment discontinuation, with a maximum of 28 consecutive days of treatment. Treatment with lenograstim should be discontinued at least 24 hours before starting a course of cytotoxic chemotherapy, since lenograstim-induced proliferation of bone-marrow precursor cells could theoretically enhance susceptibility to cytotoxic chemotherapy, increasing toxicity to the myeloid lineage.

If patients are receiving dose-intensified chemotherapy, they should continue lenograstim treatment until two consecutive ANC measurements of $>1 \times 10^9/L$ are obtained.

▼ Bone-marrow transplantation: lenograstim should be administered as a 30-minute intravenous infusion, diluted in isotonic saline solution, starting the day after transplantation. Dosing should continue until the expected nadir has passed and the neutrophil count has returned to a stable level compatible with treatment discontinuation, with a maximum of 28 consecutive days of treatment if necessary.

5 Preparation of injection

Reconstitution: Immediately prior to administration, lenograstim should be reconstituted by adding the extractable contents of one ampoule of solvent (water for injections) to the lenograstim vial and agitating gently. The contents should not be shaken vigorously. Dissolution should be complete within approximately 5 seconds, and the final concentration of lenograstim in the solution is 263 µg/mL.[1]

Bolus injection: The undiluted reconstituted solution may be administered by subcutaneous injection.

Intravenous infusion: May be further diluted in 50 mL (13.4 MIU product) or 100 mL (33.6 MIU product) of 0.9% sodium chloride in glass or PVC containers and administered by intravenous infusion.[1]

Extravasation: Group 5 classification (neutral). No recommendations available.

6 Destruction of drug or contaminated articles

Disposal: Excess lenograstim may be disposed of into a drain with water. All other waste, contaminated packaging, cleaning materials and protective clothing should be incinerated as clinical waste.

Contact with skin: There have been no reports of problems following skin contact. General measures such as removal of contaminated clothing and washing thoroughly with soap and water should be taken.

Contact with eyes: Irrigate with an appropriate eyewash solution, and obtain medical advice.

References

1 ABPI (1999) *ABPI Data Sheet Compendium 1999–2000*. DataPharm Publications Ltd, London, 308–10.
2 Chugai Pharma UK (1998) *Data on File*. Chugai Pharma UK, London.

Prepared by Andrew Stanley

MESNA

1 General details

Approved name: Mesna.

Proprietary name: Uromitexan.

Manufacturer or supplier: ASTA Medica Ltd.

Presentation and formulation details: Clear glass ampoules containing an aqueous solution of mesna, 400 mg in 4 mL and 1000 mg in 10 mL.[1]

Each ampoule also contains disodium edetate 0.25 mg/mL and sodium hydroxide as buffer.

Storage and shelf-life of unopened container: When stored below 30°C and protected from light, mesna has a shelf-life of 5 years.[1]

2 Chemistry

Type: Sulphydryl compound (not cytotoxic).

Molecular structure: Sodium 2-mercapto-ethanesulphonate, HS-CH-CH-SO.Na.

Molecular weight: 164.2.

Solubility: Water soluble.

3 Stability profile

3.1 Physical and chemical stability

Mesna degrades by oxidation to form dimesna. Mesna should be protected from light, but it is stable under normal lighting conditions during administration.[2]

Container compatibility: Compatible with glass, PVC and polypropylene.

Compatibility with other drugs: Compatible with ifosfamide in 0.9% sodium chloride, 5% glucose and Ringer's lactate infusions.[2]

3.2 Stability in clinical practice

Mesna is stable for up to 24 hours in a solution of 0.9% sodium chloride or in a solution of ifosfamide in 0.9% sodium chloride.[1] Mesna (3.3 g/L and 5 g/L) and ifosfamide (also at concentrations of 3.3 g/L and 5 g/L, respectively) were admixed in 5% glucose solution and Ringer's Lactate Solution for Injection. Mesna exhibited approximately 5% decomposition over 24 hours, while ifosfamide showed no decomposition during this period.[2]

Admixtures of mesna (40 mg/mL) and ifosfamide (50 mg/mL) in water for injections (10 mL) were stable in polypropylene syringes at 4 and 20°C over 28 days, with less than 5% loss of each component present.[3] At 50 mg/mL the admixture was stable for 24 hours at 37°C,[4] thus enabling ambulatory continuous infusion of this regimen. The undiluted formulation of mesna was found to be stable when stored in polypropylene syringes at 5, 24 or 35°C for at least 9 days.[5] (Mesna was also stable for at least 1 week when diluted 1:2 with various syrups for oral use and stored at 24°C.[5] Dilutions of mesna ranging from 1:2 to 1:100 in a variety of carbonated drinks, fruit juice and milk which were stored at 4°C showed no clinically significant change in drug concentration.[5])

3.3 Stability in specialised delivery systems

Ifosfamide in combination with mesna (each at 50 mg/mL) was stable for 24 hours at 37°C in Graseby 9000 Medication devices.[4]

4 Clinical use

Indications: Reduction of urotoxic side-effects of ifosfamide or cyclophosphamide.

Dosage: This is dependent on the dose and dosing schedule of ifosfamide or cyclophosphamide. The Data Sheet[1] should be consulted for detailed information to determine the optimum mesna dose and schedule in each case. Special schedules apply, for example, to children and patients receiving pelvic irradiation. Details of oral use of mesna injection are also described (mesna is also available in oral form as tablets containing 400 or 600 mg mesna as the sodium salt).

5 Preparation of injection

Dilution: Use undiluted for bolus administration. Add to oxazaphosphorine infusion for 24-hour infusion regimens. For oral administration, mesna should be taken in a soft drink immediately after opening the ampoule.

Bolus administration: Mesna is given over 15 minutes as 20% of the oxazaphosphorine dose and is repeated after 4 and 8 hours.

Intravenous infusion: Mesna is given as a concurrent infusion. Initially 20% of the oxazaphosphorine dose is given by intravenous bolus injection, followed by the oxazaphosphorine dose over 24 hours. A further infusion of 60% (w/w) of the oxazaphosphorine dose is then given over 12 hours.

Extravasation: Group 5 classification (neutral).

6 Destruction of drug or contaminated articles

Mesna is not cytotoxic.

References

1 ABPI (1999) *ABPI Data Sheet Compendium 1999–2000.* DataPharm Publications Ltd, London, 92–3.
2 Trissel LA *et al.* (1985) *Investigational Drugs: pharmaceutical data.* National Cancer Institute, Bethesda, MD.
3 Adams PS *et al.* (1987) Pharmaceutical aspects of home infusion therapy for cancer patients. *Pharm J.* **238**: 476–8.
4 Sewell GJ *et al.* (1994) Stability of drug infusions in ambulatory infusion devices. *Aust J Hosp Pharm.* **24**: 102–10.
5 Goren MP *et al.* (1991) The stability of mesna in beverages and syrup for oral administration. *Cancer Chemother Pharmacol.* **28**: 298–301.

Prepared by Graham Sewell

MOLGRAMOSTIN

1 General details

Approved name: Molgramostin.

Proprietary name: Leucomax.

Manufacturer or supplier: Novartis plc, Schering Plough Ltd.

Presentation and formulation details: White freeze-dried powder in glass vials for parenteral use, containing 1.67, 3.33 or 4.44 million international units (MIU) (150, 300 or 400 µg, respectively) of molgramostin for reconstitution. Each vial also contains mannitol, citric acid, dibasic sodium phosphate, polyethylene glycol and human albumin.[1,2]

Storage and shelf-life of unopened container: The product must be stored at 2–8°C and protected from light.[1,2]

2 Chemistry

Type: Recombinant human granulocyte macrophage-colony-stimulating factor (rHuGM-CSF).

Molecular structure: Water-soluble non-glycosylated protein produced by recombinant techniques.

Molecular structure: Not available.

Molecular weight: Not available.

Solubility: Freely soluble in water.

3 Stability profile

3.1 Physical and chemical stability

The manufacturers indicate that molgramostin is stable for 24 hours after reconstitution if stored at 2–8°C.[1,2]

Container compatibility: Molgramostin may be adsorbed on to containers and administration sets after reconstitution and dilution. The manufacturer recommends that molgramostin should not be diluted below 0.08 MIU/mL (7 µg/mL) when prepared for intravenous infusion, to avoid losses due to adsorption. Such solutions are compatible with glass or plastic containers and administration sets.[1,2]

Compatibility with other drugs: No information available.

3.2 Stability in clinical practice

Molgramostin is stable after reconstitution in water for injections for up to 24 hours if stored at 2–8°C. Molgramostin is also stable after further dilution in 0.9% sodium chloride or 5% glucose to a concentration of not less than 0.08 MIU/mL after dilution, for 24 hours at 2–8°C.[1,2]

3.3 Stability in specialised delivery systems

Molgramostin is incompatible with the Port-A-Cath device reservoir, due to adsorption.[1,2]

4 Clinical use

Type: Granulocyte macrophage-colony-stimulating factor (rHuGM-CSF).

Main indications: Molgramostin is indicated for reducing the risk of infection by decreasing the severity of cytotoxic chemotherapy-induced neutropenia. It is also used to accelerate myeloid recovery following bone-marrow transplantation.

Dosage: In cancer chemotherapy, the recommended dosage regimen is 0.06–0.11 MIU (5–10 µg)/kg/day by subcutaneous injection, initiated 24 hours after the last dose of chemotherapy, and continuing for 7 to 10 days.[1,2] In bone-marrow transplantation, the recommended dose is 0.11 MIU (10 µg)/kg/day by intravenous infusion, commencing the day after bone-marrow transplantation, for a maximum duration of 30 days.[1,2]

5 Preparation of injection

Reconstitution: Reconstitute by adding 1 mL of diluent (water for injections) to each vial and agitate gently to dissolve the contents.[1,2]

Bolus administration: The reconstituted solution of molgramostin may be administered by subcutaneous injection.

Intravenous infusion: The required dose, after reconstitution, is diluted in 25–100 mL of 0.9% sodium chloride or 5% glucose and infused over 4–6 hours through a peripheral or central venous line.[1,2]

6 Destruction of drug or contaminated articles

Incinerate as special clinical waste.

Contact with skin: Wash with copious amounts of water.

References

1 ABPI (1999) *ABPI Data Sheet Compendium 1999–2000.* DataPharm Publications Ltd, London, 991–2.
2 ABPI (1999) *ABPI Data Sheet Compendium 1999–2000.* DataPharm Publications Ltd, London, 1488–9.

Prepared by Yaacov Cass